ELVIN F. DONALDSON, Ph.D., The Ohio State University, is Professor of Finance in the College of Commerce and Administration, The Ohio State University. Dr. Donaldson is the co-author (with John K. Pfahl) of *Personal Finance*, Fourth Edition, and is a contributing editor to the *Financial Handbook*, Fourth Edition, both published by The Ronald Press Company.

JOHN K. PFAHL, Ph.D., The Ohio State University, is Professor of Finance in the College of Commerce and Administration, The Ohio State University. Dr. Pfahl has had wide experience as an investment, financial, and real estate consultant. He is the co-author (with Elvin F. Donaldson) of *Personal Finance*, Fourth Edition, and is a contributing editor to the *Financial Handbook*, Fourth Edition, both published by The Ronald Press Company.

CORPORATE FINANCE

Policy and Management

ELVIN F. DONALDSON

Professor of Finance, The Ohio State University

and

JOHN K. PFAHL

Professor of Finance, The Ohio State University

SECOND EDITION

THE RONALD PRESS COMPANY · NEW YORK

[1963]

Library of Congress Catalog Card Number: 63–13746
PRINTED IN THE UNITED STATES OF AMERICA

To Our Families

Preface

This book has been written to explain the principles underlying the financial policies, practices, and management of the modern business enterprise. It is designed primarily for college courses and has developed out of many years of teaching and close association by the authors with the financial community.

The First Edition has been widely used in leading schools and colleges throughout the country and has acquired the reputation of being a complete, authoritative, and readable treatment of the subject. In this edition the authors have conscientiously strived to retain these virtues and at the same time condense the treatment of some subjects and also add new material particularly in the changing area of financial management. We have retained the basic analytic and evaluative approach in order to provide the student with a solid base upon which to build his study of such important areas of management concern as profitability, return on investment, cost of capital, and internal and short-term financing. In this material we stress throughout the relationship of financial management activities to corporate objectives and the decision-making processes of financial managers.

To include and properly develop this new substantive content, we have necessarily reorganized, condensed, and rearranged much of our earlier work. Our question material completely covers the content of each chapter. In order to further stimulate student interest through involvement in problem-solving situations that require the application of basic principles, additional problems have been inserted at the end of each chapter. We have also provided Selected Reading lists with each chapter.

v

It would be impossible here to acknowledge adequately the advice, counsel, and guidance of those many colleagues who assisted us. We do wish, however, to express our special thanks to Professor Ronald S. Foster, who taught the previous edition for several years, for his helpful suggestions and constructive criticism.

ELVIN F. DONALDSON
JOHN K. PFAHL

Columbus, Ohio
March, 1963

Contents

CHAPTER   PAGE

Part I
FORMS OF BUSINESS ORGANIZATIONS

1 Finance **3**
AREAS OF FINANCE: Public Finance. Private Finance. THE
FINANCE FUNCTION IN BUSINESS: Nature of the Finance
Function. Importance of the Finance Function. The Place
of Financial Management. FINANCE AND RELATED FIELDS:
Accounting and Finance. Law and Finance. Taxation and
Finance. FINANCE IN AN ECONOMIC SOCIETY: Financial Mar-
kets. Macro and Micro Finance.

2 Non-corporate Forms of Business Organizations . . **16**
THE INDIVIDUAL PROPRIETORSHIP. THE GENERAL PARTNER-
SHIP: Agency Power of Partners. Partnership Name. Nature
of Partners' Liability. Sharing of Profits. Status of Partners'
Loans to Business. Liability of Outgoing Partners. Liability
of Incoming Partners. Partnership Lacks Stability. Provi-
sions for Stability. Taxation of the General Partnership.
Partnerships Taxed as Corporations. Corporations Taxed as
Partnerships. Taxation of Partnerships and Corporations
Compared. Use of the Partnership Form of Organization.
THE LIMITED PARTNERSHIP: Nature of the Limited Partner-
ship. Limited Partner's Interest is Assignable. Use of the
Limited Partnership. THE PARTNERSHIP ASSOCIATION. THE
MINING PARTNERSHIP. THE JOINT VENTURE. THE JOINT
STOCK COMPANY. TYPES OF TRUST ARRANGEMENTS: Living
Trust. Testamentary Trust. Investment Trust. Voting Trust.
Combinations Formed by Trust Device. THE MASSACHU-
SETTS TRUST: Formation of the Massachusetts Trust. Liabil-
ity of the Shareholders. Taxation. Use of the Massachusetts
Trust.

3 The Corporation **40**
HISTORY: Development of General Incorporating Laws. Corporation Laws in the United States. TYPES OF CORPORA-

vii

TIONS: Public and Private Corporations. Profit and Stock. Ordinary Business Corporations. ATTRIBUTES OF THE COR- PORATION: Legal Entity. Permanent Life. Transferability of Shares. Limited Liability. Representative Management. SELECTING STATE OF INCORPORATION: State Taxes. Restric- tions Imposed by Laws. Whether Statutes Have Been Tested. INCORPORATION PROCEDURE: The Charter. The By- laws. Organization Meetings. TRANSACTING BUSINESS IN OTHER STATES: Qualification in Foreign State. Penalties for Non-Compliance. Interstate vs. Intrastate Commerce. Meet- ing the Requirements.

4 **Corporate Management** 61
THE STOCKHOLDERS: Stockholders' Rights. Voting Rights of Stockholders. Straight Voting. Cumulative Voting. Proxy Voting. Class Voting. Fractional and Multiple Votes. Non- voting Stock. Methods of Continuing Control. Pre-emptive Right of Stockholders. Inspection of the Books. THE DIREC- TORS: Qualifications of the Directors. Powers of the Board of Directors. Board Committees. Liabilities of Directors. Avoidance of Liability. THE OFFICERS: Qualifications for Officers. Powers and Duties of the Officers. Liability of Officers.

Part II
CORPORATE SECURITIES

5 **Capital Stock** 83
Nature of Corporate Stock. Authorized, Issued, and Out- standing Stock. Capital Stock. Capital. STOCK CERTIFI- CATES AND STOCK TRANSFER: Transfer of Stock. Stockholder Entitled to Dividends. Stockholder Entitled to Vote. Liability of Stockholders. TREASURY STOCK: Reasons for Reacquiring Stock. Ways of Reacquiring Stock. Legal Right of Corpora- tion to Reacquire Shares. PAR AND NO-PAR STOCK: Par Value as a Measure of Liability. Disadvantages of Par Value. Adoption of No-Par Stock Laws. Stated Value of No-Par Stock. Advantages of No-Par Stock. Tax Disadvantage of No-Par Stock. OTHER STOCK VALUES: Book Value. Current- Asset Value. Market Value. Real Value.

6 **Types of Stock** 103
COMMON STOCK. PREFERRED STOCK: Why Preferred Stock is Issued. Legal Nature of Preferred Stock. PREFERRED DIVIDENDS: Preference. Cumulative Dividends. Non-cumu- lative Preferred Stock. Right To Participate in Dividends.

VOTING RIGHT OF PREFERRED. PREFERREDS' LIQUIDATION
RIGHTS. PROTECTIVE PROVISIONS IN PREFERRED STOCKS: Re-
strictions on Further Issues. Maintenance of Certain Ratios.
Surplus and Dividend Reserves. Other Provisions. REDEMP-
TION OF PREFERRED: Callable Feature. Compulsory Redemp-
tion of Preferred Stock. Preferred Stock Sinking Funds. Con-
vertible Preferred Stock. SUMMARY OF PREFERRED STOCK
RIGHTS: Investment Worth of Preferred Stock. OTHER TYPES
OF STOCK: Classified Stock. Guaranteed Stock. Prior-Lien
Stock. Bankers' Shares. Deferred Stock. Founders', Promot-
ers', and Management Shares. Debenture Stock.

7   Corporate Bonds   130
Bonds Compared With Stocks. Practical Difference. BOND
FEATURES: Denomination of Bonds. Maturity of Bonds.
BOND YIELDS: Computing Bond Yields. Bonds Quotations.
Relationship Between Bond Prices and Interest Rates. REG-
ISTERED AND COUPON BONDS: Registered Bonds. Coupon
Bonds. Registered-Coupon Bonds. TRUSTEE AND INDEN-
TURE: Duties of the Trustees. The Bond Indenture. REA-
SONS FOR SELLING BONDS: To Secure Capital. Financial
Condition of the Company. Condition of the Market. Control.
Wider Market. Cost of Funds. Trading on the Equity. Federal
Income Tax. BOND RETIREMENT. REDEMPTION: Redemption
Before Maturity. Methods of Redeeming Bonds Before
Maturity. Disadvantages to Bondholder of Redemption. RE-
FUNDING: Reasons for Refunding. Savings on Fixed Charges
Through Refunding. Inducements to Refund. EXTENSION
OF MATURITY. SINKING FUNDS: Reasons for Sinking Fund.
Determining Amount of Sinking Fund Installments. Sub-
stitutes for Sinking Fund Payments. Corporation's Obliga-
tion for Sinking Fund Payments. Sinking Fund Trustees.
Types of Sinking Fund Investments. Methods of Acquisition
and Disposition of the Bonds. Distinguished from Sinking
Fund Reserve. SERIAL BONDS: Advantages to Issuing Cor-
poration. Advantages to Investor. Callable Serial Bonds.
Market Aspects of Serial Bonds.

8   Types of Bonds   164
MORTGAGE BONDS: Nature of a Mortgage. Nature of Junior
Mortgages. Assuming a Mortgage. Closed-End Issues.
Open-End Mortgage. Limited Open-End Mortgage. Restric-
tions on Open-End Issues. After-Acquired Property Clause.
Avoiding the After-Acquired Property Clause. TYPES OF
MORTGAGE BONDS: First Mortgage Bonds. Divisional Bonds.
Special Direct-Lien Bonds. Prior-Lien Bonds. Second,

Third, etc., Mortgage Bonds. General, Consolidated, and
Refunding Mortgage Bonds. COLLATERAL TRUST BONDS:
Reasons for Issuance. Payment of Interest, Dividends, and
Principal on Pledged Securities. Voting Pledged Stock.
Substitution of Pledged Securities. EQUIPMENT OBLIGA-
TIONS: Equipment Mortgage Plan. Conditional Sale Plan.
Philadelphia Plan. Terms of the Lease. Security Behind the
Obligations. Investment Worth of Equipment Obligations.
Use in Other Fields. LAND TRUST CERTIFICATES. LEASEHOLD
MORTGAGE BONDS. ASSUMED BONDS. GUARANTEED BONDS:
Lease. Financing a Subsidiary. Consolidation. Other In-
stances. Investment Worth. Guaranteed Bonds and Guar-
anteed Stocks Compared. JOINT BONDS. RECEIVERS' AND
TRUSTEES' CERTIFICATES. DEBENTURE BONDS: Protective
Provisions in Debenture Issues. Subordinated Debentures.
Secured Debentures. INCOME BONDS: Interest Provisions in
Income Bonds. Income Bonds Compared With Preferred
Stocks. Recent Uses. Quotations. PARTICIPATING BONDS.

9   Convertibles, Warrants, and Options   197
CONVERTIBLE BONDS: Extent of Use. Why Sold. Disadvan-
tage to Issuer. Advantages to Buyer. Disadvantages to
Buyer. Conversion Ratio. Price Pattern of Convertible
Bonds. Determining When To Convert. Adjustment for In-
terest and Dividends. Uneven Number of Shares. Conver-
sion Period. Protection Against Dilution. Hedge for Short
Sellers of Stock. Conclusion on Convertibles. STOCK PUR-
CHASE WARRANTS: Type of Securities Carrying Warrants.
Reason for Use. Purchase Price of Stock With Warrant. De-
tachability of Warrants. Duration of Warrants. Antidilution
Provisions. Warrants Compared With Convertible Privilege.
Price of Detachable Warrants. Use as Hedge in Short Sale.
Hybrid Form. Other Uses of Warrants. STOCK OPTIONS:
Given to Investment Bankers. Given to Corporate Promoters.
Given to Corporate Officials. Tax Status of "Restricted"
Stock Option. Problems in Connection With Warrants and
Options.

Part III

FINANCING THROUGH SECURITIES

10   Promoting and Financing a New Business   225
Promotion of a Company in a New Field. Promotion of a
Company in an Established Field. Promotion of a Combina-
tion of Two or More Existing Companies. Promotion of Other
Major Changes. THE PROMOTER: Types of Promoters. Legal

Position of the Promoter. Liability of Promoter. Compensation of the Promoter. STAGES IN PROMOTION: Discovery of the Idea. Investigation of the Proposed Project. Planning and Obtaining Financing. Assembly of the Factors of Production. LEGAL ASPECTS OF PROMOTION: Leases. Options. Patents. Copyrights. PURPOSE OF PROMOTION.

11 Capital Structure 244

Importance of Capital Structure. FACTORS IN CHOOSING A CAPITAL STRUCTURE: Legal Form of Organization. Whether Outside Capital is Needed. Size of the Business. Age of the Business. Stability of the Earnings. Nature of the Business. Nature of the Assets. Level of Interest Rates. Taxes. Control. Government Regulation. Preference of Investors and Investment Bankers. CAPITAL STRUCTURE PRINCIPLES: Issue Weakest Security First. Make Capital Structure Simple. The Safer the Security to the Buyer, the Lower its Cost. Leverage Offers Higher Profit, but Involves More Risk. THE CHOICE: Risk. Cost. Control. Flexibility. CAPITAL STRUCTURE PATTERNS: Industrials. Public Utilities. Railroads. Finance, Insurance, and Real Estate Corporations.

12 Valuation, Capitalization, and Recapitalization . . 264

PRINCIPLES OF VALUATION: Cost. Market. Income. VALUATION OF AN ENTIRE COMPANY: Asset Value. Market Value. Earning Power Value. Valuation by Use of Both Assets and Earnings. CAPITALIZATION: Bases of Capitalization. Overcapitalization. Undercapitalization. RECAPITALIZATION: Common-Stock Recapitalization. Preferred Stock Recapitalization. Debt Readjustment. Recapitalization for Overcapitalized Companies. Recapitalization for Undercapitalized Companies.

13 Privileged Subscriptions 287

REASONS FOR USE: Legal Obligation. When Not Subject to Pre-emptive Right. Practical Reason for Privileged Subscription. PROCEDURE: Subscription Warrants and Rights. VALUE OF RIGHTS: Explanation of Value of Rights. Quotation of the Rights. Determining Value of Rights With Stock Ex-Rights. Actual Price of Stock and Rights. Long-Run Effect on Stock Price. What To Do With the Rights. Action by Outsiders. TAXATION: Rights Valued at Less Than 15 Per Cent of Stock Value. Rights Valued at 15 Per Cent or More of Stock Value. CONDITIONS FOR SUCCESS: A Favorable Outlook for Business and Stocks. The Money Used for Profitable Purposes. Wide Distribution of Old Stock. New Issue Rela-

tively Small. Price of New Stock Relatively Low. UNDER-
WRITING PRIVILEGED SUBSCRIPTIONS. SALE OF PREFERRED
STOCK AND BONDS.

14 Investment Banking 307
INVESTMENT BANKING: Services Performed by Investment
Banker. Advantages of Bankers to Investors. Types of In-
vestment Bankers. Departments of a Large Investment
Bank. SYNDICATES: Syndicates or Groups. Purchase Group.
Selling Group. Compensation Paid to Investment Bankers.
Price Stabilization. COMPETITIVE BIDDING: Advantages of
Competitive Bidding. Disadvantages of Competitive Bidding.
PRIVATE PLACEMENT: Reasons for Development of Private
Placement. Advantages of Private Placement. Disadvantages
of Private Placement. Brokerage Fees to Bankers. REGULA-
TION OF SECURITY ISSUES. STATE LAWS: Exempt Securities.
Exempt Transactions. Weaknesses of State Laws. Securities
Issued by Public Utilities and Financial Institutions. THE
FEDERAL SECURITIES ACT OF 1933: Basic Purpose. Adminis-
tration. Principal Provisions. Exempt Securities. Exempt
Transactions. Registration Statement. Effective Date of Reg-
istration Statement. The "Red-Herring" Prospectus. The
Prospectus. Penalties Provided. Persons Liable. Avoidance
of Liability. Value of Civil Liability Provisions. Evaluation
of the Securities Act of 1933.

15 The Stock Market 339
OVER-THE-COUNTER MARKET. SHAREHOLDERS IN THE UNITED
STATES. THE STOCK EXCHANGES: The New York Stock Ex-
change. Advantages of Listing to the Issuing Corporation.
Advantages of Listing to the Investor. Composition of NYSE
Membership. American Stock Exchange. National Stock Ex-
change. The Regional Stock Exchanges. SECURITIES
EXCHANGE ACT OF 1934: Registration of Exchanges. Regis-
tration of Securities. Margin Requirements. Manipulation
Prohibited. Segregation. Information on Stock Holdings.
Short-Term Profits of Insiders. Proxy Regulations. Periodic
Reports. Termination of Registration. Over-the-Counter
Markets. BUYING AND SELLING: Types of Orders. Buying on
Margin. Buying and Selling Odd Lots. Short Selling. Brok-
ers' Commissions. Stock Transfer Taxes. Monthly Investment
Plan. Dollar Averaging. Secondary Distributions. Other
Block Offerings.

16 Mutual Funds—Investment Companies 368
GENERAL NATURE: Early History. American Experience.
TYPES OF INVESTMENT COMPANIES: Face-Amount Installment

Certificate Companies. Unit or Fixed or Semi-Fixed Companies. Closed-End Companies. Open-End Companies. CLASSIFICATION ACCORDING TO NATURE OF PORTFOLIO: Balanced Fund. Bond Funds. Preferred Stock Funds. Diversified Common-Stock Funds. Funds Specializing in One or More Industries. "Special Situation" Funds. Funds for Foreign Securities. INVESTMENT COMPANY CHARGES: Market Price of Closed-End Companies. Management Fees. INVESTMENT IN INVESTMENT COMPANIES. ACCUMULATION AND WITHDRAWAL PLANS: Accumulation Plans. Reinvestment of Dividends. Systematic Withdrawal Plans. REGULATION AND TAXATION: The Investment Company Act of 1940. Taxation of Investment Companies and Their Shares.

Part IV

FINANCIAL MANAGEMENT

17 Organization and Objectives 391

THE FINANCIAL ORGANIZATION: The Relation of Finance to Other Functions of a Business. The Organization Level of the Finance Function. The Internal Structure of the Finance Organization. Duties of Financial Executives. OBJECTIVES: Service. Profit. Permanence. Financial Management Objectives. PROFITABILITY: Measurements of Profitability. SOLVENCY: Meaning of Solvency. Planning and Controlling Solvency. Credit Rating from the Creditor's Viewpoint. THE FINANCIAL MIX.

18 Return on Investment and Cost of Capital 412

DETERMINING THE AMOUNT OF THE INVESTMENT: Stock Purchase. New Equipment Purchase. Valuation of Entire Corporation. Valuation of a Division. DETERMINING RETURN: Future Returns. Past Returns. RELATING RETURN TO INVESTMENT: Relate Like Things. Selection of Standards. The Triangular Relationship. TIME VALUE IN RETURN ON INVESTMENT: Timing Patterns. Timing and Profitability. Time-Value vs. Accounting Method. USES OF PROFITABILITY MEASUREMENTS: Capital Budgeting. External Standard of Comparison. Internal Standard of Comparison. Measure of Product Performance. Profit Planning. Control. COST OF CAPITAL: Bonds. Preferred Stock. Common Stock. Retained Earnings. Average Cost of Capital.

19 Financial Management Tools 442

Creditor Analysis. Owner Analysis. Other Decision Elements. ACCOUNTING DATA: Stewardship Accounting. Uses

of Accounting Data. FINANCIAL STATEMENTS: The State-
ment of Financial Position. The Income Statement. The
Flow of Funds Statement. RATIO ANALYSIS: Uses of Ratio
Analysis. Standards for Comparison. Limitations of Ratio
Analysis. Types of Ratios. BUDGETING: The Budget as a
Planning Tool. The Budget as a Control Tool. Importance
and Function of Budgets. Forecasting. Budget Prepara-
tion. Flexible Budgeting. Budget Limitations. Types of
Budgets. CASH BUDGET: Cash Receipts. Cash Disbursements.
Cash Balance. Uses of the Cash Budget. Limitations of the
Cash Budget. Proforma Statements.

20   Asset Management   473
Asset Level Requirement. Types of Assets. Working Capital.
CASH: Reasons for Holding Cash. Minimum Cash Level.
Cost of Cash Investment. Aiding Cash Flow. Short-Term
Investment. RECEIVABLES: Proper Level of Receivables.
Credit Granting. Credit Terms. Collection Policies. Cost of
Credit Selling. Measurement of Receivables Management.
INVENTORY: Proper Level of Inventory. Costs of Carrying
Inventory. Types of Inventory. Inventory Turnover. Inven-
tory Valuation. FIXED ASSETS: Costs of Fixed Assets. Valua-
tion of Fixed Assets.

21   Unsecured Current Financing   502
Advantages of Current Financing. Disadvantages of Current
Financing. Determining Amount of Current Financing.
Temporary and Permanent Needs and Sources. SPONTANE-
OUS SOURCES: Trade Credit. Accruals and Deferred Items.
SUPPLIERS: Cost. Credit Terms. Risk, Control, and Flexi-
bility. UNSECURED COMMERCIAL BANK CREDIT: Line of
Credit. Cost. Risk, Control, and Flexibility. Selecting a Bank.
COMMERCIAL PAPER HOUSES: Operations. Advantages. Dis-
advantages. OTHER UNSECURED SOURCES.

22   Secured Current Financing   523
Reasons for Use. TYPES OF COLLATERAL: Accounts Receivable. Inventory. Securities. Fixed Assets. Bankers' Acceptances. Other Asset Pledges. Comakers or Indorsers.
SOURCES OF SECURED CURRENT FINANCING: Secured Bank
Financing. Finance Companies. Factors. Government. Consumer Finance Companies.

23   Intermediate Financing   542
Reasons for Use. Advantages and Disadvantages. TERM
LOANS: Characteristics of Term Loans. Protective Provisions.
Cost. Other Arrangements. Term Loans from the Borrower's

Point of View. Sources of Term-Loan Financing. INSTALL-
MENT FINANCING OF FIXED ASSETS: Costs. Risk. LEASING:
Leasing as an Alternative to Ownership of Assets. Characteristics of Leases. Advantages to the Lessee. Disadvantages
to the Tenant. Sale and Leaseback.

24 Depreciation Policies   563

MAINTENANCE POLICIES: Maintenance and Repairs. Replace-
ments. Additions and Betterments. Disposal. DEPRECIATION
ACCOUNTING POLICIES: Allocating Expense to Accounting
Period. Proper Valuation of Assets. Subjective Nature of
Charge. Effect on Income Tax. Effect on Replacement. Use
of Assets Resulting from Depreciation Charges. Experience
of American Manufacturing Corporations. METHODS OF
CHARGING DEPRECIATION: Production Method. Straight-Line
Method.   Fixed-Percentage-of-Declining-Balance   Method.
Sum-of-the-Year's-Digits Method. First-Year-Extra-Allowance
Method. Investment Tax Credit. Sinking-Fund Method.
Other Methods. Choice of Method. OBSOLESCENCE: Obso-
lescence and Depreciation. Accounting Procedures. DEPLE-
TION: Accounting Procedure. Depletion and Income Taxes.
When Assets Are Not To Be Replaced. AMORTIZATION.

25 Net Income and Retained Earnings   591

The Meaning of Net Income. THE INCOME STATEMENT:
Sales. Cost of Goods Sold. Other Operating Expenses. Non-
operating Income. Non-operating Expenses. Federal Income
Taxes. Effect of Net Income on the Balance Sheet. Profit
Distortion. Profit Improvement. Fixed and Variable Costs.
RETAINED INCOME AND SURPLUS: Meaning of Surplus. Mean-
ing of Deficit. Earned Surplus or Retained Earnings. Capital
Surplus. Uses of Surplus. RESERVES: Valuation Reserves.
Liability Reserves. Surplus Reserve. DEFICITS. REINVEST-
MENT: Purpose of Reinvestment. Preinvestment of Earnings.

26 Dividends   615

Cash Dividends. Property Dividends. Scrip Dividends. Bond
Dividends. STOCK DIVIDENDS: Reasons for Paying Stock
Dividends. Practical Advantages to Shareholders. Taxability
of Stock Dividends. Fractional Share Warrants. Stock Divi-
dends Paid from Capital Surplus. Readjustment of Capital
Account. Rescission of Stock Dividends. New York Stock
Exchange Rules on Stock Dividends. STOCK SPLITS: Stock
Splits and Taxation. Advantages of Stock Splits. Reverse
Stock Split-ups. DIVIDEND TERMINOLOGY: Regular Divi-
dends. Extra Dividends. Interim and Final Dividends. Spe-

cial Dividends. Liquidating Dividends. DECLARATION OF DIVIDENDS: Declared Dividends Are Debts. Remedies for Improper Dividends. FACTORS AFFECTING DIVIDEND POLICIES: Common Law. Statutory Law. Restrictions Imposed by Commissions and Regulation. Contractual Arrangements. Nature of Company Business. Age and Size of Company. Stock Distribution. Tax Considerations. Earnings. Cash Flows and Liquidity. Attempt To Maintain Stable Dividends.

Part V
EXPANSION AND ADJUSTMENT

27 Expansion 645

Purpose of Expansion. Measures of Expansion. Advantages and Disadvantages of Expansion. TYPES OF EXPANSION: Internal and External Expansion. Methods of Financing Expansion. Direction of Expansion. FINANCIAL MANAGEMENT AND EXPANSION: Expansion Problems for Financial Management.

28 Combinations 664

Historical Development of Combinations. FORMS OF COMBINATIONS: Purchase of Assets. Mergers and Consolidations. Holding Companies. Leases. Other Forms of Combinations. COMBINATIONS AND THE LAW: The Sherman Anti-Trust Act of 1890. The Clayton Act of 1914. The Public Utility Holding Company Act of 1935. The 1950 Legislation. Anti-Trust Exemption. Present Status of Combinations and the Law.

29 Failure and Equity Receivership 689

FAILURE: Economic Failure. Financial Failure. Real vs. Apparent Causes of Failure. Causes of Failure. External Causes of Failure. Non-financial Internal Causes of Failure. Internal Financial Causes of Failure. COMPROMISES: Extensions. Composition. Assignments. Creditors' Committee. EQUITY RECEIVERSHIP: Equity Receivership Procedure. Powers and Duties of Receiver. Receivership Compared With Compromise Settlements. Procedure Following Receivership. REORGANIZATION FOLLOWING RECEIVERSHIP: Reorganization Procedure. Shortcomings of Equity Reorganizations.

30 Reorganization, Bankruptcy, and Termination . . . 713

The Bankruptcy Act of 1898. THE CHANDLER ACT: Appointment of Trustee. Duties of the Trustee. Protective Committees. Work Preliminary to Plan. Mandatory Provisions of Reorganization Plan. Objectives To Be Accomplished. Treatment of Interested Parties. Control. Procedure Under Chapter X. Receivership Under Chapter X Compared With Equity Receivership. Advantages of Reorganization Under the Bankruptcy Act. Arrangements Under Chapter XI. RAILROAD REORGANIZATION: The Mahaffie Act. TERMINATION WITHOUT FAILURE: Reasons for Voluntary Dissolution or Liquidation. Procedure of Voluntary Dissolution. Dissolution Initiated by State. Partial Liquidation. TERMINATION FOLLOWING FAILURE: Friendly Liquidation. Compositions and Assignments. Liquidation Following Receivership. BANKRUPTCY: Purpose of Bankruptcy. Initiating the Action. Acts of Bankruptcy. Further Procedure. Priority of Claims. Debts Not Affected by Discharge. Bankrupt's Exemptions. Advantages of Bankruptcy. Shortcomings of Bankruptcy.

Index 733

I

FORMS OF BUSINESS ORGANIZATIONS

1

Finance

To a person who is not acquainted with the subject, a mention of the term *finance* might bring to mind a variety of different concepts. Each individual gives the word a somewhat different connotation, based on his own experience. Some people would immediately think of such personalities as J. P. Morgan or John D. Rockefeller and would conclude that finance was a subject of interest only to the very wealthy. Others might think of the consumer finance company with an office on Main Street and associate finance with the lending of money to individuals. Still others would picture the commercial bank or savings and loan association, thinking that finance was concerned primarily with large financial institutions dealing in huge sums of money. Some businessmen use the term finance only when they are thinking of selling stock or borrowing money; others think in terms of the need to finance their customers. Many people interested in government would immediately think in terms of the many problems of governmental finance. The recurring gyrations in the stock market might cause many individuals to associate the term primarily with investing and speculating in stocks. The considerable public attention devoted to the problem of inflow and outflow of gold would lead others to think of this area when discussing finance.

Actually all of the above are examples of the topics which are included under the general heading of "finance." The following discussion will attempt to narrow the field of finance and define that portion of the field which is covered in the general subject matter of "business or corporate finance."

AREAS OF FINANCE

The field of finance can be divided into a number of different subsidiary areas. These areas are presented schematically in Figure 1–1. The most important division of the field is between *public* and *private* finance.

It is to be noted, however, that these two areas are not completely independent. As indicated in Figure 1–1, private finance supports public finance through taxation and is in turn supported by public finance through certain kinds of spending and service. In addition, both private finance and public finance deal with the same financial institutions in the same financial markets. In fact, finance, in a private profit system, is the major equalizing force in the determination of the distribution of resources between the general areas of public and private operation and within the different subclassifications of these two areas.

Public finance may be subclassified in a variety of ways, but the most common is by the type of institution involved—whether international, federal, state, or local. Private finance is also subdivided in a variety of ways of which the most common also deals with the institution involved—whether business, consumer, or non-profit. Profit business finance may be broken down into corporate and non-corporate finance.

Public Finance

Public finance can be defined as the procurement, control, and spending of money by governmental bodies. In the early history of our nation, the subject of public finance was of much greater importance than that of private finance because our government and foreign governments were important suppliers of capital to all segments of the society. With the development of the nation, the accumulation of savings, the rise of the modern corporation, and reinvestment of earnings by business, private individuals and institutions took over a major portion of the role of supplying capital. Except during war periods or war financing, government for many years was a relatively minor factor in financial markets and in financial decisions.

Beginning with the depression of the 1930's, government became increasingly important in the allocation of capital and the distribution of resources. In recent years, the general field of public finance has accounted for about 20 per cent of our total national product. Public bodies are important elements in financial markets and certain financial institutions deal almost exclusively in the general area of public finance. The federal government's debt of approximately $300 billion added to the debts of other governmental agencies requires a significant amount of financing through the financial markets. Public taxation and public spending are influential in determining the future course of action of private bodies as well as public institutions.

This book is not concerned with public finance—our interest lies in the field of private finance. This is not to underemphasize the importance of public finance, but merely to point out that the problems of public finance are so significantly different from private finance that they require separate study. In studying private finance, however, one cannot ignore the interrelationships between public and private finance and the effect of the whole public sector of the economy on the activities of the private units being analyzed.

Private Finance

Generally speaking, the area of private finance covers the activities of raising and managing money by non-governmental units. Private finance frequently is divided into three categories: business finance, personal finance, and financing of non-profit organizations. The study of personal or consumer finance is concerned with the financial aspects of decisions made by individuals. The financing of non-profit organizations encompasses the financial problems encountered by such organizations as hospitals, research foundations, educational institutions, churches, and charitable institutions. The study of business finance deals with the financial problems of private business concerns which strive to earn profits.

The field of real estate finance is sometimes segregated from other business and consumer finance. However, private profit businesses, non-profit institutions, and consumers deal in the field of real estate finance. Therefore, since this book deals with private profit business finance, insofar as real estate must be financed for private profit businesses, this area is discussed. If the general area of private finance were subclassified on the basis of the asset being financed rather than the institution, real estate finance would be an important classification. Other classifications would be inventory finance, receivables finance, consumption finance, automobile finance, etc.

Finance is important to all types of businesses—whether corporate or non-corporate. While the title of this book is *Corporate Finance,* most of the discussion will have general application to various kinds of business undertakings and to all forms of business organizations. The non-corporate forms of business organizations are more restricted in available sources of capital than are corporations. The problems connected with the administration of corporate funds are much more complex than those encountered in other forms of organizations. Therefore, an understanding of corporate finance would include an understanding of the less complicated subject of non-corporate finance.

The field of corporate finance may be subdivided in several ways. One of the most common is according to the type of corporation involved. Businesses are sometimes classified into two broad groups: industrial and commercial. The former consists of manufacturing companies and extractive firms and the latter consists of all other types of business concerns. In the stock market, the common breakdown of corporations is: railroads, public utilities, financials, and industrials. This latter group

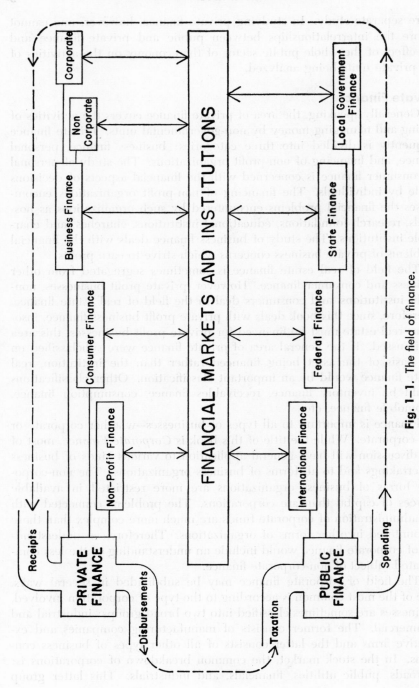

Fig. 1-1. The field of finance.

includes all types of companies which do not come under one of the other three headings. Because this classification is the one most commonly used in financial circles, it will be used in this book.

The term *private finance* is sometimes used to mean the financing of "privately owned" businesses. These are firms whose stock is not owned by a large number of stockholders—the public. The term *publicly owned corporations* is often used to apply to those corporations which do have a large number of stockholders. The financing of both privately owned and publicly owned corporations properly comes under the heading of corporate finance. The financing of a publicly owned business should not be confused with the field of public finance.

It should be noted that there is considerable overlapping among the various areas within the field of finance. For example, the selection of the corporate securities that an individual should buy is normally considered to be within the study of personal finance or consumer finance. The type of securities that a corporation might issue to finance its needs is, however, a portion of the study of corporate finance. When a governmental agency such as the Small Business Administration supplies funds to a business concern, both business finance and public finance are simultaneously involved. While the primary concern of this book is with the field of business finance, other areas of finance will be examined when the discussion carries naturally into these areas.

THE FINANCE FUNCTION IN BUSINESS

In both public and private finance, the use of the word *finance* implies providing the capital factor of production, primarily in money form. Thus, the field of public finance covers governmental receipts of money —primarily through taxation—and governmental spending. Private finance deals with the providing of capital to meet the requirements of private individuals and institutions. The finance function in business is basically to provide the capital needed, usually in cash form, to operate the business.

Nature of the Finance Function

The primary objectives of most businesses are to make a profit for owners and to perform a service for society. The accomplishment of these objectives is not achieved by mere chance. It is the task of management to perform the managerial functions of planning, organizing, and controlling all of the activities of the firm to the end that these business objectives are attained. Planning may be defined as the act of deciding in advance on an action which is to be undertaken. Organizing is concerned with the work of providing the resources and conditions that are necessary to execute the plans which have been formulated. Controlling has to do with seeing that the work gets done according to plan.

The functions of a business, particularly an industrial concern, are often divided into only two broad groups: production and distribution (selling). Included in these are detailed functions such as accounting, advertising, financing, purchasing, research, etc. The task of management is to administer the various departments or functions of the business. Every act of management relates directly or indirectly to one or more of the various functions of a business.

The importance of good management cannot be overstressed. With proper management the problems of all the departments will be solved, and without it a business cannot be a success for any extended period of time. It should be appreciated, however, that production management, financial management, sales management, etc., are all parts of "management."

The function of finance in a business simply refers to the activities concerned with the planning, organizing, and controlling of the funds used in the business. The primary activities necessary for the successful management of the finance function of any business are (1) financial planning, or estimating and planning for the future flow of cash receipts and disbursements; (2) financial organizing, or raising the funds needed to carry on the operation; and (3) financial controlling, or checking the financial operations to insure that the cash flows are proceeding according to plan and that the deviations are handled in a manner that is compatible with continued financial health and long-run profit maximization of the firm.

The basic aspects of the finance function are essentially the same in all of the various types of business concerns. Most of what is said in this book, therefore, will have general application to the different kinds of business undertakings. However, we will not generally be concerned with the peculiar problems of businesses that are subject to special laws and regulations such as railroads, public utilities, or financial corporations. Our primary interest, therefore, lies in industrial concerns—manufacturing, wholesaling, retailing, and service companies.

Importance of the Finance Function

All of the various functions of a business must be properly managed if the firm is to be successful for any extended period of time. The importance of good financial management cannot be overemphasized. The success of a business and even its survival are to a very considerable degree determined by its financial management.

A business may have good production and sales departments, but it may be doomed to failure if it has been financed improperly at the time of its establishment. Or, the improper use of bank or trade credit may result in failure. The unwise purchase of equipment or inventories might prove to be disastrous. Improper control of expenses may shoot costs up to the point where failure is inevitable. The inability to float a bond or stock issue at a particular time may result in complete failure. And in general, the inability to meet debts as they come due will force any company to the wall. The point should be stressed that all of these are *financial management* problems.

The Place of Financial Management

The tasks of financial management must be performed in all business organizations regardless of size and type. These tasks are extremely important to the continued well-being of a firm and to the accomplishment of its objectives. However, financial management does not always receive the same attention from students of business as does management in certain other functional areas such as marketing and production.

There are several reasons for this. One is that there are ordinarily not many people involved in performing the financing function of a typical business concern, and the other is that in the great majority of businesses there is no "finance department." The accounting and credit departments carry on detailed and routine operations of a financial character, and the purchasing department is entrusted with the spending of considerable amounts of money, but these departments are not directly responsible for the financial management of a company.

In an individual proprietorship the owner is the financial manager. In a partnership or small corporation one of the owners or perhaps all of them take on the financial function. In some instances part of the work is done by a treasurer, secretary, bookkeeper, or credit manager. Financial management becomes more involved as the size of the business increases, just as is usually the case with the other business functions. In a large corporation the board of directors is charged with the responsibility of policy making. In some instances a "finance committee" of the board, which may act between board meetings, determines financial policies, which policies are usually adopted by the entire board at its next regular meeting.

The chairman of the board of directors, when active in the affairs of a corporation, may devote a considerable amount of time to financial matters. The chief executive officer appointed by the board is the president of the company. In some companies, or at certain times in any company, the president will be directly occupied with financial management. The chief financial officer of the corporation, also appointed by the board of directors, is commonly the treasurer. A vice-president in charge of finance may be the principal financial officer of the company. In some companies the controller (sometimes spelled "comptroller," but pronounced the same), or auditor, is charged with some financial management. In some instances all of these officers get together to formulate financial policies, which are recommended to the board of directors. A budget committee, which may be composed of some or all of these officers, may be appointed to aid in the determination of financial policies. In some companies this is a committee of the board.

The financial management of a company may thus be carried on by various officers or committees within the company. The financial policies adopted by those in charge reach out and affect every department of the company.

FINANCE AND RELATED FIELDS

Because finance is an integral part of business operation, it is closely related to all other business subjects. The activities of marketing and production cannot be undertaken unless the necessary financing is provided. Furthermore, the results of marketing and production activities produce the profits which aid future financing and which are the objective of the firm. It is perhaps unfortunate that it is necessary to study business in its functional segments in order to have manageable subject matter; an understanding of the interrelationships of these functional areas is as important as a knowledge of each of the areas alone.

There are certain academic fields which are particularly closely related to the subject of business finance. A study of finance cannot be undertaken separately from the study of business law. Because accounting statements are the major tools used in financial management, it is unwise to study the field of finance without a knowledge of accounting. Because the objectives of the finance area of the business are the same as the objectives of the total business and because business operates within an economic society, it is a necessary prerequisite for any student of finance to have some understanding of the economic theories under which our system operates. The problems of taxation have become so important and complex that some understanding of taxes is also required in a study of business finance. The authors have assumed that the majority of the readers of this book will have an adequate background in the areas of economics and accounting. The text attempts to provide the necessary knowledge of law and taxation insofar as it applies directly to the problems of corporate finance.

Accounting and Finance

Accounting is indispensable and very closely related to financial management. The financial results of operations are recorded in the accounting books, and from these books are taken the data on which financial decisions are based. A good accounting system properly administered is essential to efficient financial management. In the section of the book dealing with the determination of income, depreciation, dividend policy, undistributed profits, and surplus reserves, we will be utilizing accounting methods.

Law and Finance

As business has developed and become more and more complex, the impact of laws is felt to an increasing extent. A study of corporate finance would be impossible without delving into the law. From the formation of a business organization through all its life, including its dissolution, the procedures must strictly follow the law. Securities sales, rights of the stockholders and bondholders, powers and liabilities of the officers and directors, the declaration and payment of dividends, etc., are all governed by the law. There are three types of law: (1) common law, (2) statutory law, and (3) administrative law.

Common Law. Common law represents the prevailing legal opinions and attitudes of the people as laid down by the judges in court decisions. It is an elastic system of law which can apply to an infinite variety of circumstances. It represents the thinking of many learned individuals over a long period of time. Where there are no statutes dealing with a particular situation, the common law is applicable. Each state has its own court decisions, and therefore its own common law. Generally speaking, the common law of the various states is about the same, but there are some differences.

Certain forms of business organizations, such as the individual proprietorship and the general partnership (in some states), which will be discussed later, are formed merely by contract among the members and are therefore referred to as common-law forms of organizations.

In former times in England when an individual thought that the common law was too rigid and did not give him relief, he sometimes appealed to the king for justice. The king eventually was compelled to refer these actions to the chancellor. This developed into the chancery courts. Today in this country we refer to such courts as *equity courts,* and the actions brought in these courts are called *equity* actions. Certain types of actions will be brought in *equity,* whereas others will be brought in the *law* courts. An injunction to prevent the occurrence of a wrongdoing, for example, would be brought in equity, but a suit for damages in a contract action would be brought in law. In most instances in the United States the same court hears both legal and equity actions. The term *equity* is sometimes used synonymously with *justice.* In some instances the term is used to refer to "ownership," such as the stockholder's *equity* in the corporation, or *equity* securities.

Statutory Law. The common law has certain weaknesses. It is slow to develop and therefore is inadequate for the rapidly changing economic and social systems. In some instances conflicting decisions on the same issue have been handed down by different judges. The legislatures of the various states and Congress have therefore enacted *statutory* law to supersede the common law in certain fields, or to apply in situations in which there was no common law. In some instances the statutes merely codify the existing common law, or clarify it. Statutory law represents a less elastic but more definite system than the common law. In the event of conflict between the common law and the statutes, the latter will prevail, unless they are declared unconstitutional. The corporation and certain types of partnerships, which will be discussed later, are formed under statutory law.

Administrative Law. Out of some statutes has developed what has come to be known as *administrative law*. Administrative bodies or commissions are sometimes set up by the state legislatures or by Congress to carry out some specific statute or statutes. For example, the Federal Trade Commission administers some of the antitrust laws, and the Internal Revenue Service administers the federal income tax laws. These bodies will adopt rules and regulations governing the procedure for carrying out the statutes or passing on certain actions which may or may not be taken under the particular statutes. The rulings of the commissions have the force of law, until or unless the parties affected appeal to courts and get a contrary ruling. In most instances the rulings of the commissions will not be appealed, and when they are, it is probable that they will be upheld. It is thus apparent that these administrative commissions, which are executive in character, assume or take on powers that are really legislative or judicial in nature. As business develops it is becoming more and more subject to regulation by various types of commissions.

Taxation and Finance

Tax administration is normally a part of the finance function in most businesses. This means that financial management has the responsibility for determining tax liabilities and for meeting tax payments. The increasing importance of taxes as an expense of business in our society requires that special attention be paid to the general area of taxation. Certain actions can be taken by financial management which have the effect of reducing the tax liability to government. The complexity of the tax laws makes the determination of business tax liability a very specialized subject. Tax laws are written in such a way that management decisions on financing, investment, accounting techniques, etc., can influence the amount of the tax liability. As a result, considerable attention is given to the tax effect in the making of financial management decisions.

FINANCE IN AN ECONOMIC SOCIETY

The United States and most of the Western world operate as capitalistic societies. An understanding of the theory of capitalism is necessary for an appreciation of the activities of finance in this kind of society. Basically, the capitalistic system allows private ownership of capital, and decisions on use of capital are made by large numbers of individual capitalists operating for themselves or for groups of other people. This system assumes economic objectives for our society. These objectives are the creation of additional values which will lead to higher standards of living and the production of profits which will allow additional capital investment.

Inherent in the system is freedom of choice on the part of the individual suppliers and users of capital. It is assumed that the decision makers arrive at their choice of actions on the basis of the greatest economic gain to the individual or group decision maker. Thus, the capitalistic system is market oriented.

Financial Markets

Financial markets are an important element in a capitalistic system. It is through these markets that financial resources are allocated to the various individuals, businesses, governments, or other institutions seeking capital. Suppliers of capital go to the capital markets to judge the alternatives for investment of their capital. As indicated in Figure 1–1, all the various types of finance are interrelated by the functioning of financial institutions and financial markets. The theory of the capitalistic society is that the marketplace will determine which users of funds will receive funds and the rates which they will have to pay.

In order to make a market system work, both the users and suppliers of the capital must act rationally and must be in a position to judge the potential outcomes of various investments. While no decision maker has complete knowledge of the future, it is apparent that estimates of the future are necessary to make the market work properly. The more restrictions placed on the marketplace, the less is the freedom of choice for the decision makers. The capitalistic system assumes that there will be a large number of individual decision makers. Practical experience indicates that certain of these are much more important than others. These would be the managers of the very largest corporations and financial institutions and those who make the decisions for government—particularly federal government—as well as labor union leaders.

Macro and Micro Finance

In economics, the term *macro* applies to the study of the total economic system and *micro* deals with study of individual economic units within a system. Thus, macro finance deals with the over-all financial effects on society and micro finance with financial problems of the individual economic unit. This book is concerned primarily with micro finance. However, the two are closely interrelated. Economic theory assumes that the individual economic units in making their decisions will influence the total economic system. It is important that each individual micro unit act rationally and take a long-run point of view for the total macro system to work. In our society, the long-run profit motives of the micro units lead to the best economic results for the macro society. Thus it is important that business financial management take a profit point of view in its decisions and that these decisions be approached as scientifically and rationally as possible.

If a particular business can make more profit than other businesses, more resources should be channeled in its direction since society is willing to pay more for its service than for the services of other businesses. Highly profitable firms should attract more capital to their operations. It is equally important that the unprofitable firm be willing to give up some of its capital so that it may be invested in a more profitable operation—thereby contributing more of what society desires. To make the macro system work, individual decision makers must be willing to allocate their capital to the place in the economy which provides the highest return consistent with the risk. If the businessman cannot invest his capital at sufficient return in his present operations, he must either move into new fields or give the capital back to its owners so that they can invest it in new fields.

It should be emphasized that this discussion is based on a long-run point of view for decision makers. It is often difficult for business to take actions with the long run in mind. Certain short-run activities can completely defeat the long-run purposes of the business and of society. The long-run point of view is a prerequisite to good business financial management decision making.

QUESTIONS

1. Differentiate public and private finance.
2. What is the interrelationship between public and private finance?
3. Is the financing of publicly owned businesses part of public finance?
4. What is the place of finance in the business unit?

5. Do you believe that more job offerings are available in production or distribution than in finance? If so, how do you account for this?
6. Indicate the importance of accounting in the study of corporate finance.
7. Explain why taxation is of special importance in the study of finance.
8. List and briefly explain the various kinds of laws. Do these same kinds of laws affect you as an individual? Explain.
9. What is the relationship between economic theory and the subject of corporate finance?
10. Define macro finance and micro finance.

SELECTED READINGS

AMERICAN MANAGEMENT ASSOCIATION. *The Financial Executive's Job.* New York: American Management Association, 1952.

BROWN, ALVIN. *Financial Approach to Industrial Operations.* New York: Society for Advancement of Management, 1957.

DAUTEN, CARL A.; SAGAN, JOHN; WESTON, J. FRED; VAN ARSDELL, PAUL M.; HOWARD, BION B.; WILLIAMS, CHARLES M. "Toward a Theory of Business Finance," *Journal of Finance,* May, 1955, pp. 107-51.

DEAN, JOEL. *Managerial Economics.* Englewood Cliffs, N. J.: Prentice-Hall, Inc., 1951.

EELLS, RICHARD. *The Meaning of Modern Business.* New York: The Columbia University Press, 1960.

WESTON, J. FRED. *Readings in Finance From* Fortune. New York: Holt, Rinehart and Winston, Inc., 1958. Section 1.

2

Non-corporate Forms of Business Organizations

This book is concerned mainly with the corporation and corporate finance. In order to have a complete study of the field of business finance, however, it is appropriate to discuss briefly in this chapter the other forms of business organizations. At the beginning of this chapter the extent of the use of the corporate form will be mentioned in order that the relative importance of the various forms of organizations may be understood. Later in the chapter the income tax status of the corporation will be discussed, again in order that a comparison may be made with the other important forms of organizations.

THE INDIVIDUAL PROPRIETORSHIP

The oldest, simplest, and most commonly used form of organization is the *individual proprietorship*. It is sometimes called the *individual enterprise* or *entrepreneurship, sole proprietorship,* or merely, the *proprietorship*. The business is owned, managed, and controlled by a single person. For legal purposes there is really no distinction between the proprietor and the proprietorship.

The individual proprietorship is the most easily formed of the various forms of organizations. If a person starts a business by himself and takes no steps to start another form of organization, the law will say that he has an individual proprietorship. No organization papers need be drawn up, nor are there any organization taxes and fees to be paid.

The federal income tax must always be reckoned with in the formation of any type of organization. In the case of the individual proprietorship the tax laws do not distinguish between the proprietor and the proprietorship. The business income is reported on the individual's income tax form, and this is true regardless of whether any of the income is withdrawn from the business. The example given later in the chapter of the taxation of a general partnership will apply equally to the individual proprietorship.

One of the most important disadvantages of this form of organization from the viewpoint of the proprietor is that of unlimited liability. If the business assets are insufficient to satisfy the firm's creditors, they may proceed against the individual's personal property. Thus, the proprietor subjects all his personal property to the risks of his business. Property which is held in his wife's name, however, cannot be attached, provided the title to such property was not transferred to her in anticipation of action by the creditors.

Although the corporation overshadows the individual proprietorship in terms of wage earners and value of product, nevertheless the individual proprietorship is still the most commonly used form of business organization in the United States. It leads by a wide margin in the professions and in agriculture. Other strongholds of this form of organization are in retailing, service establishments, construction, small trucking concerns, and real estate firms. (See Table 2–1.)

Table 2–1. Sole Proprietorships, Partnerships, and Corporations—Percentage Distribution by Industry Classification

Industry	Sole Proprietorships	Partnerships	Corporations	Total
Agriculture, forestry, and fisheries....	95.7	3.9	0.4	100.0
Construction	82.9	8.6	8.5	100.0
Finance, insurance, and real estate....	47.0	19.5	33.5	100.0
Manufacturing	47.8	12.3	39.9	100.0
Mining	56.7	21.7	21.6	100.0
Services	88.0	7.1	4.9	100.0
Trade—Wholesale and Retail........	75.9	11.5	12.6	100.0
Transportation and utilities..........	82.3	5.2	12.5	100.0
Nature of business not allocable......	63.3	15.2	21.5	100.0
Total	81.9	8.5	9.6	100.0

SOURCE: *Statistical Abstract of the United States* (Washington, D. C.: U. S. Government Printing Office, 1962), p. 488.

THE GENERAL PARTNERSHIP

The *general partnership* may be defined as an association of two or more persons carrying on as co-owners a legal business for profit. It is referred to as a common-law form of organization, although at the present time most of the states have statutes relating to it. In thirty-three of the states the Uniform General Partnership Act has been adopted. These include most of the leading commercial and industrial states. In most of the others, special statutes cover certain phases of partnership activity.

The general partnership is based on a contract between two or more persons. It is advisable that the contract be in writing and signed by the partners, but it may be oral, or even implied. When written articles of partnership are drawn up, adequate provisions relating to the following should be included:

1. Name of the partnership
2. Names of the partners
3. Nature of the business to be conducted
4. Capital contribution of each of the partners
5. Method to be followed in dividing profits and losses
6. Agency powers of the partners
7. Procedure for admitting new partners
8. Procedure for partners' withdrawal from the firm
9. Amount, if any, of salaries, or interest on investment, to be paid to the partners
10. Procedure to be followed, and how assets should be distributed upon dissolution

For business purposes the partnership is looked upon as a firm or company. At law, however, it is not treated as a legal entity. In contrast to the partnership, the corporation is considered a legal entity, with a life separate and apart from that of the individuals who own it.

Agency Power of Partners

In the absence of agreement to the contrary, each partner has full authority to enter into *ordinary business* contracts for the firm. Such contracts bind the other partners just the same as if they had made the contracts themselves. Partners, however, cannot bind their partners on personal contracts. Any agreements in the articles of partnership restricting or limiting the contractual rights of a partner are not effective against innocent third parties such as firm creditors. The other partners, however, have a legal claim against a partner for losses sustained by them as a result of the particular partner's breaking his agreement.

Unless otherwise provided in the articles, each partner has one vote in connection with the internal management of the firm, regardless of the amount of his capital contribution. For *extraordinary* matters, such as taking a new partner, amending the articles, changing the firm name, selling all the assets, etc., unanimous consent of all the partners is necessary.

Partnership Name

Unless the statutes of the state provide otherwise, the partnership may adopt any name it desires. The statutes of some of the states provide that if the firm name does not contain the names of the partners, the partnership must file with the proper county or state officials the name of the firm and the names of the partners.

Some people think, mistakenly, that whenever the word *company* is included in the name of a business, the concern is incorporated. It is true that the various states require that *company, corporation, incorporated,* or their abbreviations appear in a corporate name, but it does not follow that a partnership cannot use the word *company.*

If a business firm, including a partnership, adopts a name which is so similar to that of another firm previously formed that material confusion results, certain legal actions may follow. The first firm to use the name may bring an injunction action to restrain the continued use of the name on the part of the other company, or it may sue for damages or for part of the profits of the newer firm.

Nature of Partners' Liability

One of the principal disadvantages of the partnership form of organization is the liability of the various partners for debts or wrongdoings on the part of their partners or themselves. In an individual proprietorship, the liability of the owner is not limited to the assets of the business. Partners in a general partnership likewise have unlimited liability. But in a partnership this is more severe than in an individual proprietorship, since a partner is not only unlimitedly liable for debts which he himself contracts, but is also liable without limit for those contracted for the firm by his partners. This grows out of the fact that each partner is considered an agent of the firm and can bind it and its partners on all matters concerned with the business.

The liability of a partnership is spoken of as a *joint liability* or *joint and several liability.* In a technical sense, partners are said to be liable *jointly and severally* for torts (wrongdoings) committed by their partners. Thus, if one partner in the course of ordinary business operations injures a person, action may be had against all the partners or any of the partners. In respect to business debts, partners are said to be *jointly* liable. That is, action is brought against all the partners. But having done this and obtained judgment against all the partners, a creditor may proceed to collect against any or all the partners. Thus, in final analysis, this may also result in a *several* liability.

From what has been said, it is evident that a particular partner may lose all his personal property as a result of a partnership debt contracted by one of his partners.

Partners are never liable for the personal debts contracted by their partners. Personal creditors may, however, proceed against the partnership assets to collect a personal debt of one of the partners, but the most they could obtain would be that particular partner's equity in the partnership. According to the court decisions and statutes in some of the states, however, before such creditors could collect from the partnership assets, the firm's creditors would have to be paid.

A partnership creditor could, after having received judgment against the partners, come against either the partnership assets or the personal assets of any or all the partners. A different situation exists when the two classes of creditors file their actions at the same time, or when the business is being dissolved under court authority, or is bankrupt. Then the court will allow the personal creditors prior right against the personal assets of the respective partners, and the firm creditors prior right against the partnership assets. In the event that the creditors are not fully satisfied from such assets they may then proceed against the other class of assets (provided there are any left). This is referred to as the *rule of marshaling of assets*. But, as stated above, the right of personal creditors is limited to the particular partner's equity in the firm assets.

If one partner is unable to stand his pro rata share of a partnership debt or loss, such loss must be borne by the other partners according to their profit-and-loss-sharing ratio. When one partner is forced to stand more than his pro rata share of a loss, he has what is called a *right of contribution* against the other partner or partners for their pro rata share.

Unless otherwise provided, profits and losses are divided equally by the partners. If they so desire, they can provide in the articles of partnership that profits be divided according to capital contribution, or in any other agreed-upon ratio.

The foregoing can perhaps best be understood by an example. Assume that three partners enter into a general partnership and agree to share profits and losses equally. After several years of unsuccessful operation the business is dissolved under court authority. Neither the partnership nor the personal creditors had previously received judgment against the partners. No profits or losses have been divided among the partners. Partnership debts existed in the amount of $6,000. Upon court sale of the partnership property the assets bring only $3,000. The original contributions to the partnership capital, and the personal assets and personal debts of the partners are as follows:

	Adams	*Brown*	*Clark*
Partnership capital	$6,000	$8,000	$10,000
Personal assets	5,000	5,000	15,000
Personal debts	1,000	8,000	1,000

Since this is a dissolution under court authority, with neither class of creditors having prior judgment, the court will allow the partnership creditors first claim against the firm assets, and the personal creditors first claim against the personal assets.

Thus, the $3,000 from the firm assets would be applied toward the partnership debts of $6,000. This leaves a deficiency of $3,000. The personal creditors would then be paid from the personal assets. This would leave Adams $4,000 in assets, Brown would still owe $3,000, and Clark would have assets of $14,000 left.

The next step is to determine the amount of the profit or loss. Since the business started out with a capital of $24,000 and lost all of this and still owed $3,000, the total loss of the business amounted to $27,000. Since the losses are to be borne equally, each of the partners should stand a loss of $9,000. If this could be done then Adams should put in an additional $3,000, Brown should contribute $1,000, and Clark should get back $1,000. Such a settlement would provide the $3,000 to pay the deficiency to the firm creditors. After paying off his personal creditors, Adams has $4,000 left, so he could contribute the $3,000 which he owes. But Brown used all his personal assets and still owes his personal creditors $3,000. Since Adams and Clark stood losses equally, they will have to stand Brown's $1,000 partnership deficiency equally. Thus, Adams will have to contribute an additional $500, and Clark will get back $500 instead of $1,000. The $3,500 collected from Adams will thus pay the firm creditors their $3,000, and Clark will get $500. Adams and Clark will then each have a *right of contribution* against Brown for $500.

If Brown later comes into possession of property the partners could come against him for the amount owed. The personal-deficiency-judgment creditors of Brown, however, would have to be satisfied first before the partners could satisfy their claim.

The above indicates the final settlement. As a practical matter, the firm creditors may have proceeded against Clark for the entire deficiency of $3,000. If this had been done, Clark would have a right against Adams for $3,500, and against Brown for $500. (If Brown had $1,000 in personal property left, Clark would go against him for $1,000 and against Adams for $3,000.)

Sharing of Profits

In the absence of agreement otherwise, profits and losses are shared equally by the partners. Let us assume that after all the business debts were paid the partnership in the above example ended up with $51,000. Since it started out with a capital of $24,000, it follows that the business made a profit of the difference between these two figures, or $27,000.

Unless provision to the contrary was made, this profit would be divided equally among the partners. Thus, each partner would receive a profit of $9,000. Then the original capital investment of the partners would be returned. Thus, settlement would be made as follows:

	Adams	Brown	Clark	Total
Original capital	$ 6,000	$ 8,000	$10,000	$24,000
Share of profits	9,000	9,000	9,000	27,000
Total	$15,000	$17,000	$19,000	$51,000

Status of Partners' Loans to Business

When a partnership is in need of additional money, some or all of the partners may add to their capital contribution, or they may lend money to the firm. Such loans may or may not draw interest, depending upon the agreement. In event of dissolution of the business the firm creditors, sometimes called *outside* creditors, must be paid in full before the partners' loans (called *inside* creditors) are paid. After these business creditors are paid off, the partners' loans must be paid before there can be any distribution of profits or return of capital.

Liability of Outgoing Partners

If a partner withdraws from the business, he retains full liability for all debts existing at the time of his withdrawal. This holds true even if the remaining partners have agreed with him to assume his share of the debts. If such an agreement is made and the withdrawing partner is forced to stand some of the debts, he may have recourse against the other partners. The withdrawing partner can be assured of relief from existing debts only by agreement with the creditors themselves.

May the withdrawing partner be held liable for debts contracted by the partnership after his withdrawal? That all depends. If the proper procedure is not followed the withdrawing partner may be held liable by creditors who thought that he was still a partner. What the withdrawing partner should do is to notify existing creditors, or those with whom the firm has done business in the past, of his withdrawal from the business. But this gives no notice to other persons who have known of his presence in the firm. To take care of these possible future creditors, a public notice of withdrawal should be inserted in a newspaper in general circulation in the community.

Liability of Incoming Partners

According to common law, if a new partner enters an existing partnership he is not liable for the debts that are on the books at the time he comes into the firm. In those states which have adopted the Uniform

General Partnership Act, however, he is liable for existing debts, but the law provides that this liability can be satisfied only from his interest in the partnership. If an incoming partner agrees with the partners to stand a pro rata share of existing debts, then as far as the partners are concerned he could be held to his agreement.

Partnership Lacks Stability

The legal doctrine of *delectus personae* applies to the general partnership. This means that each partner has a right to choose the partners with whom he wishes to engage in business. At common law any change in the personal composition of the partnership will legally terminate it. Thus, the withdrawal of any partner, or the admission of a new partner will legally dissolve the old partnership, although from a practical standpoint a new partnership will begin the next moment. Although the old partnership may be dissolved, the partners, of course, remain liable for the debts owed.

Death, bankruptcy, or insanity of any of the partners will likewise terminate the partnership. The executor, trustee in bankruptcy, or guardian, as the case may be, can compel the remaining partners to account to him for the particular partner's equity in the business. In order to do this it may be necessary to dissolve the firm. It follows from this that the wife of a deceased partner does not step into her husband's shoes as a member of the partnership. However, she could compel the remaining partners to account to her for her husband's interest in the firm.

General partnerships are sometimes formed also for a definite period of time. Where this is the case, the termination of this period would dissolve the partnership. The Uniform General Partnership Act, as adopted in a number of states, provides that the sale by a partner of his interest in a general partnership does not of itself dissolve the partnership. The assignee, however, would not become a partner unless the other partners wanted to admit him to the firm. If not admitted, he has no right to interfere with the management of the partnership nor is he permitted to inspect the books, but he does have the assignor's rights to any profits, and in event of dissolution he is entitled to the assignor's interest.

From what has just been said it is apparent that as a practical matter partners cannot sell their interests to others without the consent of the other partners. This shortcoming causes some people to hesitate to invest money in a general partnership.

Provisions for Stability

Liquidation sometimes results from the death of a partner because of the inability of the remaining partners to buy out his interest. An increasing use is being made of partnership life insurance for this purpose.

Each partner takes out life insurance for an amount up to the value of his interest in the firm. The other partners are made the beneficiaries of the policies. Upon the death of a partner the remaining partners will get the necessary cash to buy out the deceased partner's interest or to pay part or all of the firm's debts, or the proceeds may be used in part for both purposes.

Another arrangement used by many partnerships is the *buy-and-sell agreement*. Each partner agrees in writing that upon his death the remaining partner (assuming two partners) may buy out his interest at a stipulated price. This agreement is properly signed by both partners and each retains a copy. This settles the disposition of the partner's interest in the firm upon his death. Furthermore, it establishes the value of his interest. Partnership life insurance, as described above, may enable the surviving partner to buy the deceased partner's interest from his estate or from his heirs. Another advantage of the buy-and-sell agreement is that the valuation of the partners' interests specified in the agreement is usually accepted as the value of the interest for purposes of the inheritance and federal estate taxes. The provisions of the buy-and-sell agreement will take precedence over any stipulations made in a will.

Taxation of the General Partnership

Like the individual proprietorship, the general partnership does not have to pay any organization tax or any annual franchise tax. In this respect it has an advantage over the corporate form of organization.

At first glance the general partnership might appear to have an advantage over the corporation in respect to the federal income tax. The latter has to pay the corporation income tax, but the general partnership is not subject to this tax. (However, the partnership must file a tax form.) In addition, any dividends paid by the corporation are subject to the personal income tax (after giving effect to the dividend exclusion and credit), in the hands of the recipient stockholder.

In the case of the general partnership each partner anually reports his share of the partnership profits on his personal income tax form, regardless of whether any of the profits are withdrawn from the business. A partner may or may not enjoy an advantage over a stockholder in a corporation, depending upon the particular circumstances.

If practically all the business profits are going to be paid out to the owners every year, from the income tax standpoint the partnership would be preferred over the corporation. If, however, a substantial part of the earnings are going to be retained in the business, the owners of a partnership might find it difficult to secure the necessary amount of cash to pay their income taxes. If the business was incorporated, the earnings for that year would be subject to the corporate income tax and this would, of course, be paid from the corporate earnings. The part not paid out, however, would not be subject to the personal income tax.

Another consideration relates to the size of the individual's income. If an individual's personal income is relatively large for a particular year, his share of the partnership profits would be subject to a higher tax rate than the corporate rate. If the business was incorporated and relatively small so that the particular individuals had control over the dividend policy, they might refrain from paying any dividends in those years in which their personal incomes were large. During these years, then, only the corporate income tax would have to be paid. In those years in which their personal incomes were small, and their incomes subject to the lower tax rates, they could distribute the corporate accumulated earnings to themselves in the form of dividends. The combination of the corporate tax and the personal tax on the dividends might in this case be smaller than what they would have had to pay each year if the business had been formed as a partnership. A word of caution, however, should be injected here. If a corporation retains earnings beyond the reasonable needs of the business, such earnings may be subject to an additional tax.[1]

In most instances, however, particularly in the case of small businesses, the partnership form of organization enjoys a tax advantage over the corporation. Thus, unless there is some other reason why the corporate form should be used, such as to secure limited liability, or to secure capital, etc., it is not recommended.

Partnerships Taxed As Corporations

The Internal Revenue Code of 1954 permits certain partnerships (as well as other non-corporate forms of organizations) to elect to be taxed as corporations. To make such election the business must not have over fifty members, and it must be one in which capital is a material income-producing factor (this would include most manufacturing and mercantile firms), or in which the principal income is derived from brokerage commissions or profits from the sale of commodities, real estate, or securities. This provision of the law would benefit those firms that wish to retain a substantial part of the earnings, and for which the corporate tax rate would be less than the personal tax rate. Subsequent withdrawals of earnings from the business will be subject to the personal income tax the same as corporate dividends. Having elected to be taxed as a corporation, the business cannot switch back to its former tax status unless there is a change in the ownership of 20 per cent or more.

---

[1] In any year in which a corporation retains earnings "beyond the reasonable needs of business," it may be taxed 27½ per cent on the first $100,000 of "unreasonably retained" earnings plus 38½ per cent on any excess over that amount. Up to $100,000 of total accumulated earnings, however, is exempt. Sections 531–537, Revenue Act of 1954, as amended in 1958.

Corporations Taxed As Partnerships

As a relief to "small business," Congress in 1958 enacted legislation which permits certain small corporations to elect to be taxed as partnerships. The following are the principal requirements to qualify under this statute. The corporation must have only one class of stock outstanding and there must be not more than 10 individual shareholders. The corporation's gross receipts from rents, royalties, dividends, interest, annuities, and gains from the sale of securities cannot exceed 20 per cent of its total gross receipts. The consent of all the shareholders is necessary to obtain this tax treatment.

A corporation being taxed as a partnership may elect to be taxed as a corporation in subsequent years if all the shareholders agree to the change. If the election is made in the first month of the taxable year the business will be taxed as a corporation for that particular year, but if the decision is made after the first month, the changed tax status becomes effective at the beginning of the next taxable year.

Taxation of Partnerships and Corporations Compared

A better understanding of the relative tax burdens of partnerships and corporations can perhaps best be gained from an example. We will assume that the partnership has not elected to be taxed as a corporation and that the corporation has not elected to be taxed as a partnership. Although tax rates are changed frequently, we will use definite rates—those applicable for the year 1962. If these rates are changed, the reader can substitute the existing rates.

We will assume that Mr. Adams and Mr. Brown have capital investments in a business of $100,000 and $500,000 respectively. The 1962 net income of the business before owners' salaries and taxes was $70,000. Each owner by agreement is entitled to an annual salary of $5,000. Aside from salaries and business income, Adams had taxable personal income of $5,000, and Brown had $245,000. Each is married and has one dependent child, and takes the "standard deduction" of $1,000. We will assume that their wives have no income, and that each files a joint personal income tax return. We will assume that the owners share profits according to their capital investment. To bring out the desired points, we will assume that in Case A (next page), no business profits are withdrawn by the owners, and that in Case B, all of the available profits are distributed. We will proceed to determine how much in federal income taxes would be paid in Case A and Case B if the business were operated as a general partnership, and as a corporation.

If Business Operated As a Partnership. By agreement each partner takes a salary of $5,000. Subtracting total salaries of $10,000 from the business profits of $70,000 leaves $60,000 profits. Adams is entitled to one-sixth of this, or $10,000, and Brown is entitled to five-sixths, or $50,000. In a general partnership each partner must report his share of the business income on his personal income tax return *regardless of whether it is withdrawn from the business*. Therefore, the taxes paid in Case A and Case B would be the same.

The income tax for each partner would be computed as follows:

	Adams	Brown
Salary	$ 5,000	$ 5,000
Other personal income	5,000	245,000
Share of business profits	10,000	50,000
Adjusted gross income	$20,000	$300,000
Less: Deductions	1,000	1,000
	$19,000	$299,000
Less: Exemptions (3 × $600)	1,800	1,800
Taxable income	$17,200	$297,200
Taxes due on this income	$ 4,328	$221,148

In computing the taxes, if the partnership profits are considered to be the top part of the individual's income, it is found that the highest rate which is applied to Adams' share is 34 per cent, and the highest rate applied to Brown's share is 89 per cent. Considering Case A, when no business profits except salaries are distributed, it might be difficult for Adams to pay personal income taxes of $4,328, when his total cash income was only $10,000. If no salaries were withdrawn, the situation would, of course, be still worse. Since the taxes have already been paid on the partnership income, however, no further taxes would be paid in the future if the partners withdraw some or all of these profits from the business. Thus, taxes on the partnership income are paid only once, at the time the income is earned by the business, and it is a personal income tax only that is paid.

If Business Operated As a Corporation.

Case A: No Dividends Paid

Net corporate income before salaries	$70,000
Less: Salaries	10,000
Taxable net income	$60,000
Taxes on first $25,000 @ 30 per cent	$ 7,500
Taxes on balance of $35,000 @ 52 per cent	18,200
Total corporate taxes	$25,700

After paying the taxes of $25,700, a balance of $34,300 would be retained in the business. No personal tax would be paid on this unless sometime in the future it was distributed as dividends to the owners. The personal tax for Adams would be only $1,504 (computed on an adjusted net income [before deductions and exemptions] of $10,000), and Brown's personal tax would be $176,648 (computed on an adjusted net income of $250,000). But since these two people are the sole owners of the corporation, the corporate tax in effect comes out of their pockets. Since the partners share profits in the ratio of one-sixth and five-sixths, we will assume that the corporate tax burden is felt in this same ratio. Therefore, of the total corporate tax of $25,700, Adams stands $4,283 (to nearest dollar), and Brown stands $21,417. Adding this to the personal tax paid in Case A, the total tax burden would be $5,787 for Adams, and $198,065 for Brown. Comparing this with Case A for the partnership, it is seen that the tax burden for Adams would be more in the case of the corporation, but less for Brown. Again, the point should be stressed that if any of the retained corporate profits are distributed as dividends in the future, such dividends would be subject to the personal income tax.

CASE B: ALL CORPORATE PROFITS (AFTER TAXES) DISTRIBUTED AS DIVIDENDS

	Adams	Brown
Dividends received (⅙ and ⅚ of $34,300)...........	$ 5,717	$ 28,583
Less: Dividend exclusion	50	50
Dividends reported	$ 5,667	$ 28,533
Salary	5,000	5,000
Other personal income	5,000	245,000
Total	$15,667	$278,533
Less: Deductions and exemptions................	2,800	2,800
	$12,867	$275,733
Taxes on this income	2,980	202,043
Less: Dividend credit (4 per cent of reported dividends)	227	1,141
Personal taxes due	$ 2,753	$200,902

In Case B, for the corporation it is obvious that part of the business income is taxed twice. The corporate tax comes out first, and then the remaining part of the income which is paid in dividends, less the dividend exclusion and dividend credit, is subject to the personal income tax. Again since Adams and Brown own the corporation, they feel the effect of the corporate tax. To get the true tax burden we should add their respective shares of the corporate tax and their personal taxes.

	Adams	Brown
Share of corporate tax..............	$4,283	$ 21,417
Personal tax	2,753	200,902
Total tax burden.............	$7,036	$222,319

Comparing this computed tax burden with the amount of taxes that would be paid if the business were operated as a partnership, it is seen that the tax burden for Adams is considerably more when the business is operating as a corporation, and only slightly more for Brown. If it is intended that the business profits should be distributed each year to the owners, the partnership would be the preferred form of organization, *from a tax standpoint.* There may be other reasons, which will be discussed in Chapter 3, why these partners may still prefer the corporate form of organization. If profits are not to be distributed, or only a small portion of them paid out, people in the high tax bracket, such as Brown, might prefer the corporate form of organization in order to escape the high personal taxes that would have to be paid if the business were operated as a partnership. Furthermore, with the corporate form of organization, owners might retain the profits in the business until years in which their other income was small, and then pay themselves dividends— which would be taxed at lower rates because of the smaller total income of the shareholder.

Use of the Partnership Form of Organization

The general partnership, like the individual proprietorship, is often used in the case of retail and wholesale establishments, service businesses, small manufacturing concerns, and the professions. It is used also by many stock brokerage and investment banking firms. The rules of the New York Stock Exchange prior to 1953 provided that memberships could not be held by corporations. A brokerage firm that owned a seat on the Exchange therefore had to use the individual proprietorship form of organization, the general partnership, or the limited partnership.

THE LIMITED PARTNERSHIP

In all businesses that are formed by contract among the members, such as the general partnership, the owners are subject to unlimited liability for the firm's debts. Thus, it can be said that all common-law forms of business organizations (with the possible exception of the Massachusetts trust, discussed later in this chapter) have unlimited liability. The only way a business can secure limited liability is to organize under statutes which specifically provide for it. Almost all of the states have statutes permitting the organization of the limited partnership.

The laws of the particular state must be strictly adhered to in the creation of this form of organization. The usual method of formation is to file articles or certificates of limited partnership with a county official. No organization tax other than filing fees must be paid. There is also no annual franchise tax. For federal income tax purposes it is treated the same as a general partnership.

Nature of the Limited Partnership

Such a partnership must contain one or more *general* partners, who have the ordinary unlimited liability as in a general partnership, and one or more *limited,* or *special,* partners whose liability is limited to their contribution to the firm's capital.

A limited partner is entitled (1) to full information in regard to the business, (2) to inspect the books of the firm, (3) to have the firm dissolved according to the agreement or by court decree, and (4) to a share of the profits or other compensation provided for, and in event of dissolution, to a return of his contribution (after his share, if any, of firm debts are paid).

The limited partner, however, is not permitted to exercise any managerial rights. If he does so, or if he acts as an agent for the firm, or if his name is used in the firm name, or if he allows his name to be used in any way in connection with the business without clearly indicating the nature of his position, he can be held for full unlimited liability.

The statutes of some of the states provide that a certified copy of the certificate must be filed in every county in which the firm has a place of business. Outside the state of formation the limited partnership may be looked upon as a general partnership unless it files its certificate in the manner provided by the statutes of that state.

In the event of dissolution the limited partner is generally entitled to his profits and return of his contribution before the other general partners receive anything. The death, insanity, or withdrawal of a general partner will dissolve the firm unless the surviving general partners continue it according to the original agreement, or consent to continuing it.

Limited Partner's Interest Is Assignable

The interest of a limited partner may be assigned without disrupting the life of the firm. Unless otherwise provided, however, the assignee would not have the right to business information, or to inspect the books, but he would have the assignor's right to profits and to his proper share of the contribution upon dissolution. However, if the certificate so provides, or if all the remaining partners agree, the assignee will be a substituted limited partner with all the rights, powers, restrictions, and liabilities of the assignor. The assignor, however, would remain liable for any share of debts for which he was liable, within the limits of his contribution.

Death of the limited partner does not terminate the business. The legal representative of the deceased limited partner would have all of the latter's rights for the purpose of settling the estate, together with such power as the deceased had to make his assignee a substitute limited partner.

Use of the Limited Partnership

The limited partnership fits the situation where a person wishes to have an interest in a partnership without the unlimited liability. This might be an aging general partner who wishes to retire from active participation. Or it might be a wealthy person who does not want to subject his personal fortune to the risks of a general partnership. In some instances the widow of a deceased general partner would be acceptable as a limited partner, but not as a general one.

THE PARTNERSHIP ASSOCIATION

The partnership association, which is also called the "limited partnership association," is formed in a manner similar to that of the limited partnership. Articles, signed by at least three persons, are filed in the county in which the business is organized, and only filing fees must be paid. Only four states—Michigan, New Jersey, Ohio, and Pennsylvania—authorize its formation. In Ohio, the organization's life cannot exceed twenty years, and it can be formed for any purpose except banking or dealing in real estate. Under the federal income tax laws it is taxed the same as a corporation.

The interest of each owner is represented by shares. These shares are transferable only with the consent of the members. If a person buys the shares of one of the members, he must be elected to membership by a majority of the members in number and value of their shares, before he is recognized as a member. If he should not be acceptable to the others, the organization would be compelled to buy his shares.

Management of the company is vested in a board of managers or directors elected by the members. The board of managers may elect officers to carry out the policies set by them. Debts may be contracted only by one or more of the managers. Any contract involving a liability exceeding $500 must be in writing and signed by at least two managers in order to bind the firm; otherwise only the contracting manager is liable for the debt.

All the partners, or shareholders, in the partnership association have *limited* liability. That means that after they have paid for their shares in full, they will not be liable to firm creditors for any additional amount. In this respect the association is similar to the corporation. The statutes of some of the states prescribe that the word "Limited" appear in the title of the firm.

Outside the state of its formation, the organization is usually looked upon as a general partnership. In some states, however, if it registers like a foreign corporation and pays similar taxes, the limited-liability feature will be respected.

This form of organization is one that the student will encounter more frequently in textbooks than in actual business practice. The possibility of unlimited liability because of failure to conform to some provision of the law, or of operation outside the state of its formation, restricts its use. Furthermore, there have been very few court decisions to test the statutes relating to it.

THE MINING PARTNERSHIP

The partners in a mining partnership are "tenants in common" in respect to the business property, and partners with respect to the profits. It follows from this that one partner could sell his interest in the property without the consent of the others. The transfer of a partnership interest or the death or bankruptcy of a partner does not terminate the business. In some instances the property is owned by only one of the persons, but the working of the property is carried on by the mining partnership.

The partners do not have the general agency possessed by members of a general partnership. In many instances only one of the partners acts as manager. He (or they) has only the authority that is given to him, or is customary in the business. The other partners are liable for any debts properly contracted by the manager.

As would be expected, the common law on these partnerships has evolved in those states where mining and oil developments have been carried on. In some of the western states, including Idaho, Montana, and Nevada, statutes relating to the mining partnership have been enacted.

THE JOINT VENTURE

This type of partnership is formed to carry on a single or temporary undertaking. It is often called the "joint adventure," and in some instances is spoken of as a "syndicate," or "deal." Today it is perhaps most commonly used, in a special form, in connection with the underwriting and sale of securities from the issuing corporation to the public.[2]

The legal nature of this form of organization can best be described by contrasting it with the general partnership. The duration of the joint venture is limited to the period stated in the agreement. The various owners, or partners, give up their general agency power, and concen-

[2] See Chapter 14 for a discussion of syndicates.

trate the management of the undertaking in an elected manager. The latter is paid a salary or commission and the remaining profits are distributed to the owners according to their agreement. The owners possess the unlimited liability of a general partnership, but, of course, the severity of this is lessened by the fact that the partners do not have general agency power to bind the other members.

THE JOINT STOCK COMPANY

In England the business corporation grew out of the old joint stock companies. Although the joint stock companies were of some importance in the United States during colonial times, by the time there was need for a form of organization to carry on large-scale business, we had laws permitting the formation of corporations. A classic example of the joint stock company in the United States is the Adams Express Company, which is no longer engaged in the express business, but is now an investment company, sometimes called "investment trust." [3] Nevertheless, it is still operating under the joint stock company form of organization.

The joint stock company is really a type of partnership. Like the general partnership, it is a common-law form of organization. It is created by agreement among the members or owners. Ownership in a joint stock company is represented by shares of stock. By agreement among the members, these shares are made freely transferable. Any purchaser of the shares is accepted as a member. The owners, by their agreement, give up their agency powers, and concentrate the management of the company in an elected board of managers or directors. The latter have the right to appoint the executive officers to carry out their policies. This free transferability of the shares and the restriction on the agency power of the owners enable the company to secure more capital than could be obtained by the general partnership. Thus, the shares are similar to corporate stock. The joint stock company has continuous life like a corporation, unless the agreement limits it.

One shortcoming of the general partnership is present in the joint stock company—*unlimited liability*. Due to the restriction on the agency power of the owners, however, this does not constitute such a serious drawback as is the case with the general partnership. The shareholder's liability applies to those debts which were contracted while he was a member.

The joint stock company does not have to pay an organization tax, and in most states it is not subject to an annual franchise tax. It follows from this that it may go into most of the states without paying any taxes except those which must be paid by individuals. However, in some of the states,

[3] See Chapter 16 for a discussion of investment companies.

such as New York, it is required to pay the same annual franchise tax as a corporation. The joint stock company must pay the same federal income tax as a corporation. Thus, it is subject to one of the most important disadvantages of the corporation. But it lacks the very important advantage of the corporation—limited liability. This accounts for the fact that the joint stock company is not an important form of business organization in the United States today.

TYPES OF TRUST ARRANGEMENTS

A *trust* is a legal device whereby a person, or persons, called the *creator, trustor,* or *grantor,* turns over property in trust to a *trustee* or *trustees* (commonly a bank or trust company) to be held and managed by them for the benefit of the *beneficiaries* (also called the *cestui que trust,* or *cestuis que trustent*). The creator and beneficiary may be the same party.

Trusts, except those established for charitable purposes and for certain types of pension plans, cannot be made perpetual. The statutes of the various states prescribe the maximum duration and the procedure to be followed to renew the trust. In most states the trust is limited in duration to "lives in being plus twenty-one years and nine months." This means that the life of a trust can extend over a period of twenty-one years and nine months after the death of persons named in the trust agreement at the time of its creation. There are various types of trusts set up for many different purposes.

Living Trust

When a person during his lifetime turns over property to trustees to be administered for a specified time and then given back to the person creating the trust, or to another designated beneficiary, the arrangement is called a *living trust.* This may be set up by an actor or actress, or a prize-fighter, whose earnings may fluctuate greatly or may even cease entirely. In some instances people who have an appreciable amount of money and are too busy to manage their investments set up this kind of trust.

Testamentary Trust

The *testamentary trust* is one which is provided for by a person in his will and which becomes effective upon his death. In some instances, it is provided that the income from the trust investments shall go to one person for his lifetime, called the *life tenant,* and upon his death the property will go to another person, called the *remainderman.*

Investment Trust

An *investment trust* is a type of company which invests its money in stocks or bonds, or both, of other companies. It will be discussed in Chapter 16.

Voting Trust

In order to secure continuity of management for a designated period of time, a corporation may deposit part or all of its stock with a trust company, and sell instead *voting trust certificates* to the public. This type of arrangement is called a *voting trust*. This is often used by a reorganized company which desires to continue a particular management until the company has had opportunity to get back on its feet.

The trustees vote the corporate stock and receive any dividends paid on it. Such dividends are then redistributed to the holders of the certificates. The voting trust certificates are freely transferable in the market, but of course such transfer does not affect the voting right of the corporate stock which is held by the trustees. Upon termination of the trust, the voting trust certificates are taken up and the corporate stock is given to the certificate holders.

Combinations Formed by Trust Device

In the latter part of the last century some combinations, such as the Standard Oil Trust, were effected through the use of the trust device, by having the shareholders of a number of companies turn their stock over to a group of trustees and receive, in return, trust certificates. The trustees holding the controlling stock in the various companies controlled the election of directors and thus the policies of the various companies. This was really a type of voting trust, but the latter term is usually used where the stock of only one corporation is held, as was described above.

This type of arrangement was not looked upon with favor by the courts. The purpose of the combination was to control the operations of separate, competing concerns. By holding the dominating interest in these companies, the trustees could restrict output, limit territories, set prices, etc. The common law would not allow the enforcement of agreements which were in restraint of trade, and the statutes of many of the states declared them illegal. Finally the federal government, by the enactment of the Sherman Anti-Trust Act of 1890, made such combinations illegal.

Because of the early use of the voting trust arrangement to effect a combination in restraint of trade, the early monopolies came to be known as "trusts." Even today many people, including writers, use the terms *trust* and *monopoly* interchangeably. When we talk about antitrust legislation, what we really mean is "antimonopoly" legislation.

THE MASSACHUSETTS TRUST

The Massachusetts trust is created by the application of trust principles to a business undertaking. Instead of this title, it is sometimes referred to by the following names: *business trust, common-law trust,* and *business association formed under a deed of trust.*

Until 1912, the laws of Massachusetts prohibited the corporation from holding real estate for investment purposes. Thus, people wishing to engage in this form of business could not secure limited liability. To do so the lawyers thereupon created a form of business organization based on the trust principle.

Formation of the Massachusetts Trust

Like any other, this trust is formed by drawing up a deed or declaration of trust which places legal title to the property in a board of trustees. This is a purely voluntary agreement, although in Massachusetts it must be filed with the state. The owners of the business, the beneficiaries, receive transferable trust certificates. These are sometimes called "certificates of beneficial interest," or merely "shares." For all practical purposes, they are looked upon in about the same way as shares of stock in a corporation. By the terms of the agreement, subsequent share purchasers become parties to the agreement, the same as the original owners.

The management of the business is placed in the hands of the board of trustees, who can appoint officers to carry out the policies set by them. In practical analysis the trustees run the business in the same way as the board of directors operate a corporation.

The life of the firm is stated in the trust agreement. It cannot be made perpetual.

Liability of the Shareholders

An important consideration in connection with the Massachusetts trust is the liability of the beneficiaries, or in other words, the shareholders. Regarding this, a flat statement cannot be made which would hold good in all the states, but the following would be applicable to Massachusetts and some of the other states.

If the trust is properly set up, and if the trustees are the real managers of the business and cannot be removed during their terms of office, except for cause, the courts will say that the shareholders have limited liability— the same as shareholders in a corporation. The agreement should state that neither the trustees nor the beneficiaries shall have any personal liability for legitimate business debts, and that a statement to this effect should be made by the trustees in all contracts made by the business.

When the trustees are appointed for life, or for the duration of the trust, the courts are more likely to say that the shareholders have limited liability than when they are elected annually by the shareholders. Even when the trustees are elected at stated intervals, the shareholders may be able to secure limited liability by stipulations in the firm contracts referred to above, saying that the creditors can look only to the firm's assets for the satisfaction of their claims. In some of the states the shareholders will have unlimited liability regardless of how the organization is operated.

Some states look upon the Massachusetts trust as a general partnership and thus say that the shareholders' liability is unlimited. Others recognize its status as a true trust, as in the case of Massachusetts. Some treat it as a corporation, which would mean that it would have to register in the state the same as corporations. Some states appear to ignore the Massachusetts trust or at least do not give it any status.

Taxation

Massachusetts imposes an annual tax on the shares of trusts. In this state they also have to pay filing fees for their trust deeds in all cities in which they transact business. New York requires the Massachusetts trust to pay the same annual franchise tax that is paid by corporations. In states having income taxes it is usually taxed the same as a corporation. Some states require the trust formed in other states to pay the same foreign taxes as are required of corporations. The Massachusetts trust is required to pay the same federal income tax as is paid by a corporation.

Use of the Massachusetts Trust

In Massachusetts a number of public utility holding companies make use of the trust. There is a specific reason for this. According to the statutes of the Commonwealth, any public utility will be dissolved if a foreign corporation (one formed outside the state) which controls a majority of the utility's stock issues securities based upon this stock. To prevent the utility's stock from falling into the hands of such a foreign corporation, the stock is held by a Massachusetts trust formed for that purpose.

Some of the investment trusts or companies organized in Massachusetts use the Massachusetts trust structure. These are fairly certain of their status as trusts within the state, and they do not have to operate outside it. The taxes they pay are less than they would be if the companies were incorporated. Furthermore, they need not have annual meetings, which are required of corporations.

QUESTIONS

1. What are the different names that may be applied to the individual proprietorship?
2. May the word *company* be included in the name of a general partnership? Is there any reason why it should not be used? Explain.

3. Explain in detail the nature of the liability of partners in a general partnership.
4. Explain the nature of the liability of incoming and outgoing partners in a general partnership.
5. Indicate the possible advantages and disadvantages of two partners' having a "buy and sell" agreement with each other to become effective upon their deaths.
6. How are partners in a general partnership taxed under the federal income tax laws? From the tax angle, indicate when you would recommend the partnership form of organization, and when the corporation.
7. Indicate the circumstances under which a partnership may be taxed as a corporation, and when the corporation may be taxed as a partnership.
8. Indicate specifically how the income of the various forms of organizations (other than the general partnership) discussed in this chapter is taxed under the federal income tax laws.
9. Indicate the factors which might determine which of the forms of organizations discussed in this chapter would be used in a particular instance.
10. Distinguish between the limited partnership and the partnership association.
11. Indicate the nature of the liability of partners in a limited partnership and a partnership association in states other than the state of their formation.
12. Indicate the circumstances under which you would recommend the limited partnership.
13. Indicate the nature of the agency powers of partners in the general partnership, the limited partnership, and the partnership association.
14. Contrast the mining partnership with the general partnership.
15. Contrast the joint venture with the general partnership.
16. Contrast the joint stock company with the general partnership.
17. Do you think that the joint stock company is more similar to a general partnership or to a corporation? Explain.
18. Can a business trust have perpetual life? A charitable trust?
19. What is meant by a "testamentary trust"?
20. Indicate the nature of the agency powers and liability of shareholders of a Massachusetts trust.

PROBLEMS

1. Abbott, Becker, and Calhoun invested $8,000, $10,000, and $12,000 respectively, in a business enterprise. After several years of unsuccessful operation, the firm was forced to quit business. At the time of dissolution the liquidation value of the assets was only $8,000, whereas business creditors' claims amounted to $11,000. The firm members had personal property and personal debts of the following amounts:

	Abbott	Becker	Calhoun
Personal property	$15,000	$7,000	$20,000
Personal debts	0	8,000	5,000

The firm's creditors and the personal creditors filed their actions at the same time. There was no agreement made among the parties for the division of profits and losses and none had been distributed. Indicate how final settlement would be made if the business had been operated as a general partnership.

2. Allen and Burns have been in general partnership for the past five years. Burns sells out his interest to Clay for $5,000, and the business continues with

Allen and Clay as general partners. Indicate the nature of the liability, if any, of both Burns and Clay for debts existing at the time of the transfer of interest and for debts contracted after the transfer.

3. Mr. Davis and Mr. Williams invested $200,000 and $600,000 respectively in a business. The net profit of the business for the current year before partners' salaries and federal income taxes was $100,000. Each draws an annual salary of $10,000 from the business. Aside from salaries and business profits, Mr. Davis had personal income for the year of $10,000, and Mr. Williams had personal income of $200,000. Each of the owners had a wife who had no income and one dependent child. Assume that each took the "standard deduction" and filed a joint income tax return. The net profits of the business after salaries and taxes are shared by the owners according to their capital contributions. Assume in Case A that no business profits are distributed to the owners, and in Case B that all of the profits after taxes are distributed. Assume the tax laws and rates to be those for the current year. (a) Compute the amount of the personal income taxes that will be paid by Mr. Davis and Mr. Williams in both Case A and Case B, if the business is operated as a general partnership. (b) Compute the amount of the federal corporate income tax and the personal tax that will be paid by Mr. Davis and Mr. Williams in both Case A and Case B, if the business is operated as a corporation. (c) From a tax viewpoint, which of the two forms of organizations stated above would you recommend to Mr. Davis and to Mr. Williams? Explain.

4. Indicate how final settlement would be made if the business in Problem 1 was a: (a) Limited partnership with Abbott being the limited partner, (b) Limited partnership association, (c) Joint stock company, (d) Massachusetts trust.

5. The Massachusetts Investors Trust and the Adams Express Company are both investment companies. Look up these companies in the financial manuals, such as Moody's or Standard & Poor's, and report the following in regard to the companies: (a) Legal nature of the form of organization, (b) Possible reason for the adoption of the form of organization, (c) Name of the policy-making body in each company, (d) Titles of the leading executive officers of each company.

SELECTED READINGS

BOGEN, JULES I. (ed.). *Financial Handbook,* 3d ed. New York: The Ronald Press Co., 1952. Section 9.

CRANE, J. A. *Handbook of the Law of Partnership and Other Unincorporated Associations,* 2d ed. St. Paul: West Publishing Co., 1952.

DICKERSON, WILLIAM E., and STONE, LEO D. *Federal Income Tax Fundamentals.* San Francisco: Wadsworth Publishing Co., Inc., 1961. Chapters 15, 17, 18.

DORIS, LILLIAN (ed.). *Business Finance Handbook.* Englewood Cliffs, N. J.: Prentice-Hall, Inc., 1953. Chapter 23.

GUILD, ALDEN. *Professional-Partnership Purchase Plans.* Montpelier, Vt.: National Life Insurance Co., 1961.

J. K. Lasser's *Your Income Tax.* New York: Simon and Schuster, published annually.

ROHRLICH, CHESTER. *Organizing Corporate and other Business Enterprises,* 3d ed. Albany, N. Y.: Matthew Bender & Co., Inc., 1958.

ROWLEY, REED. *Rowley on Partnership,* Vol. I. Indianapolis: The Bobbs-Merrill Co., Inc., 1960.

ROWLEY, REED, and SIVE, DAVID. *Rowley on Partnership,* Vol. 2. Indianapolis: The Bobbs-Merrill Co., Inc., 1960.

3

The Corporation

The problems of the individual proprietorship and the partnership are comparatively simple; merely starting in business results in their formation. Most of their capital must be supplied by the owner or owners, who are few in number. In contrast, the corporation is a relatively complex form of organization. The raising of capital for large corporations calls for the sale of various types of stocks and bonds. Complicated problems arise in connection with its financial management, expansion, consolidation, and reorganization.

HISTORY

Today we think of the corporation as being a large private business undertaking with many stockholders. But this concept is a rather recent development. Authorities disagree as to whether the corporation can exist before it is created by a sovereign power. If we assume that a group of people acting together as a corporate body creates a corporation, then we could say that corporations existed at the time of the Roman Empire. These, however, were not private business undertakings. They were the religious societies, military groups, trade groups, and towns. Later, in England, such groups acted as corporate bodies. No stock was issued.

If we assume that the corporation must be created by a sovereign power, we would recognize the churches and monasteries, which were formed by the pope, as being the first corporations. The counterpart in civil life was the granting of royal charters by the king in England. These were first granted to ecclesiastical bodies, municipalities, and trade guilds, and later to the large trading and colonizing companies.

Development of General Incorporating Laws

Until about the middle of the nineteenth century the large business undertakings, such as the trading companies, were formed as joint stock companies. In some instances they received royal charters. But the king used his right to form corporations very sparingly, and people started applying to Parliament for special charters. Then in 1844, Parliament enacted the Joint Stock Companies Registration Act, commonly called the "Companies Act of 1844." This was a statutory body of law providing for the incorporation of companies, and started the general incorporating laws of England. This Act did not provide for limitation of liability. In 1855, however, an amendment was made which provided for limited liability if it was so stated in the deed of settlement (charter), and provided that the name of such organization should contain the word "Limited."

Corporation Laws in the United States

Prior to the Revolutionary War there were few corporations in the colonies. Those that were here were formed either by royal charter or by special charter from Parliament. After our independence the state legislatures started granting special charters. This was a slow method and in many instances became the subject of political patronage.

The next step was the enactment by the state legislature of a body of law providing for the incorporation of companies under a standard code. It was no longer necessary for the legislature to act separately on each application for incorporation. The first general incorporation act (although limited in its application) in the United States was enacted by New York in 1811. This act antedated the first English general incorporating law by thirty-three years.

The United States incorporation law is different from that in England. In England only one corporation act exists, but here we have separate laws for each of the various states. This makes the study of corporation law in the United States confusing and difficult. Since the federal government has only the powers granted to it in the Constitution, it can form corporations only to carry out these powers. Thus it is the states and not the federal government that have the right to form railroad, public utility, and ordinary business corporations. In recent years the federal government has been exerting an increasing influence over corporations through its powers to tax and to regulate interstate commerce and through its war powers; and there has been some agitation for the federal government to either charter or license corporations which are engaged in interstate commerce.

TYPES OF CORPORATIONS

Most of us are aware of different types of corporations, but if we attempted to classify them we might encounter difficulty. This results in part from the fact that there are different ways of grouping them. Various methods of classification are:

1. *According to who forms them:*
   a. Public—formed by government
   b. Private—formed by private persons
2. *According to profit:*
   a. Profit
   b. Non-profit
3. *According to stock:*
   a. Stock
   b. Non-stock
4. *According to field of enterprise:*
   a. Ordinary business corporations—manufacturing, merchandising, trading, commercial, services, etc.
   b. Public utilities—electric, gas, water, communications, etc.
   c. Railroads
   d. Financial
5. *According to operations:*
   a. Operating company
   b. Holding company
   c. Combined operating and holding
6. *According to where incorporated:*
   a. Domestic—formed in the state
   b. Foreign—formed outside the state

Figure 3–1 illustrates a detailed classification of the various types.

Public and Private Corporations

Public corporations are those formed by the government. These include cities and incorporated towns and villages, municipal water or electric companies, and those formed by the federal government, such as the Federal Deposit Insurance Corporation. The activities of public corporations, particularly those created by the federal government, are increasing in importance, but in a book of this kind they are usually not discussed.

Private corporations are formed by individuals rather than by government. The words "publicly owned" and "privately owned" are sometimes given a different connotation when used in connection with cor-

CLASSIFICATION OF CORPORATIONS

I. PRIVATE

1. With capital stock (Profit)
- a. Manufacturing
- b. Merchandising or trading
- c. Extractive—mining, quarrying, oil, timber
- d. Agricultural
- e. Construction
- f. Personal services—advertising, consulting, etc.
- g. General services — hotels, cleaners, amusements, etc.
- h. Real estate
- i. Financial — banking, insurance, investment, securities
- j. Public utilities — electric, gas, water, transportation, communications
- k. Holding companies
- l. Miscellaneous

2. With or without capital stock
- a. Mutual companies
- b. Co-operatives

3. Without capital stock (Non-profit)
- a. Educational
- b. Religious
- c. Social
- d. Charitable
- e. Trade associations

II. PUBLIC

1. Municipal
Incorporated cities and towns

2. Government-owned water and power companies, Tennessee Valley Authority, etc. (Some public corporations issue stock.)

Fig. 3–1. The classification of corporations.

porations. Some people would refer to a corporation whose stock is closely held by a few persons (a close corporation), such as the Rand Corporation, as a *privately owned* corporation, and such companies as the General Motors Corporation, whose stock is widely held, as a *publicly owned* corporation.

Profit and Stock

Corporations which are formed for the purpose of making a profit practically always issue stock, and non-profit corporations commonly do not issue stock. We will discuss in this book only the stock-issuing corporation which is formed for profit.

Ordinary Business Corporations

In our first outline, in Chapter 1, profit corporations which issue stock were grouped into four classes—railroads, public utilities, financials, and industrials, or ordinary business corporations. The latter is a large group into which belong all the business corporations that do not fall into one of the other three classes.

Most of our discussion will apply to all of these four types of corporations, but the emphasis will be on the ordinary business corporation, such as a manufacturing, merchandising, trading, commercial, or mining company. The states have special laws which apply to public utilities, railroads, and financial institutions, and it is not our purpose in this book to go into details about these laws.

ATTRIBUTES OF THE CORPORATION

A *corporation* is an artificial, or legalistic, person chartered by the state to perform the purposes stated in its charter. The definition most commonly cited in books is the one written by Chief Justice John Marshall in the famous *Dartmouth College* case in 1819, as follows:

A corporation is an artificial being, invisible, intangible, and existing only in contemplation of the law. Being the mere creature of law, it possesses only those properties which the charter of its creation confers upon it, either expressly, or as incidental to its very existence. These are such as are supposed best calculated to effect the object for which it was created. Among the most important are immortality, and, if the expression may be allowed, individuality; properties, by which a perpetual succession of many persons are considered as the same, and may act as a single individual. They enable a corporation to manage its own affairs, and to hold property without the perplexing intricacies, the hazardous and endless necessity, of perpetual conveyances for the purpose of transmitting it from hand to hand. It is chiefly for the purpose of clothing bodies of men, in succession, with these qualities and capacities, that corporations were invented, and are in use. By these means, a perpetual succession of individuals are capable of acting for the promotion of the particular object, like one immortal being.[1]

[1] The Trustees of Dartmouth College v. Woodward, 4 Wheat. 518, 636 (1819).

Legal Entity

As we can see from this quotation, the corporation itself is looked upon as a legal being, or *legal entity*, which has an existence and life separate and apart from that of the individuals who own it. Property is held in the corporate name, and suit is brought by and against the corporation. It can even sue its members, and its members can also sue the corporation. Death of a stockholder, or of all the stockholders, does not have any legal effect on the life of the corporation.

Permanent Life

We have already noted that at common law the death, bankruptcy, insanity, or withdrawal of a partner from a general partnership terminates the life of the organization. None of these things affects the life of the corporation. In most states such life is perpetual, or is made so in the charter. All the stockholders could die or transfer their stock to others, and still the life of the corporation would go on. This permanency of life is of considerable advantage to a business organization. Contracts may be made for the next hundred years or so, and bonds are issued which in some instances do not mature for several centuries. From a practical standpoint, however, it is realized that despite the permanency of life given by law, a corporation may terminate within a short time after its organization due to financial difficulties.

Transferability of Shares

Corporate shareholders can sell their shares to anyone at any time without affecting the life of the organization. No consent to the transfer is necessary. Any lawful owner of the shares is recognized as a stockholder in the corporation. This is in considerable contrast to the transfer of a person's interest in a general partnership.

Limited Liability

One of the most important features of the corporation is *limited liability* for owners. By this is meant that after the purchaser has paid the full par value, or stated value in the case of no-par stock, for his shares, he cannot be held liable for any further amount either to the corporation or to its creditors. Once this amount has been paid in to the issuing corporation, a subsequent purchaser would not be liable on the stock regardless of what he paid for it. The limited liability feature is further discussed in Chapter 5.

The corporation is the only type of organization that offers limited liability to all its members in all the states. The law on this point is clear and well understood. It would be inconceivable to even think of business organizations of the size we find in the United States today if it were not for this liability benefit. A single enterprise can collect billions of dollars from people all over the world. It would be impossible to get this amount of capital from such distances if the organization could not give its owners limited liability. Buyers know that they can lose all they put into corporate stock, but they also know that neither the corporation nor its creditors can take action against them, regardless of the financial condition of the company. This knowledge results in a more receptive mind toward the purchase of stocks.

Representative Management

Each partner in a general partnership has general agency powers to bind all the other partners on all regular matters of business. People would hesitate to enter a business firm which was composed of many owners who could render them liable for any business debts contracted. By making corporate stock subject to limited liability, part of the disadvantage of investing money in a business in which debts can be contracted by others was removed. But corporations on the average have more owners than do partnerships. It would be an impossible situation if each of several hundred thousand stockholders in a corporation had the power to contract debts for the organization—even though the shareholders did have limited liability.

Representative management is a necessity for large corporations. According to the statutes, stockholders do not have any agency powers to contract for the company. They, however, do have the right to elect a board of directors to whom management is delegated. The directors in turn are given the right to appoint officers to carry out the policies adopted by them.

In many instances a particular class of stock, such as preferred stock, may be deprived even of the right to elect directors. Even where all the stock is voting, the average stockholder's vote in the large corporation means little or nothing because of the huge number of shares that are outstanding.

SELECTING STATE OF INCORPORATION

A corporation is usually organized in the state in which it operates. This is particularly true if all the business is to be carried on in that state. If incorporated in another state, the corporation would have to pay taxes and fees in that state, and would also have to pay a foreign corporation tax in the state in which it operated. The foreign tax might be as much as the taxes it would have to pay if incorporated there in the first place.

When the company is going to operate in a number of states, or when its nature is such that it could locate in one state about as well as another (which would be the situation in the case of a holding company or investment company), then it would be advantageous to compare the laws and select the state that would best serve its purposes. Following are some of the factors that would be considered.

State Taxes

In many instances the amount of taxes due determines the state selected. The most important taxes and their effects are described in the sections that follow.

Incorporation Tax. All the states require a corporation to pay an incorporation tax at the time of organization. In most of the states the amount of the tax varies according to the amount of the authorized capital stock. In Arizona all corporations pay a flat filing fee of $25, but the publication and other fees run the total cost up to approximately $95, regardless of the size of the corporation. In a number of the states the tax is one-tenth of one per cent of the capital stock; in some it is ten cents per share. In the case of no-par stock, some states consider it to have a par value of $100 per share for tax purposes, and in other states it is taxed a specified amount per share. In some instances the tax for a no-par stock is less than that paid for a $100 par share. In most of the leading incorporating states the tax per share is gradually reduced on the higher brackets of capitalization. The minimum incorporation tax in the various states ranges from $5 to $50. (In addition there are usually filing fees.)

In Delaware, which is one of the leading incorporating states, the organization tax is as follows:

A. For par stock corporations

Tax per $100 of par	Capitalization
1¢	Up to $2,000,000
½¢	Over $2,000,000 to $20,000,000
⅕¢	Over $20,000,000

B. For no-par stock corporations

Tax per share	Capitalization (shares)
½¢	Up to 20,000
¼¢	20,001 to 2,000,000
⅕¢	Over 2,000,000

The tax rates stated above, for both the par and no-par stock, apply to the shares within the given bracket. In other words, a corporation capitalizing with 100,000 no-par shares would pay a tax of ½¢ per share on the first 20,000 shares, and ¼¢ per share on the remaining 80,000 shares. The minimum tax in Delaware is $10 and the filing fees approximate $25.

Aside from a few states, such as Arizona, the leading incorporating states of Delaware, Maryland, and New Jersey have lower organization taxes than other states, particularly for the larger corporations. Small filing fees must also be paid.

Although the amount of the tax may be considerable, particularly for large corporations, percentagewise it is not a heavy burden. Also, it is paid only once, unless the authorized capital stock is increased. For this reason, the other taxes are of more importance.

Annual Franchise Tax. In a few states, including the Dakotas and Nevada, there is no annual franchise tax although they have small filing fees. The rest of the states have either this tax or an annual income tax, or both.

The annual franchise tax is usually based on the authorized capital stock, the issued capital stock, or the book value of the stock. In some states the tax is based only on that part of the capital stock which is employed in the state, as measured by the proportion of its property located there, and of its business transacted within the state.

The annual franchise tax in Delaware is based on the authorized stock capitalization, and is as follows:

Total Tax	Authorized Shares
$5.50	250 or less
$11.00	251 to 1,000
$22.00	1,001 to 3,000
$27.50	3,001 to 5,000
$55.00	5,001 to 10,000
$27.50	For each additional 10,000 or fraction thereof

The minimum annual tax in Delaware is $5.50, and the maximum is $50,000. There is also an annual filing fee of $5.00. In addition to the franchise tax, there is an income tax of 5 per cent of taxable income from business carried on and property located in Delaware. Of the states having franchise taxes, the leading incorporating states of Delaware, Maryland, and New Jersey are among those having the lowest taxes. In Pennsylvania, which has the highest, the tax is $5 for each $1,000 of capitalization. This, however, is based on only the amount of the stock represented by the assets which are employed in the state. In addition, Pennsylvania has a 6 per cent tax on the corporate income which is allocated to Pennsylvania. The minimum annual franchise fee varies among the states from $5 to $50.

State Income Tax. Thirty-six of the states levy a corporate tax measured by income. In six of these, however, including New York, the tax is in the nature of a franchise fee for the privilege of doing business in the state. In some of the states the tax is based only on the business done within the state. The tax rate usually varies from 2 to 8 per cent, with 4 per cent being common.

Property Taxes. The amount of the real and personal property taxes varies among states, and among counties and towns. A company may locate its place of business in a certain state for lower property taxes. It may then incorporate in that state.

Where personal property tax rates vary according to city or county, companies with large holdings of personal property, such as holding companies, will often establish their "principal office" in a small town in order to lessen their taxes. Thus the Standard Oil Company (New Jersey), for example, maintains its principal office in Flemington, New Jersey, rather than Newark or Jersey City.

Restrictions Imposed by Laws

Where a choice of incorporating states is possible, promoters also consider a number of other factors in selecting the state in which to incorporate. In general they consider the various restrictions which are placed on the formation and operation of the corporation. Other things being equal, they will favor the states which have liberal business laws. Such factors include:

1. Qualifications of incorporators and directors
2. Nature of the liability of stockholders, directors, and officers
3. Whether no-par stock, non-voting stock, or classified stock is permitted
4. Restrictions, if any, on the amount of bonds that can be issued
5. Whether stockholders' and directors' meetings must be held within the state
6. Relative ease of amending the charter
7. Purposes for which a corporation may be formed

Whether Statutes Have Been Tested

Some states have lenient corporation laws, but promoters hesitate to incorporate in these states, because there have been too few court decisions in the jurisdiction to interpret or test the laws. They prefer a state with a long record of decisions.

Some states by their statutes and court decisions have shown that they want to favor or encourage the formation of corporations and the carrying-on of business. The industrialized states are generally of this type.

Some of the agricultural states on the other hand have not always taken this attitude, and in some instances it would be difficult to predict what the future attitude of some of the states might be. The reputation of the state should be taken into consideration when selecting an incorporating state.

INCORPORATION PROCEDURE

Usually a lawyer handles the organization routine in forming a corporation. But the articles or certificate of incorporation must be signed by, usually, at least three *incorporators*. Legally, it is they who form the corporation. At common law the only qualifications for incorporators were that they be natural persons and have the capacity to contract. Some of the states require that one or a majority of them be citizens of the United States, and residents of the particular state. Some states require that the incorporators subscribe to stock in the articles of incorporation. Upon the state's acceptance of the articles, the incorporators then become the first stockholders.

In many instances the incorporators are mere "dummies"—disinterested parties who have the necessary qualifications and are used as a matter of convenience.

The Charter

In order to be formed, a corporation must be granted a *charter* by the state. The people wishing to incorporate fill out or have filled out a form usually called *articles of incorporation, certificate of incorporation,* or *articles of association.* After acceptance by the state, this becomes the charter of the corporation. In a technical sense, the charter includes not only the articles, but the state statutes and all higher law. For convenience, however, we will use the term "articles of incorporation" or "certificate of incorporation" interchangeably with "charter."

The charter is looked upon as a contract between the state and the corporation, and between the corporation and its stockholders. It follows from this that any change that is made in the charter will have to be made with the consent of both the state and the stockholders. The usual contents of the articles or certificate of incorporation are as follows.

Name. Since the corporation is a legalistic person it must have a name. The statutes of the various states require that the name be stated in the articles, and that it contain the words, "Corporation," "Incorporated," "Company," or abbreviations of them. Some states require either these words or others such as "Association," "Syndicate," or "Limited." It must be written in English letters, although it may be a foreign name. The words "Bank," "Trust Company," etc., cannot be used unless it actually is a bank or a trust company.

The state will not approve any name too similar to the name of a corporation previously formed there, or a foreign corporation registered in the state, except with the written consent of the other corporation. If it later develops that the name is so similar that material confusion results, the fact that the state approved the name is no defense. If the name of a firm is infringed upon so that material confusion results, proper legal actions may be brought against the offending firm.

Location of Principal Office. The city or town where the "principal office" is located must be stated in the articles. Some states require the street address as well. It is thus known where to reach the corporation in event of suit, or in sending out tax notices. This "principal office" that is required in the state may not be the place where the corporation transacts its business. Since the low tax rate on personal property often dictates the choice of some small community, a law firm or trust company may serve as the office of hundreds of corporations.

Purpose. An important part of any charter is the *purpose clause*. A common-law organization can carry on any kind of lawful business. A corporation, on the other hand, comes into being with only the powers which are granted to it in the charter. It is therefore advisable to use care in drawing up the purpose clause. Lawyers have form books which contain standard purpose clauses for almost any kind of business operation. In addition to the expressed powers granted in the charter, a corporation has the power to do things that are implied or incidental to the stated purpose.

If a corporation performs acts beyond the stated purpose, or beyond its implied or incidental powers, these are called *ultra vires* acts. Formerly the law said that a corporation lacked the capacity to perform such acts, but more modern law recognizes the power of a corporation to perform them, and any objection will be from the standpoint of the corporation's lack of authority to perform them. Only interested parties, such as the stockholders or the state, have the right to object to the performance of an *ultra vires* act.

Capital Stock. The total number of shares authorized for issuance is stated in the charter. If these have a par value, the amount of it is indicated; if there is no par value, this must be made clear. In some instances the "stated value" of the no-par stock is shown. If the stock is classified, this too must be specified, as must any preferences, limitations. or restrictions on any class of stock.

Some of the states place a minimum of $500 to $2,000 on the amount of the authorized stock. Although some of the others do not set a minimum, they require that a certain amount, such as $500, or $1,000, must be paid in before the corporation can transact business. None of the states places a maximum on the amount of stock that can be issued. Some, however, limit the amount of preferred in relation to the common stock.

Duration. Many of the states require that the corporation's duration be stated in the charter. Usually life can be perpetual, but a few states place a limitation of 20 to 100 years. The maximum life permitted is generally stated in the charter. Where the life is limited to a designated number of years, charter renewals are easily obtained. In some states, such as Ohio, if there is no specific statement otherwise, life is assumed to be perpetual.

Other Provisions. Many states specify that the minimum amount of capital which will be paid in before the corporation transacts business must be stated in the charter. If business is transacted before this amount has been paid in, the directors can be held personally liable on any debts contracted up to this amount.

In New York the certificate of incorporation must also contain the number of directors, and the names of directors who are going to serve until the first annual stockholders' meeting.

Certain states permit "special charter provisions." These define or limit the exercise of authority of the corporation or the directors, officers, or stockholders.

In addition to the articles, a number of the states require that the corporation also file a form designating the agent to accept *service of process* (notice of suit).

The Bylaws

Bylaws are the rules or regulations governing the internal operation and management of the corporation. They are subordinate to the charter, so that in case of a conflict between the two the charter provisions will prevail. The bylaws are usually drawn up by a lawyer before the corporation is formed, and then the stockholders in their first meeting accept them. The directors may also draw up bylaws relating to their own sphere of activity. These must not conflict with those adopted by the stockholders.

In some states, the term *bylaws* applies to the rules adopted by the directors, and the term *regulations* (or, *code of regulations*) is used for those adopted by the stockholders. When the term *bylaws* is used in this book it will apply to the rules adopted by the stockholders, unless otherwise indicated.

Since the bylaws relate to the internal affairs of the corporation, they may be amended by the same body that adopted them. Consent of the state is not necessary as it is in the case of the charter, unless the state statutes require it.

The bylaws contain provisions relating to the following topics.

Stockholders' Meetings. For these, bylaws provide for:

1. Time, place, and purpose of the annual meeting; notice of meeting
2. Special meetings; call and notice of meeting
3. What constitutes a quorum at the meeting
4. Method of voting the stock; proxy and cumulative voting
5. Inspectors of election
6. Order of business

Directors and Directors' Meetings. The bylaws adopted by the stockholders may adequately cover the directors' meetings. If separate bylaws are adopted by the directors, the detail will be stated there. The following relate to the directors:

1. Number
2. Qualifications
3. Term of office
4. Classification
5. Filling vacancies
6. Powers and restrictions on powers
7. Meetings: regular and special, call and notice, quorum, officers of meeting, order of business
8. Compensation, if any

Committees of the Board. The bylaws of the larger corporations usually provide for the appointment of committees of the board to assist the board. An executive committee and a finance committee are often appointed. The duties, responsibilities, etc., of the committees are stated.

Officers. The board of directors is given the power to appoint officers to carry out the policies it has adopted. The following details are usually included in the bylaws:

1. Officers to be appointed
2. Qualifications
3. Term of office
4. Powers and duties
5. Salaries

Stock. The following are specified in the bylaws relating to stock:

1. Form of the stock certificate
2. Transfers of stock

3. Lost and stolen certificates
4. Transfer agent and registrar
5. Inspection of the stock records

Finances and Dividends. The details covering these items are as follows:

1. Fiscal year
2. Reserves
3. Bank accounts
4. Signature on checks and notes
5. Dividend dates, stockholders entitled to dividends

Miscellaneous. In addition to the above, the bylaws may contain provisions relating to the following: Form of the corporate seal, inspections of the financial records, surety bonds required of officers, and signatures required on contracts.

Amendment. The bylaws usually end with provisions pertaining to how and by whom they may be amended.

Organization Meetings

To complete the formation of the corporation it is necessary to have the organization meetings. These consist of the first meeting of the stockholders and the first meeting of the board of directors. Actually, these meetings may never be held. The lawyer may write up the minutes and have the stockholders and directors sign them.

TRANSACTING BUSINESS IN OTHER STATES

The federal government, through its Constitution, has been given the power to regulate *interstate* commerce. A state therefore cannot tax a corporation formed in another state or prevent it from carrying on trade in the state as long as the business is interstate in nature.

Although the mere solicitation of orders or the maintenance of a sales office in the state by a foreign corporation is normally looked upon as interstate commerce, the Supreme Court in several recent decisions [2] upheld the right of the state to tax such business under its income tax laws. Congress, however, in 1959, passed legislation [3] which provides that no state, county, or city may impose a tax on the net income derived within its boundaries by any person from interstate commerce, provided the only business activities are the solicitation of orders for the sale of

[2] Northwestern States Portland Cement Co. v. State of Minnesota; Williams v. Stockham Valves and Fittings, Inc., 358 U.S. 450, 79 Sup. Ct. 357 (1959) (the *Northwestern-Stockham* cases).

[3] Public Law 86–272.

personal tangible property. It is uncertain at the present time just what additional acts done in interstate commerce might subject a corporation to a particular state's income tax law.

But a state can require a foreign corporation (one formed outside the state) to pay taxes and meet its other requirements if the business is *intrastate* in nature. The opening up of a store in the state is one illustration of intrastate commerce. A corporation's charter usually gives it the right to transact business both within and outside the state. This means only that as far as the state of organization is concerned, the corporation has the power to transact business in the other states. A state's authority, however, extends only to its own boundaries, and therefore it is up to the other states to give the corporation the right to enter their jurisdiction.

Qualification in Foreign State

Before a corporation can lawfully transact intrastate commerce within a foreign state, it must *qualify* as a foreign corporation there—that is, follow the corporation laws of that state.

Corporations formed in a particular state (domestic corporations) must file their articles and pay their taxes and fees in that state. It is therefore only fair to the state's own corporations that the same be required on the part of a foreign corporation that is transacting business within the state. In order to qualify in a foreign state a corporation must usually:

1. File a copy of its articles of incorporation, financial statements, and whatever other papers are required
2. Pay filing fees, and a tax similar to the organization tax
3. Appoint an agent to receive service of process (suit)
4. Pay a tax similar to the annual franchise fee, and whatever other taxes are levied by the state

Penalties for Non-Compliance

Qualification would probably not be entered upon unless penalties were inflicted in event of non-compliance. The states vary somewhat in regard to these penalties, but the following are the basic types.

Fines Against the Corporation. According to the statutes of most of the states, a foreign corporation will be subject to a fine if it transacts intrastate commerce business before qualification. The amount of these fines varies from $10 to $10,000. In some instances the fines can be levied for each offense, and in some states the corporation can be fined a stated amount for each day or each month in which it transacts business before qualification.

Fines Against Officers and Agents. A number of the states have statutes which specify fines against the officers or agents who transact the business. The officers whose duty it was to qualify the corporation are also sometimes fined. The amount of the fine varies among the states from $10 to $2,000. In some states the penalty can be levied for each business transaction. Although they are on the books, such fines are rarely applied, and where they are, the trend is toward leniency.

Imprisonment of Officer or Agent. Ten of the states provide in their statutes for jail sentences for officers and agents of a corporation that transacts intrastate commerce business before qualifying. The jail term varies among the states from thirty days to six months. This penalty, however, is rarely applied.

Personal Liability for Debts. The statutes of eight of the states provide that the officers or agents who transact business before qualification can be held personally liable for the corporation's debts. A few of the states extend this personal liability also to the stockholders.

Contracts Unenforceable. One of the most common types of penalty in the various states is that of declaring unenforceable any contracts made by an unqualified foreign corporation. This may be very severe in many instances. A corporation may sell a large quantity of goods in a foreign state, and then if the bill is not paid, it finds itself denied the use of the state courts in attempting to collect.

The states which have this type of penalty can be divided into two classes. One class takes the attitude that although the foreign corporation may not sue as long as it is not qualified, it may, after the transaction of business has occurred, qualify and then sue. The other states hold that if an act is wrong when done, later qualification will not enable the corporation to sue. Although the unqualified corporation cannot sue, the other party to the contract can always sue the corporation.

Contracts Void. Nine of the states have a more severe penalty than saying the contracts of an unqualified foreign corporation are unenforceable. The statutes of these states provide that the contracts are void—that is, void on behalf of the foreign corporation, but enforceable against it. In these states later qualification would not enable the corporation to sue on any contracts made prior to qualification.

Interstate vs. Intrastate Commerce

We have indicated what must be done in order to qualify in a foreign state. The penalties for non-compliance have also been stated. A real problem often arises when we try to distinguish between *interstate* and *intrastate* commerce.

Interstate commerce is that which takes place between two states, while intrastate commerce takes place within a particular state. If part of the transaction is interstate in nature, but part is intrastate, the courts will look upon the entire act as being intrastate. The courts often used the phrase "doing business" to indicate intrastate commerce.

In addition to determining whether a particular act constitutes doing business within the state in order to know whether qualification is necessary, there are two other reasons why this is important: (1) to determine whether the penalties are applicable, and (2) to determine whether the corporation is subject to *service of process* in the state.

If a corporation is transacting only interstate commerce between its own state and the foreign state, it is not subject to suit in the foreign state. In other words, it cannot be served with summons or process. But if it is transacting intrastate commerce within the foreign state, then it is subject to service of process in that state and can be sued there.

A study of legal cases involving the question as to whether an act is interstate or intrastate appears to show some conflict among the states and even within a particular one. Some cases arose over the application of the penalties, and some of them on the question whether the company was subject to service of process in the state. Usually a corporation does not have to do as much in the state in order to be held to be doing business for the purpose of service as it does for the purpose of determining whether it is subject to the penalties. In many instances, however, it appears that the court rules the same acts interstate or intrastate regardless of the reason for the origin of the case. The types of transactions listed below would probably be held the same regardless of whether the case arose with respect to the application of penalties or service of process.

Interstate Commerce. The following acts on the part of a foreign corporation are usually held to constitute interstate commerce.

1. Solicitation of orders by traveling salesmen subject to approval at the home office from which the goods are shipped to the purchaser
2. Maintenance of a sales office to facilitate the solicitation of orders of the kind stated above
3. Keeping in the state samples which are never sold
4. Collection for goods sold in interstate commerce
5. Consignment sales
6. Purchasing in the state subject to approval of the home office
7. Installation of a complex product that requires the services of an expert from the factory
8. A single or isolated act, unless it appears to be the first of a series of acts, or unless prohibited by statutes

Intrastate Commerce. Many courts say that in order to be doing business (intrastate) there must be some permanency or continuity in the corporation's business operations. The following acts would usually be held to be intrastate commerce:

1. Completion of contracts in the state
2. The sale of samples kept in the state
3. Selling goods after they have come to rest in the state
4. Maintenance of a warehouse within the state where goods are sold and delivered
5. Maintenance of a principal office
6. Maintenance of a store in the state
7. Making adjustments in the state without being subject to approval of the home office
8. The installation of simple products
9. Construction work
10. Isolated act if it appears to be the first of a series of acts, or if prohibited by statutes

Meeting the Requirements

Many corporations that are now transacting intrastate commerce within foreign states, and are thus running the risk of the penalties, could in many instances change the nature of the business to interstate by making slight changes. For example, if the salesmen can accept the orders in a foreign state, a clause could be printed in the contract form making them subject to approval at the home office. Warehouses could be given up and a new system of distribution effected.

Where it is imperative that business be carried on in the state, a small corporation could be organized to operate within the state as a domestic corporation. Interstate sales could be made to it by the foreign parent company. The taxes for the small subsidiary would probably be less than the qualification taxes of the large foreign corporation. In some states, such as Texas, for example, if the officers and directors of the two corporations are the same they might hold this to be a subterfuge and tax the subsidiary the same as the parent corporation.

The state officials do not usually go about looking for foreign corporations for the purpose of levying fines. The situation comes to light commonly when a bill is not paid and the foreign corporation attempts to sue a resident of the foreign state. In most instances people pay their honest debts, and therefore some corporations feel that it is cheaper to run the risk of not being able to collect on some debt than to pay the foreign corporation taxes and fees.

Many corporations are illegally doing intrastate commerce business in foreign states simply because they do not know that qualification is necessary.

QUESTIONS

1. Is the community in which you live incorporated? Is your college or university incorporated? If so, what kind of corporations are they?
2. Trace briefly the development of corporation laws.
3. Indicate six different ways of classifying corporations.
4. List the advantages and disadvantages of the corporation as compared with the general partnership.
5. List the factors which may have an influence on the selection of the state of incorporation. Which of these usually decides the issue?
6. List the items that appear in the articles or certificate of incorporation.
7. (a) What are the requirements and restrictions in regard to the corporate name? (b) If one corporation infringes on the name of another corporation, what action may be had by the latter?
8. (a) What is meant by *ultra vires* acts? (b) What is the attitude of the laws in regard to *ultra vires* acts?
9. Distinguish between the charter and the bylaws of a corporation.
10. What is meant by a foreign corporation? Is this the same as an alien corporation?
11. Indicate the nature of the right, if any, of a corporation to carry on business beyond the boundaries of the state in which it is incorporated.
12. What must a corporation do in order to "qualify" in a foreign state?
13. What penalties may be inflicted against an unqualified foreign corporation for the transaction of business within the various states?
14. Indicate whether the following acts on the part of an unqualified foreign corporation are interstate or intrastate commerce: (a) Completion of contracts, (b) Consignment sales, (c) Maintenance of an office, (d) Maintenance of a warehouse, (e) Purchasing, (f) Installation, (g) Isolated acts.
15. If a corporation finds out that it is transacting intrastate commerce business in a foreign state, what might it do to make its business transactions legal without qualifying as a foreign corporation?
16. Explain what is meant when it is said that corporate shareholders are subject to double taxation. (Reference to federal income taxes.)
17. Indicate the various types of taxes that must be paid by a corporation.
18. Explain the various reasons why a business may incorporate even though it does not need to sell stocks or bonds to obtain capital.

PROBLEMS

1. Mr. Watts bought 100 shares of The Quality Corp. common stock directly from the issuing company at its par value of $10 per share. Subsequently the corporation failed and after its assets were exhausted, the company still owed creditors the sum of $8,000. Can Mr. Watts be held liable for any of these debts? If prior to the failure Mr. Watts had sold the stock to Mr. Lamp for $5 per share, would the latter be liable for any of the company's debts? Explain.

2. The Atlantic Corp. was organized in Delaware with an authorized capitalization of 1,000,000 shares. What would be the amount of the organization tax if: (a) The stock had a par value of $50 per share? (b) The stock had no par value? What would organization tax be in your state?

3. The "Drive It Yourself" company had been organized and operating in a particular city for a period of one year when the "U-Drive-It" was formed and started operating in the same city. Shortly thereafter the former company brought an injunction against the latter to restrain it from continuing to use its name. Do you believe that the injunction should be granted? Why or why not?

4. Look up the ordinary business corporation laws in your state and indicate the following: qualifications for incorporators and directors; minimum paid-in capital to begin business; maximum duration of corporation; penalties which may be inflicted on an unqualified foreign corporation for doing business in the state.

5. Assume that a corporation pays dividends equivalent to 100 per cent of its earnings after taxes, and that both the corporation's income and the shareholders' dividends are taxed at the highest bracket applicable. Indicate how much of each dollar of corporate earnings before taxes is paid in federal corporate and personal income taxes for shareholders (joint filing assumed) who have the following taxable incomes after deductions, exemptions, and dividend exclusion. (Disregard the "dividend credit" provided for in the Internal Revenue Code.) (a) $5,000, (b) $10,000, (c) $50,000, (d) $100,000, (e) $500,000.

SELECTED READINGS

BEAMAN, WALTER H. *Paying Taxes to Other States*. New York: The Ronald Press Co., 1963.

BERLE, A. A., JR. *The Twentieth Century Capitalist Revolution*. New York: Harcourt, Brace & World, Inc., 1954.

CAPLIN, MORTIMER M. *Doing Business in Other States*. New York: United States Corporation Co., 1959.

Corporation Course. Englewood Cliffs, N. J.: Prentice-Hall, Inc., 1960.

Corporation Manual. New York: United States Corporation Co. Published annually.

FLETCHER, WILLIAM MEADE. *Cyclopedia of the Law of Private Corporations,* Permanent ed. Chicago: Callaghan & Co., Vol. 1 (1931), Vol. 6 (1950 rev. vol.), Vol. 17 (1960 rev. vol.), Vol. 18 (1955 rev. vol.).

LATTIN, NORMAN D. *The Law of Corporations*. Brooklyn: The Foundation Press, Inc., 1959.

OLECK, HOWARD L. *Modern Corporation Law*. Indianapolis: The Bobbs-Merrill Co., Inc., 1960.

ROHRLICH, CHESTER. *Organizing Corporate and other Business Enterprises,* 3d ed. Albany, N. Y.: Matthew Bender & Co., Inc., 1958.

STEVENS, R. S. *Handbook on the Law of Private Corporations,* 2d ed. St. Paul: West Publishing Co., 1949.

What Constitutes Doing Business by a Corporation in States Foreign to the State of its Creation. New York: The Corporation Trust Co., Latest edition.

4

Corporate Management

The theory of corporate management gives the authority for most corporate decisions to the board of directors. The board may, in turn, delegate authority to officers it selects. The stockholders of the corporation elect the board. Each of these three major elements in corporate management is discussed below.

THE STOCKHOLDERS

The average stockholder in our large corporations takes little or no part in the management of the business. A certain percentage of them send in their proxies and the proxy committee elects the board of directors. If the stockholder becomes dissatisfied with the management of the firm, he will probably register his disgust by selling his stock. The average stockholder is interested directly in the prospect for an appreciation in price of his stock, or in the dividends.

Recent years, however, have witnessed an increasing number of instances in which displeased shareholders have taken steps to oust the management. This results in proxy fights with the corporate management in an attempt to secure the support of the shareholders.

Despite the relatively unimportant place which the average stockholder occupies in corporate management, he has certain rights which, if not respected, will give him a legal claim to redress.

Stockholders' Rights

Stockholders' rights can be divided into two classes: (1) general rights, and (2) collective rights. The general rights are those which accrue to him individually by virtue of being a stockholder, such as the right to a stock certificate, and the right to transfer his stock. The collective rights

61

are those which the stockholders as a body possess, such as the right to elect the board of directors. In our discussion we will not distinguish between these two groups of rights.

If a stockholder's right is not respected by the corporate management, he usually does nothing about it. Perhaps this is the most practical course to follow. A stockholder owning relatively few shares can do little or nothing if the management does not respect his rights. If attempts are made to take advantage of certain rights, the management may use legal obstacles and the stockholder will probably cease his efforts, for fighting corporate managements costs more money than the average stockholder possesses. Delaying tactics are often used which may cause the stockholder to give up in disgust. The management can use the corporation's money (really the stockholders') to hire its counsel, but the stockholder has to pay for his out of his own pocket.

Management is placed in control of the corporation and is charged with the responsibility of looking after the interests of the stockholders as a group—not of a single stockholder. Sometimes the interests of the two are not the same.

Following is a list of the rights of stockholders. A brief discussion of rights needing further elaboration follows the listing.

1. To receive a certificate or certificates representing the number of fully paid shares held
2. To transfer this stock at any time
3. To be notified of meetings and to vote at these meetings, either in person or by proxy
4. To receive dividends when and if declared by the board of directors
5. To share in new issues of stock subject to the restrictions stated below
6. To share in the assets upon dissolution
7. To inspect the corporate books subject to the limitations stated below
8. To elect the board of directors
9. To vote upon amendments to the charter or bylaws, and for dissolution, sale of the assets, merger or consolidation of the corporation

Voting Rights of Stockholders

Theoretically, it might be said that the stockholders, through their right to elect the board of directors, control the corporation. This, however, would be true only in the case of very small corporations, where a relatively large percentage of the stock is held by one or a few individuals. As the size of the company increases, the average stockholder owns a smaller percentage of the total stock, he is less acquainted with the business, and he has little knowledge of the personal qualifications of the directorial candidates. In corporate giants, once a board of directors is in power it can through the proxy system perpetuate itself in office. Even so, it takes the collective vote of a specified percentage of the shareholders or their proxies to elect the directors.

At common law each stockholder has one vote on each matter that comes before the meeting regardless of the number of shares he possesses. This is a carry-over from the partnership and the early corporation. We now look upon the corporation as a collection of capital, rather than a collection of individuals, and the statutes in the various states now give the stockholder the right to cast one vote for each share unless otherwise qualified or restricted.

Straight Voting

In the election of directors a stockholder has the right to cast one vote per share for each vacancy to be filled. Thus, if a person had ten shares and there were five directors to be elected, he could cast ten votes for each of five candidates. The criticism of this kind of voting, which is called *straight* voting, is that a faction controlling one more than half the total shares could elect all the directors, and the other faction which had only one less than half the shares would be unable to elect any of the directors. For example, if there were 100 shares of stock voting at the meeting, and five directors to be elected, the faction holding 51 shares could cast 51 votes for each of their five candidates, while the faction holding 49 shares could cast only 49 votes for each of their five candidates. The result is that the bare majority would fill all the vacancies on the board.

Cumulative Voting

In order to overcome the shortcomings of the straight voting system, the statutes (or constitution) of a number of the states now provide that the stockholders may *cumulate* their votes. Under this system of voting for the directors a shareholder is given as many votes per share as there are directors to be elected. Of course, this is no more votes than he had under straight voting. But under *cumulative* voting the stockholder can concentrate these total votes on as few candidates as he wishes.

To refer to the above example, if a faction held 49 shares, it would, when there are five vacancies to be filled, have a right to cast a total of 245 votes (5 times 49). These 245 votes could be concentrated on two of the minority's candidates, thus giving each one 122 votes. To prevent them from being elected the majority would have to cast at least 122 or 123 votes for at least four candidates, since the five receiving the highest number of votes would be elected. But the majority has only 255 votes

(5 times 51). If it concentrated these votes on four of its candidates, each would receive only 63 votes. Thus the minority would be certain of getting in at least two of its candidates.

If, in the above example, the minority cumulated its votes but the majority did not, the minority could elect four of the five directors. With its 245 votes, the minority could cast 61 votes for each of four candidates. If the majority did not vote cumulatively, it would cast only 51 votes for each of five candidates. The statutes usually require that stockholders notify the company a specified number of hours ahead of the meeting if they are going to cumulate their votes. This puts the other stockholders on guard, and they likewise can cumulate their votes. In the above example, the majority should concentrate its votes on three of its candidates, casting 85 votes for each, in order to insure getting a majority of the board.

A formula can be used to determine the exact number of shares necessary to elect a given number of directors, as follows:

$$\frac{\text{Total number of shares voting} \times \text{Number of directors desired}}{\text{Total number of directors to be elected} + 1} + 1 = \text{Number of shares necessary}$$

In using the formula any fractional part of one in the answer is dropped. Referring again to the example used above, if a person wants to know how many shares he needs to own in order to be sure of electing one person, or himself, to the board of directors, he could ascertain the number by substituting in the formula, as follows:

$$\frac{100 \times 1}{5 + 1} + 1 = 17\frac{2}{3}, \text{ or } 17$$

We can prove the result just obtained. If a person had 17 shares he could cast a total of 85 votes (5 times 17) for one director. In order for this candidate not to be elected it would be necessary for the other shareholders to cast at least 85 or 86 votes for five directors. But the other shareholders have only 83 shares, and therefore could cast only 83 votes for each of five directors. If we take a number less than 17, say 16, for example, we find that this would not be sufficient. With 16 shares a person could cast a total of 80 votes for one candidate. The remaining shareholders, however, would have 84 shares, and therefore could cast 84 votes for each of five candidates, and thus elect all of them.

The formula can also be used, of course, to determine how many directors to concentrate on when a given number of shares is held. If a person held 35 shares and wanted to vote in such manner as to be sure of electing the largest number of directors possible, he could determine this by letting x represent the unknown quantity in the formula.

$$\frac{100 \times x}{5+1} + 1 = 35$$

$$\frac{100x}{6} = 34$$

$$x = 2$$

Thus, the person holding 35 shares should cast 87 votes for each of two candidates and they would be sure of being elected.

In the formula it should be noted that it is the total number of shares actually voting which is used, and not the total number of voting shares the corporation has outstanding. A person may have less than half the total number of voting shares outstanding, but if that represents more than half of the shares that are present at the meeting and voting, he would have control of the meeting.

At common law a stockholder could not cumulate his votes, but forty-three of the states now have constitutional provisions or statutes relating to it. These are of two types: (1) those that specify that shareholders shall have the right to cumulate their votes (this right cannot be taken away from them by the corporation), and (2) those that give the shareholders the right only if it is so provided in the articles or certificate of incorporation or in the bylaws. In twenty-two of the states, cumulative voting is mandatory if the stockholder wishes to do so. These include the important incorporating states of Illinois, Pennsylvania, Ohio, and Michigan. The others are Alaska, Arizona, Arkansas, California, Hawaii, Idaho, Kansas, Kentucky, Mississippi, Missouri, Montana, Nebraska, North Dakota, South Carolina, South Dakota, Washington, West Virginia, and Wyoming.[1] Cumulative voting is permissive if included in the articles or bylaws in the District of Columbia and twenty-one of the states, which include the favorite incorporating states of Delaware, New Jersey, and New York. The others are Colorado, Indiana, Louisiana, Maine, Maryland, Massachusetts, Minnesota, Nevada, New Mexico, North Carolina, Oklahoma, Oregon, Rhode Island, Tennessee, Texas, Utah, Vermont, and Virginia.[2] The remaining seven states have no constitutional provisions

[1] Leland C. Whetten, "Cumulative Voting for Directors: Its Origin and Significance," *Studies in Business and Economics,* Bulletin No. 2, Bureau of Business and Economic Research, School of Business Administration, Georgia State College of Business Administration, Atlanta, Georgia, 1959, pp. 6, 12, and 13.

[2] *Ibid.,* pp. 6 and 13.

or statutes authorizing cumulative voting; these are Alabama, Connecticut, Florida, Georgia, Iowa, New Hampshire, and Wisconsin.

When such voting is followed there should be only one ballot for the election of all the directors. The ones receiving the highest number of votes, or in other words, a plurality, are elected, regardless of whether this represents a majority of the votes. If separate ballots were taken to fill each vacancy on the board, it would defeat the purpose of cumulative voting, as the majority could always cast more votes than the minority. If a tie results, however, additional ballots should be taken.

It should be noted that cumulative voting is used only in the election of directors.

Proxy Voting

At common law a shareholder had to be present at the meeting in order to cast his votes, but the statutes of the various states now permit him to vote by proxy. The term *proxy* applies to both the written authorization and the person or committee to whom it is sent. In the case of our large corporations which have hundreds of thousands of stockholders scattered throughout the country it would be impossible ever to secure a quorum at a meeting if proxy voting were not permitted.

A proxy can be revoked at any time prior to the time when it is voted, unless it is coupled with an interest. An example of the latter is one in which a shareholder puts his stock up as collateral for a loan and gives the lender his proxy.

It is the custom for large corporations to send out notices of the stockholders' meetings and to enclose a proxy form for the shareholder to fill out, giving several of the corporate officers, who constitute the *proxy committee*, the right to vote the stock. The Securities and Exchange Commission has adopted rules and regulations relating to the solicitation of proxies on all listed securities. These require the corporation to give the shareholders a considerable amount of detailed information. (The more important of these requirements are stated on pages 351–352.)

Class Voting

Corporations can qualify or limit the voting rights of stockholders by appropriate provisions in the charter and bylaws. This becomes part of the contract under which people purchase the stock. One of these changes from the ordinary procedure is to provide that the stock will vote as a class.

Some corporations issue their stock under a contract which specifies that the preferred stock voting as a group or class shall be entitled to elect a designated number of directors, and the common stock as a group shall be entitled to elect a specified number of directors. This method insures representation on the board of directors for the preferred stock even though the number of shares of preferred outstanding is much less than the number of common shares. An example of class voting can be illustrated with the $1.50 cumulative convertible $25 par preferred stock of Mid-West Refineries, Inc. The contract provides that the preferred shall vote equally with the common, one vote per share, but it is further provided that:

. . . if total assets (excluding goodwill, deferred charges, and prepaid items) after deducting total liabilities other than contingent liabilities, on two successive quarterly financial statements, shall be less than 133 per cent of the aggregate par value of the preferred stock outstanding, and/or if four quarterly dividends on the preferred stock are in arrears, the preferred stock as a class shall be entitled to elect a majority of the board of directors until the assets over liabilities, as stated, exceed 133 per cent of the par value of the preferred stock, and if four quarterly dividends shall have been in arrears, all arrears of dividends shall have been declared and paid or funds set aside therefor.

Fractional and Multiple Votes

When there is more than one class of stock, it is occasionally provided that the stock of one class shall be entitled to only a fraction of one vote per share, or that it shall be entitled to a specified number of votes per share.

Non-voting Stock

Many corporations make their preferred stock *non-voting*. Such stock, however, sometimes by virtue of statutes or charter provision, has what amounts to a *vetoing* power, in that it is given the right to vote on specified matters such as the creation of a bonded indebtedness, issuance of additional preferred stock, consolidation, merger, or dissolution of the company. Non-voting preferred stock is often given *contingent* voting power. An example of this is a case in which it is given the right to vote (as a class or otherwise) if the dividends on it are in arrears for a stated number of quarterly periods.

Some companies have *classified* common stock outstanding. One class of the common may vote, and the other class may be made non-voting. People have not objected to the issuance of a non-voting preferred stock, since the purchaser is often looked upon as at least a semi-investor, and is willing to sacrifice the voting right for a preference as to dividends. But the non-voting common stock is not so well received. Traditionally it is the common stockholders who bear the greatest risk and who have the right to elect the board of directors. Since 1926, the New York Stock Exchange has refused to list a non-voting common stock.

Methods of Continuing Control

There are a number of ways in which a board of directors which does not own a majority of the stock may perpetuate itself in office. Some of these have been mentioned before but are listed below in summary form.

Minority Interest Often Controlling. It usually does not take 51 per cent of even the voting stock of a corporation in order to get control. If a faction held only 40 per cent of the total voting stock, but all of it was fully represented at a meeting at which there was only 75 per cent of the total stock represented, this 40 per cent would obviously be the controlling interest.

When a majority vote is required to pass a measure at a meeting, it is usually taken to mean a majority of the votes cast, assuming a quorum to be present. If 100 per cent of the stock was represented at the meeting, but only 75 per cent of it voted, the faction holding 40 per cent of the stock could carry a measure.

When a majority of the stock is widely scattered in the hands of many stockholders, none of whom owns an appreciable amount, the votes may also be scattered over many candidates for directors, with the result that a concentrated minority may be able to control. Cumulative voting may be used in this way by the minority in order to get control. There is also the probability that some of the votes of this unorganized majority will fall to the candidates or proposals of the controlling minority interest.

If we carry this point one step further, we will arrive at the situation we see in our large corporations today. The management holds a small minority of the total stock (or even a negligible amount), but by working together and collecting the proxies of the scattered majority, they end up with a majority of the votes.

Failure To Elect New Directors. According to common law and the statutes in the various states, failure to elect new directors results in the old ones' continuing. In some instances management fails to call a meeting or send out notices of the annual meeting, in order to accomplish this objective. The failure to send notices, however, is contrary to the statutes of many of the states.

Sometimes, where not prohibited by statutes, the charter or bylaws may specify that a two-thirds or three-fourths vote of the entire outstanding stock is necessary to elect the directors. It may be impossible to get that amount of the stock represented at the meeting, or, if it is represented, to secure that percentage vote. This would result in the original board's continuing in office.

Holding Company. A *holding company* which owns a majority or all the voting stock of another company can control the latter company.

Whoever has control of the holding company can therefore control the subsidiary companies. The holding company is discussed in Chapter 28.

Voting Trust. Control is sometimes effected through the use of the *voting trust*. In this setup the stock is held by a group of trustees for a specified number of years. This was described in Chapter 2.

Good Management. A method of perpetuating the management which might be so obvious as to be overlooked, is for the management to be so efficient that the company enjoys good earnings and pays liberal dividends. Such managers are usually re-elected.

Reduction in Size of Board of Directors. Where cumulative voting is followed, a reduction in the size of the board of directors results in an increase in the percentage of the shares needed in order to elect one director and to effect a change in the control of the company.

Staggered Terms for Directors. When the terms of office of the board of directors are staggered, it is sometimes referred to as *classification* of the board. For example, the charter or bylaws may call for a board of nine persons. Upon organization of the company, three directors would be elected for one-year terms each, three for two-year terms, and three for three-year terms; each year thereafter three directors would be elected for three-year terms each. This prevents a complete turnover of the board in any one year. In many non-profit corporations the directors' terms are staggered in order to provide for continuity in management. Some profit corporations' boards also are staggered, but the legality of this where cumulative voting is practiced, and the wisdom of it for profit corporations, are subject to some question. Those acquiring controlling stock interests in a corporation may be compelled to wait several years before they can get control of the board of directors.

If a corporation has a nine-man board and each director is elected each year for a one-year term, under cumulative voting a minority interest of one share more than 10 per cent could elect one director. But if the board was classified into three groups with each group being elected every three years for three-year terms in a staggered fashion, it would require one share more than 25 per cent of the total voting shares to elect one director.

The Supreme Court of Illinois in 1955 ruled that the Illinois statute providing for the staggering of directors' terms was unconstitutional because it conflicted with the cumulative voting rights of stockholders which are provided for in the state constitution.[3] The Supreme Court of Ohio, however, in 1956, held that classification of the board could be used

[3] Wolfson v. Avery, 6 Ill. 78, 126 N.E.2d 701 (1955).

despite the fact that shareholders had the right to cumulate their votes.[4] The Ohio statutes provide that shareholders may cumulate their votes and that this right may not be restricted or qualified by the articles or code of regulations. They further state that the articles or code may provide for classification of the board of directors. The Supreme Court of Pennsylvania in 1956 [5] held that the statute providing for classification of the board did not violate the constitutional provision conferring cumulative voting rights. The Supreme Court of Appeals of West Virginia in 1958,[6] however, held that a corporate bylaw providing for classification of the board vitiates the cumulative voting right conferred by the constitution and statutes of the states and was therefore invalid. The legal status of staggered terms for directors in most of the states that provide for cumulative voting has not been adjudicated.[7]

Pre-emptive Right of Stockholders

Another right of a stockholder is to share in new issues of stock in the same proportion that his old stock represents to the total stock. This is known as the *pre-emptive right*. This enables the stockholder to maintain his degree of control in the company and his equity in the surplus. This being the case, the right would accrue to only those stockholders whose stock is voting or participating in dividends (entitled to dividends beyond a stated rate), or in assets upon dissolution. This right will be more fully explained in Chapter 13.

Inspection of the Books

The stockholders are the owners of the corporation. Since they elect the directors to carry on the business it is only proper that the stockholders should have the right to examine the corporate records. At common law the shareholders have the right to examine the records at a reasonable time and place and for a proper purpose. They cannot demand the right of inspection to gratify mere idle curiosity, for speculative purposes, or

---

[4] Humphrys v. Winous Co., 165 Ohio St. 45, 133 N.E.2d 780 (1956).

[5] Janney Appellant v. Philadelphia Transportation Co., 387 Pa. 282 (1956).

[6] State *ex rel.* Jack E. Syphers v. Harry B. McCune, 101 S.E.2d 834 (1958).

[7] Leland C. Whetten, *op. cit.*, states that he found only three cases bearing on this question prior to 1955. A California case decided in 1885 (Wright v. Central California Water Co., 8 Pac. 70) held invalid under the constitutional requirement of cumulative voting a resolution providing for the election of seven directors, one at a time, at the same meeting. A New York court decision in 1910 (Bond v. Atlantic Terra Cotta Co., 122 N.Y. Supp. 425), and a Common Pleas Court decision in Allegheny County, Pennsylvania, in 1950 (Hepps and Cohen v. A. M. Byers Co.) both held that cumulative voting did not preclude classification of the board. Whetten points out that many state statutes specifically provide for classification of the board, including nine of the thirteen states where mandatory cumulative voting is a matter of constitutional law. He further states that only three states—Alabama, California, and Wyoming—have statutes specifically prohibiting classification.

for purposes hostile to the best interests of the corporation and its other stockholders.

The common-law right of inspection applies to all the corporate records. This would include the bylaws and regulations, stock books, financial or account books, and the minutes of the stockholders' and directors' meetings. A proper purpose must always be present before right of examination has to be given; if the right is demanded because of suspected fraud or mismanagement, very good proof would have to be submitted.

Statutes or constitutional provisions in some of the states confirm, limit, or enlarge the right of examination. Some statutes specify that the stockholders shall have the right to examine the stock books, but say nothing about the right to examine the other records. Where this is done, the stockholders still have their common-law right to examine the other records. The right given by statute may make it more absolute. If no qualifications are made relative to the statutory right of examination of the stock books, then the stockholder might have to show more cause for attempting to exercise his common-law right of examining the account books than in his demand to inspect the stock books. In New York the statutes provide that a stockholder in order to examine the records must have been a stockholder of record for at least six months, or he must hold at least five per cent of the outstanding stock.

This right to examine the corporate records is seldom exercised. Most stockholders do not have enough interest in the management of the company to want to examine the records. If they are dissatisfied with the way things are going they usually sell their stock. If a stockholder applied for the right to inspect the records, he would probably be refused by the management. To attempt to enforce his legal right would probably take more time and money than the average stockholder would want to devote to the cause.

When statutes specify inspection rights, they often provide penalties for wrongfully refusing to permit the examination. In some instances the statutes provide that the financial statements must be sent to stockholders upon request, and if the officials do not comply with the request they are subject to a fine of a specified amount for each day of default.

THE DIRECTORS

In a small corporation the stockholders and the directors may be the same persons, but in the case of the large corporations with many stockholders, the management must be concentrated in the hands of a relatively small number of people. Despite any shortcoming that may be stated relative to the delegation of management, it would be inconceivable even to think of a situation in which thousands of persons could directly manage a business.

The statutes in most of the states prescribe that there shall be at least three directors, and do not place a limitation on the number. The term of office is usually stated to be one year, or until their successors are elected. When *classification* of the board is carried out, the term is longer than one year.

Qualifications of the Directors

At common law the only qualifications for directors are that they be natural persons and have the capacity to contract. The statutes in some of the states require that they be shareholders, and from one to a majority of them citizens of the United States, or residents of the state.

In addition to the common-law and statutory qualifications, the directors should, of course, possess such special abilities as are required in the particular situation. A large stock interest in the company does not necessarily qualify a person for the director's job, but of course that helps him to get elected. Other things being equal, stock ownership is usually advisable because the director might take a greater interest in the business.

Powers of the Board of Directors

The management of the corporation is to be exercised not by the stockholders or the officers, but by the board of directors. Whatever power is granted to the corporation in its charter is really the power of the board. This power is not to be exercised by a single director, or by the various directors acting separately, but only by the board acting as a body in meeting.

It is the power and duty of the board to do all things necessary and proper in carrying on the purposes of the corporation. But it does not have the right to take extraordinary actions without the approval of the stockholders, or to do things which were not properly authorized in the charter. More specifically, the board has the power to do the following:

1. Formulate policies to carry out the purposes for which the corporation was formed
2. Appoint executive officers to carry out these policies
3. Appoint committees of the board to act in the intervals between board meetings
4. Adopt bylaws for their own convenience, which, however, cannot be inconsistent with those adopted by the shareholders
5. Declare dividends from appropriate sources
6. Inspect all the corporate records
7. Ratify important contracts
8. Adopt or approve budgets

9. Adopt or approve financing plans, expansion plans, etc.
10. Initiate proposals to amend the bylaws and charter

Board Committees

The board of directors has the power to appoint committees from the board. Small corporations usually do not have such committees. Larger ones often have an *executive committee,* and sometimes one other, such as a *finance committee* or *sales committee.*

The executive committee is ordinarily composed of directors who are also active officers in the corporation and therefore are convenient in the event that decisions must be made in the intervals between board meetings. Generally speaking, the executive committee has the power to make the same kind of decisions as the board itself on all ordinary matters, but they cannot act on extraordinary matters, such as the declaration of dividends, expansion, etc., which require the action of the entire board. In order that no question may be raised in regard to the action taken by the committees, it is common practice for the board in its next meeting to approve the actions taken by the committees.

Liabilities of Directors

A considerable amount of power and responsibility is entrusted to the board of directors. The shareholders may have millions and even billions of dollars invested in the corporation. A director occupies a position of trust. The law takes the attitude that a fiduciary relationship exists between him and the corporation and between him and the shareholders as a body. Such a relationship demands a high degree of care and prudence on the part of the directors. This being the case, it is only natural to expect that the law would provide penalties for failure to live up to this trust. Certain penalties or liabilities are imposed by common law, and the statutes have added to them. Directors can be held liable for the following:

1. Losses resulting from fraudulent acts
2. Losses resulting from illegal acts, or those which are *ultra vires* (beyond the corporation's powers)
3. Losses resulting from negligence
4. Losses resulting from willful mismanagement, or mismanagement resulting from negligence
5. The payment of dividends from unauthorized sources
6. Wrongfully refusing stockholders the right to examine the corporate records
7. Failure to make required reports
8. Signing statements or reports known to be false
9. Causing or permitting entries in the corporate books which are known to be false

10. Making transfers of property for the purpose of preferring or defrauding creditors when the corporation is insolvent
11. Conversion, embezzlement, larceny, and misapplication of the corporate property
12. Certain acts specified in the Securities Act of 1933, and the Securities Exchange Act of 1934. (These Acts are discussed in Chapters 14 and 15.) Among the more important of these are the following:
    a. False statements of material facts, or omission to state material facts in the registration statement
    b. Failure to report, or incorrect reporting, of amount of stock held
    c. Profit made by the purchase or sale of company stock within a period of less than six months. (Action must be instigated by the corporation or stockholders to recover this profit.)
    d. The Securities Acts also prohibit the directors from making short sales or manipulation of the company stock, and solicitation of company proxies except as provided in the Act.

Avoidance of Liability

A director should accept his position only if he feels qualified, and can devote the necessary amount of time to the job. He should attend the directors' meetings regularly, and faithfully discharge his duties. Occasional absence from the meetings is permissive, but continued willful absence may result in liability for negligence for some acts committed or omitted by the board.

If certain actions are taken by the board which a particular director believes are wrong, he should see to it that a record is made in the minutes indicating his disapproval. When he is absent from meetings, it is advisable for him to read over the minutes and have his disapproval recorded on any questionable action.

An attempt is sometimes made to relieve the directors from liability for certain acts by a statement to this effect in the articles of incorporation. Examples of this would include provisions of the following type: that the directors will not be liable for profits made on transactions with the corporation; that they will not be liable in any way for contracts made with other corporations in which they are directors or shareholders; that loans may be made by the corporation to its directors or officers. If an act of a director would make him liable, probably most courts would hold him still liable despite the presence of such clauses in the articles.

THE OFFICERS

The statutes of most of the states provide that the board of directors shall appoint or elect a *president, secretary,* and *treasurer.* They may also provide for vice-presidents, and assistant secretaries and treasurers. The articles or bylaws may provide for additional officers such as *general manager* or *controller*.

Such appointees or electees are called "officers" or "executive officers." Some confusion may exist when the term "officer" is used because it is not known whether reference is made to the executive officers or the directors. The latter are sometimes called "officers" but they are not executive officers. The directors can act only through meetings, but the executive officers have individual duties assigned to them. Both are referred to as agents of the corporation. In addition to the directors and executive officers, there may be other agents, such as a sales manager, or a purchasing agent. These agents and the officers are employees of the corporation, but in contrast, the directors as such are not considered employees.

Qualifications for Officers

Some state statutes provide that some or all the corporate executive officers shall be stockholders. Some specify that the president shall be a member of the board of directors. Also, the articles or bylaws may state additional qualifications.

As a practical matter it is realized that the officers should have the necessary experience or fitness to carry out their duties.

Powers and Duties of the Officers

The powers of the officers are stated in the statutes, the bylaws, and in some instances, in the charter of the corporation. The board of directors may also grant certain powers to them. In addition, the officers have incidental, apparent, and inherent powers. Since officers are agents they, like other agents, have the *incidental* power to do those things which are necessary. *Apparent* powers are those which the officers have by virtue of the corporation's holding out to innocent third parties that they have the power to perform certain acts. An *inherent* power is one that an officer has by virtue of the nature of his office. For all practical purposes there is not much difference between an "incidental" power and an "inherent" power. Their nature can best be understood by briefly stating the powers of each of the executive officers.

President. The president is the chief executive officer of the corporation. Although he along with the other officers is appointed by the board of directors, the president has authority over the other officers. The statutes of some of the states require that he sign or countersign the stock certificates and other corporate instruments. He presides at the stockholders' meetings and, in event that there is no board chairman, at the directors' meetings—the latter is considered an inherent power. In some instances the offices of president and chairman of the board are vested in the same person.

Courts are more and more often taking the attitude that the president has the power to do any act which the board of directors could authorize or ratify. In fact, in most corporations the president, or some other executive officer, takes the initiative, formulates policies and carries them out, and later has the board of directors ratify the acts. In many instances, of course, the president recommends policies to the board, gets its approval, and then executes them.

The statutes of some states provide for an office of *chairman of the board of directors*. Even in the absence of such statutes this could be done in the bylaws. Sometimes the question is raised whether the president or the chairman of the board is the more important officer of the corporation. No definite answer can be given to this question since it depends upon the particular company and the personalities of the individuals. Since the board, in theory at least, formulates the policies for the officers to carry out, the chairman of the board could be the more important. He presides at the board meeting and might be able to sway the directors to his way of thinking. Furthermore, his vote would be the deciding one in event of a tie. In many corporations the board chairman is undoubtedly the more important officer.

When the board merely approves what the officers do, the board chairman would not be so important. In a number of corporations, the office of chairman is more or less an honorary title which is given to a retiring president. In this way he may still be kept on the payroll. In many instances, however, the president may be too old to engage actively in the everyday activities of the management; but he may be the most valuable man possible for the post of chairman.

In some organizations, such as trade associations, the operating head is commonly called "secretary" or "executive secretary," and the title of "president" is more or less honorary, and is given to one of the active members.

Vice-President. About all that need be said about the vice-president is that he takes over the president's powers and duties in event of absence, incapacity, or death of the president. Other than that, he has no inherent duties by virtue of his office. If there are first and second vice-presidents, etc., the former would take over if the president were incapacitated, and the second would carry on in the event that something happened to his immediate superior.

In some corporations an employee of the corporation, such as the sales manager, might be given the title of "vice-president in charge of sales." Or the manager of one of the plants or of a company division, such as the export department, might be given the title of vice-president. In some instances these titles are handed out rather freely in order to impress the public, or the particular employee himself.

Secretary. The secretary does not have an inherent power to act for or bind the corporation. The board of directors, however, may assign him such specific powers. The usual duties of the secretary as prescribed by statutes and bylaws are: to keep minutes of the stockholders' and directors' meetings; have custody of the corporate seal; sign stock certificates, documents, and reports to stockholders and the state; give notice of meetings; and keep the stock books. In the larger corporations the actual details of these duties are handled by other employees, though the responsibility is the secretary's.

Treasurer. The usual power or duty of the treasurer is custody of the corporate funds. His duties or part of them may be found in the statutes, but they are commonly listed in the bylaws. Unless specifically authorized to do so, the treasurer cannot bind the corporation on contracts, but some courts have held that by virtue of his office he could execute corporate notes. The usual powers or duties of the treasurer are as follows: to take care of all the funds and securities; deposit money in banks approved by the board of directors; indorse checks and other financial instruments received; sign notes, checks, and drafts; supervise the company's financial books; prepare the financial and tax reports; and advise the board of directors on dividends, financial plans, and budgets.

In large firms the treasurer may be in charge of all of these items, but the actual work would be carried on by subordinates. Sometimes the office of "secretary-treasurer" is given to one person.

Other Officers. Besides the officers listed above, some corporations have additional ones. An increasing number of firms have a *controller* (same as "comptroller"). His duties are set forth in the bylaws. Practice varies considerably as to the nature of his duties. In some instances he is chosen by the board of directors; in other cases the executive committee of the board may appoint him. In some corporations he is hired by the president or other executive officer, and has the same rank as a department head. The duties of the controller vary widely among companies, but generally speaking, he takes over many of the treasurer's duties. Quite commonly he is in charge of the company's financial books and the budget.

Many corporations have an *auditor*. He may be the chief accounting officer of the corporation, but in some cases he is independent of the accounting department and checks on the records, and reports directly to the treasurer or the president. When there is no controller, he often carries on the work of one. Where there are both of these officers the auditor sometimes reports to the controller. In the case of ordinary business corporations the auditor is usually only an employee and not an executive officer of the company.

Some companies, particularly manufacturing firms with several plants or locations, have an officer who is called the *general manager*. The statutes do not provide for this office, so when it exists it would be specified in the bylaws. For the particular plant or division, the general manager may be the most important company employee. He is usually looked upon as an important department or divisional head, rather than an officer. Sometimes the title of general manager is given to the president.

Liability of Officers

The law looks upon the executive officers as occupying a fiduciary relation to the corporation and to the shareholders as a group, in a manner similar to that of the directors. Some courts have even held the executive officers, who received salaries and were active in the business, to a higher degree of diligence than the directors, who were serving gratuitously. Because of the similar trust position, the liabilities of the executive officers are practically the same as stated for the directors above.

The liabilities imposed on the officers by the Securities Act and the Securities Exchange Act are the same except that the liability for incorrect statements or omissions of material facts in the registration statement applies to only the officers who signed the statement. The following apply to officers of companies whose stock is listed. They are not permitted to sell the stock short, or to engage in its manipulation. They, as well as the directors, must report all their purchases and sales of the company stock to the Securities and Exchange Commission. Any profit made on company stock owned for a period of less than six months can be recovered by suit by the corporation or by its stockholders.

QUESTIONS

1. What part do the shareholders play in the management of large corporations in the United States?
2. List the rights that are possessed by corporate shareholders.
3. At common law how many votes does a shareholder possess? Has this been changed by the statutes? Explain.
4. (a) Is cumulative voting permitted at common law? (b) Do the statutes of the various states give shareholders the right to cumulate their votes, or do they merely permit it if so specified in the articles of incorporation? (c) What is the purpose of cumulative voting? (d) Give an example of cumulative voting. (e) Is cumulative voting used for any purpose other than the election of directors? (f) When cumulative voting is followed, how many ballots can be taken in the election of directors? Explain. (g) Do you believe cumulative voting should be permitted in all corporations? Explain.
5. (a) Is proxy voting permitted at common law? (b) What objections might be raised to proxy voting? If proxy voting were prohibited would this overcome the objections?
6. Explain what is meant by class voting and why it is sometimes provided for.

7. Indicate the various ways in which control of a corporation may be obtained without the ownership of a majority of the stock.

8. What is meant by the pre-emptive right of shareholders?

9. (a) Indicate the nature of the common-law right of a shareholder to inspect the books of his corporation. (b) How have the statutes of some of the states modified this right? (c) Of what practical value is this right? Explain fully.

10. (a) Indicate the common-law and statutory qualifications for corporate directors. (b) What is meant by classification of the board of directors? Why is it sometimes done? Is classification of the board legal when cumulative voting is followed? Explain. (c) List the powers possessed by the board of directors. (d) How may a director avoid many of the liabilities which the law imposes on directors?

11. (a) Distinguish between the directors and the officers of a corporation. (b) Who is the most important officer in a corporation?

PROBLEMS

1. Assume that the Standard Corp. has 1,000 shares of voting stock outstanding but only a total of 700 shares is represented at the meeting called for the purpose of electing a board of three directors. Each share has one vote for each director to be elected. How many shares would you have to own or control in order to insure the election of yourself to the board if: (a) Straight voting is followed? (b) Cumulative voting is followed?

2. If 1,000 shares vote cumulatively at a meeting called to elect five directors, what is the maximum number of directors that you could be sure of electing if you owned or controlled 280 shares?

3. The New Process Corp. has 10,000 shares of stock outstanding of which you own 1,500 shares. Each share has one vote on each matter of business. The board of directors consists of nine persons. How many directors would you be sure of electing if: (a) Straight voting is followed? (b) Cumulative voting is followed? (c) Cumulative voting is followed, but the board has staggered terms with three directors being elected each year for three-year terms?

4. On January 2, Mr. Smith purchased three shares of stock of the Reliable Corporation. One week later he appeared at the company's offices and demanded the right to examine the books of the company. (a) If you were in charge would you permit the examination? Why or why not? (b) If the right of examination is refused what could Mr. Smith do about it?

5. Look up the statutes of your state in regard to the following: (a) Right of shareholders to inspect the corporate books. (b) Is cumulative voting permitted? If so, must it be so provided in the articles of incorporation? Must notice of intention to cumulate votes be given to the corporation? (c) Whether classified stock is permitted. (d) Whether a voting trust is permitted, and if so, the maximum duration.

SELECTED READINGS

BERLE, A. A., JR., and MEANS, G. C. *The Modern Corporation and Private Property.* New York: The Macmillan Co., 1933.

BOGEN, JULES I. (ed). *Financial Handbook,* 3d ed. New York: The Ronald Press Co., 1952. Pp. 368–403; 421–35.

BRADSHAW, T. F. "The Place and Status of the Financial Executive Today," *The Financial Executive's Job,* Financial Management Series, No. 99. New York: American Management Association, 1952. Pp. 14–22.

FLETCHER, WILLIAM MEADE. *Cyclopedia of the Law of Private Corporations,* Permanent ed. Chicago: Callaghan & Co., Vol. 3 (1947 rev. vol.), Vol. 5 (1952 rev. vol.).

The Duties of Financial Executives, Studies in Business Policy, No. 56. New York: National Industrial Conference Board, 1952.

The Financial Executive's Job, Financial Management Series, No. 99. New York: American Management Association, 1952.

WESTON, J. FRED. "The Finance Function," *Journal of Finance,* September, 1954, pp. 265–82.

WHETTEN, LELAND C. *Cumulative Voting for Directors: Its Origin and Significance.* Studies in Business and Economics, Bulletin No. 2. Atlanta: Bureau of Business and Economic Research, School of Business Administration, Georgia State College of Business Administration, 1959.

―――――. *Recent Proxy Contests: A Study in Management-Stockholder Relations.* Bulletin No. 6. 1959.

―――――. *The Influence of Recent Proxy Contests on Social and Economic Trends.* Bulletin No. 11. 1961.

WILLIAMS, C. M. *Cumulative Voting for Directors.* Cambridge, Mass.: Graduate School of Business Administration, Harvard University, 1951.

II

CORPORATE SECURITIES

5

Capital Stock

In an unincorporated organization, such as the general partnership, there is no such thing as "stock." The respective partners own a fractional part of the business, which can be ascertained by looking at the articles of partnership or the financial books of account. No certificates are issued to represent this interest in the business.

Nature of Corporate Stock

The stock of a corporation is divided into units called *shares*. These may have a par value, for example $100, or there may be no nominal dollar value assigned to them. The latter is called no-par stock.

Stock itself is invisible—no one has ever seen it. What we see is the certificate which evidences the stock. When a person buys stock he merely buys a bundle of legal rights, such as the right to vote the stock, to receive dividends, to share in the assets upon dissolution, etc. There is nothing inherent in stock which will enable it to earn dividends or to advance in price in the market. Its performance depends upon the success of the corporation's business.

In order to raise millions of dollars from hundreds of thousands of people it is absolutely necessary that the ownership of the corporation be divided into a large number of shares with a small denomination each.

Authorized, Issued, and Outstanding Stock

The *authorized* stock is that amount which the corporation is permitted in its charter to issue. At the time of organization it merely represents a permit on the part of the state. No money may have been paid on the stock, and in fact, maybe the stock certificates are not even printed. To increase the authorized stock calls for action on the part of the stockholders and the state, since the charter is a contract between these parties.

That part of the authorized stock which has been subscribed to by the shareholders and accepted by the corporation or sold to the stockholders is called the *issued stock*. This remains issued until canceled by appropriate action on the part of the corporation.

Outstanding stock is that part of the issued stock which is in the hands of the stockholders. If the corporation reacquires part of its stock this is called *treasury stock*. As long as this remains treasury stock and is not canceled by the corporation, it is still included in the issued stock, but it is not included in the outstanding stock. Thus all outstanding stock is issued stock, but not all issued stock must be outstanding.

Capital Stock

The term *capital stock* is commonly used to refer to the aggregate of corporate stock. When *preferred stock* is issued, the other class of stock is called *common stock*. But when only one type of stock is issued it is commonly called *capital stock* on the books of the company and in the balance sheet.

Capital

There are various meanings of the word *capital*. The economist defines it as wealth used for further production. This may be satisfactory for his purposes, but it is a little too indefinite for us.

In legal works the terms *capital* and *capital stock* are commonly used synonymously. In other words, lawyers and judges often say that the capital of a corporation is the aggregate of the par value of the stock, or the stated value in the case of no-par stock. This meaning can be illustrated by the legal rule that dividends cannot be paid from *capital*. It is realized, of course, that dividends are never paid from the capital stock. What is meant is that dividends cannot be paid when the effect of payment would be to reduce the net assets to a figure below the capital stock. Since the term *capital stock* is well understood, while the term *capital* has different meanings to different individuals, it is suggested that when referring to the aggregate of the stock, we use the term *capital stock* rather than *capital*.

The other common use of the term *capital* is to apply it to the total assets of the corporation. This is the use which is here recommended.

STOCK CERTIFICATES AND STOCK TRANSFER

The ownership of stock is evidenced by a *stock certificate*. Most people look upon this as the stock. It is of practical importance to distinguish between the stock and the certificate because if a person loses a stock certificate or it is destroyed, he has not lost the stock. A new certificate will be issued if he puts up an indemnity bond with the company to protect it if the old certificate, properly indorsed, turns up in the hands of an innocent purchaser for value.

The following are contained on the face of a stock certificate: name of company and state of incorporation; serial number of the certificate; number of shares represented; in case of par stock, the par value; name of the registered owner; date of issue; signature of the appropriate corporate officers; seal of the corporation; signatures of the transfer agent and registrar.

One certificate can represent one share or a number of shares. Since 100 shares is the smallest unit of trading for most stocks on the floor of the New York Stock Exchange, most of the certificates transferred there are for this number.

Transfer of Stock

Since the certificate evidences the stock, when a shareholder wishes to sell or transfer his stock he must transfer the certificate by signing the assignment form on the reverse side (see Figure 5–1), having the signa-

---

For value received, _____
hereby sell, assign and transfer unto _____
_____ (   ) shares of the
_____ Capital Stock represented
by the within certificate and do hereby irrevocably constitute and appoint
_____ attorney
to transfer said stock on the books of the within named Company with full
power of substitution in the premises.

Date _____ 19_____

In presence of:

Fig. 5–1. Stock assignment form on reverse side of stock certificate.

ture witnessed, and inserting the proper date. It is not necessary to write in the name of the buyer, nor of the person to whom one gives power of attorney to transfer the stock.

The issuing corporation looks to the stockholder of record as the owner of the shares. Stock is properly transferred on the books of the company by someone who is authorized to do so by the registered owner. The transfer agent of the issuing company inserts his name in the blank space left by the owner.

If only part of the shares represented by the certificate are being transferred, the number being sold can be inserted in the appropriate space. The transferee's name would be inserted or a letter to the agent would instruct him to transfer over the given number of shares to the transferee. A certificate would be made out to him for the appropriate number of shares and a new certificate would be sent to the transferor for the number of shares being retained by him.

Many large companies appoint a trust company as their transfer agent. Such a company handles all the details in connection with the issue and transfer of the stock. It may also appoint another trust company as registrar. The latter checks on the transfer agent and prevents an overissue of stock. The New York Stock Exchange requires that all companies whose stock is listed must maintain a transfer agent and a registrar in the financial district of New York. These are commonly trust companies. The registrar cannot be the issuing company or the transfer agent. All stock sold on the New York Stock Exchange must be transferred in that city. A company may maintain transfer offices also in other cities.

If a stock certificate is placed with a bank as collateral for a loan, it is advisable not to sign the form on the reverse side of the certificate, because after the loan is paid off and the certificate returned to the owner, it would bear his indorsement and a finder or thief could pass good title to it. Instead the owner should execute a separate assignment form, called a *stock power of attorney,* and attach this to the certificate.

Stockholder Entitled to Dividends

When directors declare dividends they make them payable to stockholders *of record* several days or weeks in the future, and the dividend is paid several weeks or a month after the record date. A typical example would be as follows. The directors meet January 15, and declare the dividend to stockholders of record February 1, with the dividend payable February 15.

When stock is sold about the same time as the record date, the question may be raised whether the seller or the buyer gets the dividends. Stock sold "regular way" on the New York Stock Exchange calls for delivery on the fourth full business day following the sale. Unless otherwise specified by the Exchange, the stock will sell *ex-dividend* three full business days before the record date (if the record date falls on Saturday or a holiday, the stock will sell ex-dividend four full business days before the record date). When a stock sells "ex-dividend" it means that the seller, rather than the buyer, will be entitled to the dividend. In the example above where the record date was February 1, the stock would sell ex-dividend on January 29 (January has 31 days). The stock would sell *cum-dividend* through January 28. This means that the buyer would be entitled to the dividend.

If a person bought the stock prior to the ex-dividend date, but did not get it transferred to his name by the record date, the company would pay the dividend to the stockholder of record, which would be the seller, but the buyer could demand that the seller turn over to him the amount of the dividend.

This procedure results in the dividend's going to the person who is entitled to it. The seller has his money tied up in the company and is therefore entitled to receive the dividend. If the buyer acquires the stock a few days before the ex-dividend date and gets it transferred to his name by the record date, he will get the dividend. But the stock would have been selling cum-dividend, and the buyer would have paid a price that included the dividend.

If the market in general is rather stable, a good investment stock will tend to sell off on the ex-dividend date by approximately the amount of the dividend. If the stock closed down (as compared to the close the previous day) on the ex-dividend date by an amount equivalent to the dividend, the "net change" column in the newspaper will show no change for the day.

If the board of directors declares a dividend without specifying the record date, then the dividend will be payable to stockholders of record the day the dividend is declared.

Stockholder Entitled to Vote

In the past it was a common practice of corporations to close their stock transfer books some days in advance of a meeting in order that a list of the stockholders entitled to vote at the meeting could be obtained. Although some still do this, the larger corporations now usually provide that the stockholders of record of a particular hour on a given day in advance of the meeting are those entitled to vote.

Some states, such as New York, require that if a person buys stock after the record date but before the meeting date, the seller must upon demand turn over a proxy to the buyer.

Liability of Stockholders

If a person has not paid for his stock in full, he is subject to calls by the directors for the unpaid amount. In the event that a corporation is insolvent, creditors may come against the stockholders for the amount owned.

If partly paid stock is transferred, the question arises as to whether the transferor or the transferee is liable for the unpaid amount. It is difficult to generalize on this point because of differences in state laws and in the circumstances. In most of the states the transferee would be liable for calls made on the stock after the transfer, if he took the stock knowing that it was not fully paid. In some states, however, the transferor is liable to those who became creditors prior to the transfer.

It is common practice now not to issue the stock certificate until the stock is fully paid. The stock certificate usually states that the stock is "fully paid and non-assessable." If an innocent purchaser for value acquired such a certificate, he would not be liable for any assessments on the stock. In this event the liability would either be lost or would be retained by the seller, depending upon the state law, when the call was made, and when the debt was incurred. In some states the innocent purchaser for value would have no liability even if the certificate were not marked "fully paid."

Once the full amount of the stock has been paid to the issuing corporation, a purchaser of the stock in the market has no liability on it regardless of the price he pays.

The Uniform Stock Transfer Act, which has been adopted in all the states and the District of Columbia, gives stock certificates the same negotiable qualities that the Uniform Negotiable Instruments Act gives to negotiable instruments. This means that if a certificate has been properly indorsed, an innocent purchaser for value acquires good title despite the fact that it may have been lost or stolen. If a stock certificate is lost or stolen, the company and its transfer agent should be notified immediately. If the certificate had been indorsed, the loser may still have title to it unless it is held by an innocent purchaser for value. But if the registered owner's name is forged on the certificate, title still remains in him, even against an innocent purchaser for value.

TREASURY STOCK

Treasury stock is uncanceled stock which a corporation has issued and then subsequently reacquired through purchase or gift. Such stock does not vote, nor does it receive dividends. If the treasury stock is canceled or reissued, it ceases to be treasury stock. Treasury stock is included in the *issued* stock, but of course it is not *outstanding*.

When treasury stock is acquired, accountants usually recommend that it be shown on the balance sheet as a deduction from the outstanding stock. Since the other balance sheet items are not affected by the donation of the stock back to the corporation, it is necessary to credit a donated surplus account with the same amount as is subtracted from the capital stock. If the treasury stock is sold for less than the amount that was credited to the surplus account, the surplus will have to be charged or debited with the difference.

Many corporations carry treasury stock as an asset on their balance sheets. It is true that it may be sold for cash, but it is usually recommended that it be not listed on the asset side of the balance sheet.

Reasons for Reacquiring Stock

There are various reasons why a corporation might reacquire part of its issued stock.

For Debt Owed by Stockholders. A corporation sometimes sells its stock on the installment plan. In the event the stockholder is unable to pay for the stock, he may be compelled to forfeit it to the corporation.

Sale to Officers and Employees. Many corporations have a plan of selling stock to officers and employees at a price below the existing market price. In some instances the stock sold is unissued stock, but in other cases it is stock which the corporation has acquired in the market. If the stock is being sold below the par value, the question of liability would arise in case the stock were unissued stock; but if it were treasury stock, it could be sold as fully paid stock regardless of the price which was paid for it. The corporation may take advantage of low market prices which exist from time to time to acquire the stock. Some stock option plans do not allow issuance of unissued stock. Pension plans are another reason and source of funds for stock reacquisitions.

Redundant Cash. At certain times a corporation may find that it has cash on hand which is not needed in the immediate future. The current dividend rate may be rather high at the time, but the corporation may be unable to obtain a high return from investments. Despite these conditions, the market price of the stock may be reasonable. Perhaps the best investment for the corporate funds at this time would be to purchase back part of its stock.

To Reduce Future Dividend Requirement. This point is similar to the preceding one. In fact, one of the reasons a corporation may use its surplus cash to buy back its stock is in order to reduce the cash that will be needed in the future to pay the regular dividend rate.

To Eliminate Burdensome Requirements. A corporation may have outstanding a type of stock, such as a cumulative and participating preferred stock (to be discussed in the following chapter), which may prove burdensome, particularly at a time when earnings are low. When the stock is selling for a reasonable price in the market and the corporation has surplus cash, it may buy back the stock and thus eliminate the burdensome features. In this way the common stockholders will benefit both in lean and prosperous years.

Market Support. When a corporation's stock is slipping in the market, it may feel that it would be to the best interests of both the corporation and its stockholders to go into the market and buy up part of the stock in order to stabilize the price. Before doing this a corporation should look into the legal question of whether it has the right to buy the stock for this purpose. It is not in furtherance of the purpose for which the corporation was formed, nor would it be to the best interests of the shareholders to buy back the stock at one price and be forced to sell it at a lower price.

Ways of Reacquiring Stock

Following are the various ways in which a corporation may reacquire its stock.

Forfeiture from Stockholder for Debt. This was mentioned above in connection with the reasons for acquisition.

Donation of Treasury Stock. Stockholders may wish to aid the company by donating some of their shares.

Purchase from Individual Stockholders. A corporation will sometimes negotiate with individual stockholders for the purchase of part or all of their stock. Those approached usually hold a large block of stock. The advantage of purchasing directly from individual stockholders is that the corporation will thus not force the market price of the stock up by its purchases.

Purchase in the Open Market. In some instances the corporation will go into the open market and purchase its stock. The disadvantage of this method is that the corporation by bidding for the stock will tend to push up the price it will have to pay. Sometimes it will have a broker gradually buy up the stock in such a way that the extra demand will not increase the price appreciably.

Stock Tenders. Another method used to reacquire stock is for the issuing corporation to advertise for *tenders* of its stock. The corporation agrees to pay not over a specified price per share for a given number of shares or for a specified amount of money available for the purchase. A time limitation is placed on the tenders. The stockholder sets the price which he will accept, commonly the maximum price set by the corporation. Some stockholders, however, will specify a lower price in order to insure a sale. In the event that more shares are offered than the corporation can purchase, those offering the lowest price will be taken up first.

Legal Right of Corporation to Reacquire Shares

There is no legal objection to a corporation's acquiring treasury stock through donation by the shareholders. But when it comes to purchasing or canceling the stock, the corporation should be careful to follow legal requirements.

Stock can be canceled only by statutory authority. The board of directors usually initiates the cancellation. Statutes usually require a vote of either a majority or two-thirds of the shares to effect the reduction in the stock. Since a cancellation involves an amendment to the charter, the procedure for amending should be followed. This requires assent on the part of the state also.

When a corporation buys back its stock there may be two parties harmed—the stockholders and the creditors. Stockholders may be injured because part of the corporation's funds are being removed from the business, and furthermore, the corporation may pay too high a price for the stock. In addition, the proportionate ownership and control of the corporation may be changed by purchasing the stock from only part of the shareholders, or purchasing it from all, but not in proportion to the amount of stock held by each. If the repurchase is permitted, the corporation should see to it that purchase from fewer than all the shareholders, or other than in proportion to the total amount of stock held by each, is permitted.

A more serious objection relates to the possible impairment of creditors' rights. The stockholders are the owners of the business, and they collectively, as the corporation, owe the creditors. If the company had the unrestricted right to buy back its stock, it is conceivable that all of the corporate assets might be used to retire the stock and the creditors would be left with nothing.

There is in law what is known as the *trust fund theory*. According to this, the capital stock of a corporation is a trust fund for the benefit of creditors. This title is a misnomer for several reasons. In the first place the capital stock is not a "fund." And in the second place, if it were, it would not be a *trust* fund. What is meant by the law is that the corporation cannot use its assets to reduce voluntarily the net assets (assets less liabilities) below the capital stock figure. The reasoning behind this is that when extending credit, the creditors look to the balance sheet and see a definite amount opposite the caption "Capital Stock," and they thereupon grant credit to the company on the faith that net assets at least equivalent to this amount will be retained in the business for the security of the debt. It is true that operating losses may reduce the net assets below this figure, but the corporation should not voluntarily reduce it by such actions as paying dividends or buying back part of the stock and canceling it.

When the reduction of stock is permitted, the statutes either expressly or by implication provide that such reduction could not be made if it would impair the ability of the corporation to meet its debts.

PAR AND NO-PAR STOCK

The early English corporation had par values of various amounts, and some of the corporations formed here during colonial times issued stock with varying par values. There are a few isolated early cases in the United States of corporations issuing a type of no-par stock under special statutes. But most stock issued by corporations in the United States prior to 1912 had a par value.

Since stock represented a fractional ownership of the corporate property or the corporation, it seems only natural that a fixed dollar amount, or "par value" should be assigned to a share. A par value of "$100" was a convenient figure to use. It was also customary in former times to sell par stock at its par value. Thus, the purchaser or prospective purchaser looked upon the aggregate par value of his shares as the value of his equity in the business.

Par Value as a Measure of Liability

The aggregate of the par value of a corporation's shares is ordinarily the figure at which the capital stock is carried in the balance sheet of the issuing corporation. If a person buys a share of stock from the issuing corporation for less than par, he can be held liable for the difference between what he paid and the par value. Thus, the par value has served as a measure of liability for the shareholders.

Before proceeding, however, we should not overlook this exception to the above: according to common-law decisions in a number of the states, if a corporation has tried to sell its stock at par but is unable to do so, and if the money is needed to keep from failing, and not for expansion purposes, the corporation may sell its par stock at the best price obtainable and no liability will be attached to it even if it is sold below par. This common-law rule has been written into the statutes in some of the states.

Disadvantages of Par Value

Some of the disadvantages of par stock will be discussed since it was because of these that no-par stock laws were enacted.

Difficulty in Obtaining Equity Capital. When a corporation is in need of additional funds, its stock may be selling in the market for less than its par value. But the corporation either cannot legally sell additional stock below par, or if it is legal, the public will not buy the stock because of the possible future liability. No one will pay par for new stock when he can buy the same old stock in the market at a discount.

Narrow Market. Generally speaking, the lower the selling price of a stock, the wider the market. Other things being equal, a corporation can sell stock at $50 a share to more people than if the price were $100. If the state law requires a par value of $100, which was usual in the past, it thus narrows the potential market and makes financing charges higher. Today, however, the most common par value among industrials listed on the New York Stock Exchange is $1 per share, and the next most popular par is $5.

Difficulty in Obtaining Paid-in Surplus. In many instances corporate promoters would like to put part of the consideration received from the stock in the surplus account and thus start out with what might be thought of as a good showing. To do this would necessitate selling the par stock at a premium, which might be difficult to do.

Status of Bonus Stock. Some corporations may want to give common stock as a bonus in connection with the sale of preferred stock or bonds. Sometimes employees or management are given some of the company's stock. If this is unissued par stock, and nothing is obtained for it, the person to whom it is given might be held liable for the par value, unless the statutes specifically authorize the practice.

Par Value is Misleading. When a share of stock carries a par value many people believe that the stock is worth that amount, or was originally worth that amount, or will some time in the future be worth that amount. To this extent the par label is misleading. A stock is rarely worth its par value even at the time it is sold. Even if the stock is worth its par value at the time it is sold, operating losses or profits may alter the situation so much that there may be absolutely no relation between the par of a stock and its actual value.

Adoption of No-Par Stock Laws

Because of some of the shortcomings stated above there was agitation for the adoption of laws that would permit a corporation to issue stock which did not possess a par value. New York, in 1912, was the first state to enact such legislation, and since then all the states, except Nebraska,[1]

---

[1] Not only must all stocks have a par value in Nebraska, but it is required that all the stock of the same corporation must have the same par value per share. Registered public utility holding companies are not permitted to issue no-par stock without SEC approval.

have adopted statutes which permit the issuance of no-par, as well as par, stock. Certain types of corporations, such as banks, trust companies, insurance companies, and savings and loan associations, however, are not permitted to use no-par stock in a number of the states. Probably about one-third or less of the stocks listed on the national exchanges are no-par.

At the same time the states were enacting no-par statutes, many of them changed their laws to permit stock with a par of any amount, or of any amount from $1 up to $100 per share. Some of the disadvantages of $100 par stock have been overcome by the adoption of a low par value.

Stated Value of No-Par Stock

The statutes of some states provide that the no-par stock shall have a *stated value*. This is an arbitrary value that is assigned to the stock and is found either in the charter or as a resolution in the minutes of the directors' meeting. Where a stated value is contained in the charter, it is similar to a par value, except that this stated value may not appear on the stock certificate.

In most instances the stated value is determined from time to time by the board of directors. To the extent that a shareholder knows the stated value, if he buys the stock at less than this price, he may be held liable for the difference between what he paid and the stated value. As a practical matter, however, the directors always set a stated value at or below the sale price of the stock.

In other states there is no necessity to establish a stated value. This is more truly no-par stock than when a stated value must be set. The directors merely determine from time to time the price at which new issues of the stock are to be sold. In some states the stated value, or all the consideration received from such stock, must be carried to the capital stock account, but in others part of the consideration may be put in a surplus account, provided a statement to this effect was made at the time the stock was sold.

Advantages of No-Par Stock

Most of the advantages of no-par stock are obviously the same as the disadvantages of par value stock stated above, so the advantages will merely be listed.

1. Capital may be easier to obtain from the sale of the stock since there is no requirement that a par amount be obtained
2. There is little chance that stockholder liability will exist after the subscription price has been paid
3. A wider market may be obtained for the stock than if a relatively high-value par stock is sold

4. It may be easier to acquire a paid-in surplus from the sale of the stock than if par stock is used
5. There is less likelihood that any liability will attach to bonus stock
6. There is less chance that the investing public will be misled as to the actual value of the stock

Tax Disadvantage of No-Par Stock

Practically the only disadvantage of no-par stock relates to taxation. In some of the states the organization tax on each no-par share is the same as the tax on each $100 of par value. No-par stock is almost invariably sold for less than $100 a share, so that a larger percentage of the sales price goes to the state. In other words, if one corporation sold its no-par share for $10, and another corporation sold a $10 par stock at the same price, the no-par corporation would have to pay ten times as much in taxes per share as the par stock corporation. In New York, for example, the organization tax is 5¢ per $100 of par authorized, but 5¢ on each no-par share authorized.

Another tax that may be felt more by no-par stock corporations is the annual franchise tax for domestic and foreign corporations. In some of the states which base this tax on the authorized or the issued stock, it is assumed that each no-par share has a value of $100, or some fixed amount ranging from $10 to $100. This would be a greater burden than the organization tax, since it must be paid each year.

Formerly the federal issue and transfer taxes were more on no-par shares than on low-par shares, but since 1958 the two types of stock have been taxed the same.

OTHER STOCK VALUES

Book Value

The book value of stock is the amount shown on the financial books as represented by the assets less the liabilities. Another way of saying this is that the book value is represented by the amount shown in the net worth section of the balance sheet.

Where there is only one class of stock the book value per share would be calculated by dividing the net worth of the corporation by the number of shares outstanding. Many companies do not place a value on their intangible assets such as goodwill, patents, and franchises, so their value would not be reflected in the book value. Where these are valued in the balance sheet, the financial services usually subtract them from the net worth in obtaining the book value. They then commonly refer to book value as the "tangible-asset value" or "net tangible-asset value." When "book value" is referred to it is not always known whether the intangibles have been deducted. The conservative way is to deduct them.

When there is both preferred and common stock outstanding the calculation of the book value is a little more involved. To calculate the book value per share of the *preferred* stock one would divide the total net worth (less intangible assets) by the number of preferred shares. As a practical matter, the book value of the preferred means little or nothing, particularly since all of the net assets, including those represented by the common stock, are assigned to the preferred stock. If there is more than one class of preferred outstanding, the book value of each class is calculated by subtracting from the net worth (less intangible assets) the par value (or equivalent) of each class senior to the one under consideration.

The book value of the *common* is calculated by subtracting the preferred stock from the net worth (less intangible assets). To get the book value per share this figure would be divided by the number of common shares. This raises the question as to what figure would be used in subtracting the preferred stock. In many instances subtracting the preferred at its par value would be satisfactory. If there are any accumulated dividends on the preferred stock, these should be added to their par value before subtracting.

If the par value of the preferred, however, has little relation to the worth of the stock, another figure should be used. For example, a preferred stock with a nominal par value of $1 per share may have been sold for $100 a share. The stock may be entitled to $105 and accrued dividends in event of involuntary liquidation, and $110 and accrued dividends in the event that it is voluntary, and it may be callable by the company at $120 a share. The dividend rate specified on the stock may be $6 a share. A book value of the common derived by subtracting the preferred at par would be very misleading, to say the least. Some of the financial services use the involuntary liquidation price, and it is suggested that the reader use this figure. Any accrued dividends would be added.

To illustrate computation of book value of stock we will assume that the preferred stock in the balance sheet on page 97 is entitled to $105 a share plus accrued dividends in the event of involuntary liquidation. We will assume that one year's dividends of 6 per cent have accrued on the stock. Two methods of arriving at the book value will be illustrated.

In the past considerable importance was attached to the book value of a company's stock but in recent years it has been given little attention. This is undoubtedly the right attitude for several reasons. In the first place, assets might be carried on the books at a figure far different from the cost. At the time of organization the assets are usually inflated. Later the book figure may be cut down considerably below cost less depreciation in order to be conservative, or to reduce depreciation charges, and thereby increase the net earnings.

BALANCE SHEET

The Standard Corporation
As of December 31, 1962

Assets		*Liabilities*	
Current assets	$ 2,220,000	Current liabilities	$ 500,000
Goodwill	1,000,000	Bonds	2,000,000
Fixed assets	15,000,000	Preferred stock ($100 par)	2,000,000
		Common stock ($100 par)	10,000,000
		Surplus	3,720,000
Total	$18,220,000	Total	$18,220,000

CALCULATION OF BOOK VALUE

Total Assets			$18,220,000
Less:			
Goodwill		$1,000,000	
Current liabilities		500,000	
Bonds		2,000,000	3,500,000
Net tangible assets (book value of preferred)			$14,720,000

$14,720,000 divided by 20,000 equals $736, book value per
share of the preferred stock.

Net tangible assets			$14,720,000
20,000 preferred shares @ $105		$2,100,000	
6% accrued dividend		120,000	2,220,000
Book value of common stock			$12,500,000

$12,500,000 divided by 100,000 equals $125, book value per
share of the common stock.

Alternative method:

Net worth (preferred and common stock and surplus)		$15,720,000
Less:		
Goodwill		1,000,000
Book value of preferred stock		$14,720,000
Less: Preferred @ $105 plus accrued dividend		2,220,000
Book value of common stock		$12,500,000

$12,500,000 divided by 100,000 equals $125, book value per
share of the common stock.

Even if the assets are carried at their cost, there is not necessarily any
relationship between the book value of the stock and the market value.
Some companies acquire assets in appreciable amounts at a time when
prices are high. Others purchase them when prices are low. But the
earning power of a given asset would be the same regardless of whether
it was acquired at a high or at a low price. Furthermore, operating losses
or profits retained in the business would either lower or increase the
value of the company's assets.

The most important reason why the book value does not indicate the
real worth of a stock is that the worth depends upon anticipated future
earnings. Two companies may have identical book values for their stock,

but one of them may have such better management and location that it can earn considerably more and pay larger dividends than the other company. The anticipated earning power and dividend payments are the factors that determine the stock's real value.

Current-Asset Value

It may be of some importance to calculate the *current-asset value* of a stock. When only common stock is outstanding this is found by subtracting from the current assets *all* the liabilities. The current-asset value per share could then be found by dividing by the number of shares outstanding. If preferred stock is outstanding, the same procedure as described above is followed. This is really another type of book value, being the current-asset book value of the stock.

Book values are sometimes used to determine the liquidating value of the stock. If fixed assets are sold at a forced sale, they usually bring only a small percentage of the book value. The current assets bring a much higher figure. The cash and perhaps the securities would, of course, yield 100 per cent. The current-asset value of a stock might truly represent the liquidating value better than the book value including fixed assets.

Market Value

The easiest of all values to determine is the market value of a stock. For stocks which are listed on the leading stock exchanges, the last sale price or closing price fairly well indicates the market value. If there were no sales for several hours before the market closed, the "bid-and-asked" prices would show the worth of the stock at the time the market closes.

The market price of a stock is a resultant of the forces of supply and demand. People want to buy stocks either for the dividends, or for the anticipated appreciation in the price of the stock, or both. These result from the future earnings of the company. Therefore, the future earning power of the company has more influence on the market price of a company's stock than any other single factor. But no one knows definitely what the future earnings of any company will be. A number of factors, including the past and present earnings and the trend of the income, are used in attempting to predict the future earnings.

The *price-earnings* ratio is a convenient formula used by many to determine whether they think the market price is high or low in relation to present earnings per share. This ratio expresses how many times its earnings a share is selling in the market. The *earnings per share* is not the dividends the stockholder gets, but rather it is the net profit (after taxes) of the company divided by the number of shares outstanding. If a company is earning $10 a share on its stock, and the stock is selling in the market for $100, the stock would be said to be selling for 10 times its earnings ($100 divided by $10). If a non-participating preferred stock is outstanding, the preferred dividend is subtracted from the net earnings to get the earnings on the common stock.

In recent years stocks comprising the leading industrial averages and indexes have been selling in the neighborhood of 16 to 20 times earnings. This has been due in part to the fact that the investing community expects inflation to continue.

If the stock is selling at three or four times earnings a person might think it to be a good buy. On the other hand he may refuse to buy a stock at 25 times earnings. But if a stock is selling for only four times earnings it is an indication that the future prospects for the company are not bright. Conversely a 25-times ratio would indicate that people are discounting the prospect for favorable future earnings. One of the shortcomings of the price-earnings ratio is that it compares present stock prices with past or present earnings. Stock prices at any one time reflect the prospective *future* earnings.

Real Value

We sometimes hear people say that a particular stock is selling at more, or less, than its real value. What do we mean by *real value?* In the case of a listed stock the market value commonly goes up and down in the course of a day, week, month, or year. In times of prosperity stock prices soar to extreme heights, and then when depression hits they fall to excessive depths. The prices appear to go too far in either direction and then correct themselves and go too far in the opposite direction. They are as much overpriced at the peak as they are underpriced at the bottom of a depression.

The book value or the earnings per share of a stock will not change much, if at all, in a day's time, but the price of the stock may fluctuate violently due to technical factors, such as an overbought or oversold market. The real or intrinsic worth of the stock may not have changed at all. This is one of the reasons why it is said that the market price of a stock does not necessarily indicate the real value. Also, in some instances something which will favorably affect the stock in the future is not generally known and therefore its real worth may be more than it is selling for in the market.

There are many types of property which have a real value to us far in excess of the price we could get if we sold the property. But when it comes to stocks, it is difficult to escape the conclusion that a stock is worth what you can get for it. In other words, generally the market price reflects the real value.

QUESTIONS

1. Why do sole proprietorships and partnerships not issue stock? Why do corporations issue it?
2. (a) Distinguish between stock and a stock certificate. (b) Of what practical value might it be to distinguish between the stock and the certificate?
3. Distinguish between the authorized, the issued, and the outstanding stock of a corporation.
4. Distinguish between the capital, and the capital stock of a corporation.
5. If a company has only one class of stock outstanding, what is it usually titled on the balance sheet?
6. (a) Why is it advisable not to indorse a stock certificate which is put up as collateral for a loan? (b) What would be done in lieu of an indorsement?
7. (a) When stock is transferred near a dividend date, what determines whether the transferor or the transferee is entitled to the dividend? (b) If the directors of Company X, whose stock is listed on the New York Stock Exchange, declare a dividend to stockholders of record January 15, when will the stock go ex-dividend?
8. When stock is transferred near the time of the annual meeting, what determines whether the transferor or the transferee is entitled to vote the stock?
9. (a) Indicate briefly the nature of the liability of corporate shareholders. (b) Who may be held liable when partly paid stock is transferred?
10. (a) What is meant by treasury stock? (b) Who votes treasury stock? Who receives dividends on it? (c) Indicate the reasons for the origin of treasury stock and the circumstances under which it might be acquired.
11. (a) List the reasons why a corporation might reacquire its own stock. (b) List the various ways by which a corporation might reacquire its own stock. (c) Indicate briefly the nature of the legality of a company's purchasing its own stock.
12. (a) What are the reasons, if any, for corporate stock to have a par value? (b) What are the shortcomings, if any, of par-value stock to the issuing corporation?
13. What are the advantages of no-par stock from the viewpoint of the issuing corporation?
14. What are the possible disadvantages of no-par stock from the viewpoint of the issuing corporation?
15. (a) Must no-par stock have a "stated" value? (b) If a stated value is required for no-par stock, is it necessary to specify it in the articles or certificate of incorporation?
16. At what value should no-par stock be carried in the balance sheet of the issuing corporation?
17. (a) Distinguish between the following stock values: par value, book value, net tangible-asset value, and real value. (b) Give a hypothetical example of an abbreviated balance sheet of a corporation which has preferred stock outstanding, and compute the per-share book value of the preferred and the common stock. (c) Indicate several circumstances under which the determination of the book value of stock would be of considerable practical value.

18. (a) Give a hypothetical example of the computation of the price-earnings ratio. (b) Of what practical value is the price-earnings ratio? (c) Why should too much emphasis not be placed on this ratio?

PROBLEMS

1. The board of directors of the Standard Corp. on January 10 declared a dividend of $1 per share, payable on February 20, to stockholders of record as of January 24. Assume that you purchase one share of this stock from Mr. Adams on January 21 for regular-way delivery on the New York Stock Exchange. (a) When would the stock go ex-dividend? (b) Who would get the dividend check?

2. The following is a balance sheet of the New Corp. as of December 31, 19x1:

Assets		Liabilities and Net Worth	
Cash	$ 50,000	Payables	$ 200,000
Receivables	100,000	Preferred Stock	1,000,000
Inventory	300,000	Common Stock	2,000,000
Plant	3,250,000	Surplus	1,500,000
Goodwill	1,000,000		
Total	$4,700,000	Total	$4,700,000

The preferred stock bears a 7 per cent cumulative dividend, and both it and the common have a par value of $100 per share.

(a) Assuming that the preferred and common share alike in assets upon dissolution, and that all accumulated dividends have been paid on the preferred to date, what is the book value per share of the common stock? (b) If the preferred stock is entitled to its par value only upon dissolution, what is the book value per share of the common? (c) If the preferred stock is preferred over the common in respect to assets upon dissolution to the extent of $110 per share and accrued dividends, and no dividends have been paid on it for the past two years, what is the book value per share of the common? (d) What is the book value per share of the preferred stock?

3. The articles of incorporation of the Amalgamated Corp., filed at the Secretary of State's office on January 2, 19x1, provided for the issuance of 50,000 shares of common stock with a par value of $100 per share. The following day Mr. Hopkins, Mr. Chase, and Mr. Douglas turned over the property to the corporation, and each received $1,000,000 in stock in payment for the property.

The next day each donated to the corporation $200,000 of the stock, which was not canceled by the corporation. On January 5, $400,000 of this stock was resold to Mr. Stone for $320,000 in cash. On the same day Mr. Reynolds contracted to purchase $100,000 of the donated stock from the corporation on February 1 at the price of $75 per share, payment to be made on February 1. On January 6 Mr. Harlan and Mr. Holmes each subscribed for 1,000 shares at par, paying 20 per cent down and agreeing to pay the balance on call. The following day these subscriptions were accepted by the directors. On January 10 the directors called for another 20 per cent to be paid on the stock. Mr. Harlan met the call but Mr. Holmes was unable to do so, and the corporation canceled his subscription by appropriate resolution adopted by the board of directors.

On January 11 Mr. Hughes contracted to purchase 1,500 shares of this un-issued stock at par. It was agreed that he was to deposit 20 per cent of the contract price with the company immediately and 20 per cent additional each month for 4 months, at the end of which time the stock certificate was to be delivered to him. In the meantime the company agreed to pay him 3 per cent interest on the money deposited.

Assume that you are called upon to submit a report to the treasurer of the company on January 12 showing the status of the company's stock at that time. Indicate the amounts that you would show under the following heads:

(a) Authorized stock   (d) Unissued stock
(b) Issued stock   (e) Full-paid stock
(c) Outstanding stock   (f) Partly paid stock
                 (g) Treasury stock

4. A company has assets of $600,000; liabilities of $100,000; capital stock of $400,000; and surplus of $100,000. The stock, which has a par value of $100 per share, is given up by the shareholders for no-par stock with a stated value of $50 per share, the exchange being on a share-for-share basis.

(a) Indicate three different ways in which the no-par stock may be shown on the balance sheet. (b) As a stockholder in the company, which of these methods would you favor? Why? (c) If you were a creditor of the company, which method would you prefer? Why? (d) Which method would be considered the best accounting practice? Why?

5. The Standard Corp. was organized June 1, 19x1, with an authorized capital stock of 10,000 shares of no-par stock. On June 3, 5,000 of these shares were sold to the public for $40 per share. On September 1 of the same year an additional 2,000 shares were sold for $30 per share.

(a) Do you think that it was legal to sell the 2,000 shares at this relatively low price? (b) Do you think that it was fair to the shareholders who purchased the first shares sold? Why? (c) Would the last 2,000 shares sold have to be first offered to the original shareholders before they could be sold to the public? Explain.

SELECTED READINGS

BOGEN, JULES I. (ed.). *Financial Handbook,* 3d ed. New York: The Ronald Press Co., 1952. Section 10.
Corporation Course. Englewood Cliffs, N. J.: Prentice-Hall, Inc., 1960.
Corporation Manual. New York: United States Corporation Co., published annually.
DORIS, LILLIAN (ed.). *Business Finance Handbook.* Englewood Cliffs, N. J.: Prentice-Hall, Inc., 1953. Chapter 17.
FLETCHER, WILLIAM MEADE. *Cyclopedia of the Law of Private Corporations,* Permanent ed. Chicago: Callaghan & Co., Vol. 11 (1958 rev. vol.), Vols. 12 and 12a (1957 rev. vol.), Vols. 13 and 13a (1961 rev. vol.).
LATTIN, NORMAN D. *The Law of Corporations.* Brooklyn: The Foundation Press, Inc., 1959.
OLECK, HOWARD L. *Modern Corporation Law.* Indianapolis: The Bobbs-Merrill Co., Inc., 1960.
ROHRLICH, CHESTER. *Organizing Corporate and Other Business Enterprises,* 3d ed. Albany, N. Y.: Matthew Bender & Co., Inc., 1958.

6

Types of Stock

The principal types of stock are *common* and *preferred*. Although common stock is much more important than preferred in terms of the number of companies issuing the stock and the aggregate market value, most of our attention in this chapter will be devoted to preferred stock. This is because the technical features of preferred stock are more complex and varied than in the case of common stock. The other forms or types of stock and stock terminology will be briefly discussed in the final part of the chapter.

COMMON STOCK

The *common* stockholders are the residual claimants of the corporation. When there are other classes of stock outstanding, the common shareholders are the last ones to receive dividends, and are usually the last ones to receive the assets in event of dissolution. If only one class of stock is outstanding it is necessarily common stock, although many corporations call it "capital stock" on the balance sheet. (All kinds of stock are included in "capital stock.") In England common shares are referred to as *ordinary shares*. In a few instances *ordinary stock* has been issued by companies in the United States.[1]

In 1890, the Great Northern Railway Co. reacquired all of its common stock, leaving only the preferred stock outstanding.[2] Although titled

[1] The Alabama Great Southern Railroad Co. (controlled by the Southern Railway Co.) has an issue of *ordinary stock* outstanding, which is listed on the American Stock Exchange. It is preceded by an issue of $3 cumulative preferred stock which participates equally share for share with the ordinary stock in any dividends after the ordinary has received $3 per share in any one year.

[2] In 1898, the preferred was designated as $6 non-cumulative preferred, and in 1935, it was changed from $100 par to no-par through a share for share exchange.

preferred stock, this really became common stock, since it was not preferred over any other stock. Due in part to the misunderstanding, the company finally on July 2, 1954, reclassified the preferred as no-par common, and issued the shareholders two new common shares for each old preferred share.

When preferred stock is issued it is commonly limited to a specified dividend, and is non-voting. When earnings are large the common stand to gain more than the preferred. Thus the common stock usually fluctuates more in the market than does the preferred.

There has grown up in recent years what is known as the *common-stock theory of investment*. This theory embraces the idea that a well-selected and diversified list of common stocks held over a long period of years will turn out better than a similar investment in preferred stocks or bonds. Corporations usually pay out only part of their earnings in the form of dividends, and the balance is plowed back into the business. This increases the equity of the common stockholders and gives the company an increased investment which will increase earnings still further in the future.

Common stock is looked upon as a hedge against inflation. As prices rise, the worth of the corporate property increases. Earnings and dividends also usually increase with inflation. In view of these conditions several states in recent years have changed their laws to permit life insurance companies and trustees to invest a certain percentage of their assets in common stock.

Despite all the factors which argue for the purchase of common stock, the average person will probably continue to lose money on it. The ordinary individual does not have the necessary background, experience, and temperament to enable him to select successfully the companies that will probably turn out well in the future. Even if he is possessed of all these qualities, it is still exceedingly difficult properly to determine just when to buy the stock and when to sell it.

PREFERRED STOCK

As its title indicates, *preferred stock* is a type of stock which is preferred over common stock in some way. In England, the term *preference* is used instead of *preferred*. In practically all, if not all, preferred issues outstanding, the stock is preferred over the common in respect to dividends. It usually is preferred over the common also in respect to assets upon dissolution. In recent years most of the preferred issues have been cumulative in respect to dividends. Commonly the voting right is restricted in some way.

The specific rights, preferences, or limitations depend upon the statutes of the state in which the company is incorporated, and upon the provisions relating to it in the articles of incorporation, the bylaws, and the stock certificate. We, therefore, cannot make general statements regarding the rights of preferred stock and have them apply to all preferreds. The rights of any specific preferred stock depend upon the specific contract under which it is issued.

Preferred, like common, stock may be no-par or par value. Unlike the common, preferred stock must have a specified dividend rate since it is entitled to this amount before any dividends can be paid to the common. (Some companies by custom pay a fixed amount on the common each year, but this rate is not specified in the contract.) When the preferred is no-par, the dividend rate must be expressed in dollars and cents, but when the stock is par value it may be stated in per cent. The latter might, however, be misleading unless the particular par value is known. For this reason the annual dividend rate on par preferreds is generally expressed in dollars per share and this rate is used in the title of the particular stock in order to identify that issue. (Some companies have a number of different preferred issues, each with a different dividend rate.) Following are the titles of three selected issues: Atchison, Topeka and Santa Fe $2.50 Non-cumulative Preferred, Pacific Gas and Electric $1.50 Cumulative Preferred, and Union Pacific $2 Non-cumulative Preferred. The Atchison stock has a par value of $50, and a dividend rate of 5 per cent, Pacific Gas and Electric has a $25 par and a dividend rate of 6 per cent, and Union Pacific has a par value of $50 and a dividend rate of 4 per cent.

Why Preferred Stock Is Issued

Many people do not want to assume the risks that go with common stock, and they are desirous of a regular and fixed dividend. Bonds are a type of security which offer greater safety and a more regular return than common stocks, but because of these favorable features, the rate of interest paid on bonds is relatively low. Preferred stock is a sort of compromise security which offers less risk and greater certainty of return than common stock, but a higher return than can be obtained on a bond of the same company. Preferred stock appeals more to the investor or semi-investor than does common stock. The speculator, as distinguished from the investor, may be more desirous of buying common stock.

The reason a corporation sells any type of security is to get money. Quite often at the time a company is formed the common stock is handed out to the promoters and organizers for their services, and for the property, if any, which they turn over to the corporation. Preferred stock is then sold to the public to secure the additional capital needed.

Many preferred stock issues, particularly in the railroad field, have arisen at the time of reorganization. Some of the bondholders were usually asked to turn in their bonds and accept preferred stock in exchange. The preferred stock might appeal to them more than common stock, so the company offered this type of security to induce them to give up their bonds.

At times the market may be more favorable to stocks than to bonds, but for some reason the company does not want to sell common stock, or the public may want something other than common stock, so preferred stock is sold. Preferred stock is sometimes a suitable type of security to issue in connection with a consolidation or merger. It is often used at this time in exchange for securities of other companies, or sold for the additional capital needed.

From the standpoint of the common stockholders and the issuing corporation, preferred stock provides a means of getting additional cash without letting the new shareholder participate in the management or in future abnormal earnings. Since the dividend rate is usually limited, any earnings on the stock in excess of this rate will add to the common stockholders' equity. This is called *trading on the equity*, or *leverage*, and will be fully discussed in Chapter 7. Preferred is sometimes given to shareholders for their accrued dividends. Some corporations have given preferred stock as a bonus in connection with the sale of bonds or common stock.

Legal Nature of Preferred Stock

In Chapter 4 the rights of stockholders were listed. Among these were the right to vote and the right to receive dividends when declared by the board of directors, and the right to assets upon dissolution. Owners of preferred shares are stockholders and therefore are entitled to all of their rights, unless the contract provides otherwise. As far as the law is concerned, all of the shareholders, regardless of what type of stock they hold, are treated equally, unless otherwise provided. It follows from this that the preferred shareholders have the same rights as those having common shares if such rights have not been altered in the contract under which the stock was issued.

The fact that we call the stock "preferred" implies that some preference over the common has been given to it in the contract. Where it is specified that the stock is voting, or that it is cumulative with respect to dividends, it is then clear what rights are possessed by it in respect to these features. Many preferred stock contracts, however, specifically state some of the rights of the preferred, but they are silent concerning other features. The question then arises how the preferred ranks as compared with the common with respect to these unmentioned features.

PREFERRED DIVIDENDS

Preference

Preferred stocks which are outstanding have a stated dividend rate. If the stock is called "preferred" and has a stated dividend rate the courts will hold that it is preferred over the common with respect to dividends, even though the contract does not specifically state this. In the discussion, it will be assumed that the stock being considered has a stated dividend rate.

To understand the rights of preferred stock it is necessary to distinguish between interest and dividends. Interest on a debt owed is a fixed charge of the company—a debt—and it must be paid regardless of whether the company earns any profits. Dividends, on the other hand, constitute a distribution of the profits. There must be profits either current, or accumulated from the past, or a surplus arising from some other source, before the board of directors can legally declare a dividend. After a legal dividend has been declared it constitutes a debt of the corporation.

Even if the company has a profit or surplus from which dividends can be paid, the board of directors is under no legal obligation to declare dividends to the preferred or other stockholders. In fact, if the profits are small or the corporation needs the money for future uses, the board of directors may pass the dividend. The only compulsion that exists is that the directors must pay the preferred its dividend in any one year *if* they wish to declare dividends to the common. The preferred shareholders cannot compel the directors to pay them anything as long as the board is acting in a fair manner.

Table 6–1. Preferred Stock Yield Averages, 1957–1961, Moody's 10 High Grade Industrials

Year	Yield (per cent)
1961	4.60
1960	4.71
1959	4.62
1958	4.34
1957	4.48

SOURCE: *Moody's Industrial Manual*, 1962.

The board of directors is usually elected by the common shareholders or their proxies, either because the preferred is not voting, or because the number of common shares greatly exceeds the number of preferred shares. In many instances, the directors are owners of large blocks of the company's common stock. It would seem natural to expect that directors would tend to favor the common shareholders, even at the expense of the preferred shareholders.

From a legal standpoint, then, it would appear that the preferred shareholders do not have a very secure position as regards dividends. Actually, however, a board of directors will usually declare the preferred dividends where there are profits sufficient to pay the dividend without seriously jeopardizing the future operation of the company. To pass the dividend under these circumstances would probably affect the market for the company's stock and produce an adverse effect on the company's credit.

The principal advantage of the preferred over the common is the preference as to dividends. If the company has large earnings and can pay dividends on both the preferred and the common, then there is not much advantage in having the right to get the dividends first. In many instances, however, the preferred shareholders get regular dividends while the common shareholders receive them only spasmodically. Also, the rate paid on the preferred is sometimes higher than that paid on the common.

Cumulative Dividends

If dividends on a particular preferred stock are *cumulative,* it means that if dividends at the stated rate are not paid in any year they accrue into subsequent years, and must be paid *before* any dividends can be paid to the common.

If a company issued a preferred stock which did not have a stated dividend rate, it undoubtedly would not be held to be cumulative by the courts since there is no way of knowing at what rate to cumulate the dividend. But preferred stocks as a practical matter have a specified rate stated in the contract. If the contract further states that the stock is cumulative or non-cumulative, or words to this effect, then it is clear as to the stock's rights. But assume that the stock has a stated dividend rate but nothing is said in the contract concerning cumulation. Will the courts hold it to be cumulative or non-cumulative? The courts reason that if a definite per-annum rate is stated, such as 5 per cent, and there is no statement that it is non-cumulative, the stock should be entitled to this amount *each* year, and that if it is not paid in any year, the dividend will *cumulate* into subsequent years. Most preferred stocks outstanding today are cumulative.

Even if the stock is cumulative, the dividends on it do not have to be paid. The only compulsion is that the cumulated dividend must be paid *before* any dividends can be paid to the common shareholders.

Although the cumulative feature in a preferred stock is desirable from the viewpoint of the investor, its value should not be overestimated. If a company can pay regular dividends on its preferred stock, it will generally do so regardless of whether the stock is cumulative or non-cumulative. If the company earns nothing the dividend is usually not paid. The value of the cumulative feature comes into play when the company after some lean years during which the dividends are passed, runs into prosperous years and has to pay the arrears on the preferred before it can pay any dividends to the common.

If the dividends on the preferred have accrued for a number of years the stockholder rarely receives the full amount in cash. To attempt to pay the arrears may mean that the common will have to go without dividends for many years even after the company's earnings increase. This affects the market for its stock, and may make it difficult for the company to borrow money, or if it can secure loans, it may be at a relatively high interest rate.

Various methods or compromises are used to get rid of the accumulated dividends. In some instances the corporation offers the shareholders new preferred or common stock for the dividends. The new preferred may be an issue with different rights from the stock on which they are paying the dividend. Sometimes the shareholder is asked to take part of the dividend in cash and the balance in stock. In a few cases the directors have promised to resume current dividends on the preferred if the preferred shareholders would give up their right to the accrued dividends. The preferred stockholders cannot be compelled to accept the compromise settlement. In practice, however, the preferred shareholders are usually not organized and are therefore in a weak bargaining position, and they commonly accept the plan advanced by the management.

Non-cumulative Preferred Stock

If a preferred stock is *non-cumulative* it means that if the dividend is not paid in any year it is gone forever, and the shareholder will have no claim to it in subsequent years. Some court decisions in the past, however, held that even if a preferred stock was made non-cumulative by contract, it would, nevertheless, be cumulative in those years in which profits sufficient to pay the dividend had been earned. The United States Supreme Court in 1930, in the famous *Wabash Railway* case, however, held that if a stock is non-cumulative, it remains so even if the company earns profits sufficient to pay the dividend. The words of the court on this point were as follows:

We believe that it has been the common understanding of lawyers and business men that in the case of non-cumulative stock entitled only to a dividend if declared out of annual profits, if those profits are justifiably applied by the directors to capital improvements and no dividend is declared within the year, the claim for that year is gone and cannot be asserted at a later date.[3]

Since non-cumulative preferred stock does not appeal to the investing public, we find that it has been used mainly in the reorganization of insolvent companies, recapitalization of solvent concerns, and as a stock dividend.

Right To Participate in Dividends

A preferred stock is said to be *participating* when it has the right to share with the common in some way after the stated rate on the preferred has been paid. When we speak of a *non-participating* stock we are referring to one which has no further right to dividends in any one year after its stated rate (plus any accrued dividends in the case of cumulative stock) has been paid.

A question that arises is this: Is the statement of the dividend rate to be construed not only as a statement of preference, but also as an implied statement of limitation? The courts are not in agreement on this point, so we cannot make a definite statement and say that it is one way or the other. But we can say this: The great weight of authority holds the stock to be *non-participating*.

In Pennsylvania, however, the courts have definitely held that when the stock was not made non-participating by contract, it would be *participating*. The reasoning behind this is the point previously stated, that preferred stock has all the rights of common unless otherwise changed. If the preferred received its stated rate and the common got all the rest, this would be putting a limitation on the preferred if the amount paid to the common exceeded that which went to the preferred.

The high-court decisions in the other states which have decided on this point and in England, however, have held that the preferred is *non-participating* unless it is specifically made participating by contract. These courts take the attitude that when a preferred stock is given a stated preference as to dividends, this impliedly is a statement of limitation as well.

Several other arguments are presented by the courts in holding the stock to be non-participating. One is that in their opinion most people when buying preferred stock think that it is entitled to only its stated rate in any one year. Furthermore, in some of the cases which came before the courts, the company had in some of the years paid the preferred its stated rate, and then paid the common a larger amount. The preferred stockholders had not objected to this practice in the past, so they evidently

[3] Wabash Ry. Co. v. Barclay, 280 U.S. 197, at 203 (1930).

believed that their stock was non-participating. In a few of the cases some of the directors who voted for the larger common dividends were preferred stockholders.

Another point which is made by the courts is that the stated preference as to dividends is given to the stockholders in lieu of the right to participate in dividends equally with the common. Looking at it from the standpoint of the common stockholders, the common shareholders give the preferred stock first chance to any dividends, and frequently first claim as to assets upon dissolution, so they are taking more risk than the preferred. This being so, the common shareholders should be the ones to reap the returns if the company is unusually successful.

As a matter of practice, the great bulk of the preferred stocks outstanding are non-participating.

If the dividend in question is one payable in stock of the company, special consideration should be given to it. Let us assume in a particular case that the amounts of preferred and common stock outstanding are the same. We will assume also that the preferred is voting and that it has equal rights with the common in respect to assets upon dissolution. If, after the preferred and common had received the stated rate of dividends, the company paid an additional dividend in stock to the common only, the right of the preferred in regard to control and in regard to its share in the assets upon dissolution would be altered. It was pointed out in Chapter 4 that shareholders had the pre-emptive right to get new stock in the corporation in order to maintain their degree of control and their equity in the company. The courts in some of the states have therefore held the preferred to be participating under circumstances similar to these when the dividend was a stock dividend. In some of the cases holding this way, the preferred was specifically made non-participating by the particular contract.

There are three different types of participating preferred stock which may be provided for in the contract. They are described in the sections that follow.

Simple Participation. When the preferred gets its stated rate and the common a like rate or a fixed amount per share, and then the balance of the dividend is split equally per share (or at the same percentage rate) between the preferred and the common, it is called *simple participation* (sometimes also referred to as *fully participating*). An example of simple participating preferred stock is the Moody's Investors Service $3 Cumulative Participating Preferred. This stock has a preference of $3 cumulative dividends ahead of the common, and then after the common receives $2.25 in dividends in any year, the preferred participates with the common share for share in any further dividends declared.

Immediate Participation. The contract under which the stock is issued sometimes states that the preferred is entitled first to its fixed rate, and then if any more dividends are paid, the preferred immediately participates on an equal basis per share or designated amount with the common. In other words, the common does not get a stated rate before the preferred participates. This is called *immediate participation*. An example is the Arden Farms Company $3 Cumulative Preferred Stock. This stock is entitled to a $3 cumulative dividend ahead of the common, and then whenever a dividend is declared on the common, each share of the preferred is entitled to an amount equal to one-fourth of the dividend declared on the common share, but the additional dividends on the preferred are limited to $1 per share in any calendar year.

Special Participation. Any type of participation other than the two mentioned above would be called *special participation*. The different types used in practice are too numerous to mention, but the following would indicate the extremes. The preferred is entitled to a preferential dividend of 6 per cent, and then after the common has received a similar rate, the preferred is entitled to all the additional amount paid that year. Or, the preferred is entitled to its stated rate of 6 per cent, then the common is paid the same rate, if declared by the directors, and if any more dividends are declared that year, the preferred gets an additional 2 per cent and the common gets the balance.[4]

VOTING RIGHT OF PREFERRED

Unless the voting right is taken away from preferred stock, it has the same right to vote as common stock. According to the statutes in the various states this would mean one vote per share on each matter that came before the meeting.

It is common practice to restrict the voting right of the preferred, but it is usual to provide that the preferred will have the right to vote on certain questions, or under certain conditions. In some instances the contract provides for class voting which gives the preferred the right to elect a designated number of directors. The voting rights of the General Motors Corporation $3.75, and $5.00, preferred stocks, stated below, are typical of an industrial concern.

The shares have no voting power except if dividends are in default for a period of six months, when holders of the preferred shares would have the right to elect one-fourth of the board of directors so long as the default continues. The

[4] The Bunker Hill Company 6 Per Cent Cumulative Preferred (par $100) is an example of special participation. This stock has preference as to dividends of 6 per cent, plus a bonus of an amount per share per quarter equal to dividends paid on common in excess of $1.50 for each 4 shares for the previous quarter, such bonus in no event to be less than 50 cents a share per quarter on stock owned by employees.

preferred also have the right to vote on selling, conveying, transferring, or otherwise disposing of the property and assets of the corporation as an entirety, and the creation of mortgages.

Practically all of the "non-voting" preferred stocks have the right to vote for directors (either ordinary voting or class voting) if dividends are in default for a specified period of time, or the right to vote on mergers, consolidations, sale of assets, etc., or to vote on the issuance of additional preferred stock or bonds.[5]

One of the reasons that "non-voting" preferred stock is practically always given some contingent voting right is to add to its marketability. Investment bankers may insist on the inclusion of such rights. Another is the fact that the New York Stock Exchange will no longer list a preferred stock unless it has at least the following voting rights: (1) right to elect not less than two directors if the dividends are in arrears for the equivalent of six quarterly periods, and (2) a two-thirds affirmative vote of the preferred as a class on any charter or bylaw amendments which materially affect the position of the preferred stock.

The restrictions which are placed on the general voting right of preferred stock are not too serious. Most stockholders, whether they be common or preferred, do not take an interest in the corporate management. Furthermore, the preferred stockholders are usually interested in their stock as an investment and not as an instrument for controlling the corporation. Even where the preferred stock has ordinary voting powers, the number of common shares outstanding generally exceeds the number of preferred shares, so that the vote of the preferred would mean little. In the case of class voting, however, this would not be the situation.

It is only fair that the preferred should be given the right to vote as a class on all matters that would affect their relative position in the corporation. Since the main advantage of the preferred is to receive a preferential dividend, it seems proper that they should, as a class, be

[5] A study of 1,094 preferred stocks listed on the New York Stock Exchange showed that only 5.7 per cent had no voting rights at all. W. H. S. Stevens, "Voting Rights of Capital Stock and Shareholders," *The Journal of Business of the University of Chicago*, October, 1938, pp. 311–40. A study of 250 *industrial* preferred stocks issued in 1944–1946 revealed that *none* of them was denied the voting right completely. A total of 25 per cent of them had full voting rights, but the remaining 75 per cent had the right to vote for directors if dividends were in arrears for a specified period, to vote on mergers, etc., and the issuance of senior securities. J. F. Bradley, "Voting Rights of Preferred Stockholders in Industrials," *The Journal of Finance*, October, 1948, pp. 78–88. A more recent study of 72 preferred stocks issued by various types of industries, including public utilities, during 1946–1950, showed that only 18 per cent had general voting rights. But 86 per cent of them had various types of voting rights in event dividends were in arrears for a specified period, 87½ per cent could vote on major changes such as mergers, sale of assets, etc., and approximately 89 per cent had the right to vote on the issuance of senior securities. Donald A. Fergusson, "Recent Developments In Preferred Stock Financing," *The Journal of Finance*, September, 1952, pp. 447–62.

given the right to receive representation on the board of directors when the dividends are in arrears for a specified period of time.

PREFERREDS' LIQUIDATION RIGHTS

In the event of dissolution of a corporation, the claims of the creditors always come first. If there is anything left, it is distributed to the shareholders. If the statutes of the state and the contract are silent as to the right of the preferred, then the common law says that the assets shall be divided evenly per share between the preferred and the common stock. In other words, the preferred has no preference in respect to assets, and also it is not limited as compared with the common.

Preference as to assets upon dissolution is rare among railroad preferreds, but a majority of the preferreds issued by public utilities and practically all the industrial preferreds have this preference. The extent of the preference varies, but quite commonly it is preferred up to the par value, or stated value, of the stock. In some instances the preferred is entitled to par in the event of involuntary dissolution, but par and a slight premium in case of voluntary liquidation. A $100 preferred stock, which may be callable at $110, may be entitled to $110 in event of voluntary dissolution and $105 in case of involuntary liquidation.

Of the stocks which have a preference as to assets, close to 90 per cent call for a preference not only up to the par value, or a specified amount, but also in respect to any accrued dividends. This preference may also be given effect if the company is merged into another company, or when it is reorganized.

Several legal questions are involved in connection with the preference as to assets. If a particular preferred stock calls for par, or a stated amount in the case of no-par stock, and accrued dividends, but at the time of dissolution there are no profits or surplus, is the preferred stock entitled to the accrued dividend before anything is paid to the common? Some courts have held that the preferred is not entitled to the dividends, while others have held that the stock is entitled to the preferential dividend.

This question cannot be said to have been settled in the United States, but the weight of authority is that the preferred is entitled to the preferential dividend upon dissolution even if not earned. It should be kept in mind that we are here referring to a stock which has specifically been given a preference in respect to dividends upon dissolution. If no such preference is given, the preferred would not be entitled to it, unless such dividends were declared by the board of directors, and a surplus would have to be present before they could declare a dividend. But if the preferred contract calls for par and accrued dividends ahead of the common upon dissolution, most courts take the attitude that this relates to a return of capital, and not profits, and that a corporation can contract for the return of capital in any way that it desires.

Does the stated preference as to assets impliedly limit the stock to the preferential amount? The courts in the United States are not in accord on this question, but most of the decisions have held that the stated preference as to assets impliedly limits the stock to this amount. In other words, the weight of authority is that the stock is *non-participating in assets* where it has been specifically given a stated preference as to assets. Of course, if the stock specifically stated that it was participating in assets in addition to being preferred as to assets, this would control. An example is the Moody's Investors Service $3 Cumulative Participating Preferred. The contract provides that this stock is first entitled to $50 per share and accrued dividends in event of liquidation, and then after the common gets $50 a share, the preferred participates equally share for share with the common in any further distribution of assets.

The preference as to assets is given in order to increase the marketability of the stock. But the practical importance of this right is overestimated by the average buyer. A corporation does not fail because it has stock outstanding. Debts are what cause failure. Creditors always have the right to be paid in full before anything is distributed to the stockholders. In many instances, after they are paid, nothing remains for the shareholders. In such a case the preference of the stock would mean nothing. As long as the company continues to operate, the preference never comes into play.

Perhaps we have been a little too critical of the value of the preference as to assets feature. We have been speaking only of failure and liquidation. The preference as to assets feature has been respected in some instances when a corporation has been merged with another, reorganized, and in the case of a public utility, dissolved under the Public Utility Holding Company Act.

PROTECTIVE PROVISIONS IN PREFERRED STOCKS

Preferred stock is quite commonly sold as the senior security of the company. If additional preferred stock having the same or a prior claim to dividends is issued, the status of the original preferred would be materially altered. The status of the stock might also be changed materially by incurring more debt or by the depletion of cash or surplus by excessive dividends to the common, or the use of current assets for expansion purposes. Since the preferred is ordinarily non-voting, or if it is voting, the common nevertheless usually controls, the holders of the latter are not in a position to protect themselves against the actions that might be taken by the common shareholders and the directors. For this reason investment bankers commonly insist that certain protective provisions be inserted in the preferred stock contract. The following are illustrative of the various types of such provisions.

Restrictions on Further Issues

The contract may provide that no bonds or preferred having the same or prior claim may be issued. A more common provision is that no such securities may be issued without the consent of two-thirds or three-fourths of the preferred shares. This provision is often contained in the contract even though the preferred is non-voting on ordinary matters. In the General Motors Corporation preferred stock contracts, referred to earlier in the chapter, it is provided that the company without the consent of 75 per cent of the preferred shares cannot create any bonds, mortgages, or specific liens on its properties except existing obligations on hereafter acquired property and renewal of such obligations, and the pledging of securities to secure cash advances maturing within three years.

In some instances the preferred might be helped by the issuance of a prior-lien stock. This might enable the corporation to secure needed funds which would prevent its failure.

Maintenance of Certain Ratios

The contract may call for minimum requirements in any one or more of the following types of ratios.

Current Ratio. In some instances it is provided that directors cannot pay dividends or otherwise voluntarily use cash for expansion when it would result in a reduction in the current ratio (ratio of current assets to current liabilities) below $2\frac{1}{2}$ or 3. Or, such action cannot be taken if it would reduce the net current assets (current assets less current liabilities) below a certain percentage, such as 150 per cent, for example, of the preferred stock.

Ratio of Assets to Preferred Stock and Bonds. The contract may provide that dividends on the common cannot be paid if it would reduce the total assets to less than twice, for example, the amount of bonds and preferred stock outstanding.

Ratio of Earnings to Preferred Dividends. Another type of provision is that no dividends may be paid on the common unless the company is earning its preferred dividend by a stated number of times, such as, for example, three times. Or it may be provided that no new preferred stock can be issued unless the company is earning the dividend on its present preferred and the amount which it contemplates issuing at least, for example, $2\frac{1}{2}$ or 3 times.

Ratio of Preferred to Common Stock. In order to have a substantial buffer of common stock behind the preferred, it is sometimes provided that the amount of preferred outstanding cannot at any time exceed, for example, one-half the amount of common stock.

Surplus and Dividend Reserves

Occasionally the contract under which the stock is issued states that no dividends may be paid to the common if it would reduce the surplus below a specified figure, or below a stated ratio of the preferred stock. In some instances a specified reserve for dividends on the preferred must be set up and maintained before any dividends may be paid to the common.

In the contract under which the General Motors Corporation preferred shares are issued the corporation covenants not to pay any cash dividends on the common stock unless aggregate of common and surplus shall exceed $335,700,600 by an amount not less than $100 for each share of preferred outstanding in excess of 1,875,366 shares, and net current assets are more than $75 for each share of outstanding preferred.

Other Provisions

The right given to preferred (which has been made non-voting) to vote for directors if dividends are in arrears, and the right to vote on unusual matters such as mergers, consolidations, and liquidation, are sometimes classed as protective provisions. Stipulations in the contract calling for the gradual retirement of the preferred, or the setting up of redemption funds for preferred are also considered as protective clauses.

REDEMPTION OF PREFERRED

Callable Feature

Unless the contract under which the stock is issued provides otherwise, a corporation cannot force the stockholder, either common or preferred, to give up his stock. It is the usual practice, however, in the case of industrial preferreds to make the stock callable by the company at any time. When callable, it is usually at a premium of from 5 to 20 per cent over the par value, or stated value or issue price in the case of no-par stock.

At the time the stock is issued the company may have been able to sell only preferred stock. And it may have been necessary to give it a preference not only with respect to dividends and assets, but other protective features which might in the future result in some embarrassment to the corporation or hamper its future financing. Later on, the company may have a good market for its common stock, or its earnings may have produced an amount sufficient to retire the preferred stock. Anticipating such events, industrial companies commonly make their preferred callable.

From the standpoint of the shareholder, the call feature may prove to be a disadvantage. The interests of the preferred stockholder and the corporation are not the same. The corporate policies are determined by the directors, who are usually elected by the common shareholders. What benefits the preferred may be at the expense of the common, and vice versa. When the corporation's credit improves, or its earnings increase it may decide to exercise the call feature. At this time the preferred would be a better investment than when it was originally sold.

The call price is usually at a premium in order not to detract too much from its marketability, and to soften the blow when the privilege is exercised. It will be found in practice that the market price of a preferred stock will rarely exceed its call price. It should be kept in mind that the call feature is at the option of the corporation, not the stockholder.[6]

Compulsory Redemption of Preferred Stock

A number of preferred stock issues, particularly in the industrial field, contain provisions which compel the issuing corporation to buy back a certain amount of the preferred stock annually. The amount to be purchased usually varies according to the earnings of the company. There are several reasons for the inclusion of such a clause in the issue. Among industrial companies, as distinguished from railroads and public utilities, senior issues of securities, such as bonds and preferred stock, are commonly looked upon as a temporary method of raising funds. When the opportunity of paying them off arises they should be retired. Furthermore, if the corporation is buying back a certain amount of the preferred stock annually, this will create an additional market for the stock, and thus tend to keep the price up. Also, as the issue is being retired, the shares remaining outstanding will have a relatively more secure position. The retirement of the preferred also improves the position of the common stock.

[6] The $5 Cumulative Preferred stock of the General Motors Corporation, mentioned several times in the chapter, is entitled to $100 and accrued dividends in event of liquidation of the company, but it is callable at $120 and accrued dividends. The General Motors $3.75 Cumulative Preferred is also entitled to $100 and accrued dividends upon liquidation. (These two issues of preferred are no-par and they have a *pari passu* [equal] preference over the common both with respect to dividends and assets upon liquidation.) The $3.75 General Motors Preferred is callable through November 1, 1966 at $102; through November 1, 1971 at $101; and thereafter at $100.

An obligatory redemption clause in the preferred stock contract raises a serious legal question. Can a corporation be compelled to buy back its preferred stock even if it has agreed to do so in the contract? An answer to this question necessitates an examination of the statutes of the states, the court decisions, the ability of the corporation to pay its debts, and the surplus position.

We have already referred to the "trust-fund theory," which holds that the capital stock is a trust fund for the benefit of creditors. Although this is a misnomer, it is nevertheless true that a corporation cannot use its funds to retire its stock when it would impair the company's ability to pay its debts, or cause insolvency. If the firm used its "surplus" to retire the stock there would be no violation of the trust-fund theory. But even here, the stock should not be retired if it would seriously affect the ability to pay debts, or cause insolvency.

The statutes of the leading states permit a corporation to retire its stock. The fact that a redemption clause was in the contract at the time the stock was issued would strengthen the right. In some instances the statutes state that the stock can be retired only from surplus. In some states the corporation would have this right even in the absence of such statutes. The statutes of some of the states, however, provide that a corporation may redeem its preferred stock so long as the remaining assets are at least equal to the liabilities plus the par or stated value of the remaining stock. Under such statutes preferred could be redeemed even if there was no surplus (or deficit) on the books, provided, of course, that a premium over the par or stated value did not have to be paid to acquire the preferred. Redemption would not be permitted, however, if the company was insolvent or if the redemption worked a fraud on the creditors.

In order to redeem the stock a company may buy it in the market, or if it is callable, exercise the call feature. Since the stock will probably not be selling in the market for more than its call price, the company might buy it in the market. Furthermore, when stock is called in it is usually the entire issue which is so treated, although it may be callable by lot. In some instances the stock is retired by asking for tenders on the part of the shareholders.

Preferred Stock Sinking Funds

A considerable number of industrial preferred stock contracts call for the corporation to set up a *sinking fund* or *retirement fund* for the retirement of the stock. This is particularly true where the retirement is compulsory. A sinking fund constitutes a separate account to which funds are transferred for the express purpose of retiring the stock. It will be discussed more fully in Chapter 7 in connection with bonds.

In some instances the setting-up of the sinking fund is compulsory, while in other cases it rests with the discretion of the board of directors. What was stated above relative to the unenforceability of compulsory redemption clauses under certain circumstances, applies with equal force to compulsory preferred stock sinking funds.

While the presence of a sinking fund tends to strengthen the position of the preferred and make a better market for the stock, if the money put into the fund is needed in the business, the fund might be of questionable value to the preferred stockholders.

Convertible Preferred Stock

Many preferred issues, particularly those sold by industrial companies, contain a clause which gives their holders the right to *convert* them into common according to the terms of the contract. In contrast to redemption, conversion is at the option of the stockholder.

Table 6–2. Selected List of Convertible Preferred Stocks Listed on the New York Stock Exchange

Issue	Number of Common Shares Per Preferred Share	Call Price of Preferred
Allis-Chalmers Mfg. Co. $4.08	3⅓	104
American Airlines, Inc. $3.50	4.838	103
Chesapeake & Ohio Railway Co. $3.50	1.6	105
Crucible Steel Co. $5.25	3.448	103
Curtiss-Wright Corp. $2.00	1	40
FMC Corp. $3.25	4.189	101
Hilton Hotels Corp. $1.37½	0.66⅔	26¼
Lone Star Gas Co. $4.84	6	103
Reynolds Metals $4.50	2	103
Safeway Stores, Inc., $4.30	6.52	100
Schenley Industries, Inc. $0.50	0.25	10
Whirlpool Corp. $3.40	1⁵⁄₁₁	80

NOTE: In some instances the call price of the preferred and the number of common shares obtainable upon conversion are different from those stated in the table for 1965, or subsequent years.

The principal reason for the inclusion of such a clause is to add to the marketability of the preferred stock. At the time the stock is sold, the company may not have had a market for its common, but people would buy the preferred because of the advantage in dividends and cumulative features. But many of these same persons would like to have the common stock if the credit of the company improved and if the earnings increased. The common might then be more attractive than the preferred because it might increase in price on the market, and the dividends may be more than those paid on the preferred.

From the standpoint of the issuing company, the conversion feature may have been necessary in order to sell the stock, or to sell it with the designated dividend rate at the particular price. In other words, the cost of the financing would be less. But if the preferred holders exercise the conversion right, it would be at a time when the company would probably choose to have the preferred remain outstanding rather than have more of the common out. In the long run, however, the conversion of the preferred might benefit the company because it would eliminate the preferential cumulative dividend, and if they were present in the contract, eliminate any provisions which might restrict the future sale of senior securities.

Approximately 35 per cent of all publicly offered preferred stock issues sold from 1933 to 1952 had some sort of conversion privilege attached.[7] Industrials accounted for almost 89 per cent of the convertible preferred issues.[8] The contract may provide that conversion can be made at any time, or it may limit the time for conversion. A study of preferred shares sold in the period 1948–1952 showed that 64 per cent of the convertible issues had a time limit for conversion which averaged about ten years.[9]

When a convertible preferred stock is issued, the contract contains a stated price at which the common may be acquired upon conversion, or the number of shares of common which may be obtained for each share of preferred. This is called the *conversion ratio*. Thus a particular contract may state that the conversion price is $50, or it may state that 2 shares of common can be obtained upon the conversion of one share of preferred.

When a stated conversion price is given, this indicates the price that will have to be given for each share of common. In the case of par stock, the preferred is used in exchange value at its par value. Thus, if the preferred had a par value of $100, and the conversion price was $50 (this means that the common can be acquired at $50 a share), the shareholder could obtain 2 shares of common for each share of preferred converted.

Splits or stock dividends in the common stock would dilute the value of the conversion privilege. For that reason convertible preferred stock contracts usually contain an *antidilution* clause which provides that if the company splits its common or pays stock dividends on the common, the preferred upon conversion will receive a proportionately larger number

---

[7] C. James Pilcher, *Raising Capital With Convertible Securities,* Bureau of Business Research, University of Michigan, Ann Arbor, Michigan, 1955, p. 6. This study included public offerings in excess of $300,000 each.

[8] *Ibid.,* p. 19.

[9] *Ibid.,* pp. 48–49. These preferred stocks included practically all of the convertible preferreds issued in 1948–1952, for which a prospectus accompanied the New York Stock Exchange Listing Application.

of shares. For example, if the contract provides that a preferred share is upon conversion entitled to 2 shares of common, and the company has a 2-for-1 split or a 100 per cent stock dividend, according to the antidilution clause, the preferred would then be entitled to 4 shares of common. The subject of conversion will be discussed in more detail in Chapter 9, when we consider convertible bonds. Most of the discussion there will apply with equal force to convertible preferred stock.

SUMMARY OF PREFERRED STOCK RIGHTS

We have been discussing the common-law and statutory rights of preferred stock, and also provisions which may be included in the contract to alter these rights. Since preferred is practically always, if not always, preferred as to dividends, the listing below will pertain to a preferred stock which has specifically been given this preference.[10]

Common-Law Rights	*Rights of Typical Preferred Stock*
Cumulative	Cumulative
Non-participating (most states)	Non-participating
Voting	Non-voting (unless dividends are in arrears. Also right to vote on corporate changes and issuance of senior securities.)
Not preferred as to assets	Preferred as to assets
Participating in assets	Non-participating in assets
Non-callable	Callable
No sinking fund	Sinking fund (industrials)
Non-convertible	Non-convertible

Investment Worth of Preferred Stock

It is difficult to generalize on the investment worth of any type of security. Some preferred stocks are excellent investments, others poor ones. But in concluding our discussion on preferred it might be of some

---

[10] The voting rights of a sample of 72 preferred stocks issued in 1946–1950 were stated in the footnote on p. 113. The percentage of these stocks possessing other features are as follows:

Contractual Rights	*Per Cent*
Cumulative	100
Participating	1
Convertible	29
Liquidation preference	100
Callable	100
Sinking fund provision	51
Limitation on common dividend	82

Donald A. Fergusson, "Recent Developments in Preferred Stock Financing," *The Journal of Finance,* September, 1952, p. 452.

value to compare it as a class with common stock and bonds. Bonds represent debts of the issuing corporation. The company is obligated to pay the interest on the bonds and the principal amount upon maturity regardless of whether it has any earnings.

In comparing preferred stock with the other types of securities, we will assume that the preferred stock has the rights, preferences, and limitations usually given it. That is, we will have in mind a stock which is cumulative, but non-participating in dividends, non-voting on ordinary matters, callable, and preferred, but limited in assets upon dissolution.

It is sometimes said that a preferred stock is midway between a common stock and a bond. That is, the dividends are apt to be more certain and regular than those on common stock, but they do not constitute a debt as is the case with bond interest. The dividends on the preferred are limited in amount as compared to the common, which makes it somewhat similar to a bond in this respect. The preferred dividend, however, would be expected to be larger in amount than the interest paid on bonds. The common is voting, but the preferred is similar to a bond in that it is non-voting, at least on ordinary matters. The common is not redeemable or callable, whereas the preferred may be by the terms of the contract. This compares somewhat with the call feature and maturity of bonds.

Despite what has just been said, we cannot escape the fact the preferred stock is stock. The preferred shareholder is an owner in the business and not a creditor. Dividends can be paid only if there is a surplus, and even then whether they are paid rests with the discretion of the board of directors.

A somewhat exaggerated statement is that preferred stock has the disadvantages of both bonds and common stocks and the advantages of neither. That is, it is limited in return similar to the bond, and like the common, is not sure of getting dividends. Not being a credit instrument, there is no obligation to pay the dividend or the principal amount back to the shareholder, and unlike the common stock, it ordinarily is non-participating and therefore does not share in any abnormal success which the company may have.

Other things being equal, it would be better to own a preferred stock of a company that has no bonds outstanding, and where the consent of two-thirds or three-fourths of the preferred voting as a class would be necessary before any bonds could be issued. Naturally, it would be better to own the preferred stock of a good company, even if bonds were outstanding, than the preferred of a weak company. There are a number of preferreds that have bonds ahead of them which are excellent investments.

OTHER TYPES OF STOCK

Classified Stock

This is usually designated as Class A and Class B stock. The A stock is preferred over the B in respect to dividends, but usually the A stock does not possess the right to vote, or at least does not vote as long as dividends are being paid on it. In some instances the dividend is *cumulative,* but in other cases it is non-cumulative. In some cases after the A stock has received its specified dividend and a liberal dividend has been paid to the B, the A stock may be *participating,* i.e., it is allowed to participate with the B stock in any additional dividends declared. The A stock is also generally preferred over the B in respect to assets upon dissolution, and often is made *callable* by the company. Both classes are usually no-par stocks.

If a company has no preferred stock outstanding, the Class A is really a preferred stock. Even if there is a preferred issue out, the Class A may be considered a junior type of preferred.

An example of classified stock is the Class A $1 par stock of the Curtiss-Wright Corporation. This stock is entitled to a $2 non-cumulative dividend before anything can be paid to the common stock. The A stock, however, is entitled to the same voting rights as the common (one vote per share) and the same liquidation rights. It is convertible into one share of common, and is callable at $40.

Guaranteed Stock

This is a stock the dividends on which have been guaranteed by another company. It commonly arises in railroad consolidation where Company A leases the lines of Company B, and as one of the provisions of the lease, A guarantees the dividends on B's stock. This could be either common or preferred stock.

If the dividends on the guaranteed stock are not paid, the shareholders have a claim against the guaranteeing company the same as any other unsecured creditor. Since the principal amount of stock does not represent a debt, they would have no claim against the guaranteeing company with respect to the principal amount. If the latter should fail and be unable to pay anything, the stockholders would have no claim against the issuing company in respect to dividends or principal. In other words, they are just ordinary stockholders so far as the issuing company is concerned.

Preferred stock without a guaranty is sometimes called guaranteed stock. This is incorrect, since a company cannot guarantee the dividends on its own stock.

Table 6–3. Selected List of Guaranteed Railroad Stocks

Stock	Par Value	Guaranteed By
Allegheny & Western Ry. 6%	$100	Baltimore & Ohio R.R.
Bessemer & Lake Erie R.R. 6% Pfd.	50	Carnegie-Illinois Steel Co.
Boston & Albany R.R. 8¾%	100	New York Central R.R.
Cleveland & Pittsburgh R.R. 7% Reg.	50	Pennsylvania R.R.
Delaware R.R. 8%	25	Pennsylvania R.R.
Erie & Pittsburgh R.R. 7%	50	Pennsylvania R.R.
Nashville & Decatur R.R. 7½% Orig.	25	Louisville & Nashville R.R.
Northern Central Ry. 8%	50	Pennsylvania R.R.
Pittsburgh, Ft. Wayne, & Chicago Ry. 7% Pfd.	100	Pennsylvania R.R.

Prior-Lien Stock

Prior-lien stock is placed ahead of other stock in respect to dividends, or assets, or both. It is thus a type of preferred stock. It should be distinguished from *senior* stock. If a company issued both common and preferred stock at the same time, the preferred would be considered senior stock, but it would not be a prior-lien stock. If a new issue of preferred stock were subsequently put in ahead of the old preferred stock this new issue would be a prior-lien stock, and it would also be a senior stock. An example of a prior-lien stock is Minnesota Enterprises, Inc. (name changed from Twin City Rapid Transit Company in 1962), 5 Per Cent Convertible Prior Preferred Stock (par $50) issued in 1945, at which time the 7 Per Cent Preferred was redesignated as 7 Per Cent Second Preferred Stock.

In order to place an issue of stock ahead of another issue it would, if so provided in the contract, or in the statutes, necessitate the consent of a prescribed number of the shares. This is sometimes done when a corporation is in financial difficulty and can secure new capital only by getting the old stockholders to subordinate their issue to a new one.

Bankers' Shares

If a company's stock sells at too high a price, the market for it will be restricted, with the result that in relation to the earnings or assets of the company the stock might be selling for too low a price. If the company were to sell additional stock at this time, it would be relatively expensive financing in view of the dividends being paid.

Instead of selling the new shares directly to the public, the issuing company places them with a bank or trust company. The financial institution issues non-voting certificates of beneficial interest against the deposit of the company's shares. These certificates are called *bankers' shares,* or *subshares.* A much larger number of these certificates are issued than the number of shares deposited. Dividends are paid by the issuing company to the trust company. The latter then prorates these dividends to the holders of the bankers' shares.

The bankers' shares, which greatly outnumber the corporate shares, can be sold at such a relatively low price that a much wider market can be obtained than if the stock was directly sold to the public. Thus, in relation to the dividends being paid, the company obtains cheaper financing. Bankers' shares are rarely issued.

Deferred Stock

This type is one on which dividends are deferred until the expiration of a stated period or until after the happening of a particular event. The dividends on this stock are usually not paid until after they are paid on one or all the other stock issues. Using the term in a broad sense we could say that when both common and preferred are outstanding the common is a deferred stock. But the term *deferred stock* ordinarily applies to a stock that does not receive dividends until after they have been paid not only on the preferred, but on the common as well. This type of stock is used much more in England than in the United States.

Founders', Promoters', and Management Shares

In some instances a special class of stock called *founders' shares, promoters' shares,* or *management shares* is given to the promoters of a corporation or to some of the top management. This is really another name for deferred stock. Dividends are not paid on it until after a specified amount has been paid to all the other classes of stock. When this type is issued the number of shares is much less than in the other classes of stock. In some instances all the profits, after a specified rate is paid to the other types, may go to these shares. In some cases the profits are divided evenly between this type of stock as a class and the other classes. Since the number of founders' shares is relatively small, the *per-share* dividends would be relatively large. These shares are used more commonly in England than in the United States.

Debenture Stock

This term is rarely used in the United States, but when such a stock has been issued it has been a type of preferred that came ahead of the other stock of the company.[11] The term is more commonly used in Eng-

[11] An example is the Dennison Manufacturing Company 8 Per Cent Cumulative Debenture Stock. This stock has a preference in respect to dividends over the A common and the voting common. In liquidation it is entitled to $160 and dividends ahead of the other stock. The stock is callable also at $160 and accrued dividends. It has no ordinary voting power unless dividends are $12 in arrears, when it has the right to elect approximately two-thirds of the board of directors, and to exercise ordinary voting rights with the voting common, each debenture share to have ten votes, and each voting common share to have one vote. These voting rights continue until all accumulated dividends have been paid.

land where it applies to a *bond,* and not a stock. In some instances the bond is secured by a mortgage and in other cases it is not secured.[12] In the United States the word "debenture" is used to apply to a bond which is not secured by property. But we call these obligations *debenture bonds,* and not debenture stocks.

QUESTIONS

1. What is meant by the "common-stock theory of investment"?
2. (a) Why might a corporation issue preferred stock rather than some other type of security? (b) Why might a person buy preferred stock rather than some other type of security?
3. In general, what rights are possessed by preferred stock as compared with common?
4. If a company issued a stock labeled "7 per cent preferred stock," and no other preferences or limitations are stated in the contract or the statutes of the state, indicate the rights of the preferred as compared to the common in relation to the following points: cumulation; participation rights, if any, with respect to dividends; right to assets upon dissolution; and voting rights, if any.
5. Is there any legal or moral obligation on the part of the board of directors to declare dividends on the preferred stock? Explain.
6. What preferences and limitations, as compared with common stock, are possessed by the typical preferred stock?
7. From the standpoint of the shareholder, what is the practical value of the cumulation as to dividends feature of preferred stock?
8. Indicate various types of participation in dividends features which may be provided for in preferred stock contracts.
9. Indicate the nature of contractual features that are sometimes placed in the preferred stock contract relating to voting rights.
10. If the preferred stock contract specifies that in event of dissolution the stock is entitled to its par value and accrued dividends ahead of the common, must a "surplus" be present on the books before the preferred is entitled to the accrued dividends? Explain.
11. Does the giving of a preference as to assets upon dissolution impliedly limit the preferred stock to that amount? Explain.
12. Ascertain whether the statutes of your state give any preferences or place any limitations on preferred stock. If so, indicate what they are.
13. Indicate the various types of "protective provisions" which are sometimes placed in the contract for the protection of preferred stock.
14. Indicate the right, if any, of a corporation to call in its preferred stock. Are sinking funds ever provided for the redemption of the preferred stock?
15. If a preferred stock which is selling in the market for $80 a share, and which has a par value of $100, is convertible into common stock at $60 a share, how high would the common have to go in order that a person would break even by converting? Assume the price of the preferred remains the same as stated above.
16. Indicate in general the investment worth of preferred stock as compared to bonds and common stock.

[12] The Canadian Pacific Railway Company has outstanding a secured perpetual bond issue which is called a "4 Per Cent Consolidated Debenture Stock" issue.

17. Indicate what is meant by each of the following: classified stock, guaranteed stock, prior-lien stock, bankers' shares, deferred stock, founders' shares, and debenture stock.
18. Is the British terminology concerning corporate stock any different from that used in the United States? Explain.

PROBLEMS

1. Assume that the New Electronics Co. had 2,000,000 shares of capital stock outstanding and that it earned after taxes $6,000,000 for the past fiscal year. The company paid a dividend of $2 a share for the year. If you purchased a share of this company's stock at $45 and the stock is selling at this same price today: (a) What is the price-earnings ratio for this stock? (b) What is your yield?

2. The Modern Translucent Co. has 1,000,000 shares of capital stock outstanding which has a book value of $40,000,000. The company is currently earning 20 per cent on its book value and it expects this rate of earnings to continue. The company later sold 500,000 additional shares of its capital stock at $60 per share to the general public. Initially, however, it was able to earn only 10 per cent on its new money.

(a) How was the book value per share of the stock affected by the sale of the new stock?

(b) How were the earnings per share affected by the sale? (Assume that the company continued to earn 20 per cent on the old stock equity.)

(c) Would you conclude that the sale of the new stock was harmful to the old shareholders? Why or why not?

3. The Standard Corp. was organized on January 2, 19x1, and within a few days sold $2,000,000 of 7 per cent preferred stock and $2,000,000 of common stock, both having a par value of $100 per share. The stock was sold at par, and there was no paid-in surplus. Net earnings after taxes for the first 5 years were as follows:

Year	Earnings
19x1	$ 25,000 (deficit)
19x2	5,000 (deficit)
19x3	0
19x4	310,000
19x5	840,000

All the available earnings were paid out in the form of dividends each year to the extent permitted by law. If you owned one share of the preferred and one share of the common stock, how much in dividends would you receive on each share for each of these years if the preferred stock was:

(a) Non-cumulative and non-participating? (b) Non-cumulative and participating? (c) Cumulative and non-participating? (d) Cumulative and participating? (e) If the statutes of the state and the contract were silent as to cumulation and participation features?

4. The preferred stock in the preceding question was issued under a contract that stated that it was entitled to par and accrued dividends ahead of the common in event of dissolution of the company. Assume that the company merely broke even on its operations for the year 19x6, but at the end of that year it sold out to a competitor for $5,140,000 in cash that was distributed to

the shareholders. If you owned one share of preferred and one share of common stock how much would you get for each share? (Assume that the dividends stated in the preceding question have been paid.)

5. The New Corp. has outstanding $3,000,000 in common stock; $2,000,000 in 7 per cent non-cumulative, non-participating preferred stock; and $1,000,000 in 6 per cent first mortgage bonds. Mr. Astor said that he would not purchase any of the preferred stock because it had the weakness of the common stock without its advantage and the weakness of the bonds without their advantage.

(a) What did Mr. Astor probably mean by that statement? (b) Do you think he was correct? Explain.

SELECTED READINGS

BARNES, LEO. *Your Investments.* Larchmont, N. Y.: American Research Council, published annually.

BOGEN, JULES I. (ed.). *Financial Handbook,* 3d ed. New York: The Ronald Press Co., 1952. Section 10.

———. "The Importance of Equity Financing in the American Economy," *Journal of Finance,* June, 1950, pp. 170–78.

"Dividend Rights of Non-Cumulative Preferred Stock," *Yale Law Journal,* February, 1952, pp. 245–52.

DORIS, LILLIAN (ed.). *Business Finance Handbook.* Englewood Cliffs, N. J.: Prentice-Hall, Inc., 1953. Chapter 17.

FERGUSSON, D. A. "Recent Developments in Preferred Stock Financing," *Journal of Finance,* September, 1952, pp. 447–62.

FLETCHER, WILLIAM MEADE. *Cyclopedia of the Law of Private Corporations,* Permanent ed. Chicago: Callaghan & Co., Vol. 11 (1958 rev. vol.), Vols. 12 and 12a (1957 rev. vol.), Vols. 13 and 13a (1961 rev. vol.).

SANTOW, LEONARD JAY. "Ultimate Demise of Preferred Stock as a Source of Corporate Capital," *Financial Analysts Journal,* May–June, 1962, pp. 17–54.

STEVENSON, HAROLD W. *Common Stock Financing.* Ann Arbor: University of Michigan, 1957.

7

Corporate Bonds

Although all corporations secure at least part of their capital from the sale of stock, many of them, particularly railroads and public utilities, borrow part of it. When an individual borrows money from a bank, savings and loan association, or finance company, he executes a note in favor of the lending institution, promising to pay the amount borrowed at a specified time with interest at a stated rate. But when a corporation wants to borrow millions of dollars, no one individual or company has that amount to lend, or if they did, they would not want to lend it to one company.

When the corporation borrows a substantial amount of money, therefore, it is necessary in most instances to borrow it from a number of different persons or companies. The instrument given to the lender which embodies the promise to pay the debt is called a *bond*. So, when a corporation sells bonds it is borrowing money. These bonds are similar to notes except that they are generally of longer maturity than notes and there is more formality surrounding their issue.

Bonds Compared With Stocks

Stocks and bonds are both referred to as *securities*, but there is a considerable difference between these two types of securities. Following is a summary of their principal differences.

1. *Bonds represent debts.* The stockholders are the owners of the business, whereas the bondholders are its creditors. Upon dissolution of a corporation, the bondholders must be paid in full before anything can be given to the stockholders.

2. *Bonds must be paid off.* Since the bonds represent a debt, they must be paid upon maturity, or some compromise settlement may be

worked out. But as a legal matter they must be paid or the bondholders can take steps to foreclose the corporate property for the satisfaction of their claims. Stocks, in contrast, do not come due. Preferred stocks may be callable, but they do not have a due date.

3. *Interest on bonds a debt.* The corporation is also obligated to pay the interest on the bonds semiannually or annually, according to the terms of the agreement. It is practically always provided that failure to pay the interest will also make the principal amount of the bonds due. Except for "income bonds" (Chapter 8), this obligation to pay interest is present regardless of whether the corporation has any earnings. In contrast, dividends on stocks cannot be paid unless there are earnings or an accumulated surplus, and they are paid only if declared by the board of directors.

4. *Interest is a fixed amount.* The amount of the interest on a bond is fixed at the time the bond is issued and remains the same throughout its life. The dividends on stock may fluctuate.

5. *Bonds are non-voting.* The bondholders have no voice in the management of the company; in other words, bonds are non-voting. Stock carries the right to vote unless such right is restricted by the contract. Upon failure or insolvency of the company the bondholders may dictate to the directors under threat of foreclosure.

Practical Difference

The paragraphs above represent the legal differences between bonds and stocks. In some instances the contract will give the bonds certain features that are possessed by stocks; these will be pointed out later in our discussion. Preferred stocks, as we have already seen, may have a stated cumulative dividend, may be made non-voting, and upon dissolution may be preferred, though limited, in the distribution of assets. These features tend to make the preferred stock somewhat similar to bonds. But despite these features, there still remains the principal distinction that the stockholders are owners and the bondholders are creditors.

The actual legal rights accruing to the bonds are not always enjoyed by the bondholders. The latter are frequently unorganized and do not press for the strict observation of their rights. As a practical matter, it is often realized by the bondholders that if the corporation has to default in the payment of the interest, they may gain more in the long run by permitting it to operate rather than by exercising their legal right to foreclose. When large corporations fail they are rarely liquidated. The usual procedure is for the corporation to go into the hands of a receiver or trustee in bankruptcy. This will prevent the bondholders from foreclosing on the corporate property. Following this the concern will commonly go through a reorganization rather than a liquidation. The treatment accorded the bondholders will depend upon the types and amounts of securities outstanding, the seriousness of the failure, and the bargaining power of the security holders. So, in actual practice the difference between bonds and stocks may be relative rather than absolute.

Table 7–1 shows the amount of bonds, preferred stock, and common stock offered for cash sale in the United States for the years 1956–1961.

Table 7–1. New Corporate Bonds and Stocks Offered for Cash Sale 1956–1961

| Year | Millions of Dollars | | | | Percentage Distribution | | | |
	Bonds	Preferred Stock	Common Stock	Total	Bonds	Preferred Stock	Common Stock	Total
1961	$9,425	$449	$3,273	$13,147	71.7	3.4	24.9	100.0
1960	8,081	409	1,664	10,154	79.6	4.0	16.4	100.0
1959	7,190	531	2,027	9,748	73.8	5.4	20.8	100.0
1958	9,653	571	1,334	11,558	83.5	5.0	11.5	100.0
1957	9,957	411	2,516	12,884	77.3	3.2	19.5	100.0
1956	8,002	636	2,301	10,939	73.2	5.8	21.0	100.0

SOURCE: *Moody's Industrial Manual,* Moody's Investors Service, Inc., New York, 1962, p. 17.

BOND FEATURES

Denomination of Bonds

The usual *denomination* of a bond is $1,000. This is commonly called the *face value,* or *par value.* This represents the amount that will be paid to the bondholder upon maturity of the bonds. Bonds may originally be issued for more or less than their face value, and the amount that must be paid for them after original issue depends upon the market. In many instances bonds are callable by the issuing corporation at a slight premium from the face value.

Bonds may be issued with a face value of more or less than $1,000. Some corporations have issued them with a face value of $500 or $100. The Series E United States Savings bonds have a face value as low as $25. Bonds with a face value of $100 or less are sometimes referred to as *baby bonds.*

The relatively high face value of most bonds prevents their purchase by the general public. Bonds are usually purchased by investors who have considerably more than $1,000 to invest. Corporations feel that the printing, selling, and transferring costs would be too high relative to what they would obtain to issue them in denominations of less than $1,000.

Maturity of Bonds

When corporations borrow from commercial banks for a period of 30, 60, or 90 days they execute a *note* to the bank which contains their promise to pay the principal and interest. They also sometimes borrow on notes for periods up to five years, or ten years, or longer. These notes are similar to bonds but usually there is less formality surrounding their issue. When a corporation obtains a large loan from an insurance company it may execute notes with maturities greatly in excess of ten years.

Those bonds which have a maturity of from five to fifteen years are commonly called *short-term* bonds. When the maturity runs over fifteen years and up to forty years, they are referred to as *medium-term* bonds. *Long-term* bonds have a maturity in excess of forty years.

Long-term bonds are more commonly found in the railroad field than among public utilities and industrials. Many of these were issued in reorganizations, in exchange for shorter-term securities. Examples of long-term railroad bonds are the Northern Pacific Railroad Company's 3 per cent general lien bonds, which mature in the year 2047, and the New York Central Railroad Company's 4½ per cent refunding and improvement mortgage gold series A, which come due in 2013. An unusual case is the Elmira and Williamsport Railroad Company's 5 per cent income bonds which mature October 1, 2862.[1]

There have been a few isolated cases where perpetual bonds have been issued. The Green Bay & Western Railroad Company's Non-Cumulative Income A and B Debenture Bonds have no maturity date, but the contract provides that they will become due only upon sale, liquidation, or reorganization of the company. The Canadian Pacific Railroad Company has outstanding a Perpetual 4 Per Cent Consolidated Debenture Stock which, despite its title, is a perpetual bond.[2] The British Consols are a well-known example of perpetual bonds. The latter are callable by the government, but they have no maturity date. In regard to the principal amount, a perpetual bond is more like a stock than a bond, but it is similar to other bonds in respect to interest. The idea of borrowing money without providing for its repayment is contrary to our accepted principles of debt. Perpetual bonds could benefit either the issuer or the holder depending upon their face rate of interest, and the future trend of interest rates in general.

[1] These bonds were issued in 1863; hence from the time of issue they have a life of 999 years. Furthermore, these bonds are non-callable. They are guaranteed as to interest by the Pennsylvania Railroad Company, and they are traded in the over-the-counter market.

[2] This bond issue is listed on the New York Stock Exchange. It is non-callable. By legislation it has been given a first lien on all the company's assets and earnings. The fact that it is called a "Debenture Stock" issue is probably due more to British practice than to the fact that the issue does not have a maturity date.

BOND YIELDS

Bonds have a fixed rate of interest which must be paid the same as any other debt on the dates due. Interest on bonds is usually due semi-annually on the first or fifteenth of the month, such as January 15, and July 15, although in some instances the interest is paid annually. The rate of interest is expressed as a percentage of the face value of the bond. When the interest is paid semiannually the amount paid each six months is one-half the stated rate. The face rate of interest is called the *nominal yield*.

The rate of interest a bond bears is set at such an amount that the bond can be sold by the issuing company at or near its face value. The rate of interest which a corporation must pay on its bonds depends upon the general interest rates prevailing in the market at the time the bond is issued, the supply and demand of money, the general credit of the company, the nature of the particular bond issue, the length of maturity of the bonds, and the price at which the corporation proposes to sell the bond in the market.

After giving due consideration to the above factors, investors will pay such a price for a bond that the rate of return on their money, which is called the *yield,* will be the amount demanded. The following factors would tend to make the face rate of interest relatively low: low prevailing interest rates in the market, large supply of loanable funds, high credit rating of issuing company, a well-secured senior bond, and a short-term bond. When interest rates are relatively low, the shorter the maturity of the bond, the lower will be the yield demanded by investors. When bonds are sold at a premium or discount the loss or gain in the principal amount at maturity (or at call date) is considered a deduction from or addition to the current interest being received by the holder.

Table 7–2 shows the cost of borrowed capital in the United States for the years 1957–1961 as measured by the average yields of newly issued railroad, industrial, and utility bonds. Table 7–3 shows the yields on bonds and on preferred and common stocks for the years 1956–1961.

Computing Bond Yields

If a person buys a bond at its face value and sells it at the same price, his *yield* will be the same as the face rate of interest. If, however, he pays more or less than the face value, or if he pays the face amount and sells it for something different, the yield will be more or less than the face rate of interest.

Let us assume that a person bought a 4 per cent 10-year $1,000 face value bond for $1,086.25. The fact that a premium was paid for the bond

Table 7–2. Average Price of Borrowed Capital 1957–1961
(Moody's Weighted Average of Yields on Newly Issued Domestic Bonds)

Year	Railroad	Industrial	Utility	Corporate Average
1961	4.88%	4.70%	4.70%	4.70%
1960	*	4.67	4.84	4.82
1959	*	4.67	4.97	4.94
1958	4.56	4.31	4.21	4.26
1957	5.01	4.46	4.74	4.26

* No new issues.
SOURCE: *Moody's Industrial Manual*, Moody's Investors Service, Inc., New York, 1962, p. a18.

Table 7–3. Yields on Bonds, Preferred Stock, and Common Stock
1956–1961

Year	Moody's Composite Corporate Bonds	Moody's Preferred Stock Series *	Moody's 200 Common Stocks
1961	4.66%	4.67%	3.07%
1960	4.73	4.80	3.60
1959	4.65	4.78	3.31
1958	4.16	4.57	4.05
1957	4.21	4.75	4.33
1956	3.57	4.24	4.07

* Average of 10 high-grade and 10 medium-grade industrials and 10 high-grade and 10 medium-grade utilities in the low-dividend series.
SOURCE: *Moody's Industrial Manual*, Moody's Investors Service, Inc., New York, 1962, pp. a18, a25.

indicates that the corporation could borrow money at less than 4 per cent interest. The purchaser will get $40 a year interest on the bond. But if he holds the bond until maturity, he will get back only $1,000. Thus, he will lose $86.25 of his principal. The actual yield on the bond will obviously be less than 4 per cent for two reasons. First, the 4 per cent face rate is based on the face value of the bond and not the purchase price, and second, the premium is lost. We can determine the approximate *yield to maturity* with the following formula.

$$\frac{\text{Annual interest} - \text{Annual amortized premium (or, } + \text{ Annual amortized discount)}}{(\text{Cost price} + \text{Maturity value}) \div 2} = \frac{\text{Approximate yield}}{\text{to maturity}}$$

Substituting the above figures in the formula we get the following:

$$\frac{\$40 - \$8.625}{(\$1,086.25 + \$1,000) \div 2} = 3 \text{ per cent}$$

If the bond was bought at a discount from the face value, the annual amortized discount would be added to the annual interest, as indicated in the formula. This formula does not give the exact yield but it is close enough for ordinary purposes. The actual yield can be found in standard bond tables which are available in banks, brokerage offices, and libraries.

If a premium bond is callable by the company before its maturity date, then the purchaser should consider his *yield to call date,* instead of maturity. The call price would then be used instead of the maturity value in the formula. There are two reasons why the yield on a premium bond should be computed to call date rather than maturity. First, the fact that the bond is selling at a premium indicates that the corporation's current borrowing rate is less than the face rate on the bonds. Therefore, it would be cheaper for a corporation to call in its bonds and put out an issue with a lower face rate. So the probability is that a corporation will exercise the call feature on a premium bond. The purchaser should, therefore, be realistic and compute his yield to call date. The second reason for doing this is that it is conservative practice since it gives a lower yield.

If a callable bond is selling at a discount it is indicative that the corporation's current borrowing rate is more than the face rate on the bond, and therefore it is probable that the bonds will not be called in. Therefore, the yield should be computed to the maturity date. Furthermore, computing the yield on a discount bond to maturity will give a lower yield, therefore it is the more conservative method to use.

The *current yield* is determined by dividing the amount of the annual interest by the current price of the bond. To use the figures in the above example, if a person bought a 4 per cent bond for $1,086.25, the current yield would be little more than 3.68 per cent. If a bond which has only a short time to run until maturity is selling at a substantial discount, it is probable that it will not be paid at maturity, so it would be advisable to use the current yield rather than the yield to maturity.

If it is probable that the bonds will be paid off at maturity, the price of both discount and premium bonds will gradually work toward the face value as the maturity date approaches.

Bonds Quotations

Corporate bonds are ordinarily quoted in percentage of their face value. Thus a quote of 98 for a particular bond means a price of $980 ($1,000 face value assumed). The buyer must pay the seller the quoted price plus any accrued interest. In other words, the quoted price of bonds does not include any interest which has accrued since the last payment date. This is in contrast to stocks whose quoted price reflects any anticipation of dividends. Corporate bonds sold for "regular-way delivery" on the New York Stock Exchange call for delivery the fourth business day following the sale. Regular-way delivery on government bonds, however, is the next day following the sale. Accrued interest is computed from the last interest payment date up to, but not including, the day of delivery.

In computing accrued interest on corporate bonds, a 360-day year (30 days in each month) is assumed (on United States Government securities the actual number of days is used). If a 6 per cent corporate bond on which interest is paid semiannually on January 1 and July 1, is purchased at 98 ($980) on April 27, it will be delivered regular way on May 1. Thus the buyer must pay to the seller $20 for the accrued interest (four months) in addition to the $980. In computing his yield on the bond the buyer should use the figure $980.

There are two instances when bonds are quoted flat, i.e., when the quoted price includes any accrued interest. These are income bonds (with a few exceptions), which will be described later, and bonds that are in default.

Relationship Between Bond Prices and Interest Rates

A particular 4 per cent bond may originally sell for its face value. If the credit of the issuing company remains about the same, but interest rates in general drift lower in the market, people may be willing to invest their money at a lower rate of interest than formerly, so they may bid up the price of the 4 per cent bond to a premium.

Conversely, if interest rates in general would advance, then people could get a higher rate of return. If they could buy a 4½ per cent bond at its face value, they would pay less than that for a bond similar in nature, but which bore a face rate of only 4 per cent. In other words, a rise in interest rates would cause a drop in the price of existing bonds. It is thus seen that bond prices result from people's demanding a particular yield.

Regardless of how bond prices, and thus yields, may fluctuate in the market, however, the yield to a particular individual is always computed on the purchase price of the bond.

Although *yields* on short-term and long-term bonds tend to move together, the short-term yields follow the business cycle more closely and go to greater extremes in both directions than do the yields of long-term bonds. The *prices* of long-term bonds, on the other hand, fluctuate more than do the prices of short-term bonds. The following indicates the prices at which a 3 per cent bond would sell to yield 4 per cent, and the prices at which a 4 per cent bond would sell to yield 3 per cent. As is noted, when the bond is selling at a discount or a premium, the longer the maturity, the greater is the discount or premium.

Maturity in Years	Price of a 3% Bond in a 4% Market	Price of a 4% Bond in a 3% Market
5	95.51	104.61
10	91.82	108.58
20	86.32	114.96
30	82.62	119.69

If market interest rates would decline from 4 to 3 per cent, investors would pay the face value for a 3 per cent bond. This would result in an increase in the price of the 30-year, 3 per cent bond, of 17.38, but a rise of only 4.49 in the price of the 5-year maturity. Referring now to the last column above, if the market rate of interest would rise, from 3 to 4 per cent, the price of the 4 per cent 30-year maturity would fall 19.69, while the price of the 5-year maturity would fall only 4.61.

It should be kept in mind that in the above example we were assuming that people would buy the various maturities on the same yield basis. This was done in order to show the comparative effects on the prices of long-term and short-term bonds of a change in market interest rates. As a practical matter, investors usually demand different yields on different maturities. When interest rates are comparatively low, long-term securities sell on a higher yield basis than do short-term securities. In order not to sacrifice too much in the way of yield by buying a short-term bond, and not run the risk of losing too much on the price of a long-term bond resulting from an increase in interest rates, the medium-term bonds are recommended for the average investor.

REGISTERED AND COUPON BONDS

Registered Bonds

With respect to the payment of interest and principal, bonds are classified as (1) registered, (2) coupon, or (3) registered-coupon. A fully *registered bond* is one which contains the name of the owner on the bond, and which is registered in his name on the company's records (usually maintained by the registrar). This is similar to the registration of stocks.

Interest on a fully registered bond is paid by check directly to the registered holder. When the principal is due it is paid to such holder upon presentment of the indorsed bond. If a holder wants to transfer it, he must indorse it. For the purchaser to be recognized by the issuer as the owner, it will be necessary to surrender the indorsed bond to the transfer office of the company and have a new one issued in his name.

If a person buys an unindorsed registered bond, he does not necessarily get title. If the indorsement is forged, then no one can acquire title to it. The advantage of a registered bond thus lies in its safety. A thief or finder cannot pass good title to an unindorsed registered bond. It is also less trouble to receive the interest by mail than to clip the coupons and present them for payment, which must be done with a coupon bond.

The disadvantage of a registered bond is that it is more trouble to transfer than a coupon bond because of the necessity for indorsement, and the fact that the buyer has to get it registered in his own name. As a result, the registered bond will usually sell for slightly less than a coupon bond of the same issue.

If a registered bond is put up as collateral for a loan the banker will want the right to have the bond transferred to his name in event of default in the loan. If the bond is indorsed then it would still have the owner's indorsement on it after it is returned to him when the loan is paid. Rather than indorse the bond, it would be better for the owner to attach to it a signed *bond power of attorney*. This would give the bank the right to have it transferred to its name in event the loan is not paid.

The registered bond may be preferred by an institutional investor, such as an insurance company, which might contemplate holding it until maturity. The treasurer of a company or a trustee might prefer it because of the relative safety from loss or theft.

Coupon Bonds

The coupon bond contains a series of dated coupons which are clipped by the owner on the appropriate dates and sent to the issuing company or given to a bank for collection. The coupons are payable to bearer. Unless the bond is registered as to principal, the principal amount is also payable to bearer. Title to this bond passes by delivery. It is not necessary to indorse it, nor does the buyer have to get it transferred to his name. An innocent purchaser for value gets good title to the bond.

The coupon bond usually sells for slightly more than the registered bond. The usual price differential is from one quarter of a point to one point ($2.50 to $10.00 on a $1,000 bond). Most buyers of corporate bonds (and U. S. Treasury bonds) prefer the coupon bond.

The principal disadvantage of the coupon bond may be inferred from the above. There is greater danger in holding the bond because of the possibility of loss or theft. For this reason coupon bonds should always be kept in a safe place, such as a safe deposit box. It is advisable for a person to keep a record of the serial numbers of all types of bonds he owns, particularly coupon bonds, in order to aid in identification of the bonds in the event that they are lost or stolen. The list of the numbers should be kept in a different place from where the bonds are kept.

If a person loses a bond he should immediately notify the company or its registrar, giving full particulars. In order to secure a new bond, however, the issuing company will usually require that he put up a surety bond to protect the company in event the bond shows up in the hands of an innocent purchaser for value.

Another possible disadvantage of the coupon bond is the trouble of clipping the coupons. This may not seem to be much of a job to the average reader, but in the case of large institutional investors, and also for some individuals, it is quite a task. Furthermore, since the coupons may come due at different times on different bonds, an extensive investor may find it quite troublesome to have to make frequent trips to the bank to get the coupons and send them in for collection. Furthermore, if the coupons are not sent in on time, the bondholder will lose the opportunity of getting interest on the interest due. In the case of registered bonds the interest is always sent on time, so the bondholder can invest the interest. Since the company does not have the names of the coupon bondholders, it will be necessary for them to watch the financial newspapers for any announcement of a call. This is another disadvantage of coupon bonds.

In the case of large bond issues, both registered and coupon bonds are usually issued. It is then generally provided that the registered and coupon bonds can be exchanged for each other at the option of the holder. Usually a charge of from $1 to $2 per bond is made for the exchange. If such an issue is listed on the New York Stock Exchange, all purchases and sales are assumed to be the coupon bonds.

Registered-Coupon Bonds

Corporations sometimes issue a bond which is registered as to principal but coupon as to interest. Or the bond may originally be sold as a purely coupon bond but with the owner being given the right to have it registered as to principal at his option. Such bonds are sometimes called *registered-coupon bonds.* The interest coupons are payable to bearer, but otherwise the bond is treated as registered. The owner's name appears on the back of this type of bond.

TRUSTEE AND INDENTURE

When an individual borrows money there are only two parties involved—the borrower and the lender. But when a corporation borrows by selling bonds there are three parties to the agreement—the borrowing corporation, the bondholders, and a *trustee.* The trustee is supposed to represent the interests of the bondholders. The borrowing corporation deals with the trustee rather than with the individual holders. When the bond issue is secured by a mortgage on the corporate property, legal title to the property is transferred to the trustee (in some states the trustee holds a lien) who holds it in trust for the benefit of the bondholders. It would be impractical to give separate mortgages to thousands of individual bondholders. Trustees are used, however, even if the issue is not a mortgage one, to facilitate the dealings between the bondholders and the corporation.

The trustee is selected by the company or the investment banker who is selling the issue, or they may jointly make the decision. The trustee is usually a trust company which has experience in this work and which has a permanent staff to take care of the details. In some instances an individual is appointed as a cotrustee. The trust company, being a corporation, may not have the authority to transact business in other states in which some of the corporation's property may be located, but an individual trustee can represent the corporation in all states. The trust company, on the other hand, does not have the limited life of an individual.

In the past, trustees often neglected the interest of the bondholders and favored the corporation which selected them. As a result, the federal government in 1939, adopted the Trust Indenture Act. This Act applies to all security issues which must be registered with the SEC (Securities and Exchange Commission) except foreign government bond issues and corporate issues of $1,000,000 or less. The following are among the more important provisions of the Act relating to trustees.

1. One of the trustees must be a corporation with capital and surplus of not less than $150,000, organized in the United States and authorized to exercise corporate trust powers, and subject to supervision or examination by federal, state, or territorial authority. The Act provides that individuals may be appointed cotrustees.
2. In a situation where a conflict in interests would arise such as where the trustee is acting under another indenture of the same issuer, or where the trustee or its officers are affiliated with the issuer or underwriter, the trustee must either resign, remove the conflicting interest, or notify the security holders and let them exercise their powers of removal.
3. The issuing corporation is required to furnish a list of bondholders to the trustee at stated intervals, which lists must be made available by the trustee to individual bondholders upon demand.
4. The trustee must submit an annual report to the bondholders indicating the nature of any advances made by the trustee to the corporation, the condition of the property held in trust, and other relevant matters.
5. The trustee must notify the bondholders of all defaults within ninety days.
6. In the event of default the trustee must exercise his defined powers and rights with the same degree of care and skill as a prudent man

would exercise or use under the circumstances in the conduct of his own affairs.

Duties of the Trustees

The duties of the trustees vary according to the indenture (the latter is described below) but the following are typical.

1. *Authentication* of the bonds. In order to give protection to the bondholders against overissue and forgery, the trustee authenticates the bonds by signing a statement such as the one below, which is called the *certification of the trustee.*

> This bond is one of the bonds described in the within mentioned deed of trust.
>
> ————————————————— Trust Company
>
> By ————————————————
> Trust Officer

2. *Collection and disbursement* of interest and principal. It is the duty of the trustee to collect the money from the corporation and disburse the interest and principal payments to the bondholders.
3. *Sinking fund.* If the indenture provides for a sinking fund to retire the bonds, it is usually the duty of the trustee to secure the money from the corporation and acquire the bonds.
4. *Protection of security.* If the bonds are issued under a mortgage, it is the duty of the trustee to see to it that the mortgaged property is not dissipated. When other securities are pledged as collateral behind the bonds, the trustee is the custodian of the collateral. He must also attend to the substitution of the collateral in the event that some of the securities pledged are retired.
5. *Protection of bondholders.* It is the duty of the trustee to make the corporation observe all the provisions included in the indenture for the protection of the bondholders. In the event of default, the trustee must take the steps indicated in the indenture.

The Bond Indenture

The three-way agreement between the issuing corporation, the trustee, and the bondholders is contained in a rather elaborate contract called the bond *indenture.* Other titles used for this document include the following: *trust agreement, deed of trust,* and *mortgage and deed of trust.* In general the indenture contains all the details in connection with the bond issue and the relationships between the corporation, the trustee, and the bondholders.

Following are the provisions which are usually contained in the indenture.

1. The indenture starts out with the names of the parties to the agreement. These are the issuing corporation and the trustee. The bondholders are the beneficiaries under the trust.
2. Next is the preamble which states the purposes of the indenture, the legal authorization for the issuance of the bonds, the form of the bonds and of the interest coupons, if they are coupon bonds, and the certification of the trustee.
3. The granting clause which contains a detailed description of any property mortgaged, or any securities put up as collateral.
4. A statement of the maximum amount of bonds to be issued under the indenture. If all the bonds are not to be issued at once, a statement of the amount to be issued immediately will usually be stated, followed by a statement of the conditions under which the additional bonds may be issued.
5. Clauses, or *covenants*, for the protection of the bondholders. These include the following: agreement of the corporation to keep its mortgaged property in proper repair, to maintain insurance on the property, to set up depreciation reserves, to pay property taxes, and agreement not to place a prior lien on the property.
6. The procedure to be followed by the bondholders to levy on the mortgaged property in case of a mortgage issue, or to pursue their rights as general creditors.
7. An *acceleration clause* which states that if any default in interest payments occurs, the principal of the bonds will become due and payable.
8. Any provisions for a sinking fund to retire the bonds.
9. Any provision for calling the bonds before their maturity.
10. Rights, if any, to convert the bonds into other securities.
11. Any provision for the maintenance of minimum working capital requirements before dividends can be paid to the stockholders.
12. Definition of the powers, duties, and liabilities of the trustee. These were dealt with above.

Registration of a security issue is not complete until an indenture which complies with the provisions of the Trust Indenture Act of 1939 is filed with the SEC. The Commission's responsibility is to see to it that the indenture conforming to the Act is properly filed. But the Commission does not thereafter have any powers with respect to the enforcement of the provisions of the indenture. The indenture is enforceable by the parties thereto. The requirements of the Act, however, make it mandatory to include in the indenture certain provisions for the protection of the bondholders in event of negligence or misfeasance on the part of the trustee, and forces the corporation to exercise greater responsibility. Failure on the part of the trustee or the corporation to comply with the provisions of the Act, however, means little unless the bondholders initiate action against them.

REASONS FOR SELLING BONDS

To Secure Capital

The obvious reason why any corporation sells bonds is to secure money. Our present interest is why corporations sell bonds instead of, or in addition to, the sale of notes and stocks, or instead of borrowing from a bank.

Financial Condition of the Company

There are many instances where because of financial weakness of the company the market would not absorb a stock issue, but a bond issue could be sold. The company under such circumstances has no alternative in securing new capital but to issue bonds.

Condition of the Market

A corporation follows the preference of the public for bonds or for stock and would issue what is more economical under the circumstances.

Control

The matter of participation in control is sometimes an important factor in determining whether a public stock issue or bond issue will be sold. Bonds do not possess the right to vote, but stocks, with the exception of some classified issues and some preferred issues, do.

Wider Market

Stocks and bonds are to some extent not purchased by the same class of buyers; in general, speculators tend to favor stocks, while investors prefer bonds.

Many institutions such as banks, trust companies, trustees, and life insurance companies are either prohibited by the law from buying stocks, or if permitted, the percentage of their resources that can be invested in stocks is relatively small. Thus, a corporation may have more classes of bond buyers than stock buyers.

Cost of Funds

Bonds ordinarily are sold in denominations of not less than $1,000, while stocks are usually sold at considerably less than $100 a share. Furthermore, bonds are ordinarily sold in much larger dollar amounts than stocks, and are a much safer investment than stocks of the same company.

Because of these facts, the selling costs connected with a bond issue of a given amount are lower than the costs of a stock issue of the same amount.

In addition to the above, the annual interest charges that a corporation must pay out on bonds are ordinarily less than would have to be paid in dividends on stock. Since bonds constitute a debt of the issuing corporation, while stock represents ownership, a person will ordinarily lend money to a corporation at a lower rate than he would demand from stock.

Many growth stocks, however, sell on a lower yield basis than bonds issued by the same company, but due consideration must be given to the tax savings resulting from the bond interest; this is discussed below.

Trading on the Equity

The term *equity* is used in different ways, but in corporation finance it means *ownership*. Thus, we speak of stocks as being *equities,* or *equity securities.* If a corporation has only common stock outstanding and it sells additional common stock at its book value, but the *rate of earnings on the stockholders' investment* remains the same, the *earnings per share* on the old stock would remain the same. But if instead of selling more stock, the corporation obtained the same amount of additional money by the sale of bonds, the rate of interest on which is less than the rate the company is earning on its capital, then the earnings per share on the stock would be increased. This process or procedure of using the stockholders' equity as a basis for borrowing money at a lower rate than the corporation hopes to earn on the bondholders' money is called *trading on the equity.*

Let us assume that a company has $1,000,000 in stock outstanding, and an equivalent amount invested in assets. To simplify the example, we will assume that there are no liabilities, and also no surplus. For the time being we will consider the earnings before federal income taxes. If the company earns, after all expenses, $100,000 a year, the earnings per share on the stock would be 10 per cent.

We will assume that the corporation wants to raise another $1,000,000, through the sale of either common stock or bonds. If it sells the stock, and continues to earn 10 per cent on its capital, the total earnings would increase to $200,000, but the *earnings per share* would remain at 10 per cent. But if the company raised the $1,000,000 through the sale of a 3 per cent bond issue, the earnings on the common stock after the bond interest was paid would amount to $170,000. This represents earnings per share of 17 per cent on the stock, instead of only 10 per cent.

We can carry the above example further to illustrate the effect of trading on the equity. If the company increased its *rate of earnings* on its capital from 10 to 15 per cent, the earnings per share on the common

Table 7–4. Effect of Leverage on Stockholders' Equity (Before Taxes)

Item	Capitalization					
	Stock $2,000,000	Stock $1,000,000 Bonds $1,000,000	Stock $2,000,000	Stock $1,000,000 Bonds $1,000,000	Stock $2,000,000	Stock $1,000,000 Bonds $1,000,000
Earnings before interest	$200,000	$200,000	$300,000	$300,000	$30,000	$30,000
Interest on bonds		30,000		30,000		30,000
Earned on stock (before taxes)	$200,000	$170,000	$300,000	$270,000	$30,000	0
Per cent earned on stock	10%	17%	15%	27%	1½%	0

Table 7–5. Effect of Leverage on Stockholders' Equity (After Taxes)

Item	Capitalization					
	Stock $2,000,000	Stock $1,000,000 Bonds $1,000,000	Stock $2,000,000	Stock $1,000,000 Bonds $1,000,000	Stock $2,000,000	Stock $1,000,000 Bonds $1,000,000
Earnings before interest	$200,000	$200,000	$300,000	$300,000	$30,000	$30,000
Interest on bonds		30,000		30,000		30,000
Earnings after interest	$200,000	$170,000	$300,000	$270,000	$30,000	$30,000
Taxes (50%)	100,000	85,000	150,000	135,000	15,000	15,000
Earned on stock	$100,000	$85,000	$150,000	$135,000	$15,000	0
Per cent earned on stock	5%	8½%	7½%	13½%	¾%	0

would be increased by only the same percentage, assuming the firm secured the additional $1,000,000 through the sale of stock. But if the bonds were sold instead, and the company could increase its rate of earning on its capital from 10 to 15 per cent, the earnings on the stock would increase to 27 per cent. This is computed as follows:

Earnings before interest	$300,000	(15% on capital)
Less: Bond Interest	30,000	(3% on $1,000,000)
Earnings on stock (before taxes)	$270,000	(equals 27% on stock of $1,000,000)

Trading on the equity, however, sometimes backfires on a corporation. If the earnings fall to the point where the company is earning a smaller rate on its capital than it is paying on the bonds, the corporation would have been better off to have sold additional stock. To illustrate, let us assume that earnings fall to where they represent a return of only 1½ per cent on the capital. This means that the earnings would decline to $30,000. If the corporation had sold stock it would then be earning 1½ per cent on the stock. But if bonds had been sold, all of these earnings would be consumed in paying the bond interest, and the company would have earned nothing on its stock. If the company instead of earning something, suffers a loss, then the loss will be larger if it has to pay bond interest. From what has been said it is obvious that trading on the equity *magnifies both profits and losses.* In order to better visualize what has been said above, the comparative effects of selling stocks and bonds are summarized in Table 7–4.

Trading on the (common stockholders') equity can also be done by the issuance of a non-participating preferred stock. Since the dividend rate on the preferred would ordinarily be more than the interest on bonds, the use of preferred stock does not magnify the profits as much as when bonds are issued.

The term *leverage* is quite commonly used in practice to refer to what we have here described as "trading on the equity." Companies that have a large portion of their capitalization in the form of bonds are referred to as leverage companies. The term *leverage* is also sometimes used to apply to the situation where a corporation has a large surplus so that a slight increase in the rate of earnings on the invested capital will produce a relatively large increase in the earnings on the stock. The latter is referred to as *internal* leverage, whereas the former type is called *external* leverage.

Federal Income Tax

In our discussion of trading on the equity we ignored the federal corporate income tax in order to illustrate how leverage alone would affect profits and losses. As a practical matter, however, we cannot and do not want to ignore these taxes.

Bond interest is an expense which is deducted as such before arriving at the net profits on which the tax rate is based. Dividends on stock, on the other hand, are not expenses, but rather a distribution of the profits, and are not deducted before computing the income tax. This means that every dollar paid out in bond interest reduces by that amount the figure on which the tax is based. With a rate of taxation of 50 per cent, it means that if a corporation is enjoying a profit, the bond interest reduces the net taxable profit by the amount of the interest, so that there is a tax saving equivalent to 50 per cent of the bond interest. In other words, if a corporation sells a 3 per cent bond issue, instead of a stock issue, and is operating at a profit, the tax saving reduces the effective cost of the bonds from 3 per cent to 1½ per cent. In Table 7–5 are the same data as stated above in connection with trading on the equity after giving effect to income taxes at the rate of 50 per cent.

The reader should guard against an idea that savings can be effected by the unlimited issuance of bonds. It is not good financial management to pay out $1.00 in interest in order to save 50 cents in taxes. But as an alternative to stock financing, bonds will effect the tax savings illustrated above.

If trading on the equity is accomplished through the issuance of preferred stock, only the first example given above of the effect of leverage before income taxes would be applicable, since dividends, unlike interest, cannot be deducted before taxes.

BOND RETIREMENT

There are three methods of retiring bonds, and any of these methods may be used to eliminate the bonds either at or before maturity. These methods are as follows.

Redemption. Bonds are said to be *redeemed* when they are paid off in cash. This may occur at the maturity of the bonds or before by the exercise of the call feature or by the purchase of the bonds in the market.

Refunding. If bonds are paid off by means of another issue of bonds, they are said to be *refunded*. The new bonds may be exchanged to the bondholders for their old bonds, or the new bonds may be sold in the market and the proceeds used to retire the old bonds. The latter procedure is really a method of redemption.

Conversion. Bonds may be paid off by the holders thereof *converting* them into stock. This will be described in Chapter 9.

REDEMPTION

When the bonds are paid upon maturity it is a routine matter. The cash (actually a check) for the principal amount and the interest due for the last period is turned over to the trustee representing the bondholders and he distributes this to the bondholders in exchange for their bonds.

Redemption Before Maturity

Although the following are the reasons for redemption before maturity, some are also reasons why a corporation may be anxious to pay off its bonds upon maturity.

Elimination of Fixed Charges. The interest on the bonds must be paid regardless of the amount of earnings or cash possessed by the corporation. This fixed charge may in the future be a source of considerable embarrassment and may even cause the concern to fail. Realizing this, many corporations try to eliminate their bonded indebtedness, the principal as well as the fixed charge, as soon as the opportunity presents itself.

Reduction of Fixed Charges. In many instances corporations are forced to sell bonds at a time of high interest rates. Or, the company's credit at the time may be such that a relatively high rate was necessary in order to sell the bonds. Later interest rates may generally fall, or the company's credit may improve so that it could currently borrow at a lower rate than it is paying on its present bonds, and redeem the expensive old issues.

Elimination of Stringent Provisions. In order to add to the marketability of the bonds to be issued, the corporation may have been forced to include some protective provisions in the indenture, which it now would like to eliminate, e.g., the requirement to observe certain strict current-asset or cash ratios, before it may pay dividends; prohibitions against incurring of additional debt or bonded indebtedness; mortgage on after-acquired property, which might make future financing expensive. The redemption of such bonds will extinguish the stringent provisions.

Elimination of Inflexible Financial Plan. In many instances corporations sell an issue of bonds secured by a first mortgage against all their property, when they are still comparatively small or young. The company may later develop and need to borrow more money, but the issue of first mortgage bonds it has outstanding may be closed and the company cannot issue any more first mortgage bonds against the same property. Under these circumstances it would be desirable for the company to retire the old bonds.

Investment of Idle Cash. If operations and financial management are successful, a corporation should from time to time have cash on hand which might wisely be used to retire some of its bonds.

Bolster Market for Bonds. The bonds of a particular corporation may fall in price more than the general market. This drop in price may result in some of the company's bondholders' disposing of their bonds. Such a situation has an adverse effect on the credit of the company. If the company has the necessary cash available, it might be advisable for it to buy up some of the bonds on the market, and thus to check the price drop or reverse its direction.

Economical Method of Retirement. If a corporation's bonds are selling in the market at a price considerably below their call or face value, material savings could be effected if the corporation would buy the bonds on the market and cancel them.

Methods of Redeeming Bonds Before Maturity

The methods of redeeming bonds before they mature are as follows.

Exercise of Call Feature. It is the usual practice to insert in the bond indenture a provision giving the issuing company the right to call in the bonds before their maturity. The provision calls for a fixed time for redemption, which is commonly on an interest date. The indenture usually provides that notice, which in practice ranges from several weeks to several months, must be given to the bondholders in advance of calling in the bonds. Registered bondholders will be sent notice by mail; for coupon bonds the notice will be printed in designated financial publications.

It is commonly provided in the indenture that the issue is callable only as a whole, but in some instances it is provided that a specified amount less than this may be retired. In the latter case the numbers of the bonds to be called will usually be determined by lot. When bonds are called, interest on them ceases.

Purchase on Market Through Dealers. The corporation may secure the services of an investment banker or broker to buy up its bonds on the market. The broker or dealer can judge the market and buy in periods of weakness in such quantities that the price would not be run up.

Direct Negotiation with Bondholders. In some instances a corporation will negotiate directly with its larger bondholders for the retirement of their bonds, or advertise for tenders of its bonds at a price not to exceed a specified amount.

Disadvantages to Bondholder of Redemption

In this section we will be considering primarily bonds that are redeemed through the exercise of the call feature. Usually, when it is to the best interests of the corporation to retire its bonds before maturity, it would be to the advantage of the bondholders to continue to hold them.

Interest rates may decline, with the result that the company exercises the call feature and refunds the issue with one bearing a lower rate of interest.

Having secured his money back, the bondholder is now confronted with the problem of reinvesting at a time of low interest rates. Furthermore, there is commonly a brokerage charge or commission to be paid to buy new securities.

To offset, at least in part, these shortcomings of the call feature, corporations usually make their bonds callable at a slight *premium* over their face value.

REFUNDING

The bonded indebtedness of a corporation is called its *funded debt*. If a company *funds* its debt, it means that it replaces short-term notes or open book accounts by long-term bonds. *Refunding* a debt means to exchange one bond issue for another bond issue.

In a refunding operation the bondholders are frequently asked, or given the opportunity, to exchange their bonds for the new ones. If not all the old bondholders will do this, bonds of the refunding issue will have to be sold for cash sufficient to retire the old bonds. Commonly the issue is underwritten by investment bankers to insure its successful sale.

A bondholder cannot force a corporation to pay off its bonds before they are due; nor can a corporation force its bondholders to give up their bonds before they are due, unless the issue contains a call clause. But if bonds are called, the bondholder can insist on cash.

Reasons for Refunding

When a bond issue comes due, the issuing corporation may need its cash or liquid assets in the business, or it does not have available cash or liquid assets necessary for their payment. If a refunding issue is acceptable to the bondholders or can be sold to secure funds, the corporation may be glad of the opportunity to pay off its bonds in this manner.

Companies, such as public utilities, may prefer to have bonds outstanding. Since their rates are set so as to permit them to earn only a fair return on a fair investment, it may be to the interests of the stock-holders to have a bonded indebtedness more or less permanently. In this way they benefit from the *leverage,* or *trading on the equity.* Thus when a public utility bond issue becomes due, it is generally taken for granted that its place will be taken by a refunding issue.

Earlier in the chapter we considered the various reasons why a corporation might want to redeem its bonds before their maturity. The same reasons would apply with equal force to refunding before maturity.

Savings on Fixed Charges Through Refunding

When interest rates in general decline, or when the credit of the company increases to the point where it can borrow at a lower rate than it is now paying, at first glance large savings in interest rates may be expected from a refunding operation. But we should carefully compute the actual savings before jumping to conclusions. Let us assume that a corporation has outstanding $10,000,000 in 4 per cent bonds, which come due 20 years from now, and that it can secure the money at about 3 per cent today. If an issue of 3 per cent bonds is sold to refund the 4 per cent bonds it might appear that an annual saving of $100,000, or a total saving of $2,000,000 for the 20-year period, could be effected (compounding the interest would still increase the savings).

To compute the *actual* savings, however, we will have to consider the following factors:

1. Commissions to bankers
2. Printing costs
3. Expense to register with Securities and Exchange Commission
4. Legal fees
5. Maturity date of new issue
6. Call price of old issue
7. Income tax rates

To simplify our explanation we will also suppose that the corporation can sell the bonds to investment bankers at such a price that it will have left an amount equal to the face value of the bonds after paying bankers' commissions, printing costs, registration expenses, and legal fees. We will also assume that the refunding issue has a maturity of 20 years and that the call price on the old issue is 105. A 50 per cent corporate tax rate is also assumed.

To call in the old issue will require $10,500,000. Of this amount $500,000 represents the premium on the old bonds. This can be deducted as an expense for federal corporate income tax purposes, which will save $250,000 in taxes. So assuming that the $250,000 saved is available to apply toward the retirement of the bonds, it will be necessary to issue only $10,250,000 in new bonds.

The interest on the new bonds would be $307,500 annually, or a total of $6,150,000 for the entire 20 years. But since the interest charge is deductible for income tax purposes, the actual net cost to the company would be only half this amount, or $3,075,000. Interest on the old bonds would have been $400,000 a year, or $8,000,000 for the 20-year period. Adjusting this for taxes, the net cost for 20 years would have been $4,000,-000. Subtracting from this latter figure the net cost of the interest on the new bonds of $3,075,000, leaves a net interest savings on the new bonds of $925,000.

But if the refunding issue is sold, the company will have to pay off $250,000 more in the bonds than if they had let the old issue remain outstanding. Subtracting this amount from the net interest savings of $925,000, leaves us only $675,000 as the net savings that would be realized over the 20-year period by refunding the old issue.[3]

Inducements to Refund

In order to entice the bondholders to exchange their bonds for those of the refunding issue, corporations often have to give them some inducements. One or more of these may be offered in the same issue.

1. *Higher rate of interest.* In some instances the refunding bonds bear a higher face rate of interest than the old bonds.

2. *Cash bonus.* Occasionally a corporation will offer the bondholders a cash bonus if they will exchange their bonds.

3. *Partial redemption.* Corporations will sometimes offer to give the bondholders the chance to receive partial payments of the bond in cash, and the balance in new bonds.

4. *Sinking fund provision.* If the old issue had no sinking fund behind it, the company may provide for one in the refunding issue for the purpose of inducing the bondholders to refund.

5. *Better security.* The refunding issue may be better secured than the bonds which are being refunded. For example the old bonds may be debentures while the refunding issue may be secured by a mortgage. Or, the bonds outstanding may be secured by a mortgage on only a small part of the corporation's property, while the refunding issue has a mortgage on all the property.

[3] A more accurate analysis would take into consideration the earnings that might be realized by the company each year on the amount that is saved in interest. A compounding effect would be produced since in each successive year the company will have the use of the money saved in interest plus the amount earned on it in preceding years. Offsetting this in part, however, would be the income taxes that would have to be paid on the earnings realized from the savings.

If the bonds are purchased each year for sinking fund retirement a different result might be obtained. Also some consideration might be given to the fact that annual provision might be made for the retirement of the additional $250,000 in bonds, which would reduce by that amount the funds available for ordinary business purposes (adjusted for any earnings that might be earned on sinking fund, and for income taxes).

6. *Wider market.* The refunding issue may be a much larger one than the particular issue that is being refunded and thus will attract a wider market, which will result in a higher market price. Also the refunding issue may be listed on one of the stock exchanges (the old issue may not have been listed).

7. *Guarantee by another company.* In some instances a parent company will guarantee the refunding bonds issued by one of its subsidiaries as an inducement to the bondholders to accept them.

EXTENSION OF MATURITY

At a time when a corporation's bonds become due, they may not only be unable to pay them off, but their credit or the market conditions may be so bad that they cannot even put out a refunding issue. The company may therefore ask the bondholders to agree to an extension of the maturity of the bonds for a designated period of years. The bondholders cannot legally be forced to agree to the extension, but they may be too unorganized to act with concerted force, or they may realize that in the long run they may profit more from an extension than from foreclosure action. In some instances a minority of the bondholders will not agree to the extension, but if a sufficient amount of the bondholders do agree to make the plan successful, those not agreeing are paid off in cash.

The corporation may offer the bondholders some inducement to extend the maturity of their bonds. In some cases, however, the bondholder is asked to make some additional sacrifice in addition to the extension of the maturity.

SINKING FUNDS

A *sinking fund* consists of assets of designated amounts which a company sets aside at stated intervals for the purpose of redeeming all or a portion of the bonds of a particular issue at or before maturity. It gets its name from the fact that it is designed to "sink" the debt. The sinking fund may consist of cash, or part cash, securities of other companies, bonds of the same company but other than the issue for which the fund was set up, or bonds of the particular issue for which it was set up to retire.

Reasons for Sinking Fund

Where it is expected that the debt will be retired, a sinking fund is commonly recommended. The various reasons for setting up a sinking fund are as follows.

1. *Future difficult to predict.* A corporation may intend to pay off its bonds upon maturity by a refunding issue. But by the time the bonds come due the market conditions or the financial condition of the company may deteriorate so that the refunding issue could not be marketed or offered to the bondholders for their old bonds. At such a time a sinking fund might prevent failure of the company.

2. *Payment a financial strain.* When a corporation has need for a large sum of money in the future to retire its bonds, it would be advisable for it to provide annually out of earnings a fixed amount so that when the time comes that it has to meet the bond maturity payment, it will have the money. In this way that money would not be paid out in dividends or invested in fixed assets.

3. *Increases marketability of bonds.* The presence of a sinking fund provision increases the attractiveness of bonds, and they are, therefore, more easily marketed.

4. *Offsets property depreciation.* As time goes on, the specific security behind the bonds will depreciate in value. A sinking fund would give protection to the bondholders. Companies with wasting assets, such as mining corporations, almost invariably have sinking funds behind their bonds which provide for the retirement of the bonds as the assets of the company are being depleted.

Determining Amount of Sinking Fund Installments

The contract under which the bonds were issued would have to be consulted in order to determine whether there was provision for a sinking fund, and if so, the method that would be followed in determining how much should be put into the fund from time to time.

There are three different methods of determining the amounts of sinking fund installments.

Fixed Regular Installments. The most common method followed in the case of closed issues of bonds is the payment of a fixed amount of money, or money equivalent to a definite face amount of the bonds. Thus, if a corporation sold a $10,000,000 20-year bond issue, the sinking fund requirements could be set at $500,000 a year, or an amount necessary to buy $500,000 in face value of the bonds each year.

If the issue is an open one, comparable provisions can be made. The annual sinking fund installment can be expressed in terms of money equivalent to $\frac{1}{20}$ of the face value of the bonds, or an amount necessary to buy $\frac{1}{20}$ of the bonds.

In some cases the amount of money to be put into the sinking fund annually increases as time goes on. This is designed to conform to the ability of the corporation to make the payments. Another reason is not to burden the corporation too much during the early years when the interest charges are relatively high. In some instances the fixed annual sinking fund installments will provide for the retirement of only part of the entire issue.

Installments Varying According to Results of the Business. Sinking fund installments sometimes vary according to the volume of business or profits of the company. This is done in order to make the payments correspond to the ability of the corporation to meet the installments. Often there is a minimum annual requirement regardless of the results of the business operations. Following are the variables on which the amount of the payments is based.

1. *Gross volume of business or unit of output.* In some instances the amount of the sinking fund payments depends upon the gross volume of business done by the corporation. Commonly the amount paid into the fund varies according to, for example, the number of tons of ore removed in the case of mines, or the amount of lumber cut. The latter is usually called a "stumpage" charge. Sinking funds for bonds issued by land companies commonly call for installment payments varying according to the amount of land sold.

2. *Net income.* In some instances the amount of the sinking fund payments varies according to the net profit earned by the company. Some contracts call for a fixed amount plus a designated percentage of the net earnings. When the payments are based on net earnings, the percentage of the earnings sometimes increases during the later years.

3. *Dividends.* Some sinking funds call for a fixed amount or for a designated per cent of the earnings, plus an amount equivalent to dividends paid by the corporation in excess of a designated per cent, or plus an amount equivalent to a designated per cent of the dividends.

Optional Installments. In some instances the decisions on whether sinking fund installments are to be paid, and on the amounts of such installments, are left to the discretion of the board of directors. Such provisions occur more commonly in bonds issued at the time of reorganization of a company. In some of these issues minimum amounts are specified. Usually the indenture specifies that a certain percentage of the bonds shall be retired before their maturity date. In some instances when the installment payments are contingent or optional, they are cumulative up to a designated amount so that whenever possible any arrears must be made up.

Substitutes for Sinking Fund Payments

The indentures under which some bonds are issued provide that certain allocations of funds will be accepted as a substitute for sinking fund payments. For example, it is sometimes provided that if bonds having a senior lien or one equal to the bonds for which the sinking fund is set up, are paid off, it will be equivalent to the payment into the sinking fund of the same amount. In some instances, the contract provides that, if bonds for which a sinking fund is being established are paid off from funds other than the sinking fund, or if they are convertible into stock and have been converted, sinking fund payments equivalent to such amounts will not have to be made.

Corporation's Obligation for Sinking Fund Payments

When the indenture calls for a definite amount to be paid into the fund each year, default in the payment of a sinking fund installment may usually, according to the indenture, be treated the same as a default in the payment of the interest or principal on the bonds.

Indentures come under the provisions of the Trust Indenture Act of 1939 and require the trustees to make complete reports to the bondholders informing them of any default. Furthermore, the trustees must act under the circumstances as a prudent man would in the conduct of his own affairs. If the company was able to pay into the fund but did not do so, it would be the duty of the trustee to bring action to compel the company to act. But if, on the other hand, the company was financially unable to meet the sinking fund payments, the trustee may correctly decide that to attempt to force payment might do the bondholders more harm than good.

Sinking Fund Trustees

We have referred several times to the sinking fund trustee. In some instances the corporation which issues the bonds administers its own sinking fund. When the company must pay a fixed amount or variable amount into the fund, it is the usual custom today to appoint an independent trustee to administer the fund. Sinking fund payments are then made to the trustee and he invests the money or purchases the bonds which are to be retired. It is the general custom to appoint the bond indenture trustee as the sinking fund trustee.

Types of Sinking Fund Investments

There are three tests which should be applied to sinking fund investments. They are (1) safety, (2) fair return, and (3) liquidity. In general, there are four different types of sinking fund investments.

Improvements. The agreement may provide that the sinking fund may be invested in new property or in improvements made to the original property. Regardless of what might be said in favor of such investments, the fact remains that investment in ordinary corporate assets does not provide the funds with which to retire the bonds—and that is the real purpose of a sinking fund.

Bonds of Other Companies. In many of the older issues of bonds the sinking fund was invested in securities of other companies, to be converted into cash upon the maturity of the bonds for which the fund was set up.

Other Bonds Issued by the Same Company. A few bond issues that were sold in the past provided for the sinking fund to be invested in the company's own bonds which were senior to the particular issue for which the fund was established.

Bonds for Which the Sinking Fund Was Set Up. Investment of the sinking fund in the particular bonds for which the fund was established is the method most commonly followed today. It meets the sinking fund investment tests better than any other form of investment.

Methods of Acquisition and Disposition of the Bonds

The bond indenture will prescribe the way in which the bonds are to be obtained, which will be one of the following: (1) call, (2) purchase in the market, or (3) tenders.

When the bonds for which the sinking fund was established are acquired by the trustee, they may be kept alive in the fund, or they may be canceled, according to the provisions of the indenture. If the bonds are kept alive in the fund, the indenture may provide that they can be reissued under specified circumstances. Since the ultimate purpose of the sinking fund is to retire the bonds, the simplest procedure would be to cancel the bonds as soon as they are acquired by the trustee.

Distinguished from Sinking Fund Reserve

Thus far in the chapter we have been discussing sinking *funds*. These are, as we have seen, appropriations of *assets*. The setting aside of a sinking fund does not reduce the profits or the surplus of the company. Since in the long run, cash used for sinking fund payments is normally generated from earnings, that part of the profits or surplus equivalent to the amount of cash set aside in the sinking fund is not available for dividends to the stockholders. But the stockholder who looks at the surplus account only, and sees it constantly increasing in amount, may wonder why the directors are not paying a larger amount out in the form of dividends.

In order to give effect to the appropriation of money into the sinking fund, the accounting practice commonly followed is to set up a *surplus reserve*, equivalent in amount to the sinking fund. Thus each year the surplus or profits account is charged with a similar amount, which is put into an account called the "Reserve for Sinking Fund."

The bonds would be retired from the sinking fund. This would still leave the Reserve for Sinking Fund on the books. The amount in the Reserve account would then be put back into the Surplus account.

SERIAL BONDS

When parts of a single issue of bonds have different maturity dates, the bonds are called *serial bonds*. It should be noted that all the bonds are issued at the same time. This, plus the fact that they mature in series, distinguishes the *serial* bonds from those which are *issued in series* under an open-end indenture. Serial bonds are also quite common among municipalities. Equipment trust obligations (see pages 177–183) are practically always of the serial type, and the same is true of many privately placed issues.

In some cases all maturities of the serial bond issue bear the same face rate of interest, while in others the rate is different among the various maturities. When the face rate is the same, the different maturities can be purchased on different yield bases by paying different prices for the bonds.

Advantages to Issuing Corporation

There are certain advantages of the serial bond over the ordinary type bond with a sinking fund provision.

1. *Broader market.* Within the one serial bond issue are short-, medium-, and long-term bonds. Thus the issue may appeal to the different classes of investors according to these various maturities. This would tend to decrease the interest cost to the corporation. Furthermore, short and medium maturities generally sell on a lower yield basis than long-term maturities.

2. *Economy of redemption.* If the corporation were to redeem its ordinary bonds by exercising the call feature, it would be forced to pay the call price, which is usually at a premium over the face value of the bond. The serial bonds that come due each year, however, are retired by paying the face value.

3. *No sinking fund expenses.* When a sinking fund trustee administers the fund, the corporation must pay him a fee. There is no need for a sinking fund with a serial issue.

4. *Interest saved.* As each series matures, the total interest cost to the company is reduced.

Advantages to Investor

The advantages of serial bonds to the investor are as follows.

1. *Selection of maturities.* The investor can select whatever maturities he desires.

2. *No restraint on market price.* The market price of callable bonds will rarely rise above the call price. If the serial issue is not callable, there will not be this factor holding down its market price.

3. *Greater certainty of payment.* If a corporation has to pay off part of its bonds every year, there is a greater probability that the issue will be paid off than if it did not have any maturities to meet for, say, twenty years.

4. *Increased equity.* As bonds under the serial issued are retired, the equity behind the remaining bonds is increased.

5. *Maturity date certain.* When a person buys a callable bond, and the usual type is callable, he never knows just how long he will be able to hold the bond. With a serial bond (assuming it is not callable) he is always certain when the bond comes due.

Callable Serial Bonds

Serial bonds are in some instances callable. Where this is the case some of the advantages of the serial bond listed above would not be applicable.

In the case of callable serial bonds, the indenture frequently provides that the bonds are callable in the reverse order of their maturity. Commonly the call premium is a stated percentage for each year of the unexpired term. Calling the longer maturities benefits the corporation in two ways. It provides for the swift elimination of the entire debt, since the early maturities are being redeemed currently. Furthermore, it results in interest savings as the face rate of interest on the bonds usually increases with the length of maturity.

In some instances sinking funds have been established for serial bonds. The call feature stated above, which is in some of the serial issues, might be exercised and the bonds bought with the sinking fund.

Market Aspects of Serial Bonds

We stated above as one of the advantages of serial bonds that the various maturities would attract a wider market. Even though that is true, since the amount of bonds of any one maturity is limited, the bonds would not be so well known, and therefore, each maturity would tend to have a limited market. If the various maturities have the same face rate of interest, and they sell on a different yield basis, which is usually the case, then the prices of the various maturities would be different. For this reason serial bonds are not listed on the exchanges, because it would be necessary to quote prices for each of the maturities. It is common practice to quote serial bonds, not in terms of prices, but in terms of yield.

QUESTIONS

1. Do sole proprietorships and partnerships issue bonds? Why or why not?
2. (a) Indicate the various differences between bonds and common stocks.
   (b) In what respects do preferred stocks resemble bonds more than they do common stocks?

3. Are good bonds a hedge against inflation or deflation? Explain.
4. Are bonds issued in low enough denominations to permit the small investor to purchase a diversified portfolio of them?
5. (a) Distinguish between bonds and notes. (b) What characterizes short-, medium-, and long-term bonds? (c) In what type of industry are long-term bonds more commonly found?
6. (a) Distinguish between the following kinds of yields: nominal yield, current yield, and yield to maturity. When should each be used? (b) Indicate when the investor should compute the long-term yield to the maturity date and when to the call date in the case of callable bonds. (c) What factors determine the price at which a particular bond will sell in the market?
7. (a) If interest rates in general would advance, what would happen to the price of high-grade bonds? Why? (b) Do changes in interest rates cause long-term or short-term bonds to fluctuate more? Explain. (c) When interest rates are relatively low, will long-term or short-term bonds sell on a higher yield basis? Explain.
8. Distinguish between registered and coupon bonds. Which would you rather purchase? Why?
9. Indicate the various reasons why a corporation might sell a bond issue rather than a stock issue.
10. Illustrate what is meant by "trading on the equity." What other term is applied to the same thing?
11. (a) Can a corporation call in its bonds before they are due? Explain. (b) Can a holder force a corporation to redeem its bonds before they are due? Explain.
12. What are the various methods that are used by corporations to redeem their bonds before maturity?
13. Distinguish between funding and refunding a debt.
14. Indicate how the premium paid to call in a bond issue is treated for federal income tax purposes.
15. Assume that the federal corporation income tax rate is 50 per cent. A company is considering the relative advantages and disadvantages of issuing a 4 per cent bond issue, or a 6 per cent preferred stock issue. Indicate the advantage of the bonds relative to the actual cost of the money.
16. What are the various reasons for setting up a sinking fund for a bond issue?
17. Indicate the various ways of determining the amount of the sinking fund installments. Which of these do you think is best? Explain.
18. Distinguish between the sinking fund and the sinking fund reserve. What purpose is accomplished by setting up each?
19. What are the advantages to the issuer of a serial bond issue?
20. Are serial bonds listed on the securities exchanges? Why or why not? How are they usually quoted in the market?

PROBLEMS

1. The Transitron Corp. was organized in the early part of 19x1 with a capitalization consisting of $1,000,000 in 6 per cent bonds; $2,000,000 in 7 per cent non-cumulative, non-participating preferred stock; and $3,000,000 in common stock. All the stock had a par value of $100 per share. Earnings before interest charges on the bonds were paid and before taxes, were as follows (assume federal corporate income tax rate is 50 per cent):

Year	Earnings
19x1	$ 340,000
19x2	760,000
19x3	1,460,000

Because the company started out with a large paid-in surplus, all the available earnings were paid out each year in the form of dividends. Assume that you own ten shares of the common stock that you purchased at its par value.

(a) What percentage did you earn on your investment in each of these years? (b) If the company had been capitalized at the same amount as stated above but with common stock only, what percentage would you have earned on your stock in each of the years? (c) Expressed in terms of percentage, how much more did you earn in 19x3 under the circumstances stated in part (a) than in part (b)? (d) As a common stockholder would you prefer that there be bonds or preferred stock, or both, outstanding, or that only common stock be issued? Explain.

2. Assume that you purchased on original issue the Standard Corp. 20-year, 4½ per cent bonds for 110 ($1,100). Compute the following:

(a) Nominal yield, (b) Current yield, (c) Approximate yield to maturity.

3. Compute the three types of yield stated in Problem 2, above, assuming that you purchased the bond for 90 instead of 110.

4. If the bond in Problems 2 and 3 had been callable five years before its maturity, should the long-term yield be computed to the call or the maturity date? Explain.

5. The Dynamic Nuclear Corp. has $4,000,000 in bonds outstanding which mature in 10 years. The bonds are callable at 105 and are selling in the market for 105. The face rate of the bonds is 6 per cent. The company's credit has improved to the extent that it can sell sufficient 4½ per cent bonds of a new issue at par to retire the remaining old bonds. Disregarding selling costs and interest on the interest saved (assume federal corporation income tax rate to be 50%, and that the company is successful):

(a) Would you recommend that the refinancing be undertaken? (b) How much in new bonds would have to be issued? (c) What would be the difference in annual interest paid out to the bondholders? This would favor which procedure? Considering the excess in principal amount of the new bonds over the old, what would the annual net savings be? (d) What is the total amount which would be gained over the 10-year period by following the procedure you recommend?

SELECTED READINGS

Bogen, Jules I. (ed). *Financial Handbook*, 3d ed. New York: The Ronald Press Co., 1952. Section 11.

Dilbeck, Harold. "A Proposal for Precise Definitions of 'Trading on the Equity' and 'Leverage': Comment," *Journal of Finance*, March, 1962, pp. 127–30.

Doris, Lillian (ed.). *Business Finance Handbook*. Englewood Cliffs, N. J.: Prentice-Hall, Inc., 1953. Chapter 18.

Fletcher, William Meade. *Cyclopedia of the Law of Private Corporations*, Permanent ed. Chicago: Callaghan & Co., Vol. 6a (1950 rev. vol.).

Foster, L. O. *Corporate Debt and the Stockholder*. Hanover, N. H.: Amos Tuck School of Business Administration, 1956.

FRAINE, HAROLD G., and MILLS, ROBERT H. "Effect of Defaults and Credit Deteriora-
tion on the Yields of Corporate Bonds," *Journal of Finance,* September, 1961,
pp. 423–34.
HICKMAN, W. B. *Corporate Bonds: Quality and Investment Performance,* Occasional
Paper 59. New York: National Bureau of Economic Research, Inc., 1957.
HUNT, PEARSON. "A Proposal for Precise Definitions of 'Trading on the Equity' and
'Leverage,'" *Journal of Finance,* September, 1961, pp. 377–86.
————. "A Proposal for Precise Definitions of 'Trading on the Equity' and 'Leverage':
Comment," *Journal of Finance,* March, 1962, pp. 131–32.
KAPLAN, MORTIMER. "Yields on Recently Issued Corporate Bonds: A New Index,"
Journal of Finance, March, 1962, pp. 81–109.

8

Types of Bonds

Many different types of bonds are issued by corporations in the United States. We will first take up the general class of secured bonds and this will be followed by a discussion of unsecured bonds.

MORTGAGE BONDS

Nature of a Mortgage

When the bond issue is secured by a mortgage, the latter runs in favor of the trustee. Our discussion of a real estate mortgage will be better understood, however, if we simplify and describe it first from the standpoint of one individual giving a mortgage to another.

Let us assume that Adams borrows $100,000 from his *creditor* Brown, who will require that the *debtor* Adams give him a note or bond containing his written promise to pay the amount borrowed with interest at a specified rate and time. In order to add to the safety of the loan, Brown requires Adams to give him as security for the loan a mortgage on some real estate which, we will assume, consists of a lot and a building valued together at $200,000.

The correct meaning of the names which are applied to the parties involved is necessary for proper understanding. In the example given above, the debtor Adams, as giver of the mortgage, is called the *mortgagor,* and the creditor Brown, as receiver of the mortgage, is called the *mortgagee.*

So long as Adams makes the payments of interest and principal when due, Brown cannot make use of the mortgage. But if a default occurs, then Brown may exercise his rights to the mortgaged property for the satisfaction of the loan.

The mortgagee cannot immediately get possession of the property upon default of the mortgagor, but has to foreclose by legal proceedings the property under mortgage and have a court sale of the property at public auction to satisfy his claim. This is the way a mortgage is treated today by the courts, although in different states there still are two different "theories" as to the exact legal nature of a mortgage.

The older concept still adhered to in many states says that the mortgage transfers *legal title* to the property to the mortgagee. The mortgagor, however, retains *equitable title* to the same property. This is sometimes called his *equity of redemption.* "Equitable title" has been defined as that title which the mortgagor possesses in order to get back legal title upon the discharge of his debt. The transfer of legal title to the mortgagee, however, is not complete. After transferring such title, a later clause in the mortgage, called the *defeasance clause,* states that as long as the mortgagor lives up to his agreement, the transfer of title to the mortgagee shall be null and void. This theory is called the *conveyance of title* theory.

The other theory is that the mortgage is not a conveyance of title to property, but merely gives the mortgagee a *lien* on the property. This is the *lien theory.* The same result is obtained under both concepts. If a default occurs, the mortgagee forecloses to make his title good, or to get title to the property by virtue of his lien, depending upon which theory is followed. The court then proceeds to sell the property in order to secure the money to satisfy the claim.

In the event that there are no other bidders for the property, or if they do not offer enough, the mortgagee buys it with his claim. If, however, the property sold brings more than the amount owed to the mortgagee and court costs, then the mortgagor gets the balance. But if the sale brings less than the amount owed, the debtor is still liable on his note or bond for the deficiency.

In actual practice the mortgage bondholders of a corporation commonly do not receive satisfaction in the precise way described, because the corporation may go into the hands of a receiver or a trustee in bankruptcy, who will prevent the bondholders from foreclosing. This commonly ends with a reorganization of the company rather than liquidation, and the bondholders receive whatever treatment had been agreed upon or was forced upon them in the reorganization plan. This will be described later in the book when we consider reorganization.[1]

Nature of Junior Mortgages

In order to illustrate the nature of junior mortgages, we will again refer to the above example of where Adams gave Brown a mortgage on his property as security for the $100,000 loan. We assumed that Brown holds a *first* mortgage on the property. Adams may need additional

[1] See Chapters 29 and 30.

money at the time he gets the loan from Brown, but the latter may not be willing to lend him any more. We will assume that Clark will lend him $30,000 with the security of a *second* mortgage against the property. Adams could transfer to Clark no better title than he himself possessed: an equity in the property, or an equity of redemption, after the first mortgage of Brown. So it is this which Adams now transfers (subject to the defeasance clause) to Clark as security for the $30,000 loan. When Adams gave Brown a first mortgage on the $200,000 property as security for a $100,000 loan, Adams' interest or equity in the property was reduced to $100,000. When he gave Clark a second mortgage as security for the $30,000 loan, Adams' equity was further reduced to $70,000.

If Adams was then to borrow $5,000 from Douglas and give his equity after the first two mortgages as security for a *third* mortgage on the property, his equity would be reduced to $65,000. There is no necessity of obtaining the consent of Brown or Clark in order to give the junior mortgages that follow theirs.

Let us now assume that Adams defaulted in the payment of the loan to Brown who held the first mortgage. Brown will bring an action of foreclosure and sale. This action will be brought against Clark, Douglas, and Adams, since they all have an equity in the mortgaged property. If the property was purchased at the court sale by Edwards, the proceeds (after court costs and taxes) would be applied on the first mortgage, and this would have to be paid off in full before anything would be paid to Clark who held the second mortgage. Then the money would be applied on the second, and Douglas would get something only after the second mortgage had been paid in full.

The purchaser of the property, Edwards, would get it free of all claims. If Edwards would not pay enough for the property to satisfy the claim of Brown, who holds the first mortgage, Brown would use his claim to bid in the property and the claims of Clark and Douglas would be wiped out so far as Brown is concerned. If Clark and Douglas feel that the property is worth any more than the $100,000 which is owed to Brown, they can bid more for the property. Any mortgagee that is not fully satisfied after the sale has claim against Adams for the deficiency.

If default occurred in the second mortgage and action for foreclosure and sale was brought by Clark (against Adams and Douglas), the purchaser of the property would take it *subject* to the first mortgage. In other words, the claim of the first mortgage continues. If the purchaser thought the property was worth $120,000, he would pay only $20,000 for it since he would be taking it subject to the first mortgage. Clark, the holder of the second mortgage, would receive the $20,000, and Douglas would, of course, receive nothing. The latter would still have a right against Adams for $5,000, but no longer a mortgage against the property, and Clark would have a right against Adams for $10,000, the amount of the deficiency. If Clark thought the property was worth more than $120,000, he could use his own claim and bid $30,000 for the property subject to the first mortgage.

The effects of foreclosure by the various mortgagees are shown in Table 8–1. It is assumed that Mr. Edwards buys the property at court sale, and that the proceeds from the sale are after all court costs and expenses have been paid.

Assuming a Mortgage

In the above example we indicated that when the second or third mortgagees foreclosed, the purchaser took the property *subject to* the first mortgage, or subject to the first and the second mortgage. The property remains as security for the debt, and in case of default the mortgagee could bring action for foreclosure and sale of the mortgaged property, but the buyer would not be liable for any deficiency. The original mortgagor would still be liable on his note for this deficiency.

If instead of buying property subject to a mortgage, the purchaser bought it *assuming* the mortgage, the mortgagee could come against the buyer for any deficiency. In the event that he merely indorses the note, instead of replacing it, then both the original mortgagor and the buyer would be liable on the note. Someone assuming the mortgage assumes the obligation which is embodied in the note or bond as well as in the mortgage.

Closed-End Issues

When a corporation is authorized in the indenture to issue a fixed amount of bonds, such as $50,000,000 for example, and all of these bonds are issued at the same time, the issue is said to be a *closed,* or *closed-end* issue. The particular issue may be either secured by mortgaged property or it may be unsecured. The former is commonly referred to as a *closed-end mortgage*.

Generally speaking, the closed-end mortgage may benefit the particular bondholders, but it may be to the disadvantage of the issuing corporation. When a closed-end mortgage bond issue has been sold, no more bonds having the same lien against the particular property may be issued. Thus, the bondholders need not fear that their equity will be diluted. If the firm wants to sell additional mortgage bonds against the *same* property, the mortgage will have to be *junior* to the issue which is outstanding. This is to the disadvantage of the corporation since the new issue will have to bear a higher rate of interest than the senior issue. The company further suffers in that a number of relatively small bond issues will not have the market that would be enjoyed by one large issue.

Table 8–1. Rights Upon Foreclosure Sale of Mortgaged Property

Foreclosed by	Action Brought Against	Proceeds of sale	1st Mortgagee (Brown) of $100,000 gets	2d Mortgagee (Clark) of $30,000 gets	3d Mortgagee (Douglas) of $5,000 gets	Mortgagor (Adams) gets	Purchaser (Edwards) gets
1st mortgagee	Adams, 2d mortgagee, and 3d mortgagee	$115,000	$100,000	$15,000. Has claim against mortgagor for $15,000	Nothing. Has claim against mortgagor for $5,000	Nothing	Clear title
2d mortgagee	Adams and 3d mortgagee	$33,000	Still has 1st mortgage	$30,000	$3,000. Has claim against mortgagor for $2,000	Nothing	Title subject to 1st mortgage
3d mortgagee	Adams	$7,000	Still has 1st mortgage	Still has 2d mortgage	$5,000	$2,000	Title subject to 1st and 2d mortgage
1st, 2d, and 3d mortgagees	Each as in above	$131,000	$100,000	$30,000	$1,000. Has claim against mortgagor for $4,000	Nothing	Clear title

Open-End Mortgage

If the indenture does not specify a maximum dollar amount of bonds that may be sold, the issue is said to be *open*, or *open-end*. The bonds may be secured by a mortgage, or they may be unsecured.

The open-end mortgage may work to the disadvantage of the bond-holders in that if the corporation issued additional bonds under the same indenture, the equity of the bondholders would be diluted. From the standpoint of the issuing corporation, however, the open-end feature is desirable in that additional bonds having the *same lien* against the mortgaged property may be issued. Priority of issue under an open-end issue thus does not give priority of lien. The rate of interest that must be paid on the new bonds issued would be less than would have to be paid on a junior issue for two reasons. First, the bondholders would have an equal lien with the original bondholders, and second, the one large issue would attract a wider market than a number of different issues, particularly junior ones.

Open-end indentures provide for the bonds to be issued in *series*. Thus, designations such as Series A, Series B, etc., are indicative of an open-end issue (or limited open-end), except in the case of equipment trust obligations, which will be discussed later. The various series of bonds under an open-end issue may bear different face rates of interest, and their maturities too may differ.

Limited Open-End Mortgage

The indenture of a *limited open-end* issue permits the issuance of additional bonds up to a maximum specified amount. Under such an indenture a corporation might sell, for example, $10,000,000 of bonds today, but additional bonds under the same indenture and having the same claim could be sold at various times in the future, until a maximum of, for example, $50,000,000 in bonds had been issued. Thereupon the issue would become closed.

Restrictions on Open-End Issues

The following types of restrictions on the issuance of additional bonds under an open-end issue are often found in indentures. The bonds may be issued:

1. Up to a specified percentage, such as 60 or 75 per cent of the cost of new property which is acquired by the corporation.
2. If the company is earning at least twice the interest charges on the bonds now outstanding and those proposed to be issued.

3. If the net current assets are at least a certain percentage of all the bonds or at least equal to the bonds outstanding and those proposed to be issued.
4. If the capital stock bears a specified relation to the bonds outstanding and those proposed to be issued.

After-Acquired Property Clause

In order to market a particular issue of bonds it may be necessary for the corporation to secure them by not only the present property which is owned, but also by any property which the organization may acquire in the future. Such a clause in the indenture is called an *after-acquired property clause,* or simply an *after-acquired clause.* The present property and the type of property acquired in the future covered by the mortgage is carefully defined in the indenture. Usually, it is only the *real property* which is included.

From the standpoint of the bondholders, the presence of the after-acquired property clause in a bond issue tends to strengthen their position. From the corporation's viewpoint, however, such a provision may make future financing expensive, because it may be necessary for it to issue a mortgage bond to finance the new acquisitions, and the mortgage behind these bonds would have to be junior to the one outstanding which possesses the after-acquired property clause.

If the issue which contains such a clause is an open-end one, the clause will not be embarrassing to the company, since more bonds having the same lien may be issued (if not restricted by terms of the indenture) to finance the new holdings. Looking at it from the viewpoint of the bondholders, however, the open feature in the issue would tend to weaken somewhat the value of the clause. The open-end (or limited open-end) feature and the after-acquired property clause are commonly found in the same bond issue.

Avoiding the After-Acquired Property Clause

In the past, corporations which have had closed-end bond issues outstanding which contained such a clause have found it so much of a drawback that they have taken steps to avoid its effects. Such steps are discussed below.

Redemption of the Bonds. If the bonds can be purchased in the market at a fair price, or called, it may be advantageous for the corporation to buy back its bonds. In fact it may even be desirable to pay a substantial premium to get rid of the clause.

Lease. Where the use of particular property is desired it may be leased rather than purchased. In this way the after-acquired property clause is not operative.

Purchase Money Mortgage. To acquire property, the corporation makes a down payment and executes notes or bonds promising to pay the balance. A mortgage is retained by the seller as security for the debt.

The purchase money mortgage is placed on the property *before* the corporation acquires it, so this mortgage would have first claim against the particular property and the old bonds would have only a second mortgage on the property acquired. If the seller wanted all cash for the property, legal title to the property could be transferred by the seller to a trustee, and purchase money mortgage bonds, guaranteed by the buyer of the property, could be sold to the public through an investment banker the same as any other type of bond.

Subsidiary Corporation. In order to prevent the old bonds having the after-acquired property clause from obtaining a lien on new property, the company may form a subsidiary corporation and have that company take title to the new property. The stock of the subsidiary is acquired by the parent company. The subsidiary can then issue bonds having a first mortgage on the property as security.

The subsidiary may be a small, relatively unknown company and, therefore, may not be able to market its bonds economically. To secure the lowest possible interest rate, the parent could do one of two things. It could guarantee the principal and interest on the subsidiary's bonds, or it could acquire the bonds and put them up as collateral and issue its own collateral trust bonds. The stocks or bonds of the subsidiary would ordinarily not come under the claim of the after-acquired property clause bonds. The money obtained from the sale of the collateral trust bonds would be used to pay for the subsidiary's bonds. The subsidiary would of course use the money to pay for the new property.

Merger. We can best illustrate this with an example. Assume that Company A has bonds outstanding with this clause in the indenture. Company B buys the properties of Company A, and issues its stock to the stockholders of Company A in exchange for their stock. Company A is then dissolved. The bonds of Company A are assumed by Company B. Now if the company, which is all Company B now, acquires any additional properties, these properties will not come under the claim of the old A bonds, since Company A did not acquire any new property.

In some instances, however, it is provided in the indenture that to acquire the properties, the successor corporation would have to place future-acquired property under the claim of the bonds.

In passing we might inquire into the effect of the merger on bonds of Company B which contained the after-acquired property clause. Since this company is actually taking on additional holdings, its bonds containing this clause would have a lien on the properties of old Company A, but, of course, their claim would be junior to that of any mortgage bonds issued by Company A.

TYPES OF MORTGAGE BONDS

First Mortgage Bonds

A *first mortgage bond* has a first lien on property. When the term *mortgage* is used in connection with corporate bonds it is taken to mean a mortgage on *real* property, or *real estate*, as distinguished from *personal* property, such as stocks and bonds. When bonds are secured by a mortgage on real estate such as houses, apartments, office buildings, etc., they are commonly referred to as *real estate bonds*, or *real estate mortgage bonds*. A first mortgage bond may have a first lien on all the corporate property, or the first lien may be on only a small part of the property. It may have a second or third claim on other property of the corporation.

Despite the lien on physical property, the real or practical security for a first mortgage bond, the same as for any other type of bond, is based on the earning power of the company which issues the bond. An unsecured bond issued by a prosperous company with excellent management would be a safer investment than a first mortgage bond secured by an obsolete plant of a defunct company. Fixed assets, which are the security for mortgage bonds, bring only a small percentage of their cost or book value upon forced sale. They often possess little value unless they are used by a profitable business. The real value of any business asset, particularly a fixed asset, is usually expressed in the earning power of the company.

A mortgage bond is made up of two parts. First, the promise to pay the interest and principal which is embodied in the bond, and which is based on the general credit of the corporation, the same as any other type of bond; and second, the specific security for this promise to pay the debt which is contained in the mortgage. In the event of default on a mortgage bond, the bondholders through the trustee could proceed against the corporation on its promise to pay, and ignore the particular property which is mortgaged behind the bond issue.

After getting judgment against the corporation, the bondholders may then proceed to attach, or secure a lien on, the corporate property which is not already mortgaged. But by foreclosure of the lien which the mortgage bondholders already had against the specific mortgaged property, they would be a step ahead. Also, considering the fact that the corporation has failed, the promise to pay is not worth much since there is little or nothing behind it. So the mortgage bondholders usually find that their best course of action is to proceed against the particular property which is mortgaged.

Another point worth emphasizing is that the first claim of the first mortgage bondholders applies only to the specific property which is mortgaged. In other words, if Corporation A issued a first mortgage bond against Plant X, these bonds would not have first claim against Plant Y which is owned by the company. As regards Plant Y, the first mortgage bondholders would have no better right than any unsecured creditors of the company. From the standpoint of a going concern, however, the first claim which is possessed by the bonds really gives them a first chance at earnings which are derived from the use of both the mortgaged and the unmortgaged corporation property.

Divisional Bonds

Divisional bonds are those which are secured by a mortgage on only a section or division of the company's total property. They are found almost entirely in the railroad field. In most instances they are bonds which were originally secured by the entire property of a railroad which has since been acquired by a large railroad company or system.

Since divisional bonds are ordinarily secured by first mortgages on branches or divisions which have been consolidated into one large company or system, they are sometimes called *underlying bonds*. This means that they have a claim superior to that of later issues of mortgage bonds issued by the consolidated company against its total property. The same idea is expressed when it is said that the safest bonds are those which "lie closest to the rails."

Special Direct-Lien Bonds

When a bond is secured by some special-type property of a corporation such as a terminal, bridge, dock, or warehouse, it can be classified as a *special direct-lien bond*. It is noted that the security constitutes a smaller part of the company's property than in the case of a divisional bond. In some instances the type of security behind the bonds is indicated by the title of the bonds such as *terminal, bridge, dock,* or *warehouse bonds*.

Prior-Lien Bonds

Such an issue is one which is put in ahead of one or more other issues in respect to security. A corporation cannot issue such bonds, of course, without the consent of the existing bondholders (unless their bonds are subordinated debentures). It may be to the best interests of the bondholders to agree to such a prior-lien bond issue, as this may be the only way a corporation can secure money when it needs it. If a company has a first and a second mortgage bond issue outstanding, and the consent of the second is obtained to place a lien in just ahead of the second, the new issue would be considered prior to the second, but not prior to the first. Usually, however, a prior-lien issue takes precedence over all the other bond issues. When this is the case, the first mortgage would become a second, and the second would become a third, etc.

We have used the words "senior" and "junior" several times in connection with bond issues. A *senior* bond issue is one which comes ahead of one or more other issues from the standpoint of mortgage security. A *junior* issue is one that comes after one or more others from the standpoint of security. Thus, a second mortgage would be senior to a third, but junior to a first mortgage. The placing of a prior lien ahead of the first mortgage would have the effect of making the first mortgage bond issue junior to the senior prior lien. When a second mortgage is placed on the property it is incorrect to call the first a prior lien. Prior liens may be first mortgages, but first mortgages are not necessarily prior ones.

Second, Third, etc., Mortgage Bonds

If the company is a going concern and has not defaulted on the first mortgage bonds, and if the second mortgage bonds become due before the first, they would, of course, be paid off first.

In appraising the investment worth of a second mortgage bond the size of the first mortgage must be taken into consideration. If the amount of the first mortgage bonds outstanding is insignificant, a second mortgage would be practically as good as a first one.

Other things being equal, a company must pay a higher rate of interest on a second mortgage bond than on a first, due to the greater risk. Because of the dislike of the investing public for second or third mortgage bonds, the words *second, third,* etc., are rarely used now in the title of a bond.

General, Consolidated, and Refunding Mortgage Bonds

These titles are used for junior mortgage bonds instead of *second,* etc., for the reason mentioned above. A *general mortgage bond* is usually one that has a junior lien on all the property. The term *blanket* issue is often applied to a general mortgage bond issue. In some instances the terms *improvement* or *extension* are used in the title.

A *consolidated mortgage bond* is usually the same as a general mortgage bond. The name is derived from the fact that it is often used to secure money to refund or "consolidate" the other bond issues outstanding, or to effect a consolidation of several companies. In some instances the term *unified* is used for this type of bond.

A *refunding mortgage bond* is one which is exchanged for other bonds of the company, or is sold in order to secure the cash to retire another issue of bonds.

In some instances a combination of these names is used for the bond title; for example, *first and refunding mortgage, first refunding mortgage, first and consolidated, first consolidated and refunding mortgage,* etc.

Some corporations, particularly railroads and public utilities, have a number of bond issues outstanding. These issues were sold at different times and they may have varying rates of interest. Also, the issues may be relatively small and thus they may not enjoy a wide market. Generally speaking, the wider the market, the more economical it is for the corporation to sell the bonds. Furthermore, bondholders can secure more for their bonds of a large issue. So the fashion in corporation finance is to replace small issues with one large blanket issue of bonds which has the open-end provision and, in some instances, the after-acquired property clause.

COLLATERAL TRUST BONDS

With one exception which will be noted below, *collateral trust bonds* are secured by stocks or bonds, or both, of other companies. Although the pledged securities, which are referred to as the *collateral,* may be turned over to the trustee by means of a *chattel mortgage,* it is preferred that the word *mortgage* not be used in the title of these bonds, since it is usually understood to apply to a bond which is secured by *real* property (real estate) rather than *personal* property (of which securities are a part).

In event of default, the holders of the bonds have the right, through the trustee, to foreclose on the pledged securities, subject to the conditions stated in the indenture under which the bonds are issued. Although foreclosure would enable the collateral trust bondholders to gain possession of the collateral, it would not necessarily give them a right against the physical property of the issuer of the pledged securities. If the latter were bonds, then these bonds would have to be in default before the collateral trust bondholders could go against that corporation's physical property. If the pledged collateral consisted of stock, then the bondholders would end up being stockholders, and not creditors, in the company.

Reasons for Issuance

The reasons can conveniently be explained under the headings of the types of securities which are pledged.

Securities of Subsidiaries. In the case of a pure holding company, the only property which it owns are the securities of its subsidiaries. So, if this corporation wants to issue a secured bond issue the only kind open to it is the collateral trust type.

The parent company may also use collateral trust bonds as a way of economically financing its subsidiaries. The latter may be small, new, and unknown to the investing public. Furthermore, their bond issues might be too small to attract a wide market. Under these circumstances they either could not sell bonds directly, or if they could, the cost of the financing would be relatively high. So the bonds are bought by the parent who puts them up as collateral behind their collateral trust bond issue. In this way they are able to sell a bond which is secured by a mortgage on the physical properties of the subsidiaries, and also by the general credit of the large parent company. Furthermore, the issue may be large enough to attract a wide market.

Corporations sometimes have subsidiaries take title to property to avoid having the property covered by the lien of bonds outstanding which contain the after-acquired property clause. The securities of the subsidiary may then be acquired by the parent company and pledged behind a collateral trust bond issue of the parent.

Control of properties worth millions of dollars has been effected in the railroad and public utility fields on the investment of little money, through the use of collateral trust bonds. Stocks of holding companies controlling many subsidiaries are bought by top holding companies with the money obtained from the sale of collateral trust bonds secured by the stocks acquired.

Securities of Independent Companies. In some instances collateral trust bonds are issued against securities of independent companies which are held as investments. The question may arise why a company needing money would not sell these investment securities instead of borrowing money on them. The securities held may be those of small companies and the market for them might not be sufficiently wide to attract a good price. They may be sound bonds that will yield a good return to maturity. Also, the amount of securities held may be so relatively large that if an attempt was made to sell them all at once, the market price would break. For these reasons a company might prefer to keep its investments and borrow money.

Company's Own Bonds. Occasionally some corporations will issue their collateral trust bonds or notes secured by a pledge of their own mortgage bonds.

Payment of Interest, Dividends, and Principal on Pledged Securities

Any cash dividends or interest received by the trustee of the collateral trust bond issue are turned over to the corporation. Stock dividends or dividends that represent a return of capital rather than profit are retained by the trustee as security for the bonds. If the corporation which issued the collateral trust bonds defaults in the payment of interest or principal on the bonds, the trustee will retain any dividends and interest which are paid on the pledged securities.

When the principal of pledged bonds is paid, the trustee retains the cash until the corporation pledges additional securities of equivalent value.

Voting Pledged Stock

When the stock is in the name of the trustee, which is usually the case, he will ordinarily give proxies to vote the stock to the corporation issuing the collateral trust bonds. If the latter company defaults in the payment of principal or interest on its collateral trust bonds, the trustee will exercise the voting rights in the interest of the bondholders.

Substitution of Pledged Securities

The indenture under which collateral trust bonds are issued contains provisions for the substitution of pledged securities in event that any of the pledged bonds are called or mature. A similar provision is made in relation to pledged stock in event the issuer is merged into another company, consolidated with other companies, or reorganized.

EQUIPMENT OBLIGATIONS

Generally speaking, *equipment obligations* are issued by railroads or car manufacturers to finance the acquisition of rolling stock, such as cars and locomotives, and are secured by this equipment.

When acquiring rolling stock, the railroad will make a down payment, varying from 10 to 25 per cent of the cost of the equipment. Equipment obligations are then issued for the balance of the purchase price. The obligations are retired serially each six months or year, over a period usually of ten or fifteen years; the latter maturity has been more common in recent years. They are quoted in terms of yield rather than price. The obligations are issued under one of three plans which will be briefly described.

Equipment Mortgage Plan

The *equipment mortgage plan* of issuing equipment obligations is similar to that of issuing ordinary mortgage bonds. These obligations, which are called *equipment mortgage bonds,* are sold ordinarily through an investment banker to secure the money necessary to pay the balance due on the purchase price. The rolling stock which is pledged behind the equipment mortgage bonds is a type of personal property, and the deeding of title over to the trustee is accomplished under a chattel mortgage.

Several shortcomings are present in connection with the issuance of obligations under this plan. If the railroad has outstanding any old mortgage bond issues containing the after-acquired property clause, which many of them do, these old mortgages would attach to the property the minute the railroad acquired legal title to the property, provided, of course, that the indenture specified that rolling stock would come under the claim of the after-acquired clause. This would mean that the equipment obligations would be in the nature of *second* mortgage bonds as far as the equipment was concerned. Also, in event of failure of the railroad and the appointment of a receiver or trustee in bankruptcy, since the railroad has equitable title to the rolling stock, it would come under the jurisdiction of the receiver or trustee. Thus, the trustee representing the holders of the equipment obligations could not foreclose on the equipment, a situation which is true of any mortgage bondholders in respect to the mortgaged property. Because of the weaknesses mentioned, the equipment mortgage plan is rarely used.

Conditional Sale Plan

In the *conditional sale plan* the railroad makes a down payment on the equipment the same as in the plan discussed above, and issues its serial notes or bonds to the car manufacturer for the balance of the purchase price. According to prearranged plans the notes are sold to a bank or insurance company, or several banks or insurance companies. The railroad then makes the installment payments on the notes directly to the bank or insurance company. This procedure eliminates the costs of selling the notes through investment bankers. The conditional sale plan has rarely been used in recent years when the equipment obligations are publicly offered.

Philadelphia Plan

The great bulk of the equipment obligations outstanding are issued under the *Philadelphia Plan*. This plan was devised to overcome the weaknesses inherent in the equipment mortgage and the conditional sale plans. From a legal standpoint, the documents used in connection with the acquisition of the equipment and the issuance of the obligations are carefully worded in order that no creditor or court can say that the railroad has any title to the equipment prior to the time the last equipment obligation is retired.

Title to the equipment passes directly from the car manufacturer to the trustee. The railroad then *leases* the equipment from the trustee. That is why this plan is commonly called the *lease plan*. The railroad makes a down payment of from 10 to 25 per cent of the cost of the equipment. In effect this is really an advance rental payment. Equipment obligations are then sold through an investment banker to secure the necessary amount of money to pay the car manufacturer the balance of from 90 to 75 per cent.

The obligations sold under the Philadelphia Plan are in the nature of certificates of beneficial interest in the equipment and the lease. They are sometimes called *equipment trust certificates,* or *car trust certificates* (see Figure 8–1). To the extent that they are certificates of beneficial interest in the equipment and the lease, they are more like stocks than bonds. But the railroad which leases the equipment indorses on the certificates a guarantee that it will carry out the lease agreement and pay the proper rentals to enable the trustee to pay the dividends (really more like interest) on the certificates, and to meet the principal amount of the certificates as they mature. Because of the fixed maturity, the certificates resemble a bond. And because of the railroad's guarantee to pay the rentals necessary to meet the dividends and principal amount of the certificates, the latter are similar to bonds both in respect to the rate of return and obligation to pay back the principal amount.

Since the railroad has no title whatsoever to equipment while it is being financed, any bonds with the after-acquired property clause which it has outstanding would have no claim to this equipment. Furthermore, in the event of receivership of the road, the equipment will not come under the jurisdiction of the receiver or trustee in bankruptcy. This means that if the railroad does not keep up the rental payments even in receivership, the trustee can rent the equipment to another railroad, or sell it. The threat of this action will cause the receiver to continue the rental payments even if he has to default in other obligations issued by the railroad.

Since the Philadelphia Plan is the one which is practically always used, the discussion which follows will apply particularly to this plan.

Terms of the Lease

The equipment obligations are retired serially, that is, a fixed amount of them come due each year. Usually the same amount is retired each year beginning at the end of the first year. The rental payments are arranged to retire the amount coming due each year and to pay the return on the outstanding certificates.

In the event that the railroad defaults in its rental payments, or fails to live up to other covenants in the agreement, all of the certificates become due immediately. The railroad agrees that, if this occurs, it will at its own expense deliver the equipment to the trustee at places which he designates. The trustee can thereupon rent the equipment to another

NEW ISSUE

$7,950,000
Norfolk and Western Railway

Equipment Trust, Series H

4⅛% Equipment Trust Certificates

Non-callable

To be dated August 1, 1962. To mature in 15 annual installments of $530,000 each on August 1 from 1963 to 1977.

*Issued under the Philadelphia Plan with
20% original cash equity*

MATURITIES AND YIELDS

1963	3.60%	1970	4.30%
1964	3.85	1971	4.30
1965	4.00	1972	4.35
1966	4.15	1973	4.35
1967	4.20	1974	4.35
1968	4.25	1975	4.35
1969	4.25	1976	4.35
	1977	4.35%	

These certificates are offered subject to prior sale, when, as and if issued and
received by us, subject to approval of the Interstate Commerce Commission.

SALOMON BROTHERS & HUTZLER

DREXEL & CO.   **EASTMAN DILLON, UNION SECURITIES & CO.**

STROUD & COMPANY
Incorporated

August 2, 1962.

Fig. 8–1. Equipment trust certificate. (From *The Wall Street Journal*,
August 3, 1962.)

road or sell it to secure the money to pay off the outstanding certificates.
In addition to the rental payments, the railroad agrees to the following:

1. To keep the equipment properly repaired, and to replace any that
   is destroyed
2. To keep the equipment insured
3. To pay all taxes on the equipment

4. To indemnify the trustee for any claims arising out of the ownership and use of the equipment
5. To attach a metal plate to each piece of equipment stating the
   name of the trustee who owns the equipment
6. To deliver the equipment to the trustee in event of default in the
   rental payments or failure to abide by other covenants in the
   agreement
7. To file periodically with the trustee a statement showing the condition and location of the equipment

Upon payment of the last rental installment, the trustee agrees to
execute a bill of sale transferring title to the equipment to the railroad.

Security Behind the Obligations

Rolling stock wears out faster than other property, such as buildings.
At first thought this might make it appear that the equipment obligations
are poorly secured. But this is not the case. In the first place the obligations are issued only up to from 75 to 90 per cent of the cost of the equipment. So some margin of safety for the certificate holders exists from the
start. The rolling stock will last at least 20 years, while the obligations
are paid off over a period of 10 to 15 years. Furthermore, since the obligations are retired serially every year, they are being paid off at a faster
rate than the equipment is depreciating. In other words, despite the
relatively rapid depreciation of the equipment, the equity behind each
$1,000 of obligations increases, rather than decreases, as the equipment
wears out.

The margin of safety behind equipment trust obligations during their
entire life is illustrated by Figure 8–2. The original cost of the equipment, which is $3,000,000, is represented by the line A–X. It is assumed
that the equipment is depreciated annually on a straight-line basis over
a 20-year period (no salvage value assumed). This is represented by
the line A–Z. It is assumed that 20 per cent of the cost of the equipment,
or $600,000, is paid at the time of purchase. This is represented by the
line A–B. Equipment trust obligations in the amount of $2,400,000 are
issued to complete payment for the equipment. It is assumed that the
obligations are paid off in equal annual installments over a period of 15
years. The amount of obligations outstanding at any time is indicated
by the line B–Y.

The amount of obligations outstanding and the depreciated value of
the equipment at any time can be found quickly by drawing a line perpendicular to line X–Y and extending the line upward to intersect lines
B–Y and A–Z. The margin of safety would be represented by the part of
the perpendicular line which is between lines B–Y and A–Z. At the time
of issue there is a margin of safety of $600,000. But there is only $1.25 in

property behind each $1.00 of obligations. At the end of 10 years, there would be only $800,000 in obligations outstanding against equipment with a depreciated value of $1,500,000. Thus, the margin of safety would then be $700,000. At this time there would be $1.87½ behind every $1.00 of obligations. It is therefore evident that despite the depreciation in the property the obligations are better secured as time goes on.

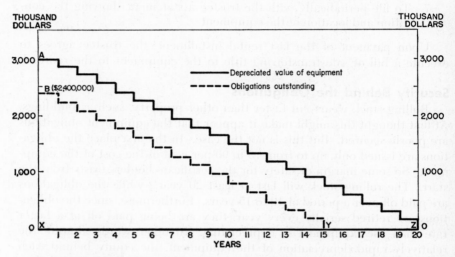

Fig. 8–2. Relationship of equipment trust obligations to depreciated value of equipment.

Investment Worth of Equipment Obligations

Equipment obligations are among the best, if not the best, railroad securities obtainable. Even roads that are financially weak have been able to secure money at a relatively low rate through the sale of these obligations. Following is a summary of the reasons why equipment obligations have such a high investment rating.

1. Rolling stock is perhaps the most valuable property possessed by a railroad. Some branch lines, terminals, shops, etc., may be abandoned, and the road can get along, but it cannot operate without cars and locomotives.
2. The equipment is standardized and can be used by other roads. Hence in event of default it might be sold to another railroad.
3. The rolling stock is built on wheels and is on a standard-gauge track and can therefore be easily transported and rented or sold to another railroad in event of default.
4. A railroad is a type of public utility and its services are essential. Thus if it fails, the receiver or trustee and later the reorganized company will need the equipment.

5. The equipment obligations are paid off faster than the equipment depreciates, so that there is an increase in the equity of the outstanding obligations.
6. If the Philadelphia or conditional sale plan is used, in event of default the trustee or seller can seize the equipment, even if the company is in the receiver's hands. Section 77 of the Bankruptcy Act specifically provides that nothing in the Act will prevent the owner from taking possession of the equipment in compliance with the provisions of a lease or conditional sale contract.

Use in Other Fields

Although the primary use of equipment obligations has been by railroads, they have also been used in other fields. Oil, coal, and steel companies have used these obligations to finance their own cars. Marine companies have used them to buy ships. Some transportation companies have financed buses with equipment obligations. In a few instances they have been used by industrial companies to finance machinery. In recent years some of the commercial airlines have used equipment obligations to finance new planes. When used for this purpose their maturity has been shorter than in the case of railroads, five years being typical.

Equipment obligations issued by industrial companies do not have the same investment standing as those issued by railroads. Several things account for this difference. The equipment behind the industrial issue is less standardized and it usually becomes obsolete faster than railroad cars. Furthermore, an industrial is subject to more competition than a railroad, and in event of failure it may be liquidated rather than reorganized.

LAND TRUST CERTIFICATES

Real estate is often financed through the issuance of *land trust certificates*. Legal title to a particular piece of land is transferred to a bank or trust company which serves as trustee. A definite number of certificates of beneficial interest representing equitable ownership of an undivided part of the land are sold to the public to obtain the money necessary to acquire the land. These certificates are similar to equipment obligations issued under the Philadelphia Plan.

Although the legal nature of land trust certificates is similar to that of stocks, in actual practice they are more similar to bonds. The usual denomination is $1,000, although in some instances it is $500, and in a few cases as low as $100. They bear a fixed rate of return similar to bonds. The money to pay the return on the certificates comes from the rental payments made by the lessee of the property. Although the certificates do not have a maturity date, the contract may give the lessee an option to purchase the land at a specified price at a designated time. In such instances a call price, usually a premium over the face value, would be stated in the certificates.

In final analysis the investment worth of land trust certificates depends upon the value of the particular land. Since the income to pay the return on the certificates comes from the rental paid by the lessee, the credit of the lessee is an important consideration. If the site is an important one, probably the lessee can profitably use the property and will be able to make the rental payments. If a default in the rental payments is made, the claim of certificate holders, through the trustee, for ground rent would come ahead of any obligations that had been issued to finance a building on the land.

If the land is such that land trust certificates may be issued, an owner may obtain much more by the sale through the certificates than by the ordinary method of selling the land. This follows from the fact that through the use of the certificates the land is sold in small units to many buyers. When a company wishes to build a building or store on the land, the land trust certificate arrangement of getting the land through a lease will obviate the necessity of providing a large amount of cash to purchase the land.

LEASEHOLD MORTGAGE BONDS

Leasehold mortgage bonds are issued to finance buildings which are erected on leased land. Many companies do not want to tie up a considerable amount of money in fixed assets, such as land. So the company, which contemplates operating a department store, for example, leases the land for a long period of time. In many instances the lessee has the right to purchase the land at a designated price. In some cases the owner wants to sell the land rather than lease it. If this is the situation, the land may be sold through the land trust certificate arrangement described above, and then the company may lease the land from the trustee.

In order to help finance the building on the leased land, the company then issues bonds which are secured by the leasehold. If only one mortgage is issued, the bonds would have a first claim against the leasehold and would be referred to as "first leasehold mortgage bonds." Provision is made for the retirement of the bonds before the termination of the lease.

Despite the fact that leasehold mortgage bonds may have a first claim against the leasehold, they are in effect second mortgage bonds. This follows from the fact that the owner of the land really has first claim against the building for the ground rent. Any shrinkage in real estate values would thus be felt by the holders of the leasehold mortgage bonds, and their equity would be wiped out before the owners of the land would be affected. Because of this the leasehold bonds as a class are not rated highly as investment securities. From what has been said it is obvious that bonds which are secured by the land as well as the improvements on the land are much better investments than those which are secured only by a leasehold.

ASSUMED BONDS

These are issued by a company which is later absorbed by another firm which takes on the obligation to pay the interest and principal on the bonds. About 80 per cent of the assumed bonds now in existence are those of railroads.

In addition to any mortgage which they may possess, assumed bonds become general credit obligations of the assuming company. Thus, they are on an equal footing with any other unsecured obligations, so far as the assuming company is concerned.

GUARANTEED BONDS

A guaranteed bond is one on which the payment of interest or principal, or as usual both, is guaranteed by another company. The guarantee is usually stated on the face or reverse side of the bond, in which case the bond may be referred to as *stamped* or *endorsed*. This is commonly done when the guarantee is direct and is made at the time the bond is issued. In the case of a lease or consolidation, the guarantee may be stated in a supplemental agreement rather than on the bond itself. Guaranteed bonds arise in one of the following ways.

Lease

Guaranteed bonds, particularly in the railroad field, have commonly arisen through a lease. Company A may lease the property or road of Company B and, as one of the conditions of the lease, guarantee the interest and principal on B's bonds.

Financing a Subsidiary

Parent companies sometimes guarantee the interest and principal on their subsidiary companies' bonds. The subsidiary may be small and relatively unknown, and thus it either could not sell its bonds or could do so only at a higher interest rate. The parent company may possess good credit, and its guarantee of the bonds would enable them to be sold at a relatively low rate of interest.

Consolidation

In some instances a company may acquire controlling interest in another company by agreeing among other things to guarantee the interest and principal on the bonds of the other company.

Other Instances

In the early history of this country many of the states guaranteed private loans that were made for the purpose of financing banks, canals, and railroads. Many of these ventures were unsuccessful and the states had to bear the loss. As a result of this experience, many state constitutions now prohibit the states from lending their credit to private business ventures.

Investment Worth

The security behind guaranteed bonds is usually considered to be dual in nature: the obligation of the issuing company and the obligation of the guaranteeing company, and for purposes of analysis we should add a third—any mortgaged property of the issuer which may be behind the bonds. In a sense this is included in the obligation of the issuer, but we want to list it separately for proper emphasis.

Guaranteed Bonds and Guaranteed Stocks Compared

In many instances when the interest and principal of a company's bonds are guaranteed, the dividends on its stock are also guaranteed by the same company. It should be noted that since stocks do not become due at any time, the principal amount represented by the stock is not guaranteed. Holders of the guaranteed stock would be in the position of general unsecured creditors of the guaranteeing company with respect to the dividend.

If the guaranteeing company fell into such financial condition that the guarantee would mean nothing, then the holders of the guaranteed bonds and stocks would revert to their original status as regards the issuing company. This means that the bondholders are the creditors and would, in event of default, have a right against the property of the issuer. The stockholders, being the owners, would come after the bondholders.

Every company is obligated to pay its own bonds; but when we speak of a guaranteed bond we refer to one which is guaranteed by *another* company. Likewise, a guaranteed stock is one on which the dividends have been guaranteed by another company.

JOINT BONDS

These are bonds on which the interest and principal are guaranteed by *two or more* companies. Like the assumed and guaranteed bonds, they commonly arise in the railroad field. When several railroads want to build and use in common some facility such as a terminal, dock, wharf, or bridge, they usually incorporate a separate company to build and operate it. This facilitates the procedure and also prevents any bond issues containing the after-acquired property clause, which any of the railroads may have outstanding, from attaching themselves to the new property.

The new corporation then issues its bonds to secure the money necessary to build the project. These are commonly secured by a first mortgage on the property. In order to make them marketable at a comparatively low rate of interest, the companies which are to use the property jointly and severally guarantee the payment of the interest and principal on the bonds. It should thus be noted that a joint bond is not jointly *issued* by two or more companies. It is issued by *one* company, but *jointly guaranteed* by the *two* or more companies. It should likewise be noted that although the joint bond is guaranteed, we reserve the term *guaranteed* to apply to a bond which is guaranteed by only *one* company. In the usual joint bond, it is *jointly and severally* guaranteed. This means that all the companies collectively guarantee the issue, and furthermore, that each one guarantees it. Thus, if any of the companies could not make good, the others could be held.

RECEIVERS' AND TRUSTEES' CERTIFICATES

When a corporation goes into the hands of a receiver in equity or trustee in bankruptcy because of failure or threatened failure, it is practically always in dire need of cash. While in the courts' hands, the corporate officials would not be permitted to sell new securities. Furthermore, considering the financial condition of the company at this time, no one would buy ordinary corporate securities. But additional cash may be a necessity in order to operate.

The solution of the problem is the issuance of receivers' or trustees' certificates. *Receivers' certificates* are issued when the company is in equity receivership, and *trustees' certificates* when the company is undergoing reorganization under the Bankruptcy Act.

Such certificates are short-term notes issued by the receiver under authority of the court which is administering the receivership. The money necessary to pay them may come from the earnings of the company, or from the proceeds of a sale of new securities, or from an assessment of old security holders.

Their claim depends upon what specific priority the court gives them. It is customary for the court to give them a claim ahead of all securities which are in default and which will probably have to undergo some sacrifice in the reorganization. But they ordinarily would not be given priority over a senior issue of bonds which was not in default and which would be "undisturbed" in the reorganization.

The court will see to it that the certificates are paid off or that adequate provision has been made for their retirement, before receivership will be lifted. In some instances the failure is so serious that the holders of the receivers' certificates will be asked to accept inferior securities in exchange for their certificates.

Receivers' certificates are commonly made callable before their maturity date. In some instances the maturity date has been extended by authority of the court. Because of the priority given them, receivers' certificates ordinarily sell on a relatively low yield basis.

DEBENTURE BONDS

Bonds which are secured only by the general credit of the issuing company, and thus have no claim on specific property, are called *debenture bonds*. The absence of specific mortgaged security is not necessarily a sign of weakness in the bonds; in final analysis the real security of all bonds is the general credit of the company. If a company which has only debenture bonds outstanding defaults in the payment of interest or principal, the bondholders through their trustee can take proper legal steps to secure a lien against the company's property. After this has been done the bonds may really become mortgage bonds. So, from the standpoint of security, debenture bonds are only a step behind mortgage bonds. If a company has both mortgage and debenture bonds outstanding, any lien on mortgaged property that would be obtained by the debenture bonds would be junior to that possessed by the mortgage bonds.

Mortgage bonds have a senior claim only in respect to the particular property which is mortgaged. In respect to unmortgaged property the mortgage bondholders and debenture bondholders would stand on an equal footing.

Debenture bonds usually have a shorter life than mortgage bonds because of the difficulty of determining the ability of a corporation to pay off its general credit obligations in the distant future. They are issued more commonly by industrial corporations than by railroads and public utilities.

It is sometimes said, and with some truth, that debenture bonds are a sign of either weakness or strength. If a company has already outstanding a number of mortgages against its properties, a debenture issue would sell about as well as a third or fourth mortgage. If a company, on the other hand, has no mortgages against its property and is in a strong financial condition, it may be able to market a debenture issue at a relatively low rate of interest without placing a mortgage against its properties. If a bond issue is sold by some types of corporations such as merchandising companies which do not own any real estate, it would have to be a debenture issue.

Protective Provisions in Debenture Issues

Following are the more commonly used restrictions or safeguards.

1. *Restrictions on mortgage indebtedness.* Investment bankers and investors commonly insist on a provision in the debenture agreement giving the bonds an equal claim on the property with any mortgage bonds subsequently issued.

2. *Restrictions against additional indebtedness.* A common type of such provision provides that additional indebtedness can be incurred only if the company's average earnings for a designated number of years have been at least equal to 3 or 4 times the interest on the debt outstanding plus the additional debt which is contemplated. In some instances the contract provides that the net tangible assets must at least be equal to $2\frac{1}{2}$ or 3 times the bonded indebtedness, including the proposed new issue.

3. *Restrictions on dividends.* Another type of provision is that of preventing the payment of cash dividends on the stock unless certain ratios are maintained. For example, the current ratio may have to be at least 2 or 3 (this means that the current assets would have to be at least 2 or 3 times the current liabilities), or the net current assets (current assets less current liabilities) would have to be at least a stated amount.

Subordinated Debentures

In recent years subordinated debentures have been used to an increasing extent by corporations, particularly finance companies, to secure additional capital. A *subordinated debenture bond* issue is one which, according to the terms of the indenture, cannot be paid in event of liquidation, dissolution, bankruptcy, or reorganization, until payment has been made to the senior creditors. Senior creditors may be described in the indenture to include existing bank creditors, and holders of bonds and notes, or those who subsequently become such creditors. Debts such as accounts payable, dividends payable, and certain other types of current liabilities are usually described in the indenture as not constituting senior debt.

Subordinated debentures are issued in order to obtain additional capital, and at the same time broaden the base for future senior borrowing. A company may have outstanding the maximum amount of bank loans and other senior debt permitted in relation to the equity structure of the company. The money obtained from the sale of subordinated debentures will increase the base or security in a manner similar to the issuance of additional stock. Thus, in the future, the company may be able to obtain additional funds from bank loans or other senior debt at a relatively low rate of interest. The particular company may favor the subordinated debentures over the issuance of preferred or common stock for the following reasons. Since the bonds have a fixed rate of interest, the benefit of leverage may be obtained. Also, the interest rate on the bonds would probably be lower than the rate of dividends that would be paid on a preferred stock issue. Furthermore, the bond interest is deductible for income taxes, whereas dividends are not. And, of course, control is not affected by the issuance of bonds, whereas this is a possibility if additional stock is sold. From the market standpoint, insurance companies, pension funds, and other institutional buyers might, either because of law or practice, favor bonds over stocks. In order to add to their marketability, most subordinated debenture issues have been made convertible into stock of the issuing company.

Secured Debentures

After seeing debenture bonds defined, one may be surprised to see the term *secured debenture*. This title is sometimes used for a bond which is secured by some property, either real or personal, or both, but where the amount or value of the security is so small in relation to the face value of the bonds, it is thought advisable not to call the obligation a mortgage or collateral trust bond.

INCOME BONDS

Income bonds are those on which the interest payments do not constitute a fixed charge unless earned, and which therefore do not have to be paid unless the company has earnings sufficient to pay them. The principal, however, comes due at a stated time and must be paid (or otherwise legal action may be taken to collect it), regardless of whether there are earnings. When issued in a reorganization, income bonds in some cases have been called *adjustment bonds,* and in a few instances *preference bonds.*

Income bonds first arose in railroad organizations. In the case of practically all railroad failures, the amount of the bond interest, called *fixed charges,* is excessive in relation to the earnings. About the only way the reorganized company can get back on its feet is to cut down the amount of these charges. So the reorganization plan usually calls for the issuance of income bonds in exchange for some of the junior bonds of the company. Most of the income bonds issued by railroads have been mortgage bonds, but their mortgage is usually a junior one.

Interest Provisions in Income Bonds

The exact nature of the interest payments on an income bond depends upon the particular contract under which it is issued. The general statement made above that the interest is a fixed charge only if earned would apply in practically all cases. In some instances even if the interest is earned it must be declared by the board of directors, in a manner similar to the declaration of dividends on stock, before the bondholders can claim it.

Considering the inexactnesses that are present in the science of accounting, there may be some question from time to time whether there are earnings, and if so, their exact amount. If the company has earnings, but an amount insufficient to pay the full rate, the indenture may provide that the amount earned shall be paid. In such instances it is commonly stated that the rate paid must be a multiple of even fractions, such as ½ per cent.

In the older railroad income bonds the interest was non-cumulative, or non-cumulative for the first few years and cumulative thereafter, but many income bonds issued in more recent years have been cumulative from the time of issue. Any accumulated interest on income bonds must be paid before any dividends can be declared on the stock, or at the maturity of the bonds.

Income Bonds Compared With Preferred Stocks

From what has been said above it is apparent that income bonds are somewhat like preferred stock. But there are several important differences between these two types of securities. Preferred dividends do not constitute a fixed charge, and do not have to be paid even if the company has earnings. Interest on income bonds, as we have seen, however, becomes a fixed charge if earnings sufficient to pay the interest are earned in any particular year. The principal of the bonds becomes due the same as any other debt of the corporation, whereas preferred stocks do not come due, although they may be callable by the issuing company.

From the standpoint of the issuing company, there are several reasons why it may prefer income bonds to preferred stock.

1. *Security holders prefer bonds.* The fact that the security can be called a "bond" would have a psychological advantage and the old bond-holders would be more ready to accept a reorganization plan if they were offered bonds instead of stock. Furthermore, the interest on the income bonds constitutes a fixed charge and must ordinarily be paid in those years in which the interest is earned.

2. *Restriction on stock ownership.* Life insurance companies have in the past been large holders of railroad bonds; these firms were prohibited from owning stock. Bonds, even though they are income bonds, could be held by the insurance companies. In recent years many state laws have been changed to permit limited holdings of stocks, both common and preferred, by life insurance companies.

3. *Income tax savings.* Bond interest is an expense and can thus be deducted before arriving at the figure on which the income tax is based. Dividends, on the other hand, are not deductible since they constitute a distribution of the profits.

Recent Uses

In recent years an increasing number of solvent companies, including railroads, have issued income bonds to secure new money or to retire preferred stock issues. The main advantage to the issuing company of the income bond as compared with preferred stock is the tax savings. Furthermore, institutional investors may purchase the bonds. In some instances, the income bonds have been subordinated debentures; in other cases they possess the conversion feature.

Quotations

Income bonds are ordinarily quoted *flat*. This means that any interest accrued or expected on the bond is included in the quoted price. When the bonds attain an investment status such as those of the Atchison, Topeka and Santa Fe Railway 4s of 1995, the bonds are quoted "and accrued interest," the same as ordinary bonds.

PARTICIPATING BONDS

As the term is ordinarily used in corporate finance, a *participating bond* is one which bears a fixed rate of interest, like an ordinary bond, and in addition is entitled to participate along with the stockholders in additional earnings to the extent provided in the contract. They are also called *profit-sharing bonds*. They have rarely been issued in the United States, but are more common in Europe. The participating feature is similar to that which appears in some preferred stock issues, but it should be remembered that the initial rate on the bonds is a fixed charge which must be paid regardless of whether there are earnings. Some participating bonds are secured by a mortgage, while other are debenture issues.

QUESTIONS

1. (a) When a corporation issues a mortgage bond, who is the mortgagor, and who the mortgagee? (b) What is the exact nature of the security behind a mortgage bond?
2. If mortgaged property sells for less than the face value of the bonds secured by the property, is the mortgagor liable for the balance? What instrument makes him liable?
3. Indicate the difference between buying property and assuming a mortgage, and buying the property subject to the mortgage.
4. (a) Distinguish between open- and closed-end mortgage bond issues. Which type would the investor ordinarily prefer? (b) What restrictions are commonly placed on the further issuance of bonds under an open issue?
5. (a) Indicate what is meant by the "after-acquired property" clause? (b) Indicate how corporations sometimes avoid the effects of the after-acquired property clause.
6. What type of property is ordinarily behind mortgage bonds?
7. Explain what is meant by each of the following types of bonds: purchase money mortgage bonds, divisional bonds, special direct-lien bonds, prior-lien bonds, first general mortgage bonds, and consolidated mortgage bonds.
8. Distinguish between funding and refunding a debt.
9. (a) How do collateral trust bonds differ from mortgage bonds? (b) If it becomes necessary for the holders of collateral trust bonds to foreclose against the collateral, can they then foreclose against the real property of the issuer of the securities which is deposited as collateral? Explain. (c) What are the various reasons why a corporation might issue a collateral trust bond rather than another kind of bond issue? (d) Who is entitled to vote corporate stock which is pledged as security for a collateral trust bond issue?
10. (a) Explain the difference among the three plans under which equipment trust obligations may be issued. (b) Why do equipment trust obligations, particularly those issued under the Philadelphia Plan, rate so highly as investment securities? (c) Would you recommend equipment obligations for the average investor? (d) How do you account for the way equipment trust obligations are quoted in the market?
11. (a) Indicate the nature of land trust certificates and explain the circumstances under which they are issued. (b) Why might an investor prefer land trust certificates over the purchase of the land directly?
12. Indicate the nature of leasehold mortgage bonds and the circumstances under which they are leased. Do they have first claim against a building which is erected on the leased land? Explain.
13. (a) Is there any security behind an "unsecured" bond? Explain. (b) Are unsecured bonds more risky than secured bonds? Explain. (c) Considering the various types of bonds that are outstanding today, would you say that the safest ones are really unsecured bonds? Explain.

14. Explain the following relative to assumed bonds, guaranteed bonds, and joint bonds. (a) Circumstances under which they arise. (b) Nature of the security behind them. (c) Their relative investment status.
15. Compare the relative status of guaranteed bonds and guaranteed stocks.
16. Indicate the nature of the security behind receivers' or trustees' certificates.
17. (a) Distinguish between the terms *debenture* and *indenture*. (b) What type of provisions is often inserted in the indenture of a debenture bond issue for the protection of the bondholders?
18. (a) Indicate the nature of income bonds. What other title is often used for them? (b) Are most income bonds debentures or mortgage bonds? (c) Of what importance would the mortgage feature of an income bond be?
19. Is there any reason why both the issuing corporation and the investor might prefer an income bond over a preferred stock? Explain.
20. Explain what is meant by a participating bond.

PROBLEMS

1. Mr. Flint borrows $5,000 on a first mortgage and $2,000 on a second mortgage to buy a house and a lot. In addition to giving the mortgagees mortgages on the property, he, of course, gives them his personal notes for the amounts stated. When Mr. Flint is unable to continue interest payments on the money borrowed, the creditors foreclose against the property. The property is purchased by Mr. Drew at the court sale. Indicate the liability, if any, of Mr. Flint after the sale, the nature of the title received by Mr. Drew, the amount received by the first mortgagee, by the second mortgagee, and by Mr. Flint if the following amounts were realized at the sale following the foreclosure action instigated by the mortgagee indicated. (Disregard court costs, taxes, etc.)

Foreclosed by	Amount obtained from sale
(a) First Mortgagee	$3,000
(b) First Mortgagee	6,500
(c) Second Mortgagee	1,500
(d) Second Mortgagee	2,500

2. The following was the last balance sheet presented by the Electronic Nuclear Corp. prior to its liquidation:

Assets		Liabilities and Net Worth	
Accounts receivable	$ 100,000	Accounts payable	$ 100,000
Inventory	300,000	Notes payable	200,000
Plant	1,000,000	First mortgage bonds	400,000
Deficit	200,000	Second mortgage bonds	200,000
		Preferred stock	200,000
		Common stock	500,000
Total	$1,600,000	Total	$1,600,000

Newer methods introduced by competitors caused a sharp decline in the earnings of the Electronic Nuclear Corp. in recent years, and the creditors forced the company into receivership. After studying the business for some months the receiver reported to the court that liquidation of the business appeared to be the solution rather than reorganization, especially since that met with the approval of the creditors. It was thought desirable to sell the assets piecemeal rather than for a lump sum. The bonds possessed a mortgage against the plant. The preferred stock had a preference over the common in respect to assets upon dissolution to the extent of $110 per share. All the stock had a par value of $100 per share.

(a) How much and what percentage on the dollar would be received by each class of creditors if the particular assets were sold for the following amounts?

Accounts Receivable	$ 60,000
Inventory	180,000
Plant	500,000

(b) Do you think that the assets were carried on the last balance sheet at an inflated figure? Why or why not?

3. The Southern R. R. Co. issued $9,600,000 in car trust certificates to finance the acquisition of $12,000,000 of rolling stock. The obligations are to be paid off in 15 equal annual installments. The average life of the rolling stock is 20 years. What is the equity behind each dollar of obligations: (a) At the beginning of the first year? (b) At the beginning of the sixth year? (c) At the beginning of the eleventh year? (d) At the beginning of the fifteenth year?

4. The entire assets of the Metal Steel Co. and the All Products Co. were purchased by the United Steel Corp. The first-mentioned company had mortgage bonds outstanding against its plant amounting to $1,000,000, and the All Products Co.'s plant was mortgaged to the extent of $2,000,000. Both of these issues were assumed by United Steel. The bond issue of the Metal Steel Co. contained the after-acquired property clause.

The United Steel Corp. then issued $2,000,000 in mortgage bonds to get cash for further expansion purposes. This issue was secured by a first mortgage on United's old plant, and contained an after-acquired property clause. United then acquired the plant of the Strip Co. and used a purchase money mortgage of $1,000,000 as part payment for the plant.

Several years later the United Co. failed, and the following amounts were received for the properties at the court sale:

Metal Steel plant	$ 800,000
All Products plant	1,400,000
Old United plant	1,500,000
Strip plant	1,300,000
Other assets of United Corp.	
(unmortgaged)	400,000

(a) Indicate the exact nature of the liens of the various bond issues prior to the court sale. (b) Indicate the amounts that would go to the designated classes of bonds and what percentage on the dollar would be realized by each class of bondholders.

5. The Subsidiary Corp. was capitalized with $1,000,000 in first mortgage bonds, which were secured by a mortgage on its plant; $1,000,000 in 6 per cent preferred stock; and $2,000,000 in common stock. The Parent Corp., which had guaranteed both the interest and principal on the bonds and the dividends on the preferred stock of the Subsidiary Corp., was capitalized with $2,000,000 in first mortgage bonds, which were secured by a mortgage on the Parent new plant; $1,000,000 in 7 per cent debenture bonds; $1,000,000 in 6 per cent preferred stock; and $4,000,000 in common stock.

The dividends on both preferred stocks have not been paid for the past 5 years. Upon default in the principal on all the bond issues, the bondholders brought action that ultimately resulted in a court sale of the properties. The following amounts were realized from the particular assets indicated:

Subsidiary plant	$ 700,000
Parent new plant	1,200,000
Other assets of parent (unmortgaged)	1,200,000

(a) Indicate the nature of the lien or claim of each class of securities before the court sale. (b) Indicate the amount that will go to each class of security holders, and state the percentage on the dollar that each receives. (For purposes of solving this problem, assume that dividends on the preferred stock have accrued for 5 years, there is no accrued interest on the bonds, and disregard any court costs.)

SELECTED READINGS

BOGEN, JULES I. (ed.). *Financial Handbook*, 3d ed. New York: The Ronald Press Co., 1952. Section 11.

DORIS, LILLIAN (ed.). *Business Finance Handbook*. Englewood Cliffs, N. J.: Prentice-Hall, Inc., 1953. Chapter 18.

FLETCHER, WILLIAM MEADE. *Cyclopedia of the Law of Private Corporations;* Permanent ed. Chicago: Callaghan & Co., Vol. 6a (1950 rev. vol.).

HICKMAN, W. BRADDOCK. *The Volume of Corporate Bond Financing Since 1900*. National Bureau of Economic Research, Inc. Princeton, N. J.: Princeton University Press, 1953.

JOHNSON, ROBERT W. "Subordinated Debentures: Debt That Serves as Equity," *Journal of Finance*, March, 1955, pp. 1–16.

ROBBINS, SIDNEY M. "A Bigger Role for Income Bonds," *Harvard Business Review*, November–December, 1955, pp. 100–14.

STREET, DONALD M. *Railroad Equipment Financing*. New York: Columbia University Press, 1959.

9

Convertibles, Warrants, and Options

CONVERTIBLE BONDS

As the name indicates, a *convertible security* is one which can be converted into another type. In practically all instances the option to convert rests with the holder rather than with the issuing company. In most instances the convertible security is a relatively sound one with a more or less fixed or limited income return, and it is convertible into a more speculative security which lacks a fixed return but which has the right to reap the benefits of any future success the company may have. Thus convertible bonds are usually exchangeable for either preferred or common stock, and convertible preferred stock can usually be exchanged for common stock. The convertible security and the one into which it is convertible are issued by the same company. Convertible preferred stock was briefly discussed in Chapter 6. Much of what is stated in this chapter will apply also to convertible preferred stock.

In a few instances bonds have been convertible into securities of other companies which were held by the company issuing the convertible bonds. Isolated instances have occurred where preferred stock has been convertible into bonds issued by the same company. There have been a number of cases among railroads and public utilities where short-term notes have been convertible into long-term bonds which were put up as collateral behind the note issue.

Extent of Use

In a study that covered all bonds issued from 1933 to 1952, it was found that slightly over 9 per cent of the total number of issues were convertible. Table 9–1 shows the total number of all publicly offered security issues during this period, including preferred and common issues, and what percentage of them were convertible issues.

Table 9–1. Public Offerings; Convertible Issues Relative to Total, 1933–1952 (Offerings in Excess of $300,000 Each, and Excluding Equipment Trusts)

	Total Number of Offerings	Number of Convertible Offerings	Per Cent Convertible
Bonds	1,959	182	9.3
Preferred stocks	1,399	494	35.3
Total senior issues	3,358	676	20.1
Common stocks	1,764	–	–
Total	5,122	676	13.2

SOURCE: C. James Pilcher, *Raising Capital With Convertible Securities*, Bureau of Business Research, University of Michigan, 1955, p. 7. Data for the table were from Sullivan & Cromwell, *Issuer Summaries, Security Issues in the United States—July 26, 1933 to December 31, 1949;* Ad Press Ltd., 1951, Vols. I and II; and *Investment Dealers' Digest*, Jan. 22, 1951; Jan. 21, 1952; and Jan. 26, 1953.

As might have been expected, the number of industrial convertible preferred stock and convertible bond issues greatly exceeded those issued by utilities, railroads, and financial institutions. The relative importance of convertible issues among these industries for the period 1933–1952 is shown in Table 9–2.

Table 9–2. Industry Use of Convertible Securities, 1933–1952 (Public Offerings in Excess of $300,000 Each, Excluding Equipment Trusts)

	Preferred Stocks		Bonds	
	Number of Convertible Offerings	Percentage of Total	Number of Convertible Offerings	Percentage of Total
Industrials	438	88.7	134	73.7
Utilities	49	9.9	40	22.0
Railroads	1	0.2	7	3.8
Banks	2	0.4	1	0.5
Insurance companies	4	0.8	0	0.0
Total	494	100.0	182	100.0

SOURCE: C. James Pilcher, *Raising Capital With Convertible Securities*, Bureau of Business Research, University of Michigan, 1955, p. 19. Data for the table were from Sullivan & Cromwell, *Issuer Summaries, Security Issues in the United States—July 26, 1933 to December 31, 1949;* Ad Press Ltd., 1951, Vols. I and II; and *Investment Dealers' Digest*, Jan. 22, 1951; Jan. 21, 1952; and Jan. 26, 1953.

Why Sold

A good investment bond does not ordinarily need a conversion privilege attached in order to sell it. In most instances this privilege is attached to a junior grade bond in order to add to its marketability.

In some cases, however, companies with exceptionally strong credit will issue convertible bonds in order to sell the bonds at a relatively low rate of interest, and also to prevent a depression in the price of the stock which might result if stock rather than the convertible bond was sold. For example, the American Telephone and Telegraph Company since the end of World War II has sold to its shareholders through privileged subscription in excess of $10 billion of convertible bonds.

Unless otherwise provided, shareholders have a pre-emptive right to buy convertible bonds before they can be sold to the public. The purpose in selling any kind of security is to obtain money. But our interest at the present is why the conversion feature is added to the bonds, or why the company does not sell stock rather than convertible bonds to obtain the money. The reasons follow.

1. *Cheaper financing.* The conversion feature adds to the attractiveness of the bond. People will give more money for a bond with a given rate of interest if the conversion privilege is attached. In other words, the company can sell such bonds on a lower yield basis than if they were not convertible. This speculative feature enhances the market for the bonds. As would be expected, the conversion feature is added to bonds more commonly during the upswing of the business cycle when the stock market is bullish. People at that time hesitate to buy fixed dollar investments. The conversion feature permits them, if they should decide to convert, to share in the future earnings of the company, and to hedge against inflation by becoming owners in the business.

2. *Inability to market stock.* Although the convertible bonds may be sold during a period of rising stock prices, the particular company may not at the time have a market for additional stock. A market for the stock may exist, but considering the size of the new issue contemplated, the sale of additional stock instead of bonds might depress the market price of the stock too much.

3. *Elimination of bonded indebtedness.* If the bondholders convert, it will eliminate the bonds and substitute additional stock instead. Generally speaking, a company prefers to have stock rather than bonds outstanding.

4. *Selling the stock for more than its worth.* Considering the price that is obtained for the bond which is later converted into stock, the net result is that the company obtains more cash per share of stock eventually outstanding than if the stock was sold originally. Perhaps we can best illustrate this with an example. Let us assume that a company's

stock is selling in the market for $75 a share. It sells for $1,000 a bond which is convertible into 10 shares of stock. If the stock subsequently rises to more than $100 a share the bondholder might convert. If he does convert, it results in the company's having obtained $100 for each share of stock which is exchanged for the bonds. Had the company sold the stock originally instead of the bonds it would have obtained only $75 a share. This means that the company by issuing the convertible bonds which are later converted, obtains 33⅓ per cent more money than if the stock had been sold instead of the bonds. If the company is paying a dividend of $6 a share, it means that the money obtained from the security sale is costing it 6 per cent instead of 8 per cent if stocks had been sold.

Disadvantage to Issuer

Although some or all of the above listed advantages of convertible bonds may be experienced by the issuing corporation, it may also encounter certain disadvantages. These are as follows.

1. *It may dilute earnings per share.* The shareholders who become such from the conversion of bonds would share in the earnings and dividends along with the old stockholders. Considering the fact that the interest rate on the bonds may have been relatively low, the result of conversion may be that the earnings per share and thus the dividends paid may be less than before the bonds were converted.

2. *Surplus may be diluted.* Since the bondholders upon conversion would share in the surplus of the company in the same manner as the old stock, the surplus attaching to each old share may be reduced.

3. *Price of stock may fall.* Because of the two points stated above, conversion may result in a drop in the market price of the stock.

4. *May be expensive.* Conversion would eliminate the *leverage* (trading on the equity) which had been experienced from the bonds. This is similar to the first point stated above.

5. *Conversion occurs at wrong time.* The bondholders would convert only when they would profit from the exchange. Looking at it from the viewpoint of the issuing corporation, what would benefit the bondholder would probably harm the corporation. At the time the convertible bonds were sold the public probably demanded bonds rather than stock, due to the fact that the company's credit position, earnings, or prospects for the future may not have been good. At this time the company would probably prefer a stock issue over a bond issue. Later when the earnings increase and the stock rises in the market, the bondholders convert. This is the time that the company could better stand the bond issue and it would prefer that the bondholders not convert their bonds. But the option rests with the bondholder and not with the corporation.

6. *Control may be altered.* The bonds, of course, do not possess the voting right. When the bondholders convert into stock they usually would be entitled to vote in the same manner as any other stockholder. This might result in the shifting of control from the existing management.

7. *Taxes increased.* Since bond interest is an expense, it is deducted before arriving at the profit figure on which the federal and any state income taxes are based. The conversion of the bonds would eliminate this deduction and thus increase the taxes, since the dividends on the stock cannot be deducted for tax purposes. The corporation would also have to pay an additional state tax on the increase in stock similar to the organization tax. In many states the annual franchise tax is based on the amount of stock outstanding, so this would be higher after conversion takes place.

Advantages to Buyer

From what has been stated above the advantages and disadvantages of convertible bonds from the viewpoint of the buyer might be apparent, but for the sake of completeness they will be briefly discussed.

1. *Security of a bond.* The holder of a convertible bond is a creditor of the company and thus occupies a more secure position than the stockholders. If the price of the stock does not advance to the point where it would be profitable for him to convert, he can retain his creditor position.

2. *Chance for profit on bonds.* The higher the stock goes the greater will be the rise in price of the convertible bond. In fact, the price of the bond will probably advance before the stock rises to the place where it would be profitable to convert since a further rise in the price of the stock will be anticipated. While the bondholder is experiencing a rise in the price of his bond comparable to the rise in the price of the stock, he nevertheless has the relatively secure position of a creditor.

3. *Chance for profit on stock.* After the price of the stock advances beyond the break-even point, the bondholder can convert into the stock and make a profit by selling it. Or, he may hold on to the stock anticipating a further rise. Also, the dividends being paid on the stock will probably be larger than the bond interest he had been receiving. Furthermore, he may for tax purposes take the dividend exclusion and dividend credit.

A further advantage of converting, although more theoretical than practical, is that the former bondholder thereafter has the voting rights possessed by the stock.

Disadvantages to Buyer

As is true of all types of securities, there are certain disadvantages to the buyer. These are as follows.

1. *Pays higher price for the bonds.* The principal reason the issuing corporation adds the convertible feature to the bond is to enable it to secure more money for the bond. The bond buyer pays a higher price for the bond, or (saying the same thing) he gets a lower yield on the bond, than if the convertible privilege had not been present. If the price of the stock does not advance, the amount paid for the convertible feature is money lost.

2. *Pays higher price for the stock.* The stock could have been acquired at a lower price at the time the bonds were purchased. Thus, whether he wants to be a stockholder in the company or a bondholder, he is paying a relatively high price in either instance.

3. *Instability of bond prices.* After the price of the stock has advanced beyond the point at which it would be profitable to convert, any further movement either up or down in the price of the stock will be followed by a proportionate change in the price of the bond. Whether he wanted to or not, the bondholder will find that he has become a speculator. Paper profits in either the bonds or the stock may be wiped out if the security is not sold at the right time.

4. *Conversion eliminates security.* Once the bondholder converts he gives up his status as a creditor of the company and becomes a stockholder. The price of the stock may fall to relatively low levels, and the dividends on the stock may be cut or eliminated entirely.

Conversion Ratio

The *conversion ratio,* which is stated in the bond contract, expresses the amount of stock which may be obtained by the conversion of the bond. It may be expressed in terms of the number of shares of stock which can be obtained from the conversion of one bond. Technically speaking, this would be a *ratio,* or as it is sometimes called, *conversion rate.* In other instances the contract states the price at which the stock can be acquired. This is termed the *conversion price.* When a conversion price is stated, the exchange value of the bond is its face value. When the stock has a par value it may be provided that the bond can be converted into stock with a par value equal to that of the bonds. Thus a $1,000 (face or par value) bond might be convertible into 10 shares which have a par value of $100 each. This is merely another way of stating a conversion price. When no-par stock is used, a conversion price or ratio would have to be stated.

It should be kept in mind that the conversion ratio stated in the contract remains the same regardless of the fluctuation in the market price of the bonds or the stock. For example, if the conversion price of the stock is $125, a $1,000 (face value) bond can always be converted into

8 shares of stock, regardless of what may be the market price of the bond or the stock. The market prices are of importance, of course, when it comes to determining whether it would be profitable to convert.

In some instances the contract calls for an increased conversion price at the end of each successive period of years. Occasionally it is provided that the conversion price will increase after a stated fractional part of the bond issue has been converted. Sometimes the bondholders must pay some cash in addition to turning in their bonds, in order to get the stock; an example of this is the American Telephone and Telegraph bonds mentioned previously.

Price Pattern of Convertible Bonds

In most instances, at the time convertible bonds are issued, the price of the common would have to rise before it would be profitable to convert. The market value of the bond is made up of two component parts which we may call the investment value and the conversion value. The *investment value* of the bond is a resultant of the worth of the bond as a credit obligation of the company. It bears a fixed rate of interest, and is secured by the general credit of the issuing company and any other security that may be pledged behind the bond. Although no profit could ordinarily be made by converting at the time the bond is sold, people will give a little more for the bond because it has the conversion privilege attached. This added value can be called the *conversion value*. After the stock has risen in price to the point where it would be profitable for the bondholder to convert, the bonds would also go up in price as a result of their conversion value. The market price at this time would reflect the conversion value rather than the investment value of the bond. Any drop in the price of the stock would be accompanied by a proportionate drop in the price of the bonds. But the bonds will follow the price of the stock down only to the point where the price of the bonds would represent their investment worth. Perhaps this can best be illustrated with the following example.

Assume that a company sells at their face value, 3 per cent bonds which are convertible into stock at $100 a share. If the conversion feature had not been attached to the bond issue perhaps the company could have obtained only 95, instead of 100 for the bonds. The investment value of the bonds would thus be considered to be 95 ($950 for a $1,000 bond) and the additional 5 points would be the conversion value. We will assume that the stock into which the bonds are convertible was selling in the market at $75 at the time the bonds were issued.

If the stock would advance in price to $100 a share, the bondholder would break even by converting. So we may call this the *break-even point.* If the stock did make this advance in price the bonds would probably also rise in price because of the anticipated profit that could be made if the stock continued to advance in price. To illustrate better the price relationship between the stock and the bonds, however, we will be somewhat theoretical and assume that the price of the bonds remains at 100 while the stock is advancing to $100. If the price of the stock should advance from $100 to $110, it would be expected that the price of the bonds would also go up 10 points. This is true because one $1,000 bond could be converted into 10 shares of stock with a total worth of $1,100. So the bond would be expected to advance 10 points, or $100 in price. If the stock would advance to $150, for example, the price of the bonds would be expected to rise to $1,500. It is thus seen that after the price of the stock advances beyond the *break-even price,* the market price of the bonds will be determined solely from their *conversion value.*

If the price of the stock would fall, we would expect the price of the bonds to follow a similar course. For example, if the price of the stock fell from $150 to $120, we would expect the price of the bonds to drop from $1,500 to $1,200. But if the price of the stock should fall below $100, we would expect the price of the bonds to drop only to about $1,000, since this price represents the *investment value* of the bond, plus something additional for the speculative future value of the conversion feature. If the financial condition of the company would deteriorate to the point where it would appear improbable that the stock would ever get back to the place where it would be profitable to convert, the price of the bond would probably drop to about 95 ($950), which is what we assumed was the *investment value* alone of the bond. Of course if the condition of the company was such that the ability of the company to pay the bond interest and retire the bonds at maturity was questionable, the investment worth of the bonds might become considerably less than 95 ($950).

Determining When To Convert

It would be profitable to convert whenever the market value of the total stock obtained exceeded the market value of the bonds to be converted. If the market price of the bonds is 100 ($1,000 for a bond with a face value of $1,000), and the conversion price is $100, in other words one bond is convertible into 10 shares of stock, it would be profitable to convert whenever the price of the stock went above $100. For every dollar the stock advanced, we would expect the bond to go up 1 point ($10 for each $1,000 bond). When the conversion price is not a round figure such as $100, and when the market price of the bond is not an even $1,000, it may be a little more difficult to determine the profitableness of conversion. For that reason it is desirable to set up a rule or formula to determine this.

The break-even price of the stock can be determined as follows:

$$\text{Break-even price of stock} = \frac{\text{Market price of bond}}{\text{No. of shares of stock obtained}}$$

It would be profitable to convert only when the market price of the stock exceeded the break-even point. To illustrate the use of the formula let us assume that a particular $1,000 bond, which is selling at $1,200, is convertible into stock at $125 a share. We will assume the stock is selling for $130 a share. Would it be profitable to convert now? With the above conversion price it is obvious that one bond could be converted into 8 shares of stock ($1,000 divided by $125). Substituting in the formula we get the following:

$$\frac{\$1,200}{8} = \$150, \text{ Break-even price of stock}$$

This shows us that it would not be profitable to convert until the stock went above $150 a share (assuming the bond price remained at $1,200). We can easily test the accuracy of the formula. It obviously would not be profitable to convert until the market value of 8 shares exceeded $1,200, the price of the bond. To just equal the market price of the bonds, the shares would obviously have to sell at $150. If conversion was made when the stock was selling for $120, the bondholder would get only $960 in stock. He would thus lose $240 in conversion.

Perhaps a simpler way to get the break-even point is to multiply the conversion price of the stock by the market price of the bonds expressed in percentage of their face value.

$$\text{Break-even price of stock} = \frac{\text{Market price of bonds (expressed in per cent)}}{\times \text{ Conversion price of stock}}$$

Substituting the above figures in the formula we get the following:

120 per cent $\times$ $125 = $150, Break-even price of stock

It might be of some value to determine what the *conversion* value of the bonds would be when the stock was selling at a particular price. This can be computed as follows:

$$\frac{\text{Conversion value of bond}}{\text{(expressed in per cent)}} = \frac{\text{Market price of stock}}{\text{Conversion price of stock}}$$

Assuming the stock was selling for $175 a share, and that its conversion price was $125, by substituting in the formula we get:

$$\frac{\$175}{\$125} = 140 \text{ (per cent), Conversion value of bond}$$

If the bond was selling for 140 per cent of its face value (it will be remembered that the market quotation for bonds is expressed in percentage of face value) that means that the market price for a $1,000 (face value) bond would be $1,400. We can get the same result by the obvious round-about method. Since 8 shares of stock can be obtained from the conversion of one bond, with a market price of $175 a share, the bondholder would get $1,400 in stock. So this would represent the conversion value of the bond.

Adjustment for Interest and Dividends

Price relationships between convertible bonds and the stock into which they are convertible do not work out exactly as indicated above. One of the reasons for this is that, as we have previously seen, bonds are quoted "and accrued interest," while stocks are quoted "flat." The market price of the bond thus does not reflect any interest which may be accrued on it, while the market price of the stock includes any accrued or anticipated dividend.

The particular contract under which the bonds are issued should be examined to determine what, if any, consideration has been given by the company to accrued interest and dividends. Some contracts provide that the bondholder is entitled to any interest accrued to the time of conversion. But specific provision for accrued dividends is less common. Of course, if the former bondholder can get the stock registered in his name before the dividend date, he will receive the dividend, unless otherwise provided in the contract.

In some instances the contract provides that upon conversion the bondholder will be credited with any interest accrued on his bonds, but charged for any accumulated or accrued dividends at the regular dividend rate, and that any balance either way will be settled by cash payment.

Uneven Number of Shares

In order to simplify the explanation above we assumed conversion prices which were evenly divisible into the face value of the bonds. But in actual practice things do not work out so precisely. For example, the conversion price may, instead of being $100, or $125, be some price such as $110. With the latter price one $1,000 bond could be converted into 9 shares of stock, but what becomes of the unused $10 part of the bond? The following alternate methods have been used in different instances.

1. Commonly the bondholder receives a warrant for $10. He could then buy up warrants worth $100 in the market and send them all in to the company in exchange for an additional share of stock, or, he could sell his warrant on the market.
2. The bondholder could send in his warrant plus $100 cash and get the additional share.

3. The company could refund him $10.
4. The contract may provide only for an even exchange. Thus the bondholder would lose the $10, unless he held bonds in multiples of $11,000, which amount could be converted into an even 100 shares of stock.

Conversion Period

The period during which bonds are convertible is specifically stated in the contract under which the bonds are issued. The conversion period

Table 9–3. Selected Convertible Subordinated Debenture Bonds Listed on the New York Stock Exchange

Issue	Standard & Poor's Rating	Convertible into Common Stock at (dollars per share) *	Call Price *
American Distilling Co., 4⅜s, 1986	BBB	$47.50	104⅛
American Optical Co., 4.40s, 1980	BBB	59.05	104½
Atlantic Refining Co., 4½s, 1987	A	58.00	103
Avco Corporation, 5s, 1979	BB	11.50	104
Boeing Co., 4½s, 1980	BB	50.00	104
Brunswick Corporation, 4½s, 1981	BB	51.00	103½
Burroughs Corporation, 4½s, 1981	BBB	38.96	103⅝
Dow Chemical Company, 3s, 1982	AA	42.59	103
Food Fair Stores, Inc., 4s, 1979	BB	32.94	102.40
General American Transportation Co., 4s, 1981	BBB	40.00	102¼
International Telephone & Telegraph Co., 4⅞s, 1983	BB	18.50	104
Macy (R. H.) & Co., Inc., 5s, 1977	BBB	32.00	103½
Phillips Petroleum Co., 4½s, 1987	AA	50.00	103⅞
Xerox Corp., 4½s, 1981	BBB	105.00	104

* In some instances the call price of the bonds and the conversion price of the stock are different from those stated in the table for 1965, and subsequent years.

may be from the issue date of the bonds until their maturity date. In event the bonds are called in under a provision in the contract (usually 30 or more days' notice of redemption is given), it is usually provided that conversion can be made for a specified number of days, such as from 5 to 30, before the call date. When bonds are reflecting their conversion value in the market, many companies force conversion by exercising the call provision.

In the case of short-term bonds, which are more frequently issued by industrials and public utilities, the conversion period is commonly from issue date to maturity date, or a specified time approximating this period. In railroad bonds, which are more commonly long-term, the conversion period may begin some years after issue date, and terminate some years before the maturity date. In a survey of bond issues listed on the New York Stock Exchange during the period 1948–1952, it was found that 80 per cent were convertible at any time during the life of the bonds.[1]

Where the conversion privilege is of value to the bondholder and the conversion period expires before the maturity of the bond, the holder should either sell his bonds or convert into the stock before the termination of the period. Otherwise he may lose a sizable amount of money. We will illustrate this, using the same example that was used before. Assume that the investment value of a bond is about 95 and that it is convertible into stock at $100 a share. If the stock is selling in the market for $125 a share, the bond should be selling at about 125 ($1,250 for a $1,000 bond). The market price reflects the conversion value of the bond rather than the investment value. Now if the conversion privilege were to expire, the market price of the bonds would drop to about 95 ($950), the pure investment value of the bond. Conversion should also be made under these circumstances if the bond is called or if it matures.

If the company issuing the convertible bonds is merged into another company and thus loses its identity, the conversion privilege will thereby terminate. Where the privilege is of some value, conversion should be made before the merger. The contract under which the bonds are issued sometimes contains provisions which require a successor company to recognize the privilege.

Protection Against Dilution

Unless provision to the contrary is made in the contract, the value of the conversion privilege may be weakened or destroyed by the company issuing stock dividends, or having stock split-ups. For example, let us assume a conversion price of $100 for the stock. The bond would have conversion value when the price of the stock went above $100. If, when the stock approached the price of $100, the company had paid a 100 per cent stock dividend, or issued two new shares for each old share (split-up), it would tend to reduce the market price of the stock to $50 a share. Now the stock would have to climb 100 per cent more in price before the conversion privilege would be of any value. This is comparable to a price of $200 for the old stock. And a price of that amount for the old stock would have meant a market price of 200 ($2,000) for the bond.

Most convertible issues sold in recent years contain antidilution clauses which protect the bondholders against the weakening of the value of the privilege. Such clauses state that the bonds would be entitled to the number of shares comparable to the old stock. Thus, in the example above, if the company had a 100 per cent stock dividend, or a two-for-one split, the bondholder could convert into 20, instead of 10 shares.

[1] C. James Pilcher, *Raising Capital With Convertible Securities,* Bureau of Business Research, University of Michigan, Ann Arbor, 1955, p. 48.

Similar clauses may be contained in the indenture to protect the bond-holders from the dilution of the value of the privilege by issuing stock to the stockholders at a price below the existing market price. In some instances the contract will provide protection to the bondholders from such actions as the following: issuance of stock having a preference in respect to redemption or dissolution over the particular stock into which the bonds are convertible, issuance of another convertible security convertible into the stock at a lower price, and distribution of assets to senior security holders.

Hedge for Short Sellers of Stock

Short selling in stocks means selling stock which is not owned by the seller at the time of the sale. When a person sells the stock short he borrows the same number of shares and makes delivery to the purchaser. Later he will purchase the stock in the market and return it to the lender of the stock.

If the stock should advance in price the short seller would lose. But if he owned a bond convertible into the stock he might prevent the loss by acquiring the stock through conversion instead of by purchase in the market. Short selling is discussed in Chapter 15.

Conclusion on Convertibles

The conversion privilege is apt to be attached to a junior-grade bond. The mere presence of the privilege may be an indication that the bonds are not of the highest security, or that the credit of the issuing company may not be of the highest standing, otherwise the bond might perhaps have been sold without adding the conversion privilege. A prospective purchaser should be on guard and thoroughly investigate the company before buying any kind of bonds. In some instances, however, such as the American Telephone and Telegraph Company, the issuer is a strong company.

The buyer of a convertible bond is trying to get on both sides of the fence at the same time. The convertible bond attempts to carry with it the security of a bond, but the speculative opportunities of stock. As a bondholder he pays for the privilege which may never be worth anything, or he may not take advantage of it at the opportune time. If he does convert, he would have found it more profitable to have bought the stock originally instead of the bond. Furthermore, even if he converts when the stock is selling at a relatively high price, there is no assurance that the stock will be sold at a price which will return him a profit. The stock may later go down to the point where he would rather not have converted. But having once converted, he cannot later convert back to being a bondholder again.

Despite the criticisms stated above, there is something to be said in favor of convertible bonds. Granted that it may be a junior-grade bond, is it any worse off by having the conversion privilege attached? About the only disadvantage at the time is that the purchaser has to pay a slightly higher price for the bond. But this higher price may be justified. The holder is not compelled to convert. If the company is successful and the price of the stock rises to the point where it would be profitable to convert, the bondholder can make a profit on the stock. If he does not want to become a stockholder, he can sell his bond and make a profit. The money could then be invested in other bonds. If he retains the bonds or the stock after he converts, he may profit still further if the price of the stock continues to advance.

If the bondholder converts he may find that the annual dividends received on the stock will be greater than the interest he had been receiving on the bond. There also may be a tax advantage. Any profit made on the sale of the bond, or on the stock after conversion, would be considered a capital gain, and if the security has been held for at least six months this is considered a long-term gain, and the taxes on it would be less than on ordinary income. Furthermore, a stockholder is entitled to the dividend exclusion and dividend credit for income tax purposes.

STOCK PURCHASE WARRANTS

The term *stock purchase warrant* is used by some to refer to different types of contracts, and in some instances several different words or phrases may be used to apply to any one of these various kinds of contracts. Using the term in its generally accepted meaning, a *stock purchase warrant* is a contract which is attached to a security at the time of its sale giving the holder of the warrant the right to purchase another type of security issued by the same company. We will use the term with this meaning.

Type of Securities Carrying Warrants

In most instances the securities to which the warrants are attached are bonds or preferred stocks. The warrants usually call for the purchase of common stock, but in a few instances the warrants attached to bonds call for preferred stock. In a few cases the warrants have been attached to one class of common stock and give the holder thereof the right to buy another class of common stock. The bonds carrying warrants are usually debentures. Generally speaking, warrants are more frequently attached to bonds and preferred stocks of inferior quality. They have been more frequently used by industrials, investment companies, and public utility holding companies than by other types of companies.

Reason for Use

The reason for the use of stock purchase warrants is probably apparent—they are "sweeteners" to facilitate the sale of the securities to which they are attached. In this respect they are similar to the conversion feature.

Purchase Price of Stock With Warrant

The price at which the warrant holder can acquire the common stock is higher than the price of the stock at the time the warrant is issued. Thus the price of the common stock would have to advance before it would be profitable for the holder to exercise the warrant. This is comparable to the situation with convertible securities.

Detachability of Warrants

Some warrants are non-detachable from the security to which they are attached, or non-detachable for a specified period and detachable thereafter. In the case of the non-detachable warrant, only the holder of the security to which it is attached can exercise the warrant. To do so he must send the security with warrant attached and the money to buy the stock to the issuing company or a designated trust company representing the company. The company or its agent then sends him the stock and the old security after having detached the warrant.

In most instances the warrant is detachable from the security. The holder thereof can detach the warrant himself and either exercise it and buy the stock, or he can sell the warrant in the market, provided, of course, that it has a market value. Such warrants are payable to bearer.

Investment bankers and investors prefer detachable warrants, since they can sell the warrants without the security to which they are attached. The issuing company might prefer the non-detachable warrants since they would continue to improve the market for the security until the warrant was exercised.

Duration of Warrants

The duration of warrants depends, of course, upon the terms of the contract under which they are issued. In most instances the time within which they may be exercised is limited to a period stated in the contract. Ordinarily in the case of bonds, the life of the warrant is less than the life of the bond. In some instances the price to be paid for the stock upon exercise of the warrant increases as time goes on.

If the security to which the warrant is attached is called by the company before the warrant has expired, the contract may provide that the warrant shall continue for the period stated. If the warrant becomes void upon redemption of the security, it is usually provided that the warrant can be exercised within a stated number of days before the redemption date. If the life of the warrant continues after redemption, a non-detachable warrant would become detachable.

Table 9–4. Selected List of Stock Purchase Warrants

Company	One Warrant Buys This Number of Common Shares	Subscription Price per Share of Common	Warrant Expires On	Where Traded [a]	
				Stock	Warrant
Allegheny Corporation	1	$ 3.75	Perpetual	NYSE	ASE
Atlas Corporation	1	6.25	Perpetual	NYSE	ASE
Investment Co. of America...	10.97	10.48	Perpetual	O-C	O-C
Mack Trucks ('61)	1	46.00	4–1–71	NYSE	O-C
Martin-Marietta	2.73	16.48	11–1–68	NYSE	ASE
McCrory Corporation	1	20.00	3–15–76	NYSE	ASE
Textron Inc.	1	25.00[b]	5–1–84	NYSE	ASE
Trans World Airlines, Inc.	2.7	20.00[c]	12–1–73	NYSE	O-C
Tri-Continental Corporation...	1.27	17.76	Perpetual	NYSE	ASE
Webb (Del E.) Corporation..	1	6.25	12–1–75	O-C	O-C

[a] NYSE—New York Stock Exchange; ASE—American Stock Exchange; O-C—Over the Counter.
[b] Subscription price raised to $30 on 5/2/64.
[c] Subscription price raised to $22 on 6/2/65.

Unless otherwise provided, if the company issuing the securities with warrants attached is merged into another company and thus loses its identity, the life of the warrants would terminate. The same would result from dissolution of the company.

In some instances no limitation is put on the life of warrants. In other words they are perpetual, unless, of course, their life is terminated by redemption of the security to which they are attached, or the company is merged into another one, or is dissolved.

Antidilution Provisions

The warrant calls for the purchase of stock at a definite price per share, whatever that share may turn out to be at the time it is exercised. Such things as stock dividends and stock split-ups will dilute the value of the privilege in the same manner as was discussed in connection with convertible issues. In recent years the contract has usually provided that the purchase price of the stock with the warrant shall be reduced proportionately in event of a stock dividend or stock split-up.

Protection against other things, such as the issuance of stock with a claim senior to that which can be purchased by the holder of the warrant, the issuance of the stock to others at a price lower than the subscription price to the warrant holder, etc., may also be provided in the contract.

Warrants Compared With Convertible Privilege

Warrants and the conversion privilege are attached to the securities for the same reason—to increase the marketability of the particular issue.

They both are usually attached to a security giving the holder the right to acquire another security junior to it. In most instances the security to be acquired will have to advance in price before it would be profitable for the holder to exercise the privilege. The exercise of both privileges tends to dilute the equity of the existing common stockholders. In other respects the privileges differ. We will assume the privilege is attached to a bond giving the holder the right to acquire common stock.

When the bondholder converts, the particular bonded indebtedness is extinguished and its place is taken by common stock. Thus, the fixed interest charge and the obligation to pay the principal of the bonds are eliminated. No new money is brought into the corporation. In contrast to this, when the bondholder exercises the warrant, he retains his bonds and buys common stock. Thus, the company's obligation to pay interest and principal remains, and its capitalization is increased by the common stock. The purchase of the stock brings new money into the corporation.

If the holder of the convertible bond wants to profit on the privilege he must either sell the bond and thus cease to hold any securities in the company, or he must convert it into stock and cease to be a bondholder. The warrant holder, as stated above, retains his bonds upon exercise of the warrant. Also, if the warrant is detachable, he may profit by selling the warrant alone and retaining his bonds.

The warrant holder will exercise the privilege only when the company is prospering and the price of its stock is high. This may be the very time when the company is not in need of additional funds, but it has no control over the exercise of that privilege. Furthermore, when a company does need funds for expansion, etc., it needs a considerable amount of money at one time. Warrants may be exercised in small amounts over a relatively long period of time.

From what has been said above it is obvious that some bondholders would prefer the warrants over the conversion privilege. The only disadvantage of the warrant is that its exercise calls for the outlay of additional cash. But if the holder does not want to buy the stock, he can profit on the warrant by selling it in the market.

Price of Detachable Warrants

Since the warrant adds value to the security to which it is attached, even though the stock of the company is not selling sufficiently high to make the exercise of the warrant profitable, it is obvious that the market puts a value on the warrant even before it has any exercisable value. The fact that it is being sold detached may give it more value than if it were still attached to the security.

One warrant ordinarily gives a person the right to acquire one share of stock. This is the way it is usually quoted in the market. If a person owns a bond which entitles him to buy 10 shares of stock there would be attached to his bond one certificate evidencing 10 warrants. Antidilution clauses, however, may result in the warrant's being good for an uneven number of shares.

A detached warrant which gives the holder the right to buy one share of stock at $20 a share would have no exercisable value if the stock was then selling at, for example, only $10 a share in the market. But actually the warrant may be selling in the market for $1 or $2. The stock may be advancing in price and speculators see the possibility that it may go above $20 in the near future, so they will bid up the price of the warrants in order to have a call on the stock if it should advance sufficiently in price. An example of this is the Tri-Continental Corporation warrants which carry the right to purchase 1.27 shares of the stock of the company at $17.76 a share.[2] In 1953 when the stock was selling on the New York Stock Exchange for only $16, the warrants were being sold on the American Stock Exchange for $4. In 1962, when the stock was selling at 39⅛, the warrants were quoted at 29½.

Part of the explanation of the above is that it takes less money to speculate indirectly in the stock through the use of the warrant than to buy the stock directly. This can be illustrated by the following hypothetical example. Let us assume that a company has detached warrants outstanding which enable the holder thereof to buy company's stock at $48 a share. We will assume that the stock is selling for $50 a share in the market. A warrant would obviously have a theoretical value of $2. Actually the warrant would sell for more than this for reasons stated above. But we will assume for illustrative purposes that it is selling for only $2. Now if the stock price should increase to $52, a rise of only 4 per cent, the price of the warrant would increase by at least $2 (actually it would probably increase more than this amount). This would be an increase of 100 per cent. So with a given amount of money a person could make a much greater profit by buying the warrant than by purchasing the stock.

Use as Hedge in Short Sale

Warrants can be used as a hedge in connection with a short sale of stock in a manner similar to convertible bonds.

Hybrid Form

In some instances corporations have issued bonds which carried warrants for the purchase of stock and the contract provided that the face value of the bonds *can* be used in whole or in part instead of cash to purchase the stock. Where all of the bond is used to pay for the stock it is really a convertible bond regardless of what it may be called.

[2] The odd figures are a result of the operation of an antidilution clause.

Other Uses of Warrants

The only kind of warrants mentioned above are those which are attached to a particular issue of securities at the time it is sold. This was the first use of warrants and still continues to be an important one. But in recent years there have developed a number of other uses of stock purchase warrants. These will be briefly discussed below.

Reorganizations. The use of warrants in reorganizations did not begin until about 1920. In the past when a company failed in many instances the stock interest was "wiped out" and the stockholders were not made a part of the reorganized company, unless they paid an assessment, which is another way of saying they were asked to buy new stock in the company. The practice then developed of giving these shareholders, who had gone through the financial troubles of the company, but who had little or no equity left, warrants entitling them to buy stock of the reorganized company at a price higher than its value at the time the company emerged from the reorganization.

In some instances when a corporation goes through a drastic financial readjustment, in order to sell a new issue of stock, it will be necessary to attach warrants to these shares giving the stockholders the right to buy additional stock of the same class in the future at stepped-up prices. As an inducement to get investment bankers to handle the issue, they also may be given warrants in addition to their commissions. These are more commonly called "options."

Refunding Operations. The success of a refunding issue depends upon a fairly large percentage of the bondholders' accepting the new issue. As an inducement to get the bondholders to accept the new bonds, it may be necessary to attach stock purchase warrants to the bonds giving the bondholders the right to buy the stock of the company at prices usually higher than existing at the time the bonds are sold. This, of course, is similar to the use of warrants to aid in the sale of new securities.

STOCK OPTIONS

We have used the term *warrant* to apply to the contract which is attached (although it may be detachable) to a new issue of securities giving the holder thereof the right to buy another class of security. We will use the term *stock option* to apply to a contract for the purchase of stock which is *not attached* to any issue of securities, although it may be used in connection with the sale of an issue of securities.[3] These options

[3] The term *stock option* is also used to apply to other types of contracts used in stock market operations. These are *puts, calls, spreads,* and *straddles,* which will not be taken up in this book, but which the reader can find discussed in books dealing with the stock market.

are usually not transferable. Some writers refer to these contracts also as "warrants," but in practice they are usually called "options."

The term *warrant* is sometimes used to apply to the piece of paper which evidences the right to acquire stock. Thus, it may be said that warrants are issued giving the holder the "option" to acquire the stock. When *stock rights* are issued under a privileged subscription, which will be discussed in Chapter 14, the contract evidencing the right may also be called a "warrant." When stock dividends are paid or stock of another class or another company is exchanged for a particular stock, a person may be entitled to a fractional share or a number of shares plus a fractional share. The company may issue "warrants" evidencing these fractional shares. We will now briefly discuss the various uses of stock options.

Given to Investment Bankers

Options are sometimes given to investment bankers as part of their compensation for selling a new issue of securities for a corporation. The options call for the purchase of common stock usually at a price higher than the selling price of the stock at the time they are given. They are usually not transferable.

Where the options permit the purchase of a substantial amount of stock, or more stock than the company has outstanding, control of the company could easily be acquired by the bankers, if they did not already have control. The probable dilution in the surplus and the earnings per share from the exercise of the options should be given serious consideration by any prospective purchaser of the stock under these circumstances. There has been a relative decline in the amount of options given to bankers.

Given to Corporate Promoters

In addition to being given stock in a new corporation, promoters are sometimes given options to purchase additional stock in the future at prices higher than the original offering price of the stock. As is true with options issued to other parties, they do not cost the company anything, and if the company proves to be successful they furnish a means for the promoter to receive additional compensation for his work.

Courts have upheld the giving of options to promoters, provided the conditions in connection with their use are fair and reasonable. In the past in many instances the number of options outstanding and their terms were not made public. Companies that must register their securities under the Securities Act of 1933 are now required to state in their registration statement and prospectus any options outstanding or to be created in connection with the particular security issue, and the specific terms of the options. The Act also requires that the names and addresses of all persons who are to receive more than 10 per cent of the options be filed.

Given to Corporate Officials

There has been a tremendous increase in recent years in the number of corporations which have given options to their leading officers. The reasons for giving them options usually fall under one of the following heads:

1. To induce a particular person to accept a position
2. To help retain an executive who is already employed by the company
3. To augment the other compensation received by an executive
4. To augment the pension plan for executives
5. To spur the executives on to make larger profits for the corporation

Although there are many able businessmen in the United States, those capable of successfully running our leading corporate giants are limited. This often results in considerable competition among companies for the services of these top-flight executives. Salaries, bonuses, and commissions constitute ways of obtaining or retaining the services of an expert. But considering the attitude of stockholders, labor unions, customers, and the general public, there seems to be some limit on the amount that can be paid to executives in the form of salaries, bonuses, and commissions. Furthermore, income taxes take the major part of such compensation.

Options to purchase the company's stock have become rather common as a means of giving greater compensation to executives, without necessarily impairing the company's public relations. Publicity is not given to the issuance of options in the same way as in the case of salaries. Furthermore, it does not cost the company anything, at the time, to issue options for the purchase of the company's stock at the same price or at a higher price than the stock is selling at the time the option is issued.

In some instances both the company and the executive look upon options as an addition to the regular pension plan operated by the company. The stock may not rise in price sufficiently high to make it profitable to exercise the options until the executive has retired or is about to retire. The stock so acquired may pay dividends of an appreciable amount during the remaining lifetime of the retired executive. Or, he could take a profit on the sale of the stock and invest the money in some other way.

It is questionable whether a corporate executive would work harder if he were to receive more compensation. He is supposed to be putting forth his best efforts regardless of the amount of his salary. But having options to purchase the company's stock at what may prove to be relatively low prices in the future will certainly not cause him to work less.

In most instances perhaps the interests of the corporation and those of the stockholders are one and the same. But sometimes the corporate officials will take advantage of their position and take actions which might benefit them in the future even if they are not in the best interests of the stockholders. For example, the directors may retain profits in the business which really should be distributed to the shareholders in the form of dividends. This should result in an increase in the book value and market value of the stock. If the officials hold a substantial amount of stock in the company and have options to buy more stock in the future at prices higher than those existing at the time the options are given, they would tend to benefit from this action.

Tax Status of "Restricted" Stock Option

The income tax status of stock options varies according to the terms and conditions of their issuance. The most favorable (from the standpoint of the option holder) tax treatment is accorded the *restricted* stock option. To qualify as a restricted option, and get the best tax treatment, it must meet the following requirements: [4]

1. The option must be granted for reasons connected with the person's employment
2. The option price of the stock must not be less than 95 per cent of the market price of the stock at the time the option is granted
3. The stock must be held for at least six months after it is purchased
4. The stock cannot be sold within two years from the date of the option
5. The option can be exercised only while the optionee is still employed by the granting corporation, its parent or subsidiary, or within three months after leaving the company
6. The option must be exercised within a period of 10 years from the time it is granted
7. The option is non-transferable, except at death [5]

With the restricted option no income tax is paid at the time the option is granted or at the time the stock is purchased. When the stock is sold, the difference between what is paid for it and the price obtained from its sale is reported as a capital gain.[6] The maximum tax on a long-term capital gain is 25 per cent. This compares with a tax of 91 per cent that would be paid on ordinary income if the executive had an income

---

[4] Internal Revenue Code, Section 130A (d) (1).

[5] A further requirement is that the employee cannot own more than 10 per cent of the total combined voting power of all classes of stock. If he owns more than this, the option price of the stock must be at least 110 per cent of the market price of the stock at the time the option is granted. The 110 per cent options must be exercised within five years from their issue date.

[6] If the option meets the requirements of a restricted stock option stated above, but the option price is at least 85 per cent but less than 95 per cent of the fair market value of the stock when the option is granted, then the holder at the time of sale of the stock will be taxed at ordinary income rates in an amount equal to the lesser of the two following differences: (1) the fair market value of the stock at time of grant of the option less the option price, and (2) the fair market value of the stock at the date of its disposition, or at the holder's death, less the option price.

in excess of $200,000. If a joint return is filed, the tax on the top part of ordinary income of a person who has a total income in excess of $200,000 would be 89, 90, or 91 per cent, depending upon the size of the income. It is thus apparent that a much greater part of the income derived from the sale of stock purchased by the exercise of a restricted stock option may be retained by the executive than if the same amount were paid in salary.

Problems in Connection With Warrants and Options

The statutes of some of the states specifically permit the issuance of warrants and options under the conditions set forth in the law. In some states corporations have sometimes issued them without any specific authorization in the laws.

Before issuing these privileges perhaps the corporation should have sufficient authorized, but unissued, stock on hand to enable it to meet the demands of the holders of the privileges. In the meantime, this ties up that amount of authorized stock. If the corporation has no authorized stock to meet the demands of the holders of the warrants or options, the shareholders cannot be forced to authorize it. In this event the holders of the privileges could not demand specific performance of the contract, but they would have a right in damages against the company for the difference between the option price of the stock and its market value.

In the case of par value stock, if the warrant or option gives the holder the right to buy the stock at a price below its par value, it would appear that he could be held liable in event of insolvency of the company for the difference between what he paid and the par value of the stock, unless it was treasury stock that was sold. Frequently it is treasury stock. Mergers, consolidations, reorganizations, recapitalizations, and the issuance of additional securities might complicate the legal rights of holders of the privileges.

Even though the requisite vote of the shareholders (or their proxies) has been obtained to grant stock options to executive officers, minority shareholders' suits have sometimes been troublesome to some companies. The management should not take any action which would result in harm to the corporation or to its shareholders. But where the stock options are granted as a type of compensation, and where the executive might remain with the company for a reasonable length of time before he can profit from the option, the company and its shareholders may actually benefit from their use. In such instances minority shareholders have no right of action against the corporation or the executives.

Unless the statutes provide otherwise, where the pre-emptive right is present, shareholders would have to waive their right to the unissued stock before it could be sold to the officers under stock options.

QUESTIONS

1. List the various reasons why convertible bonds are issued.
2. Why has the American Telephone and Telegraph Co. made frequent use of the convertible bond since the end of World War II rather than stock issues?
3. Explain what is meant by the statement that the buyer of convertible bonds pays more for the bond or stock into which it is convertible than the real worth of the bond or stock.
4. Explain the effects on the issuer and its shareholders of conversion of bonds into stock.
5. What is meant by the conversion ratio?
6. Assume that a bond which is convertible into stock at $80 a share is selling in the market for 90. (a) How many shares of stock would you get by converting one $1,000 bond? (b) What is the "break-even" price of the stock? (c) If the stock advanced in price to $100, what would be the "break-even" price of the bond? (d) If the bond was selling in the market at 120, what would be the probable market price of the stock?
7. Indicate how accrued interest and dividends complicate the computation of "break-even" prices in the convertible bond and stock.
8. Can the holder of a convertible bond do anything about the company's diluting the value of a share of stock through stock dividends and stock splits? Explain.
9. Explain how convertible bonds might be used as a hedge in connection with short selling.
10. Indicate in general whether you would recommend the purchase of convertible bonds and state your reasons.
11. Indicate the relative advantages both to the issuing company and to the investor of bonds convertible into stock, and bonds which have warrants attached for the purchase of the stock.
12. Indicate the relative advantages of non-detachable and detachable warrants from the viewpoint of both the issuing corporation and the investor.
13. Is the warrant holder given any protection against the dilution in the value of the shares of stock caused by stock dividends or splits? Explain.
14. Indicate the circumstances under which warrants might be used as a hedge in connection with short selling.
15. Indicate the various circumstances under which, or reasons why, warrants are issued.
16. Why might a warrant have a market value even though the stock can be purchased in the market at a lower price than through the exercise of the warrant?
17. Why might a speculator prefer trading in warrants rather than the stock which can be purchased through the exercise of the warrants?
18. Are warrants ordinarily attached to the better-grade investment securities?
19. Indicate the distinction made in the text between warrants and options. Is this always observed in practice? Explain.
20. Indicate why corporate executives might prefer stock options over a salary increase.

PROBLEMS

1. Mr. Leland purchased twelve 6-per-cent debenture bonds of the New Era Co. on March 16, 19x1, at 98. These bonds had a face value of $1,000 per bond and were convertible into common stock of the company at any time between January 1, 19x4, and December 31, 19x9, at $125 per share. At the time the bonds were purchased the stock of the company was selling in the market for $108 per share. The fluctuations in the price of the stock follow:

Year	High	Low	Year	High	Low
19x1	110	53	19x6	100	70
19x2	61	32	19x7	137½	80
19x3	38	16	19x8	200	187½
19x4	49	30	19x9	150	125
19x5	60	50	19x0	150	137½

(a) How many shares of stock would Mr. Leland get if he converted his 12 bonds? (b) If the market price of the bonds remained at the sale price, would it have been profitable for Mr. Leland to convert his bonds in 19x4? Why or why not?

(c) If the price of the bonds remained at the sale price, how high would the stock have to get in order for him to break even on the conversion? Express this by the use of a formula in which:

a = price of the bonds (expressed in per cent of face value)
b = conversion price
x = break-even price

(d) What do you think should have been the theoretical high and low prices of the bonds in the following years: 19x7; 19x8; 19x9? (e) Relative to their 19x1 and 19x8 prices, what do you think should have been the market price of the bonds in 19x0?

2. Look up the following convertible bonds: Lockheed 3¾s, 1980, and Dow Chemical 3s, 1982 (both listed on the New York Stock Exchange), and ascertain the following for each bond: (a) Terms of conversion. (b) Number of shares into which one bond is convertible, or conversion price of the common stock. (c) Market prices of the bonds and the stock into which the bond is convertible as of the same day this week. (d) Considering the conversion price of the stock and the market price of the bonds and stock, how much, if any, must the stock advance in price in order that a bondholder would break even by converting?

3. The Modern Aircraft Corp. was formed in 19x6 with an authorized capitalization of 2,000,000 shares of no-par common stock, and $20,000,000 of preferred stock with a par value of $100 per share. The preferred was 7 per cent non-participating and non-voting. At the time of organization, 1,000,000 shares of the common stock were sold at $40 per share. In the Autumn of 19x8 the entire $20,000,000 in preferred stock was sold at par, and each share carried with it a warrant entitling the holder to purchase one share of common stock at $50. At the time the preferred was marketed the common was selling at $43 per share.

In the early part of April, 19x9, the market price of the common stock had gone up to $80. The company's surplus account had increased to $20,000,000.

Orders sufficient to keep the plants operating three shifts a day for the next three years were on the books.

(a) Why do you think these warrants were issued by the company? (b) If the warrants were non-detachable, at what price do you think the preferred should be selling in April, 19x9? (c) If the warrants were detachable, how much would you pay for a warrant in April, 19x9? (d) Would the warrants sell for more or less than their "theoretical" value? Why? (e) Do you think that the market price of the warrant in April, 19x9 would depend upon the number of warrants outstanding? Explain. (f) From the standpoint of the issuing company, do you think the warrants should be detachable or non-detachable? Why? (g) As a director of the company, would you vote for the issuance of the warrants as stated above or for an alternative proposal to make the preferred stock convertible? Give your reasons. (h) Does the preferred stockholder who exercises his warrants and buys the common stock at $50 when it is selling in the market for $80 have any liability on the common stock? Explain. Would your answer be the same if the common had a par value of $100 per share? (i) Do you think the issuance of these warrants was fair to the old common stockholders? Why or why not?

4. The following relate to the warrants issued by the Allegheny Corp., which are traded on the American Stock Exchange:

(a) How many shares of stock may be purchased with one warrant? (b) At what price can the stock be obtained through the exercise of a warrant? (c) Look up the closing price of the warrants and the stock (the latter is listed on the New York Stock Exchange) of a particular day during the past week. How can you explain the reason for the market price of the warrants?

5. Mr. Ralph Rolls, who is in the 91 per cent tax bracket, has been offered a position with a competitor company, effective January 1, 19x1. In an attempt to retain his services, the corporation he is now working for has offered him a salary increase of $100,000 annually, or restricted options to purchase 1,600 shares of the company's stock at 95 per cent of the present market price. The stock is now selling for $50 a share. It is expected that the price of the stock will increase in price annually approximately $10 a share for at least the next four years. If Mr. Rolls decides to stay with the company, which of the alternatives would you advise him to accept? Explain fully. (Assume maximum capital gain tax rates to be 25 per cent.)

SELECTED READINGS

BARNES, LEO. *Your Investments.* Larchmont, N. Y.: American Research Council, published annually. Sections on convertibles and warrants.

BOGEN, JULES I. (ed.). *Financial Handbook,* 3d ed. New York: The Ronald Press Co., 1952. Sections 10 and 11.

DORIS, LILLIAN (ed.). *Business Finance Handbook.* Englewood Cliffs, N. J.: Prentice-Hall, Inc., 1953. Chapters 17 and 18.

FRIED, SIDNEY. *The Speculative Merits of Common Stock Warrants.* New York: R. H. M. Associates, Latest ed.

PILCHER, C. JAMES. *Raising Capital With Convertible Securities.* Ann Arbor: Bureau of Business Research, University of Michigan, 1955.

SKELLY, WILLIAM S. *Convertible Bonds—A Study of Their Suitability for Commercial Bank Bond Portfolios.* New York: Salomon Bros. & Hutzler, 1959.

WARE, THOMAS M. "The Stock Option is Vital to Our Economy's Success," *The Commercial and Financial Chronicle,* August 3, 1961, pp. 491 ff.

III

FINANCING THROUGH SECURITIES

10

Promoting and Financing
a New Business

The term *promotion* has many meanings. Its most common use in business is probably in connection with sales promotion. In addition, it refers to the advancement of an individual to a higher position. In this chapter, the term will be used in connection with the promotion of a business opportunity. In this sense, the term *promotion* refers to the discovery or conception of a business opportunity and the marshaling together of men, money, and any required materials and machines for the purpose of exploiting the idea. The more widely discussed promotions are those which involve the development of a business opportunity into the creation of a new company. However, promotions also result in material changes in existing companies.

The heart of promotion is not the creation of a new company; instead, it is the business opportunity which is promoted. Business opportunity is basically some form of an idea. The types of ideas most commonly promoted are new products or services, new production techniques, new sales methods or channels of distribution, and new financing techniques. The idea of selling an existing product through new channels of distribution is a business opportunity which requires promotion just as much as the invention of some new product.

The development of business opportunity ideas has undergone radical change in the past century. Before World War I, most new products were discovered by individuals working under their own auspices. It was up to the individual to promote his discovery or to find someone else to help him promote it. New concepts of service or new business techniques were generally developed by individuals and required a selling job to existing business organizations or the development of new business organizations to institute the concepts.

Today, the great majority of new business opportunities are discovered or created by individuals working for existing business organizations. Modern American business has recognized the importance of development and promotion of new business opportunities and is spending significant sums of money each year to help accomplish this aim. Thus, the majority of our really important discoveries are made by groups of individuals working under sponsorship of some organization. The organization usually takes the idea developed and integrates it into that organization's present operation. No promotion by outsiders is needed for the implementation of new business ideas developed in this manner. While the idea created sometimes is transferred or sold to another business for implementation or sometimes must be "sold" to others within the organization, there is not the requirement for a "promoter."

While the majority of new business opportunities today are developed internally, a sufficient number are created by independent elements so that the problem of promotion and creation of new business units is still an important one. Every new company is a promotion because each new company has some new idea with which it is involved. Perhaps the "new" idea is nothing more than a new location for a grocery store or the idea that new management will do a better job than managements of similar existing companies. Nonetheless, these are promotions. The remainder of the discussion of this chapter is concerned basically with the promotion of a new company rather than with the promotion of a business opportunity in an existing one. However, stages in promotion of ideas would be the same regardless of whether a new company is created. We are including major changes in existing business units within the categories of new companies.

Promotion of a Company in a New Field

Whenever a new product or service is discovered or created, a company may be formed in this new field in order to exploit it and to gain the profits which might be forthcoming. Promotions of this type in recent years would include transistor radios, complete home maintenance services, and espresso shops.

As would be expected, promotions of this type are hazardous undertakings. The market for the product or service is unknown, and it is extremely difficult to predict costs. Moreover, the best price at which to sell the product is not known. In many instances expensive advertising or selling forces may have to be utilized in order to build up a market for the product or service.

When a new product is to be exploited it is sometimes advisable to turn over the manufacturing operations to other companies that have the equipment and personnel necessary to make the product; also the selling may be done by established agencies. Later, after the product has become established, the new company might consider taking over the manufacturing and selling operations.

Promotion of a Company in an Established Field

This is perhaps the most frequent type of promotion. Examples of this kind of promotion would range from the establishment of a new corner grocery store, to the formation of a new sales finance company such as Ford Credit Corporation.

Despite the fact that the particular industry is established, there is considerable hazard in starting a new company in competition with those which have been established for some time. Pitfalls into which a new company may fall have probably already been encountered and avoided by the established concern, or the management has the necessary experience to avoid falling into similar ones in the future. The older companies will have the experience in management, manufacturing, selling, and financing which may enable them to do better than the new company. A strong financial condition and a large research staff may be further advantages of the established company.

With a system of private enterprise such as exists in the United States, the probability is that the various established industries have sufficient companies operating within their fields to supply the existing demand for their product or services. As the demand increases, more products can be sold, but most existing companies can expand their production to take care of the increased demand. It is easier for the established companies to expand than for new companies to enter the field.

Promotion of a Combination of Two or More Existing Companies

Promotions of this kind have the advantage of a past record of earnings of the constituent companies. This enables the promoter to determine with some degree of accuracy the probable future earnings of the combination. Also, excellent management can be provided for the combination from the best executives of the various companies entering the combination. Furthermore, the separate companies have established and trained labor forces. The goodwill that has been built up by the constituent companies can carry over to the new combination.

Effecting combinations of existing concerns is not an easy task. Many companies hate to give up their independence. The managements have to be sold on the idea, and they in turn must sell the stockholders on the combination. Many legal problems arise which must be solved. We will discuss combinations at some length in Chapter 28.

Promotion of Other Major Changes

In addition to mergers or combinations, other major changes take place in existing enterprises which result in a substantial change in the enterprise. This would include a complete change of product line of a company. It would involve change in ownership of the company by selling all of the shares of a privately owned business to the public. A complete change in management brought about by outside influences would be considered a promotion. Bringing about a complete change in an existing business involves most of the same problems as creating a new business. Decisions have to be made on what portions of the existing business will be retained and what portions will be dispensed with. It is difficult to determine in advance the results which a material change in the business will bring in the future.

THE PROMOTER

The person who brings together the men, money, materials, and machines necessary for the planned organization is called the *promoter*. The promoter performs a useful service to society when he brings into existence a needed product or service, or an improvement in some existing product or service, or an improvement in business techniques which would allow existing companies to make more profits or to lower prices.

We are sometimes inclined to use the term *promoter* for somebody who is prowling around trying to swindle the public out of money. There are such people, but in most cases the promoters of our business enterprises accomplish a considerable amount of good. We would be without the use of much of our wealth of goods and services today if it were not for the promoter. Somebody has to take the initiative. Many of our industries which supply us with what we today consider essentials were looked upon as rank speculations at the time they were started.

The promoter must have the imagination to see the need for the product or service in the future, and the courage to see the promotion through to completion when others are perhaps skeptical as to the success of the undertaking. He must have a practical turn of mind and foresee the profitableness of the venture. Another requisite of a successful promoter is an impressive personality. He must be a successful salesman, radiating success, as it will be necessary for him to sell and resell his idea to other people. A promoter must cooperate and be able to give and take.

He must also be an organizer. It is not common to find selling and organizing ability in the same person, but a promoter must possess both these qualities. The successful formation of a new company calls for proper organization of the men, money, and property into a workable unit. This is not an easy task.

Another factor of considerable aid in the promotion of a new company is money. Although the bulk of the funds for the formation of a company may finally come from other sources, it is often necessary for the promoter to have sufficient money of his own to finance all the preliminary investigations which are necessary before he can enlist the financial help of other people.

Types of Promoters

The kind of people with the necessary qualifications for successful promoters could come from any walk of life, but especially in recent years they generally belong to certain categories. Following are the various types of promoters responsible for new business undertakings.

1. *Professional promoters.* Many businesses, particularly large combinations which were formed during the latter part of the last century, were promoted by what may be called *professional promoters*. The professional promoter does not stay with the organization permanently. He effects the organization, takes his stock and such other compensation as he can obtain, and leaves to seek new fields to conquer. In some instances he aids in securing finances for the organization. The professional promoter for business enterprises is almost a thing of the past. Perhaps one of the best examples existing today is the promoter of sporting events. There are some firms or groups of people who specialize in promotions today, but relatively few individuals.

2. *Owners.* The great bulk of our businesses, particularly the smaller concerns, were started by the person who owns them or by his ancestors. One has only to look at the small retail stores, service establishments, and small manufacturing plants to realize this. Perhaps most people have the idea that they would like to become independent and "to go into business for themselves." And many of them attempt this one or more times before they die. But it is frequently discovered that starting and operating a business is not as easy as was visualized, and that independence is not commonly attained. Many of these businesses fall by the wayside shortly after they have been promoted.

3. *Business executives.* Somewhat similar to the owner promoter is the *business executive promoter*. A separate classification is needed here, however, because the executive can be a salaried employee and not an owner, or he may own only a small amount of the stock of the company

for which he is working. A person may conceive the idea of starting his own company after gaining experience from working for someone else for a number of years. Promotions of this kind are often very successful.

4. *Engineers, consultants, and lawyers.* Engineers or consultants often promote the formation of companies or combinations. Some of these got their start by being called in for consultation or investigation work by other promoters and investment bankers. In some instances they enter the field with experience gained from conducting a business management service.

There is a considerable amount of legal work connected with the promotion of a new company or the combination of two or more companies. Usually a *lawyer* must be consulted at one or more stages of the promotion. In many instances, he is busy with all stages of the promotion. This does not necessarily qualify him as a promoter, but in many instances he is prominent enough in the work to so classify him.

5. *Inventors.* We owe a considerable amount of credit to the inventors who thought up or perfected the necessities and luxuries of life, which we enjoy today. Certainly, an inventor is an important person in the promotion of a company to manufacture his product. But usually genius and good business judgment do not go hand in hand. It is also well known that most inventors, particularly at the time of their first inventions, do not have the necessary finances to produce and commercialize their product. In some cases a promoter appropriates the idea of the inventor for his own personal advantage, and in other cases, the inventor may work with a promoter. Thus the inventor is usually not the promoter of his own idea.

6. *Investment bankers.* In the promotion of large companies or combinations it is customary to contact investment bankers to have them take over the sale of the securities necessary to provide the needed money. When they merely handle the financing, they are not acting as promoters. But some investment bankers initiate and carry through large combinations of existing companies; thus they become true promoters.

7. *Venture capital firms.* In very recent years there have been several venture capital organizations formed. These include the Enterprise Development Corp., J. H. Whitney & Co., and Rockefeller Brothers, Inc. These firms do not directly initiate a project. People with ideas and plans for a new company approach them to secure aid. If after a thorough investigation the project appears practical, the firm will advance the money and take stock in the new company. A well-known and successful company, the Minute Maid Corp., was financed by J. H. Whitney & Co. These firms are not really promoters, but they finance the new company. They play an important part in promotion.

Legal Position of the Promoter

The promoter of a new business is in a peculiar legal position relative to the business during the period of the promotion. Strictly speaking, he is not an *agent* for the proposed corporation since the latter is not yet in existence. Thus, he is not assured that the corporation, once it comes into existence, will act as he has planned, and he cannot bind the corporation in advance.

Since the proposed corporation is in no position to protect itself, the law requires the promoter to exercise the degree of care and prudence exacted from a *trustee,* or *fiduciary.* He is thus required to exercise the utmost good faith toward the corporation which he is promoting. The fiduciary relationship exists from the time the promotion is begun, and lasts until it is completed. Thus it would apply from the time the promoter conceived the idea of the promotion until the corporation's management is in the hands of an independent board of directors.

Liability of Promoter

The promoter remains liable on all pre-incorporation contracts until the corporation accepts or ratifies them. He may be liable even after the corporation has accepted the contract. If the promoter represented himself as a promoter at the time of making the contract, after the corporation is formed and accepts the contract, the promoter is relieved of any liability. But if on the other hand the second party to the contract thought that he was dealing with the promoter in his own personal capacity, then the promoter could still be held liable on the contract after the corporation had agreed with the promoter to accept the contract. Naturally if the second party wants to release the promoter and look solely to the corporation, he would no longer be liable.

Promoters may also be held liable for violations of the securities laws (called "blue-sky" laws) which are found in most of the states. They may also be liable under the Securities Act of 1933 for misstatements of facts or omissions to state material facts in a registration statement signed by them. Promoters are liable for any secret profits made by them in connection with the promotion of a company.

Compensation of the Promoter

Only a minority of promotion efforts for new corporations result in the actual establishment of a business. In those cases in which the proposed corporation is not formed, the promoter and his financial backers probably lose all the money that has been expended in connection with the promotion. Thus, promotion involves a high degree of financial risk.

Because of this, the amounts expended before the new business is brought into existence are relatively small and most outlays for the new business will be made after it comes into existence. Nonetheless, the investment by the promoter may still be a substantial portion of *his* total assets. In addition, he invests a great deal of his time which could have been devoted to other activities. Because of the very high risk involved in promotions, the potential gain from promotions must also be high in order to have people perform this important function in our society.

Normally, the only compensation to the promoter comes in those situations where the new business is organized and operates. In these cases, the resulting corporation is not bound by anything which is not contained in the statutes or in the charter of the company.

The corporation, therefore, from a legal standpoint, does not have to pay the promoter anything for his services. As a practical matter, however, it will usually agree to pay him because it recognizes the value of his services, or because this is necessary in order to get the promoter to turn over his contracts, etc., to the corporation, or because the promoter is in control of the board of directors.

Due to the fiduciary nature of the promoter's position, he is not legally entitled to a *secret* profit. In order for a promoter's profit to be legal therefore, he must disclose the amount of the profit to all the original subscribers to the stock, or if the organization of the corporation is complete, it must be disclosed to an independent board of directors. To get the profit then, it will of course be necessary for it to be approved.

If the promoter makes a secret profit and is later found out, the corporation may maintain one of the following actions against him:

1. Rescind the contract, return the property to the promoter, and receive back whatever was paid for the property
2. Retain the property and sue the promoter for the secret profit, or sue him for damages

The promoter often takes, or is forced to take, stock in the new company as part or all of his personal compensation. On the other hand, he is generally reimbursed for the money outlays he made during the period of the promotion. Because of the extreme subjectivity in judging the value of the promotion, it is difficult to determine a reasonable dollar amount of compensation for the promoter. Only the future of the company and its continued existence and profits determine the real value of the promotion. Because of this, stock in the company becomes an ideal method for reimbursement of the promoter. If the company is successful, the stock will rise in value and the promoter will receive compensation. On the other hand, if the company is unsuccessful the promoter's stock will be worthless and he will not be compensated for performing a service which turns out to be valueless to society.

STAGES IN PROMOTION

While each new business opportunity presents different problems in promotion, there are certain similarities in all promotions which can be discussed in general terms. For convenience, we have divided the process of promotion into four stages. They are discovery of the idea, investigation of the proposed project, planning and obtaining financing, and assembly of the factors of production.

Discovery of the Idea

There are various ways in which the idea for a promotion may originate. An inventor may suddenly hit upon a new idea or product, or a prospector may discover a deposit of ore, or a geologist may find a new pool of oil. Sometimes the research staff of a large organization may develop a new product or compound unexpectedly, or the invention may be the result of a well-planned and long worked-out process.

In most instances the conception of the idea is not so spectacular. A person or group of persons, while working for another company, may have given some thought over a long period to starting their own business. Or the gradual expansion of a flourishing business may give rise to the need for new organizations to carry on special phases of the production and selling of the product. The pressure of competition may often result in a combination which had been planned and worked out over a period of months or even years.

Investigation of the Proposed Project

A proper investigation is a most important step in promotion. While it would seem that investigation follows naturally after the conception of an idea, many promotions have failed because of inadequate or superficial investigation of the idea. While some people can be sold almost anything, relatively few moneyed people will put substantial sums into a new enterprise unless there is some assurance that it will be an economic success. Investment bankers are not willing to help finance a promotion unless they have some assurance of future profits for the firm. Ideas mean little from an economic standpoint unless they have a practical nature and can be profitably put into operation.

The investigation might involve two parts. First, the determination of the feasibility of the idea, and second, the determination of the potential profits which might be made from the business application of the idea.

The Feasibility of the Idea. A study of feasibility could be of three types. First, there is physical or engineering feasibility. That is, can the product or service really be produced? If the idea is a new machine, will it run after it is produced? Will this new machine in turn produce the desired results in its usage?

A second area of feasibility is a study of potential resources needed to convert the idea into a productive enterprise. Are the natural resources and materials which will be necessary available for production of this product? Can the necessary manpower with the appropriate skills be obtained? Is management available which can properly guide the new organization? Can funds be obtained to finance the project? This latter question is of such importance that it will be discussed separately. However, it should be recognized that many promotions fail because of lack of availability of resources other than finance.

A third area relating to feasibility is the study of demand for the potential product or service. Will people want this product after it is produced? Will the product or service perform some useful function in society? Many new products or services are brought into existence for which there is no real demand. As a result, these promotions fail. It seems to be human nature for people to be optimistic about the practical value of their own ideas. Their minds picture the favorable factors and possibilities but fail to see the inherent shortcomings. Investigation of feasibility would include consultation with engineers, lawyers, financiers, management, and other qualified groups of people.

Estimating Profit. Any new promotion must not only be feasible; it must offer potential profit to the future owners and the promoters. Part of the investigation of the idea includes determination of future profit potentials. A determination of profit begins with a determination of expected gross revenues. Not only must the feasibility of the demand for the product be determined, but one also must decide how many of the products can be sold and at what price. The volume of sales will often depend upon the selling price. The selling price, in turn, will depend upon operating costs or prices charged by competitors, and also on volume of sales.

In order to estimate future profits, estimated costs must be subtracted from estimated revenues. The costs of doing business can, as a rule, be estimated more accurately than the volume of sales. Costs, however, depend in part upon the number of products sold, so that for their estimate it is necessary to assume a definite volume of production.

In the case of a manufacturing company, the costs would be broken down into materials, direct labor, factory overhead, administrative, and selling costs and taxes. The materials cost can be determined accurately, but, of course, changes in the price of raw materials would affect it. The direct labor costs can also be determined in advance with a fair degree of accuracy. In estimating the overhead costs attention will be given to the following: whether the factory building is owned or rented; the rate of depreciation on the building and equipment; cost of light, heat, power, and supplies; amount of supervision needed, etc.

The administrative expenses are made up of the salaries of executives and office workers, supplies, postage, telephone and telegraph, depreciation on office equipment, rent, heat, and light, and other office expenses. Assuming a certain scale of operations, these administrative expenses can be estimated fairly accurately.

Selling costs are difficult to estimate for a new company. When the products are to be sold on strictly a commission basis, the unit selling costs of course are known after the rate of commission is determined. If the marketing is to be done by salaried salesmen the costs are definite, assuming a predetermined number of salesmen and a set salary scale. But to sell a given number of products may require more salesmen than originally contemplated.

It cannot be determined in advance how much advertising will have to be done in order to sell a given volume of goods. But commonly a definite amount of money is allocated for advertising, and a program is worked out for the spending of this amount. Thus the advertising expense at first can be a definite predetermined amount.

In making estimates it is common to overestimate sales and underestimate expenses. Many expenses arise which cannot be forecast in advance. After a schedule of expenses has been worked out, it is therefore advisable to add to this an amount for unpredicted items.

After the company gets started, adjustments will have to be made when it is apparent that the estimates have been wrong. In some instances this means the appropriation of additional funds for certain expenses, while in other cases an attempt may be made to cut down on certain expenses. Future budgets can be made in line with the operating results.

Planning and Obtaining Financing

Because we commonly use money to obtain other factors of production, the planning for and obtaining of financing often precede the assembly of the other factors of production. An important part of any promotion is the estimate of the amount of funds that will be needed to start the business. Sometimes the amount of money that is put into a business is actually just the amount that a particular person or group of persons have or are able to obtain.

Few businesses fail because of too much money. But a common cause of failure is insufficient capital. In many instances the lack of cash is merely a symptom of some other fault, but in some cases it is because too little capital was put into the business originally. Since it is common to overestimate income and underestimate expenses, proper allowance must be made for these factors or the funds raised to carry on operations may later prove to be insufficient.

It is easier to raise money before a company starts than after it has run into financial difficulties. If a company is raising several millions of dollars, it would probably be easy to secure several thousand additional at the same time. But if this was not obtained and later the company was hard pressed for cash, it might find it could not secure any additional funds. Thus, ample funds should be raised before the concern starts its operations. In determining the amount of funds that will be needed, consideration should be given to the following.

Promotional and Organizational Expenses. In many instances the promoter pays the promotional expenses out of his own pocket before there is any sale of securities. But he will expect to be reimbursed for these expenses. In other cases the money for much of the promotional expenses must be advanced by others. The amount that goes to pay the promoter personally can be determined, but the amount that will be necessary for all the expenses incurred by him is difficult to estimate. Included in these is the compensation that may go to lawyers, accountants, engineers, marketing research firms, etc. The promoter may need a considerable amount of money in order to buy options on property which the company proposes to acquire.

The organizational expenses can be calculated fairly accurately. An understanding can be had with the lawyer in regard to his fees. The amount of the organization tax can be calculated when it is known what the capitalization of the company will be. If the company is going to have subsidiaries operating in other states, or will register in those states and pay the foreign corporation tax, this will have to be figured out. All expenses connected with the sale of securities will have to be given due consideration.

Fixed Assets. The amount of money that will have to be raised to acquire the fixed assets varies greatly depending on the type of business, scale of operations, whether the plant or office space is to be owned or rented, etc. A company formed to build and operate a public utility or a large manufacturing plant will obviously need more money for fixed assets than would be needed by a selling organization. Offices and plant facilities may be rented rather than purchased. If the product involves manufacturing operations, perhaps this or part of it can be done by other manufacturers. In the case of merchandising companies the renting rather than purchasing of real estate will materially lessen the amount that must be raised for fixed assets.

Current Assets. Although most of the funds raised by a business are in the form of cash and, therefore, are current assets, when we speak of the current asset requirement we mean the amount that will be more or less permanently invested in current assets after the fixed assets have been acquired. A point often overlooked is that the initial working capital (current assets) needs will be greater than the regular working capital. After a concern has been in existence for some time the production, selling, and collecting cycle will have been completed, and the company will need only a fixed minimum amount in working capital. But this fixed minimum is really a more or less permanent investment in the business. The problems connected with financing the current assets are discussed in Chapter 20.

Sources of Funds. Once the estimate is made of the amount of funds needed by the business, the sources of these funds must be determined. The most common source of funds for existing businesses is retained earnings, but it is not available in new businesses. Therefore, new business must rely entirely on outside sources. The majority of the funds would come from sales of securities but some additional amounts may be obtained from short-term financing. Determination of the sources of the funds in the development of the capital structure is the subject of the next chapter.

Assembly of the Factors of Production

Normally, the promoter attempts to determine the availability of money before he acquires the other factors of production. He should, however, have determined the availability of these other factors before going so far as to actually acquire large amounts of money for his promotion. The various factors of production include labor, management, and capital. The formation and organization of the company normally take place as these factors are acquired.

While the obtaining of money was discussed above, other forms of capital must be acquired with part of the money obtained. The promoter must know what kinds of equipment will be necessary and how and where he can obtain this equipment. Availability of raw materials must be determined and suppliers of all types should be lined up to deal with the new enterprise. It should not be assumed that the required types of physical capital will always be available when desired by the promoter. Most promotions take place in boom periods of business. Boom times are often times of shortages of various factors of production.

Perhaps the most important element in any company is the management. The selection of the executives that are to manage the company may thus be the most important part of promotion. In the case of small enterprises the people who are doing the promoting may themselves constitute the management. In other instances, particularly for the larger concerns, it is necessary to select salaried executives who are not connected with the promotion of the company. Key executives of established companies in the same line of business are always a possibility. Added compensation, of course, usually has to be offered to induce them to come with the new company. This may be a higher salary, or they may be offered stock in the new company, or options to purchase the stock at a price which might later prove to be a bargain.

Good employees are another requirement for a successful business operation. If only unskilled labor is required, it is generally available in most markets in sufficient quantity. However, if skilled labor is also needed, the promoter should not assume that he can automatically obtain it. Often it is necessary to import skilled labor from other communities, or the new business may be located in a community where skilled labor is known to be available. In times of full employment, it may be very difficult to acquire good labor. Regardless of the quality of the labor obtained, a period of training in the new process or new policies of the business is almost always necessary. An initial period of lower than expected output normally results.

LEGAL ASPECTS OF PROMOTION

The legal position of the promoter was discussed above. There are a number of other legal aspects to promotion which should be considered here. Certain of the more important of these are discussed below.

Leases

In some instances the amount of money necessary to purchase real property which will be needed by the new company is enormous. When the use of the property may be acquired through a *lease*, this procedure might be advisable. Many merchandising concerns lease their real estate instead of purchasing it.

The company which gets the use of the property under a lease is called the *lessee*. The individual or company which owns the property is called the *lessor*. It is commonly provided that the lessee will pay all taxes and insurance on the property and keep it in proper repair.

The shortcoming of the lease is that the lessee may lose the use of the property at the termination of the lease. This is commonly overcome by the inclusion of the following provisions in the lease.

1. A long lease period so that for all practical purposes the company using the property is in about the same position as if it owned the property
2. An option to renew the lease for a specified period of years at a stipulated rental
3. An option on the part of the lessee to purchase the property at a specified price upon termination of the lease

Options

Frequently the promoter does not have the necessary amount of cash to purchase property, title to which is necessary for the proposed corporation. Or, if he does have the requisite amount of capital, he may not want to tie it up in the property until it is assured that the promotion and financing of the corporation will be completed.

A possible solution to this dilemma is for the promoter to secure *options* to purchase the property from the owners for a definite price. The property owner who sells the option is called the *optioner*, while the promoter, or purchaser of the option, is called the *optionee*. The option will give the optionee the exclusive right to buy the property for the period of time covered by the option. Where the option is taken by the promoter, rather than by the corporation, it will give him the right to assign the option. If the option is not exercised, the money paid for it will be lost. If, on the other hand, the property is purchased, the contract may provide that the amount paid for the option will be applied toward the purchase price of the property. It is to the interest of the promoter to see to it that the necessary amount of money be forthcoming to exercise the option.

The question sometimes arises as to the rights of optionees in relation to innocent third parties. Let us assume that *A* sells to *B* an option to purchase a particular piece of property. Before the expiration of the option and before it is exercised, the property is sold by *A* to *C*. What are the rights of *B*? The answer depends upon the knowledge possessed by *C*, whether the particular state accepts options for recording, and whether the option has actually been recorded. If *C* had knowledge of the existence of the option, then *B* may still obtain the property. If *C* had no knowledge of the option, and it was not recorded, *C* would have good title to the property. *B* then would have a right in damages against *A*. Generally speaking, the amount of the damages would be the difference between the option price and the existing market value of the property. If the state accepted options for recording, which is the usual case, and the option was recorded, then *C* is assumed to have had knowledge of the option, and *B* could obtain good title to the property.

When the optionee, or the person to whom he has assigned the option, has a legal right to the property, and the optioner refuses to sell the property, the optionee may sue in a court of equity for specific performance of the contract.

Patents

The promotion of some projects may be successful only if competitors are prevented from manufacturing and selling the particular product. Some inventions or products lend themselves to protection through the obtaining of a patent. A *patent* is a grant by the federal government of the exclusive right to the use of a certain process for a period of 17 years. Renewal of a patent is rare since it can be obtained only by special act of Congress.

It is impossible to secure a patent on an idea or a particular product. A patent can be obtained only on the device or process of carrying out the idea or making the product. Thus even though a patent is obtained on the process of making a new product, a competitor may make, and obtain a patent to make, the same product in another way. When securing a patent it is, therefore, important to patent not only the process which is desired, but all other novel processes which might be used to make the product.

Engineering talent is valuable in working out a particular process for manufacturing a product and in thinking up possible substitutes for this process which are also included in the patent. The services of skilled patent attorneys are commonly needed to determine whether the process is in conflict with other patents, and to describe the processes which are to be patented.

The obtaining of a patent on a particular process does not insure success of the promotion. The patented process must be one which lends itself to economical production of the product; the company must be properly organized, efficiently managed, and the product properly sold before its operations are successful. In many instances the promotion is of such a nature that no patents may be obtained.

Copyrights

Where the promotion depends upon the protection of a literary or artistic work such as a book, a song, a play, or a motion picture, a *copyright* may be obtained from the federal government for a small fee. Copyrights run for a period of 28 years and may be renewed for a like period. Somewhat similar to the obtaining of a patent or copyright is the registration of a trade name, trade mark, or slogan with the Patent Office.

Patents, copyrights, and registration of trade marks do not automatically give protection to the owner. If some other person or company infringes upon these rights, it is necessary for the owner to go to court in order to protect his property. This may involve a considerable amount of money even if it is proved that there was an infringement.

PURPOSE OF PROMOTION

Since the decision to promote a new business or a new idea is made by someone we have called the promoter, it is necessary to study the promoter's motives in discussing the subject of the purpose of promotion. However, since a promoter must deal with a large number of people in developing a successful promotion, the motives of these people must also be considered. The promoter himself normally undertakes the process because of his desire for personal profit. He is interested in receiving some kind of fee or compensation which will pay him for the time and money he has devoted to the promotion. Under certain circumstances, it is possible for the promoter to obtain personal profit even though the promotion itself may be unsuccessful.

Certainly the suppliers of the permanent capital in the enterprise have profit as their purpose also. However, the profit to these permanent suppliers of capital comes about only through the creation of profits by the firm itself. Thus, from an economic point of view, profitability of the firm becomes an objective of most promotions. The future profit of the firm is often determined by actions taken during the process of promotion. It is extremely important that the promotion be properly handled in order that profits will accrue in the future.

Some of the most common errors made during the early stages of promotion are in selecting sources of funds. In order to be profitable in the long run, the firm must continue as a going concern far in the future. In order to do this, it must be reasonably financed so that the creditors will not demand repayment at a time when the firm is unable to repay. The long-run solvency of the firm must, therefore, be carefully considered by the promoter in planning his sources of funds. This balance between profitability and solvency is a major element of most business decisions and will be discussed later. However, it is important to recognize here that future profitability and solvency of a business are often determined at the time of the promotion of the business.

QUESTIONS

1. Define promotion.
2. Differentiate the promotion of an idea from the promotion of a new company.
3. How are most new business opportunity ideas promoted today?
4. What is a promoter?

5. In what form should a promoter be compensated for his services?
6. Indicate the various types of promoters we have had in the past. Which type do you think makes the best promoter?
7. Can a promoter make a profit on his promotion? Explain fully.
8. If a promoter makes a secret profit, what action may be taken?
9. Explain the right, if any, of a promoter to compensation for his services.
10. Explain the nature of the liability of a promoter, both before and after acceptance by the corporation, on contracts which he made before the corporation was organized.
11. Indicate how in a general way you would proceed to ascertain whether or not a grocery store would be successful in a particular locality.
12. Indicate how the amount of money needed for the promotion of a small machine shop might be kept at a minimum.
13. Assume that A sells B an option to purchase some real estate. Despite this A sells the property to C. Indicate the rights of both B and C with respect to the property, and what action might be taken against A. State any assumptions made.
14. Indicate the nature of patents and copyrights.
15. Justify promotion from the point of view of society.

PROBLEMS

1. Mr. Calvin Wolf has promoted a new company to produce a new product invented by Mr. Benjamin Rank. Mr. Rank owns the patent on his product. Mr. Wolf, on the other hand, has performed all the normal tasks of promotion and has financed the promotion up to the time of the creation of the new corporation. The corporation has sold securities to obtain the funds required to go into operation. How should Mr. Wolf be compensated? How should Mr. Rank be compensated? What positions could and should these men serve in the new firm?

2. You are a large stockholder in a company recently established to produce a new product. This company purchased the patent for a new product from Mr. Robert Jones, the promoter of the new company. Mr. Jones claimed that he paid $100,000 for the patent and has agreed to resell it to the corporation for that price. You later discover that Mr. Jones actually paid only $3,000 for the patent. What action can you take?

3. Supposing you developed a new type automatic razor which did not require the use of electricity and was used for dry shaving. Describe the steps you would take in promoting this new business opportunity.

4. Mr. Landski, a mechanic employed by one of the larger automobile manufacturing companies, has perfected a device for registering the quantity of oil in the crankcase of the motor. The registering part of the device is to be installed on the dashboard of the car. Mr. Landski, who is now twenty-eight years old, immigrated to this country when he was eighteen and, after working at laboring jobs for several years in the East, finally went to Michigan, where he has been employed most of the time by several automobile manufacturers.

Work on perfecting this device has been done entirely by himself in his spare time outside the shop. His friends consist mainly of shopmen engaged in work similar to what he is doing. Although Mr. Landski has earned a relatively high wage for some years, he has saved little money and therefore does not have funds to promote this device. A new man, who, by his spending, appears to have some funds, heard of Mr. Landski's device from another shop man and offered to promote it if Mr. Landski would let him have complete charge of the promotion and give him half the profits.

(a) Do you think there is a need for a product of this kind? (b) How would you go about determining whether the device was salable? (c) Should the device be patented? (d) Do you think Mr. Landski should form his own company to manufacture and sell the product? (e) Should Mr. Landski accept the offer of the other shop man? (f) Do you think the company should start out on a small scale and branch out only by reinvesting profits, or do you favor large-scale operations immediately in order to secure the advantages of reduced unit costs? (g) Do you think that the company that is paying Mr. Landski's wages should be given the device without paying him anything for it? Why? (h) What would you advise Mr. Landski to do?

5. On January 2, 19x1, Mr. Adams turned over to the Standard Corporation, for which he was acting as a promoter, two lots and received $5,000 (par value) in stock in payment for each lot. Lot A was purchased by Mr. Adams for $2,000 about five years before he sold it to the corporation. Lot B was purchased by him for $3,000 about two years before the sale, and shortly after he started acting as the promoter for the corporation. At the time it was purchased by Mr. Adams it was intended that Lot B would be turned over to the corporation.

(a) Is Mr. Adams justified in accepting $5,000 for each lot? Explain. (b) What action might be taken against Mr. Adams? (c) Is there any way that Mr. Adams would be legally justified in accepting $5,000 for Lot B? Explain.

SELECTED READINGS

BOLLINGER, LYNN L. *Management of New Enterprises.* Homewood, Ill.: Richard D. Irwin, Inc., 1954.

DONALDSON, ELVIN F. *Business Organization and Procedure.* New York: McGraw-Hill Book Co., Inc., 1938. Chapter 9.

DUN & BRADSTREET, INC. *Getting Ahead in Small Business.* New York: Dun & Bradstreet, Inc., 1954.

KELLY, PEARCE C., and LAWYER, KENNETH. *How to Organize and Operate a Small Business.* Englewood Cliffs, N. J.: Prentice-Hall, Inc., 1949.

MURPHY, THOMAS P. *A Business of Your Own; How to Select, Finance, and Start it Successfully.* New York: McGraw-Hill Book Co., Inc., 1956.

WATERMAN, M. H., and others. *Essays on Business Finance,* 2d ed. Ann Arbor: Masterco Press, 1953. Chapter 1.

WESTON, J. FRED. *Readings in Finance from* Fortune. New York: Holt, Rinehart and Winston, Inc., 1958. Section I.

11

Capital Structure

The *capital structure* of a corporation consists of its issues of bonds and stocks and its surplus accounts. These items are generally considered the permanent sources of capital for the corporation.

The term *capital structure* refers not only to the total amount of the permanent financing, but also to the nature and amounts of the various types of securities and surpluses. Analysis of a firm's capital structure, therefore, involves a breakdown of the total structure into its various components and a determination of the relative importance of these components. The term *financial structure* or *financial plan* is sometimes used instead of *capital structure*.

The inclusion of *surplus* in the capital structure is necessary because of several factors. Par value stock is frequently sold for an amount in excess of its par value. The excess over the par is carried to the surplus account, normally a capital surplus account. No-par stock also is often carried in the capital stock account at a lower amount than the consideration received for it. The difference is also credited to the surplus account. It is thus evident that there is as much reason for including this surplus in the capital structure as for including the capital stock. The part of the earnings that is not paid in dividends or absorbed by operating losses goes into the surplus account. This becomes part of the owners' equity the same as the capital stock. The surplus account is treated about the same as if it were part of the capital stock account when it comes to the determination of whether a corporation can obtain a bank loan or float a bond issue.

Planning the capital structure is an integral part of the organization of a new corporation, but it also is a matter of constant importance to the going concern. What follows will apply to both new companies being formed and those which are already in existence.

Importance of Capital Structure

One of the most important phases of promotion is the determination of the capital structure. Many businesses fail, particularly in their early years, because of an unbalanced capital structure. The capital structure could be deficient because the amount of funds raised from permanent sources is insufficient for the requirements of the business or because the particular sources selected involve too much risk.

Most promoters are naturally optimistic and tend to overestimate the income and underestimate the expenses. Such a situation will result in failure within a short time. In working out the capital structure, therefore, it is imperative that it provide for sufficient money to enable the company to carry on operations. Although the estimate of the amount of money that will be needed may turn out to be substantially correct, an error may be made in the determination of how this money should be raised. Generally speaking, a stock issue will not cause a company to fail, but a bond issue may do so. The company is not obligated to pay dividends on the stock or to repay the principal. But both the interest and principal of the bonds must be paid, regardless of the earnings, or the bondholders may take legal steps to foreclose on the corporate property. In some instances the company could stand a bond issue of moderate amount, but an error is made in issuing too many bonds and not enough stock.

A constant review of the capital structure is necessary after the promotional stage of the business. One important item added to that capital structure of a going concern is reinvested earnings or earned surplus. Companies which have been in existence for many years can make the same kinds of errors determining their capital structure as can the promoter for the new and untried business. Generally speaking, most firms tend to become more conservative in their capital structure as they mature. This is due primarily to the build-up of reinvested earnings.

FACTORS IN CHOOSING A CAPITAL STRUCTURE

Our principal interests in this chapter are the determination of the kinds of securities that should be issued to obtain needed capital under various circumstances, and a general consideration of the relative amounts of these securities which should be used. There are many factors which influence management's decisions on the make-up of the capital structure. While the basic decision for a new business rests with the promoter, and with management for an existing business, there are many outside factors which play a part in the decision. Some of the factors influence potential suppliers of funds to make certain decisions relative to whether to invest in the corporation. Others more directly influence the management in its decision on the desirability of various sources of funds. If the management cannot sell the securities of its choice, however, it must either sell those which investors will buy or not obtain funds.

Any one or more of the following may influence the total amount and form of a capital structure:

1. Legal form of organization
2. Whether outside capital is needed
3. Size of the business
4. Age of the business
5. Stability of the earnings
6. Nature of the business
7. Nature of the assets
8. Level of interest rates
9. Taxes
10. Control
11. Government regulation
12. Preference of investors and investment bankers

Legal Form of Organization

From the discussion in Chapters 2 and 3, it can be seen that the form of organization selected by the firm has a direct bearing on the sources of permanent capital which the firm may utilize. Proprietorships and partnerships, by their very nature, cannot look to the sale of stock or bonds as a part of their capital structure. Taxation on reinvested earnings is different for different forms of organization. Generally, it can be said that the corporation offers potential for much more variety in its capital structure than does the proprietorship or the partnership.

Whether Outside Capital is Needed

If the business does not have to appeal to the public for funds, the probability is that it will issue only one class of securities—common stock. Even when some securities have to be sold—perhaps to relatives or friends, or to local investors—when the issue is too small to appeal to investment brokers, common stock only will be issued. Risk to the company is much less in selling common stock, and buyers of securities might prefer a chance to share in future profits. As time goes on, surplus is also included in the capital structure. Retaining earnings, however, does not require going outside the firm for capital.

The company need not be small to confine its capital structure to common stock and surplus. Some of our large companies have only common stock outstanding. If the small company has reached large-scale production by expanding through the reinvestment of earnings, it may now be a large company with common stock as the only class of securities outstanding.

The question whether outside capital is needed is influenced by the rate of expansion of the company, the rate of earnings, and the dividend policy of the company. Concerns that expand very slowly may be able to rely on reinvestment of earnings for the needed capital. Companies that expand rapidly may be forced to go to the capital markets for funds, but the extent to which they must obtain outside capital would depend upon their rate of earnings. Even if a company is earning a good rate of return on its stock, if a substantial part of this is used for dividend payments the reinvestment of earnings may not provide all the capital needed.

Size of the Business

Very small concerns are practically always capitalized with only common stock bought by the few owners or friends or relatives in order to share in any future success of the business. A non-participating preferred stock would probably not appeal to them. There would be no market for bonds of a small company. Small businesses generally retain a large per cent of earnings as they grow, but because earnings are small, it takes some time for retained earnings to become an important part of the capital structure. As the business reinvests substantial amounts, it is no longer small, and it is able to sell other types of securities.

Age of the Business

New companies, particularly in the industrial field, should be formed with a conservative capitalization; this means common stock and only common stock. A new enterprise should be prepared for rough going. Starting out with debt may prevent future financing and result in failure of the company. The broader the common stock base at the beginning, the greater is the chance of obtaining new capital in the future.

Older companies are established in the trade, have experienced management, and have a record of earnings and an earnings trend. This past experience is used as a means of predicting the possible future trend. With this background it can be ascertained with some degree of accuracy whether the company can stand a bond issue or whether it should attempt to sell additional stock. As a company ages, it adds earned surplus as a significant part of its capital structure.

Stability of the Earnings

The relative stability of the earnings may be an important factor in determining whether the corporation wants to issue preferred stock or bonds, and also whether the investment bankers or the public would want to buy them.

Generally speaking, a company which is not sure of earnings in the future should issue only common stock. If the earnings are fairly sure, but fluctuating in amount, a small preferred stock issue might be sold. If the earnings are fairly sure and certain in amount the company might safely issue bonds. If a company is already established, the past earnings records will be available and preferred stock or bonds might be safely issued.

Nature of the Business

The nature of the business frequently has a bearing on the stability of earnings and therefore on the kinds of securities which should be issued. Public utilities are more stable in their earnings than are industrial companies. Companies selling low-priced goods or services tend to have greater stability of earnings than companies selling high-priced articles.

Nature of the Assets

If the company is in the retail merchandising business and does not own any real estate, it will probably not issue bonds, for it would have no assets that could be mortgaged as security. Steel producing companies, on the other hand, have large investments in fixed assets and commonly issue bonds.

Level of Interest Rates

If interest rates in general are high, a company may attempt to issue stock rather than bonds. Or if they are high, a short-term issue may be sold with the hope that at the maturity of the issue interest rates will be more favorable to long-term financing. On the other hand, when interest rates are relatively low, a corporation might favor a bond issue since the interest paid may be much lower than the dividends that might be paid on a similar amount of stock. Furthermore, the costs of selling bonds are usually lower than in the case of stock.

Taxes

In an earlier chapter we discussed the tax savings which are effected through the issuance of bonds. Bond interest is an expense which is deducted before arriving at the net taxable income, whereas dividends on stock are a distribution of the profits after the taxes have been computed on those profits. With a 50 per cent corporate tax, this means that a 4 per cent rate of interest on bonds would cost the issuing company only 2 per cent in view of the tax savings.

Control

The promoters or management commonly give consideration to the question of control when issuing securities. The amount of money needed may be so large that if common stock were sold, the organizers or present owners might not be able to retain control. Thus non-voting preferred stock or bonds may be sold to the public instead of common stock. In some instances a non-voting common stock may be issued.

In case a large amount of voting stock is to be sold, and the question of control arises, it is better to sell to many small investors throughout the country. In this way, control may be retained by the ownership of an exceedingly small amount of stock since the average stockholder sends his proxy to the proxy committee, which is controlled by the management.

Government Regulation

The public utilities commissions in some of the states, the Securities and Exchange Commission in respect to companies that come under its jurisdiction, and the Interstate Commerce Commission in the case of railroads, insist upon a proper balance between the amounts of bonds, preferred stock, and common stock issued by public utilities and railroads. New security issues of these regulated companies must be approved by the proper governmental body.

Preference of Investors and Investment Bankers

In many instances the kind of securities that will be issued by a new company is limited to what the investment bankers think the public will buy. During a period of business prosperity people prefer common stocks, but in a depression they may hesitate to buy any kind of security, or if they will invest their money, they will insist upon bonds only. Sometimes, people may be willing to take a chance on preferred stock when they would not buy common stock.

When the prices of stocks are rising, although the public may not want common stock at the time, they may insist that any bonds or preferred stocks they buy be convertible into the common stock, or that they carry warrants giving them the right to buy the common stock.

CAPITAL STRUCTURE PRINCIPLES

The above factors relate to the conditions of the business, its suppliers of funds, and the economic society within which the business operates. They do not take into account the features of the various sources of funds which make up the capital structure. It may be that a study of the above factors might leave management with only one possible choice for a source of funds. However, this is not normally the case. Whenever several sources are possible, the decision on which to use revolves around a study of the possible sources with emphasis on the risk involved, the cost, the control aspects, and the flexibility. In considering these features, there are certain general principles which might be applied. Four of these principles are discussed below.

Issue Weakest Security First

A company never fails because it issues common stock. But many of them fail as a result of selling bonds. The conservative thing to do at the time of promotion is to issue only common stock. A company should save to the last those securities which are easiest to sell.

At the time of promotion a company may be able to sell any kind of securities. But later on, it may run into financial difficulties, and as a result, the public may not be willing to buy any kind of its securities except a first mortgage bond. If such a bond had been issued at the start, the company would be unable to obtain any additional financing, and as a result it may fail. But if only common stock had been issued at the time of promotion, the company might be able to raise more money later by selling a senior issue such as a first mortgage bond. Although a company does not anticipate financial difficulties at the time it is formed, experience has shown that most companies have financial trouble sometime during their life, and in many instances this comes soon after they are promoted. The issuance of stock, rather than bonds, broadens the base against which future financing may be effected.

Make Capital Structure Simple

Many companies do their financing in a piecemeal fashion, with the result that they have a number of different stock and bond issues outstanding. The tendency, however, has been to simplify the capital structure. The presence of many different types of securities is confusing to the investor, and may cause him to wonder why the company had to issue so many. One stock issue, or one common and one preferred issue and one large open-end blanket issue of bonds is preferred over a large number of small issues. Furthermore, the financing costs may be lower per unit on the one large issue. A simple financial plan allows greater flexibility in the future.

The Safer the Security to the Buyer, the Lower Its Cost

In selling an issue of securities, two different costs must be considered. One is the payment to investment bankers or others for selling the securities and the other is the annual cost of the capital to the company. Ordinarily, the safer the issue (from the point of view of the supplier of funds), the lower is the amount that must be paid to the middlemen selling the securities. It is also generally true that the safer the issue to the investor, the less is the amount that will have to be paid annually to the investor for the use of his money. A senior bond, for example, will sell on a lower yield basis than a junior bond (same maturity assumed) of the same company. Preferred stock would normally carry a higher dividend rate than the interest rate on the same company's bonds. Common-stock dividends of companies that pay regular dividends may in normal times be larger percentagewise than the preferred dividends.

Leverage Offers Higher Profit, but Involves More Risk

Closely connected with the cost of financing is the leverage factor. This was discussed in Chapter 7. If conditions are favorable for the issuance of bonds, it is usually found that the rate of earnings on the stock will be more than if additional stock was issued instead of the bonds. However, in poor times, the bonds may cause financial difficulty for the company.

THE CHOICE

The final choice of the types of financing to be included in the capital structure depends upon the objectives of the management and the desires of the individuals or institutions that supply the funds. Management determines those sources which would be most desirable to it and then attempts to obtain the funds in the market. By affecting availability, the suppliers of the funds help determine the capital structure of the firm. The above factors and principles set the framework within which management on one hand and the suppliers of funds on the other make the decision on the capital structure of the firm.

Considering the objectives of both the user and the supplier of funds, the common decision on capital structure requires a balance between the factors of *risk, cost* or *income, control,* and *flexibility* or *liquidity*. Table 11–1 ranks various permanent sources of capital in relation to these factors.

It must be emphasized that risk is an important consideration to both the supplier and the user of the capital, but what is risk from one's point of view is safety from the other's point of view. Risk to the user is commonly in inverse relationship with risk to the supplier. The same relationship applies to the control factor taken from these two points of view. It should also be noted that cost to the using firm, with such minor exceptions as initial cost of selling securities, becomes income to the supplier of capital. Again, the desirability exhibits an inverse relationship from the two points of view.

As this text is concerned primarily with financing from a business firm's viewpoint, the following discussion is from the point of view of the user rather than the supplier of capital. The viewpoint of the supplier creates a fifth major factor for consideration of the user—*availability*. Within those sources available, however, the user would generally make his selection on the basis of an attempt to balance the advantages of low risk vs. the advantages of low cost and the future effects on control and flexibility.

Table 11–1. Factors of Consideration in Selecting Various Permanent Sources of Capital, By Relative Rank to the Firm and to the Supplier of Capital

Using Firm [a]				Financing Media	Supplier of Capital [b]			
Risk	Cost	Control	Flexibility		Risk	Income	Control	Liquidity
G	A	F	D	Secured Bonds	A	G	C	[c]
F	B	E	C	Unsecured Bonds	B	F	D	[c]
E	C	D	B	Subordinated Debentures or Income Bonds	C	E	E	[c]
D	D	C	E	Preferred Stock	D	D	F	[c]
B	G	B	F	Common Stock (non-voting)	G	A	G	[c]
C	F	G	G	Common Stock (voting)	G	A	A	[c]
A	E	A	A	Retained Earnings [d]	G	A	A	[c]

[a] Rankings are A for most desirable source, to G for least desirable source from users' point of view.

[b] Rankings are from A for most desirable investment, to G for least desirable investment from suppliers' point of view.

[c] Ranking depends on market availability which varies more with company than with type of security.

[d] Source is considered to be existing common stockholders.

NOTE: The rankings are based on generalizations about the various sources of funds as most commonly used. This is not meant to imply that the relative risk, cost, control, and flexibility would always be in this order under any given circumstances.

Risk

The word risk suggests the exposure of something to loss or injury. The term *financial risk* in turn refers to the potential loss of money or its equivalent value. It is primarily financial risk in which the firm is interested.

Financial risk is derived from uncertainties. These could be economic uncertainties, natural uncertainties, or human uncertainties. The major management task is to reduce uncertainties wherever possible. Uncertainties exist and vary with the choice of type of business, markets, management, financing, etc. In planning the capital structure, it is the risk of the choice of financing which creates uncertainty.

From the firm's point of view, the variation in risk between different permanent sources of capital is based on the possibility that the supplier of capital will take some adverse actions against the firm. Basically, these are legal actions and may lead to partial liquidation or dissolution of the firm. Thus, risk to the firm correlates closely with the legal position of the supplier of capital. The strong legal claims against the company are present in high-risk sources of funds and those with weak legal claims are low-risk sources of funds.

Within those sources which have strong legal claims (creditors), the timing of the claim is probably more important than variation in legal rights. A creditor may take legal action only under certain circumstances —basically *default*. Default occurs only when a maturity or payment of interest has been missed. Thus, those sources which involve payment in the distant future will have no occasion to change the course of the business in the immediate future. The highest risk creditor sources are, therefore, those with the nearest maturities or nearest required payments of some amount such as interest or periodic principal payments.

Cost

The lowest risk sources are normally the highest cost sources. The cost of the various sources of capital is discussed in Chapter 18. It should be noted here that cost includes more than required legal payments. The real cost is the expected future payment for the use of the source of funds. This is normally considerably higher for common stock than for bonds. The selling cost and other costs associated with acquiring a source of funds are also included in their total costs but are normally much less important than the periodic costs incurred from the constant use of permanent sources. Table 11–1 indicates the general inverse relationship between risk and cost of the various sources of permanent capital.

Control

Control was mentioned above from an owner's or promoter's point of view. Here we are thinking of control from management's point of view. The separation of owner and manager in today's economic world requires a special look at control from the manager's point of view. Control is exercised by owners through the right to vote for the board of directors. Other than the right to vote for directors, voting owners exercise relatively little control.

Control can be exercised by creditors and others through contractual agreements which cause management to act in certain ways, although it would act otherwise if the contractual agreements were not there. It is difficult to generalize about the relative effect of various sources of capital on control. Table 11–1 gives the authors' opinions of the most common effect on control of using various sources of funds. The least control is exerted by retained earnings because no contractual provisions are involved and because there is no potential change in the voting stock structure of the organization. The greatest effect on control is thought to be by voting common stock but there are many instances where creditors exert much more control over the organization through contractual provisions than do owners through voting.

Flexibility

It is also difficult to generalize about the relative degree of flexibility allowed by various sources of funds. Commonly, almost all temporary sources of funds offer a greater degree of flexibility to the firm than do permanent sources. However, within the permanent sources, more flexibility is offered by some than by others. By flexibility, we mean the ability of the firm to vary its use of this source of funds at its own discretion.

In most cases, it becomes very difficult for a firm to reduce the amount of common stock outstanding unless the stockholders are willing to sell stock back to the firm. Thus, common stock does not offer much flexibility. Creditor obligations may be reduced at the time of maturity without the approval of the creditors. A change in the use of this source before maturity is more difficult. Retained earnings are listed as having the most flexibility because the decision to retain or not to retain is entirely up to the management (board of directors) of the organization.

CAPITAL STRUCTURE PATTERNS

The capital structures of corporations vary significantly depending upon the specific external situation and the decisions of the firm and of the suppliers of funds at the time funds were obtained. The varying effect of the nature of the business, stability of earnings, and type of assets can be seen from Table 11–2. This table gives the capital structure for all corporations by major industry groups. Long-term debt in public utilities is much more important than in any other industry group. Relatively, it is two and one-half times as important as in manufacturing.

The relative unimportance of preferred stock for all industry groups is also indicated by this table. Public utilities make more use of this source than do other industry groups.

The extreme importance of surplus as a source of funds, particularly for manufacturing, mining, and trade, is apparent from Table 11–2. The reduced emphasis on the reinvestment of earnings and increased emphasis on sales of senior securities by public utilities account for the fact that surplus is relatively unimportant for these firms. The lower level of earnings in agriculture, forestry, and fishing would account for the relatively less important position of surplus for these firms.

Table 11–2. Capital Structure of All Corporations, By Major Groups, in the United States, 1960, in Per Cent

Industry Group	Long-Term Debt	Preferred Stock	Common Stock	Surplus	Total
Agriculture, Forestry, and Fishing	25.6	2.6	41.7	30.1	100.0
Mining	21.8	2.0	21.0	55.2	100.0
Construction	21.1	2.3	28.5	48.1	100.0
Manufacturing	16.6	3.3	22.2	57.9	100.0
Public Utilities	43.5	4.8	24.7	27.0	100.0
Trade	17.7	3.1	27.2	52.0	100.0
Finance, Insurance, and Real Estate	30.4	1.5	17.3	50.8	100.0
Service	39.0	2.5	22.3	36.2	100.0
Other	25.5	4.4	54.4	15.7	100.0
All corporations combined	26.9	3.1	22.3	47.7	100.0

SOURCE: Based on figures obtained from U. S. Treasury Department, *Statistics of Income for 1960*. Corporation Income Tax Returns, Table 1 (Washington, D. C.: U. S. Government Printing Office, 1962).

Table 11–2 indicates certain similarities among mining, construction, manufacturing, and trade. The discussion which follows groups all of these industries into the industrial classification. On the other hand, the varying nature of capital structures within the public utility classification has caused us to look at railroads separately from other public utilities. Variations in capital structure and some of the causes for these variations for major industry groups are discussed below.

Industrials

The term *industrials* is sometimes taken to mean only manufacturing industries, but it is generally used in financial circles to cover all types of industries and companies other than railroads, public utilities, financial organizations, and real estate ventures. The greater part of this group is made up of companies engaged in the extractive, manufacturing, and merchandising business. Industrial companies are more numerous and have a greater total invested capital than railroads or public utilities.

Variation in capital structure in existing firms within the broad "industrial" classification, categorized by major industry group, was given in Table 11–2. Table 11–3 indicates rather significant variation among the industries within the manufacturing classification. Tobacco companies stand at one extreme in the use of senior securities, while motor vehicle manufacturers are at the other extreme. This may be due to the fact that motor vehicle manufacturers have large amounts of special-purpose fixed assets and also have rather substantial fluctuations in earnings, whereas tobacco firms finance large amounts of inventory over longer periods of time than do most industrial firms, and sales and profits of tobacco firms have been more stable than for other manufacturing firms.

Table 11–3. Capital Structure of Corporations in Selected Manufacturing Industries in the United States, 1960, in Per Cent

Industry	Long-Term Debt	Preferred Stock	Common Stock	Surplus	Total
Beverages	19.6	4.2	16.5	59.7	100.0
Chemical Products	17.8	4.1	18.4	59.7	100.0
Electrical Machinery	18.6	2.6	20.2	58.6	100.0
Food and Kindred Products ...	16.5	4.9	24.7	53.9	100.0
Motor Vehicles	9.8	3.1	10.7	76.3	100.0
Paper Products	19.4	3.1	20.7	56.8	100.0
Petroleum Refining	14.7	1.0	29.9	54.4	100.0
Primary Metals	22.7	4.7	18.4	54.2	100.0
Rubber and Plastics	23.4	3.5	15.2	57.9	100.0
Textile Mill Products	12.3	3.2	22.0	62.5	100.0
Tobacco	21.3	7.0	22.1	49.6	100.0

SOURCE: Based on figures obtained from U. S. Treasury Department, *Statistics of Income for 1960*, Corporation Income Tax Returns, Table 1 (Washington, D. C.: U. S. Government Printing Office, 1962).

As a group, industrials are more speculative than the other types of industries. They are not protected by monopoly conditions as are the railroads and public utilities, and thus competition is always a factor to be reckoned with. The success or failure of an industrial is closely correlated with management. The average company is small and thus is not able to secure funds from the sale of securities through investment bankers.

Due to the factors mentioned above, the typical capital structure of an industrial concern consists of only common stock and surplus. Funds for expansion commonly come from the reinvestment of earnings and depreciation charges. Even if bonds or preferred stock could be sold, the security buyer may prefer common stock. This is due to the fact that there is considerable risk in buying any type of industrial security, and if the buyer is going to assume this risk, he wants at least the opportunity to reap the rewards in event the company prospers. Preferred stock and bonds are found more commonly among the large corporations than among the small ones.

Due to the great differences among industrial companies, it is difficult to state when bonds can safely be issued or what is the maximum amount that should be issued. If the circumstances are such that bonds can be issued, they should be limited in amount so that the company would be able to earn the interest charges at least seven times before taxes (this applies to investment grade.) It would also be advisable that the bonds of the typical industrial company (assuming it is the type that can issue bonds) should not exceed the excess of current assets over current liabilities. Another rule of thumb for industrial mortgage bonds is that the bonds should not exceed 50 per cent of the replacement value (less depreciation) of the particular mortgaged property.

Although bond debt is looked upon as a permanent part of the capitalization of a railroad or public utility, this is not the case in the typical industrial. At the time bonds are issued, provision should be made for their retirement. They are commonly callable and have sinking fund provisions attached. When earnings permit, industrial bonds are commonly retired.

A corporation that could safely issue bonds could also safely issue preferred stock. Since the preferred dividends are not a fixed charge, some corporations would qualify for a preferred stock issue when they should not issue bonds. But a company should be fairly sure that the earnings would adequately cover the bond interest and preferred dividends. The earnings, before taxes, should be at least seven times the sum of the interest charges and twice the preferred dividends to qualify the preferred stock as investment grade. The conversion feature is used more frequently with industrial preferreds than with other types of preferred stock.

It should be emphasized that the capital structures of various types of industries and companies shown in the tables in this chapter are for companies that are in existence. Many of these companies have been established for years and have been able to accumulate large surpluses. It will be noted that in the case of manufacturing industries in most instances the surplus comprises over 50 per cent of the capital structure. In many cases the bonds were issued only after the companies had become firmly established and were able to show steady earning power. The fact still remains that the typical industrial concern should issue only common stock.

Public Utilities

Public utilities include communication companies, electric companies, gas companies, transportation companies, and water companies. While railroads are included in the general category of transportation, in most financial discussions of public utilities, railroads are considered separately, and they will be so considered here.

Public utilities operate under certain monopoly conditions. While there is some degree of competition, such as between electric and gas companies, the government-granted monopoly and the government regulation of the industry are what cause it to be classed as a public utility. Differences exist among the various classes of public utilities, but they are not so great as those found among industrials. Table 11–4 gives the

Table 11–4. Capital Structure of Selected Types of Public Utilities in the United States, 1960, in Per Cent

Type of Utility	Long-Term Debt	Preferred Stock	Common Stock	Surplus	Total
Communications	34.6	1.5	52.3	48.2	100.0
Electric and Gas Companies and Systems	52.3	8.5	21.1	18.1	100.0
Transportation	37.3	1.9	20.9	39.9	100.0
Water	48.2	7.9	23.2	20.7	100.0

Source: Based on figures obtained from U. S. Treasury Department, *Statistics of Income for 1960,* Corporation Income Tax Returns, Table 1 (Washington, D. C.: U. S. Government Printing Office, 1962).

capital structure of selected types of public utilities. The importance of bonds and preferred stock for electric and gas companies and water companies as opposed to reinvested earnings is apparent from this table.

Water companies are the oldest and most stable type of public utility. Many water companies are governmentally owned, and hence there is a relatively small amount of water company stocks and bonds on the market. Because of the stability of their operations, water companies can stand a higher percentage of their capital structure in bonds than can most other types of utilities.

Telephone and telegraph constitute the major portion of the communications industry. Because of its large size, the American Telephone and Telegraph Company alone is a significant portion of the total communications industry. The trend for AT&T and for other communications companies has been toward a reduction in the amount of bonds and preferred stock relative to reinvested earnings and the sale of common stock. AT&T has used convertible bonds as an important means of financing so that the long-run effect as the bonds are converted is a movement from long-term debt to common-stock capitalization.

By far the most important type of public utility, both from the standpoint of total assets and the amount of securities on the market, is the electric and gas industry. These companies have shown a remarkable growth and are continuing to expand. The financial structures of electric and gas companies were complicated in the past by the formation of large holding companies on top of the operating companies and a substantial amount of pyramiding. Under the Public Utility Holding Company Act of 1935, a number of unnecessary holding companies have been forced to dissolve and many others have had to simplify their financial structure. As a result, analysis of existing electric and gas companies is simplified.

Electric and gas companies utilize a substantial amount of leverage. A high degree of stability of earnings has enabled them to meet the requirements of senior securities in poor times as well as in good times. Because of the low rate of return allowed these companies on total investment by regulation, the leverage factor is utilized to increase the return to common stockholders.

To make the bonds of an electric and gas company a safe investment, the company should have earned its total interest charges at least four times before taxes. If preferred stock is issued, the company should earn the sum of the bond interest and twice the preferred dividend at least four times before taxes. Preferred dividends are doubled because taxes must be paid on the earnings before dividends are deducted.

Railroads

The composition of the capital structure in the transportation industry is given in Table 11–4. Railroads are by far the largest portion of the total transportation industry; therefore, these figures are indicative of railroads as a group.

The failure and competition of the railroads resulted in the combination of many lines into large systems. Since the various companies had their own bonds, common stock, and in some instances preferred stock, outstanding, the financial structure of the integrated system became very complicated. The large company which acquired the others would then either guarantee or assume, depending upon the method of combination, the securities of the combined roads. As the need for additional funds arose, new bonds of the combining company were sold. Since the properties of the small companies were mortgaged behind closed issues which had been sold at the time they were formed or reorganized, the new issue of the parent would have to be a junior blanket issue on the entire properties. In most instances the investing public expects railroad bonds to be secured by a mortgage on the physical property.

Many of the bonds issued by railroads contained the after-acquired property clause. In order to avoid its effects until after the newly acquired property had been paid for, it became the common practice for railroads to finance their rolling stock through the issuance of equipment trust obligations. The joint bond was also issued to finance common terminals, bridges, docks, etc., in part to avoid the after-acquired property clause, and in part because of the expediency of having joint-use property owned and operated by a separate corporation. The typical financial structure of the large railroads is thus a complex one.

Although early reorganizations in many instances resulted in the issuance of additional bonds, in later years the companies emerged with fewer bonds and a less complicated financial structure. Since 1920, the Interstate Commerce Commission has had authority over the issuance of railroad securities, both in reorganization under the Bankruptcy Act and otherwise. This has resulted, particularly in the case of reorganizations, in a reduction in the amount of bonded indebtedness and fixed charges, and also in the elimination of worthless stock.

The large earnings of certain roads over a long period of time has in many instances overcome the original overcapitalization. During World War II, extraordinary earnings enabled many roads to retire an appreciable part of their bonded indebtedness.

Railroad expansion has been over for some time. In fact, total railroad mileage has shrunk in recent years. There is still need for funds, however, for maintenance and modernization of properties, and for the acquisition of new equipment. The latter is now being financed almost entirely through the issuance of equipment trust obligations. Because of the relatively poor credit of railroads and the uncertain future of the industry, there have been few new stock issues sold since the 1920's.

In order for the bonds and preferred stock of railroads to be investment grade, Graham [1] states that in the case of bonds the interest should be earned at least five times before taxes, and in the case of preferred stock the sum of the interest charges and twice the preferred dividends should be earned at least five times before taxes.

Finance, Insurance, and Real Estate Corporations

There are many types of financial corporations, but we will confine our attention here to banks, savings and loan associations, insurance companies, and investment companies. Table 11–5 gives the capital structure of the major industry groups in the field.

Generally speaking, financial corporations issue only one type of security—common stock. By nature these companies are engaged in what is considered to be a conservative line of business, and they, therefore, follow conservative practice in the obtaining of funds. Furthermore, institutions such as banks, savings and loan associations, and insurance companies in a sense owe money to the depositors, savers, or policyholders

---

[1] Benjamin Graham, *The Intelligent Investor,* rev. ed. (New York: Harper & Row, Publishers, 1954), p. 141.

and it is felt that these people should have the first and only claim against the company.

Mutual savings banks, all federal savings and loan associations, and savings and loan associations formed in all except a few states have no permanent stock. They are mutual undertakings and are thus owned by the holders of the savings accounts. Mutual insurance companies are likewise owned by the policyholders.

Investment companies will be discussed in detail in Chapter 16. The open-end trusts, which have become so popular with the investing public in recent years, issue only common stock. Some of the closed-end trusts issue preferred stock and bonds.

Table 11–5. Capital Structure of Finance, Insurance, and Real Estate Corporations in the United States, 1960, in Per Cent

Industry	Long-Term Debt	Preferred Stock	Common Stock	Surplus	Total
Banking	1.2	.1	23.8	74.9	100.0
Credit agencies other than banks	56.5	.2	12.0	29.3	100.0
Insurance	.5	.1	10.3	89.1	100.0
Real estate	61.5	1.6	17.4	19.5	100.0

SOURCE: Based on figures obtained from U. S. Treasury Department, *Statistics of Income for 1960*, Corporation Income Tax Returns, Table 1 (Washington D. C.: U. S. Government Printing Office, 1962).

In most instances a railroad, public utility, or industrial corporation finances the acquisition of real estate by the issuance of its own bonds. In some cases, however, such as for a merchandising company, a separate real estate corporation will be formed to hold title to the property, and it will be financed separately from the merchandising company. Real estate projects such as apartment buildings are often financed by a separate corporation which is formed for that purpose, and which holds title to the property.

Real estate corporations will often issue the maximum amount of bonds they can sell, which is frequently equivalent to the cost of the property. Or, bonds and preferred stock will be issued for the full cost of the property. The common stock is then retained by the promoters and commonly represents no tangible investment. Since real estate developments commonly occur during a period of prosperity, the building costs are usually inflated. The drop in prices in the subsequent deflationary period may result in the value of the property being less than the amount of bonds outstanding against it. Not only is the stock interest wiped out, but considerable sacrifices may be suffered by the bondholders.

QUESTIONS

1. Define capital structure.
2. What factors determine the nature of the capital structure?
3. What influence does the legal form of organization have upon the capital structure?
4. How do the nature of the company and the business to be transacted influence the type of capital structure?
5. Under what circumstances should the tax factor influence the nature of the capital structure?
6. What are some "principles" that might be formulated in regard to capital structure?
7. How does the point of view of the investor differ from the point of view of management in capital structure decisions?
8. Describe financial risk and discuss risk as a factor in selecting sources of funds.
9. What relationship exists between risk and cost in selecting sources of funds?
10. Under what circumstances should the matter of control be given considerable weight in the formulation of the capital structure?
11. Discuss availability and flexibility as influences on the company's capital structure.
12. Indicate how the capital structure of a new industrial company would probably differ from that of a new electric power and light company.
13. Describe the differences which might exist in capital structure between a new manufacturing company and a well-established manufacturing company.
14. What factors have played a part in the capital structure that we find existing today for many railroads?
15. Indicate the nature of the capital structure of financial corporations, and account for it.

PROBLEMS

1. Using Moody's Manuals for Industrials, Public Utilities, and Railroads, select two companies from each manual. Determine the percentage breakdown of the capital structure for each of the companies you have selected. Attempt to explain the reasons for the differences between the capital structures of these companies.

2. Will Jones has developed a new vacuum product for cleaning swimming pools. Several people with capital are interested in supplying funds to a new corporation which Will is planning to establish to produce his new product. What kinds of securities would you recommend that Will offer his suppliers of capital? Why do you make this recommendation?

3. Obtain a percentage breakdown of the capital structure of the American Telephone and Telegraph Co. Do the same for this company's structure five years ago, ten years ago, and fifteen years ago. Account for the changes in the capital structure breakdown and describe how they came about.

4. The American Corp. presented the following balance sheet as of December 31, 1951:

Assets		Liabilities and Net Worth	
Cash	$ 50,000	Accounts Payable	$ 200,000
Accounts Receivable	150,000	Bonds Payable	1,000,000
Inventory	600,000	Capital Stock	2,000,000
Machinery	1,000,000	Surplus	1,600,000
Land and Buildings	3,000,000		
Total	$4,800,000	Total	$4,800,000

(a) Which items might be considered the "capital" of the corporation? Which interpretation do you prefer? Why? (b) Which items might be included in the capital structure of this company? Which interpretation do you prefer? Why?

5. The Illuminated Power and Light Co. is contemplating the issuance of $10,000,000 in 4 per cent first mortgage bonds, and $5,000,000 in 6 per cent preferred stock. The combined common stock and surplus is expected to be about equal to the amount of preferred stock issued. What would the earnings have to be in order that the company could earn its combined interest and preferred dividends twice?

In working the problem please give effect to the following: Assume a federal corporate tax rate of 50 per cent. To earn the preferred dividend once after taxes it therefore would be necessary to earn it twice before taxes. (Taxes are, of course, computed after interest has been deducted.)

SELECTED READINGS

ALEXANDER, S. S. *Changes in the Financial Structure of American Business Enterprise, 1890–1940.* New York: National Bureau of Economic Research, 1943.

AMERICAN GAS ASSOCIATION. *Financing Utility Capital Requirements.* New York: American Gas Association, 1949.

CHUDSON, W. A. *The Pattern of Corporate Financial Structure.* New York: National Bureau of Economic Research, 1945.

DOBROVOLSKY, S. P. "Economics of Corporate Internal and External Financing," *Journal of Finance,* March, 1958, pp. 35–47.

EDISON ELECTRIC INSTITUTE. *The Electric Light and Power Industry in the United States.* Washington, D. C.: U. S. Government Printing Office, Annual numbers.

FEDERAL POWER COMMISSION. *Statistics of Natural Gas Companies.* Washington, D. C.: U. S. Government Printing Office, Annual numbers.

FEDERAL POWER SYSTEM. *Statistics of Electric Utilities in the United States.* Washington, D. C.: U. S. Government Printing Office, Annual Numbers.

FOSTER, LOUIS O. *Corporate Debt and the Stockholder: The Effects of Borrowing on Rates of Return.* Hanover, N. H.: Amos Tuck School of Business Administration, 1956.

GRAHAM, BENJAMIN, DODD, D. L., and COTTLE, SIDNEY. *Security Analysis,* 4th ed. New York: McGraw-Hill Book Co., Inc., 1962.

HICKMAN, W. B. *Trends and Cycles in Corporate Bond Financing.* New York: National Bureau of Economic Research, 1952.

HUNT, PEARSON. "A Proposal for Precise Definitions of 'Trading on the Equity' and 'Leverage,'" *Journal of Finance,* September, 1961, pp. 377–86.

KOCH, A. R. *The Financing of Large Corporations, 1920–1939.* New York: National Bureau of Economic Research, 1943.

SCHWARTZ, ELI. "Theory of the Capital Structure of the Firm," *Journal of Finance,* March, 1959, pp. 18–39.

WESTON, J. FRED. *Readings in Finance from Fortune.* New York: Holt, Rinehart and Winston, Inc., 1958. Section II.

12

Valuation, Capitalization, and Recapitalization

Because a balance sheet always balances, the book value of the assets of any company is always equal to the total claims against those assets. These claims are the total capital structure plus the current liabilities of the firm. However, balance occurs only because the owners' equity account is adjusted by additions or subtractions to surplus, to equal changes in value of net assets.

Part of the problem in establishing a capital structure and in planning for future changes in the capital structure is a problem of evaluation of the company and its assets. In promoting a new business, the initial total capital structure should equal the value of the asset requirements of the business. For an existing business, new security issues are often related to a desire to acquire certain assets. As the assets to be acquired take a variety of forms, it is necessary to determine the amount of securities to be raised by placing some kind of dollar value on the assets to be acquired. In the purchase of an entire business, it is necessary to plan the capital structure of the acquiring business in light of the evaluation placed upon the company being acquired. Thus, there is a very close relationship between capital structure planning and valuation.

The problem of valuation arises in business in two areas. One is the question of the worth of specific assets. A substantial amount of literature is devoted to the problem of valuation of assets for accounting purposes. Markets have been developed in which assets are valued for exchange purposes. Businessmen, through their capital budgeting processes, devote a considerable amount of time to determining the value of assets for future earning purposes. Valuation of assets is an important financial management decision as well as a most important decision for sellers of assets.

Aside from the problem of specific asset valuation, it is necessary for many groups of people to value entire companies. While the same principles may be applied in evaluating a company as in placing a value on its specific assets, applications may be quite different. Company managements are sometimes interested in a total value of their organization, but more commonly the problem of valuation of a total company is a problem for the investors in that company. In the case of merger or consolidation, management is also very interested in total company valuation.

Because of changing asset values of a company, or changing value of the total enterprise, it is often necessary to adjust the capital structure. Any adjustment in capital structure which involves some change in the amount, type, or value of securities outstanding is called a recapitalization. Because of the relationship of valuation and recapitalization, the latter part of this chapter is devoted to the subject of capitalization and recapitalization.

PRINCIPLES OF VALUATION

Whether valuing specific assets or total companies, there are certain basic approaches which are commonly taken. Almost all accepted approaches to the determination of value can be categorized into one of three major classes. These are *cost, market,* and *income.* Many appraisers in determining value of a company or of a specific asset often look into all three of these basic approaches and the final determination of value is based on some combination of the different methods used. A discussion of each of these three major approaches to valuation follows.

Cost

Original cost, replacement cost, reproduction cost, substitution cost, cost less depreciation, replacement cost less depreciation, etc., all come under the general heading of cost methods of valuation. The cost method is based on determination of a value by studying the cash outlay required to acquire the item being valued.

Original cost is the cash outlay at the time of acquisition. *Replacement cost* is the cash outlay which would be necessary today to replace exactly an item which is already owned. Either of these costs less depreciation involves making an adjustment for a decline in value due to time and use since the time of acquisition. Because the cost figures generally refer to new properties, due consideration must be given to the present deteriorated state of the existing properties. *Substitution cost* is the present cost (could be after depreciation) of acquiring properties which would turn out the same quantity and quality of products and possess the same utility as the present properties but which might not be identical.

At the time of acquisition of a property, original cost, replacement cost, substitution cost, and market value would all be equal. It is most important to keep this fact in mind in determining which method of valuation to use under given circumstances. If there are no technological changes or effects on value other than due to use and time, cost less depreciation, replacement cost less depreciation, substitution cost less depreciation, and market cost for used items of equal use and age should all be the same. Under these circumstances, the use of original cost and original cost less depreciation as methods of valuation are very suitable.

However, in practical situations over a period of time, dollar values change and significant technological progress takes place. Thus, the longer the period or the greater the change in the value of the dollar itself or the greater the technological change, the greater is the variation which occurs between the cost approach and the market approach to value. The cost approach is suitable if one is taking a backward look to judge the results of some previous action. However, the original cost approach is not as useful in terms of comparing future alternatives for values tied up in present assets or companies.

Market

The *market valuation* method requires an analysis of existing markets to determine the price at which the given property would change hands. At the time the property was originally acquired, original cost was the market value. Cost values represent past market values. In looking to the present market, one is relying upon estimates of others of value at a given point in time. Value to one person is not necessarily equivalent to value to another. Since the market price is the price where supply and demand are equal, market value represents a composite of the value determination of all the people in the market. It is not necessarily the worth to any one person in the market.

When one is forced to sell in existing markets, market value and *liquidation value* are equal. Market value is particularly important when buying or selling is going to take place in the market. If this is the situation, the quality of the market is not important in determining the market value. In using market value as a measure of worth in a situation which does not require buying or selling in the market, certain limitations are found. Foremost of these is the fact that the majority of our markets are not "perfect" markets. Many people in the market have not taken a rational approach to determining the price at which they are willing to buy and sell. Many markets have insufficient buyers or insufficient sellers to give a resulting market price which is a good composite of buyers' and sellers' decisions. Not all buyers and sellers have good knowledge on which to make valuation decisions for their own actions in the market. Markets are commonly influenced by many short-run factors which might cause them to vary from real values to a significant degree. In the better established markets, speculators are normally active and influence market prices at least in the short run.

Income

The *income method* of valuation determines present worth of a property by the flow or stream of future earnings which that property is expected to produce. This approach to valuation is useful only in business or income producing properties. In business properties, the major reason for acquisition or for holding would be to produce future return. Thus, the income approach is closely related to the objective for which the valuation method is being used. Income as an objective is more thoroughly discussed in Chapter 17. However, its importance is emphasized throughout this text. The problems in using any income method for valuation of business assets basically revolve around the difficulty of determining future income and the recognition that different uses of the property involved could significantly influence the future flow of income.

VALUATION OF AN ENTIRE COMPANY

Companies may be valued for purposes of buying or selling securities in the company, for purposes of buying or selling the total company, for measures of the efficiency of management, and for decision by all types of people who have an interest in the organization including its creditors, suppliers, customers, and employees. A number of the approaches currently in use for valuing a total company are discussed below.

Asset Value

The problem of valuing a company can be different from the problem of valuing a specific asset. However, one approach to the valuation of the total company is the sum of the values of its assets. The sum of the values of specific assets depends upon the method of valuation used for each of the assets. This could be reproduction cost, substitution cost, original cost less depreciation, market value, etc. The most common method would determine the value of the assets to be the figures at which they are carried on the books of the company. This usually means that fixed assets are valued at original cost less depreciation, and current assets at original cost. When the book value procedure is followed, due consideration must be given to the depreciation policy followed by the company, the valuation of inventories and accounts receivable, and any unusual write-ups or write-downs in the valuation of the properties. Intangible assets may also be valued at the book figures, or proper adjustment in the valuation may be made in view of the facts of the particular situation.

The book value method has the advantage of being easy and quick to apply; it does not call for a field examination of the properties, and it is probably better understood by the security holders of the company than any other method.

The current assets are commonly given special consideration in determining the worth of the total assets. Certainly there can be no question raised as to the valuation of the cash account. The book figure of the accounts receivable will also be fairly close to their actual worth. The same is true of marketable securities that are properly carried on the books. The inventory may not bring the book figure, but on the other hand since it will probably be carried at cost, the amount realized from it may exceed the book valuation. In most instances the current assets, after due consideration has been given to doubtful accounts and obsolete inventory, are commonly valued at the book figures.

When a value of assets approach is taken to determine the total value of a company, it must be assumed that all of the values of the company are in its assets. Thus, no credit is given for management, employees, goodwill, etc. Today's corporation is more than a bundle of assets—it is a going concern of which assets are only a part.

Market Value

The market value of a company is determined by taking the sum of the market price per common share times the number of common shares plus the market price of the preferred stock times the number of preferred shares plus the total value of all liabilities outstanding. Publicly traded companies are given market values daily by people dealing in the security markets.

The problems of using market value for determining the valuation of the entire company are the same as those discussed above under market principles of valuation. In addition, the great majority of corporations do not have public markets which would be very realistic. As a result, in many cases where it is desired to determine the value of an entire company there is no readily available market figure. It is extremely difficult to estimate the price at which a company could be sold on the market unless there is an existing market for that company's shares.

Earning Power Value

Business property is worth what it will earn. Cost prices may have little relation to the value of business property unless that property can earn enough to justify the cost.

In the case of practically all valuations of total companies, weight is given to the probable future earnings. Since the future earnings are unknown, the past and present earnings, and the trend of the earnings, are used in estimating the probable future earnings. Certain adjustments, however, may have to be made in the earnings figures. For example, a small corporation, in order to lessen the amount of the corporate income tax, may pay out relatively large salaries to the officer-stockholder group, and small dividends on the stock. In larger companies the dividends may be relatively large in comparison with the salaries paid. The earnings figure is thus influenced by the policy followed in regard to salaries. In order to arrive at comparable figures, the excess salaries may be added back to the earnings.

Since the depreciation policies followed by companies vary widely, the charges made may be added to the earnings and then a reasonable rate of depreciation may be subtracted. Adjustment may also have to be made in the earnings figure for any expenses, such as repairs, which have been charged to betterments, and any betterments or additions which have been charged to expense. Any non-recurring profit or loss will also call for an adjustment in the earnings. The earnings used in the computation may be the figure before deduction of interest charges. It would also be before income taxes.

The next problem is the determination of the period to be covered by the earnings. The current earnings and those of the immediate past are probably more indicative of the probable future earnings than the figures of some years past, but some unusual circumstances present may make the figures not typical. Furthermore, the seasonal nature of some businesses, or the way they may be affected by the business cycle would make it advisable to use a longer period of time. The earnings are, therefore, considered for a period varying from three to ten years.

The earnings figure used may be a simple average for the period or it may be a weighted average, in order to give more emphasis to the recent experience. Let us assume that two companies show the following earnings record for the past five years:

	Earnings	
Year	*Company A*	*Company B*
19x1	$200,000	$470,000
19x2	250,000	380,000
19x3	300,000	300,000
19x4	400,000	250,000
19x5	450,000	200,000
Total	$1,600,000	$1,600,000

If we take a simple average of the above earnings we get average annual earnings of $320,000 for both companies. But, considering the trend of the earnings, it appears that Company A's future earnings would be greater than those of Company B. In order to give effect to the trend, for both companies, we might give a weight of 5 to the last year's earnings, 4 to the year previous, and so on, until the oldest year gets a weight of only 1. The weighted average annual earnings would be computed as follows:

19x1	1 × $200,000 = $	200,000	1 × $470,000 = $	470,000
19x2	2 × 250,000 =	500,000	2 × 380,000 =	760,000
19x3	3 × 300,000 =	900,000	3 × 300,000 =	900,000
19x4	4 × 400,000 =	1,600,000	4 × 250,000 =	1,000,000
19x5	5 × 450,000 =	2,250,000	5 × 200,000 =	1,000,000
Total 15		$5,450,000	Total 15	$4,130,000

After assigning these weights to the earnings, we arrive at average annual earnings of $363,333 for Company A ($5,450,000 divided by 15), and $275,333 for Company B ($4,130,000 divided by 15). Thus, Company A's weighted average earnings are nearly 32 per cent greater than those of Company B. If the value of the companies, or their assets, or shares are based on these earnings, it is thus apparent that Company A would be worth much more than Company B.

After getting the average earnings in one of the two ways stated above, the next problem is how to use these figures to arrive at a valuation of the companies, or their shares. This is usually done by the process of *capitalizing the earnings*. The nature of the business and the industry are taken into account, and a rate of return on the invested capital typical of that business is determined. The greater the risk involved, the higher would be the rate of return used in the computation. It may be decided that a rate of, for example, 20 per cent would be typical. (This is not high since, if the income taxes were 50 per cent, the earnings after taxes would be 10 per cent. Furthermore, there is no assurance that 10 per cent will be earned in the future.) We then let the average earnings, or estimated average earnings, equal this percentage, and proceed to find out what 100 per cent (the value of the business) equals. Applying this rate of 20 per cent to the weighted average earnings in the example given above, we arrive at a valuation of $1,816,667 for Company A ($363,333 divided by .20), and a valuation of $1,376,667 for Company B ($275,333 divided by .20).

In the above example it was assumed that the past earnings of these two companies was indicative of future earnings. With expectations that future earnings will be greater, these hopeful earnings may also be capitalized in arriving at the value of the various companies. If it was anticipated that a merger of Companies A and B was to take place and that a new merged company would increase the combined earnings of the two separate companies by $100,000, an additional $500,000 in value is created by the merger. This would be added to the combined values of the two companies separately of $3,193,334 for a total value of $3,693,334.

Valuation by Use of Both Assets and Earnings

In some instances both the book value (or some other method of valuation) of the net assets and the capitalized earning power are taken into consideration in determining the value of a company. The net tangible assets may be valued at the book value, and then that portion of the value, as determined by the capitalization of earnings, which is in excess of this is considered to be the valuation of the goodwill. For example, above we determined the value of Company A to be $1,816,667 by the process of capitalizing the weighted average earnings. If the book value of the net tangible assets was $1,500,000, then the goodwill might be valued at $316,667 ($1,816,667 less $1,500,000).

CAPITALIZATION

Capitalization, as used in this text, is the amount of the issued stocks and bonds. The difference between capital structure and capitalization is that capital structure includes the surplus. At the time of organization the amount of stock which the corporation is authorized in its charter to issue is referred to as the capitalization. After operations begin, how- ever, only the amount of the stock which is issued is commonly included in the capitalization. When treasury stock is present the question may arise whether the capitalization consists of the issued stock or the out- standing stock. It is recommended that the capitalization be taken to mean the issued stock. In other words, the treasury stock would be included in the capitalization. If the corporation issued bonds, the amount of such bonds would be included in the capitalization. The amount of the capitalization would thereafter be altered as more stocks or bonds are issued or are retired.

The capitalization is sometimes confused with the capital or capital stock of the corporation. The term *capital* has several meanings, but we will use it to refer to the assets of the company. *Capital stock* is the term used to apply to the total amount of stock of the company, as shown in the net worth section of the balance sheet.

Bases of Capitalization

One of the major problems in promotion is the determination of the quantity and types of securities to be issued. This decision determines the initial capitalization of the company. The three bases which might be used in determining the original capitalization of a firm are assets, earn- ings, and nominal. The decision is somewhat different in determining the valuation of an existing company as the capitalization amounts to only a portion of the total value of a company. The three bases of cap- italization are discussed below.

Capitalization on the Basis of Assets. Capitalization on the basis of assets means the issuance of an amount of securities necessary to acquire the assets. Thus if the company needs $10,000,000 to pay for promotional expenses, cost of selling securities, and fixed assets, to provide it with the necessary amount of working capital, and to cover possible initial loss, it will capitalize at $10,000,000 and sell securities in this amount. Where the company must issue securities to acquire its property, etc., it cannot be capitalized at less than the acquisition value of the assets.

If the corporation is a going concern and issues additional stock equivalent to the value of the assets acquired with the stock, the equity of the existing stockholders would not be diluted. For whatever the statement may be worth, it can also be said that capitalization on the basis of assets tends to make the book value of the stock more what it is supposed to represent than if some other basis of capitalization had been used.

Capitalization on the Basis of Earnings. Existing companies have a past record of earnings, and although there is no assurance that these earnings will continue the same in the future, the past does give some indication of what might be expected in the future. A new company never knows what it will earn, but the organizers always try to estimate the probable earnings as accurately as possible.

When a company capitalizes on the basis of earnings it issues such an amount of stock that the estimated earnings will represent a predetermined rate of earnings on the stock. For example, if it is estimated that the company will earn $1,000,000 a year, after taxes, and it is desired that the rate of earnings on the stock be 10 per cent, it will capitalize at $10,000,000. This is obviously 10 times the estimated annual earnings. This "multiplier" can be found by dividing the desired rate of return on the stock into 100. If this company hopes to earn 20 per cent on the stock, for example, it would capitalize at 5 times $1,000,000, or $5,000,000.

The question naturally arises as to how the rate of capitalization is determined. This is not an easy task. The answer depends upon a number of factors which would include the following: whether the company is already established or a new one being promoted, the nature of the industry, and the rate of return being earned by similar companies at the time.

If the company is already established and is increasing its stock, or a new company is being formed to take over a number of existing companies, the capitalization can be higher in relation to the earnings. Also the capitalization can be relatively high if there is a good assurance that the estimate of future earnings will prove to be correct.

The rate of return currently being earned on existing prices of stocks also has some bearing on the rate of capitalization that will be used by a new company. For example, in 1929, 1946, and 1957–1961 many companies' shares were selling at such a relatively high price that the rate of return, based on current earnings and market prices of the stocks, was only 5 per cent. In 1950, however, many stocks were selling at such prices in the market that the earnings were 8 per cent. Other things being equal, a new company being promoted in 1929, 1946, or 1961 could be capitalized at a higher figure in relation to earnings than in 1950.

Perhaps by this time the reader is wondering just how a corporation can issue an amount of stock which has a fixed ratio to the earnings, without giving regard to the amount of money needed to acquire the assets and set the company up as a going concern. In many instances the corporation is formed to take over the business of an individual proprietorship, or a partnership. It may be a small close corporation with only a few shareholders who are related or closely connected. In such instances the amount of stock issued is more or less immaterial. If it is decided that the desired rate of earnings on the capitalization would call for the issuance of capital stock of a given amount, it would not make any difference whether the book value of the assets was more or less than this amount.

Some people, particularly accountants, are inclined to object to capitalizing on the basis of earnings. This objection arises in part from the importance which they attach to the cost or balance sheet value of the corporate property. Legal objection may also be raised against this method of capitalization since the stock may not be considered fully paid if it is issued in excess of the cost value of the assets.

From a business standpoint, however, capitalizing on the basis of earnings appears to be practical. Business property is worth what it will earn—not what was paid for it or the value at which it is carried on the balance sheet. It is well known that when business properties are sold piecemeal under the hammer, the amount obtained from them is commonly much less than the original cost or the balance sheet valuation. Coupled with good management, these same assets in a going concern may be worth many times what they cost or the balance sheet value or what they could be sold for at a forced sale. Capitalizing on the basis of earnings may, therefore, result in the issuance of securities in amounts more nearly corresponding to the real value of the assets than if the capitalization had been based on the cost price of the assets.

Capitalization on a Nominal Basis. In some instances the amount at which a company will be capitalized does not have any relation to the cost of the assets or the earning power of the company. When this is the case we speak of the company as being capitalized on a nominal basis. A nominal capitalization might be used in any one of the following instances.

1. *Close corporations.* If a partnership is to be incorporated and no new money or new partners are coming into the enterprise, the amount of the capitalization is immaterial. Or the same may be true when only a few persons wish to start a new business. Quite often such corporations are capitalized at a figure much lower than the real value of the business. This may keep the organization tax and the annual franchise tax at a minimum.

2. *Incorporation of estate.* A corporation formed to take title to an estate is really a type of close corporation, but due to its different nature it is listed separately. The incorporation of the estate prior to the death of the individual may facilitate the administration of the estate. Corporations of this nature may be capitalized at nominal amounts.

3. *Temporary corporations.* During the early stages of promotion there may not be sufficient cash on hand to pay the organization taxes on the full amount of the capitalization. But there is need for a corporation of some kind in order to take title to options and property, make contracts, etc. So a temporary corporation with a small or nominal capitalization may be formed for this purpose. Later when arrangements are made for the sale of the securities, and the cash necessary to pay the taxes has been secured, the capitalization can be increased to the desired amount. For example, the United States Steel Corporation was first formed with a capitalization of only $3,000. In less than six weeks afterward the capitalization was increased to over $1,000,000,000.

Overcapitalization

The term *overcapitalization* is used in two different ways, to apply to the situation (1) when the amount of capital stock and bonds exceeds the value of the assets, or (2) when the amount of capital stock and bonds is excessive in relation to earnings. Either or both of these situations could be present at the same time.

The term is apt to be used in the first way at the time of organization of the company, when properties are frequently acquired at inflated values. Sometimes properties are overvalued in order to make an excessive issue of stock appear fully paid. In many cases stock must be handed out rather freely in order to effect the formation of the new company. Organization expenses and other intangibles consume their share of the stock. It is probably safe to say that a large percentage of all new corporations that sell their stock to the public are overcapitalized at the time of their formation.

Even though the amount of stock may not be excessive in relation to the value of the assets at the start of the corporation, subsequent events, such as the following, may make it so: operating losses, undercharging of depreciation or obsolescence on the property, destruction of uninsured or underinsured property, declining prices, etc.

For a going concern it is perhaps better to apply the term "overcapitalization" to the situation where the stock outstanding is excessive in relation to the average earnings. The cost or book value of the assets is given no consideration.

If a particular company is being formed in an industry where the company should be capitalized on about an 8-per-cent basis, then it would be capitalized at 12½ times the estimated earnings. Thus if the average earnings after taxes are expected to be $100,000, the company might capitalize at $1,250,000. But if it turns out that the company's average earnings are only $50,000, this would represent earnings of only 4 per cent on the capitalization. With earnings of $50,000 on the 8-per-cent basis, the company should have been capitalized at only $625,000. Thus the company to the extent of half the capitalization is overcapitalized.

The two different meanings of overcapitalization stated above may not be as different as it first appears. If a company issues more stock than the real value of its assets, it might be unable to earn a fair rate of return on the capitalization. Thus it might be overcapitalized both in respect to assets and to earnings. Or, even though a company issues stock equivalent to the cost value of the assets, if it is unable to earn a fair rate of return on these assets (and thus not a fair rate of return on the stock), then we could say that the company was overcapitalized in relation to the *real value* of the assets, as well as in relation to its earnings.

Generally speaking, overcapitalization is undesirable. It may adversely affect not only the corporation, but its stockholders, creditors, customers, and possibly the public. Overcapitalization harms a company's credit rating and may cause financial embarrassment or future financing difficulties. If a company is overcapitalized, it cannot pay a fair dividend. Sometimes there is the possibility of stockholder liability in connection with overcapitalized companies. In addition, because stock of overcapitalized companies usually sells for a relatively low price in the market, manipulation may be possible. If the overcapitalized company is operating under monopoly conditions, the tendency may be for it to charge an excessive price for its product or service in order to pay a fair rate of return on its capital.

Undercapitalization

Undercapitalization is just the opposite of overcapitalization. Thus, it may refer to either the situation where the value of the assets is in excess of the amount of securities outstanding, or where the company is earning a relatively high rate of return on its securities. If a company follows a conservative policy of retaining part of its earnings every year, the tendency will be for it to become undercapitalized.

The term *undercapitalization* is also sometimes used in a different sense. A company may have a capitalization or permanent capital sufficient to carry on its present volume of sales, but it may attempt to expand its sales rather rapidly without getting any more permanent capital into the business. The increased sales volume will call for an additional investment in inventories, accounts receivable, etc. All its working capital may be thus employed, and the company may become short of cash. It may be said to be undercapitalized.

If the undercapitalization is due to a company's earning at a relatively high rate of return on its securities or if the value of its assets is in excess of the amount of its securities, the shortcomings of undercapitalization are not nearly so great as for overcapitalization. However, there are certain disadvantages such as the fact that high earnings would lead to substantially rising market prices and may cause the market for the stock to narrow. With high prices of stock, future financing may be difficult and it may be relatively more expensive. High prices on stock may arouse suspicion among consumers and cause employees to demand higher wages; they may also invite competition from other companies.

Undercapitalization in the situation where a shortage of assets exists or where there is an overextension or overuse of current liabilities can be much more serious for the concern. Rapidly growing closely held companies are commonly undercapitalized in this sense. Many have failed in spite of high earning power because of attempts to finance permanent asset requirements on a temporary basis.

RECAPITALIZATION

The amounts and types of stock and bonds which a company has outstanding may be changed through a variety of actions. Changes in the capitalization can remedy a situation of either over- or undercapitalization. Certain changes in the capitalization such as the sale of additional securities or refinancing by selling new securities to replace old ones are discussed elsewhere in the text. In this section a narrow meaning of recapitalization is used. The term *recapitalization* in its stricter sense covers changes in the form or amount of securities outstanding brought about by voluntary action on the part of the corporation or of security holders other than through the sale of additional securities, the retirement of old securities, or refinancing. When a change in the formal amount of securities outstanding is brought about through involuntary action of creditors, it is called a reorganization; this is discussed in Chapters 29 and 30.

Some writers distinguish between recapitalization and readjustment. When the two terms are distinguished, readjustment is used to refer to more fundamental changes in the capital structure other than from the sale of new securities, refinancing, and recapitalization. Such things as lowering the rate of interest on bonds with the consent of the bondholders, the extension of the maturity date of bonds, or other changes in the contractual features of bonds or stocks are examples of readjustments. In the following discussion, we will not attempt to draw a distinction between recapitalization and readjustment.

Common-Stock Recapitalization

A recapitalization may take place with respect to common stock in a variety of ways. The methods most frequently used are discussed below.

Stock Dividends, Stock Split-ups, and Reverse Stock Split-ups. Perhaps the most common way that common-stock recapitalization takes place is through the stock dividend and the stock split-up. Since these, together with the reverse stock split-up, are discussed at some length in Chapter 26, the reader is referred to that chapter for details on these methods of recapitalization.

Changes in the Par or Stated Value. A stock split-up necessitates a change in the per-share par or stated value of the stock. For example, when the General Motors Corporation split its stock 2 for 1 in 1950, the par value per share of the stock was reduced from $10 to $5. In 1955, when the stock was again split, this time 3 for 1, the par value per share was reduced from $5 to $1⅔. A corporation, however, may reduce the par or stated value of its stock without increasing the number of shares outstanding. This would constitute a reduction in the stated capital and it would be necessary to follow the statutes carefully in order to prevent action against the company or its officers by the creditors.

When the per-share par or stated value of stock is reduced without changing the number of shares outstanding, the surplus account would be credited with the aggregate amount by which the par or stated value was reduced. In fact, this is usually the reason why the stated capital is reduced. The write-down may have been undertaken in order to eliminate a deficit. Or it may have been advisable to increase the surplus. In some cases the write-down of the capital stock account is done in order to offset a corresponding revaluation downward in the goodwill or some of the tangible asset accounts.

Occasionally a corporation will increase the par value per share by charging surplus and crediting the stock account. In this respect it is similar to a stock dividend, but it differs in that the number of shares outstanding remains the same. It differs from a reverse stock split-up in that the number of shares outstanding is not reduced, and as just stated, the capital stock account is increased and the surplus reduced.

Changes from Par Value to No-Par Value or Vice Versa. As the various states enacted no-par stock laws, many corporations by appropriate charter amendment changed their stock from par to no-par in order to facilitate the issuance of additional stock and/or to obtain some of the other advantages of no-par stock which were discussed in Chapter 5. In some states a low-par stock company would pay less in organization and franchise taxes since many of them tax a no-par share the same as if it had a par value of $100. Another reason for the change from a no-par to a low-par share has been the fact that at the time the no-par stock was originally issued the laws did not permit the issuance of shares with a lower par value than $100.

Reclassification of the Stock. By *reclassification* of the stock is usually meant the issuance of one class of stock to take the place of another class of stock. Thus common may be exchanged for preferred, or preferred may be exchanged for common. Or one class of preferred may be exchanged for several different issues of preferred that are outstanding. If the preferred to be eliminated is callable, the call privilege may be exercised. But cash would have to be given the shareholder if he would not accept the other stock issue. The exchange of one class of stock for another would have to receive the requisite consent of the shareholders and probably a charter amendment would also be necessary.

Following are the principal reasons why a corporation may effect a reclassification of its stock:

1. To simplify the capital structure
2. To enable the shareholders to sell part or all of their holdings in the market
3. To facilitate the public offering of new stock
4. To strengthen the financial structure by eliminating senior securities
5. To reduce the outstanding voting stock

Conversion of One Type of Security for Another. Convertible bonds were discussed in Chapter 9. It will be recalled that conversion is usually from a bond or preferred stock to common stock. Conversion might be considered a type of recapitalization if we were to use the latter term in a broad way. Usually, however, it is not included since conversion takes place at the option of the security holder and not of the issuing corporation.

Preferred Stock Recapitalization

Preferred stock recapitalization or adjustment may be effected by any of the methods discussed above for common stock and for the same reasons. Relatively speaking, however, such changes in the preferred stock are made infrequently. Usually the action taken with respect to preferred stock would be one or more of the following:

1. Elimination of the preferred stock issue
2. Elimination of the accrued preferred dividends
3. Reduction of the dividend rate
4. Elimination of burdensome provisions in the preferred stock contract

Elimination of the Preferred Stock Issue. Corporations sometimes wish to eliminate securities which have a senior right to the earnings in order to strengthen the financial structure and thus be better able to stand a period of reduced earnings. In some instances common stock is offered in exchange for the preferred. In some cases the preferred is bought up in the market either from the proceeds of the sale of additional common stock or from retained earnings. When a corporation has a number of different issues of preferred outstanding it may offer the various classes a new issue of preferred as a means of simplifying the stock structure. A company may retire a preferred stock issue through the exchange or sale of bonds. The reasons for this are because the rate of interest on the bonds is usually lower than the dividend rate on the stock, and the interest will reduce the income taxes since it can be deducted before arriving at net taxable income.

Elimination of the Accrued Preferred Dividends. When the cumulative preferred dividends have been accruing for a number of years, the issuing corporation is adversely affected in a number of ways. The mere presence of the accumulation is evidence that the earnings have probably been low or non-existent, and that the working capital position of the company is weak. The accrued dividends only make a bad situation worse. The company will probably find that no additional preferred stock can be sold, and since the possibility for dividends on the common is usually remote, it will also probably not be able to sell any common stock. Furthermore, the stock, both preferred and common, will probably be selling in the market at a relatively low price. All of this will adversely affect the company's credit, and it may either find borrowing impossible, or the rate of interest that would have to be paid on a loan, if obtainable, would probably make it prohibitive. Although preferred stock is commonly made non-voting by the terms of the contract, it is usual to provide that the preferred will come into voting power if dividends are in arrears for a specified number of dividend periods. Accrued dividends on the preferred may, therefore, jeopardize the management position of the common shareholders.

For the reasons stated above, a corporation is usually anxious to eliminate in some way large accumulations on the preferred. Naturally, the common shareholders are of the same frame of mind. The preferred shareholders themselves may realize that their chances of receiving the cash dividends in the future are rather slim. Various methods of eliminating the preferred arrears have been used, but they usually take one or more of the following forms.

The simplest method is that of offering common stock to the preferred shareholders for the accrued dividends. In some instances they are given new preferred stock for the accumulation. Or, the plan may call for a combination of new preferred and some common stock. In some instances no new stock is offered, but the company attempts to get the shareholders to agree to some change in the contractual features of their old stock in exchange for the cancellation of the accrued dividends. This may take the form of a higher rate of dividends, the addition of a redemption fund, making the stock convertible into common, or giving certain participation rights to the preferred shareholders.

In rare instances bonds are given in payment of the arrears. The wisdom of the latter action is subject to some question, since the burden of meeting the interest on the bonds and the principal at maturity may merely compound the situation. In some instances the preferred shareholders are asked to accept part of the arrears in stock, either common or preferred, and then the balance is offered in cash, if such a procedure is possible.

Reduction of the Dividend Rate. A preferred stock recapitalization is sometimes made for the purpose of lowering the rate of dividends. As the credit of a company improves, other things being equal, a preferred stock issue could be floated at a lower dividend rate. Also, as interest rates in general decline, the rate that would have to be paid on new preferred stock is usually lessened also. A material saving can sometimes be effected if a company calls in its old preferred stock and replaces it with an issue bearing a lower rate of dividends. If the stock is not callable, it may be purchased in the market, but this would ordinarily not involve any savings since a relatively high price would have to be paid for the stock.

Elimination of Burdensome Provisions in the Contract. In order to secure approval for a preferred stock issue, or in order to sell it, it may be necessary to place certain restrictions in the preferred stock contract. The amount of debt that may be incurred, or the amount of preferred stock that may be issued, are in some instances limited by the contract. Or the provision may take the form of requiring the maintenance of certain ratios before dividends can be paid on the common. Sometimes it is necessary to provide redemption funds for the retirement of the preferred.

When a provision such as those stated above proves to be burdensome or impractical, the corporation may want to eliminate it. If the stock is callable, this privilege may be exercised and the undesirable feature can be eliminated by canceling the stock issue. The shareholders may be asked to accept a new preferred stock, which does not contain the undesirable feature, in exchange for their shares. If the new stock is not acceptable to them, the company will secure the money necessary to exercise the call feature by selling the new preferred stock, or possibly additional common stock, in the market.

Debt Readjustment

While debt readjustment almost always takes place in a reorganization, it may take place also at the option of the company and its creditors on a voluntary basis unrelated to potential failure. Normal methods of debt readjustment are extension of maturity, reduction of interest rates, reduction of principal, and elimination of burdensome provisions in the contract.

Extension of Maturity. Corporations may be able to operate successfully and pay the interest on the bonds when due, but sometimes they have insufficient cash to meet the principal on a large bond issue that may be coming due. The market may be such that a new issue of bonds could not be sold. Judging from all the facts available at the time, it may appear probable that after a few more years the company may become able to meet the bonds, or to put out a refunding issue. If the bondholders pursued their strict legal rights, they could force the company into receivership or bankruptcy. But this might be harmful not only to the company, but to the bondholders themselves. If it appears the company has good management, and that time alone is what is needed, the management may sell the bondholders on an extension in the maturity of their bonds. The success of an extension depends upon the company's getting the assent of an appreciable number of the bondholders. As an inducement to the extension, the issuing company may add some features to the maturing bond issue, such as a sinking fund, or it may make the issue convertible, agree to restrict dividends on the common stock during the extension period, agree not to issue any senior obligations, or offer a bonus in stock or cash.

Reduction of Interest Rate. Where it appears that the rate of interest contracted for in the bond issue is too high for the company, the company's management may be successful in getting the approval of most of the bondholders to reduce the rate of interest. In some cases the fixed rate is lowered, and the payment of the difference between this and the original rate is made contingent on earnings. In order to induce the bondholders to agree to a reduction in the rate of interest the company may add some of the features stated above in connection with the agreement for an extension.

Reduction of Principal. In rare instances a company will ask the bondholders to reduce the principal amount that is owed. When this is done, however, it is usually in effect a composition settlement. In some cases the bondholders are offered part in cash and the balance in the form of other securities.

Elimination of Burdensome Provisions in the Bond Indenture. Companies may find that certain provisions in the bond indenture are burdensome or impractical, similar to the situation discussed above in connection with preferred stock, and ask that the bondholders release the company from such provisions. For example, the company may want to postpone the payment of interest which is about due, or postpone a sinking fund installment or eliminate entirely the requirement for a sinking fund. When the company is unable to obtain financing by any other method, the bondholders may be asked to subordinate their liens to a new issue which is being proposed. Or the company may want certain assets securing a bond issue released from the lien in order to pledge them for a new issue of bonds. In order to obtain such concessions, the company may find it necessary to add to the bond issue some of the inducements stated above in connection with the extension of maturity.

Recapitalization for Overcapitalized Companies

If a company is overcapitalized, certain recapitalization methods can bring the amount of stocks and bonds outstanding into line with the value of the assets or the company's earning power. A reduction in the principal amount of the bonds outstanding will reduce the total overcapitalization if the assets are not reduced correspondingly. A reduction in interest rates on bonds or dividend rates on preferreds will increase the earnings available for common and tend to alleviate the effects of overcapitalization.

A common way to reduce overcapitalization is to reduce the amount in the capital stock account without a corresponding reduction in assets. This could be accomplished by a book write-down of the capital stock account or by a transfer from capital stock to surplus. This would normally require a change in par or stated value.

Recapitalization for Undercapitalized Companies

Stock dividend payment is a common method of increasing the capitalization of a growing profitable concern. A stock dividend involves a bookkeeping transfer from the surplus to the capital stock account. The total capital structure, of course, remains unchanged. Stock split-ups as well as stock dividends would change earnings per share and thereby reduce some of the problems of undercapitalization.

If undercapitalization is due to a shortage of permanent capital, the obvious remedy is to sell more stocks or bonds.

QUESTIONS

1. Discuss the relationship among cost, market, and income as bases for determining valuation of assets.
2. Discuss the use of book value in determining the valuation of a company.
3. Indicate how the earnings of the constituent companies in a merger or consolidation might be evaluated.
4. In determining the value of a company, what weight should be given to any goodwill accounts on the books of the company?
5. Of the various methods of determining the values of the constituent companies entering into a merger or consolidation, which would you as an impartial advisor recommend? Why?
6. Distinguish between the terms *capital, capital stock,* and *capitalization.*
7. Indicate the various bases on which a new corporation might capitalize. Which one would you recommend? Why?
8. When would a company be likely to capitalize on a nominal basis?
9. Indicate the different meanings of overcapitalization and undercapitalization.
10. What are the disadvantages of overcapitalization and undercapitalization?
11. Indicate the various ways in which a recapitalization or readjustment in the common stock may occur.
12. What are some practical ways of eliminating the accumulated preferred dividends without actually paying the dividend?
13. What are the various types of debt readjustment that may take place without receivership or reorganization?
14. Explain how a period of prosperity and inflation might have the same effect on a corporation as a reduction in the bonded indebtedness during normal times.
15. Indicate how widespread stock ownership and use of the proxy system of voting make it relatively easy to effect stock recapitalizations and readjustments.

PROBLEMS

1. Two companies in the same industry, which started business some years ago, have now, because of the severity of competition, started negotiations for consolidation. They are both close corporations, and neither one has access to

the financial records of the other. Each one, however, has the latest balance sheet of the other under the date of December 31, 19x3, and the net profit of each for the past three years is publicly known. The data follow:

Balance Sheets
As of December 31, 19x3

	The Royal Co.	The Empire Co.
Cash	$ 5,000	$ 4,000
Receivables	60,000	20,000
Inventory	120,000	50,000
Fixed Assets	450,000	212,000
Goodwill	20,000	0
Payables	25,000	6,000
Capital Stock	450,000	200,000
Surplus	180,000	80,000

Net Income
For the years indicated

19x1	$40,000	$15,000
19x2	30,000	35,000
19x3	20,000	40,000

The stock of each company has a par value of $100 per share. It is proposed that the Amalgamated Corp. be formed with no-par stock only and that this stock be issued to the shareholders of the Royal and Empire companies in exchange for their shares, and the latter two companies will then be dissolved. The following proposals have been made:

Plan A. Mr. Whitelake of the Royal Co. proposed that the Amalgamated Corp. issue 18,200 shares to be exchanged for the stock of the other two companies on the bases of their book values.

Plan B. Mr. Coventry, a director of the Empire Co., proposed that 18,000 shares of the Amalgamated Corp. be issued. The average earnings for the past three years were to be capitalized on a 10 per cent basis for the purpose of valuing the stock of the two companies.

(a) Criticize each of these plans. (b) How many shares would go to a stockholder holding one share in his respective company under each of the plans stated? (c) At what valuation should the assets and the stock be carried on the books under each of these plans? Explain. (d) Indicate a plan you would recommend and your reasons.

2. Neither of the plans stated above was acceptable to the directors of the other company; so Mr. Kingington, a financial expert, was called in for advice. His plan (Plan C) was to capitalize the weighted average earnings on a 10 per cent basis to determine the value of the fixed assets. In doing this he multiplied the 19x1 earnings by one, the 19x2 earnings by two, and the 19x3 earnings by three. The three figures thus obtained were added, and this result was divided by six. The figure thus obtained was capitalized at 10 per cent.

The current assets were valued at the net current asset book value. This latter figure was then added to the capitalized earnings figure and the result was considered the valuation of the company. The intangible assets were disregarded. Mr. Kingington recommended that the Amalgamated Corp. issue 16,728 shares of no-par stock. Since the stock of the two companies was closely held in large blocks, the problem of handling warrants for fractional shares would not be difficult. (a) State your opinion in regard to this plan. (b) How many shares would go to each company? (c) How many new shares would the holder of 100 old shares in his respective company receive? (Fractional warrants will take care of uneven amounts.) (d) At what figure would you carry the assets and the capital stock on the books of the Amalgamated Corp.? Why?

3. The Smith Corp. issued $2,000,000 in stock for assets that had a resale value of $1,800,000, and the Jones Co. exchanged $1,000,000 in stock for assets that had been appraised at $1,200,000. Average annual net earnings for the first three years were $400,000 and $30,000, respectively. No securities other than those stated above were issued by the companies. (a) Is either company overcapitalized? Which one? (b) Is either company undercapitalized? Which one? (c) What disadvantages might result from being overcapitalized? Undercapitalized? (d) How could overcapitalization be corrected? Undercapitalization?

4. The Consolidated Corp. has estimated that its average annual earnings before interest charges will amount to $2,000,000. It has been decided that the company will issue four times as much stock (in amount) as bonds and that the capitalization will be based on the estimated earnings (before interest). Indicate the amount of bonds and the amount of stock that will be issued if the earnings are capitalized at (a) 10 per cent. (b) 20 per cent.

5. The following is a balance sheet of the Acme Machine Tool Co. as of December 31, 19x1:

Assets		Liabilities and Net Worth	
Cash	$ 10,000	Notes Payable	$ 400,000
Receivables	250,000	Accounts Payable	50,000
Inventory	810,000	Accrued Dividends	700,000
Fixed Assets	5,600,000	Preferred Stock	2,000,000
		Common Stock	3,000,000
		Surplus	520,000
Total	$6,670,000	Total	$6,670,000

The following is a condensed income statement for the year ending December 31, 19x1:

Sales	$10,000,000
Cost of Sales, etc.	9,575,000
Operating Profit	425,000
Interest Expense	28,000
Net Profit	$397,000

The preferred stock is 7 per cent cumulative and non-participating. The interest expense was for the annual interest paid on the notes. The latter were issued four years ago to finance the construction of one of the plant buildings that had been destroyed by fire and was uninsured. (Insurance is now carried on all the properties.) These notes are closely held and mature in one year. All the stock of the company has a par value of $100 per share and is closely held.

The company was hard hit by a recent depression, and the accrued dividends represent five years' accumulation on the preferred stock. During the late months of the present year the company received a great number of orders for machine tools from armament manufacturers and other industries. Because of the time required for "tooling up," none of these orders has been filled.

The plant facilities are wholly inadequate to take care of present orders, and if additional plant capacity were acquired at the present time a large number of additional orders would be forthcoming. The president wanted to issue $2,000,000 more in common stock to finance a new plant, but the treasurer of the company told him that they could not do this successfully until they had a financial "housecleaning," which, he said, any first-year finance student could tell was needed by taking one look at the balance sheet.

(a) Indicate specifically what you think the treasurer meant. (b) If you were called in by the company for advice, indicate specifically what you would recommend to improve the present financial condition of the company. (c) If your plan, stated in part (b), would not be acceptable to the particular class or classes affected, what would be your second plan?

SELECTED READINGS

AMERICAN INSTITUTE OF CERTIFIED PUBLIC ACCOUNTANTS. *Quasi-Reorganization or Corporate Readjustment.* New York: American Institute of Certified Public Accountants, 1939.

BONDBRIGHT, J. C. *The Valuation of Property.* 2 vols. New York: McGraw-Hill Book Co., Inc., 1937.

COTTLE, S., and WHITMAN, T. *Corporate Earning Power and Market Valuation, 1935–1955.* Durham, N. C.: Duke University Press, 1959.

FERGUSSON, DONALD A. "Preferred Stock Valuation in Recapitalizations," *Journal of Finance,* March, 1958, pp. 48-69.

GORDON, MYRON J. *The Investment, Financing, and Valuation of the Corporation.* Homewood, Ill.: Richard D. Irwin, Inc., 1962.

JONES, RALPH C. *Effects of Price Level Changes.* New York: American Accounting Association, 1956.

LEWIS, RONELLO B. *Accounting Reports for Management.* Englewood Cliffs, N. J.: Prentice-Hall, Inc., 1957.

————. *Financial Analysis for Management.* Englewood Cliffs, N. J.: Prentice-Hall, Inc., 1959.

13

Privileged Subscriptions

In the preceding chapters the importance of common stock as a method of financing, particularly for new firms, was discussed. In this chapter we are concerned with the sale of stock by an existing business to the company's own shareholders. As ordinarily used, the term *privileged subscription* applies to the additional stock which a corporation offers to the existing shareholders, in proportion to their present stockholdings in the company and usually at a price below the then existing market price per share. As a rule, the new issue is common stock, and in the great majority of the cases, the offer to buy is extended only to the existing common shareholders.

In many instances, however, the term *privileged subscription* is used whenever the company offers any kind of securities to any of its existing security holders. For example, it may be used when the shareholders are given the right to buy bonds, or when the bondholders are offered the right to purchase stock of the corporation.

REASONS FOR USE

When a corporation selects a particular method of selling its securities it is usually done only after due consideration of the relative merits of the various other methods. The advantages and disadvantages of most of these were stated in the previous chapter.

There are two reasons why the privileged subscription plan is used: (1) legally the corporation may be compelled to use this method, or (2) it may be considered to be the best method under the existing circumstances. Sometimes, however, both reasons may coincide in the same case.

Legal Obligation

In Chapter 4, it was pointed out that, subject to some qualifications, shareholders had at common law a *pre-emptive right* to be offered new stock before it could be sold to the public. The reason for this legal right is to permit the shareholders to maintain the same degree of control in the company and to preserve their equity in the surplus of the company.

To illustrate this, let us assume that a particular corporation has only common stock authorized in its charter, and that a particular person or faction owns 51 per cent of this stock. Whoever owns 51 per cent of the stock could control the election of all the directors, or if cumulative voting was followed, at least a majority of them. If the stock capitalization of this company was to be increased 100 per cent by the sale of the new stock to the public, the person or group which formerly owned 51 per cent of the stock would now find that its 51 per cent equity had been reduced to 25½ per cent. This amount of stock is not sufficient to insure control of the company.

As a practical matter, it is understood that the above stated procedure would probably not occur. The directors would either consist of the people who owned the 51 per cent, or they would be controlled by these shareholders, and thus they would probably not follow a procedure which would change the control of the company.

The other reason given for the pre-emptive right is to enable a shareholder to maintain his same equity in the surplus of the company. This can best be explained through the use of an example. Let us assume that a corporation has the following abbreviated balance sheet:

Assets	$1,600,000	Liabilities	$ 100,000
		Capital stock (par value $100)	1,000,000
		Surplus	500,000
Total	$1,600,000	Total	$1,600,000

We will assume that the market value of the stock and its book value are the same, that is, $150 a share. If this company were to sell another $1,000,000 in stock to the public at its par value, the surplus would then be spread over twice as many shares, and thus result in a reduction of the book value (and possibly the market value) per share from $150 to $125. In other words, the old shareholders would lose $25 a share, and the new shareholders would gain this amount.

If the old shareholders were given the right to buy the stock, then for every share they held they could purchase a new one at its par value, which added to their original investment worth $150, would give them two shares, each now valued at $125. In other words, the $25 lost on the old share is made up in the value of the new share.

It should be noted that a *privileged* subscription may be a misnomer on two counts: (1) being offered the right to buy the stock first is hardly a privilege if the law forces the corporation to follow this procedure, and (2) it is not necessarily a privilege for the shareholders to be allowed to invest more in order to maintain their degree of control and equity in the surplus of the company.

When Not Subject to Pre-emptive Right

The exceptions to the pre-emptive right follow.

Continuing Sale of Original Issue. Generally speaking, the pre-emptive right does not apply to the original stock authorization, particularly if it is continually being sold. If the right were applicable it would mean that whoever first bought the stock would have to be offered all the rest of it before it could be offered to anyone else. This obviously would be a highly impractical situation. Furthermore, rights of the shareholders with respect to control and equity in the surplus have not yet been established. They are, therefore, not harmed by not getting the pre-emptive right. If only part of the original authorized stock was sold at the time of promotion of the company, and some years later the rest of it is to be sold, the pre-emptive right would apply to the subsequent sale since the shareholders' rights with respect to control and equity in the surplus have been established already.

Treasury Stock. Stockholders do not have any pre-emptive rights in respect to treasury stock. The law reasons that the existing shareholders are not worse off after the treasury stock has been resold to the public than they were before the stock had been reacquired by the company. After the treasury stock has been resold by the company it is entitled to the pre-emptive right the same as any other shares of the same class.

Non-voting, Non-participating Preferred Stock. The law recognizes the pre-emptive right as a fundamental right of shareholders, and such right, therefore, applies to preferred stock, unless it is taken away by contract, statutes, or by implication. Since the reason for the pre-emptive right is to enable a shareholder to maintain his degree of control and equity in the surplus of the company, a preferred stock which is non-voting and non-participating with respect to the surplus would not at common law have the pre-emptive right.

"Non-participating" can apply to two different situations: (1) limited to stated dividend rate per annum, or (2) limited to a stated amount in event of dissolution of the company. In denying the pre-emptive right because the preferred had no equity in the surplus, the courts usually apply this to cases where the stock is limited to a stated amount in assets upon dissolution. In some instances where the preferred and common stock share alike in assets upon dissolution, the courts have allowed the preferred to "participate" in a *stock* dividend due to the pre-emptive right, although it is doubtful if they would have ruled that the preferred would have been entitled to participate (beyond their stated rate) in a cash dividend.

Stock Exchanged for Property. It is generally held that stock which is issued for property other than cash is not subject to the pre-emptive right. Thus stock can be issued for assets or in connection with a merger or consolidation without first offering it to the existing shareholders, even though the stock is of the character that would be subject to the pre-emptive right if sold for cash. If the stock exchanged in a merger had first to be offered to the existing shareholders, and they took the stock, the merger or consolidation could never be effected, unless it could be accomplished through the use of the money obtained from the sale of the stock to the shareholders. Also, presumably the stock is exchanged for property of equal value to the stock which is exchanged for it. Thus the equity of the existing shareholders in the surplus of the company would not be affected.

When Right Denied by Statutes or Contract. The statutes of many of the states prescribe if or how the pre-emptive right may be allowed or denied. A few provide that shareholders do not have the pre-emptive right, unless it is reserved for them in the corporate charter. The statutes of some of the states provide that the pre-emptive right does not apply to stock sold to employees, stock issued in connection with the conversion of another issue of securities, stock issued as a dividend, or stock on which the pre-emptive right has been waived by a designated percentage of the stock entitled to the right.

Practical Reason for Privileged Subscription

The existing shareholders of a company have a greater interest in the company than perhaps any other group, except the employees. If the company has been enjoying large earnings and paying liberal dividends, the shareholders may be anxious to purchase additional stock in the company. Particularly is this true if the stock is offered to them at a price below the existing market price at the time.

From the standpoint of the issuing company, the existing shareholders may be the best market for the new stock. The existing stock is registered in the name of the particular stockholder and the latter's name appears on the company's records. The most important point from the standpoint of the company is that the stock can usually be sold to the existing shareholders at a cheaper price than by any other method. The alternative is usually sale through an investment banker, and that would mean paying the banker a certain percentage of the proceeds. In some instances, when a corporation sells its stock directly to the shareholders, it arranges with investment bankers for a standby syndicate to take up any shares which are not sold by the company. But the cost of this is far less than if the bankers undertook the sale themselves.

PROCEDURE

The proposal to sell stock under the privileged subscription method is initiated usually by the finance committee of the board of directors, the board of directors itself, or one or more of the executive officers of the company, and sometimes upon the advice of an investment banker. The board of directors would adopt an appropriate resolution authorizing the issue. If the additional stock to be issued has not been authorized in the charter, then a stockholders' meeting would have to be called to vote upon an amendment to the charter to approve the new issue. The charter amendment would have to be approved by the state.

If the new issue is one that would have to be filed with the Securities and Exchange Commission, this must usually be done despite the fact that the sale is being made to only the shareholders. Filing with the appropriate state securities commission would also have to be done. If the particular stock is listed on a stock exchange, the exchange must also be notified of the action which is to be taken.

Subscription Warrants and Rights

The number of new shares issued under a privileged subscription is always much less than the number of old shares outstanding. The ratio may be, for example, one new share for each five or ten old shares held. The board of directors will state in their resolution that stockholders of record as of the close of business of a specified day, usually a week or two hence, will be entitled to subscribe to the new stock. This is called the *record date.* Shortly after the record date the company will mail out to the shareholders *subscription warrants,* which evidence the right of the shareholder to subscribe to a specified number of new shares. All the terms of the issue will be stated on the warrant, including the subscription price, the bank, trust company, or company office which will receive the subscription, the final date for the exercise of the subscription, and the date when the new stock will be issued. On the reverse side of the warrant is a subscription agreement which the shareholder can complete if he wishes to subscribe to the new stock, and an assignment form which will be completed in event the shareholder desires to sell the warrant to someone else. The shareholder is usually given a period of from two to eight weeks to subscribe to the new stock. If the warrant is not exercised or sold before the end of the subscription period, it becomes worthless.

The subscription warrants just described should not be confused with the stock purchase warrants described in Chapter 9.

The subscription warrant evidences the right of the shareholder to subscribe to a specified number of new shares. This warrant also evidences another kind of "right." The latter has a technical meaning. Under the privileged subscription the shareholder is given one *right* for each old share he possesses. It is these *rights* which enable the shareholder to subscribe to the new stock. The warrant is merely a piece of paper which evidences or shows the number of such rights which are possessed by the shareholder.

If the company offers the shareholders the right to subscribe to one new share for each ten old shares owned, then a person owning ten shares would receive *one* warrant evidencing his *ten* rights. If he owned fifty shares he would get one warrant representing 50 rights. It is thus to be noted that the value of a right is the value attaching to each old share and not the value attaching to each new share.

If a person does not own enough shares to entitle him to one full share of the new stock, or if he owned an odd number of shares so that he would be entitled to subscribe to a number of new shares, but have a few rights left over, the procedure to be followed will be stated in the contract. Many companies will issue fractional warrants for the odd rights. These can be sold, or the shareholder can purchase a sufficient number of additional fractional warrants to entitle him to an even share.

The privilege is quoted in the market as the price per *right* (not the price per *warrant*—the latter would be meaningless since warrants call for any number of *rights*). Rights may be bought and sold in the market just like shares of stock, and the warrants are comparable to stock certificates. If a warrant represented 50 rights, the holder could if he desired sell 20 of the rights and have a new warrant made out for the remaining 30 rights.

VALUE OF RIGHTS

Let us assume that a corporation has the following abbreviated balance sheet (for simplicity we will assume that the company has no liabilities):

Assets	$13,000,000	Capital stock (par value $100)	$10,000,000
		Surplus	3,000,000
Total	$13,000,000	Total	$13,000,000

This company wants to raise an additional $2,000,000 through the privileged subscription sale of its stock. The directors decide to offer the new stock at par to the shareholders in the ratio of one new share for each five old shares held. We will assume that the book value and market value of the stock are the same. The value of a *right* can be calculated through the use of the following formula:

$$\frac{\text{Market price of old stock} - \text{Subscription price of new stock}}{\text{Number of old shares necessary to get one new share} + 1} = \text{Value of a right}$$

Substituting the figures in the hypothetical example given above, we get the following:

$$\frac{\$130 - \$100}{5 + 1} = \$5, \text{ Value of a right}$$

In the above example we assumed that the market value and book value of the stock were the same. This was done so that the determination of the value of a right through the use of a balance sheet could be better understood. Rarely, if ever, would the two values be the same. As a practical matter, the market value of the stock rather than the book value should always be used in the formula. In the continuing analysis we will, nevertheless, assume the two values to be equal.

Explanation of Value of Rights

Perhaps a balance sheet analysis will explain what the formula gave us. After all the new stock has been sold to the shareholders in the example given above, the balance sheet will be as follows:

Assets	$15,000,000	Capital stock (par value $100)	$12,000,000
		Surplus	3,000,000
Total	$15,000,000	Total	$15,000,000

Before the new stock was sold the company had 100,000 shares of stock outstanding. Since the surplus amounted to $3,000,000, each share had an equity of $30 in the surplus. After the new stock was sold the company had outstanding 120,000 shares. Since the new stock was sold at its par value, no new surplus came into the company. Since all shares of the same class are equal in all respects, it follows that the surplus of $3,000,000 will be spread over 20,000 additional shares. Therefore, after the new stock is sold the equity of each share in the surplus is reduced from $30 to $25. If a person owned five of the old shares, the equity of each share would be diluted to the extent of $5, or a total dilution of $25. This $25 in effect attaches itself to the new share, which cost only $100, and gives it a value of $125. So what is lost on the old shares is made up in the value of the new share.

The value of a *right* can be expressed in several ways. It represents the value lost on each old share. Or, we can say that it represents the value in subscribing to the new stock. Since the value of each share is going to be reduced by $5, regardless of whether the shareholder takes the new stock (assuming that a banker or the public will buy the stock if he does not do so), and since it would be worth $25 to subscribe to a share at $100 if it was going to be worth $125 immediately, then the five rights necessary to get the new share should be worth $5 each. Or, assume a person does not own any stock in the company but he can buy *rights* on the market to subscribe to the new stock at $100. Knowing that the new stock would be worth approximately $125, he would give $25 for the rights necessary to get the new share. And, since it takes five rights to get the share, he would pay $5 for each right.

Quotation of the Rights

If the stock is listed on, for example, the New York Stock Exchange, it is probable that the rights will also be listed. Before trading in the rights can begin the Exchange makes sure that all the requirements regarding authorization for the issuance of the rights by the board of directors and stockholders of the company and, if necessary, by the SEC and Interstate Commerce Commission, have been met. The Exchange will then announce the day on which trading in the rights can begin. At this time the rights will be traded on a "when issued" basis, since they are not available at this early date. The seller will give the buyer a contract promising to deliver the rights when they are issued. In the quotation of securities on the financial page of the newspaper "when issued" will be indicated by the use of the letters "wi" immediately after the name of the *right*. As soon as possible after the warrants evidencing the rights have been mailed out to the shareholders, the Exchange will announce the day on which rights will be traded "regular way." The absence of the letters "wi" will indicate that trading is "regular way."

Until about the time of the "record date" (day on which the stockholders of record will be entitled to the rights) the old stock will sell "rights-on," or, as it is sometimes called, "cum-rights." In other words people buying the old stock while it is selling "rights-on" will get the stock recorded in their names on the books of the company in time to receive the rights. When a person buys the stock too late to get it recorded in his name before the record date, the stock will be said to be selling "ex-rights." The first day that the stock sells "ex-rights" it will be indicated by the use of the letters "xrts" following the name of the stock. The Exchange will set the "ex-rights" date, which at the present time is usually the third full business day before the record date.

We might further illustrate the quotation of stock and rights by referring to the hypothetical situation several pages back where the balance sheet was used. Assume that the privileged subscription was announced in May, and that the following dates were stated in the contract:

June 10. Record date.
June 17. Rights issued.
July 10. Rights expire.

We will further assume that the rights are listed on the New York Stock Exchange, that all requirements have been complied with, and that the Exchange designates June 2 as the date on which trading in the rights may begin on a "when issued" basis. Applying this to the previous example where the corporation offered its stockholders the right to subscribe to one new share at $100 for each five old shares owned, the rights should theoretically sell for $5 each. Since the rights were to be issued June 17, the Exchange might designate June 18 as the date on which trading "regular way" will begin. The value of the right will not change simply because it is traded "regular way." The rights would then continue to be traded in until July 10.

Since the record date is June 10, the "ex-rights" date will probably be designated as June 7. In other words, the stock will sell "rights-on" through June 6. In the example above, the stock should therefore sell at the theoretical price of $130 through June 6. On June 7, however, the stock theoretically should open at $125. Any further change in the price of the stock would be due to factors independent of the privileged subscription.

Determining Value of Rights With Stock Ex-Rights

In the formula given above for the determination of the value of a right we used the "rights-on" value of the stock since we were interested in immediately ascertaining the value of a right. After the stock sells "ex-rights," it is necessary to make a slight change in the formula. The change consists in dropping the "1" (one) which appears in the denominator. The formula would then appear as follows:

$$\frac{\text{Ex-rights price of stock} - \text{Subscription price}}{\text{Number of old shares necessary to get one new share}} = \text{Value of a right}$$

Substituting the figures given in the above example, we get the following:

$$\frac{\$125 - \$100}{5} = \$5, \text{ Value of a right}$$

The reason for dropping the "1" in the above formula is as follows. The ex-rights price of $125 expresses the per-share value of all the stock after the subscription has been completed. By subtracting the subscription price of $100 from the ex-rights market price of $125, we get the figure of $25, which represents the value of the *opportunity* to subscribe to one new share. Then we need divide by only "5" to reduce the value to a per-share basis, or in other words, to get the value of one *right*.

Actual Price of Stock and Rights

We have used the word "theoretical" several times in reference to the value of the stock and rights in the above example. The general market may fluctuate to such an extent that the price of the stock and rights of the particular company under consideration may be affected. Despite this fact it has been found that the formula is fairly accurate in determining the value of the right and the ex-rights value of the stock.

Being able to buy stock at a price below its existing market price is usually looked upon as a "privilege," and when the privileged subscription is rumored or announced there is sometimes a tendency for the stock to advance slightly in price. In attempting to ascertain any effect on the market price of the stock due consideration would, of course, have to be given to any change in the market in general and any factors independent of the privileged subscription which would affect the price of the stock of the particular company.

Rights tend to sell at their theoretical value. In other words, the price of the rights and the stock tend to sell at parity with each other. Thus, the rights tend to advance when the stock price goes up, and to fall when the price of the stock declines. In some instances, however, the rights will sell at a price higher than their theoretical value while in other cases they will sell for less than the theoretical value. Arbitrage tends to keep the prices pretty much in line.

Other factors affecting the relative prices of the rights and the stock are the comparative costs and convenience of buying the stock on the market and acquiring it through the exercise of rights. It costs more and ties up cash to buy the stock on the market since besides the price the broker's commissions must be paid. This tends to cause the rights to sell at more than their theoretical value. But it is more convenient to call up a broker and have him buy the stock on the market than to complete the blanks on the warrant and send it in to the proper office. This tends to cause the rights to sell at less than their theoretical value.

After reading about these various factors which produce opposite effects in the price of both the rights and the stock, the reader is probably bewildered as to whether the rights should or will sell at more or less than their theoretical value. If this is true, then perhaps the authors have accomplished their purpose. The only conclusion that can be drawn is that it is uncertain whether the rights will sell at parity or above or below parity. However, the prices of the rights and the stock generally move in the same direction, and the price of the rights tends to approximate the theoretical value.

Long-Run Effect on Stock Price

In the discussion above we were concerned with the price of the stock during the short period of the life of the right. A speculator or investor is also interested in what happens to the price of the stock over a period of time after the privileged subscription has ended. No definite conclusions on this point can be drawn from past experience.

At first glance it might appear that since the new stock is sold below its existing market price, the surplus per share remains diluted more or less permanently compared with what it would have been had the privileged subscription not taken place. Or similarly, the issuing company gets less for the new shares and has, therefore, less in assets per share than formerly. Consequently, the earnings per share, and possibly the dividends per share, might be less than before the privileged subscription.

But we should distinguish between the book value and the market value of the stock. The fact that stock under a privileged subscription might be offered at 30 per cent below its existing market price, does not necessarily mean that it is being offered at 30 per cent below its book value. Or, to take an example, a stock may have a par value of $25 a share, a book value of $35, and a market value of $40. Now if new stock was offered under a privileged subscription at $35 a share, there would be no dilution at all in the surplus attaching to the old shares. If the earnings on the book value of the assets continued at the same rate as before the privileged subscription, and the same percentage of earnings were paid out in dividends, there is no reason why the new stock, and of course, the old stock, would not eventually sell at the same price per share as before the privileged subscription.

Even if there is a dilution in the surplus per share as a result of a privileged subscription, it does not follow that the price of the stock will remain depressed permanently. The privileged subscription generally can be used only by successful companies. If the earnings of the company continue to increase as a result of expansion or increased business, the earnings and dividends per share might be even larger in the future. This would ordinarily cause the stock to sell for a higher price than before the privileged subscription. Of course had the new stock been sold at the market value rather than less, the earnings per share would probably have been even larger since the company would have had the use of more dollars per share.

Where the offering price under a privileged subscription is not too far below the market price, and where the proportion of new shares to old is not too great, the "ex-rights" price will not be much lower than the "rights-on" price. This slight drop can usually be made up rather quickly if the market in general continues steady or advances. In situations of this kind the issuing company usually continues the same rate of dividends per share on all the stock as was formerly paid on the old stock. Under these conditions there is no reason why the new and old stock should not sell at least as high as before the privileged subscription. The American Telephone and Telegraph Company has used the privileged subscription under these circumstances many times in the past and the stock has usually quickly made up for the drop in the price which occurred when it went ex-rights.

What To Do With the Rights

Every shareholder receiving rights under a privileged subscription has to decide what to do with them. The shareholder may take no action, sell the rights, or subscribe to the new stock.

Take No Action. It can generally be stated that a shareholder should not sit idly by and do nothing. He should either sell the rights or subscribe to the new stock. To explain the effects of the shareholder's actions with respect to the disposition of his rights we will again refer to the hypothetical situation stated above. The *right* in this case was worth $5, and the stock sold at $125 ex-rights. Since $5 worth of the company surplus will be taken away from each share, the shareholder, owning five shares, will lose a total of $25 if he lets his rights expire. Many shareholders do not understand what the privileged subscription is all about, and as a result they do nothing. Others think that it is merely a scheme to sell them more stock (which is sometimes the case), and therefore they throw away the rights.

Sell the Rights. Since the shareholder should ordinarily not let his rights expire, his alternatives are either to sell the rights or to exercise them and purchase the new stock. Which of these he should have done, only future events can reveal. But this we know: it is always better to sell the rights than to let them expire. If the rights are sold it amounts to the same thing as selling part of the stock. If the shareholder who owned five old shares sold his five rights, he would get $25 in cash (less commissions). Since in our example his old stock would decline in price $5 a share after it went ex-rights, or a total of $25 for the five shares, he would merely break even by the sale of the rights.

Subscribe to the New Stock. To exercise the rights by subscribing to the new shares, it would be necessary for the shareholder who owned five old shares to put up an additional $100. This cash together with the five rights would enable him to get one additional share. This additional share would be, according to our assumptions, worth $125. So he, in a sense, gains $25 on this share. But each old share drops $5 in price, and therefore his five old shares are worth in the aggregate $25 less. By subscribing to the new share, the shareholder merely breaks even—the same as if he had sold his rights. The shareholder may feel that he already has enough money tied up in the particular company; or he may not have any money to invest in the new shares; so he may either sell his rights, or if he has enough he may sell part of his rights to enable him to subscribe to a few new shares without putting any new money into the company.

Action by Outsiders

An outsider could also profit from the purchase of the stock in somewhat the same manner as a shareholder. If it is thought that sometime after the subscription is over the stock will work back up to its old price, anyone could purchase the stock while it is selling "rights-on," or buy enough "rights" on the market to get the desired amount of new stock. The other alternative would be to purchase the stock in the market "ex-rights." Any of these methods would result in profit *if* the stock goes up in price after its initial drop caused by its selling "ex-rights."

TAXATION

The typical stock right is not taxable under the federal income tax laws at the time it is received by the shareholder (or at the time it is exercised to buy the new stock), and the following discussion pertains to this type of a right. If valuable rights are allowed to expire, no loss may be taken with respect to either the rights or the stock.

Rights Valued at Less Than 15 Per Cent of Stock Value

If at the time of their distribution the rights have a market value of less than 15 per cent of value of the stock (ex-rights) on which the rights were issued, the shareholder has an election to make in determining the cost basis of the rights and the stock. Assume he elects to consider the cost basis of the rights to be zero. If the rights are sold, the entire proceeds therefrom are considered to be a capital gain. In determining whether the gain is a long- or short-term one, the holding period begins from the date when the stock on which the rights were paid was acquired. If the old stock is sold, its cost basis remains the original cost. If the rights are used to subscribe to the new stock, the subscription price is the cost basis for the new stock.

Or, the shareholder may elect to allocate the cost of the stock over both the stock and the rights, in the manner described in the next paragraph.

Rights Valued at 15 Per Cent or More of Stock Value

If at the time of their distribution the rights have a market value of 15 per cent or more of the value of the stock (ex-rights) the shareholder must apportion the cost basis between the stock and the rights in the ratio that the market value of each bears to the total market value of both. This can best be understood by an example. Assume that a company offers its shareholders the right to subscribe to one new share at $10 for each three old shares held. We will assume that the "rights-on" price of the old share is $30. According to the formula used above a right should be worth $5, and the "ex-rights" price of the stock should be $25 per share. Since the value of a right is more than 15 per cent of the value of the stock, it is necessary to use the apportioning method. We will assume the shareholder holds three shares which were acquired several years ago at $20 per share.

Market value of stock	$75
Market value of rights	15
Total market value	$90

$$\frac{75}{90} \times \$60 \text{ (cost of old stock)} = \$50, \text{ cost basis allocated to stock}$$
(which is $16\frac{2}{3}$ per share)

$$\frac{15}{90} \times \$60 \qquad\qquad = \$10, \text{ cost basis allocated to rights}$$
(which is $3\frac{1}{3}$ per right)

If the three rights were sold for a total of $15, a long-term capital gain of $5 would be realized. If the three old shares were sold for $75, a long-term capital gain of $25 would be realized. If the one new share is subscribed to, its cost basis would be the subscription price plus the cost basis of the three rights, or $20. The holding period (for determination of capital gains upon sale) for the new share begins on the date the rights were exercised.

CONDITIONS FOR SUCCESS

As is true of the sale of securities by any method, a corporation should be fairly sure that the privileged sale will be successful before it is undertaken. One way to insure that all the stock will be sold is to have it underwritten by investment bankers. This will be discussed later. At the present time we are concerned with requisites for a successful sale regardless of whether it is underwritten. But from a practical standpoint, the following requirements would probably have to be met before a banker would undertake the risk of underwriting the sale.

1. A favorable outlook for business and stocks
2. The money used for profitable purposes
3. Wide distribution of old stock
4. New issue relatively small
5. Price of new shares relatively low in relation to price of old shares

A Favorable Outlook for Business and Stocks

If the shareholders feel that business conditions will continue to improve and that the stock market will go bullish, they will be more inclined to buy additional stock than if the outlook for the future were gloomy. Moreover, they will have more money available for the purchase of stock during this phase of the business cycle. Companies will also have a greater need for funds when they are expanding, and despite the higher construction costs, companies commonly do their expanding during prosperous times.

The Money Used for Profitable Purposes

The shareholders will have to be convinced that the new money will be used for profitable purposes. Perhaps one of the best assurances that the shareholders can have of this is a past record of good earnings and dividends.

Wide Distribution of Old Stock

If the stock is closely held in large blocks by a relatively small number of holders the probability is that many of them will not subscribe to the new stock. Since such shareholders already have a relatively large amount tied up in the company, they may not want to put any more eggs in that basket. Each shareholder would have to subscribe to a large number of new shares in order that the sale be successful, and many of them may not have the necessary money to do this, and will sell part or all of their rights on the market. Some will sell enough rights to subscribe to a few new shares without putting up any new capital. The bigger sale of the rights on the market will depress their price, and correspondingly the price of the stock. In extreme cases the rights will cease to have any value in the market, which means that the privileged subscription would be a failure.

If, on the other hand, the stock is widely scattered the individual shareholders will not be called upon to invest much more capital in the business. They, therefore, will be more inclined to exercise the rights by subscribing to the stock than to sell them in the market. Furthermore, although some of the rights evidenced by fractional warrants will be sold in the market, there might be a demand for rights on the part of many shareholders who need only a few more in order to subscribe to a whole share.

New Issue Relatively Small

Perhaps this point can best be understood by the use of figures. Let us again refer to the example used above where the shareholder is given the right to subscribe to one share at $100 for each five shares he owns. Suppose that a person owned 50 of the old shares. At the price of $130 per share, the value of his equity in the company would be $6,500. He is now being asked to buy 10 new shares at a price of $100 each. In other words, he is being asked for only $1,000 more. But if the shareholder had been asked to subscribe to one new share for each *two* owned, it would require an outlay of $2,500 to take the 25 shares. Since the shareholder already has $6,500 invested in the company (or his investment is worth that amount), there is a greater chance of getting an additional $1,000 out of him than there is of securing $2,500.

If a company needs a considerable amount of money, it would be better to have several privileged subscriptions over a period of time, each for a relatively small amount, rather than one large one. The number of new shares issued in relation to the old shares varies in practice, but one new share for each four, each five, or each ten old shares was the most common relationship found in the past.

Price of New Stock Relatively Low

One of the most important requisites for a successful privileged subscription is that the price at which the new stock is offered to the shareholders be considerably below the existing market price of the old stock. The new stock should not normally be offered at less than a 10 per cent discount from the price of the old stock, and it would be better if the price was at least 25 per cent below the old stock.

In the example we have been using above where the market price of the old stock was $130, and the offering price of the new was $100 (one new share for each five old), the theoretical value of a right was found to be $5. But if the offering price of the new stock was, for example, $118 instead of $100, the theoretical value of a right would be only $2. A drop in the price of stock of about 9¼ per cent would result in the right's becoming worthless. (This would be a drop of approximately $12 a share, which would mean that the stock would be obtainable in the market for $118.)

Looking at the same problem from the viewpoint of the typical stockholder, the lower the offer price of the new stock as compared with the existing price of the old stock, the greater will be the bargain which he thinks he is getting.

UNDERWRITING PRIVILEGED SUBSCRIPTIONS

Since the issuing corporation is never sure that all the new issue will be taken up by the shareholders, it may have the privileged subscription underwritten by one or more investment bankers. As will be explained in the following chapter, the banker for a fee will agree to take up any stock which remains unsold at the end of the period. This would be the *standby* syndicate arrangement.

The nature of the arrangement between the issuing company and the banker varies according to individual cases, but usually the banker is paid a *standby* fee of 2 to 3 per cent of the subscription price of the entire issue to compensate him in event he has to take over part of the issue. In some instances he is paid this fee and then the contract calls for another fee of perhaps 2 per cent on all stock which he must take up. The agreement may call for additional fees ranging from 2 to 5 per cent depending upon the amount of stock which he has to take up.

The advantage of having the issue underwritten is greater than would appear from what has already been said. Investment bankers can give advice to the issuing company about the best time to offer the new stock, and the other conditions of the issue. Also, the fact that the shareholders know that bankers have underwritten the issue will give them more confidence in the stock, and they, therefore, will be more inclined to subscribe to it.

The bankers may also buy up some of the stock or rights in the market during the subscription period when the market is weak, thus tending to stabilize the price and improve the chances of a successful sale.

SALE OF PREFERRED STOCK AND BONDS

Corporations sometimes offer new issues of preferred stock or bonds to their shareholders because they feel that this is the best or cheapest way of selling the new securities. In the case of preferred stock or bonds which are convertible into common stock, courts generally hold that the common shareholders have a pre-emptive right with respect to them.

When preferred stock or bonds are offered to stockholders under the so-called "privileged subscription" method, the problem of deciding the value of a *right* is somewhat more complicated than when common stock is being offered. In the latter case the existing stock has a market price and therefore the value of the offer, or in other words, the value of the right, can be easily computed. But no preferred stock or bonds, at least of the same character being offered, may be on the market so that the shareholder does not know their worth as a straight preferred stock or as a bond. By comparing them with similar securities of the company, or similar securities of similar companies, however, a fairly close approximate value can be attached to them.

When the security being offered is a convertible, such as a convertible bond, the shareholder has the same problem as just mentioned, but it is complicated by the fact that he may not know whether to value the privilege according to the worth of the bond as a straight credit obligation, or to appraise it from the standpoint of its conversion value. Then too, another problem adds complications. When common stock is being offered under the privileged subscription, the subscription period is only a few weeks. Therefore, the dilution effect on the surplus attaching to the old shares occurs almost immediately. But the bonds may be convertible over a ten-year period, for example, and the conversion may be made gradually over that period. That raises the question whether the shareholder should appraise the conversion worth of the bond in terms of the existing price of the old stock, or whether he should give effect to the "ex-rights" price of the stock.

The most practical procedure to follow in this case, and the one that is taken by the great majority of the shareholders, is to let the market-place set the value on the right. Through competition the so-called "experts" will determine the value of the convertible bond, and thus the value of a right. If the bond is worth more as a result of its convertible feature, then the value of the right would be set accordingly. As a practical matter, the issuing company in order to sell the bonds would offer them under such conditions that there would be some advantage in subscribing to them.

QUESTIONS

1. The New Wonder Co. plans to raise $10,000,000 through the sale of additional common stock. Why might it prefer to use the privileged subscription method rather than sale of the stock through investment bankers?
2. Indicate the type of securities which are usually offered, and the type of security holders to whom they are offered, under a privileged subscription.
3. (a) Indicate the nature of the pre-emptive right of shareholders to subscribe to new stock offered by their corporation. (b) What are the exceptions to the pre-emptive right?
4. Does one "right" under a privileged subscription entitle the holder thereof to one new share? Explain.
5. Indicate when a stock will sell "cum-rights" and when "ex-rights".
6. In determining the value of a right, should the book value or the market price of the old stock be used? Why?
7. Is the privileged subscription a misnomer? Explain.
8. What should a person do with the rights which he receives in a privileged subscription? Explain thoroughly.

9. What are the requisites for a successful privileged subscription?
10. Indicate how the sale of "rights" and the sale of stock received from a privileged subscription are treated for federal income tax purposes.

PROBLEMS

1. The Midwestern Manufacturing Co., whose stock is listed on the New York Stock Exchange, presented the following balance sheet as of December 31, 19x1:

Assets		Liabilities and Net Worth	
Cash	$ 10,000	Payables	$ 100,000
Receivables	200,000	Capital Stock	3,000,000
Inventory	690,000	Surplus	2,430,000
Plant, etc.	4,630,000		
Total	$5,530,000	Total	$5,530,000

The stock has a par value of $100 per share, and its present market price is the same as its book value. Assume that you own nine shares of the stock. On January 3, 19x2, the company announced that its capital stock was to be increased 12½ per cent through the sale to present stockholders of additional shares at par. The rights are to be given to stockholders of record as of January 20, 19x2, and the new shares may be subscribed to through March 20, 19x2. It is assumed that by the latter date all the new stock has been subscribed. (a) What is the value of one "right" in this case? (b) Construct a new balance sheet giving effect to the new financing. (c) Using the data contained in the two balance sheets, prove why the right is worth the amount that is obtained from use of the formula. (d) How many rights will you get? How many shares of new stock can you acquire with these rights? (e) Compare your investment and its worth (1) before the new stock is issued, (2) after all the new stock is sold, assuming that you acquired the number of shares to which you were entitled, and (3) after all the new stock is issued but assuming that you have thrown away your rights. Assume that the stock is selling at its book value on March 30. Have you gained or lost anything by following procedure (2) or (3)? Explain.

2. When would the stock in Problem 1 above go ex-rights? What formula would you use to determine the value of a right after the stock has gone ex-rights?

3. Assume that you purchased eight shares of the stock in Problem 1 one year before the privileged subscription at $120 per share. Assume that you elect to consider the cost of the rights to be zero. Compute the amount that would be reported for federal income tax purposes under each of the following situations: (a) You sell your rights for $9 each. (b) You subscribe to one new share and one year later you sell one old share and the one new share for $192 each.

4. Compute the amount that would be reported for tax purposes in Problem 3 above assuming that you decide to allocate the cost of the stock over both the stock and the rights.

5. Indicate the circumstances under which you would prefer to elect for tax purposes to treat the cost of the rights as zero, and when you would prefer to allocate the cost of the stock over both the stock and the rights.

SELECTED READINGS

BOGEN, JULES I. (ed.). *Financial Handbook*, 3d ed. New York: The Ronald Press Co., 1952. Section 10.

DICKERSON, WILLIAM E., and STONE, LEO D. *Federal Income Tax Fundamentals*. San Francisco: Wadsworth Publishing Co., Inc., 1961. Chapter 6, p. 26, and Chapter 8, pp. 18–19.

EVANS, GEORGE H., JR. "The Theoretical Value of a Stock Right," *Journal of Finance*, March, 1955, pp. 55–61. Comments on this article by Stephen H. Archer and by William Beranek are in the *Journal of Finance*, September, 1956, pp. 363–66, and 367–70.

"Rights Prove Profitable," *Exchange*, April, 1960, pp. 9–11.

STEVENSON, HAROLD W. *Common Stock Financing*. Ann Arbor: University of Michigan, 1957.

WALKER, ERNEST W., and BAUGHN, WILLIAM H. *Financial Planning and Policy*. New York: Harper & Row, Publishers, 1961. Pp. 268–75.

WESTON, J. FRED. *Managerial Finance*. New York: Holt, Rinehart and Winston, Inc., 1962. Chapter 20.

14

Investment Banking

In this chapter we will be concerned with investment banking and the regulation of the original issue of securities. When the terms *banking* and *banks* are used the average person is apt to think of *commercial banking*. Commercial banks usually maintain both checking and savings accounts for individuals and businesses. The funds so acquired are invested in short-term obligations or loaned to business concerns, usually for a short term, for such purposes as financing inventories, paying accounts, meeting payrolls, and other working capital purposes. In some instances commercial banks will lend money to business firms for a relatively long period, but essentially they are interested in short-term loans only.

INVESTMENT BANKING

Investment banking is concerned with long-term financing—the kind that is secured by companies through sale of stocks and bonds. Furthermore, the investment banker does not *lend* the money to the company. Rather he *buys* the stocks or bonds, and then resells these securities to investors. It is to be noted that the investment banker is a principal in buying securities rather than an agent for someone else.

In addition to buying securities from the issuing corporation, some investment bankers will also buy securities which have already been issued, and sell them to other buyers. In connection with the original distribution of securities, some investment bankers will buy the securities from other investment bankers and then sell them to institutions and individual investors.

The stock brokerage business is often confused with investment banking. There is, however, a fundamental difference between them. The *broker* acts as an agent for the buyer and seller. He does not take title to the securities. He merely acts as a go-between for the buyer and seller, and collects a commission from either the buyer or the seller according to whose order he is executing. The order that goes through a broker is for securities which have already been issued by the corporation. Confusion between brokers and investment bankers is more common when the same firm, through different departments, carries on both investment banking and brokerage business.

Services Performed by Investment Banker

The services are as follows:

1. *Middleman.* There are always companies wanting capital and investors seeking investment opportunities. But without the services of the investment banker, it would be difficult for the two to get together. The corporation wanting capital is an expert in the manufacture, assembly, or sale of some particular product or service—not in securities. Individual investors are likewise engaged in their respective pursuits and have no opportunity to know the various companies that want funds. The investment banker acts like a wholesaler or retailer in that he secures the goods, in this case the securities, from the various issuers and sells them to the consumer or investor.

The cost to the issuer by selling through an investment banker is ordinarily less than if he attempted to market the securities directly to the investor. The banker has a security sales organization built up and this organization has contacts with other bankers and with the investing public.

2. *Assurance of successful sale.* If the issuing corporation attempts to sell its securities directly to the investor, it is never sure that the sale will be successful. Only part of the issue may be sold. This would have an adverse effect on the price of the securities, and furthermore, the company would not get all the money that was needed. When the sale is made to an investment banker the issuer has more assurance of selling all the securities, and also all the money will be coming in at the same time. This latter is often essential.

3. *Advice on the issue.* The investment banker is an expert in securities and the securities market. He knows what types of securities are selling and can thus advise the issuing company on the best type to sell at the particular time. He is also well acquainted with the current yields on other securities and, therefore, is in a good position to advise the company on the face rate of interest or dividend rate which would be set on the securities.

Timing is an important factor in marketing securities. The investment banker is in a position to know when the securities should be placed on the market. If the issuing company attempted to sell the securities directly, the timing may be off, with the result that all the issue could not be disposed of, or the selling price might have to be lowered considerably to sell the entire issue.

4. *Securities usually well placed.* If the issuing company attempted to sell its own securities they might be sold to the existing stockholders, the employees, or to people in the particular locality. Anything that might adversely affect the corporation may result in the securities' being thrown back on the market.

When securities are sold through an investment banker they are usually "well placed." The banker has a sales organization built up throughout the country, and contacts are usually made with the investment class rather than with speculators.

5. *Market support.* The price quotations for securities are for the relatively few which are being sold on the market. When a substantial part of an entire issue is placed on the market, at or about the same time, the tendency is for the price to fall. This has a marked influence on the price of the securities already sold and on the value of the part of the issue which is yet to be sold.

When the securities are sold through investment bankers, the latter commonly support their price by buying some of the securities on the market whenever the price weakens.

6. *Continued financial advice.* Not only may the advice of the investment banker be utilized at the time the securities are sold—he may continue to lend his aid for an indefinite time. Since the reputation of the banker is affected by the performance of the securities which he has sold, he will be interested in the future success of the company. He serves often as a financial adviser to the company during the entire time the securities are outstanding. In some instances he is made a member of the board of directors, which in some cases he insists upon.

7. *Aids the promotion of sound enterprises.* An investment banker is particular about the securities which he undertakes to sell. It is a business proposition with him. Naturally he will buy only those securities which he thinks he will be able to sell successfully. Thus companies which are not needed, or which will probably not prove to be successful, will be turned down by the banker. On the other hand, he will take over the securities of those companies which he thinks are selling a product or service that is wanted by the public.

Advantages of Bankers to Investors

The discussed functions of the investment banker were at the same time the advantages to the issuing company. The advantages of the banker to the investor are as follows:

1. *Issuer has been investigated.* Before an investment banker will take over an issue of securities, he will conduct a very thorough investigation of the issuer. Lawyers check property titles, patents, and contracts; engineers determine the value and physical condition of the properties; and accountants make a detailed check of the company's books. The production and marketing methods and labor relations are gone over. And of course, considerable weight is given to the efficiency of the management. All of this means that when an investor buys securities of an issue which has been taken over by an investment banker he is assured that a very thorough examination of the issuer has been made, and that in the opinion of the expert banker, the security issue will prove to be successful. The average investor is never in a position to make such an investigation himself.

It should not be inferred from the above that all issues which bankers handle will turn out well. Bankers vary as to the extent to which they investigate an issue, and their judgments are naturally not the same; also, it is impossible for anyone, including bankers, to know what will take place in the indefinite future.

2. *Assurance of proper security contract.* The staff of the investment banker will check the charter and bylaws of the issuer to determine if the security issue is properly authorized and that all the legal requirements have been complied with. They will have the necessary protective provisions inserted in the agreement, and these will be worded in such a way that the courts will uphold them. Although the banker is interested in the profit he will make from selling the securities for the company, he knows that the terms of the issue must be attractive to investors in order to sell the securities successfully.

3. *Maintenance of market.* This point, which will receive more attention later in the chapter, is obviously to the advantage of the investor.

4. *Advice of banker.* The investment banker's continued advice to the issuing company on financial matters would turn out to the advantage also of the holder of the securities. If a person buys securities through an investment banker, he may come to this source for future investment information. The banker is an expert in this field and is capable of giving sound advice, but he might, of course, be somewhat biased in his opinions by what securities he still has on his shelves to sell.

5. *Representative of the investors.* Security holders are usually unorganized and therefore cannot act with concerted force. If the company gets into financial difficulties or undergoes a reorganization, the investment banker that sold its securities often takes the initiative and represents the interests of the security holders. The latter, therefore, may receive better treatment in the reorganization than if the banker had not been in the picture.

Types of Investment Bankers

From the standpoint of type of organization, investment banks have been formed as individual proprietorships, general and limited partnerships, and corporations. As would be expected, corporations now carry on the greater part of the business, although there are a few partnerships left.

In the 1920's, it was characteristic of many investment banks to specialize in one type of securities, such as bonds, or stocks, or railroad securities, or municipal bonds; but beginning in the 1930's and continuing to the present, most investment banks handle various types of securities. A few, however, handle only one type of security, or specialize in that type. For example, Halsey, Stuart & Co., Inc., is the only large house of its kind in the country today that handles only bonds, while C. F. Childs and Company specializes in United States government bonds.

Some investment banks act only as wholesalers, some only as retailers, while others combine the functions of wholesaler and retailer. Such companies as Dillon, Read & Co., Inc., do not maintain a regular retail sales organization. Their primary function is to buy the securities from the issuing company and sell them to other investment bankers, who in turn sell them to financial institutions and to the public. Although these houses are classed as wholesalers, they do some selling directly to institutional investors. But this is classed as *institutional*, rather than *retail*, selling. These wholesalers handle large issues which are sold on a national scale. Some of the investment banks, such as Halsey, Stuart & Co., Inc., buy securities from issuing companies and sell them to other investment bankers, institutions, and to the public. They are thus performing both the wholesale and retail functions, as well as engaging in institutional selling.

A final type is the house that is engaged primarily in buying securities from members of the selling group or from individual investors, and selling them to someone else. They may on occasion buy a local issue directly from the issuer, and in some cases they will be members of an underwriting or selling group. Many of them also sell open-end investment company shares. The term *investment dealer* or *bond house* is sometimes applied to them. In some instances these houses merely arrange for the purchase or sale of securities for an individual, thus acting as a broker. The main business of a dealer of this kind is in the over-the-counter market.

Many of the large investment banks have branch offices in the larger cities throughout the country. Salesmen working out of these offices are assigned to call on the retail trade, banks, and other institutional investors.

Departments of a Large Investment Bank

A large investment bank that buys securities from the issuing company and sells them to other bankers, institutions, and to the public is departmentalized in a manner similar to other large concerns. These departments will be briefly described.

Buying Department. The buying department, as the term would indicate, has to do with the purchase of the securities from the issuing company. Needless to say, the work of the buying department is highly important. It is often said, and with a great deal of truth, that an issue well bought is half sold. The buying department uses the services of other departments such as the statistical and legal departments in the investigation of the issuer. Independent lawyers, engineers, and accountants are often hired to make a study of the company.

Although a particular bank may be large, the decision to buy or to refuse an issue is made by a few persons. They may be the partners of the firm or its principal officers, or a committee composed of some of the leading officers of the company.

Syndicate Department. In the case of large issues, syndicates or groups are formed both to purchase the issue and to sell it. A syndicate department selects the other members of the buying group and the members of the selling group to which the buying group will sell the securities. In some banks, however, the buying department makes up the purchase group, while the syndicate department organizes the selling syndicate.

Sales Department. When the house is not exclusively a wholesaler, it will have a selling department. This organization will have salesmen whose duty is to call on institutional and individual buyers and on other investment houses or dealers.

Trading Department. The trading department may engage in stabilizing operations after the new securities have been sold. In many instances a new issue handled by the investment banker is disposed of by taking in other securities in exchange for the new issue. It then becomes the duty of the trading department to sell these securities. The trading department also buys and sells seasoned securities in the market when it sees an opportunity for profit, maintains a secondary market in issues originally sold by the firm, and executes customers' buy-and-sell orders in the open market.

Statistical or Research Department. This department aids the buying department by making whatever studies are needed when considering a new issue of securities. It will also make studies of particular industries, companies, or securities. The statistical department will answer inquiries from investors and dealers in regard to particular securities. It will usually examine the holdings of investors free of charge, and make recommendations regarding the sale and purchase of specific securities. In some houses there is an investment advisory department which takes over some of the work of the statistical department stated above.

Accounting Department. This department handles the bookkeeping work the same as in other types of businesses. It will also keep the records in connection with buying and selling groups and aid in the settlement of these accounts.

SYNDICATES

In our discussion we have assumed that the investment banker or group of investment bankers purchases the securities outright from the issuing corporation and then sells them to other bankers or investors. This is the usual arrangement, but it is only one of the following three types of agreements between the banker and the issuer:

1. Firm commitment
2. Stand-by commitment
3. Best-effort commitment

Firm Commitment. The *firm commitment* is the type we have been discussing where the banker or group of bankers buys the securities directly from the issuing company and then sells them to investors, other bankers, or institutions. When the banker agrees to buy the securities, all the responsibility for selling them is on his shoulders. The issuing company gets its money from the investment banker before the securities are sold to the public. This type of commitment is the one most commonly used. The firm commitment syndicate is also used in connection with *secondary distributions* of securities. (This will be discussed in the following chapter.) After we have described the stand-by and best-effort commitments, the rest of the chapter will deal primarily with the firm commitment.

Stand-by Commitment. In the case of the *stand-by commitment,* the issuing company will sell its own securities, and the investment banker or group of investment bankers will merely "stand-by" and "take-up" and sell any securities which the issuing company is unable to sell. It thus becomes a firm commitment to the extent of any unsold securities. This type of commitment is most commonly made when the company attempts to sell securities to its existing stockholders under the privileged subscription. It is also sometimes used when a company offers its security holders a new type of security in exchange for the securities which they hold.

Best-Effort Commitment. In the *best-effort commitment* the invest-ment banker does not agree to buy any of the securities. He merely agrees that he will use his best efforts to sell as many of the securities as possible. Thus, he is really acting only as an agent in selling the company's securities. This type of arrangement is usually made when the issue is a speculative common stock whose sale is doubtful. This arrangement may also be used when a company wants to sell a better quality issue, but where it is not necessary that the entire issue be sold. In the case of the best-effort commitment, the banker is paid a commission only on the securities which he sells.

Syndicates or Groups

In many instances the purchase of an issue of securities may require many millions of dollars. The particular investment banker may not have available the amount of capital necessary to buy the issue, or may not want to risk an enormous amount in one company. For this reason the banker may call in other investment bankers to help him buy the issue. This group of bankers is called the *underwriting syndicate,* or *purchase group.*

In order to aid in the sale of the securities, the purchase group may or may not form a special organization called the *selling syndicate* or *selling group,* to whom the securities are sold.

Purchase Group

When the issue is large in size the investment banker who originated it may call in other investment bankers to buy a share of the issue along with him. Any of the following terms are applied to the group thus formed: *purchase syndicate, purchase group,* or *underwriting syndicate.* In order to avoid confusion with the *selling syndicate* or *group,* we will refer here to this buying organization as the *purchase group.* The invest-ment banker who originated the issue will usually serve as manager of the group.

Purchase Agreement. The *purchase agreement* is the contract that is made between the members of the purchase group and the issuer. Each of the members of the purchase group severally contracts for the purchase of his particular share of the issue directly with the issuer, although all of the participants are included in the same purchase agreement. This limits the liability of each participant both in respect to the penalties provided by the Securities Act of 1933, and in respect to the unsold securities.

The purchase agreement covers all essential matters, such as the time and place of delivery of the securities, and stipulates how and when pay-ment shall be made, conditions that must be performed by the company before the actual purchase of the securities, etc.

It is now common practice to include "market-out" clauses in the agreement, giving the purchase group the right to terminate the agreement if certain events occur before there is a public offering of the securities. Such events are, for instance, declaration of war involving the United States, closing of the stock exchanges, declaration of bank moratoriums, the discovery of a false statement in the agreement, instigation of a lawsuit against the issuing company, and other events which might adversely affect the financial position of the company. Since such "market-out" clauses have been inserted in agreements, there have been few instances where such events have occurred, but even where they have, the bankers have usually not tried to take advantage of them.

Agreement Among Purchasers. The *agreement among the purchasers* is a contract made between each purchaser and every other purchaser in the group, and also between each purchaser and the manager of the group. Following are some of the more important contents of this agreement: the amount of securities to be purchased by each member, the amount of money to be deposited immediately by each member, provisions relating to the payment and delivery of the securities, liability of the members, expenses assumed by the members, authority and compensation of the manager of the group, provisions, if any, relating to price stabilization operations, and the effective date and termination date of the agreement.

In connection with the *purchase agreement* it was indicated that it was common practice for each member of the buying group to purchase his share of the securities directly from the issuer, and that he would therefore be liable only for that amount of securities. This is referred to as the *limited liability account* or *divided account*. The agreement, however, may provide that in event not all the securities should be sold, each member would have a liability for them in proportion to his original subscription. This liability continues until the account is closed out. When the agreement provides for this type of liability it is called the *unlimited liability account* or *undivided account*.

The advantages of the divided account to the banker who has an effective sales organization are obvious. After taking down the amount of securities to which he subscribed, he has no further liability. But the divided account is not preferred by those bankers who are not sure of being able to dispose of their share of the issue. The divided account is the one usually used in the sale of corporate securities which have a common maturity date.

The undivided account, however, is widely used in the case of municipal bonds and corporate securities which have serial maturities, such as railroad equipment obligations. In the case of serial bonds, certain of the maturities can more readily be sold than other maturities. If the account was divided, some of the leading bankers would take down their allotment in the maturities which were easily marketed, leaving the less desirable ones for the other bankers. For this reason such accounts are commonly undivided, so that the banker who got the preferred maturities may still be forced to take some of the other maturities.

Selling Group

The purchase group may be the only syndicate present in the distribution of a security issue. In such a case it would be referred to in most instances as an *underwriting syndicate*. This syndicate would then sell the securities through its own sales organization to institutions, individual investors, and maybe also, to investment dealers.

The tendency in recent years has been to include a larger number of investment bankers in the originating group. Also, a larger proportion of the securities are being sold by members of this originating group without the use of the selling syndicate than was formerly the case. This is particularly true in the case of municipal issues and corporate issues that are of the best quality, or are small in amount.

In the case of corporate securities, however, there is often a group of bankers or dealers between the purchase group and the investor. Since the nature of this group differs in practice, and different terms are applied to the same type of group as well as the same terms to different types of groups, confusion abounds in the literature.

The object of the investment banking setup is to get distribution of the securities to the final investor. Generally speaking, the greater the number in the purchase group, the greater will be the number of bankers who can be prevailed upon to enter the selling group. Likewise the greater the number in the selling group, the greater will be the number of investors who can be contacted. Consideration is given to the geographic distribution of the securities in the selection of members of the purchase and selling groups.

When a selling syndicate is set up, members of the purchase group commonly also participate in the selling syndicate. Thus, they in effect receive double commissions, one for underwriting the issue, and the other for aiding in the sale. In the trade it is said that they "take down" a part of the issue for sale by their own organization. The manager of the purchase group may also set aside part of the issue for sale to institutional investors. The balance of the issue is "given up" for sale to the other members of the selling group.

The provisions relating to the sale of the securities are contained in a *selling group agreement*, which is a contract between the purchase group and the selling group. The following provisions are included in the contract: terms of sale to the selling group, and prices to be charged by them for the securities; provisions relating to the payment for and delivery of the securities; invitation to dealers to subscribe to the issue, or to confirm allotments reserved for them; and provisions relating to termination of the agreement.

One type of arrangement is for the purchasing group to allot the dealer a designated amount of the securities, and ask the dealer to confirm this by a specified time. When the confirmation is received, the dealer becomes liable on a firm commitment for that amount of securities. The other type is an offer on the part of the purchase group to the dealer to subscribe to part of the issue. In this case the purchase group reserves the right to reject part or all the subscription.

There is a distinction sometimes made between the phrases *selling syndicate* and *selling group*. The National Association of Securities Dealers, Inc.,[1] uses the term *syndicate* when the members of the organization are committed to take the securities, and the term *group* when there is no such commitment. Using the words with this meaning, selling groups are now more commonly used than selling syndicates. Despite the attempt to make a distinction between a "syndicate" and a "group," in practice the words are commonly used interchangeably.

Compensation Paid to Investment Bankers

The compensation received by the investment bankers for underwriting and selling securities varies according to a number of different factors. Generally speaking, the better the quality of the issue, the lower is the compensation. Thus, lower yield bonds carry lower compensation than higher yield bonds. The amount paid the bankers for handling bonds is less than that paid for handling a stock issue of the same size of the same company. The tendency is for the compensation to be a lower percentage for a large issue than a small one. In many instances, however, the larger issues are those of companies that are financially strong. The percentage compensation for public utility issues is lower than for mining and industrial companies.

In the case of securities that can be sold in large blocks, e.g., to institutional investors, the amount paid to bankers is usually a lower percentage. Bankers ordinarily receive a smaller percentage compensation on securities sold through competitive bidding (discussed below) than on issues which they get through negotiation. The condition of the market at the time of sale also influences the rate of commission that will be charged.

The difference between what the issuing company gets for the securities, and what the investor pays is called the "spread." This is also sometimes called a "commission" or "discount." This, of course, repre-

[1] Rules of Fair Trade Practice, Article II, Sec. 1 (g), (h).

sents the bankers' gross compensations. On manufacturing company issues sold in recent years, the approximate average bankers' commissions, expressed as a percentage of the proceeds of the public sale, on issues of from $1 to $2 million, and $20 to $50 million, were as follows: bonds 6½ and 1½ per cent; preferred stock, 8¾ and 3¼ per cent; common stock 10½ and 5 per cent.[2] The amount of the spread that goes to the various middlemen varies widely, but normally the manager of the purchase group would get about 10 per cent, the purchase group itself about 30 per cent, and the selling group about 60 per cent.

The spreads stated above represent the *gross* income from the underwriting and selling. Out of this income the bankers would have to pay all the expenses connected with the purchase and sale of the securities and their other expenses. In some instances the spread is so small that a slight change in the market may wipe out entirely the profit to the bankers. Occasionally they are forced to hold the securities for a while until the market improves. In some cases the bankers are forced to sell the securities for a lower price than they paid for them.

Price Stabilization

The price of securities that are already on the market is determined by the relatively few securities which at any one time are being bought and sold in the market. When a new issue of securities is being sold, the effect of a relatively large quantity on the market at the same time is to depress their price. If the market price of those securities which have already been sold weakens, it may jeopardize the sale of the remaining part of the issue.

In order to maintain the price of the securities, the manager of the purchase group is commonly given the right to buy and sell the securities in the market. The agreement usually limits the amount of the account to from 5 to 10 per cent of the entire issue. The manager may sell these repurchased securities in the market, or he may force the members of the purchase group to take them up in the proportion to which they originally participated in the group.

Although the manager will attempt to maintain the price of the securities at or near the offering price during the life of the syndicate, if the market slips very much, he may have to keep lowering the price offered for the securities. In some instances the price falls so low that all attempts at stabilization are abandoned.

[2] For complete data on costs see *Cost of Flotation of Corporate Securities, 1951–1955*, Securities and Exchange Commission (Washington, D. C.: U. S. Government Printing Office, 1957), pp. 9, 38–40; and Avery B. Cohan, "Cost of Flotation of Long-Term Corporate Debt Since 1935," Research Paper 6 (Chapel Hill, N. C.: School of Business Administration, University of North Carolina, 1961).

Since pegging the market is a form of manipulation, it can legally be done under the Securities Exchange Act of 1934 only with the consent of the Securities and Exchange Commission. Daily reports must be filed by the manager of the purchase group disclosing all stabilizing operations.

COMPETITIVE BIDDING

In most states public sealed bidding is required for state and municipal bond issues. United States Treasury bills are also sold in this way. Since 1941, the Securities and Exchange Commission has required, with a few exceptions, that issues of public utility holding companies subject to the Public Utility Holding Company Act of 1935, and the operating subsidiaries of such companies, be sold only by sealed bids. In 1950, the Federal Power Commission (this body has jurisdiction over public utilities which operate across state boundaries, but which are not subject to control by the Securities and Exchange Commission) issued an order requiring, with certain exceptions, public bidding for the security issues that come under its jurisdiction. In some instances the state laws also require competitive bidding for public utility issues. Since 1944, the Interstate Commerce Commission has, with some exceptions, compelled competitive bidding for public sale of all railroad issues over $1,000,000.

When investment bankers learn of an issue to be offered through bids, some of them alone or in connection with a number of other bankers will take steps toward bidding on the issue. Copies of the registration statement will be obtained from the issuer, and the latter may hold meetings at which the nature and terms of the issue will be explained and discussed. The bankers will then submit sealed bids for the issue. The banker getting the issue may then proceed to sell it through syndicates in the same way that we have described.

Advantages of Competitive Bidding

Following are the advantages of competitive bidding from the viewpoint of the issuing company.

Higher Price Obtained from the Issue. In the case of private negotiations between the investment banker and the issuing company, the latter is more or less forced to take the price for the securities offered by the banker. In the case of competitive bidding, however, each banker knows that other bankers are bidding on the issue, and thus each one will tend to bid the highest price possible in order to get the issue. It is thus argued that competitive bidding results in the lowest financing cost to the issuer. In the sale of public utility bonds in recent years investment bankers have received approximately 1 per cent of the offering price in the case of negotiated issues, but on issues handled through competitive bidding their commissions approximated only .8 per cent.[3]

Will Not Lead to Banker Control. In some instances the system of private negotiation has led to banker control of some companies. The particular banker would advise the company on financial matters and handle its security issues from time to time. The banker would often insist that a member of his firm be on the board of directors as long as any of the securities were outstanding. It is argued that under the more impersonal system of competitive bidding on each issue this banker control would not develop.

The Underwriting Business Will Not Be Concentrated in the Hands of a Few Large Bankers. It is argued by some that the private negotiation system of handling securities has resulted in a few large firms' getting most of the business, and that competitive bidding would tend to break this up.

Disadvantages of Competitive Bidding

Following are the arguments against competitive bidding.

Intimate Banker-Issuer Relationship Destroyed. Under the private negotiation system the investment banker acts as a financial adviser to the issuing company. His services are often valuable in setting the terms and conditions of the issue, and he may continue to advise the company while the securities are outstanding and even after they have matured. When a new issue is being considered, the same banker would probably be called in. It is argued that competitive bidding would break up this desirable arrangement.

Issue May Be Overpriced. Due to the competition of bankers, the price paid the company for the particular issue may be relatively high. As a result the banker might price the issue to the public at a higher price than would have been the case under private negotiation. If the issue is overpriced, it will probably fall in price later, which may thus adversely affect the issuer, the investor, and the banker. In reply to this argument it should be stated, however, that in general, investors will not pay more for the securities than they are worth.

May Result in the Issues' Being Handled by Only a Few Large Bankers. The proponents of both private negotiations and competitive bidding argue that the other method will result in a relatively few large bankers' getting most of the underwriting business. The argument against competitive bidding is that since it tends to result in a relatively high price

[3] For exact figures see Avery B. Cohan, *op. cit.,* p. 38.

to the issuer, the banker will have to keep his compensation to a minimum. This may result in the spread becoming so small that only the relatively few large bankers will get the business.

Inflexibility. When the sale takes place through private negotiation, the terms can be changed to fit the market conditions at the time the issue is put on the market. But in the case of competitive bidding the terms are set and the bankers are asked to submit their bids. In the meantime the market may advance or decline before the issue is sold.

Ineffective Under Adverse Circumstances. If the issue is a small one, or an issue of a company that is not well known, or a company that has a poor financial standing, there may be no bids submitted for it. Likewise when the market is unsettled, bankers may hesitate to bid.

PRIVATE PLACEMENT

An important trend in recent years has been the elimination of the investment banker in the sale of securities. Some institutional investors, particularly the life insurance companies, have been buying bonds directly from the issuing company. In some instances bonds have been privately placed with commercial banks and pension funds. One entire issue may be sold to one institution or a small number of such institutional buyers.

Common stocks are rarely sold through private placement. This is undoubtedly due in part to the fact that life insurance companies either are not permitted to buy them or are narrowly restricted in their purchase, and also because financial institutions prefer less speculative types of securities. More preferred stock issues have been privately placed since life insurance companies are less restricted in their purchase and because they as a class are less speculative than common stocks. The type of securities that has been commonly sold by private placement has been bonds. Since 1950 approximately 60 per cent of all industrial, financial, and service-type corporations' bonds sold for cash have been privately placed. About 30 per cent of all public utility bonds have been marketed in this way. The lower figure for public utilities is undoubtedly due at least in part to the fact that many of them are compelled to sell their securities through competitive bidding.[4] Table 14–1 shows the percentage of all debt issues which were privately placed for the years indicated.

[4] For detailed data relating to private placements see Avery B. Cohan, "Private Placements and Public Offerings: Market Shares Since 1935," Technical Paper 1 (Chapel Hill, N. C.: School of Business Administration, University of North Carolina, 1961); also latest Annual Report of the Securities and Exchange Commission (Washington, D. C.: U. S. Government Printing Office).

Table 14–1. Public Offerings and Private Placement of Corporate Debt Issues in the United States for Selected Years, Percentage of Total

Year	Public Offerings	Private Placements
1961*	57.9	42.1
1960	59.5	40.5
1959	49.5	50.5
1958	65.6	34.4
1957	61.4	38.6
1956	52.8	47.2
1950	48.0	52.0
1940	68.2	31.8

* For the first six months.

SOURCE: 27th Annual Report, Securities and Exchange Commission (Washington, D. C.: U. S. Government Printing Office, 1961), p. 215.

Reasons for Development of Private Placement

1. *No registration cost.* The Securities Act of 1933 requires that security issues which are to be publicly offered in interstate commerce must, with certain exceptions, be registered with the Securities and Exchange Commission. This entails a considerable expense to the issuing company. Securities that are privately placed do not have to be registered.

2. *No waiting period.* The Securities Act provides that no registered securities may be sold until the effective date of the registration statement. And the effective date is usually twenty days after the statement is filed with the SEC. During this period the market may break and jeopardize the successful sale of the securities. When the issue is privately placed, however, there is no waiting period that must be observed.

3. *Avoiding liability for officers and directors.* The Securities Act provides certain liability for officers and directors for any misstatements of material facts or omissions of material facts in the registration statement. Some corporate officials look upon private placement as a means of escaping this possible liability.

4. *Save bankers' commissions.* No commissions need be paid with private placement.

5. *Good investment for institutional investor.* The assets of life insurance companies have been increasing rapidly over a period of years. Interest rates were on the decline from 1932 to 1946, and insurance companies had difficulty investing their money in high-grade securities which bore a fair return. The insurance companies naturally have had to compete with each other in buying bonds offered through investment bankers. With the tremendous resources available, they started contacting

the issuing company directly. In many instances the insurance company has been able to buy the securities at a cheaper price than through an investment banker.

Advantages of Private Placement

The advantages of private placement are practically the same as the reasons for its development, which have just been stated. It will be noticed that these advantages are from the viewpoint of the issuer and the investor, and not the eliminated investment banker. Probably both benefit in many instances: the issuer may get a little more, and the investor may pay a little less than if the issue had been sold through a banker.

Another possible advantage of private placement is that, if the issuing company should run into difficulty, it might be easier to effect an adjustment with the institutional owner than if the securities were scattered among many individual investors.

Disadvantages of Private Placement

Private placement results in a loss of the underwriting and selling commissions to the investment bankers, but the following disadvantages are from viewpoints other than the banker's.

1. *Inability of issuer to buy back securities at a discount.* When securities are sold through the regular channels, opportunities often exist where a corporation can buy back its bonds on the market at substantial discounts. But when the securities are privately placed, the life insurance company will probably hold on to them until their maturity, at which time the issuer will have to pay back the full face value of the bonds.

2. *Future financing may be more difficult.* If the issue is privately placed, no general market is built up for the company's securities, and unless the same or some other institutions want to buy them, the issuer may have some difficulty in disposing of new securities.

3. *Fewer high-grade securities available for others.* It has been only the high-grade issues which have been privately placed with life insurance companies. That means that other investors, including the smaller institutional investors, do not have a chance to buy them.

Brokerage Fees to Bankers

If large institutional investors, such as life insurance companies, approach the issuing company about a new bond issue, or vice versa, the investment banker, of course, is out of the picture.

The more recent trend has been for an investment banker to act as a "finder." He will make it his duty to know companies that need financing, and insurance companies that want to invest. In some instances the investment banker is approached by the insurance company, while in others the issuing company may call him in. In acting as a "go-between" the banker receives merely an agent's or broker's fee for making the arrangement between the buyer and the seller. The fee which he receives, usually ranging from $\frac{1}{10}$ to 1 per cent of the issue, is smaller than the amount he would receive if he underwrote and sold the issue.

REGULATION OF SECURITY ISSUES

There has long been a need for laws to protect the buyers of securities. In ordinary sales of goods we have the rule or doctrine of *caveat emptor* which means, "Let the buyer beware." Under this rule of law the buyer is supposed to be able to see the goods and to judge their quality. If the seller makes any fraudulent misrepresentations in regard to the goods, the buyer has a legal right to bring suit, and if he can prove that fraud exists, he may recover the amount of his losses. But to do this he must take the initiative and prove fraud, which is usually difficult to do.

This law relating to ordinary goods proved very ineffective when it came to security selling. Securities are intangibles and it is impossible to judge their quality merely by inspection. The statements that accompany the security sale are highly important, but the average person is not capable of interpreting them. But even in cases where fraud is present and provable, relatively few buyers would take the time and spend the money that would be necessary to prosecute.

STATE LAWS

Beginning with Kansas, in 1911, all states now, except Nevada, have special laws relating to the sale of securities within their jurisdiction. These are called "blue-sky laws." [5]

In general there are three types of state securities laws. One type requires that the issuer register the security issue and receive the approval of the state securities commission before it may be sold. This type law is found in 43 of the states. Some of these states permit registration by "notification" for old well-established companies with a good earnings record, but require "qualification" for other issues. In 32 of the states the laws authorize some state official, such as the attorney general, to obtain court injunctions to prevent or stop the sale of fraudulent issues. Some of the states which have this fraud-type statute also require the ap-

---

[5] The name is said to have originated from the fact that the laws were designed to stop the sale of securities of corporations that were formed to exploit the resources of the "blue sky." In a U. S. Supreme Court case decided in 1917 the court quoted another decision which said that the laws applied to "speculative schemes which have no more basis than so many feet of 'blue sky.' " Hall v. Geiger-Jones Co., 242 U. S. 539, 550 (1917).

proval of the issue before it may be sold. Only four states, Delaware, Maryland, New Jersey, and New York, have the fraud acts exclusively. In 44 of the states security dealers and brokers must be approved and licensed by the state before they may transact business.[6] Most of the states have all three of the types of laws stated above.

Exempt Securities

When the state law requires the approval of security issues before they may be sold, there are always a number of exempt securities. These include securities which must be approved by some other state commission; government, state, and municipal bonds; and securities of other than ordinary business corporations. Following are the types of securities that usually do not have to be approved by the securities department:

1. Those issued by the United States, a state, or political subdivision
2. Stocks or shares issued by banks, savings and loan associations, trust companies, and insurance companies
3. Securities classed as "legal investments" in the state
4. Securities, such as those issued by railroads and public utilities, which must have the approval of the public utilities commission in the state
5. Real estate securities
6. Securities that are listed on approved stock exchanges
7. Securities issued by non-profit organizations

Exempt Transactions

Although the security may be one that should ordinarily be listed, the nature of the particular sale may be such that approval of the state is not necessary. The following are included in these exemptions:

1. Sale of stock to existing stockholders
2. Sale or issuance of securities in a reorganization
3. Judicial sales
4. Sales to one or a few persons

Weaknesses of State Laws

Although the state securities laws have been effective in stopping the sale of most fraudulent issues, there are certain weaknesses in the state laws. Following is a summary of the most important shortcomings.

1. *Laws applicable only to intrastate sales.* The principal weakness of the securities laws of the various states is that they apply only to sales made within the state. Many security issues are sold on a national scale. So long as the transaction crosses the state boundaries it is interstate in nature and subject to control by the federal government, and not the state.

[6] A small minority of the states have only this type of control.

Sales that are completed outside the state by mail cannot be controlled by the particular state.

2. *Incompetent officials.* In many instances the officials who are appointed to administer the securities laws are persons who have been appointed in reward for political favors granted. They are commonly not acquainted with the securities business.

3. *Fraud statutes not adequate.* The fraud statutes do not accomplish all the objectives that should be sought in a securities law. Where this is the only kind of security law in the state, it is not necessary for a company to file information about itself and the securities it plans to issue. The approval of the state is not necessary for the sale of the securities. The state only has the power to stop the subsequent sale of the securities if it believes fraud has been committed. This is somewhat like locking the stable after the horse has been stolen.

4. *Too many exempt securities.* In many of the states there are too many exempt securities and exempt transactions. In some states all guaranteed securities are exempt. Some exempt any security which is listed in designated securities manuals, or which is listed on a stock exchange.

5. *Questionable intent of some laws.* In some of the states the securities commission is given the authority to determine whether in its judgment the company will be serving a useful purpose or will be successful. It is doubtful if any commission is capable of deciding these questions. Many of our important industries and companies today would probably never have been started if a state commission had had to pass judgment on whether they thought the enterprise would be successful. Furthermore, it may be dangerous to our capitalistic economy to give anyone such power.

Securities Issued by Public Utilities and Financial Institutions

Our discussion of state regulation of securities applies in most instances to the securities of ordinary business corporations. Most of the states have public utility commissions which have the power to set rates and pass on security issues of railroads and public utilities within the state. Also, a banking (or similarly named) commission usually has the right to approve or disapprove the issuance of securities of banks and other financial institutions.

THE FEDERAL SECURITIES ACT OF 1933

Prior to 1933, the federal government, through the Interstate Commerce Commission, regulated the securities issued by railroads. In 1909,

Congress passed the Mail Fraud Act, under which the postal department was given the right to stop the sending of misleading and fraudulent statements regarding securities, and other goods and services, through the mail. Penalties were provided for the violation of the law. The postal department, however, did not have an adequate staff to enforce the law. Even if some persons were forced to discontinue sending fraudulent statements through the mail, no relief was afforded by the law to those individuals who had been defrauded.

The need for federal regulation of security issues has been realized since the end of the last century. Following World War I, several bills were introduced into Congress for such a law, but no legislation was enacted. After the stock market crash of 1929, and the start of the depression of the 1930's, however, the President, Congress, and the investing public realized the urgent need for such a law.

The practices followed by many companies and investment bankers during the late 1920's were misleading, to say the least. Aside from meeting the securities laws in the particular states, they were free to sell the securities in any manner desired. In most instances, inadequate information was given about the particular issue being distributed. Where the information was given, in many instances it was in such a form that it could not be understood by the average investor. In many cases the issuer or banker would not make any incorrect statements, but they would intentionally fail to give all the facts. Only the favorable factors would be listed. If the most recent financial statement was not favorable, an older one which showed better results might be used.

Basic Purpose

The basic purpose of the Securities Act of 1933 is to compel the issuer to give all the pertinent facts relating to the particular security issue, in order that the investing public would have a means of determining the investment worth of the issue. The law requires that not only must the information given be correct, but also that the issuer give all the material facts about the company and the issue. Thus, the truth and the whole truth must be given. At the time of its enactment, the legislation was often referred to as the "Truth in Securities Act."

The Securities Act of 1933 merely requires full disclosure of all the facts. It was not intended that the federal government should pass upon the soundness of the security issue. As long as all the pertinent information is given in a truthful fashion, the government has no power to disapprove the issue. The Act requires that the front page of every prospectus must certify that "The Commission has not passed on the merits of any securities registered with it. It is a criminal offense to represent that the Commission has approved these securities. . . ."

Administration

The Securities Act of 1933 originally gave the Federal Trade Commission the power to administer the various provisions of the law. Legislation passed the following year, the Securities Exchange Act of 1934, set up a commission called the Securities and Exchange Commission (SEC) to administer both Acts.

The SEC is composed of five commissioners who are appointed by the President with the advice and consent of the Senate. They are appointed for a term of five years. For purposes of administration, the United States is divided into nine regions with an office in each region, and branch offices in eight large cities.

Principal Provisions

The Securities Act of 1933 requires that, with certain exceptions, before any new offering of securities can be made to the public through the use of the mails or interstate commerce, the company must file with the SEC a *registration statement,* containing certain specific information about the company and the issue.

To bring the information to the attention of prospective investors, the Act requires that a copy of the *prospectus,* which contains about the same information as the registration statement, but in abbreviated form, must be made available to every buyer at or before the completion of the sale.

The fee for registering the issue with the Securities and Exchange Commission is $\frac{1}{100}$ of 1 per cent of the aggregate price of the proposed issue, but not less than $25.

Exempt Securities

When the Act was first adopted it was provided that issues not exceeding $100,000 in amount could be exempt from registration. In 1945, this limit was raised to $300,000. It was thought that the cost incident to registration would be too high in proportion to the amount of money obtained by the company when the issue was small in amount. The exemption is not automatic. It is necessary for the company to file an abbreviated registration statement, and get the approval of the SEC before the issue of $300,000 or less will be exempt.[7] Following is an outline of the exempt securities:

[7] This is governed by Regulation A. A copy of the "offering circular" must accompany the registration statement. It is required that this circular be given to buyers in connection with sales or offers to sell. After registration, a waiting period of ten days is necessary before the securities may be sold, unless the SEC shortens the period. In the case of issues of less than $50,000, the offering circular may be dispensed with except for newly formed companies and those that have had no net earnings in at least one of the two preceding fiscal years.

1. Issues of $300,00 and less, if approved for registration under Regulation A
2. Securities issued by the United States, a state, or a political subdivision of a state
3. Securities issued by any state or national bank
4. Securities of savings and loan associations
5. Securities issued by railroads
6. Receivers' and trustees' certificates
7. Short-term notes and bills with a maturity of not more than nine months
8. Securities of non-profit organizations
9. Life insurance and annuity contracts

Exempt Transactions

The Securities Act of 1933 covers only transactions involving the primary distribution of securities to the public. In the case of private sales, such as the sale of an issue of bonds to a life insurance company, or the sale of the issue to only a few persons, it is not necessary to comply with the Act.

Since the Act covers only those sales involved with the primary distribution of the securities, subsequent sales of the securities by persons, brokers, or dealers are not governed by the legislation. This is referred to as secondary distribution. Following is a summary of the type of security transactions which may take place without the necessity of registering the securities:

1. Sale of securities not involving a public offering
2. Sale of securities to existing security holders under certain circumstances
3. Exchange of securities with existing security holders
4. Resale of securities after primary distribution has taken place
5. Securities sold only to residents within the state of issuer

Registration Statement

The *registration statement* is an elaborate document, three copies of which must be filed with the SEC. The listing of the requirements of this statement is contained in 32 paragraphs covering several closely printed pages. The preparation of the registration statement and the prospectus, including the printing, often involves many thousands of dollars and may take months to prepare.

In general the registration statement covers everything that the Commission needs in order to approve the issue. Following are some of the more important requirements of the statement:

1. Names and addresses of directors, officers, promoters, underwriters, and of stockholders who own more than 10 per cent of the

company's stock, and the amount of securities held by each, and the amount of securities of the new issue to be held by each

2. Payment made or to be made to promoters, and all remuneration paid to each director and officer, and to anyone else receiving in excess of $25,000 a year

3. Filing of important documents and statements including the following:
   a. Copy of articles of incorporation and bylaws
   b. Detailed current balance sheet
   c. Detailed current income statement
   d. Statement of the amount of stock and bonds outstanding and the detailed provisions of all securities
   e. Statement of all securities covered by options outstanding, or to be created in connection with the security issue being registered, and the names and addresses of persons who are to receive more than 10 per cent of the options
   f. Terms of material contracts made, not in the ordinary course of business, including any management contract involving bonuses, and profit-sharing arrangements

4. Statement of net proceeds, offering price, and names of underwriters of any securities sold within two years preceding the filing of the registration statement

5. Elaborate detailed information relating to the particular issue being registered, including the following:
   a. Nature and amount of the security issue, and all underlying agreements relating to the issue
   b. Specific purposes of selling the issue
   c. Proposed price at which the securities will be offered to the public
   d. Estimated net proceeds which will be obtained from the sale of the securities
   e. Detailed list of itemized expenses incurred by the issuer in connection with the issue
   f. Commissions and any other type of compensation directly or indirectly received by the underwriters in connection with the sale of the securities
   g. Copy of opinion of counsel in respect to the legality of the issue, and names and addresses of counsel

Effective Date of Registration Statement

The law provides that the effective date of the registration statement shall be 20 days after it has been filed. The Commission may, however, shorten this period if it believes such action is justified by the circumstances. The securities cannot be sold or offered for sale until the effective date of the registration statement. During the 20-day period, which is known as the "cooling period," the Commission examines the registration statement to determine if it meets the requirements of the Act. If the material is satisfactory, it will be approved and will become effective automatically 20 days after the filing date.

If some of the material is incomplete or inaccurate, the Commission will issue a "stop order," and notify the issuer what additional information is needed. The stop order prevents the statement from becoming effective, until it is properly amended. Even after the registration statement becomes effective, the Commission may, after 15 days' notice, and opportunity for a hearing, issue a stop order suspending the effectiveness of the statement. The Commission will notify the issuer of any failure to conform with the provisions of the Act by means of a "letter of deficiency." Informal conferences between the Commission and the issuer, at which differences are ironed out, have largely eliminated the need for a stop order after the registration statement has been approved.

The "Red-Herring" Prospectus

One of the purposes of the cooling period is to enable dealers and the public to learn as much as possible about the issue prior to the time it is offered for sale. But the formal prospectus cannot be given to the purchaser until after the registration statement has become effective.

To supply underwriters and dealers with information about the nature of the particular issue is the function of the "red-herring" prospectus. This Preliminary Prospectus (its official title) received its name from the fact that it contains a statement printed in red lettering on the side of the page, and in language prescribed by the Commission, that the prospectus is not an offer to sell or the solicitation of an offer to buy, and that no orders can be received until after the effective date of the registration statement.

The rules set up by the Commission prescribe what can be contained in the "red-herring" prospectus. It should have a fair summary of the more important parts of the registration statement, and it should not contain an opinion or recommendation as to the investment worth of the securities. The offering price and other details are not stated in this prospectus. The Commission requires that a copy of the real prospectus must be sent to anyone who received a "red-herring" prospectus.

The Prospectus

The registration statement is available to prospective investors at the offices of the Securities and Exchange Commission, and photostatic copies of it may be obtained for a small fee. The statement, however, is a long, detailed volume and is read by few except investment bankers and large institutional investors. The fact that the buyer would have to take the initiative and secure a copy also detracts from its use.

Realizing the shortcomings of the registration statement, the Securities Act requires that a *prospectus* must be given to every buyer or person solicited either before or at the time of sale of the securities. This prospectus must contain a summary of the more important provisions of the registration statement. It is the desire of the Commission that the prospectus be in such an abbreviated form that people will read it, but considering the requirements, the fear of corporate officials and bankers that they may be held liable for failure to state the whole truth, causes them to be somewhat wordy. The result is that many prospective buyers do not read the document.

A copy of the prospectus must be filed with the Commission at the same time that the registration statement is filed. Since circulation is given to the prospectus, every effort is made to indicate that the Commission by approving the registration statement and prospectus has not put its stamp of approval on the quality of the security issue. To that end the law requires that the following statement be written in bold-face type, in capital letters, on the outside front cover page of every prospectus:

THESE SECURITIES HAVE NOT BEEN APPROVED OR DIS-APPROVED BY THE SECURITIES AND EXCHANGE COMMISSION NOR HAS THE COMMISSION PASSED UPON THE ACCURACY OR ADEQUACY OF THE PROSPECTUS. ANY REPRESENTATION TO THE CONTRARY IS A CRIMINAL OFFENSE.

In the case of securities that must be registered, the issuer and bankers must be careful not to make any offers of sale or solicitation of orders without accompanying them with a prospectus drawn up in proper form. Some announcement or advertisement which was not intended by the issuer or banker to be a prospectus or offer to sell, might be construed by the Commission to be such an offer or prospectus. The Securities Act of 1933 defines a prospectus as follows:

. . . The term "prospectus" means any prospectus, notice, circular, advertisement, letter, or communication, written or by radio or television, which offers any security for sale or confirms the sale of any security; except that (a) a communication sent or given after the effective date of the registration statement (other than a prospectus permitted under subsection (b) of section 10) shall not be deemed a prospectus if it is proved that prior to or at the same time with such communication a written prospectus meeting the requirements of subsection (a) of section 10 at the time of such communication was sent or given to the person to whom the communication was made, and (b) a notice, circular, advertisement, letter, or communication in respect of a security shall not be deemed to be a prospectus if it states from whom a written prospectus meeting the requirements of section 10 may be obtained and, in addition, does no more than identify the security, state the price thereof, state by whom orders will be executed, and contain such other information as the Commission, by rules or regulations deemed necessary or appropriate in the public interest and for the protection of investors, and subject to such terms and conditions as may be prescribed therein, may permit.[8]

It is obvious from the above stated definition of a prospectus that care must be used in what is stated in an advertisement of a registered security since any statement which is construed to be an offer to sell must be accompanied by a copy of the prospectus. The Rules and Regulations further provide what may be included in a notice, circular, advertisement, letter, or other communication.[9]

Penalties Provided

In order to induce full compliance with the provisions of the law, the Securities Act of 1933 provides for a number of penalties in event of violation of any part of the statute.

We have already referred to the fact that the Commission may issue a *stop order* if it believes the issuer has not complied with the provision of the law. In addition, if the Commission believes that any person is or is about to be in violation of the law it may apply to the federal courts for an *injunction* against the violation. The Commission may also give evidence of the violation to the Attorney General who is authorized to institute criminal proceedings against the violator.

The Act provides for both *criminal* and *civil penalties* in event of violation of the law. In regard to the first, the law provides that any person who willfully violates the Act or the rules of the Commission, or any person who willfully makes any untrue statement of a material fact or omission of a material fact in a registration statement is guilty of a crime and may, upon conviction, be fined not more than $5,000 or imprisoned for not more than five years, or both.

The *civil* liabilities are a little more complicated. If the seller fails to file a registration statement or to send a prospectus, or if the contents of the prospectus are not correct, or if the prospectus or communication includes an untrue statement of a material fact, or omission of a material fact, he can be made to return the purchase price of the security; or if the purchaser has sold the security, the latter can recover damages from the seller. It is to be noted that the penalties for these particular violations of the law run in favor of only the immediate purchaser. The purchaser would be unable to collect if it could be proved that he had knowledge of the untruth or omission. The seller could escape the liability if he could prove that he did not know of the untruth or omission and "in the exercise of reasonable care" could not have known of it.

[8] Sec. 2 (10).
[9] Rule 134 of the General Rules and Regulations under the Securities Act of 1933.

The second type of civil liability arises when the registration statement contains an untrue statement of a material fact or an omission of a material fact. This is a liability for damages for the difference between the amount paid for the security (not exceeding the price at which the security was offered to the public) and (1) the value at the time of suit, or (2) the price at which the security was disposed of in the market before suit, or (3) the price at which the security was disposed of after suit but before judgment, if the damages are less than under (1). The damages may, however, be reduced if the defendant can prove that the depreciation in the value of the security was caused by something other than the defect in the registration statement. The liability which we have just stated, in contrast to the one stated in the paragraph immediately preceding, runs in favor of not only the immediate purchaser, but all subsequent purchasers as well. Of course, if it can be proved that the purchaser knew of the defect in the registration statement, he would be unable to collect.

The original Securities Act permitted the purchaser to collect damages even if he did not rely on the misstatement or omission at the time of making the purchase. An amendment made in 1934, however, provides that if the purchaser acquired the securities after the issuer has published an earnings statement covering a period of at least twelve months beginning after the effective date of the registration statement, he would have to prove that he relied on the untruth or omission in the registration statement in purchasing the securities. In order to enforce the civil liability the purchaser must bring action within one year after the discovery of the untruth or omission, but not more than three years after the securities were offered to the public or were sold.

Persons Liable

In case of failure to file a registration statement, or failure to give a prospectus, or in the event the prospectus contains untruths or omissions of material facts, the law provides that the person who sells the security is liable. This would include the issuer and investment bankers.

When the suit is because of untrue statements or omissions of material facts in the registration statement, the following are liable:

1. The issuer
2. Every person who signs the registration statement
3. Every director who was serving as such at the time the statement was filed, or who with his consent was named in the registration statement as about to become a director
4. Every accountant, engineer, appraiser, or "any other person whose profession gives authority to a statement made by him, who has with his consent been named as having prepared or certified any

part of the registration statement, or as having prepared or certified any report or valuation which is used in connection with the
registration statement, with respect to the statement in such registration statement, report, or valuation, which purports to have
been prepared or certified by him"
5. Every underwriter

In connection with the liability of the underwriter, he is liable for
only that part of the issue which he underwrote.

Avoidance of Liability

Liability can be avoided if it can be proved that the decline in the
value of the securities was due to some cause other than the untruth or
omission in the registration statement.

Every person except the issuer may avoid liability by proving any
one of the following:

1. That he resigned from the office or relationship stated in the registration statement prior to the effective date of the statement, and
   that he notified the Commission of such resignation
2. That he had no knowledge of the particular part of the registration
   statement under consideration becoming effective, and that after
   becoming aware of the true facts he resigned, notified the Commission, and gave reasonable public notice that the registration statement became effective without his knowledge
3. That after reasonable investigation he had reasonable grounds to
   believe, and did believe at the time the registration statement became effective that the statements made were true and that there
   were no omissions of material facts

Value of Civil Liability Provisions

There have been some criticisms of the civil liability provisions of the
Securities Act. There have been relatively few instances of security
buyers bringing action, and in those that have arisen, only a small percentage have resulted in convictions. This, however, may be an indication of the value of the liability provisions. Because of the possibility of
their imposition, issuing corporations, their directors and officers, and
investment bankers have been especially careful to meet the requirements
of the law.

One weakness of liability penalties of this kind is that the purchaser
must first take the initiative before these civil liabilities will be invoked.

Evaluation of the Securities Act of 1933

The Act was never intended as a means of preventing the sale of
speculative securities. So long as the registration statement and prospec-

tus show all the facts and omit no material facts, the issue will be approved, no matter how speculative it may be. Investors will continue to lose money by the purchase of speculative securities. Moreover, losses arise from many things other than untruths and omissions in the registration statement and prospectus.

The issuing company learns many valuable things about itself because of the necessity of preparing the registration statement. This may also indirectly benefit the investor. Investment dealers who buy the securities from the underwriters and sell them to the public have a means of ascertaining much more about the securities than was possible before the adoption of the Act. Institutional investors, particularly those who buy large quantities of the securities, can determine the quality of the issue by an examination of the registration statement.

The average investor also has the information available to study the particular issue if he so desires. But most people pay little attention to the registration statement and prospectus. Nevertheless, the issuing company and the underwriters are careful to conform to the requirements of the law because of the chance of liability. The requirements of the prospectus, coupled with the desire on the part of the issuer and bankers to avoid liability, result in the prospectus' being too lengthy to be read by very many investors.

There can be no doubt that the Securities Act of 1933 has resulted in the elimination of many fraudulent issues that would otherwise have been put on the market. Most of these do not come to light now since promoters would realize their inability to get the issue registered. In other instances, when they attempt to get them qualified, the Commission issues stop orders.

QUESTIONS

1. Contrast the functions performed by commercial bankers with those carried on by investment bankers.
2. Do commercial banks ever buy and sell securities? Explain.
3. What are the possible advantages to the investor of having an investment banker take over the sale of securities?
4. Distinguish between the following kinds of agreements made between investment bankers and the issuer of securities: (a) firm commitment, (b) stand-by commitment, (c) best-effort commitment.
5. Describe the procedure followed in the organization and operation of a syndicate to handle the sale of an issue of securities.
6. Distinguish between the divided and undivided account syndicates.
7. Do you think the investor is helped or harmed by the price pegging activities of a syndicate? Explain.
8. Indicate the advantages and disadvantages of competitive bidding for securities both to the issuer and the investment banker. What type of securities are commonly sold in this way?

9. Indicate the advantages and disadvantages of private placement of securities to the various parties concerned and to investors in general.
10. Distinguish between investment bankers and securities brokers. May the same firm carry on the functions of both? Do investment bankers handle listed or unlisted securities? Explain.
11. What types of security transactions may take place in your state that are exempt from the securities laws?
12. Indicate the circumstances which led up to the adoption of the Securities Act of 1933 (hereafter referred to as the Act).
13. What are the principal provisions of the Act?
14. (a) What securities are exempt from registration under the Act? (b) What types of securities transactions are exempt from the Act?
15. Can the Securities and Exchange Commission (SEC) refuse registration of a particular security issue simply because it believes the issue to be too speculative? Explain.
16. Does the fact that the SEC has approved the registration of a particular security issue indicate in any way that it believes the securities are of good investment grade?
17. (a) Who may be held liable for the violation of the provisions of the Act? (b) What is the nature of the liability?
18. Do you believe that because of the Act the average investor has more information relating to the particular issue being sold than if the legislation had not been enacted? Explain.

PROBLEMS

1. Determine whether the channels of distribution for the sale of securities are discussed in the marketing course in your institution. Account for your findings. What similarities and differences exist between the sale of securities and the sale of "goods and services"?

2. The following is a balance sheet of the All-Metal Manufacturing Co. as of June 30, 19x1:

Assets		Liabilities and Net Worth	
Plant	$4,000,000	Capital stock	$6,000,000
Machinery	2,000,000	Less: Treasury stock	1,000,000
Inventory	1,300,000	Outstanding	$5,000,000
Receivables	800,000	Surplus	3,000,000
Cash	200,000	Payables	300,000
Total	$8,300,000	Total	$8,300,000

The stock has a par value of $100 per share and is selling in the market for $160 per share. Mr. Gary owns 1,000 shares of this stock. The directors voted to sell 10,000 shares of the authorized but unissued stock to a syndicate composed of Coon, Kobe & Co., Pillin Deed, and the City National Co., at $140 a share. The syndicate was to buy the stock outright and attend to all details in connection with its sale. Mr. Gary objected to this sale to the syndicate, but the company nevertheless closed the deal. (a) Was Mr. Gary justified in objecting? Can he do anything about it? Explain fully. (b) If it had been 10,000 shares of treasury stock that were sold to the bankers instead of the unissued stock, would your answer to (a) above be different? Explain. (c) If the 10,000 shares of unissued stock had been exchanged for the Western plant of the Eastern Steel Co., would Mr. Gary have any recourse? Explain. (d) If the stock had been purchased by the bankers at a price that enabled them to pay all expenses in connection with the sale and make only a reasonable profit, would Mr. Gary be justified in objecting? Explain.

3. Mr. Flatbush of Kalamazoo stated in a recent article that he preferred to buy his securities in the market sometime after the original sale rather than from the investment bankers at the time the syndicate was selling the securities. Why do you think Mr. Flatbush might prefer this means of purchase?

4. The following apply to the laws in your state pertaining to the sale of securities: (a) Must security issues to be sold in your state be registered with a state commission? (b) What types of security issues are exempt from registration? (c) What must be done to register an issue? (d) Does the commission have the authority to decide whether the particular issue can be sold? Explain. (e) Are security dealers and brokers required to have a license?

5. Ascertain the names of five investment banking firms in the United States. Which of these firms are incorporated? Do any of them also carry on a brokerage business in stocks?

SELECTED READINGS

Cohan, Avery B. *Private Placements and Public Offerings: Market Shares Since 1935*, Technical Paper 1. Chapel Hill: School of Business Administration, University of North Carolina, 1961.

Friend, Irwin; Hoffman, G. W.; and Winn, W. J. *The Over-the-Counter Securities Market.* New York: McGraw-Hill Book Co., Inc., 1958.

Investment Bankers Association of America. *Fundamentals of Investment Banking.* Englewood Cliffs, N. J.: Prentice-Hall, Inc., 1949.

Loll, Leo, Jr., and Buckley, Julian G. *The Over-the-Counter Securities Markets.* Englewood Cliffs, N. J.: Prentice-Hall, Inc., 1961.

Loss, Louis. *Securities Regulation.* Boston: Little, Brown & Co., 1951.

———. *Securities Regulation, 1955 Supplement.* Boston: Little, Brown & Co., 1955.

Miller, Glenn R. "Long-Term Small Business Financing From the Underwriter's Point of View," *Journal of Finance*, May, 1961, pp. 280–90.

Soldofsky, Robert M. "The Size and Maturity of Direct-Placement Loans," *Journal of Finance*, March, 1960, pp. 32–44.

Waterman, M. H. *Investment Banking Functions.* Ann Arbor: Bureau of Business Research, University of Michigan, 1958.

15

The Stock Market

Although many people immediately think of the New York Stock Exchange when the term *stock market* is mentioned, the latter is much broader than this and embraces all markets in which stocks are originally sold or later resold.

Corporations obtain capital through the *primary distribution* of their securities through investment bankers or directly to the public, their shareholders, or occasionally to their employees or executives. Companies would find it difficult to market their securities if there did not exist a market where investors could at any time sell their securities at a fair price. The resale by investors is referred to as the *secondary distribution*.[1]

The places in which securities are sold, or the channels through which they are sold, are called security *markets*. These are of two kinds: (1) the over-the-counter market, and (2) the organized security exchanges.

OVER-THE-COUNTER MARKET

The sale of securities by any method other than on the organized security exchanges is considered to be in the over-the-counter market. Since so much of the business of this type is now done over the telephone, it has been said that a more fitting name for this market would be the "over-the-telephone" market.

The over-the-counter market in this country is made up of some 2,500 securities houses and over 1,500 branch offices. Quotations on more

[1] The term *secondary distribution* is also used in a more restricted sense to refer to an *off-the-board* offering of a large block of securities which are listed on an organized stock exchange.

than 25,000 over-the-counter securities are published annually. This compares with about 3,000 securities which are listed on the exchanges. In some instances the houses merely act as brokers and collect a fee for the execution of a security transaction. In other cases they will take title to the securities purchased and resell them to other dealers or to the public. When the dealers take title to the securities the sale will be said to take place by negotiation. The dealer may be willing either to buy or to sell a particular security, and he will therefore quote bid and asked prices. These constitute the price at which he will buy and the price at which he will sell respectively. A prospective customer, however, may be successful in getting the spread between the two narrowed by "negotiation" with the dealer.

More security issues are to be found, and a greater dollar value of sales occurs in the over-the-counter market than on the organized security exchanges. All state and municipal bonds are sold only in the over-the-counter market. Although some U. S. government obligations are listed on the New York Stock Exchange, the bulk of the business in them is done in the over-the-counter market. Other securities which are either sold entirely or for which the greater part of the business is done in this market, include the following: open-end investment companies, bank and insurance company stocks, railroad equipment obligations, serial bonds, real estate securities, and in general the securities of small or medium-sized corporations.

A sizable amount of buying and selling of listed stocks and bonds takes place in the over-the-counter market by persons or firms that are not members of the registered exchanges.

Many of the dealers in the over-the-counter market are the same firms that handle the original or primary distribution of securities that are sold through investment bankers.

SHAREHOLDERS IN THE UNITED STATES

In 1962 there were 17,010,000 American shareholders in the nation's publicly held companies. This represented an increase of 36.2 per cent over the number of shareholders in 1959.[2] It is estimated that there are 2,000,000 additional Americans who own stock in privately held companies and who are not included in the 17-million figure stated above. Table 15–1 shows the increase in the number of shareholders in publicly held companies since 1952.

[2] Data relating to shareholders in this section are taken from the New York Stock Exchange study, *1962 Census of Shareowners in America*. Four such studies have been made by the Exchange since 1952.

Table 15–1. Individual Shareowners of Publicly Held Corporations in the United States, 1952, 1956, 1959, 1962

Year	Number	Percentage Increase over 1952
1962	17,010,000	162.1
1959	12,490,000	92.5
1956	8,630,000	33.0
1952	6,490,000	–

SOURCE: *1962 Census of Shareowners in America,* and *1956 Census of Shareowners,* New York Stock Exchange.

The dramatic growth in the number of shareholders is well illustrated by the increase in the proportion of adults in the United States who own stock.

In	One adult out of this number owned stock
1962	6
1959	8
1956	12
1952	16

Of the total adult shareowners in the United States 51 per cent are women, and 49 per cent men. Three out of five adult college graduates are shareowners. The average shareowner today is 48 years old, and his annual household income is $8,600. Of the total number of shareowners, 45.2 per cent had annual household incomes within the $5,000 to $10,000 bracket. Table 15–2 shows the breakdown according to income groups for the years 1962 and 1959.

THE STOCK EXCHANGES

An organized security exchange is a private organization formed and operated to facilitate the purchase and sale of securities by its members. A security exchange itself does not buy or sell any securities. The bulk of the business done on a security exchange is performed by brokers executing orders for their customers.

The membership on an exchange is more or less fixed, and if a person wants to become a member, it will be necessary to purchase a membership from a member who wants to sell. Bid and asked prices are kept on file at the exchanges for those who are interested, and may also be found in the financial press. Approval of the particular exchange, however, is necessary before any person will be admitted as a member. Only members are permitted to trade on the floor of the exchanges. Any orders to

Table 15–2. Total Shareowners of Publicly Held Corporations by Income, 1962, 1959

| Household Income | Individual Shareowners | | | | Estimated Total U. S. Population by Income | Per Cent of Each Income Group Who Are Shareowners | |
| | 1962 | | 1959 | | | | |
	Number	Per Cent of Total	Number	Per Cent of Total		1962	1959
Under $3,000	1,002,000	6.0	1,106,000	9.0	39,492,000	2.5	2.5
$3,000–$5,000	2,072,000	12.4	2,469,000	20.1	35,596,000	5.8	5.6
$5,000–$7,500	3,592,000	21.5	3,145,000	25.6	45,336,000	7.9	6.2
$7,500–$10,000	3,959,000	23.7	2,776,000	22.6	31,346,000	12.6	14.0
$10,000–$15,000	3,258,000	19.5	1,769,000	14.4	18,418,000	17.7	15.7
$15,000–$25,000	2,021,000	12.1	700,000	5.7	5,136,000	39.3	26.9
$25,000 and over	802,000	4.8	319,000	2.6	1,771,000	45.3	36.8
Sub-total	16,706,000	100.0	12,284,000	100.0	177,095,000	9.4	7.1
Not classified by income	304,000		206,000		6,117,000		
Total	17,010,000		12,490,000		183,212,000		

SOURCE: *1962 Census of Shareowners in America*, New York Stock Exchange, p. 11.

buy or sell listed securities that are received by a member of an exchange must be executed on the floor of the exchange.

There are 14 exchanges in this country that are registered with the Securities and Exchange Commission, and four others that are exempt from registration.[3] The largest of the registered exchanges is the New York Stock Exchange, and the second largest is the American Stock Exchange (formerly the New York Curb Exchange). Expressing it in round numbers, approximately 84 per cent of the market value of all stocks sold on national securities exchanges is sold on the New York Stock Exchange, and about 9 per cent is handled on the American Stock Exchange. Thus the balance of about 7 per cent is the amount that is handled by all the other exchanges.

Although the exchanges are referred to as "stock exchanges," even in their formal titles, most of them also have bonds listed.[4] But the bulk of the trading done on the exchanges is in stocks.

The New York Stock Exchange

Due to the relative importance of the New York Stock Exchange, we will describe the nature of its organization and operation. The American Stock Exchange will be mentioned only with respect to its differences from the New York Stock Exchange (which is often referred to as the "Big Board").

The New York Stock Exchange was founded in 1792. It is organized as a voluntary association, and its constitution provides for 1,375 members. (The Exchange has bought back and retired nine of the memberships.) Until 1953, only individuals were eligible for membership, but in that year the constitution was amended to permit corporations to own memberships.[5] Memberships on the Exchange are sometimes referred to as "seats."

The number of security issues listed on the New York Stock Exchange varies from year to year; on January 1, 1962, there were 1,541 stock issues and 1,186 bond issues listed. Only the large, well-established companies that have a relatively large number of shares outstanding in the hands

[3] The following are the 14 registered exchanges: American Stock Exchange, Boston Stock Exchange, Chicago Board of Trade, Cincinnati Stock Exchange, Detroit Stock Exchange, Midwest Stock Exchange, National Stock Exchange, New York Stock Exchange, Pacific Coast Stock Exchange, Philadelphia-Baltimore Stock Exchange, Pittsburgh Stock Exchange, Salt Lake Stock Exchange, San Francisco Mining Exchange, and Spokane Stock Exchange.

The four exempt stock exchanges are as follows: Colorado Springs Stock Exchange, Honolulu Stock Exchange, Richmond Stock Exchange, and Wheeling Stock Exchange.

[4] About 97 per cent of the bond trading done on the various exchanges is handled by the New York Stock Exchange. The greatest volume of bond trading, however, takes place in the over-the-counter market.

[5] As of January 1, 1962, there were 94 corporate members.

of many shareholders are eligible to have their securities listed. Following are the initial listing requirements of the New York Stock Exchange:

1. Demonstrated earning power under competitive conditions of $1 million annually, after all charges and taxes.

2. Net tangible assets of over $10 million, but greater emphasis will be placed on the aggregate market value of the common stock, where $10 million or more at the time of listing is looked for.

3. At least 500,000 common shares outstanding (exclusive of concentrated or family holdings) among not less than 1,500 shareholders, after substantially discounting the number of holders of less than 100 shares.

4. The company is required to maintain a separate transfer agent and registrar in the Borough of Manhattan.

In addition to the above, the Exchange requires a listed company to provide timely disclosure to the public of earnings statements, dividend notices, and other information which may affect security values or influence investment decisions. A company must pay an initial listing fee varying according to the number of its shares; the minimum fee is $2,000. An annual fee must also be paid for a period of 15 years after listing. The amount of this fee also varies according to the number of shares, with a minimum of $500 a year.

Once a security is listed, the issuing company cannot voluntarily remove the security without the approval of 66⅔ per cent in amount of the securities. But even if this approval is obtained, the security may not be delisted if 10 per cent or more of the individual security holders disapprove of its delisting. The Exchange, however, may take the initiative whenever it considers that continued dealings in the security are not advisable. The Exchange will give consideration to delisting a common stock of a company when there are:

1. 300 holders of record or less, after substantially discounting the number of odd-lot holders

2. 100,000 shares or less outstanding, exclusive of concentrated holdings

3. $1,000,000 or less aggregate market value, exclusive of concentrated holdings

4. $2,000,000 or less aggregate market value of outstanding common stock, or net tangible assets applicable to it, and the company's net earnings after taxes have averaged $200,000 or less for the past three years

Advantages of Listing to the Issuing Corporation

The issuing corporation cannot initially sell an issue of securities on or through the New York Stock Exchange. The issue must first be sold to the public either directly by the issuer, or through investment bankers, and adequate distribution of the security obtained before it is eligible for listing. The sales of the company's shares that take place on the Exchange thereafter represent sales made by the company's shareholders to other persons or companies.

From what has just been said the reader may conclude that listing benefits the shareholders and prospective shareholders of the company rather than the issuing company itself. Actually both benefit. The advantages of listing to the issuing company are as follows:

1. *Wider market.* If a security issue is listed on the NYSE it will enjoy a much wider market than otherwise. The wider market may give stability to the security and usually results in a higher price.

2. *Sale of new securities facilitated.* If at the time a new issue is being sold, publicity is given to the fact that application to list the securities will be made, this will improve the market and enable the company to float the new issue at a lower interest or dividend rate than would otherwise be the case.

3. *Advertising value.* Publicity connected with the listing probably improves also the market for the company's products.

4. *Indication of strength.* The fact that a company's stock is listed on the NYSE is an indication that, at the time of listing, the company was a large and successful one with bright hopes for the future. It should be realized, however, that some time after listing it may decline in importance.

Advantages of Listing to the Investor

Listing a stock on the New York Stock Exchange has certain advantages to the shareholders or prospective shareholders of the company. The principal advantages are as follows:

1. *Assurance that NYSE standards have been met.* The company must be large and must have established earning power, and the future must appear favorable. Furthermore, it is an indication of a good distribution of the stock. The investor is assured that the securities have been legally issued, that the stock certificates are probably not counterfeited, and that there will probably not be an overissue of stock certificates.

2. *Stock will sell at a higher price.* Due to the wider market for the stock and the publicity given the company, it is probable that a shareholder can get a better price when selling his securities than if they had not been listed. It should be realized, however, that for the same reason, a higher price will probably have to be paid for the securities.

3. *Ready and continuous market.* People owning securities which are not listed may be unable to sell them at a particular time or only at a relatively low price. If, on the other hand, the stock is listed, the investor knows that he may dispose of his securities at any time, and that he is getting the best price obtainable at the particular time.

4. *Higher collateral value.* Bankers are more willing to lend money on the collateral of listed securities, and a higher percentage of the market value of the security can be borrowed. This follows from the fact that the bankers know that if the loan is not repaid, they can at any time sell the collateral at the best obtainable price.

5. *Assurance of adequate information.* The investor in listed securities has the assurance that, due to the requirements of the NYSE, adequate information about the issuing company and its securities will be available at all times.

6. *Reasonable commissions.* The NYSE sets the minimum commissions that may be charged by its members to buy and sell listed securities. In practice these have become the maximum rates that are charged by members.

Composition of NYSE Membership

The "seats" on the New York Stock Exchange are owned by several different classes of members, described below.

1. *Commission brokers.* Approximately 648 members of the Exchange are classed as *commission brokers.*[6] These are members of brokerage firms who execute orders on the floor of the Exchange for their customers and charge for it the regular commission rates.

Partners of commission-broker members must agree to abide by the rules of the Exchange and are referred to as *allied* members. They, however, possess none of the rights of the regular members.

2. *Specialists.* About 360 members of the Exchange are *specialists.* As the title would indicate, these members specialize in the execution of orders of one or more different stocks. They act as brokers for other brokers. The latter commonly give the specialists orders which they have that are to be executed only at prices that are somewhat far away from the market prices existing at the time. Specialists may also buy and sell stocks on their own account. They are subject to strict rules of the Securities and Exchange Commission which are designed to prevent the specialists from taking advantage of their customers for their own personal profit.

3. *"Two-dollar brokers."* The so-called "two-dollar brokers" also execute orders for other brokers, particularly when the latter are too busy to handle the orders, and they may trade on their own account. They are also called *floor brokers.* There are 161 members of this kind. They formerly received a commission of $2 per 100 shares of stock from the broker for whom they were executing the order, and this accounted for the

---

[6] The numbers of each type of Exchange member stated in this chapter are as of July 17, 1962.

title, but rates have since been changed and now average about $3 per 100 shares.

4. *Odd-lot dealers and brokers.* In the case of most stocks listed on the NYSE the smallest unit that can be bought or sold on the floor is 100 shares. Since many people want to invest in less than this amount, several *odd-lot* firms have developed which will deal in units of less than 100 shares. Representatives of these firms hold 35 memberships on the NYSE. In order to help them carry on their business, these odd-lot houses have 82 stock exchange members who act as "associate brokers" and execute their orders on a commission basis. Thus, the odd-lot dealers and brokers account for a total of 117 memberships.

5. *Floor traders.* Floor traders buy and sell stocks on their own account on the floor of the Exchange, and do not execute orders for other persons. In recent years their number has diminished, and today there are only 30 memberships of the Exchange in this group.

6. *Bond brokers and dealers.* Bond trading is separated from stock trading on the floor of the Exchange. Those specializing in bonds may act as dealers and buy and sell bonds on their own account, or they may act as brokers in executing orders for other persons. There are 12 such members on the NYSE. (These are included in the various types of members stated above.[7])

American Stock Exchange

The American Stock Exchange (ASE; also abbreviated as Amex) is the second largest exchange in the United States. The organization and operation of the ASE are patterned very closely after the NYSE, so we will merely indicate the differences between the two exchanges.

The American Stock Exchange is newer and smaller than the New York Stock Exchange. The NYSE really has only one class of members (although partners of members are called "allied" members). The ASE has 499 *regular members* who carry on their business in a manner similar to that of the members of the NYSE. A great majority of these members are members of firms that have one or more memberships on the NYSE. In addition to the regular members, the ASE permits an unlimited number of *associate members.* At the present time there are 411 associate members. These members are not permitted to trade on the floor of the Exchange, but they may have their business transacted by regular members at a greatly reduced schedule of commission rates. Most of the associate memberships are held by persons who are members of the NYSE.

[7] The above stated types account for 1,316 memberships. As of July 17, 1962, five memberships were in the names of deceased members, two were under suspension, and the remaining 43 memberships were inactive.

Trading on the ASE takes place in both *listed* and *unlisted* stocks. Listed stocks must meet the standards set up by the Exchange before they are accepted. Unlisted stocks, on the other hand, are those which have been admitted for trading upon application of a member of the Exchange. The issuing corporation has nothing to say about it, neither does it pay any listing fee. No new stocks have been admitted for unlisted trading privileges since March 1, 1934, because the Securities Exchange Act of 1934 virtually prohibited any addition to the list. Of a total of 1,001 stock issues traded on the ASE, 797 are fully listed and 204 have unlisted trading privileges.[8]

The listing requirements of the ASE are not as stringent as those of the NYSE. The ASE will list stocks of newer, smaller, and more speculative companies than will the NYSE. In general a company to be listed on the ASE must meet the following requirements:

1. Net worth of at least $1 million
2. Demonstrated earning power of at least $150,000 after all charges and taxes
3. At least 200,000 shares of stock outstanding, exclusive of management and family holdings
4. At least 750 shareholders of whom not less than 500 must own at least 100 shares each

Many of the companies whose stocks have been listed on the ASE have developed into large and seasoned companies, and many of them have in the past been accepted for listing by the New York Stock Exchange. The ASE has more foreign issues, particularly Canadian stocks, listed than does the NYSE. The initial listing fees are also lower on the ASE, and there is no annual fee.

Bonds are traded in on the ASE in a manner similar to the NYSE. Securities which are listed on the NYSE will not be traded in on the ASE.

National Stock Exchange

The third stock exchange in New York City—The National Stock Exchange (Natex)—opened in 1962. This exchange was sponsored by the New York Mercantile Exchange, and membership in the latter is necessary for membership in the new stock exchange. In general the National Stock Exchange is designed to appeal to companies that cannot meet the listing requirements of either the NYSE or the ASE. There are no rigid listing requirements for the Natex but generally the company must have a net worth in excess of $500,000, and have at least 100,000 shares of stock outstanding in the hands of at least 500 shareholders. Stocks traded in on the NYSE or the ASE cannot be listed on the Natex.

[8] These figures are as of January 1, 1962.

The Regional Stock Exchanges

The 11 registered stock exchanges located outside New York City are known as *regional* exchanges. The largest is the Midwest Stock Exchange located in Chicago. All of the regional exchanges combined do only about 7 per cent of the total dollar value business of all the registered exchanges.

The regional exchanges were originally set up to provide an organized market for local and regional securities which were not traded in on either the NYSE or the ASE. Later many of the stocks that were listed or traded in on the NYSE and the ASE were, with the Securities and Exchange Commission's approval, given unlisted trading privileges on one or more of the regional exchanges. Today most of the business of the regional exchanges is in securities that are traded in on the NYSE or the ASE.

SECURITIES EXCHANGE ACT OF 1934

Many of the practices carried on in the securities business in the past, particularly in the 1920's, were contrary to the best interest of investors, but it took the stock market crash of 1929 and the depression of the early 1930's to force action designed to improve the situation. One thing that was needed was the regulation of the resale of securities after they had been issued, and the regulation of the stock exchanges and other markets through which these sales and purchases took place. This was accomplished by the enactment by Congress of the Securities Exchange Act of 1934.

The Act also provided for the creation of the Securities and Exchange Commission whose job it is to administer the Securities Acts. Later it was given the authority also to administer the following: the Public Utility Holding Company Act of 1935, the Trust Indenture Act of 1939, the Investment Company Act of 1940, and the Investment Advisers Act of 1940.

Registration of Exchanges

The Securities Exchange Act of 1934 requires all securities exchanges to register with the Securities and Exchange Commission. Several local exchanges have been exempt from this requirement. Registration involves the filing of a considerable amount of detail relating to the exchange and its rules and regulations, and makes the exchange subject to the provisions of the Act and the rules and regulations of the Commission.

The exchange must pay to the Commission an annual fee equal to $\frac{1}{500}$ of one per cent of the aggregate dollar amount of the sales of registered securities. The exchanges pass this fee along to the seller of securities.

Registration of Securities

Members of the exchanges are not permitted to buy or sell any security listed on the exchange unless the security has been registered with the Commission. The company whose security is listed on a registered exchange must therefore file the information required with the Commission. At the present time the data required by the Commission for registration are about the same as the NYSE requires for listing the security.

The following types of securities, however, are exempt from the requirement of registration: (1) direct obligations of the United States government, (2) obligations issued or guaranteed by corporations in which the government has an interest, (3) direct or guaranteed obligations of a state or political subdivision thereof, and (4) securities exempted by the Commission.

Margin Requirements

The Act originally set the margin requirement for the purchase of securities, but the power to decide margins later was transferred to the Federal Reserve Board. The enforcement of the minimum margin requirements, however, is left with the Commission.

Manipulation Prohibited

Before the Act was passed, the New York Stock Exchange prohibited certain types of manipulation, but the legislation added to these and provided severe penalties for their violation. In general the Act prohibits any practice or device which interferes with a free and orderly market. False or misleading statements relating to the securities are prohibited. The same is true of any artificial means of causing the price of a security to rise or fall. The Commission is given the power to decide the conditions and the circumstances under which price stabilization in connection with the issuance of new securities may take place. The Commission also has the authority to prohibit or regulate short selling.

Segregation

Many of the members of a stock exchange act as brokers in executing orders for other brokers and the public and also as dealers in buying and selling on their own account for their own personal profit. It has been felt by many that some of these members have taken advantage of the buying and selling public for their own personal advantage. It has been realized that without proper regulation this is possible and has been done in the past.

The exchanges have for many years prohibited a member from making a profit as a dealer and getting a brokerage commission on the same transaction. But the Act gives the Commission the authority to compel a member to act at all times only as a dealer, or only as a broker. This is referred to as *segregation*. For example, the Commission could prohibit all floor trading and permit the members of an exchange to act only as brokers and execute orders for others. To date, however, the Commission has not forced segregation, but it has adopted rules and regulations which closely define the trading functions of the floor trader, the specialist, and to some extent the odd-lot dealer.

Information on Stock Holdings

The Act requires that at the time of registration of the security with the Commission all officers, directors, and persons owning 10 per cent or more of any class of stock file with the Commission the amount of their holdings. Or if anyone comes into this category thereafter, he must file his holdings. Furthermore, the Act requires that all such persons stated above report to the Commission monthly any purchases or sales of their company's stock, within 10 days after the close of the calendar month. The Commission releases this information to the press.

Short-Term Profits of Insiders

The framers of the Act felt that corporate officers and large stockholders should not be able to profit from short-term speculation in their company's stock. To that end the Act provides that if any director, officer, or person owning 10 per cent or more of any class of stock makes a profit on the sale of his company's stock which he held for a period of only six months or less, a suit may be instigated by the corporation, or a shareholder acting on behalf of the company, to recover the profits for the corporation. It is to be noted that the Act does not prohibit such a profit. It only states that if a short-term profit is made by an insider, it may be recovered *if* suit is brought against the person. Officers, directors, and shareholders owning 10 per cent or more of any class of stock are also not permitted to sell the company's stock short.

Proxy Regulations

A large percentage of the voting in large corporations is done through proxies. In past years it was not uncommon for the proxy form to contain merely the announcement of the time, place, and purpose of the meeting, and the name or names of the person who would act as proxies for the shareholder. By signing the proxy and sending it in to the company, the shareholder gave his proxy the power to vote more or less as he chose.

The Commission, acting under the Securities Exchange Act, has adopted a long list of requirements for the proxy and the proxy statement. A copy of the proxy must be filed with the Commission 10 days before it can be sent out. The following are among the more important provisions that must be included in the proxy statement sent out for a listed stock.

1. Statement of who is soliciting the proxies and who is paying the cost of the solicitation.
2. If auditors are to be selected at the meeting, or a committee to select the auditors, the names of the auditors or committee nominees must be stated.
3. A clear explanation of all the matters of business that will come before the meeting.
4. Space must be provided for the shareholder to vote For or Against the various proposals that will come before the meeting. The proxy may provide, however, that if he does not express himself the vote will be cast in the way indicated.
5. When action is to be taken with respect to election of directors; bonus, profit sharing, pension or retirement, or other remuneration plan; or the granting or extension of options or special warrants or rights to purchase stock by directors to nominees for election to director, the following are required:
   a. Present occupation of directors and nominees for directors
   b. Amount of each class of equity securities of the issuer or of any parent or subsidiary owned by the directors and nominees for directors
   c. Direct remuneration paid by the issuer and its subsidiaries during the last fiscal year to each director, and each of the three highest paid officers whose direct aggregate remuneration exceeded $30,000, naming each such person, and the total amount paid to all the directors and officers as a group, without naming them
   d. Pension and retirement benefits of each director and officer

Periodic Reports

The Act gives the Commission power to require corporations to file with the Commission and the exchanges such information as may be necessary to keep the registration statement up to date. Annual financial statements are required, and the Commission has power to compel the filing of quarterly statements. These reports are available in the offices of the exchanges and the Commission. The average investor rarely would request statements from these offices. The various financial services and the financial press, however, get information from these sources and give publicity to the data.

Termination of Registration

The Commission has the power to deny registration of a security issue, or to suspend registration, or to withdraw the security from registration if in its judgment the issuing company has failed to comply with the terms of the Act or the rules and regulations adopted by the Commission.

When such action is taken the security can no longer be traded on the national exchanges. It is, however, preferred by the Commission that the exchanges themselves take the initiative in requesting such action.

Over-the-Counter Markets

Thus far our discussion of the Securities Exchange Act of 1934 has dealt with only the national securities exchanges and the securities that are listed on such exchanges. The Act did not contain specific provisions relating to the over-the-counter market, but it did give the Securities and Exchange Commission the power to make such rules and regulations as it saw fit for the regulation of this segment of the securities market. The Act was amended in 1936 to provide for the registration of all securities brokers and dealers. The Act was further amended in 1938 by the Maloney Act which provided for the formation and registration of associations in the over-the-counter market for the purpose of adopting rules and regulations for the self-government of the business. To date, only one such association has been formed, the National Association of Security Dealers.

The National Association of Security Dealers has drawn up an elaborate body of rules dealing with fair and uniform practices to be followed by its members. Members' markups or commissions must be fair and non-discriminatory. Price concessions may be made to other members of the organization, but securities dealers who are not members must be charged the same price as is charged the public.

BUYING AND SELLING

It is a very simple matter to buy and sell listed stocks and bonds. Our emphasis will be on stocks, but most of what is said would apply with equal validity to bonds. We will assume that the stock is listed on the New York Stock Exchange, but the procedure would be practically the same on any other exchange.

In order to buy stock all that is necessary is to give the order to a stock broker and put up the necessary amount of money. The local broker will wire the order to his correspondent or home office in New York. This office will immediately telephone the order to the company's telephone clerk on the floor of the exchange. The clerk will call the company's floor man and give him the order. The latter will go to the "post" at which the particular stock is sold, and, if it is a market order, buy the stock at the lowest price obtainable. A confirmation of the purchase will be sent back to the buyer. All of what has just been described (with the possible exception of the confirmation) takes place in a matter of only a few minutes.

Types of Orders

There are several different types of orders that a person may give in buying and selling stocks and each has its advantages and disadvantages. We will discuss only the more common types of orders.

Market Orders. A *market order* to buy is executed immediately at the lowest price obtainable. A market-sell order will also be executed immediately, at the highest price obtainable. When a brokerage firm's representative on the floor of the exchange receives a market order to buy a particular stock, he will go to the post at which that stock is traded and ask the specialist what the market is in that stock. The specialist may say "30 to ¼." That means he will buy the stock at 30, or sell it at 30¼. The purchaser's broker will then probably bid 30⅛ for the stock. If no one will sell it at that price, he will then buy it from the specialist, or whoever made the quotation, at 30¼. If this had been a sell order, the broker would have tried to sell the stock at 30⅛, and if he could not do so, he would then let it go for 30.

The advantage of a market order is the certainty of getting it executed immediately. Since there are always bid (buying) and asked (selling) quotations on all stocks, a person can always buy or sell immediately if he is willing to buy or sell at the "market." This is of importance if he is buying in a rapidly advancing market, or selling in a fast falling market. (Markets fall faster than they advance, so the sell market is used more commonly than the buy market order). The disadvantage of the market order is that he may pay more for the stock, and he may get less for it, than if he had specified a price at which he wanted the order executed.

Limited Orders. A *limited order* is one that specifies a price at which the order is to be executed. But it is the broker's duty to get a better price than that specified if it is possible to do so. Comparing this with the example of the market order stated above, a person may give the broker an order to buy the stock at 29¾. The floor representative of the firm would ask the specialist the market in the particular stock and if he replied, as in the above example, "30 to ¼," the broker would know that he could not buy the stock then at 29¾, since the specialist had been bidding 30. So, the broker would probably turn the order over to the specialist who would record it in his book. If the market later declined to the point where the stock could be bought for 29¾ or less, the order would be executed.

Before putting in a limited order the purchaser or seller may ask for the market on the stock, and his broker would wire through to the exchange and get the bid and asked prices (there is no charge for this service). The limited-buy order would then be put in below the market (below the asked price, or even below the bid price, as in the example just given).

The limited-sell order would be put in at a price higher than the bid price (or perhaps even higher than the asked price). For example, a limited-sell order might be put in at 30⅛, or higher. The ordinary fluctuations of the market during the day or week may lower or raise the price of the stock to the point where the limited order can be executed.

The advantage of the limited order is that a customer may pay somewhat less, and get somewhat more, than if a market order had been put in. The disadvantage of the limited order is that he may never (or at least within a given period of time) be able to buy or sell the stock. If his order is to buy, the market may keep on advancing indefinitely, and never get down to the price where his order can be executed. After the market has advanced he may put in a new order to buy the stock at a price considerably higher than if he had bought it at the "market" originally. The same reasoning in reverse applies to the limited-sell order.

Unless otherwise specified, a limited order is good only for the day it is given to the broker. If not executed that day, it will automatically be canceled. If desired, however, the order can be made "open," in which case it will, if not executed, remain alive after that day. A customer may specify the period he wants the order to remain open, such as "this week," etc.

Stop-Loss Orders. At the time an order to buy at 29¾ (or at the market) is given, an order to sell the stock at, for example, 27¾ "stop," may also be placed with the broker. Such an order is called a *stop-loss order*. It is given for the purpose of limiting a possible loss. In the above example, if the market on the particular stock should decline and there was a sale at 27¾, the stop-loss order would automatically become a market order to sell at the best obtainable price. If a sale was made at 27¾, probably the stop-loss could be executed at the same price. If so, the most that the purchaser would lose would be two points. If the stop-loss order had not been in, the price might have declined for a considerable length of time, and the purchaser may have eventually sold out at a much greater loss. That is the advantage of the stop-loss order.

The disadvantage of this kind of an order is that the market may get down to 27¾, or slightly below and the purchaser would be sold out. The market may then reverse itself and go up many points over a period of months or even years, but the purchaser does not profit from this since he has been sold out. Had the stop-loss order not been in, perhaps he would have held on to the stock and profited from the rise. The stop-loss order should not be placed too close to the existing market price, otherwise the ordinary fluctuations in the market might cause a sell-out.

Another precaution should be observed. If the stop-loss order to sell had been put in at 27¾, as in the above example, as the market declined a person might become afraid that he would be sold out, so he might cancel the order, and place a new stop-loss order at 25, for example. A further decline might give rise to a similar fear, with the result that this order might be canceled and a new one placed at, for example, 23½. The same procedure might be continued with further declines. If a person follows this practice, the stop-loss order will be of little benefit. The stop-loss order to *buy* will be discussed in connection with short selling.

Buying on Margin

When a person purchases stock and pays for it in full he is said to have bought the stock *outright*. Stocks, however, may be bought partly on credit, like many other commodities. The amount which is paid down at the time of purchase is called the *margin*. The Federal Reserve Board fixes the margin required, and at the present time the margin must be at least 50 per cent of the cost of the stock. Thus if a share of stock is bought at $100 a share, a margin of at least $50 must be deposited with the broker. The broker's correspondent office in New York uses the stock as collateral and borrows from New York banks the other $50 which is needed to buy the stock. The purchaser pays interest to the broker on the amount borrowed, which is called his *debit balance*.

With a given amount of money more shares can be purchased on margin than can be bought outright. For that reason marginal buying results in a larger percentage profit on the money invested, or if the stock goes down, a larger percentage loss is suffered than if the purchase had been outright. Of course, the profit or loss is realized only when the stock is sold.

Some people will overextend themselves in marginal buying. Should the stock decline in price, the margin will be decreased. According to the rules of the New York Stock Exchange, the broker must compel the purchaser to maintain a margin of at least 25 per cent of the existing market price of the stock. In the example given above, if the stock declined 33⅓ per cent, or from $100 to $66⅔, the margin would be decreased by the amount of the decline, or $33⅓. Thus, the margin now would be only $16⅔. The latter amount is just 25 per cent of the existing market price of $66⅔. Therefore, more margin would have to be put up if the market drops further. If the purchaser is unable to do this, the broker will be compelled to sell him out. Considerable sacrifices may have to be made by the purchaser to get additional funds to maintain the margin. If he is unable to secure additional money, he will be sold out at an appreciable loss. Had the purchase been outright, the stock could still be retained even though it had declined in price.

Marginal buying also enables a person to *pyramid* if the stock goes up sufficiently high. The purchaser may use part of the book profits which he makes as additional margin. Against this he may borrow more money and purchase additional shares. This process will result in increased profits *if* the stock continues upward since more shares are held. But if it drops in price, the loss will be greater for the same reason.

Buying and Selling Odd Lots

Most of the stocks listed on the New York Stock Exchange can be bought or sold on the floor of the Exchange only in units of 100 shares or multiples of 100 shares. To buy some stock that would cost $100 a share, for example, would require an outlay of $10,000 if the purchase is outright, and at least $5,000 if bought on a 50 per cent margin. Most people do not have this amount of money available for the purchase of stocks. Or if they do have that amount, they may not want to invest the entire amount in only one stock.

In order to take care of those who want to buy and sell in quantities of less than 100 shares, several *odd-lot* houses in New York have developed a business of buying shares in units of 100 shares on the floor of the Exchange, and then selling them to the public in any amounts from 1 to 99 shares. They likewise will buy these "odd lots" from the public, or from the brokers representing the public, assemble them in units of 100 shares, and sell them on the floor. To a considerable extent the odd-lot houses' purchases and sales of odd lots tend to balance each other so that they do not have to do much business in round lots. These odd-lot house members or their associate brokers operate on the floor of the Exchange. When a broker's telephone clerk gets an odd-lot order he will immediately send it directly to a representative of an odd-lot house for execution.

In addition to paying the regular commissions to his broker, the purchaser or seller of an odd lot of stocks must pay the odd-lot house *a differential*. This differential is ¼ of a point ($.25) per share for stocks selling at $40 and above, and ⅛ of a point ($.12½) for stocks selling below $40 a share. Following is an illustration of the execution of the three types of orders described above in odd lots.

In the case of a *market* odd-lot order, the odd-lot house representative will wait until the next sale of a round lot (100 shares or multiple of 100 shares) and then add ¼ or ⅛ to this (depending upon the price of the stock) for a purchase order, or subtract ¼ or ⅛ in the case of a sell order. Thus, if a person put in an order to *buy* 10 shares of XYZ stock at the market, the odd-lot house would charge the buyer ¼ point (if the stock sells for more than $40 a share) more than the price at which the next sale of a round lot takes place. If the next sale made on the floor after the odd-lot broker received the order was at $100, the odd-lot buyer would be charged $100¼. In addition, the buyer would have to pay the regular commission rates to his own broker. If the order had been to *sell* at the market, the odd-lot house would pay the seller $99¾.

In the case of a *limited* odd-lot order, the odd-lot broker will execute it only when he can make the ¼ or ⅛ differential. Thus, if a person put in an order to *buy* 10 shares of XYZ at $100, the odd-lot house will sell it to him at $100 only when the market (a sale of 100 shares or multiple thereof) goes down to $99¾. If the order had been to *sell* at $100, the odd-lot house will give him that for the stock only when the market goes to $100¼.[9]

The odd-lot stop-loss order will be executed whenever the market (sale of 100 shares or multiple) reaches or goes through the price specified in the order. If the order is to sell, the seller will get ¼ or ⅛ of a point (depending upon the market price of the stock) less than the price of the sale which made the order effective. Thus, if a person put in an order to sell 10 shares of XYZ at $97 "stop," the order would be executed when there was a round-lot sale at $97. The odd-lot seller would then receive $96¾.[10]

There are 262 stocks listed on the New York Stock Exchange in which a round lot is only 10 shares. These are the less active stocks. About 97 per cent of them are preferred stocks. Trading in 198 of the 10-share-unit stocks takes place on "Post 30," which is located in one corner of the new trading floor and the other 64 stocks are traded in at the other 18 posts.[11] Odd lots in these stocks would be any number of shares from 1 to 9. The odd-lot business at Post 30 is handled by two firms of specialists. A higher odd-lot differential is charged for these stocks than for the 100-share round-lot stocks.

If an order is for an amount of stock that represents both a round lot and an odd lot, the round lot will be treated as such, and the remaining shares will be handled as an odd lot. Thus, in case of the 10-share-unit stocks, if an order for 15 shares was received, 10 shares would be handled as a round lot, and 5 shares would be treated as an odd lot. In the case of 100-share-unit stocks, if the order was for 250 shares, the 200 shares would be handled as a round lot, and the remaining 50 shares would be considered an odd-lot order.

Short Selling

One of the most confusing phases of stock market activity to the beginning student is the practice of short selling. When a person sells stock which he does not own, he is said to be *short selling* or *selling short.*

[9] Slightly different rules are applicable if the effective round-lot sale is more than ¼ of a point (for stocks selling at $40 and above), or ⅛ of a point (for stocks selling below $40) from the price specified in the limited order.

[10] If the price of the stock fell from $98 to $96, for example, without hitting $97, the sale at $96 would make the odd-lot order effective, and the odd-lot seller would receive $95¾.

[11] The figures relating to 10-share round-lot stocks are as of August 13, 1962.

The most natural question that follows is: How can a person sell something which he does not possess? The answer is simple. He borrows the stock and makes delivery.

The short seller is a "bear." He expects prices or the price of a particular stock to go down. (A "bull" expects them to go up.) Like anyone else, he would like to buy low and sell high. And since he thinks prices are relatively high at the particular time, and that they will be lower later, he would like to sell at the particular time and then do his buying some time later when prices have fallen. The "bull" does or hopes to do the same, but he buys first and sells later. The short seller sells first, and buys later. The following illustrates the steps involved in short selling.

Assume that Mr. A believes that XYZ is relatively high at $100. So, he places an order with his broker to sell 100 shares of XYZ short, at $100. The broker will require him (rules adopted by the Federal Reserve Board) to put up a margin of at least 50 per cent, or $5,000. (NYSE rules require a minimum maintenance margin of 30 per cent of the existing market.) This is to protect the broker if the price goes up. Mr. A's broker sends the order through and the stock is sold to Mr. B on the floor, we will assume, at $100. Mr. B's broker will pay Mr. A's broker the $10,000.

In order to make delivery of the stock to Mr. B, Mr. A's broker will borrow 100 shares of XYZ from Mr. C. Why will the latter lend his stock? Because Mr. A's broker lends Mr. C the $10,000 which was obtained from Mr. B. Formerly Mr. C would have paid interest on the money borrowed, but in recent years the loan of the money is made without interest for the privilege of getting the stock. Occasionally, people like Mr. C will borrow the money without paying interest and in addition will demand a "premium" of $1.00 a day per 100 shares on the loaned stock. When no interest is paid for the money nor premium for the stock, the stock is said to be lending "flat." Mr. C can demand his stock back at any time, or Mr. A can demand the money back at any time upon proper notice. If Mr. C wants the stock back Mr. A can buy it in the market, or if he does not believe that it is the right time to buy the stock, he might borrow it from someone else on the same terms that he borrowed it from Mr. C, and return it to the latter.

We will assume that XYZ goes down to $95, and that Mr. A wants to close out his short sale. Mr. A will therefore buy 100 shares of XYZ from Mr. D at $95. Mr. A will then return the 100 shares to Mr. C, and the latter will return the loan of $10,000. Mr. A will use $9,500 of this to pay Mr. D for the stock. The net result is that Mr. A sold the stock for $10,000 and bought it for $9,500, thus making a profit of $500, less commissions and taxes.

Of course the market does not always move in the direction anticipated by the short seller. If the market had started up and had gone to $105, for example, Mr. A may have become afraid that it was going to continue to advance, and decided to close out the short sale at that time. If so, he would have had to pay a total of $10,500 for the stock, and thus would have lost $500, in addition to commissions and taxes.

It should be realized by the short seller that he does not know what his losses may be. When a person buys stock outright, the most that he can lose is the total investment, since the lowest the stock can go is zero. But the short seller stands to lose from the stock's advancing in price, and theoretically there is no upper limit to the price which a stock may reach.

The short seller, however, may use the stop-loss order to limit his losses in a manner similar to the buyer. At the time Mr. A sold the stock short, he might have put in an order to *buy* the stock at $103 "stop." If the market advanced to this point and there was a sale at $103, the stop-loss order would become a market order to buy at the lowest price obtainable. Perhaps this would be $103. In that event, the maximum loss that would be sustained by Mr. A would be $300, plus commissions and taxes. Or, if the stock fell to $95, and Mr. A felt that it might go lower, but he was afraid it might start back up, he might put in an order to buy at $97 "stop," and thus protect a profit of $300.

There has been considerable criticism of the practice of short selling. The Securities and Exchange Commission has the power to regulate it, or to prohibit it. To date it has seen fit only to regulate it. In an attempt to prevent short selling from accelerating a falling market, the SEC adopted a rule that short selling can take place only at a price higher than the last regular sale of the stock, or at the same price as the last sale, provided this price was higher than the last preceding different price. Perhaps this can be illustrated better than explained. Assume that regular sales of the stock occurred in the following order: $100, $99¾, $99¼. A short sale could be made only at a price of $99⅜ or higher. With the stock headed down in this manner the probability is that no one would buy the stock at $99⅜. And someone would have to buy it or otherwise a short sale could not take place. To illustrate the other part of the rule, we will assume the market moved as follows: $100, $99¾, $97⅞, $97⅞. A short sale could be made at $97⅞ (if someone would buy it) or higher, since although this is the same price as the last regular sale, it is nevertheless higher than the last preceding different price.

Short sales in round lots normally account for from 4 to 5 per cent of the total round-lot sales, and odd-lot short sales usually run from ½ to 2 per cent of the total odd-lot sales.

Brokers' Commissions

Both the buyer and the seller of stocks must pay a commission to the broker for handling the order. The New York Stock Exchange sets the minimum commission rates that may be charged by members for the execution of orders in listed stocks. If a person buys stocks and holds on to them, he will have only the buying commission to pay. But if he sells, then the commission for selling must be paid.

For purposes of computing the capital gains or losses on the sale of stocks, the commissions paid may be added to the cost of the stock, and subtracted from the amount received from the sale of the stock.

Table 15–3 shows the minimum rates charged by members of the NYSE. These rates became effective March 30, 1959.

Table 15–3. New York Stock Exchange Commission Rates on Stocks Selling for $1 per Share and Above

Money Value of 100-Share Unit	Commission Charge for 100-Share Unit
If less than $100.00	As mutually agreed (usually 6%)
$100.00 to $399.99	2% of money value + $3
$400.00 to $2,399.99	1% of money value + $7
$2,400.00 to $4,999.99	½% of money value + $19
$5,000.00 and above	1/10 of money value + $39

As noted in the table the commissions are computed on the money value per 100 shares of stock bought or sold. Assume that a person bought (or sold) 200 shares at $40 per share. The money value of 100 shares would be $4,000. Taking ½ per cent of this we get $20, to which we add $19, which gives us $39, the commission for 100 shares. Multiplying this by 2, we arrive at the total commission charge of $78 for the 200-share unit.

If the order is for an odd lot the commissions are $2 less than stated in Table 15–3. Assume that the order involved 20 shares at $40 (odd-lot differential included). The money value is thus $800. One per cent of $800 is $8, to which we add $5 ($7 less $2), giving us the total commission charge of $13. If the order is for a round lot plus an odd lot, for example 120 shares, it is treated as a round lot of 100 shares and an odd lot of 20 shares.

Notwithstanding the schedule of rates set forth in the table, when the amount involved is $100 or more, the commission cannot exceed $1.50 per share or $75 per single transaction (of 100 shares), but in any event it cannot be less than $6 per single transaction. If two or more different stocks are bought or sold, each is considered a separate transaction. Commissions must be paid both when stock is bought and when it is sold. Commission rates on the American Stock Exchange are quite similar to those on the New York Stock Exchange, but rates tend to be higher on the regional exchanges.

Stock Transfer Taxes

All sales of stock are subject to a transfer tax by the federal government. In addition, four states—Florida, New York, South Carolina, and Texas—levy a transfer tax. The transfer taxes are paid by the seller (odd-lot houses are not subject to the transfer taxes).

Federal Tax. The federal stock transfer tax is as follows: 4¢ on each $100 (or fraction thereof in excess of $50) of the actual value of the shares sold, but in no case will the tax be more than 8¢ per share. The minimum on any single transaction is 4¢.

New York Tax. The New York stock transfer tax is of particular importance since all stock sold on the NYSE and the ASE must stand the tax regardless of where the seller lives. The New York tax is as follows:

Selling Price of Stock	Tax per Share
Less than $5	1¢
$5 but less than $10	2¢
$10 but less than $20	3¢
$20 or more	4¢

Securities and Exchange Commission Fee. The Securities and Exchange Commission charges the exchanges an annual fee of $\frac{1}{500}$ of one per cent of the aggregate money value (one cent for each $500, or fraction thereof) of all sales of registered securities. The fee is paid by the seller.

Monthly Investment Plan

In 1954, the New York Stock Exchange inaugurated the *Monthly Investment Plan,* which is available through many members of the exchange. Under this plan a person may invest a fixed amount of money at regular intervals over a long period of time. The amount invested may be as small as $40 every three months, or as large as $999 a month. This amount (less commissions) is used each period to purchase a particular stock. A separate plan is arranged for each different stock that is purchased. The investor is credited with the exact number of shares or fractional shares that his money will buy. Credit is received for dividends on fractional shares as well as on whole shares. On commitments of less than $100, the commissions are 6 per cent.

Dollar Averaging

The investment of a fixed amount of money at regular intervals is called *dollar averaging* (or *dollar cost averaging*). The Monthly Investment Plan arrangement described above illustrates a type of dollar averaging. Since the fixed amount of money will buy few shares when they are high in price, and relatively many shares when they are low in price, it will be found that the average *cost* (per share) to an investor of his stock over a long period of time will be less than the average *price* of the stock during the same period. Dollar averaging takes the "emotion" out of stock buying and thus usually prevents an investor from making the common error of "buying high and selling low."

Secondary Distributions

Single transactions on the New York Stock Exchange or on any of the other exchanges, or in the over-the-counter market (after original offering), ordinarily involve only a relatively small number of shares of a particular issue. The total number of shares traded by the auction method on the exchanges for any day in fact comprise only a small percentage of the total number of shares listed of the particular stock. In some instances a relatively large number of shares might be offered for sale at one time. This might result from the sale of shares held in an estate or important holdings of shares by company officials, by investment companies, trust companies, or other institutional investors.

Whenever a relatively large block of stock is sold or is offered for sale at one time, the price will be driven down with the result that the seller by his own efforts receives less for the stock than its intrinsic worth. Before 1934, the only alternative to this was to sell the stock in small amounts over a period of time. But this would ordinarily not meet the objective of the seller, and in some instances the sale had to be made immediately. So, manipulative devices were used to bolster the stock so that the market could absorb the large block at one time without unduly depressing the price.

After the enactment of the Securities Exchange Act of 1934, manipulative practices were prohibited, and severe penalties were provided for any violation of the law. This, plus the fact that the market was "thin" in the late 1930's, led to the practice of selling large blocks of securities in the over-the-counter market after the close of the New York Stock Exchange. This is called a *secondary distribution*. The permission of the Exchange is necessary for such sale. Generally speaking, the block of securities to be sold must be at least as large as a month's balance of regular trading on the NYSE. A group of investment bankers or brokers will form a temporary syndicate or group for the purpose of selling the block of securities, and some selling pressure will be exerted. The offering price of the stock will be at or slightly below the closing price for that particular day. The sale may be underwritten by investment bankers in the same manner as a primary offering. Both members and non-members of the Exchange can buy the stock. An attempt will be made to sell the entire block of stock before the opening of the Exchange the following morning. If this cannot be done, the offering will usually be withdrawn in order not to conflict with the ordinary trading in the particular stock on the Exchange.

The original seller under the secondary distribution, which may be an investment company, receives a fixed amount for the stock, which is slightly less than the closing price for the particular day, but undoubtedly more than if the stock had been sold in the ordinary fashion. The bankers or syndicate selling the stock receive a fee which may be from two to five times the amount of the ordinary New York Stock Exchange commission. (The Exchange requires that it be at least twice the Exchange commission rates.) The buyer of the stock does not have to pay a commission. Price stabilization (for which permission must be obtained from the SEC) is usually used by the syndicate in connection with secondary distributions. Secondary distributions are sometimes called "secondary offerings," "off-the-board offerings," "dusk to dawn sales," and "block sales." [12] Secondary distributions of the type described here are also sometimes used for unlisted securities.

Other Block Offerings

As the off-the-board offerings of listed stocks became more numerous, particularly the American stocks being sold by foreign governments at the start of World War II, the New York Stock Exchange became concerned about the volume of listed stocks being sold in the over-the-counter market. This resulted in the Securities and Exchange Commission's amending its rules in 1942 to permit *special offerings* to take place on the floor of the national securities exchanges during regular trading hours. Such sales can be arranged when it is apparent that the market cannot absorb the block of stock within a reasonable time in the regular way without unduly depressing the price, and where the number of shares is not large enough to justify a secondary distribution. A special offering must be at least 1,000 shares and have an aggregate value of at least $25,000. As a general rule the number of shares should approximate two weeks' normal trading volume. The broker will announce the offering price over the ticker, and it is open to all NYSE members and their customers. Although the transactions are made on the floor of the Exchange, they are not part of the regular auction market.

In 1953, two additional procedures for handling block sales of stocks were authorized by the NYSE. One of these is the *exchange distribution*. Here the offering broker goes directly to his customers and solicits orders

[12] It should be noted that we are using the term *secondary distribution* here in a technical sense to refer to the off-the-board offering of a block of securities. We have previously used the term in a general sense to refer to the resale of stocks on the market after the original issue, such as the sales on the organized stock exchanges.

or expressed intentions to buy at a net price quite close to the prevailing market value. When enough buy orders are obtained the broker goes to the post where the particular stock is sold and *crosses,* in the auction market, the buy orders with his block sell offer; this will be at a price between the existing bid and offer prices in the regular market at the time.

The other procedure is *specialist block purchase.* A broker may negotiate a direct purchase of his block of stock, outside the regular auction market, with the NYSE specialist in that stock.

Later it was realized that in addition to arrangements for the block sale of stock, special procedures were also needed to handle the *purchase* of large blocks for institutional buyers. In 1956 the NYSE authorized what are termed *special bids, exchange acquisitions,* and *specialist block sales* to facilitate such purchases. These correspond to special offerings, exchange distributions, and specialist block purchases, described above.

A member must obtain permission from the NYSE for any of the block sales or purchases discussed above.

QUESTIONS

1. Is there any difference between the "stock market" and "market for stocks"? Indicate the nature of the over-the-counter market. What types of securities are sold in this market?
2. Do the registered securities exchanges themselves buy or sell any securities?
3. Indicate the advantages to the issuing corporation of having its stock listed on the New York Stock Exchange (NYSE).
4. Indicate the advantages to the investor of listing on the NYSE.
5. What are the requirements for listing a stock on the NYSE?
6. What different functions are performed by members of the NYSE?
7. How does the American Stock Exchange differ from the NYSE?
8. What are the principal provisions of the Securities Exchange Act of 1934?
9. (a) Can officers and directors buy and sell their own stock? What restrictions and limitations are put on them? (b) Can an officer or director make a short-term profit in his company's stock? Explain.
10. Indicate what must be contained in the proxy statement of a registered stock.
11. What are the relative advantages and disadvantages of the market and the limited order?
12. When is a stop-loss order for a round lot executed, and what price is paid or received for the stock?
13. How many shares of a stock selling at $20 a share can be purchased under existing margin requirements with cash of $10,000? How low could this stock go in the market before the broker would be compelled to call for more margin under the present New York Stock Exchange rules?
14. Indicate what would constitute the effective sale, and how much per share a person would pay for an odd-lot transaction if the order was: (a) A market order. (b) A limited order. (c) A stop-loss order.

15. Indicate the advantages and disadvantages to the investor of stop-loss orders.
16. (a) Indicate the mechanics involved in a short sale of stock. (b) Is it more expensive to buy on margin than to sell short? Explain. (c) Explain the Securities and Exchange Commission rule relating to short selling.
17. Indicate who must pay the federal and the New York stock transfer taxes on both round lots and odd lots.
18. Are odd-lot sales included in the published figures for the total sales on the New York Stock Exchange?
19. Explain fully how an odd-lot trader is at a disadvantage as compared to a person trading in round lots. What constitutes an odd lot at "Post 30"?
20. Explain the nature of the *secondary distribution* plan for secondary offerings of stock.

PROBLEMS

1. Indicate the price that would be paid for the following types of securities that are purchased at the quotations stated. (a) XYZ stock at 56. (b) ABC bond at 98. (c) U. S. Treasury Bond at 92.8.
2. The following refers to the business or financial section of your local newspaper: (a) Are the current market prices of some stocks listed on the New York Stock Exchange given? The American Stock Exchange? (b) Is the daily volume of sales on the New York Stock Exchange given? (c) Are any over-the-counter securities quoted? Which ones? (d) Are any stock averages or indexes quoted? If so, which ones?
3. What newspapers or magazines relating to the stock market are in your school library?
4. Mr. Smith puts in an order to buy 10 shares (round lot 100 shares) of a particular stock. After the order reaches the odd-lot dealer, sales of 100-share units took place at the following prices in the order indicated: 20⅛, 20, 19⅞, 19¾. Indicate which sale of a round lot made his odd-lot order "effective," and how much per share he would pay for the stock if the order was: (a) A market order. (b) To buy at 20⅛ "stop." (c) To buy at 20.
5. Compute the New York Stock Exchange commissions, federal transfer tax, and New York transfer tax on the following transactions: (a) 200 shares of stock sold at $20 a share. (b) 50 shares (odd lot) of stock sold at $80 a share. (c) 5 shares of stock sold at $400 a share. (d) 200 shares of stock sold at $500 a share. (e) 100 shares of stock sold at $1 a share.

SELECTED READINGS

BARNES, LEO. *Your Investments.* Larchmont, N. Y.: American Research Council. Published annually.
CRANE, BURTON. *The Sophisticated Investor.* New York: Simon and Schuster, 1959.
ENGEL, LOUIS. *How to Buy Stocks.* New York: Bantam Books, 1957. (A free copy may be obtained from the offices of Merrill Lynch, Pierce, Fenner & Smith.)
"General Rules and Regulations under the Securities Exchange Act of 1934," Washington, D. C.: U. S. Government Printing Office. Latest revision.
KAMM, JACOB O. *Investor's Handbook.* Cleveland: The World Publishing Co., 1954.
LEFFLER, GEORGE L. and FARWELL, LORING C. *The Stock Market,* 3d ed. New York: The Ronald Press Co., 1963.

MAYER, MARTIN. *Wall Street: Men and Money.* New York: Harper & Row, Publishers, 1955.

MERRITT, ROBERT D. *Financial Independence Through Common Stocks,* rev. ed. New York: Simon and Schuster, 1957.

New York Stock Exchange Fact Book. New York: The New York Stock Exchange. Published annually.

WALTER, J. E. *The Role of Regional Security Exchanges.* Berkeley: Bureau of Business and Economic Research, University of California, 1957.

16

Mutual Funds— Investment Companies

One type of financial institution which we want to discuss in some detail is the *investment company*. Although this form of organization is an important buyer of corporate securities, the widespread public interest in this type of company arises from the fact that its shares constitute an increasingly important form of investment for the typical small investor in the United States.

At the beginning of 1941 the combined assets of all investment companies in the United States were slightly in excess of $1 billion. By 1951 this had increased to approximately $3⅓ billion. But by 1962 the assets had reached the imposing figure of approximately $26 billion. As of January 1, 1962, there were 5.8 million investment company shareholder accounts held by 3 million shareholders (some people have more than one account). Figure 16–1 shows the growth in shareholder accounts for the period 1940–1960.

GENERAL NATURE

Investment companies are formed for the purpose of investing the proceeds of the sale of their own securities in the securities of other companies. The purpose of buying securities of other companies is investment rather than control, the latter being the objective of the holding company. The investment company, through the sale of its own shares, offers the investor a part ownership in the securities of a large number of other companies. In addition to this diversification, the investment company is in a better position, through its expert management, to decide

368

Fig. 16–1. Growth of investment company shareholder accounts.

what securities are the best to buy, and when to buy and sell them, than is the average investor.

Investment companies are sometimes called *investment trusts*. This is due to the fact that many of the early companies were formed under the Massachusetts trust form of organization. Some of those in existence today, such as the Massachusetts Investors Trust, are still operating under this form of organization. Most of them, however, are formed as corporations. When the term *investment trust* is used, however, we should interpret it as referring to the type of company rather than the form of organization which is used. The Adams Express Company, a closed-end investment company, was formed and is still operating as a joint stock association. The form of organization under which the particular investment company is operating is of little interest to the investor.

Early History

Although the modern business corporation originated in America, we must go to European history for the origin and development of investment companies. Wiesenberger [1] states that the origin can probably be traced to the Société Générale de Belgique, which was formed in 1822 by King William I of Belgium. Aside from this company and a few other isolated ones formed on the Continent, the real start of the organization of investment trusts began in Dundee, Scotland, in 1868, with the forma-

[1] Arthur Wiesenberger & Co., *Investment Companies* (15th ed.; New York, 1955), p. 19.

tion of the Foreign & Colonial Government Trust.[2] As the name would indicate this company was formed for the purpose of diminishing or diversifying the risk in the purchase of foreign and colonial government securities.

The early British trusts were fairly conservative. The emphasis was on income rather than capital appreciation. Diversification, particularly geographical diversification, was carried on to a considerable extent. Many of the securities purchased were those of the Commonwealth, or possessions, and foreign securities. Most of the companies had balanced portfolios, and they issued stock similar to our common and preferred stock, and debenture bonds.

American Experience

The first important investment company formed in the United States was the Boston Personal Property Trust, which was organized in Boston in 1894.[3] This company is still in existence today. There were few such companies formed in the United States, however, until the late 1920's. There was ample opportunity here for investors to buy the securities of operating companies which had possibilities of making greater profits for the investors than investing in the conservative investment companies.

In the late 1920's investment company formation began in earnest. Business was prosperous and stock prices were mounting. People were eager to purchase stocks with the hopes of making profit through their sale at a higher price. Possible future earnings and dividends were projected ahead some years at the same trend that had been going on, and the existing prices of stocks were discounting this future possibility.

The stock market crash of 1929 brought the expansion of investment companies to an abrupt halt. During the ensuing depression of the early 1930's a number of investment companies failed and some were bought up at relatively low prices and consolidated into larger units. The soundly conceived and well-managed companies, however, survived and some of them are among the largest investment companies today.

Because of a number of bad financial and management practices followed by some of the investment companies, the Securities and Exchange Commission in 1936, under a Congressional mandate, began a study of investment companies which culminated in the Investment Company Act of 1940, which will be discussed later in this chapter.

After the depression of the 1930's was over, a slight pickup occurred in the development of investment companies, but big expansion did not

[2] Rudolph L. Weissman, *The Investment Company and the Investor* (New York: Harper & Row, Publishers, 1951), pp. 1, 3.
[3] Wiesenberger, *op. cit.*, p. 20.

occur until after the conclusion of World War II. Since 1950 the development has been phenomenal. As noted in Table 16–1, the total assets of all investment companies increased from $3,402,525,000 in 1951, to a total of $25,994,089,000 at the beginning of 1962. This represents an increase of 664 per cent. During this period the closed-end companies' assets increased from $871,962,000 to $3,205,277,000, or an increase of 268 per cent. But during the same time, the open-end companies' assets increased from $2,530,563,000 to $22,788,812,000, which is an increase of approximately 800 per cent! Part of the net gain in assets has been due to the increase in stock prices, but in the case of the open-ends particularly, it has resulted in large measure from the increase in the number of shares outstanding.

Table 16–1. Growth of Investment Company Assets, Total Assets (Beginning of Year)

Year	Open-End	Closed-End	Total
1962	$22,788,812,000	$3,205,277,000	$25,994,089,000
1961	17,025,684,000	2,083,898,000	19,109,582,000
1959	13,242,388,000	1,931,402,000	15,173,790,000
1957	9,046,431,000	1,525,748,000	10,572,179,000
1955	6,109,390,000	1,246,351,000	7,355,741,000
1953	3,931,407,000	1,011,089,000	4,942,496,000
1951	2,530,563,000	871,962,000	3,402,525,000

SOURCE: Arthur Wiesenberger & Co., *Investment Companies* (New York: 1962), p. 26.

TYPES OF INVESTMENT COMPANIES

There are several different ways of classifying investment companies. One is according to the form of organization used. Another distinction is based on the nature of their portfolio. Still another method of classification, which we will discuss now, is according to the fundamental way in which they are set up for the sale, and in some instances for the repurchase, of their shares and the general operation of their business.

Face-Amount Installment Certificate Companies

Face-amount certificate companies contract with the investor for the sale to him on the installment plan of a certificate with a face or maturity value of a specified amount, such as $1,000. Payments are made in fixed amounts at specified dates over a period of from 10 to 15 years. Dividends are credited against the certificates, and these together with the installment payments build up the worth of the certificate to its face value at maturity. If cashed in before maturity, the certificates will have a surrender value, but during the first few years, when lapses are relatively high, there will either be no surrender value, or if there is one, it may be less than the investor has paid in. The investor pays a high selling cost for this installment type certificate, and it is not recommended for the average person. There are only a comparatively small number of these companies in existence in the United States.

A similar type of company is the installment investment plan company. Like the face-amount company, it is of relatively minor importance.

Unit or Fixed or Semi-Fixed Companies

The unit trust, or as it is sometimes called, the "fixed" trust was of some importance in the late 1920's and the early 1930's, but it is practically obsolete today. Under this plan a fixed group of securities or "unit" of securities was deposited by the sponsor with a bank or trust company, and against these, certificates of beneficial ownership in the unit of securities were sold to the public. The list of securities deposited remained "fixed," and could not be altered. In the case of the "semi-fixed" trusts, the management was given limited powers for the substitution of securities. According to the terms of the contract, the holder of the trust shares could convert them into cash equivalent to the value of his undivided portion of the securities deposited, or if he possessed sufficient certificates, he might convert them into a unit of deposited securities.

The *fixed trust* (more appropriate title since the certificates were not issued by a company) represented an effort to protect against poor management, and it was relatively popular for several years following the stock market crash in 1929. Naturally, it lacked the advantages of good management.

Closed-End Companies

Closed-end companies are so called because they have a relatively fixed amount of securities outstanding. They may from time to time sell additional securities, the same as any other type corporation. Also they may occasionally purchase some of their securities in the market like other companies do. The shares issued by the larger closed-end companies are listed on the New York Stock Exchange, or other exchanges, and are bought and sold by investors through brokers the same as securities of ordinary corporations. The prices of these shares are therefore dependent upon the law of supply and demand, similar to other listed stocks. A few closed-end shares sell at a premium over their book value, but the majority of them sell at discounts below their book value.

Some of the closed-end companies issue preferred stock and bonds, in addition to common stock, while others confine themselves to the issuance of only common stock. Most of the closed-end companies invest in a broadly diversified list of common stocks.

The closed-end companies were patterned after the British companies. Practically all of the leading closed-end companies in the country today were formed in the 1920's.[4] The largest closed-end company today is Tri-Continental Corporation, which was organized in 1929. The second largest company is The Lehman Corporation which was formed in the same year. The shares of both of these companies are listed on the New York Stock Exchange. The assets (less current liabilities) of these companies at the beginning of 1962 were $494,151,096, and $353,-812,122, respectively.

Open-End Companies

The *open-end* investment companies stand ready at all times to sell new shares to investors and to buy back the shares outstanding. They are often called *mutual companies,* or *mutual funds.* Sales are made at the then existing book value of the shares plus a loading charge, which will be explained later. A few of the companies do not add a loading charge. They purchase the shares back usually at the existing book value. It is this constant sale and repurchase of the shares that distinguishes these companies from all others. The shares of the open-end companies are not listed on the stock exchanges. They are bought and sold through selling agents of the issuer or brokers who specialize in them, or they may be handled by ordinary brokers. Part of the loading charge goes to the broker. In some instances they are sold and bought directly by the issuing company.

The open-end companies, with a few exceptions, have only one class of stock outstanding. They do not issue preferred stock, nor do they sell bonds. The Investment Company Act of 1940, which will be discussed later in the chapter, forbids the creation of any new open-end companies with senior securities.

Although some of the open-end companies confine their investment portfolio to a list of common stocks of a particular industry, others have a broad diversified list of common stocks. Many of the open-ends have a balanced portfolio consisting of common stocks, preferred stocks, and bonds. Some of the open-end companies invest only in bonds, while others buy only preferred stocks.

The open-end company had its origin in the United States. The first open-end company to be formed was the Massachusetts Investors Trust, which was organized in Boston in 1924. This company, which had assets (less current liabilities) of $1,799,875,825 on January 1, 1962, is the

[4] Wiesenberger, *op. cit.,* p. 232.

largest diversified common-stock investment company, and the second largest investment company in the country. The largest balanced open-end company, and also the largest investment company, is Investors Mutual, Inc., which was formed in 1940 by the Investors Diversified Services, Inc., of Minneapolis. On January 1, 1962, it had net assets of $1,915,069,611.

Both closed-end and open-end companies are classed under the head of *management investment companies*. This terminology results from the fact that in the case of both of these types of companies the management has full discretion in the selling or buying of securities for the portfolio. This is in contrast to the situation present in the unit or fixed investment trust.

CLASSIFICATION ACCORDING TO NATURE OF PORTFOLIO

Some investment companies diversify their portfolios more than others. The companies are sometimes classified as follows on the basis of their investments.

Balanced Fund

Balanced funds are found among the open-ends, but rarely among closed-ends. This type of fund has part of its investments in preferred stock and bonds as well as common stocks. In some instances government bonds and cash will form part of the portfolio. The average investor does not have sufficient capital to diversify between bonds and stocks. If he buys all stocks the risk is maximized, and he has no protection against deflation. If he buys nothing but bonds, his return will be relatively low, and he will have no protection against inflation. The balanced fund offers the small investor a part ownership in a wide list of both stocks and bonds. He thus is somewhat hedged against both inflation and deflation, his risk is less, and the average return should not be excessively low.

There is no law that governs the proportion of bonds and stocks. The management may tend to work out of stocks somewhat as the market advances, and buy more heavily in bonds. After a decline in the prices of stocks, the investment procedure may be reversed. As would be expected, the balanced fund is more conservative than a common-stock fund. Balanced funds differ as to emphasis on income and appreciation. The following are among the leading open-end balanced funds:

Axe-Houghton Fund B	Investors Mutual
Boston Fund	Loomis-Sayles Mutual Fund
Commonwealth Investment Co.	National Securities Dividend Series
Diversified Investment Fund	Scudder, Stevens & Clark Fund
Eaton and Howard Balanced Fund	Wellington Fund
George Putnam Fund of Boston	

Bond Funds

There are several investment companies whose investment portfolios consist only of bonds. In some instances these are investment-grade bonds, while others have more speculative ones. The securities offered by such companies have the advantages and disadvantages of purchasing bonds, but of course, the small investor can get a wide diversification and good management. An example of bond funds is the Keystone Custodian Funds, B-1, B-2, B-3, and B-4.

Preferred Stock Funds

There are a few investment companies specializing in the purchase of only preferred stock. Similar to the bond funds, the shares issued by these companies have the advantages and disadvantages of purchasing preferred stock, but like any other investment company, the investor gets the advantage of expert management and diversification. An example is National Securities, Preferred Stock Series.

Diversified Common-Stock Funds

The majority of the investment companies come under the classification of diversified common-stock funds. In some instances these companies will purchase some speculative bonds or preferred stocks, and in some cases a small amount of high-grade senior securities, but the great bulk of their investments consists of common stock. There is a wide variation, however, in the objectives of the companies and the type of common stock which they purchase. Some keep their funds fully invested in high-grade dividend paying stocks. Some stress both dividend return and appreciation in the principal. Some put more emphasis on "growth" possibilities and seek capital appreciation perhaps more than dividend returns. Others specialize in speculative low-price shares that generally move faster, both ways, than the general market.

Among the leading diversified common-stock funds are both open-end and closed-end companies. Following are some of the leading companies:

Open-End	*Closed-End*
Affiliated Fund	Adams Express
Dividend Shares	Consolidated Investment Trust
Fidelity Fund	General American Investors
Fundamental Investors	Lehman Corporation
Incorporated Investors	Madison Fund
Keystone Custodian Funds,	Tri-Continental
S-1, S-2, S-3, and S-4	U. S. & Foreign Securities
Massachusetts Investors Trust	
One William Street	
United Funds, Accumulative Fund,	
and Income Fund	

Funds Specializing in One or More Industries

Some of the investment companies specialize in the securities of companies within one industry, or within a few industries. Some of them are common-stock funds, while others have a more balanced portfolio. Both closed-end and open-end companies are found in this classification. In some instances the particular company has several funds of a somewhat different character.

Open-End	*Closed-End*
Atomic Development Mutual Fund	Abacus Fund
Century Shares Trust	Electric Bond & Share
Chemical Fund	Newmont Mining
Gas Industries Fund	Petroleum Corporation
Television-Electronics Fund	Transamerica Corporation
United Science Fund	United Corporation

"Special Situation" Funds

These funds acquire controlling stock interests in particular companies and take an active part in their management. They may later sell their holdings and purchase controlling interests in other companies. The two largest special situation companies are Alleghany Corporation, which is listed on the New York Stock Exchange, and Equity Corporation, which is on the American Stock Exchange.

Funds for Foreign Securities

A number of investment companies have been formed in recent years to specialize in Canadian and other foreign securities. In order to secure tax benefits, some of them have been organized and operated in Canada but at least 95 per cent owned by non-Canadians. Leading among these *non-resident-owned* (NRO) open-end companies are the following: Investors Group Canadian Fund, Canada General Fund, Scudder Fund of Canada, Canadian Fund, New York Capital Fund, and Loomis-Sayles Canadian and International Fund.

A few closed-end investment companies have been formed in recent years to invest principally in European and other foreign securities. Among these have been American-South African, and Eurofund, both of which are listed on the New York Stock Exchange.

INVESTMENT COMPANY CHARGES

All except a few of the open-end investment companies are sold through dealers who charge a selling fee which is included in the price the investor pays for the shares. The typical open-end company computes the book value of its shares (net assets based on market price of investments divided by total shares outstanding), twice daily. The investment company shares will in most instances be offered to the investor at the book value plus the selling charge, or as it is commonly called, the "loading charge." Most companies have a loading charge of 7½ per cent of the selling price. In recent years, however, a number of companies have increased the charge to 8½ per cent.

If a company has a loading charge of 7½ per cent, and its shares are offered at $20, it means that 7½ per cent of this, or $1.50, is the amount the investor is paying to the distributors of the shares. The book value of the shares would therefore be only $18.50. Some erroneously believe that a loading charge of 7½ per cent means 7½ per cent of the book value. If $1.50 is charged when the book value is $18.50, the selling or loading charge is almost 8.11 per cent of the book value of the share. (An 8½ per cent charge is 9.28 per cent of book value.) When the investment company's shares are sold through a wholesale distributor, he may get ⅓ of the loading charge, and the broker or retail seller will get ⅔ of it.

Investment companies will buy back their shares usually at the then existing book value. In the above example, it is apparent that the market price of the stock would have to rise $1.50 before the investor would be even with the board. Since the investor can sell the stock at its book value, that means the stock would have to go up approximately 8.11 per cent (not 7½ per cent).

If a person buys shares of an ordinary corporation, or a closed-end investment company, he does not have to pay a loading charge, but he will have to pay a broker's commission to buy the stock, and another broker's commission to sell it. A comparison of the relative costs of buying an open-end share and a closed-end share should, therefore, take that fact into consideration. The price of closed-end company shares depends, of course, on the market price as set by buyers and sellers, rather than on the book value. The amount of the broker's commissions depends upon the money value of the shares purchased and the shares sold. In most instances, where 100 or more shares are bought, the commission would average less than 1 per cent on each transaction. If less than 100 shares are purchased, the odd-lot differential must also be taken into consideration. If a person purchased 40 shares of a closed-end company's stock that was selling for $18.50 (we will assume this is the book value) in the market, he would pay broker's commissions and odd-lot differentials totaling $17.45. The same amount would be paid if he sold the stock at the same price. Thus, the total buying and selling charges would be $34.90. This would be equivalent to a charge of $.87 a share, or approximately 4.7 per cent. This is only about half the cost of buying and selling shares of an open-end company.

If bought at book value (or lower), the yield on the closed-end shares would tend to be more. In the above example, the purchaser of the closed-end shares would pay a total of $18.95 a share ($18.50 plus odd-lot differential and commissions of $.45). The yield would be computed on that price, while in the case of the open-end company it would be computed on the purchase price of $20 a share (assuming book value of $18.50 and charge of 7½ per cent).

Some of the open-end companies reduce the selling charge on large orders. Massachusetts Investors Trust, for example, has the following schedule of selling charges:

Sales Charge (per cent)	For Purchases of
8.50	Up to $25,000
5.75	$25,000
4.00	$50,000
3.25	$100,000
2.50	$250,000

Several of the open-end companies, however, do not include any loading or selling charge in the price of their shares. They sell the shares directly to the public at the book value, and purchase them back also at the book value.[5]

Market Price of Closed-End Companies

The prices of closed-end companies seek their own level in the market the same as any other type of stock listed on the exchanges or sold over-the-counter. Since part of the income of the companies is used to pay the management and other expenses of the company, the typical closed-end company's shares have in the past sold at substantial discounts below the book value of the shares. Also, in the past it was customary for the percentage discount to widen as the stock market in general went down, and to narrow as the general market went up.

Beginning with the stock market rise in 1949 and continuing to the end of 1961, the percentage discount of the leading companies has steadily narrowed. From 1951 to 1956, the average discount of 15 leading closed-end companies was approximately 15 per cent. From 1957 to 1960 it averaged about 10 per cent. Since then the percentage discount has further narrowed and by January 1, 1962, it had practically disappeared for the leading companies. In fact, as noted in Table 16–2 a number of the leading open-end companies were selling at a premium over the book value on January 1, 1962. Another interesting point is, with the drastic stock market decline in the first half of 1962, the discounts became smaller

---

[5] Among the companies which have no selling charge are the following: Energy Fund; De Vegh Mutual Fund; Johnson Mutal Fund; Loomis-Sayles Mutual Fund; Haydock Fund; Scudder, Stevens & Clark Common Stock Fund; Scudder, Stevens & Clark Fund; Rittenhouse Fund; Stein, Roe and Farnham Balanced Fund; Stein, Roe and Farnham Stock Fund; and T. Rowe Price Growth Stock Fund. Several of these companies, however, have a redemption fee of 1 per cent.

(or the premium larger). This is the reverse of past experience. The amount of the discount (or premium) usually reflects the past or expected future management performance.

Table 16–2. Percentage Discounts (Below Book Value) at Which Closed-End Investment Companies Were Selling, at Beginning of Year, 1957–1962

Stock	1962	1961	1960	1959	1958	1957
Equity Corp.	42	41	41	39	57	33
American-South African	39	30	11	6	Co. started Sept. 1958	
Alleghany Corp	22	30	37	46	54	48
U. S. & Foreign Securities	16	22	18	13	18	9
Tri-Continental	13	23	21	17	24	40
Electric Bond and Share	12	19	27	12	16	23
General American Investors	10	19	3	4	4	20
United Corp.	5	4	2	P5	P16	1
Dominick Fund	4	17	17	20	22	25
Adams Express	3	14	8	4	11	20
National Aviation	3	P2	10	11	P8	P8
Carriers & General	2	12	13	3	11	18
Standard Shares	P1	3	5	P1	5	6
Abacus Fund	P2	2	5	P2	7	17
Lehman Corp.	P5	P1	1	P11	P14	P14
Niagara Share	P6	12	8	16	20	29
General Public Service	P12	13	17	11	16	11
Madison Fund	P23	2	14	14	23	32

NOTE: P indicates premium over the book value.

SOURCE: Arthur Wiesenberger & Co., *Investment Companies* (New York: 1962), p. 272.

Management Fees

The principal item in the operating expenses of investment companies is the fee paid to the management. In the typical company the management is paid an annual fee of ½ of 1 per cent of the average value of the net assets. Some of the large companies reduce this percentage on higher brackets of assets. This is usually computed quarterly. The other expenses include taxes, legal and auditing fees, and fees to the custodian of the portfolio, the registrar, and the transfer agents. The total expenses average usually from ½ to ⅔ of 1 per cent of the net assets, and between 12 and 18 per cent of the gross income of the company.

INVESTMENT IN INVESTMENT COMPANIES

If a person directly owns the securities of operating companies he will get 100 per cent of the dividends paid. But if he buys the shares of an investment company that owns these same securities, the investment company will get these dividends, and from them, it will have to pay the expenses and management fee. The investor will receive whatever the investment company pays out in dividends. Usually this is substantially all of the income of the investment company after expenses have been paid.

It is sometimes argued that the investor would be better off to buy the shares of operating companies directly, rather than indirectly through the investment company, and thus receive 100 per cent of the dividends paid by the various companies whose shares are held. However, it should be realized that the average investor does not have sufficient capital to get the wide diversification that an investment company offers. Furthermore, he receives the advantage of expert management in the selection of the securities held by the investment company and in the timing of buying and selling. In some instances the so-called "expert management" has not been able to do much better than the performance of the stock averages, and some people have wondered at times whether the management was worth the price being paid for it.

A criticism of the type just made, however, may not be a fair one. An investor has no assurance that he would do as well as the performance of the stock averages. He might, for example, not buy stocks that moved the same way or as much as the stock averages. Furthermore, even if he had sufficient capital to buy the stocks that comprise one of the averages, he might trade in them with the result that any gains made might not be as much as if he had held the stocks and not traded.

Even though an investor can get diversification and expert management in buying the shares of investment companies, the performance of different companies varies widely. The average person might not select the right company. But even if he does pick a good company, he might do the same thing that he would do if he were buying shares of operating companies directly—he might buy the investment company shares high, and sell them low. In other words, even though the investment company is being expertly managed, the individual investor still has to decide when he is going to buy and when he is going to sell the investment company shares.

ACCUMULATION AND WITHDRAWAL PLANS

In order to take the emotion out of stock buying, and thus obviate the possibility or probability of buying at relatively high prices, some people follow the procedure of investing a fixed amount of money in stocks at regular intervals of time. This is called *dollar averaging*, and was discussed on pages 362–363.

Accumulation Plans

Almost all of the open-end investment companies have an "accumulation investment program," or "systematic investment program," whereby a person can invest an initial amount, ranging from $50 to $250, and then invest a fixed amount, usually from $25 to $70 monthly or quarterly or at some other specified regular periods, to gain the advantages of dollar averaging.

Some companies will apply the entire amount of the periodic investment toward the purchase of their shares and fractional shares. Others will sell the maximum number of whole shares, and credit the investor's account with the balance, which will be used at the time of the next periodic investment in purchasing additional whole shares. Usually certificates representing the shares purchased are not sent to the investor unless he requests them, or until 100 shares have been accumulated.

Some of the accumulation plans are purely voluntary. The shareholder invests whatever amounts he desires subject to minimum installment limitation provided. Other plans are *contractual*. The investor signs up to make regular installment investments of a fixed amount at regular intervals, such as monthly. The plan may run from 5 to 15 years, with 10 years being common. The contractual plan may be *with* or *without penalty*. With the former, no penalty is assessed against the investor if he fails to invest the fixed amount on the definite dates prescribed. The regular selling charges are added to each installment purchase.

The trend in recent years has been toward a contractual plan in which one-half of the first year's investment is applied toward the selling charges to be made for the entire contractual period, such as, for example, 10 years. (This constitutes the penalty for dropping out.) The balance of the selling charges are apportioned evenly over the remaining installments. This is referred to as the "prepaid charge" or "front-end load" plan. Should the investor drop out of the plan during the early years he would get back less than he invested, even if the value of the company's portfolio remained at the same value. For this reason many people will not sign up for this plan, and in some of the states it cannot be used. Some individuals, however, favor this plan because it more or less forces them to stick with the periodical installment purchases. Figure 16–2 shows the relative importance of several types of plans or accounts.

Some of the contractual plans permit the purchase of declining term life insurance with a face value equivalent to the unpaid balance of the specified investment goal.

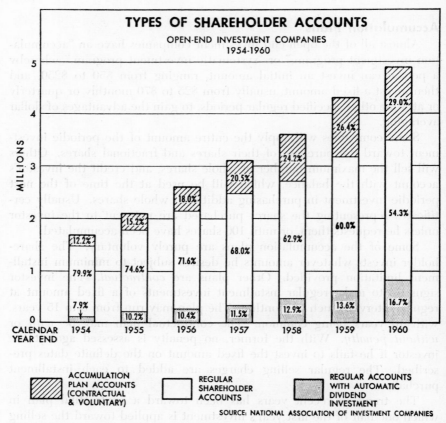

Fig. 16–2. Different types of accounts in open-end investment companies.

Reinvestment of Dividends

Practically all of the open-end companies will automatically reinvest dividends paid by the company if the shareholder so specifies. Such an arrangement is practically always made in an accumulation or contractual plan.

Practically all open-ends will reinvest dividends paid from capital gains at the net asset value of the shares, but many of them add the selling charge for shares purchased from ordinary income dividends. Reinvestment of capital gains dividends particularly is recommended since it preserves the principal of the investment, and if the current income is not needed, reinvestment of ordinary income dividends is advisable in order to get the effect of compounding.

Only five of the closed-end companies now have plans for the automatic reinvestment of ordinary and capital gains dividends, but a number of others give the shareholder an option of taking capital gains dividends in cash or in shares.

Systematic Withdrawal Plans

A majority of the open-ends now offer an arrangement whereby the investor may at a given time start withdrawing his investment in regular monthly or quarterly installments. The amount of the regular withdrawal may be a fixed amount of dollars, or it may consist of the proceeds of the sale of a specified fixed number of shares. When the entire investment is exhausted the payments, of course, cease. In some instances the investment may be used to purchase a life annuity or another type of annuity. Many of them require ownership of at least $10,000 in shares to start such a plan.

REGULATION AND TAXATION

The Investment Company Act of 1940

Due to the bad practices which had been followed by many investment companies, and as a result of a study made by the Securities and Exchange Commission, Congress, in 1940, enacted the Investment Company Act. Following are the principal features of the Act. (Face-amount certificate companies are subject to some other requirements not stated here.)

All investment companies are required to register as such with the Securities and Exchange Commission, which administers the Act. Investment companies must have a minimum capital of $100,000 before they can publicly sell shares. Open-end companies formed after the Act can issue only one class of securities—common stock. Closed-end companies can issue bonds and preferred stock, but any such bonds must be covered three times by the assets, and preferred stock must be covered twice. Only one class of bonds and one class of preferred stock may be issued by the closed-ends. Any preferred stock issued must be voting.

The registration statement that must be filed by the investment company with the Securities and Exchange Commission must contain a description of the company, the method of operation, and the investment policy it intends to follow. A statement of the investment policy must be included in the prospectus or other material given to prospective investors. Semiannual financial statements must be sent to the shareholders. When dividends are paid the shareholders must be informed what part, if any, represents capital gains or other special sources of income.

The Act provides that a majority of the board of directors or the board of trustees cannot be connected with the investment banking firm or brokers who handle the sale or purchase of the company's shares. At least 40 per cent of the directors must be persons who are not officers of the investment company or investment advisers of the company. Investment companies formed after the adoption of the Act are prohibited from buying sufficient shares in other investment companies to obtain working control of the other companies.

The sale of new shares is subject to the provisions of the Securities Act of 1933. The Investment Company Act further regulates the sale of investment company securities. In practice this has been done largely by voluntary action through the National Association of Security Dealers, which is subject to the jurisdiction of the Securities and Exchange Commission.

Taxation of Investment Companies and Their Shares

Unless registered with the Internal Revenue Service as a "regulated investment company," an investment company would pay the same corporate taxes that are paid by any other type of corporation. That means that all of the interest income received, except that earned on tax-exempt bonds, must be reported. But in order to lessen the amount of double taxation, investment companies, like other corporations, are required to report only 15 per cent of the dividends received on the stock which they own. Capital gains, which are profits made on the sale of securities held in the portfolio, are reported as such. The tax rate on the long-term capital gains (made on securities held for more than six months) is 25 per cent.

The investor owning shares in a non-regulated investment company would pay the same income taxes that are paid by a shareholder of any other type of corporation. Some companies cannot qualify as a "regulated investment company," and are, therefore, taxed as any ordinary type of corporation because they do not pay a sufficient amount of their earnings out to the shareholders in the form of dividends. Other companies could qualify but wish to remain "non-regulated" in order to gain certain tax advantages for their shareholders arising from the incurring of capital losses from the sale of securities which have been acquired at relatively high prices.

The terms "non-regulated" and "regulated," as used above, are perhaps misleading. All investment companies are "regulated" by the Securities and Exchange Commission in the administration of the Investment Act of 1940. But when we use the term in connection with taxation, we are using it in a different sense. It is realized by the government that when investment companies are taxed as ordinary corporations, triple taxation to some extent results. That is, the ordinary corporation whose shares are owned by the investment company pays the corporate

rate on its income. The investment company then must pay the corporation tax on the dividends (income) received on the shares of this corporation which it owns (subject, however, to the 85 per cent credit). Thus far, it is double taxation. Then the owner of the investment company shares would have to pay the personal income tax on the dividends received on his shares. Now we have triple taxation.

To lessen the tax burden, if an investment company, either open- or closed-end, can qualify, it may register with the Internal Revenue Service as a *regulated investment company.* One of the requirements for a regulated company is that it must pay out in dividends at least 90 per cent of its net income, exclusive of capital gains, for any taxable year. We will state the other requirements later. A regulated investment company does not have to pay any corporation income taxes on that portion of its income, whether obtained from ordinary income or capital gains, which is paid out in dividends to its shareholders. But it pays the regular corporate tax on the portion retained. (It is still allowed an 85 per cent credit on dividends received.) Any gains arising from the sale of securities are considered capital gains and are taxed as such (if not paid out in dividends).

The shareholder of the regulated investment company pays the regular personal income tax on the dividends received. Any part of the dividend which represents a capital gain, however, is taxed as a capital gain. (The maximum tax on a long-term capital gain at the present time is 25 per cent.) In some instances only a portion of the dividends received by a shareholder in a regulated investment company may be subject to the dividend exclusion and the dividend credit.[6]

In the past the *retained realized* long-term capital gains of a regulated investment company were in effect taxed twice—first when the company paid the tax upon realizing the gain, and again when the shareholder sold his investment company shares at the augmented value resulting from the capital gain. This double taxation was eliminated by an amendment to the law in 1956.[7] As before, the company will pay the 25 per cent tax on realized retained long-term capital gains. The company will notify the shareholder as to the amount of the gain which is applicable to his shares, and he will report the capital gain on his personal tax form. The

[6] If the dividends *received* by the investment company constitute less than 75 per cent of its gross income (capital gains excluded), the portion that is entitled to the exclusion and credit may be computed as follows:

$$\frac{\text{Dividends received by investment company}}{\text{Investment company's gross income}} \times \text{Dividends received from investment company}$$

[7] Public Law 700, Sec. 852(b)(3)(D), July 11, 1956.

shareholder, however, can take credit for the tax which is paid by the company. (If the 25 per cent exceeds the amount of taxes that would be applicable to the particular shareholder's capital gains, figured at his top bracket rate, he can apply the balance of the credit against other gains, or he can apply for a refund.) The amount of the retained capital gain (less the 25 per cent tax paid by the company) is added to the cost basis of the stock for the purpose of determining capital gains or losses upon sale of the stock by the shareholder.

In addition to the requirement that at least 90 per cent of the ordinary earnings be paid out in dividends annually, the other qualifications for a regulated investment company are as follows. At least 90 per cent of the gross income for any taxable year must be from dividends, interest, and gains from the sale of securities, but not more than 30 per cent of the gross income may be derived from gains on securities held for less than three months. Not more than 5 per cent of the company's assets may be invested in the securities of any one company, and not more than 10 per cent of the voting securities of any company may be acquired. Once a company has elected to be treated as a regulated investment company, it must continue the same status every year thereafter.

QUESTIONS

1. How do investment companies differ from ordinary business corporations? What other title or titles are sometimes used for them?
2. What was the first real period of development of investment companies in the United States? Were they as a class at first successful? Why or why not?
3. Indicate the various types of investment companies found in the United States today. Which is the most numerous? Why?
4. Distinguish between the open- and closed-end management investment companies. Which of these is the most numerous? Why?
5. Indicate clearly what determines the price an investor would pay for the stock of most open-end investment companies and the price he would get when he sells the stock.
6. (a) Look up the bid and asked prices of the following stocks as of a recent date: Eaton and Howard Balanced Fund, Incorporated Investors, Massachusetts Investors Trust, and Wellington Fund, Inc. Calculate what percentage of the book value of the stock of each company is added as a selling or loading charge (small purchase assumed). (b) Look up the book value of as recent date as available and the market price, of approximately the same date, of the following companies: Adams Express, General American Investors, Lehman Corporation, and Tri-Continental. At what percentage under or over the book values was each selling? If you purchased and sold 20 shares of any two of these stocks what would the total commissions be, expressed as a percentage of the book value for each stock? (c) What conclusions might you draw relative to open- and closed-end companies by a comparison of the answers to (a) and (b)?

7. Indicate the relative advantages of balanced funds and common-stock funds.
8. How do you account for the tremendous increase in the assets of open-end companies during and after World War II?
9. Explain the nature of the cumulative investment plans offered by many of the open-end companies. Do you think they are a good thing for the average investor?
10. State the principal features of the Investment Company Act of 1940.
11. (a) What is meant by a "regulated" investment company? (b) Explain definitely how the income of a regulated investment company is taxed as compared with a non-regulated company. (c) How are the dividends from an investment company taxed in the hands of the recipient shareholders?
12. What are the advantages and disadvantages of buying investment company shares from the standpoint of the average investor?
13. Do you believe that investment companies will continue to grow in the United States? Explain.

PROBLEMS

1. Assume that on January 2 you purchased some shares of an open-end regulated investment company for $10 per share. This price includes the company's selling charge of 8½ per cent. Further assume that the same day you purchased some shares of a closed-end regulated investment company which had a book value (net asset value) per share exactly the same as the open-end company, but that you bought them at a discount of 10 per cent below the book value plus a commission of 2 per cent. How much per share did you pay for the closed-end company shares? Assume that at the end of the year each company paid a dividend equivalent to 3 per cent of the net asset value per share at the beginning of the year. What was the yield to you on your shares in each company? Expressed in percentage, how much greater was your yield on the closed-end company shares than on the open-end company shares?

2. From Wiesenberger's *Investment Companies* (or other source) ascertain the names of at least two mutual funds in which arrangements may be made by the shareholder for the systematic withdrawal of his investment upon retirement. Indicate the nature of the plans. Do any of the closed-end companies have such a plan?

3. Ascertain the names of at least two mutual funds that offer the "front-end load" plan. Find out from the securities department or division of your state whether such plans can be sold in your state.

4. Assume that you purchased an open-end regulated investment company share for $20, and that the price included the customary loading charge of 7½ per cent. At the time you purchased the stock 50 per cent of its book value was made up of appreciation in the value of its portfolio. If the company sold these securities in which it had a book profit and distributed the long-term capital gain to its shareholders, how would you stand on your investment after you paid a 25 per cent tax on the capital gain?

5. (a) Explain the difference, if any, among the following: corporation, Massachusetts trust, joint stock company, investment company. (b) Explain the difference, if any, among the following: financing company, holding company, investment company.

SELECTED READINGS

"A Haven When Stocks Slump" (relating to closed-end investment company shares). *Business Week,* April 21, 1962.

BARNES, LEO. *Your Buying Guide to Mutual Funds and Investment Companies.* Larchmont, N. Y.: American Research Council. Latest edition.

————. *Your Investments.* Larchmont, N. Y.: American Research Council. Published annually.

BULLOCK, HUGH. *Story of Investment Companies.* New York: Columbia University Press, 1959.

CHRYSLER, EDWIN W., JR. "Growth of the Mutual Fund Industry," *Financial Analysts Journal,* January–February, 1962, pp. 31–38.

DOANE, C. RUSSELL, and HILLS, EDWARD J. *Investment Trusts and Funds From the Investor's Point of View.* Great Barrington, Mass.: American Institute for Economic Research. Latest edition.

Forbes. The August 15 issue of the magazine each year has a performance record of the leading mutual funds.

Investment Companies Fact Book. New York: National Association of Investment Companies, 1961.

JOHNSON, HUGH A. *Johnson's Investment Company Charts.* Buffalo: Hugh A. Johnson. Published annually.

MEAD, STUART B. "Investment Companies or Mutual Funds: Which?" *Business Topics,* Graduate School of Business Administration, Michigan State University, Winter, 1961.

————. "Mutual Funds as an Investment," *Business Topics,* Graduate School of Business Administration, Michigan State University, Spring, 1960.

National Association of Investment Companies Annual Report. New York: National Association of Investment Companies. Published annually.

STRALEY, JOHN A. *What About Mutual Funds?* rev. ed. New York: Harper & Row, Publishers, 1958.

WIESENBERGER, ARTHUR. *Investment Companies.* New York: Arthur Wiesenberger & Co. Published annually.

IV

FINANCIAL MANAGEMENT

17

Organization and Objectives

Previous sections of this book have discussed forms of organization, corporate securities, and techniques for financing through securities. This section deals with the internal financial management of a firm. The functions of finance are to provide the funds needed by an enterprise to facilitate production and distribution and to work toward effective utilization of these funds to accomplish the ultimate objectives of the organization.

There are both managerial and operative functions to be performed in the finance division of a firm. The operative functions are relatively less significant and consist mainly of carrying out financial policy. Managerial functions, however, are extremely important. *Financial management* is defined as planning for, providing, and controlling a firm's capital to achieve its over-all objectives. This definition encompasses the development of financial plans as well as financial policies, a financial organization, and techniques for controlling operations.

THE FINANCIAL ORGANIZATION

Establishment of the financial organization within a firm requires a determination of the relationship between the finance function and other functions of the business. Various levels in the organization must be designated for different types of decision making on financial management problems. Responsibility for financial decisions must be clearly placed in the organization. While the development of the financial organization within a specific firm varies substantially with the conditions of the firm (sales volume, product lines, sources of capital, form of organization, etc.), certain general observations can be made which are useful in developing all types of financial organizations.

The Relation of Finance to Other Functions of a Business

Once the over-all objectives for a business have been clearly and concisely set forth, the functions which must be performed in order to achieve these objectives can be determined. The first functions to become evident are the organic functions—those which are so vital to the functioning of a firm that it would cease to exist if they were not performed. They are given different names in different businesses. In the typical manufacturing firm they might be called production, sales or marketing, finance, and personnel. If business organizations are to attain an objective of providing economic values to their customers, they must create and distribute these values or economic utilities. Thus, the creation and distribution of utility are two organic functions. A third organic function—the provision of capital—is commonly added, because without it the first functions cannot be performed in a capitalistic society. For purposes of completeness, a fourth organic function—the provision of labor—is added, since the creation and distribution of utility require labor as well as capital.

Finance is intimately related to the other three organic functions of the business. The production function performs the operations necessary to produce an item, and then turns it over to the marketing or sales function which, through a series of activities, gets the product into the hands of the consumer. This process is a continuous one, and throughout the entire process, capital and labor are necessary. Thus, both the finance and personnel functions must be integrated with all stages of the process. It should be noted, however, that they do not directly create and distribute utility. Rather, they make possible or facilitate the production and sales functions which do create and distribute utility. The fact that finance is facilitative in nature indicates that it is a staff activity which has evolved for the purposes of aiding, advising, and assisting the line organization. Authorities in the field, however, are not in agreement on this point, and many consider finance a line activity.

Whether finance is thought of as a staff or line activity, it must be performed in any firm. Actually, it can be performed as a secondary responsibility by those individuals who are primarily concerned with the creation and distribution of utility. This would ordinarily occur in a small organization. As a business grows, the amount and complexity of finance activities begin to require so much of other functional executives' time that a department is established to carry out these activities. This is, of course, staff evolution.

As the organization continues to grow and the finance department becomes more clearly defined, some of the activities of the finance function become the basic responsibility of administrators handling this financial department. An example of such an activity is that the finance department typically has the primary responsibility for seeing that the firm does not run short of funds. Other activities, however, remain a joint responsibility with those in charge of other phases of the business. Budgeting, for example, is commonly shared with other line and staff departments. Another shared responsibility would be the development of credit policies. The objectives of a finance department as distinguished from the finance function itself could be described as providing advice and service to line management and to other staff departments on matters involving securing, safeguarding, handling, recording, investing, measuring, evaluating use of, and paying out capital in any of its forms.

The Organization Level of the Finance Function

The discussion above dealt largely with the lateral relationship of finance to the other functions in the firm. Consideration is now given to the organization level of the finance function. A single decision at the financial policy-making level can spell the difference between success and failure. In addition, top management exercises various types of financial controls regularly to check the effectiveness of its operations. Therefore, the finance function is normally accorded a high place within the company. Boards of directors commonly reserve for themselves more decisions on finance than on most other functional areas. Thus, major financial management policies are determined at very high levels in the organization, possibly even above the level of the chief financial executive.

In looking at the finance organization [1] it should be noted that in most cases the chief financial officer reports either to the president or to the president and the board of directors. In addition, the chief financial officer normally participates in the administrative management of the company and contributes to the decision-making processes of the organizational units above his level. It is the duty of the chief financial officer to see that the financial implications of broad decisions are clarified and understood by those who must make these important decisions. The financial officer must understand the business and keep in touch with all phases of its operation. Probably no functional area of the business is so intimately interrelated with the other areas as is finance.

The finance function is usually less decentralized than other functions in the company. Even when a general policy of decentralization exists, finance is commonly used as a major control device; thus, the finance function still tends to remain centralized. In a highly decentralized or-

---

[1] The term *finance department* is not commonly used just as the term *marketing department* is not a common one. Finance in a large firm would include a number of departments so we will use the term *finance organization* to cover the firm's organizational structure devoted to financial activities.

ganization, a divisional finance officer often is under the direct supervision of the finance officer at the home office.

The Internal Structure of the Finance Organization

While the size of the firm is particularly important in the development of an internal financial organization, it should be noted that many other factors also influence this development. These other factors would include the product or service of the organization, the legal form of organization, the objectives of the company, and certain geographic and personnel factors. The discussion which follows, however, will be based mainly upon the influence of changing size.

In a very small company in which the finance function has not yet evolved out of the line and no separate finance organization exists, the president or owner-manager is the chief financial officer, and the more routine and detailed aspects of finance are performed within the marketing or production line functions, generally by the heads of these departments. As the firm grows, finance staffing is set up to relieve the line executives of most of the burden of financial work. Finance at this stage of the company's growth is commonly organized with a distinct treasury orientation. The chief financial officer is normally given the title of "treasurer," and he performs both a treasurer's and a controller's activities. These activities are outlined in detail later in a discussion of large firms. The treasurer of a small company, and any clerical personnel that he might have working with him, perform all of the same activities as the treasurer of a large firm. Some of the activities might be performed at more irregular intervals or on a more informal basis than in large firms, but nevertheless they are all performed.

When a company's operations become voluminous and complicated due to increased size, a division of responsibility within the finance organization often appears. It is here that the controller (sometimes called "comptroller") makes his appearance alongside the treasurer. There is no real uniformity as to the use of the titles "treasurer" and "controller," nor as to whether the treasurer reports to the controller or the controller to the treasurer or whether the two are equal in authority. Use of these titles is not really essential to an understanding of the ordinary organization developed to handle the finance function.

In large companies, functional devolution and specialization within the financial department are carried still further due to the increased complexity of the finance function. In many large companies, financial policy decisions are taken out of the hands of the treasurer and controller and are made by the vice-president of finance or the chairman of the finance committee (sometimes the same person). Figure 17–1 portrays a possible organization of a finance department for a very large company.

In this example, the treasurer and controller report to the vice-president in charge of the financial staff, who in turn reports to the executive vice-president, who is chairman of the financial policy committee.

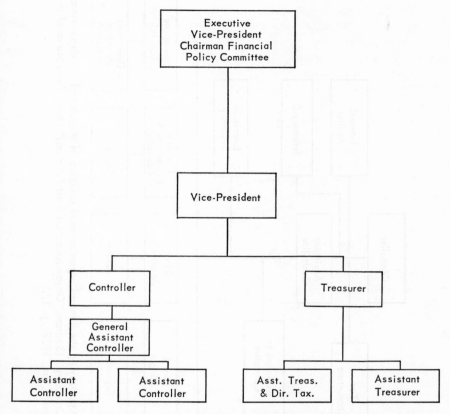

Fig. 17–1. Chart portraying the organizational structure of the financial staff of the General Motors Corporation. (Source: "Organization Of Staff Functions" [New York: National Industrial Conference Board, Inc., 1958], p. 10.)

Duties of Financial Executives

The activities of the finance organization in a large firm are many and varied. They would include accounting, auditing, banking relations, budgets, capital expenditures, cash management, claims, contracts, credit management, custody, financial planning, financial statements, financing, government requests, insurance, inventories, investing surplus funds, payrolls, real estate, signature, statistics, and taxes. It should be noted that many of these activities become the joint responsibility of finance with other functional areas of the business.

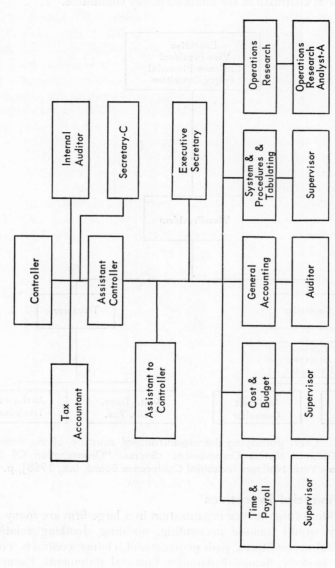

Fig. 17–2. Chart portraying the internal organizational structure of the controller's department of the Lukens Steel Company. (Source: "Organization Of Staff Functions" [New York: National Industrial Conference Board, Inc., 1958], p. 17.)

In an attempt to divide the activities of the finance department into those which might more commonly be considered treasury activities and those considered controller activities, certain problems are encountered. Single definitions of these titles do not have universal acceptance. However, it can validly be said that the activities of the treasurer's organization are concerned with custody, cash and banking, credits and claims, and financing. The activities of the controller's organization include accounting, interpretation, and control. More specifically, the controller may have the entire responsibility for all elements of accounting and auditing. If the finance organization handles budgeting, it would most commonly come under the controller as would preparation of tax forms and supply of information to government. The treasurer on the other hand would perform custody and signature activities which might include responsibility for insurance, real estate, and cash management. In addition, the treasurer would normally determine sources of funds and make financing arrangements. Figures 17–2 and 17–3 portray the structure of the controller's and treasurer's organizations in a large manufacturing firm. The organizational structure indicates the types of activities handled in each area.

OBJECTIVES

It is a generally accepted principle of good management that the objectives of any segment of the business should be consistent with and contribute to the objectives of the total organization. Thus, in discussing financial management objectives, it is necessary first to consider the objectives of the total organization.

Service

Most management authorities begin their discussion of business objectives with the primary *service* function. This service function is a service to society in the form of creation and distribution of utility to customers. The increasing acceptance of the service concept is indicated by the emphasis given service in most published statements of objectives of large American corporations.

The corporation is created by the State. Obviously, in agreeing to its creation, the State must have been satisfied that the corporation would make a contribution to society—in this case to the citizens of the State. This contribution comes about through the performance of some business activity. In a capitalistic economy, service and its performance benefit those performing the service as well as the customers or recipients. This benefit to the provider of the service is, of course, profit. It is generally agreed that, in the long run, no firm makes a profit if it does not perform

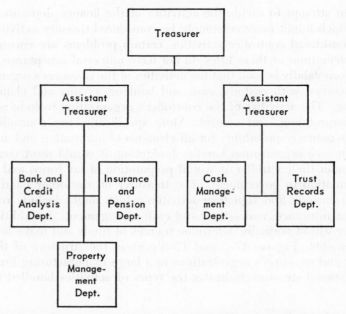

Fig. 17–3. Chart portraying the internal organizational structure of the treasurer's department of a large manufacturing firm. (Source: "Organization Of Staff Functions" [New York: National Industrial Conference Board, Inc., 1958], p. 14.)

a service. It is not so generally agreed that the converse of this statement is also true. The emphasis on the service objective differentiates the objectives of the business from the objectives of those persons making decisions for the business—its management and owners. Other objectives besides service must also be considered in any decision-making process within the business organization.

Profit

The *profit* motive is fundamental in a private profit economy. It is not expected that owners of capital would give up the use of their capital without some return. (This return is commonly called profit if the suppliers of the capital take an ownership position in the firm to which they transfer their capital.) Thus, the objective of the owners is profit, but intelligent ownership recognizes that it must perform service in order to make profits in the long run, and therefore its decisions are geared toward service as well as profit. However, it is generally agreed that profit is the motivating factor behind owners' decisions relative to business units. The profit motive, therefore, is sometimes called a collateral objective for the firm, and the primary objective for the owners and managers of the firm.

It should be noted that owners and managers, rather than the firm itself, make decisions for the firm. Therefore, profit becomes a major motivating factor in most business decisions.

Permanence

The possibilities of taking a short-run rather than a long-run point of view on business objectives require a consideration of still another specific objective. If a firm is to provide service, it must stay in existence. Therefore, as long as service is provided, there is a concept of *permanence* for the organization. If the decision makers in the organization believe they can provide service to customers in the long run, then permanence of the organization becomes a collateral objective. The same analysis applies to the profit concept. If the owners and managers are interested in profit in the long run, it is necessary to keep the business unit operating; therefore, permanence becomes a collateral objective here also. A short-run point of view in the operation of any business may lead to quite different conclusions on these matters; however, the discussions in this text assume a long-run point of view.

Since permanence implies continued operation, an approach to the objective of permanence is to counteract those forces which could possibly cut off operations of the business. Thus, a shortage of management, labor, or materials could lead to the decline of the business and to its loss of permanence. However, under normal conditions, the shortage of these factors is not a common cause of loss of permanence for business organizations. The major factor which has led to the closing down of business units has been legal action or potential legal action on the part of those who are in a position to take it. Legally, the creditors have the strongest position in the firm and are the group most likely to cause a firm to lose its permanence. Therefore, the accomplishment of the permanence objective of a firm is closely related to meeting the requirements of creditors so that legal actions are not taken against the firm to force sale of its assets, liquidation, or dissolution.

Financial Management Objectives

Financial management of a firm tends to be more closely associated with the problems of permanence than are most other areas of the company. Specifically, a very important financial management problem is the problem of solvency—maintaining the permanence of the organization by satisfying creditors, so that legal actions will not arise. The finance department of the business is commonly the area which is most responsible for maintaining solvency of the organization. In addition, finance and financial management are generally concerned with the profit and service objectives also. However, most financial decisions would tend to be made on the assumption that if long-run profits are possible, service will be performed. Thus, the emphasis in financial decisions is more on profit than on service. While all areas of the business share the responsibility for the development of reasonable profits, it is the financial area which must measure profit and determine its reasonableness. Finance, therefore, is a strong influencing factor in many decisions geared toward the profit objective of the firm.

The major financial problem of the modern corporation is a problem of balance between *profitability* and *solvency*. Obviously, long-run solvency is necessary for long-run profitability; however, in the short run, emphasis could be given to one or the other of these factors to such an extent as to cause the complete lack of accomplishment of the other. A major dilemma of financial management in the short run is to maintain a proper balance between the objectives of profitability and solvency.

PROFITABILITY

The word *profit* was used above to describe a major objective of the business firm. The authors prefer the use of the term *profitability*. Profit is generally considered an accounting term and is used more in looking backward than in looking forward. In fact, accounting normally only recognizes "profit" when it is "realized." For purposes of financial management objectives, the decision-making process always deals with future potentials rather than with past results. Past results are useful in helping to judge the future, but the past cannot be changed. The results of decisions affect the future only. Therefore, the major application of profit as an objective is in terms of forward planning and future actions. In this sense, the financial planner is more interested in the "ability" to profit than in profit realized to date. Thus, the term *profitability* is more applicable in financial management.

In addition, profitability, as utilized today, implies not only a forward look but also a concept of reasonableness of profit. Thus, the emphasis is not merely on being "in the black" but on how far a company is "in the black" in order reasonably to meet objectives. Thus, any measurements of profitability utilized in financial management require a determination of what is a reasonable amount of profit to anticipate.

Since profit legally belongs to the suppliers of capital, and since it is either paid to them or credited to their account on a pro-rata basis relative to the amount of capital contributed, it would appear reasonable to begin with a measurement of profitability relative to the amount of capital contribution. It is obvious that General Motors Corporation would have a very poor year if it profited only $1,000,000 whereas the corner grocery store would have an outstandingly successful year relative to its profit objective if it earned $50,000. General Motors Corporation needs to experience much larger profits to justify the much greater investment level. Profitability is a measure of investment worth in terms of future expectations. The dollar return on an investment should closely correlate with the amount of the dollars invested. Varying sizes of investment are unimportant in comparing alternatives. The reasonableness of the dollar profit can be determined only by first comparing the amount of the dollar profit to the value of the investment.

While this section is devoted primarily to applications of profitability in financial management, the reader should note that outside investors have always used a profitability measure in judging the value of their investment. Thus, bond or stock yield is a measure of profitability and its reasonableness. Yield is merely a relationship of the return to the amount of the investment. Stockholders buy in expectation of certain yields in the future. The price-earnings ratio for stock investment, which has become so popular in recent years, is also a measure of profitability. It describes the amount which one must currently pay for each dollar of expected corporate earnings.

Measurements of Profitability

A number of generally acceptable alternative yardsticks of investment worth are available for use by management and have received considerable publicity in recent years. Among these, the five major ones are postponability, pay-back, operating ratio, profit margin, and return on investment.

Postponability. A commonly used standard for choosing among investment proposals is *postponability* or necessity. Postponability estimates how long a project can be put off. If there is an excess of budget requests for investment funds over the amount of available funds, many companies use postponability as a screen to reject projects which can be deferred, even though postponement means foregoing the profits that would be made possible by the additional investment.

This method of selecting investment is not very logical. It is not likely to lead to allocation of investable funds in such a way as to produce maximum profitability. An investment which might yield large savings and high profits could be put off almost indefinitely by this approach. Postponability does not consider alternatives and therefore is likely to result in a stagnant operation. By placing a "must" label on a proposal, its originator says in effect that there are no alternatives to taking this action.

Postponability is not really measurable. It does not measure the earning power of an individual project. If any project is a "must" project, the real urgency is in its effect upon the earnings of the organization. Other measures of profitability will tend to push these "must" projects to the fore through a direct consideration of earnings and investment levels. Postponability does not reflect productivity of capital nor does it permit an objective comparison in ranking of projects. As a result, present management tends to use measures of profitability and investment worth other than postponability.

Pay-Back. Another measure of investment worth that is often used is *pay-back*—the number of years it will take the gross earnings (before depreciation) of a project to return the original outlay. For example, if a new piece of equipment is to cost $400 and it is expected that by installing this new piece of equipment net savings from reduced labor costs and maintenance would be $150 per year, the pay-out or pay-back period would be 2.67 years. This method has the advantage of being relatively simple to apply; it is based on estimates of earnings and investment outlays alone and does not require an estimate of the life of the project. This method is useful for highly profitable projects where the obvious life of the investment is substantially in excess of the pay-back period. Pay-back measures the rapidity with which the return will replenish the original capital fund. The pay-back period is, therefore, essentially a cash concept concerned solely with cash outlay and cash return.

By itself, the pay-back period does not measure profitability in the sense of a return on investment. Hence it is not much help in selecting among alternative investments. In limited pay-out investments, no fixed relationship exists between pay-back period and profitability. A one-year pay-back would not be profitable if the investment is worthless at the end of one year. On the other hand, a three-year pay-back may be highly profitable if the investment would continue to pay back at the same rate for three more years after the pay-back period. Pay-back ignores the duration of earnings beyond the pay-back period and weights immediate earnings too heavily. The pay-back approach penalizes new products or project investments when initial losses might be high but long-term rewards very great.

Operating Ratio. The *operating ratio* is the ratio of expected operating expenses to expected operating revenue. Although called a "ratio," like many other ratios it is expressed as a percentage. It is computed as follows:

$$\frac{\text{Operating expenses}}{\text{Net sales}} = \text{Operating ratio}$$

The operating ratio shows the percentage of each dollar of sales or revenue that is spent in operating expenses. It thus measures the efficiency of operations. Generally speaking, the lower the ratio, the greater is the efficiency of the company. Proper consideration must be given to the particular industry studied, since the ratio varies widely among industries. The operating ratio excludes non-operating items such as income from sale of fixed assets, bond interest, and income taxes. As a result, it does not measure the efficiency of all activities of the company but only those which would generally be considered "operations."

The difference between the operating ratio and 100 per cent is the ratio of net operating income to sales. The lower the operating ratio, the higher the percentage of net operating income to net sales. These measures are not good measures of investment worth or profitability. In addition to measuring only those aspects of the company which are "operations," there is nothing in this ratio which judges reasonableness of investment. A 10 per cent net operating income on sales is not necessarily a 10 per cent return on investment. In fact, this would be the case only where sales and investment were equal, and this is not normally the circumstance. In many companies and industries, sales are substantially in excess of investment; whereas in other situations, investment may be substantially in excess of sales. The operating ratio is a measure of efficiency of operations in terms of outlay per dollar of sales, but it is not a measure of profitability.

Profit Margin. The *operating profit margin* is the relationship of net operating income to net sales. The *profit margin* of the firm is the relationship of net income to net sales. By using net income rather than net operating income, the effects of all activities of the firm are considered rather than just those which would normally be called "operations." However, the use of profit margin also completely ignores the variations of different amounts of investment for different activities.

In meeting a reasonable profit objective, there are three essential factors—sales, expenses, and investment. A sound relationship among all three is necessary to accomplish profit objectives. The ratio discussed here concerns only two—sales and expenditures. The expansion of plant and current asset investment cannot be made without recognizing the fact that increased investment carries with it a responsibility for increased earnings. In fact, the failure on the part of the operating management to relate volume and profit performance to the capital required to produce them can easily result in excessive plant investment and abnormally high inventories. If profit margin constitutes the only basis of measurement, multi-line companies may give emphasis to product lines with high margins but with very low return on investment rather than to those with high return on investment. It is unfortunate that the basis for computing profitability most commonly used by many firms has been profit margin. In comparison with return on investment, the profit margin ratio is inadequate in the sense that it tells how much profit is realized from sales without taking into account the amount of investment which is responsible for producing those sales.

Return on Investment. The above discussion leads to the conclusion that the only really acceptable measure of profitability is a relationship between the amount of the profit anticipated and the value of the investment. None of the other measures discussed is actually a measure of profitability of investment. The relation between the return and the investment outlay becomes the measure of the productivity of capital. The acceptance of *return on investment* (ROI) as the major measure of financial management is based on the assumption that the principal goal of the organization is profit and that the purpose of this profit is to give a reasonable return to investors.

It is further assumed that management has a *responsibility* to realize earnings on investors' capital and that the amount earned should be sufficient relative to alternatives to justify the investment on the part of the investors. If management cannot earn a reasonable return for the investors, the investors should recover their investment, if possible, and put it to other more productive uses. Return on investment as a measurement of profitability is accepted by the authors as the most meaningful of the various profitability measurements. The problems of determining return on investment and applying it to business decision making are discussed in the next chapter.

SOLVENCY

While most authorities discussing corporate objectives consider service and profitability, it is apparent that neither of these objectives could be accomplished in the long run if the firm did not stay in business. Therefore, another objective of almost every business organization is permanence or continued operation in the future. If the service and profit objectives are considered from a long-run point of view, the long life of the organization becomes a basis for the accomplishment of these objectives. While it is possible to envision businesses established to perform a service or to meet a profitability objective in the short run only, most statistics available indicate that businesses generally are interested in long-run operation. Those corporations or proprietorships or partnerships which die of natural causes, i.e., decision on the part of the owners or managers that the firm should be closed, are considerably less in number than those which go out of business due to pressure by creditors.

Except for certain illegal operations, the only circumstance in which outsiders can force dissolution or liquidation of a corporation is when the latter defaults on its contracts. In other words, the most important out-side element in determining the life of the corporation is the creditor. Any outside element, such as employees or government, with a money claim against the corporation which could be legally enforceable to the extent of causing the dissolution of the organization, would automatically become a creditor. If a firm is solvent, it can meet creditors' claims, and therefore it can reach its permanence objective.

Another term sometimes used in financial management for solvency is *liquidity*. Liquidity is described later in this book and is concerned with ability to convert asset values into liquid (specifically money) form. *Solvency* as used here is a broader term. Therefore, the authors prefer the use of the term *solvency* in discussing financial management objectives.

Meaning of Solvency

Solvency may have two different meanings. First, it is considered as the ability of a going concern to meet its obligations as they become due. Inability to do so is referred to as technical insolvency (sometimes called "financial failure"). The second approach to solvency is from a more permanent point of view. In this sense, solvency is the ability of the firm to pay all of its debts if it liquidated. Inability to do this is considered actual or total insolvency. It should be recognized that neither category is exclusive of the other.

A firm can be technically insolvent while being actually or totally solvent from a total-asset-to-debt point of view. The firm's assets might be worth enough to meet the requirements of creditors in an orderly liquidation, but the assets might not be in sufficiently liquid form for the firm to be able to repay creditors immediately or to meet debts as they come due without either a significant readjustment in the firm or liquidation. On the other hand, a firm could be technically solvent and actually insolvent in that it could have sufficient cash on hand to meet immediately maturing obligations but not sufficient total asset values to meet its total liabilities.

The problem of technical insolvency tends to appear first in most operations and it is the one with which the financial management must be constantly concerned. An important problem of financial management is that of managing operations in such a manner as to insure that immediately maturing obligations can be met—thus preventing technical insolvency. The long-term position is also important but it is less subject to frequent and rapid changes than the short-term solvency situation which varies with seasonal and other short-term factors.

One major source of money to maintain solvency is the liquidation of certain assets. This can be in the normal operation of business through collection of accounts receivable, or it could be through liquidation of certain assets outside of normal operations. The second major source of money to meet problems of technical solvency is a store of cash already on hand. A third major readily available source of money is funds from outsiders—primarily short-term creditors. The problem of solvency of a technical nature becomes the problem of ability to keep cash flowing in the organization in such a way as to meet all obligations. The maintenance of sufficient cash flow depends upon the liquidity of assets, the cash reserves on hand, and the ability to obtain funds from outsiders as needed.

Various measurements of solvency are used by outsiders in making decisions on whether to advance funds to the firm. These measures involve a study of financial position and past payment record. Some ratios which have been developed to help a creditor measure solvency are discussed in Chapter 19.

Planning and Controlling Solvency

Planning and controlling solvency should be relative to the three sources of cash stated above. The liquidity of assets and the rate at which they would normally convert to cash are important elements of financial management and are discussed in Chapter 20. Cash as a store of value is also discussed in Chapter 20. The use of the cash budget and other techniques for planning and controlling solvency from an asset-flow point of view are discussed in Chapter 19. The third source of cash, the ability to obtain funds from outsiders, is discussed below.

It is extremely difficult for any firm to maintain a sufficient cash store to meet emergency solvency requirements which might arise in the future. Thus, conversion of assets and obtaining of funds from outsiders basically maintain the solvency of most organizations. Any firm must maintain a reasonable credit rating to remain technically solvent in the long run.

Since technical solvency involves a short-run point of view, time is of the essence. It is normally difficult to obtain owner funds quickly. Reinvested earnings obviously require time to acquire. Thus, the major source of new funds to maintain technical solvency for a firm is from creditors—particularly short-term creditors. The decision whether the firm can obtain the funds it needs is one made by its creditors on the basis of their interpretation of the firm's credit rating. The importance of maintaining a good credit rating cannot be overemphasized.

Credit rating is an intangible concept which becomes established in the minds of creditors or potential creditors and which refers to the future ability and willingness of the debtor to pay his debts. The credit rating of the debtor may vary substantially over periods of time. Various credit rating institutions may assign a different rating to the same debtor. The credit rating indicates the ability to obtain credit on satisfactory terms.

A firm with a good credit rating finds little difficulty in borrowing to meet short-term capital needs, but one with a poor credit rating may be unable to borrow when the need arises or may have to pay extremely high interest rates or agree to unreasonable terms to obtain a loan.

Credit Rating from the Creditor's Viewpoint

Underlying an understanding of how to maintain a good credit rating is an appreciation of the factors considered by creditors in establishing the credit rating for a firm. These are the four C's of credit: *character, capacity, capital,* and *collateral. Character* includes the willingness of the debtor to pay his debts. If a debtor has been prompt in paying his bills in the past, it is assumed that he will continue to be so, unless conditions change. A debtor who has consistently been slow in payment of accounts will generally have a very poor credit rating regardless of his financial condition or capital. Creditors look to experiences of others in granting credit. This information is readily obtainable through credit interchange bureaus and such organizations as Dun & Bradstreet, Inc. Slow payment of an account does not affect a firm's credit rating with only that particular creditor. Generally, all other creditors, or potential creditors, will know all about the slow-pay account. Failure to pay a bill may cause cancellation of credit by other creditors as well as by the one involved.

Capacity implies the earning ability of the company. Capacity will be judged by an analysis of the firm's financial statements. Earnings records will be studied and probable trends in earnings determined to judge the ability of the business to repay debt. The ability of the management, amount of competition in the industry, general industry conditions, and the stage of the business cycle will all be taken into account in attempting to judge future earning power. The purpose for which the capital obtained on credit will be used is considered in its effect on the probable future earning power of the business.

Capital has to do with the worth of the business and, therefore, is another indication of its ability to pay. Not only total capital is taken into account, but also owners' equity, liabilities outstanding, liquidity of capital items, and use being made of capital. The amount of debt outstanding is important as it limits the claim of a new creditor on the assets in the event of financial difficulty. In addition to the amount of other debt, the lien involved and the maturity dates are important to a new creditor in determining his position in event of liquidation as well as his chances of repayment under normal circumstances. The working capital position is of particular importance, as it tends to indicate liquidity and ability to meet short-term loans. If the net working capital is relatively small, firms will be reluctant to grant credit or make loans as they will question the ability of the company to pay. The nature of the working capital items, and their turnover rates, are important in this regard.

Collateral is of importance to certain creditors. Collateral involves a pledge of specific property and gives the creditor obtaining the pledge an advantage in collection over other creditors with no specific claim against property. If collateral is involved, the value and liquidity of the property pledged is of importance. The value of the pledged property to the operation of the concern is also considered. Even if collateral is pledged, the ability of the corporation to pay based on its earning power or current position is generally a more important credit-rating consideration due to the expenses and difficulty of foreclosure on pledged property.

Another factor which creditors will consider in determining credit rating of debtors might be called "conditions." This would include the present status of the business cycle and general credit and business conditions throughout the country. In addition, credit is always limited by the ability of the creditor to lend and how well the proposed loan fits into the creditor's maturity and diversification plan. Creditors require substantial financial information from the debtor and the ease with which this information is obtained may influence the granting of credit.

THE FINANCIAL MIX

It should be recognized that profitability and solvency in the short run do not necessarily go hand-in-hand. In fact, the major dilemma of the financial manager is to maintain balance between profitability and solvency.

In selection of sources of funds, the manager could select very low-cost sources to improve profitability. Low-cost sources are generally those which have early maturities, such as short-term loans obtained from financial institutions. Short-term loans require payment in the very near future and therefore affect future cash requirements and solvency. On the other hand, the selection of long-term higher-cost sources of funds such as sale of stock would reduce the profitability of the firm but would definitely contribute to its technical solvency because the stock never comes due. Selection of source of funds, which is discussed in other chapters, becomes primarily a problem of balance between profitability and solvency.

Another example of the interrelationship of profitability and solvency is in the investment of funds. Cash is the lowest yield investment which the firm can normally make. In fact, cash in a checking account yields no return to the firm. One way of meeting solvency problems, however, is to have large amounts of cash available in checking accounts. If this is done, the profitability of the firm is significantly reduced. On the other hand, solvency in the short run is very much improved. Maintenance of large amounts of short-term low-yield investments to meet potential emergencies is a recognition of the requirements of solvency but is contrary to the objective of profitability. Profitability would require the investment of these funds in less liquid but much higher yielding assets.

The above discussion is related to the short-term conflict between profitability and solvency. It is important to note that in the long run these two must go hand-in-hand, and that there cannot be long-run profitability without solvency. Also, there is little point in having solvency without meeting the other objectives of profitability and service. Thus, the long-run problems in the relationship of profitability and solvency are not nearly as great. However, financial management is faced with the problem of making day-to-day decisions. The great majority of these decisions have short-run implications in which the gains for profitability must be weighed against the potential effects on the solvency of the firm. This balance between solvency and profitability becomes the *financial mix* of the organization.

QUESTIONS

1. What level in the organization has the ultimate authority and responsibility for finance decisions? On what level is the chief financial officer placed in most corporate organizations?
2. Differentiate the duties of the controller from the duties of the treasurer as these activities are commonly separated.
3. Relate the service and profit objectives.
4. Why is permanence a collateral objective for most firms?
5. Define *profitability*. Differentiate profitability from profit.
6. Discuss the following as measures of profitability: (a) Postponability. (b) Pay-back. (c) Operating ratio. (d) Profit margin. (e) Return on investment.
7. How is pay-back determined?
8. Define *profit margin*. Of what use is this concept in financial management?
9. What is the relationship between operating ratio and profit margin?
10. Distinguish between technical and total insolvency.
11. What are the three major ways to meet technical solvency needs?
12. What is the importance of maintaining a proper credit rating?
13. What are the four C's of credit?
14. Differentiate capacity and collateral.
15. What is meant by financial mix?

PROBLEMS

1. The McWilkin Co. is a rapidly growing manufacturer of electronic components. The finance function within the company has been handled primarily by the president of the organization. The president in the past has also carried the title of "treasurer." The board of directors has decided to hire a full-time

financial officer to take over part of the financial responsibility. The board is considering a title of "controller" for this new executive. How would you suggest that the finance function be divided between the president-treasurer and the controller?

2. Make up a statement of corporate objectives for a small manufacturing firm which you own and manage. Determine how these objectives affect the financial management of the firm.

3. The Anderson Co. is considering the purchase of a new piece of labor-saving equipment. It is estimated that this new equipment will save $5,000 per year in wages and related expenses. The new piece of equipment costs $35,000. How would you measure the desirability of this purchase from a postponability point of view? Determine the pay-back on this piece of equipment.

4. The income statement of The Little Co. is as follows:

	Year Ending 12–31–x1	Year Ending 12–31–x2
Sales	$1,464,321	$1,531,012
Cost of Goods Sold	987,243	1,032,419
Gross Margin	477,078	498,593
Selling, General, and Administrative Expenses.....	346,246	347,798
Operating Profit	130,832	150,795
Non-operating Income	31,267	19,108
	162,099	169,903
Non-operating Expense	27,312	38,299
	134,787	131,604
Federal Income Taxes	67,498	65,988
Net Profit	$ 67,289	$ 65,616

Determine the operating ratio and profit margin for each year. Why do they move in opposite directions? What use could you make of these two measures?

5. The balance sheet of The Little Co. is as follows:

	Year Ended 12–31–x0	Year Ended 12–31–x1	Year Ended 12–31–x2
Current Assets	$ 632,381	$ 732,423	$ 748,200
Fixed Assets	640,638	636,490	663,812
Total Assets	$1,273,019	$1,368,913	$1,412,012
Current Liabilities	$ 268,421	$ 327,026	$ 334,509
Fixed Liabilities	200,000	200,000	200,000
Net Worth	804,598	841,887	877,503
Total Liabilities and Net Worth....	$1,273,019	$1,368,913	$1,412,012

Using the information in Problem 4, determine the profitability of The Little Co. in the year 19x1 and the year 19x2.

SELECTED READINGS

ANTHONY, ROBERT N. *Management Accounting*, rev. ed. Homewood, Ill.: Richard D. Irwin, Inc., 1960.

BIERMAN, HAROLD, JR. *Managerial Accounting*. New York: The Macmillan Co., 1959.
———, and SMIDT, SEYMOUR. *The Capital Budgeting Decision*. New York: The Macmillan Co., 1961.

Brown, Alvin J. *Financial Approach to Industrial Operations.* New York: Society for Advancement of Management, 1957.

Dale, Ernest. *Planning and Developing the Company Organization Structure.* Research Report No. 20. New York: The American Management Association, 1952.

Davis, Ralph C. *Industrial Organization and Management,* 3d ed. New York: Harper & Row, Publishers, 1957.

———. *The Fundamentals of Top Management.* New York: Harper & Row, Publishers, 1951.

Dean, Joel. *Managerial Economics.* Englewood Cliffs, N. J.: Prentice-Hall, Inc., 1951.

Eells, Richard. *The Meaning of Modern Business.* New York: The Columbia University Press, 1960.

Gordon, Myron J. *The Investment, Financing, and Valuation of the Corporation.* Homewood, Ill.: Richard D. Irwin, Inc., 1962.

Heckert, J. Brooks, and Willson, James D. *Business Budgeting and Control.* New York: The Ronald Press Co., 1955.

Lewis, Ronello B. *Financial Analysis for Management.* Englewood Cliffs, N. J.: Prentice-Hall, Inc., 1959.

Marting, Elizabeth. *Management for the Smaller Company.* New York: American Management Association, 1959.

National Industrial Conference Board, Inc. *Organization of Staff Functions.* New York: National Industrial Conference Board, Inc., 1958.

———. *The Duties of Financial Executives.* New York: National Industrial Conference Board, Inc., 1952.

Wipflar, Earl J. *Return on Investment.* Financial Series No. 103. New York: American Management Association, 1953.

18

Return on Investment
and Cost of Capital

Because of their importance as financial management concepts, return on investment and cost of capital have been selected as the subjects for a separate chapter. Both concepts are closely related to the profitability objective of the firm and are particularly useful as measuring devices for determining the degree of accomplishment of this objective.

In the previous chapter, we concluded that return on investment (ROI) is the only really acceptable measure of profitability for financial management's use. The problems inherent in applying this measure and its specific applications are discussed below.

DETERMINING THE AMOUNT OF THE INVESTMENT

Before a relationship between return and investment can be determined it is necessary to place a value on the investment base. This value depends upon the use for which the return on investment is being computed.

Stock Purchase

For a stock investor, the investment base is normally considered to be the cost price of the security at the time he is making a decision to purchase. Thereafter, the most accepted investment base would be the current market price of the security because this is the amount for which it could be sold to obtain funds to make other investments. Some authorities prefer to use the original cost base after the security has been acquired to judge the results of the original purchase. However, this is not useful for comparison with current alternative investments.

New Equipment Purchase

Determining the investment base in a decision relating to investment in a new piece of equipment is considerably easier than determining the investment base for a total enterprise. In judging the profitability of any planned specific investment, the investment base is normally taken as the net cash outlay required to begin to produce a profit from the new investment. Thus, in replacing one machine with another, the net cash outlay would be the result after subtracting the salvage value on the old machine and after adding installation costs of the new machine to the investment base. Depreciated book value of the old machine would be ignored in determining the investment base of the new one except insofar as it would affect cash tax outlay. If a tax saving is to be gained by replacing the old machine with a new one through a write-off of book values on the old machine, this saving would be subtracted from the investment base.

Valuation of Entire Corporation

In determining the investment base for an entire corporation, a variety of accepted approaches are available. If the purpose is to measure profitability to owners, the owners' equity or net worth may be used as the investment base. If the purpose is to measure profitability to common stockholders alone, preferred stock values should be deducted from total equity. If the purpose is to judge profitability to the firm rather than to the owners, some broader investment base must be used. Three generally accepted bases are total assets, total operating assets, and total assets less current liabilities (same figure as the capital structure).

It should be recognized in using any investment base for the total enterprise that substantial judgment factors determine the book value of the assets or of the equity and that an alternative or opportunity value could be significantly different. The advantage of working with cash outlay as an investment base is that there are substantial alternative uses for cash and it is in cash form that other investments are made. Thus, in determining the desirability of any investment, the use of cash outlay as the investment base offers a comparison for other potential uses for the same cash. This direct comparison does not exist in using book figures.

Return on Stock Equity. The common-stock investor could use the book value (value on the company's books) of his investment in determining profitability by relating the dividend or earnings per share to this value. This gives him a measure of the success of his investment based on the books of the company but it is not useful in terms of judging alternatives. If he uses the current market value of his investment and relates current dividends or earnings to it, he has a figure which is considerably more meaningful, because it is possible to sell the stock at current market value and to take the cash received and invest it elsewhere. Thus, return on current market value must be sufficient to justify retention of the stock regardless of the return on the book value or on his original cost value. It can be concluded that return on book equity is not very useful to the stockholder. Better measures are available for management's use in judging operations; these are discussed below.

Return on Total Assets. In determining the efficiency of the management or the accomplishment of the objectives of the total firm rather than of the owners, it must be recognized that all businesses employ funds in excess of owners' investment. These additional funds may be obtained through buying on credit, bank borrowing, accruals, or funded debt. Regardless of the source of the funds, management has responsibility for their application and for returns made through employing them.

For purposes of comparisons with other competitive companies, the use of stockholders' equity as an investment base in computing the return on investment is impractical. The most logical step is to turn to the other side of the balance sheet and consider total assets used in the business as a base against which the profit might be computed. It would seem logical to measure the efficiency of management on the basis of total assets under its direction regardless of the source from which these assets were obtained. Where the money comes from is not significant since the concern here is only with how these funds are utilized. For these purposes, the total assets or capital employed supplies a common base or denominator for comparison of competitive results and eliminates the confusion which might arise through attempting to use a net equity figure, since companies accumulate funds used in their businesses in different ways.

In accepting an asset base for investment, certain controversies arise in the measurement of asset values. Three possible approaches are depreciated value of assets, replacement value, or acquisition value. The use of depreciated value, particularly in companies where old equipment is used, would normally develop a very high return on investment. The use of depreciated values would also result in distortions in periods of fast write-offs. On the other hand, depreciated values are more indicative of amounts available for alternatives than are original acquisition costs. The use of depreciated or net book values and the return computed thereon is of significance particularly in the appraisal of a return on investment for the total firm. However, it is of little value in determining divisional operating returns on investment and in establishing a yardstick which is capable of appraising past, present, and future operating results.

Although the use of replacement values in determining return on investment provides interesting and valuable economic information, the possibilities of varying pricing practice on the basis of replacement value would generate complexities in the administration of return on investment for operating purposes. Where replacement value is determinable and where obsolescence is not substantial, worthwhile use may be made of this base in judging departmental or divisional return. In other cases, in periods of relatively stable prices, the gross assets method provides a more useful base and gives a more accurate trend picture for use in making long-term plans.

The problem of value of assets is applicable only in judging past performance. In any future investment in which a cash outlay base is used, original cost, replacement cost, and net assets or depreciated cost are all equal. This is why return on investment is so much more useful and applicable in judging future investments than in measuring the results of past activities.

Return on Operating Assets or Capital Structure. Some firms use operating assets rather than total assets as an investment base. This is suitable if operations alone are being judged. However, in judging a total firm and its management's efficiency, it should be noted that the firm owns its non-operating as well as its operating assets. Further, management is committed to a return on all assets regardless of type. It is usually due to a management decision that the firm has non-operating assets (unrelated securities and real estate, for example), and thus management should earn an adequate amount on these assets *and* on the operating assets.

The use of capital structure as a base is an attempt to remove seasonal effects on assets and to think toward a requirement of return to permanent suppliers of funds only. It is reasoned that temporary suppliers of funds were used for temporary needs only. Thus, judging management in the long run would exclude a requirement to do more than meet interest payments (if any) to these creditors and to repay them when due.

Valuation of a Division

Because the capital structure of a firm applies to the total corporation only, it is normally impossible to determine the capital structure of a division of the company or the type of financial structure used for a product line or a geographical operation. Return on equity in any segment of the business cannot be used to measure profitability because the amount of the equity is unknown. Thus, return must be measured relative to assets—either total assets, operating assets, or permanent assets. For most divisions, total assets and operating assets would be equal; non-operating assets are usually controlled by the firm's headquarters.

The asset base for measurement of return on investment is consistent with the concept of control and assigned responsibility. In this case, the operating managers are judged on the results of the employment of assets entrusted to their care. The above discussion on acquisition value, replacement value, or depreciated value of assets in establishing a base for measuring profitability of the entire firm applies also in establishing a base for use in division measurements.

DETERMINING RETURN

The determination of the return figure to be used in a return on investment problem involves a subjective evaluation of the amount of gain obtained from the use of capital. In judging the profitability of past performance, a return figure is commonly obtained through the application of principles of accounting to the operations of a business. In judging profitability for investment alternatives in the future, return involves an estimate of future gains to be obtained from one investment alternative vs. another. Because of the difficulties of predicting the future, determination of return in the future is even more subjective than return in the past.

Future Returns

In estimating future returns, a reduction in costs is considered the same as additional income. In a problem of replacing one piece of equipment with another, an estimate must be made of the annual expense outlays with the old piece of equipment vs. those with the new one. Reduction in annual cash outlays in operating the new equipment would be considered the return. In analyzing the return potential on a new product, the gross receipts from the production and sale of the new product must be determined and all operating expenses relative to that product subtracted to give a net gain from the product per year.

Past Returns

In judging past performance a variety of accounting figures can be used for return. It is obvious that the return figure to be used is always the gross income less certain charges inherent in the operation. The question arises as to the treatment of such items as bond interest, bank interest, taxes, and depreciation. If gross asset values are used in the investment figure, the return should be before the subtraction of depreciation charges. Income taxes present a particularly difficult problem because of the way in which they are determined. It is generally accepted that income taxes are really an expense of doing business, and that the return on capital is only after subtraction of income taxes. However, because of the differentiation in the accounting net-profit figure based on the type of financing used, it is common in judging the efficiency of a business as a whole to use net profit before income tax and before other payments for the use of capital, such as interest. By using a before-tax figure, the variation in return for large and small businesses is more comparable since the tax requirement varies with the size of the business and with certain managerial actions.

For most decisions relative to a specific investment for an existing company, the return figure would be the net annual cash gains resulting from making the investment vs. operating under present conditions before the payment of income taxes, interest, dividends, or any other payment for the use of the capital invested in the project.

RELATING RETURN TO INVESTMENT

The above discussion centered on determining the amount of the investment and the amount of the return. A way of measuring return on the investment then would be to relate the expected return to the expected investment and to state return as a per cent of investment. For example, net operating income divided by operating assets equals the percentage return on investment. In judging return for stockholders, net profit for the company after tax would be divided by the stockholders' equity in the company. A stockholder himself might relate net earnings per share to market value of his stock. These relationships emphasize return and investment.

Relate Like Things

The most important point of caution to be recognized with respect to earning-power percentages is that the return figure utilized should be related to its associated investment figure. Thus, if owners' equity is taken as the investment, the accounting net-profit-after-tax figure should be taken as the return. If total permanent assets or capital structure is used as investment, the return figure should include not only profit to owners but interest to permanent creditors. If total *operating* assets is the investment figure, net *operating* income should be the related return figure.

To illustrate the above point, assume the following simplified financial statements for the ABC Company.

Annual Income Statement

Sales	$1,000,000
Cost of Goods Sold	600,000
Gross Profit	400,000
Expenses	300,000
Net Operating Profit	100,000
Non-operating Income	10,000
Interest Expense	(10,000)
Net Profit before Income Taxes	100,000
Income Taxes	50,000
Net Profit	50,000
Dividends Paid	30,000
Addition to Retained Earnings	$ 20,000

BEGINNING BALANCE SHEET

Current Assets	$ 500,000	Current Liabilities	$ 300,000
Fixed Assets	300,000	Fixed Liabilities	200,000
Non-operating Invest-		Common Stock	200,000
ments	200,000	Retained Earnings	300,000
		Total Liabilities and	
Total Assets	$1,000,000	Net Worth	$1,000,000

Note that the beginning balance sheet is used for simplicity. It would be considered better than the ending balance sheet, but an average of the two might be most meaningful. The following relationships can be developed.

1. Total assets are $1,000,000. The corresponding return figure is net profit plus interest ($60,000), or net profit plus taxes plus interest ($110,000) for earnings of 6 per cent after taxes and 11 per cent before taxes.

2. Owners' equity is $500,000. The corresponding return figure is net profit ($50,000) for a return of 10 per cent.

3. Operating assets are $800,000. The corresponding return figure is net profit plus interest less non-operating income ($50,000), or net profit plus interest and taxes less non-operating income ($100,000) for a return of 6.25 per cent after tax and 12.5 per cent before tax. These returns are higher than on total assets because the return on the non-operating assets is not as great as the return on the operating assets.

4. Capital structure is $700,000. The corresponding dollar returns are the same as for total assets (it is assumed that all interest is for the fixed liabilities) for a return of 8.5 per cent after tax and 15.71 per cent before tax.

5. If 20,000 shares of stock are outstanding, and earnings per share are $2.50 and dividends per share are $1.50, and if the stock is selling in the market for $40 per share, the earnings yield is 6.25 per cent and the dividend yield is 3.75 per cent. Both of these yields are measures of return on investment to the stockholder.

Selection of Standards

Most companies set a standard for minimum return in the future. Usually this standard is the return on investment the company has experienced in the past. If the firm manages to do as well in *percentage* return in the future, its owners and managers may be satisfied. Of course, the asset base would rise as the firm expands and reinvests earnings, so dollar earnings would also have to rise to maintain the same percentage return on investment.

If the same method of computing return on investment is used for the standard as for the operation being judged (and it certainly should be), the choice of method becomes much less important. The relationship from the past to the present is likely to be the same under any method of computation chosen.

The Triangular Relationship

The above relationships of return and investment overlook the basic service of the business unit—its sales. A firm does not make profits unless it has sales. As a result, a commonly used approach to relating return to investment is a combination known as the *triangular relationship*. The three sides of the triangular relationship are investment, sales, and earnings. An industrial enterprise earns by turning over its investment and making a profit on its sales. As a result, the earning power of this enterprise is a product of two factors: capital turnover and profit margin. Sales divided by assets equals capital turnover, and earnings divided by sales equals profit margin. Multiplying the profit margin by the turnover gives the return on investment. This formula is stated as follows:

$$\frac{\text{Sales}}{\text{Investment}} \times \frac{\text{Earnings}}{\text{Sales}} = \text{Return on Investment}$$

While the result of application of the above formula is the same as would be obtained by merely dividing earnings by investment, the use of this formula tends also to emphasize the importance of sales in the total process of the profitability of the firm. The triangular relationship gives an analytical tool by which the factors contributing toward the over-all return on investment may be emphasized. This formula applied to the ABC Company described above would be:

$$\frac{\$1,000,000}{\$1,000,000} \times \frac{\$110,000}{\$1,000,000} = 11 \text{ per cent}$$

TIME VALUE IN RETURN ON INVESTMENT

In the above discussion, no differentiation was made as to the timing of the return. It was assumed that the average annual net return would be related to the average investment over the life of the investment. This has been the common approach to return on investment and is the so-called "accounting method." If a specific investment has a useful life of 9 years and its average return is $10 per year with a total return of $90, the accounting approach would use the figure $10 per year regardless of the timing of the return within the 9 years.

Timing Patterns

Figure 18–1 indicates three types of patterns of timing of return, all of which give a total return over life of $90 and an average return of $10 per year. The question now arises: "Are these three patterns equal in value?" The answer is "No" if it is assumed that there are always alternative investments. Assuming that the returns given in the three pat-

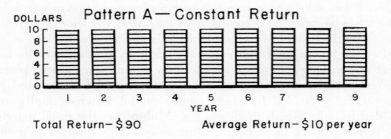

Pattern A — Constant Return

Total Return—$90   Average Return—$10 per year

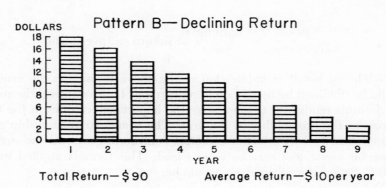

Pattern B—Declining Return

Total Return—$90   Average Return—$10 per year

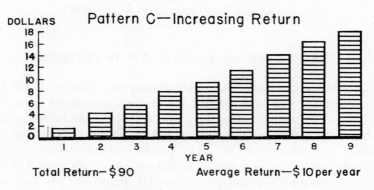

Pattern C—Increasing Return

Total Return—$90   Average Return—$10 per year

Fig. 18–1. Patterns of return.

terns in Figure 18–1 are all in cash form, at the end of the first year under pattern A the investor would have $10 to invest in some other alternative for the remaining 8 years of this total project. Under pattern B, he would have $18 to invest for the remaining 8 years, and under pattern C, he would have only $2 to invest for the remaining years. Obviously, he could earn more in the remaining 8 years by reinvesting $18 than he could by reinvesting $2. Thus, if the returns are in cash form, pattern B would be much more desirable than pattern A, and pattern C much less desirable than either of the other two. Under pattern B, the investor has $60 in gain in 4 years. Under pattern C, it takes almost 8 years for the same amount of gain. Thus, under pattern B he can be reinvesting the return and earning more during the intervening years than he could in pattern C. The conclusion is that time does influence economic value. A dollar today is worth a dollar in terms of alternative investments. A dollar 10 years from now is worth something less than a dollar invested today for the intervening 10 years.

Figure 18–2 is further indication of the influence of time on economic value. If it is possible to earn a 25 per cent rate of return, $20 received 10 years hence is worth only $2.14 today. Or $2.14 invested at 25 per cent compounded annually and the return reinvested would give $20 ten years from now. On the other hand, $20 five years from now at a 25 per cent return would be worth $6.56 today, and $20 one year from now would be worth $16 today. It must be kept in mind that all emphasis placed on the timing of receipts of income in usable form for other investment assumes that other investment alternatives are always available. This would seem to be a reasonably practical assumption in today's economy.

Timing and Profitability

Because of the influence of timing of receipts, a number of applications of the return on investment approach in measuring profitability take into account the timing of receipts as well as the average amount of receipts. Thus, for new investments, a normal approach would be the cash-flow approach, which takes total cash outlay required immediately as the investment and then discounts to present values the cash receipts or gains expected in each year during the life of the investment. Tables 18–1 and 18–2 can be used in determining the value of a return at any number of years in the future at a given capitalization rate, or in determining the rate of return which a constant flow of dollars over a given period of years produces on a time-value basis.

Figure 18–3 indicates the difference between the *accounting method* and the *time-value method* in determining return on investment. It also indicates the differences which could accrue in the accounting method based upon decisions as to what portion of the outlay to capitalize.

HOW TIME INFLUENCES ECONOMIC VALUE

25% RATE OF RETURN   LEVEL ANNUAL RECEIPTS

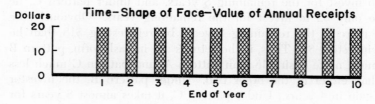

Time–Shape of Face–Value of Annual Receipts

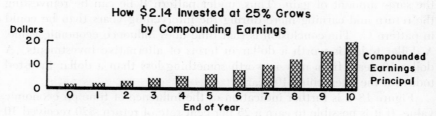

How $2.14 Invested at 25% Grows
by Compounding Earnings

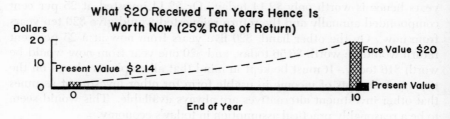

What $20 Received Ten Years Hence Is
Worth Now (25% Rate of Return)

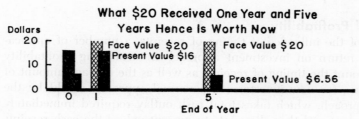

What $20 Received One Year and Five
Years Hence Is Worth Now

What Each Future Years Annual
Receipt Is Worth Now

Fig. 18–2. How time influences economic value.

EFFECT OF CAPITALIZATION POLICY ON RATE OF RETURN

Case	Motor Truck Purchase Life 10 yrs. Capitalized 100% Depr. Rate 10%				Track Relocation Project Life 10 yrs. Capitalized 50% Depr. Rate 10%				Either Project Life 10yrs.	
Method	ACCOUNTING METHOD				ACCOUNTING METHOD				TIME-VALUE METHOD	
Time Period	Net Cash Flow	Book Write Off	Book Profit	Aver. Book Invest	Net Cash Flow	Book Write Off	Book Profit	Aver. Book Invest	Net Cash	Receipts Discount. at 28%
0	−20				−20	10	−10		−20	−20.00
0-1	6	2	4	19	6	1	5	9.5	6	5.20
1-2	6	2	4	17	6	1	5	8.5	6	3.94
2-3	6	2	4	15	6	1	5	7.5	6	2.98
3-4	6	2	4	13	6	1	5	6.5	6	2.25
4-5	6	2	4	11	6	1	5	5.5	6	1.70
5-6	6	2	4	9	6	1	5	4.5	6	1.28
6-7	6	2	4	7	6	1	5	3.5	6	.96
7-8	6	2	4	5	6	1	5	2.5	6	.72
8-9	6	2	4	3	6	1	5	1.5	6	.55
9-10	6	2	4	1	6	1	5	.5	6	.42
Total	40	20	40	100	40	20	40	50	40	0.00

Average Profit 4 Average Investment 10	Average Profit 4 Average Investment 5	Average Profit 4
RETURN 40%	RETURN 80%	RETURN 28%

Fig. 18–3. Effect of capitalization policy on a rate of return.

Table 18–1. Present Value of $1

Years Hence	1%	2%	4%	6%	8%	10%	12%	14%	15%	16%	18%	20%	22%	24%	25%	26%	28%	30%	35%	40%	45%	50%
1	0.990	0.980	0.962	0.943	0.926	0.909	0.893	0.877	0.870	0.862	0.847	0.833	0.820	0.806	0.800	0.794	0.781	0.769	0.741	0.714	0.690	0.667
2	0.980	0.961	0.925	0.890	0.857	0.826	0.797	0.769	0.756	0.743	0.718	0.694	0.672	0.650	0.640	0.630	0.610	0.592	0.549	0.510	0.476	0.444
3	0.971	0.942	0.889	0.840	0.794	0.751	0.712	0.675	0.658	0.641	0.609	0.579	0.551	0.524	0.512	0.500	0.477	0.455	0.406	0.364	0.328	0.296
4	0.961	0.924	0.855	0.792	0.735	0.683	0.636	0.592	0.572	0.552	0.516	0.482	0.451	0.423	0.410	0.397	0.373	0.350	0.301	0.260	0.226	0.198
5	0.951	0.906	0.822	0.747	0.681	0.621	0.567	0.519	0.497	0.476	0.437	0.402	0.370	0.341	0.328	0.315	0.291	0.269	0.223	0.186	0.156	0.132
6	0.942	0.888	0.790	0.705	0.630	0.564	0.507	0.456	0.432	0.410	0.370	0.335	0.303	0.275	0.262	0.250	0.227	0.207	0.165	0.133	0.108	0.088
7	0.933	0.871	0.760	0.665	0.583	0.513	0.452	0.400	0.376	0.354	0.314	0.279	0.249	0.222	0.210	0.198	0.178	0.159	0.122	0.095	0.074	0.059
8	0.923	0.853	0.731	0.627	0.540	0.467	0.404	0.351	0.327	0.305	0.266	0.233	0.204	0.179	0.168	0.157	0.139	0.123	0.091	0.068	0.051	0.039
9	0.914	0.837	0.703	0.592	0.500	0.424	0.361	0.308	0.284	0.263	0.225	0.194	0.167	0.144	0.134	0.125	0.108	0.094	0.067	0.048	0.035	0.026
10	0.905	0.820	0.676	0.558	0.463	0.386	0.322	0.270	0.247	0.227	0.191	0.162	0.137	0.116	0.107	0.099	0.085	0.073	0.050	0.035	0.024	0.017
11	0.896	0.804	0.650	0.527	0.429	0.350	0.287	0.237	0.215	0.195	0.162	0.135	0.112	0.094	0.086	0.079	0.066	0.056	0.037	0.025	0.017	0.012
12	0.887	0.788	0.625	0.497	0.397	0.319	0.257	0.208	0.187	0.168	0.137	0.112	0.092	0.076	0.069	0.062	0.052	0.043	0.027	0.018	0.012	0.008
13	0.879	0.773	0.601	0.469	0.368	0.290	0.229	0.182	0.163	0.145	0.116	0.093	0.075	0.061	0.055	0.050	0.040	0.033	0.020	0.013	0.008	0.005
14	0.870	0.758	0.577	0.442	0.340	0.263	0.205	0.160	0.141	0.125	0.099	0.078	0.062	0.049	0.044	0.039	0.032	0.025	0.015	0.009	0.006	0.003
15	0.861	0.743	0.555	0.417	0.315	0.239	0.183	0.140	0.123	0.108	0.084	0.065	0.051	0.040	0.035	0.031	0.025	0.020	0.011	0.006	0.004	0.002
16	0.853	0.728	0.534	0.394	0.292	0.218	0.163	0.123	0.107	0.093	0.071	0.054	0.042	0.032	0.028	0.025	0.019	0.015	0.008	0.005	0.003	0.002
17	0.844	0.714	0.513	0.371	0.270	0.198	0.146	0.108	0.093	0.080	0.060	0.045	0.034	0.026	0.023	0.020	0.015	0.012	0.006	0.003	0.002	0.001
18	0.836	0.700	0.494	0.350	0.250	0.180	0.130	0.095	0.081	0.069	0.051	0.038	0.028	0.021	0.018	0.016	0.012	0.009	0.005	0.002	0.001	0.001
19	0.828	0.686	0.475	0.331	0.232	0.164	0.116	0.083	0.070	0.060	0.043	0.031	0.023	0.017	0.014	0.012	0.009	0.007	0.003	0.002	0.001	
20	0.820	0.673	0.456	0.312	0.215	0.149	0.104	0.073	0.061	0.051	0.037	0.026	0.019	0.014	0.012	0.010	0.007	0.005	0.002	0.001	0.001	
21	0.811	0.660	0.439	0.294	0.199	0.135	0.093	0.064	0.053	0.044	0.031	0.022	0.015	0.011	0.009	0.008	0.006	0.004	0.002	0.001		
22	0.803	0.647	0.422	0.278	0.184	0.123	0.083	0.056	0.046	0.038	0.026	0.018	0.013	0.009	0.007	0.006	0.004	0.003	0.001	0.001		
23	0.795	0.634	0.406	0.262	0.170	0.112	0.074	0.049	0.040	0.033	0.022	0.015	0.010	0.007	0.006	0.005	0.003	0.002	0.001			
24	0.788	0.622	0.390	0.247	0.158	0.102	0.066	0.043	0.035	0.028	0.019	0.013	0.008	0.007	0.005	0.004	0.003	0.002	0.001			
25	0.780	0.610	0.375	0.233	0.146	0.092	0.059	0.038	0.030	0.024	0.016	0.010	0.007	0.005	0.004	0.003	0.002	0.001	0.001			
26	0.772	0.598	0.361	0.220	0.135	0.084	0.053	0.033	0.026	0.021	0.014	0.009	0.006	0.004	0.003	0.002	0.002	0.001				
27	0.764	0.586	0.347	0.207	0.125	0.076	0.047	0.029	0.023	0.018	0.011	0.007	0.005	0.003	0.002	0.002	0.001	0.001				
28	0.757	0.574	0.333	0.196	0.116	0.069	0.042	0.026	0.020	0.016	0.010	0.006	0.004	0.002	0.002	0.001	0.001	0.001				
29	0.749	0.563	0.321	0.185	0.107	0.063	0.037	0.022	0.017	0.014	0.008	0.005	0.003	0.002	0.002	0.001	0.001					
30	0.742	0.552	0.308	0.174	0.099	0.057	0.033	0.020	0.015	0.012	0.007	0.004	0.003	0.002	0.001	0.001	0.001					
40	0.672	0.453	0.208	0.097	0.046	0.022	0.011	0.005	0.004	0.003	0.001	0.001										
50	0.608	0.372	0.141	0.054	0.021	0.009	0.003	0.001	0.001	0.001												

SOURCE: Robert N. Anthony, *Management Accounting*, rev. ed. (Homewood, Ill.: Richard D. Irwin, Inc., 1960), p. 656.

Table 18–2. Present Value of $1 Received Annually for N Years

Years (N)	1%	2%	4%	6%	8%	10%	12%	14%	15%	16%	18%	20%	22%	24%	25%	26%	28%	30%	35%	40%	45%	50%
1	0.990	0.980	0.962	0.943	0.926	0.909	0.893	0.877	0.870	0.862	0.847	0.833	0.820	0.806	0.800	0.794	0.781	0.769	0.741	0.714	0.690	0.667
2	1.970	1.942	1.886	1.833	1.783	1.736	1.690	1.647	1.626	1.605	1.566	1.528	1.492	1.457	1.440	1.424	1.392	1.361	1.289	1.224	1.165	1.111
3	2.941	2.884	2.775	2.673	2.577	2.487	2.402	2.322	2.283	2.246	2.174	2.106	2.042	1.981	1.952	1.923	1.868	1.816	1.696	1.589	1.493	1.407
4	3.902	3.808	3.630	3.465	3.312	3.170	3.037	2.914	2.855	2.798	2.690	2.589	2.494	2.404	2.362	2.320	2.241	2.166	1.997	1.849	1.720	1.605
5	4.853	4.713	4.452	4.212	3.993	3.791	3.605	3.433	3.352	3.274	3.127	2.991	2.864	2.745	2.689	2.635	2.532	2.436	2.220	2.035	1.876	1.737
6	5.795	5.601	5.242	4.917	4.623	4.355	4.111	3.889	3.784	3.685	3.498	3.326	3.167	3.020	2.951	2.885	2.759	2.643	2.385	2.168	1.983	1.824
7	6.728	6.472	6.002	5.582	5.206	4.868	4.564	4.288	4.160	4.039	3.812	3.605	3.416	3.242	3.161	3.083	2.937	2.802	2.508	2.263	2.057	1.883
8	7.652	7.325	6.733	6.210	5.747	5.335	4.968	4.639	4.487	4.344	4.078	3.837	3.619	3.421	3.329	3.241	3.076	2.925	2.598	2.331	2.108	1.922
9	8.566	8.162	7.435	6.802	6.247	5.759	5.328	4.946	4.772	4.607	4.303	4.031	3.786	3.566	3.463	3.366	3.184	3.019	2.665	2.379	2.144	1.948
10	9.471	8.983	8.111	7.360	6.710	6.145	5.650	5.216	5.019	4.833	4.494	4.192	3.923	3.682	3.571	3.465	3.269	3.092	2.715	2.414	2.168	1.965
11	10.368	9.787	8.760	7.887	7.139	6.495	5.988	5.453	5.234	5.029	4.656	4.327	4.035	3.776	3.656	3.544	3.335	3.147	2.752	2.438	2.185	1.977
12	11.255	10.575	9.385	8.384	7.536	6.814	6.194	5.660	5.421	5.197	4.793	4.439	4.127	3.851	3.725	3.606	3.387	3.190	2.779	2.456	2.196	1.985
13	12.134	11.343	9.986	8.853	7.904	7.103	6.424	5.842	5.583	5.342	4.910	4.533	4.203	3.912	3.780	3.656	3.427	3.223	2.799	2.468	2.204	1.990
14	13.004	12.106	10.563	9.295	8.244	7.367	6.628	6.002	5.724	5.468	5.008	4.611	4.265	3.962	3.824	3.695	3.459	3.249	2.814	2.477	2.210	1.993
15	13.865	12.849	11.118	9.712	8.559	7.606	6.811	6.142	5.847	5.575	5.092	4.675	4.315	4.001	3.859	3.726	3.483	3.268	2.825	2.484	2.214	1.995
16	14.718	13.578	11.652	10.106	8.851	7.824	6.974	6.265	5.954	5.669	5.162	4.730	4.357	4.033	3.887	3.751	3.503	3.283	2.834	2.489	2.216	1.997
17	15.562	14.292	12.166	10.477	9.122	8.022	7.120	6.373	6.047	5.749	5.222	4.775	4.391	4.059	3.910	3.771	3.518	3.295	2.840	2.492	2.218	1.998
18	16.398	14.992	12.659	10.828	9.372	8.201	7.250	6.467	6.128	5.818	5.273	4.812	4.419	4.080	3.928	3.786	3.529	3.304	2.844	2.494	2.219	1.999
19	17.226	15.678	13.134	11.158	9.604	8.365	7.366	6.550	6.198	5.877	5.316	4.844	4.442	4.097	3.942	3.799	3.539	3.311	2.848	2.496	2.220	1.999
20	18.046	16.351	13.590	11.470	9.818	8.514	7.469	6.623	6.259	5.929	5.353	4.870	4.460	4.110	3.954	3.808	3.546	3.316	2.850	2.497	2.221	1.999
21	18.857	17.011	14.029	11.764	10.017	8.649	7.562	6.687	6.312	5.973	5.384	4.891	4.476	4.121	3.963	3.816	3.551	3.320	2.852	2.498	2.221	2.000
22	19.660	17.658	14.451	12.042	10.201	8.772	7.645	6.743	6.359	6.011	5.410	4.909	4.488	4.130	3.970	3.822	3.556	3.323	2.853	2.498	2.222	2.000
23	20.456	18.292	14.857	12.303	10.371	8.883	7.718	6.792	6.399	6.044	5.432	4.925	4.499	4.137	3.976	3.827	3.559	3.325	2.854	2.499	2.222	2.000
24	21.243	18.914	15.247	12.550	10.529	8.985	7.784	6.835	6.434	6.073	5.451	4.937	4.507	4.143	3.981	3.831	3.562	3.327	2.855	2.499	2.222	2.000
25	22.023	19.523	15.622	12.783	10.675	9.077	7.843	6.873	6.464	6.097	5.467	4.948	4.514	4.147	3.985	3.834	3.564	3.329	2.856	2.499	2.222	2.000
26	22.795	20.121	15.983	13.003	10.810	9.161	7.896	6.906	6.491	6.118	5.480	4.956	4.520	4.151	3.988	3.837	3.566	3.330	2.856	2.500	2.222	2.000
27	23.560	20.707	16.330	13.211	10.935	9.237	7.943	6.935	6.514	6.136	5.492	4.964	4.524	4.154	3.990	3.839	3.567	3.331	2.856	2.500	2.222	2.000
28	24.316	21.281	16.663	13.406	11.051	9.307	7.984	6.961	6.534	6.152	5.502	4.970	4.528	4.157	3.992	3.840	3.568	3.331	2.857	2.500	2.222	2.000
29	25.066	21.844	16.984	13.591	11.158	9.370	8.022	6.983	6.551	6.166	5.510	4.975	4.531	4.159	3.994	3.841	3.569	3.332	2.857	2.500	2.222	2.000
30	25.808	22.396	17.292	13.765	11.258	9.427	8.055	7.003	6.566	6.177	5.517	4.979	4.534	4.160	3.995	3.842	3.569	3.332	2.857	2.500	2.222	2.000
40	32.835	27.355	19.793	15.046	11.925	9.779	8.244	7.105	6.642	6.234	5.548	4.997	4.544	4.166	3.999	3.846	3.571	3.333	2.857	2.500	2.222	2.000
50	39.196	31.424	21.482	15.762	12.234	9.915	8.304	7.133	6.661	6.246	5.554	4.999	4.545	4.167	4.000	3.846	3.571	3.333	2.857	2.500	2.222	2.000

SOURCE: Robert N. Anthony, *Management Accounting*, rev. ed. (Homewood, Ill.: Richard D. Irwin, Inc., 1960), p. 657.

425

Two different investments are considered in the example in Figure 18–3. Both require a cash outlay of 20 ($20.00 or any multiple thereof) and both yield a net cash flow of 6 per year for 10 years. In using the standard accounting method for determining the return on investment of the motor truck purchase, the total outlay of 20 is capitalized and amortized over the 10-year life. Thus, the annual write-off is 2 and the average investment each year is halfway between beginning book value and ending book value that year (an original value of 20 less 2 write-off in the first year gives a value of 18 at the end of year 1 and an average value for the year of 19). Average investment over 10 years is 10. An average return of 4 on an average investment of 10 is 40 per cent.

In the track relocation project, one-half of the original investment is written off immediately as an expense. The remaining 10 in value is amortized over 10 years at the rate of 1 per year. Thus, average investment in the track relocation project over the 10 years is 5. An average return of 4 on an average investment of 5 is 80 per cent.

Using the time-value method, no attention is paid to accounting amortization. Initial cash outlay is considered as well as annual cash return. A return of 6 per year for 10 years gives a rate of return of 28 per cent on an investment of 20. Both projects in Figure 18–3 are equal under the time-value method. Each 6 to be received in the future is discounted to present value at the rate of 28 per cent (see Table 18–1).[1] The present value of the total to be received during the life of the project equals the initial cash outlay. Therefore, the rate of return is 28 per cent.

Time-Value vs. Accounting Method

Both the accounting method and the time-value method measure the productivity of capital, but the accounting method has certain limitations which have led to an increasing acceptance of the time-value method. First, the accounting method requires determination of the cost value of the investment. The time-value method uses net cash outlay as the cost value. Second, in the accounting method, the project earnings would vary substantially with the choice of amortization and depreciation policies. The time-value method, since it considers only cash funds, does not present this problem. Third, the accounting method ignores the time patterns of investment and earnings and therefore does not take into account the additional earnings from reinvesting cash.

The major problems in application of the time-value method are its lack of familiarity, its complexity to the uninitiated, and the fact that it

[1] The 5.20 in Figure 18–3 for the first year is higher than the 4.686 (6 x .781) derived from Table 18–1 because the six (dollars) is received throughout the year, rather than all at the end of the year, which is the situation in Table 18–1 (same for other years).

does not correspond to generally accepted accounting concepts. The time-value method is particularly recommended when the timing of receipts would vary significantly from year to year, when the life of the project is relatively short, and when the value of the investment does not remain constant (it declines due to depreciation or obsolescence). If the value of the investment were to remain constant throughout its life and the return in cash flow each year were also constant, the time-value and accounting approaches would give the same result. An illustration of this is the purchase of bonds at par to be held to maturity. Both approaches would give the stated rate of interest as the return on investment.

USES OF PROFITABILITY MEASUREMENTS

Some of the general uses of return on investment as a measure of profitability have been discussed above. These include potential use in judging investment by stockholders and creditors as well as by management. The discussion below is concerned only with return on investment as a measurement of profitability used by internal management.

Capital Budgeting

Within the framework of business conduct, there is a phase of budgeting for income and expense that is not accounted for in the income statement. Some items of income and expense involve a longer period of time than the 12 months commonly used in income statements. They reflect such items as additions, improvements, replacements, plant and equipment, major repairs, and research. Current repairs can generally be listed as expense on an income statement and would fit within normal income and expense budgeting operations. Similarly, current research is normally covered in annual income and expense budgeting. Capital research embraces that type of research which is of such a different nature as to result in a new product, or whose end results are as yet unknown. In acquisition of capital assets, in major repairs, and in research, investments are made for which return is expected in future accounting periods rather than in the current period. As a result, budgeting for these investments involves fundamentally different general principles from those used in planning for current expenditures and income.

In budgeting for capital items (in most firms this would include only outlays for plant and equipment since research and repairs are considered current outlays) estimates must be made of the timing of the returns related to the investment being considered. A *capital budget,* therefore, is an estimate of investment value and the returns and timing of the returns related to that investment. The most significant characteristic of capital budgeting is that each project constitutes a distinct venture that is considered by itself. There are as many capital budgets as there are special projects.

Preparation of capital budgets requires an estimate of the amount of cash outlay required for the investment, and of the potential returns to be received and the timing of these returns. As a capital budget is prepared for each potential investment project, the profitability of the potential investment can be determined by relating the return and its timing to the amount of the investment. The selection of which investments to make is the final result of the budgeting process and is based on a comparison of the relative rates of returns of the alternative investments and of the risks involved in each of these investments. Return on investment becomes the basic deciding factor in most capital budgeting decisions regarding selection of investments.

Of all decisions of management, capital budgeting is among the foremost in its importance to the success of the firm. In deliberations on capital budgeting, a wide variety of possible investments should be considered by management. The selection of the right investments in capital assets is the most important function of management for it is these decisions which mold the future course of the business and spell the differences between success, mediocrity, and failure.

The capital budgeting process or technique is no better than the methods used in determining the profitability advantages of the alternative proposals. For most internal investment decisions, the time-value return on investment would seem to be the most desirable approach. The estimates of potential returns and of the net cash outlay required are subjective and can involve rather substantial error. However, the capital budgeting process forces management to a formal and relatively detailed estimate of outlays and of incomes, and thus does not allow management to jump to an over-all decision that a certain investment would be profitable without collecting the available facts and attempting to weigh them in light of other alternatives.

External Standard of Comparison

Return on investment for the entire company can be used as a standard of measurement of the efficiency of management as a whole. If the investment values used are reasonable, the return relative to these values should be sufficient to justify the investment in this company. Management can use this over-all company standard in comparing itself with other companies and in setting standards for its future operations. Investors might also use it to measure management's efficiency.

Internal Standard of Comparison

Because of the better data available and because of fewer problems in measuring worth of the investment, return on investment is more meaningful for internal comparisons than for external ones. The return on investment is a measurement of profitability and can well be applied to divisional operations within a company. This requires an allocation of company resources to the various divisions and an allocation of company net incomes to these divisions also. Certain reasonable and accepted approaches can be used to allocate assets and earnings to various divisions so that divisional return on investment can be determined.

Certain limitations are inherent in any approach of this nature. First, the return-on-investment figures are no better than the allocations which were used to determine them. Second, relative efficiency is a long-run concept and no single year's operations should be used as a sole measure of efficiency. Third, in using this approach to place responsibility on divisional management for potential compensation purposes, the influence of external factors over which divisional management has no control must be seriously considered. In addition, the influence of over-all corporate policies which the divisional management did not determine must be considered.

Measure of Product Performance

The return on investment standard can be used to measure product performance in much the same way as it is used to measure the performance of operating divisions within the corporation. If each individual product is made by a different operating division, the application of return on investment would be the same as it is in measuring divisional results. In the event that more than one product is being made by a single operating unit, allocation of total investment to each product presents some difficulty. Once investments are allocated to various products and annual returns are also allocated, return on investment by product can be determined. This requires that definite product costs must be established, and expenses and revenues must be segregated by products. Even when the judgment limitations in these allocations are recognized, certain obvious and substantial variations in return on investment might be significant enough to cause a reconsideration of certain products or at least to change emphasis on certain products or product lines in the operation of the firm.

The addition of new products or the expansion of the products in an existing line can be decided upon after determining a potential return on the additional investment required to produce these new products or new lines. The older approach to making decisions on products or product lines emphasizes primarily the gross profit margin on each product or line. The return on investment approach forces management to take into consideration also the amount of the investment required. This leads to recognition that a high gross or net profit margin line is not necessarily the most profitable if it also requires a very high investment, and that a low profit margin line might be very profitable if it requires a relatively insignificant investment.

Profit Planning

Granted that profit performance can be diagnosed more readily by examining the business in terms of margin and turnover, it can be shown that the return on investment approach takes margin and turnover into account and can be used for purposes of profit planning. Sound planning calls for the establishment of long-range profit and volume objectives for the business as a whole and for each product line. Such long-term goals are usually established for share of the market, dollar sales volume, profit in dollars, and return on investment. If return on investment has been established as the key objective, and if it has been expressed in terms of specific profit margin and asset turnover, it becomes apparent that the marketing and production programs in support of the objectives must necessarily be directed at one of the following: (1) to increase volume, (2) to increase margin by reducing the costs, or (3) to minimize asset investment in relation to volume.

If performance goals with respect to each of these three factors have been established, the gap between present performance and the goal can be quantitatively expressed for each factor. By means of such expression, actions necessary to close the gap can be planned more precisely. Various functional programs developed in support of a profit improvement plan can be materially improved in direction and timing if each program is consciously identified with one of the three methods of improving the return on investment. If these specific programs are aimed toward improvement of one of the three elements in return on investment, it becomes easier to evaluate their impact on the over-all performance—thus assuring that the programs are closely meshed to the performance objectives that they are designed to support.

Each management policy can be considered in the light of its potential effect on the three factors of return on investment. For example, a change in credit policy which would lead toward liberalization of credit terms would have to have the potential to produce enough additional return to justify the increased investment in accounts receivable. Approaching the question of credit policy from this point of view forces a determination on the part of the advocates of policy change of the amount of return which the policy change will produce, and also requires an estimate of the amount of the additional investment. The channeling of the decision along these lines forces it to be made in the light of its effect upon potential return on investment for the organization as a whole.

Control

The acceptance of return on investment as a basic financial management objective leads to an appreciation of the importance of certain factors in the control necessary to meet the objective. Figure 18–4 indicates the relationship of factors affecting return on investment. Each of the factors mentioned in this illustration becomes a control point which must be watched if the over-all objective of a reasonable return on investment is to be obtained. The emphasis on sales is indicated by the fact that it appears twice at the third level of factors. A breakdown of investment into permanent and working capital and a further breakdown of working capital indicate those points which are more subject to control during the day-to-day operation of the business. The same is true of obtaining earnings by an analysis of sales minus cost of sales and a further breakdown of cost of sales into those areas which are most subject to control.

From a control point of view, it should be noted that a reduction in any of the factors on the fifth level of the chart would lead to an increase in the percentage return on investment. On the other hand, an increase in any of these factors without a corresponding change elsewhere would lead to a reduction in return on investment. It should be further noted that if sales increased without a change in either total investment or operating income, there would be no effect on the ultimate return on the investment. From a control point of view, the importance of judging the effect of changing sales upon the investment requirement as well as on the cost of sales is clearly indicated.

COST OF CAPITAL

The importance of determination of return on investment in financial management has already been indicated. The use of return on investment in relating one alternative investment to another is well-accepted. However, the mere relationship of one alternative investment to another does not give a clear picture of the reasonableness of return. If two potential investments were available and one yielded 1 per cent annually and the

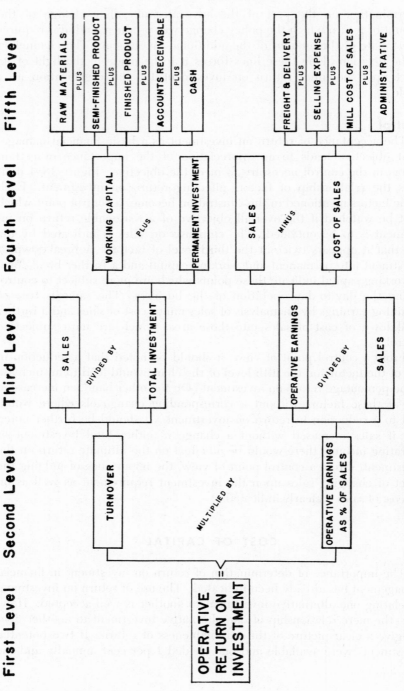

Fig. 18–4. Relationship of factors affecting return on investment.

other 2 per cent annually, a mere comparison of alternatives would lead to an acceptance of the 2 per cent return on investment.

It might be generally agreed that 2 per cent annually is not a reasonable return. A third alternative is always available—the alternative of no investment. If capital is available and there is no reasonable investment in sight for the company, the capital should be returned to its owners so that they can find reasonable investments for its use. Therefore, it becomes necessary to determine some cut-off point or minimum standard of return on investment below which the company would not make investments.

The reason that 1 and 2 per cent returns are not satisfactory in the long run is that the investors in any company can earn more than this on their own at a substantially lower risk by buying government bonds or depositing in savings accounts. This suggests that other alternatives to be considered should include alternatives for the investors as well as alternative investments for the firm itself. This is sometimes difficult to do and a more common approach to the problem of determining a minimum standard for return is to determine the *cost of capital*. In other words, return on any investment made by a firm should at least equal the cost of the capital which the firm uses in that investment. In this application, return on investment is an operating return before any payment for the use of capital.

Another approach would be to consider the cost of capital as a cost of the investment, and, therefore, no investments would be made unless the return after subtracting cost of capital were something in excess of zero. This leads to the acceptance of the full-cost approach to business investment. That is, investments should yield enough to cover all costs of operation including all accounting costs plus the cost of the capital invested even though normal accounting procedures do not consider this a cost. Stated differently, no investment is satisfactory if it merely shows some dollar amount of profit; i.e., operates "in the black." The amount of profit must be sufficient to justify the investment on the part of those making it or, in effect, the investment is not covering all of its cost and thus is an unsatisfactory one.

Operating on the assumption that there are always alternative uses for capital, every source of capital for a firm involves a cost. While standard accounting recognizes as a cost only those payments for capital which are legally required, financial management must accept as a cost some amount for the use of owners' funds as well as creditors' funds. The company should make no long-run or permanent investment that would not yield an amount sufficient to reasonably compensate the owners for the use of their funds as well as to meet interest requirements of creditors.

Because all costs of capital are not labeled expense from an accounting point of view, the measurement of the average cost of capital for the firm involves a deviation from standard accounting policy. Nonetheless, this deviation is necessary for purposes of management decision making in regard to alternative investment and repayment of sources of capital. It is not possible to determine average cost of capital until the cost of each individual source of capital is determined. Therefore, the following discussion considers the determination of the cost of individual sources of capital before determining an average cost of capital for the firm.

Temporary sources are often excluded in determining costs of capital because they are not considered relative to the permanent investment in the firm. Also temporary sources tend to fluctuate substantially in quantity so that it is difficult to get a concept of the permanent cost of these sources. Furthermore, as discussed in Chapter 21, the more permanent of the so-called temporary or spontaneous sources tend to be of no cost to the firm when compared with other alternatives the firm may have. For these reasons, only the permanent sources of capital will be considered here in determining an average cost of capital.

Bonds

The determination of the costs of funds obtained from bondholders is similar to that for all types of long-term creditors. The basic problem is one of determining the net amount received from this source and the average annual cost of the source. The net amount received is not necessarily the face amount of the bonds or the amount entered in the bonds payable account in the balance sheet. The cost of bond capital should be related to the actual amount of capital received by the firm, for which it is paying this cost. Thus, the firm would not normally use the face value of the bonds being sold in its determination of the cost of bond capital. Instead, the price to the public (which might vary from the face value) would be considered and from it would be subtracted the spread to the underwriters in order to obtain the proceeds to the company. From this would be subtracted other costs of the issue in order to get *net* proceeds to the company. This amount, which is normally less than the face value of the bonds, is the amount of the capital received and the amount to which costs must be related.

The annual costs would be the interest paid out on the bond issue. It should be noted that the costs of sale of the issue were subtracted from the investment rather than considered as a cost in determining cost of capital. The relationship of the interest paid out to the amount of capital received would give the cost of capital if the maturity value of the bonds was the same as the amount received from their sale. If the maturity value differs, the additional outlay at the time of maturity (if the amount received was less than the maturity value) would have to be considered a cost. Taking into account the time value of the money, the present worth of the annual outlays could be determined as well as the present value of the future principal payments. The same approach could be used if the amount received was in excess of the final maturity value to be paid.

Because the amount of capital received does not normally vary significantly from the required maturity outlay, the accounting approach of amortization of the premium or discount and of average value of the investment does not yield a significantly different cost from the time-value approach. This is particularly true for long-term obligations. For very short-term obligations or in situations where the premium or discount is significant, it is recommended that the time-value approach be used and that the present value of each annual outlay in the future, including the present value of the payment of principal at maturity, be considered in arriving at the cost of bond capital. In other cases, the premium or discount should be amortized over the life of the bond issue and the premiums subtracted from the annual interest cost or the discount added to the annual interest cost. This average annual cost should be related to the average amount of bonds outstanding which would be the net proceeds from the sale of the issue plus the amount to be paid out at maturity divided by two.

Preferred Stock

The determination of cost of capital obtained from preferred stockholders is less complex than for bonds because preferreds have no maturity date. Thus, there is no problem of amortization of premium or discount and no problem of a payment at maturity. In this case, the net proceeds would be determined the same as in the bond issue and the annual dividend related to these net proceeds in order to get a percentage cost of capital. If it was the intention of the issuer to call the preferred stock at some determined date in the future, the premium or discount (compared to net proceeds from sale) at the time of redemption would have to be considered in determining the cost of capital.

Sinking funds and conversion features complicate the problem of determining the cost of capital of both bonds and preferred stocks. In the case of the sinking fund requirement, when the sinking fund is able to earn exactly the cost of the capital without a sinking fund, or when it is used immediately to retire the bonds, the over-all cost is no different. On the other hand, sinking funds normally earn less than the cost of the capital obtained and therefore the requirement of the sinking fund often increases slightly the cost of the specific source of capital being considered.

In convertible issues, cost determination problems become twofold. Costs can be determined for the issue assuming conversion would not take place and, therefore, conversion would have no effect on costs. If it is assumed that conversion will take place, and this is the more logical assumption, then costs have to be determined in light of the cost of the capital after conversion. Usually this would be the same as determining the cost of common-stock capital if the preferred issue or bond were convertible into common. In this sense the firm would experience two different costs: one, a cost of preferred stock or bonds for the issue as long as it remained outstanding; and two, a different cost after time of conversion, which would be the same as common-stock cost.

Common Stock

Determination of the cost of common-stock capital is considerably more subjective than that of either preferred stock or bonds. If we accept the assumption that the firm has an obligation to earn for its owners a reasonable return on their investment in light of their other alternatives, we have the problem of determining what is the potential return obtainable on their alternatives. The alternative rate attainable becomes, in effect, the cost of common-stock capital to the firm, since the owner would presumably give his capital to the firm only if at least this return were anticipated.

The problem of determining cost of common-stock capital is particularly complex because the owner can get his return in two ways—through dividends or through price appreciation. Primarily because of the current tax situation, the dividend payment by corporations to owners is not indicative of the kind of return owners expect to make in the long run. As a result, the relationship between the expected dividend pay-out and the amount of capital received is not a very effective measure of the cost of common-stock capital. It is, however, a measure of the outlay necessary to obtain this capital over some short period of time in the future. Dividend payment usually does not meet the requirement of earning a reasonable return for owners in light of other alternatives. Therefore, considerably more emphasis is placed on the earnings of the firm in determining the cost of common-stock capital than upon its expected dividend pay-out. Actually, it is not the earnings which the firm experiences but the expectation of its earnings on the part of its owners which really is the cost of common-stock capital.

With the emphasis on earnings in today's stock market, one approach to the determination of cost of common-stock capital is to relate the anticipated earnings per share on the part of the owners to the net price obtained on the new stock. The net price obtained is the selling price to the public minus the spread to underwriters and other costs of the issue. This is relatively easy to determine at the time of a sale of new common stock. The much more difficult determination is the anticipated earnings per share expected by owners. In normal market times, the price-earnings ratios on similar securities might be used to measure owner anticipation. However, in times of very high or very low market prices for securities, existing price-earnings ratios are not very indicative of owner expectations. To determine the cost of common-stock capital, therefore, it is necessary to determine some longer-range expectation of earnings, on the part of owners. Long-run analysis of returns and stock prices leads one to the conclusion that it is not unreasonable to use a 10 per cent after-tax figure as an expectation for owners in companies of medium risk and an 8 per cent return after tax for lesser-risk investments.

It should be noted that the costs of common stock and preferred stock as determined above are after-tax costs to the company. In order to compare these to the cost of bond capital and other creditor capital, the corresponding tax requirement would have to be added to the cost. Thus, 10 per cent after-tax cost of common stock is approximately 20 per cent before-tax cost at existing federal income tax rates. It is certainly true that in times of high market prices for securities, companies may raise common-stock money with earnings substantially below those which a 10 per cent cost would indicate as a requirement. It is the authors' contention, however, that this is a temporary situation due to market conditions and expectations of market price appreciation, and that the firm must still consider itself successful only if it earns a reasonable long-run expectation regardless of what the owner happens to obtain or expect through profits made in the security markets.

Retained Earnings

Since the retained earnings are legally credited to the stockholders' account, it is generally assumed that a firm withholds earnings from the stockholder only if it can expect gains on these earnings to be equal to or greater than the amount which the shareholder himself could earn. Even though it is difficult for shareholders significantly to influence dividend policy, it would appear that in the long run stockholders would not allow the firm to withhold earnings if they received no additional gains in the future from the firm after the earnings were withheld. Thus, whether the shareholder makes an investment in the firm through his initial purchase of the stock or whether he reinvests annually through the firm's retention of earnings, he would tend to have the same expectation of a percentage return on the value of his investment.

The reinvestment of earnings should lead to an increased value of the stockholders' investment because of the expectation of future earnings on the reinvested earnings. If this is the case, it would appear that the cost of retained earnings would be equal to the cost of common-stock capital with the exception of the savings which would accrue through the fact that no cash outlay is required for costs of issuing the common stock and for spread to underwriters. Since these amounts are generally relatively small in relation to the amount of the issue, it could be said that, in general, the cost of retained earnings is approximately equal to the cost of common stock.

Some authorities take into account the stockholders' tax position in determining the cost of retained earnings. It is their contention that if the earnings were paid out to the stockholders in the form of dividends, they would have to pay income taxes on these earnings and they would, therefore, have some lesser amount available for investment in other alternatives. Thus the firm would need to earn less on the amount retained than on the original investment in order to offer the stockholder the same opportunities he would have elsewhere. For example, if a stockholder required a 10 per cent return on his initial investment in the firm, the firm would have to earn $1.00 after tax to justify a $10.00 investment. On the other hand, if the firm retained the $1.00 earned in the first year in the business rather than paying it to the owner, it might have to earn only $.075 on that $1.00 the next year to justify retention in light of the owners' alternatives. If the firm had paid the $1.00 to the owner in the form of dividends and the owner had to pay 25 per cent of this in taxes, he would have $.75 left available for investment elsewhere or for purchases of additional stock in the same firm. If he expected the same 10 per cent return on his investment, this $.75 of new investment would yield $.075 per year in coming years. While this approach seems reasonable in determining the cost of retained earnings from the point of view of stockholder alternatives, it is extremely difficult to apply because of the substantial variation in tax position of stockholders. Many stockholders pay no income tax and others might pay as high as 91 per cent on top bracket income. It does not seem reasonable that management should capitalize on the tax position of its stockholders, and therefore, the authors assume that the cost of retained earnings is equivalent to the cost of common-stock capital regardless of the tax position of the owners.

Average Cost of Capital

The cost of the various sources of capital should be determined in any analysis used in selection of sources of capital. Thus, in a decision to issue bonds, the cost in the future of the bonds as a source of capital should be related to the cost of other alternatives such as preferred and common stock. It is obvious that the lowest cost sources are not always selected. In fact, the decision becomes one of a balance between cost and risk. The ordinarily higher cost common-stock and retained-earnings sources are very low risk to the company and are, therefore, often selected in spite of their higher cost.

For purposes of determining a minimum return on investment which must be earned to justify business use of capital, the cost of each individual source of capital is not very meaningful. If a firm were borrowing funds at a bank to invest in a certain project, and the cost of these funds was 6 per cent, the firm would need to earn only 6 per cent before payment for the capital for that project. If this bank borrowing was accomplished and the loan was still outstanding, and the next year the firm was considering other projects and therefore had to go to common stockholders or retained earnings at a cost of 20 per cent, then any project selected that year would have to yield at least 20 per cent. It is obvious that in this case a low yielding project could be selected in one year and a high yielding project turned down the next year. Therefore, decisions on minimum level of return required for any investment should be based on the average cost of capital rather than the cost of the specific source which is used in connection with a specific investment.

The cost of capital is an important element in the pricing of the product of the firm. The firm should price its product to cover all costs including its cost of capital. One product of the firm does not use one source of capital and another product another source. Instead, all products use all sources. It seems reasonable, therefore, that each product should be charged with the average cost of capital based on the amount of capital that product requires rather than with the cost of only one type of capital.

It would also seem reasonable to conclude that the average cost of capital utilized in financial management decisions should be a weighted average. That is, the cost connected with the most important source of capital in quantity should be given the greatest weight and the cost connected with the least important source the smallest weight. For example, if the firm had costs of capital of 5 per cent for bonds, 12 per cent before tax for preferred stock, and 20 per cent before tax for common stock and retained earnings, its weighted average cost would not be 5 plus 12 plus 20 divided by 3 or $12\frac{1}{3}$. Instead, its weighted average cost of capital would be based on the percentage used of each of these four major sources. If the firm planned to have approximately 20 per cent in bonds, 10 per cent in preferred stock, 30 per cent in common stock, and 40 per cent in retained earnings, the costs would be determined as follows:

Bonds	$5\% \times .20 = .01$
Preferred Stock	$12\% \times .10 = .012$
Common Stock	$20\% \times .30 = .06$
Retained Earnings	$20\% \times .40 = .08$
Weighted Average Cost of Capital	.162 or 16.2%

In this example, if the firm assumes that the capital structure break-down given above is realistic for it in the future, and that the costs determined are reasonable, it should turn down any investment opportunity which does not yield 16 per cent before tax and before payment for the use of capital. Many industrial firms use a standard before-tax investment return cutoff of 20 per cent.

For orderly operation of rate of return and determination of selection of alternative investments, management needs an objective and realistic standard of minimum acceptability. This should generally be based on the company's average cost of capital.

QUESTIONS

1. How is the investment base determined for problems of judging return on investment?
2. What return figures correspond to the following investments? (a) Total assets. (b) Operating assets. (c) Owners' equity. (d) Capital structure.
3. How would you recommend measuring profitability of a division?
4. What standards of performance might management use in judging its own efficiency?
5. What is meant by the triangular relationship? What is the importance of this concept?
6. Discuss turnover and profit margin as they apply to return on investment.
7. What is meant by time value in return on investment?
8. Define *capital budgeting* and state its uses in financial management.
9. Discuss the use of return on investment for the following purposes: (a) External standard of comparison. (b) Internal standard of comparison. (c) Measure of product performance. (d) Product planning.
10. What is meant by the cost of capital?
11. How is the cost of bond capital determined?
12. How is the cost of preferred-stock capital determined?
13. How is the cost of common-stock capital determined?
14. How is the cost of retained-earnings capital determined?
15. What is meant by the average weighted cost of capital? Of what use is this concept?

PROBLEMS

1. Determine return on investment for General Motors Corp. using: (a) Total assets. (b) Operating assets. (c) Capital structure. (d) Equity.

2. The Anderson Co. is considering the purchase of a new piece of labor-saving equipment. It is estimated that this new equipment will save $5,000 per year in wages and related expenses. The new piece of equipment costs $35,000. If the equipment had perpetual life, what would be the potential return on investment?

3. Determine the return on investment for the piece of equipment described in Problem 2 if it is expected that the equipment will have a life of 5 years and a salvage value of $25,000.

4. Determine the return on total assets as well as the return on common-stock equity last year for General Electric Co. and Standard Oil Co. of New Jersey.

5. In the 1961 balance sheet the Florida Power and Light Co. indicated the following sources of capital:

Current Liabilities and Deferred Credits	$ 63,000,000
3% First Mortgage Bonds	20,000,000
3⅛% Bonds	21,000,000
3¼% Debentures	9,000,000
3½% Bonds	41,000,000
3⅝% Bonds	10,000,000
3⅞% Bonds	25,000,000
4⅛% Bonds	28,000,000
4⅜% Bonds	15,000,000
4⅝% Bonds	15,000,000
5% Bonds	25,000,000
5¼% Bonds	20,000,000
4½% Preferred	26,000,000
4.35% Preferred	10,000,000
No-Par Common Stock	178,000,000
Earned Surplus	62,000,000
Surplus Reserves	29,000,000

The company had a net income in 1961 of $30,000,000. Estimate the average weighted cost of capital for the Florida Power and Light Co.

SELECTED READINGS

ANTHONY, ROBERT N. *Management Accounting*, rev. ed. Homewood, Ill.: Richard D. Irwin, Inc., 1960.

BIERMAN, HAROLD, JR. *Managerial Accounting*. New York: The Macmillan Co., 1959.
————, and SMIDT, SEYMOUR. *The Capital Budgeting Decision*. New York: The Macmillan Co., 1961.

BODENHORN, DIRAN. "On the Problem of Capital Budgeting," *Journal of Finance*, December, 1959, pp. 473–92.

BROWN, ALVIN J. *Financial Approach to Industrial Operations*. New York: Society for Advancement of Management, 1957.

DEAN, JOEL. *Managerial Economics*. Englewood Cliffs, N. J. Prentice-Hall, Inc., 1951.

DOBROVOLSKY, S. P. "Economics of Corporate Internal and External Financing," *Journal of Finance*, March, 1958, pp. 35–47.

GORDON, MYRON J. *The Investment, Financing, and Valuation of the Corporation*. Homewood, Ill.: Richard D. Irwin, Inc., 1962.

HECKERT, J. BROOKS, and WILLSON, JAMES D. *Business Budgeting and Control*. New York: The Ronald Press Co., 1955.

LEWIS, RONELLO B. *Financial Analysis for Management*. Englewood Cliffs, N. J.: Prentice-Hall, Inc., 1959.

LYON, PAUL W. *Operating Return on Operating Investment*. Financial Series No. 111. New York: American Management Association, 1956.

WIPFLAR, EARL J. *Return on Investment*. Financial Series No. 103. New York: American Management Association, 1953.

19

Financial Management Tools

Decision making is the most important activity of financial management. The processes of planning, organizing, and controlling involve decisions on the part of the manager. The acceptance of a plan is a decision. Organization requires decisions on how to organize, what types of direction are necessary, staffing problems, etc. The function of control requires decisions on what kinds of controls to use, when control indicates an activity is out of line, what to do to bring operations within control limits, etc. The decision process used by financial management is the same as for any other functional management—only the area in which the decisions are made separates financial management from other management activities.

After accepting an objective such as profitability or solvency or a combination of the two, decisions must be made on how to accomplish these objectives in the best possible manner. Decisions commonly made in business are between alternative actions, but "no action" must always be recognized as one of the alternatives. Decision making involves a determination of the possible outcome of each of the various actions which might be taken, of the probability that certain outcomes will occur, and of the degree to which these possible and probable outcomes will bring about the objectives to be accomplished. Managements vary in their approach to the decision-making process, the data they use in making the decision, and their evaluation of the data. The concept of the need for a decision and the need for judging future outcomes is, however, inherent in any management application.

No decision is any better than the data on which it is based. Not only must the data be reliable; they must be properly applied to the problem at hand. "Scientific" management has developed a number of techniques or "tools" which are used in collecting and integrating data in usable form for the decision-making process. The major financial management tools to be discussed in this chapter are financial statements, ratio analysis, and financial budgeting. These are not exclusively the tools of financial management; the same tools are used also by other elements in society whose objectives are quite different from those of internal financial management. It is not at all uncommon to find management, creditors, government, and stockholders applying the same tools in arriving at a decision, even though the objectives of each of these four groups are different. Since this is the case, it is most important to recognize at the beginning of any discussion on financial management tools that the application of a tool depends upon the purpose for which the tool is being used. Common purposes of various interested parties utilizing financial tools are discussed below. The objectives of financial management were discussed in the preceding chapter.

Creditor Analysis

Creditors are very frequent users of various financial tools. In fact, certain tools used by financial management today were developed primarily for use by creditors in making their various lending and investment decisions. Management's use of these tools, however, is not exactly the same as the creditors' use. If a creditor could have a crystal ball which would absolutely predict the future for him, he would need to ask only one question regarding each lending decision: "Will I be paid as agreed?" If he had the answer to this question, he would have no need to worry about current ratios, flow of funds, cash balances, equity-to-debt relationships, and other considerations which are part of a normal credit analysis. However, the creditor cannot determine the future through a crystal ball, and therefore he uses a series of tools to help him determine the probability of his being paid as agreed.

The creditor is normally only interested in profitability insofar as it affects the firm's ability to pay in the future. Short-term creditors, particularly, place little reliance on profitability since it takes time to realize profits and the firm will have to find other means for repayment of the loan before significant profits are on hand. There are certainly many instances where creditors lend to firms which are currently unprofitable and are expected to continue to be unprofitable in the short run.

Creditors would normally be very much interested in the liquidity of a firm's assets and in its short-run solvency. But it is almost a truism that a firm which is most ideal from the creditors' point of view would not be considered a very well-managed firm from the managers' or owners' point of view. This firm would be highly liquid and conservatively financed and, therefore, would not be as profitable as it could be under other conditions.

The tremendous emphasis placed on solvency and liquidity by creditors has led them to develop tools to measure past and present liquidity as a guide to estimates of future liquidity and solvency. The major decision to be made by creditors is whether a loan should be made or not. Additional decisions would involve the terms that should be included in the loan, what should be done in the event of default on the loan, and what is the future possibility of additional lending on a satisfactory basis to this customer.

Owner Analysis

A typical stockholder's decisions are directed toward the objective of making a return on investment. This return normally comes from two sources—dividends and/or market gains. The investor's crystal ball would require an answer to the question: "How much will I make from this investment?" The answer to this question would enable him to decide whether to buy a security, or, if he already owns it, whether to hold on to it, buy more, or sell.

Investors' objectives may vary to some extent from those of the corporation as a whole. Many investors do not take a long-run point of view toward their investments. Because the investor has an opportunity for market gain as well as gain from dividends, his analysis of his position is invariably somewhat different from the internal analysis of the position of the company by management.

Other Decision Elements

Other parties interested in financial analysis of the firm would include government, customers, employees, and suppliers. Government's particular interests are taxation and regulation. The decisions to be made by government revolve around the questions: "Is the company paying its proper taxes to government?" and "What regulation should be exerted over this company?" Answers to these questions are partially based on analysis of financial tools.

Customers also have an interest in the long-run stability and survival of the firm. With permanence in mind, a customer's approach to the subject of financial analysis of the firm may be very different from that of other interested parties. The federal government, as a customer of many major defense contractors, has made the greatest use of financial analysis tools in making customer decisions. The important decisions are: "Should we deal with this supplier?" and "If so, at what price?"

Employees are beginning to take more interest in the long-range aspects of the firms for which they work. In addition, particularly in union bargaining, employees are interested in the profit position of the firm insofar as it affects the firm's ability to pay higher benefits. In the bargaining process, employees may rely on financial analysis of the firm and utilize many of the same tools which financial management would use, but their application is of a very different nature.

Suppliers may be interested in financial analysis of customers, particularly in situations where franchise arrangements and exclusive distributorships are in effect, or where supplies are limited and the supplier prefers to sell to the firm that has the greatest long-run potential. Determination of the potential of the firm is based in part on analysis of financial tools.

ACCOUNTING DATA

Accounting may be defined as "the act of recording, classifying, and summarizing in a significant manner and in terms of money, transactions and events which are, in part at least, of a financial character and interpreting the results thereof." [1] In simpler terms, accounting is the process of collecting, organizing, and interpreting financial data relating to the activities of an enterprise. The accounting process involves a very special-purpose information system based on accepted rules and practices concerning the application of financial resources and the earnings therefrom. Accounting includes the measurement of values of resources, claims against these resources, and financial effectiveness of their application.

Accounting is certainly not an end in itself; it is a language which combines financial factors, dissimilar tangible and intangible assets, and claims, to arrive at financial measurements. Accounting is the language in which most of the data used in financial analysis decisions are presented. Because of the importance of accounting in the financial management decision process, it is singled out here for special discussion. Space limitations allow discussion of only a few of the many important elements in accounting systems which should be understood by the user of accounting data. [2]

Stewardship Accounting

Most practitioners of accounting consider themselves professional people in giving unbiased, knowledgeable judgment concerning financial values and results of business operation. Professional accountants abide by a certain ethical code designed to protect an "outside" user from fraudulent or misleading accounting data. The early development of the recognized profession of accounting resulted from the need of creditors and owners to receive information about concerns with which they dealt which was presented in such a way as to remove the biases of the original preparers of the data. Data were normally prepared by management and were based on an objective different from that of the outside users

---

[1] American Institute of Certified Public Accountants, Committee on Terminology, Accounting Terminology Bulletin No. 1, Review and Resume (New York: The American Institute of Certified Public Accountants, 1953), p. 9.

[2] For this reason a basic understanding of accounting is a prerequisite to a study of the general area of finance and financial management. It is assumed that the reader of this book has this background.

of the data. Potential stockholders and creditors desired to be protected against overenthusiasm on the part of the promoters or managers of a firm and, therefore, from the overstatement of the firm's values or prior earnings.

It should be recognized that application of accounting principles to a particular firm involves a considerable exercise of judgment. The determination of values of assets and of earnings is entirely a matter of subjective judgment, and bias in any direction can result in substantially misleading accounting data. Thus, a competent and disinterested party, the professional accountant, is called in to determine if the data are free from management and promoter bias and whether they are not significantly misleading.

The principal factors inherent in stewardship accounting are timeliness, consistency, objectivity, and comparability between firms, along with a substantial element of conservatism. All of these elements are important in providing reliable and accurate information to outside parties. Timeliness is necessary for the data to be useful. Objectivity presents the data from a disinterested party's point of view. Comparability allows the user of accounting data to relate them to data from other operations. Consistency allows a comparison to prior periods. Conservatism is designed to give the user information which says that, where value judgments are difficult to make, the data should tend in the direction of understatement of asset values and of earnings. If this understatement misleads the investor or creditor, at least it does not cause him losses through investing or lending. The assumption inherent in this approach is that a decision not to do something which might prove to be worthwhile is not nearly as bad as a decision to do something which might turn out badly.

The above discussion indicates some of the potential problems in using a single accounting system for a variety of different purposes. Because most firms at least begin with a single accounting system with a common approach to the integration of data, the basic principles under which the data are collected and integrated must be recognized and a determination must be made as to whether these principles meet the requirements of the objectives to be served in using the data. There is certainly nothing to prevent management from collecting any kind of data it wants, under any system of data collection and with any approach to data integration it desires. In fact, a recognition of the problems inherent in a rigid, universal accounting system would normally lead to a conclusion that for certain management decision purposes, data must be developed differently.

A particularly difficult problem in accounting in the post-war period has been changing price levels. Accepted approaches to stewardship accounting include an assumption of a constant value of the dollar. All values are stated in terms of dollars and no attempt is made to differentiate dollars of one year from dollars of another. Certainly, 1939 dollars are not the equivalent of 1963 dollars. Yet, in standard accounting systems these dollars carry equal weight. This problem is most acute where important elements of value in the firm were acquired at prices substantially different from current prices. When significant variation in price level has occurred and when large amounts of values in the firm are based on price levels that are different from those that are now current, adjustments might well be made in order to meet the particular user's objectives.

The element of conservatism creates a problem for management's use of accounting data. For management purposes, the most accurate and most reasonable data should be used rather than the most conservative. If the system produces only "conservative" data, for certain applications, adjustments must be made in the data before it can be used in the decision-making process. An example would be securities carried on the books at original cost which are now selling at three times their original cost in the market. Any decision regarding holding or selling of these securities should take market value into account rather than their original cost (except insofar as original cost affects potential tax payment).

Uses of Accounting Data

In spite of the potential problems mentioned above, standard accounting data are the most useful information available for most financial decisions. Accepted accounting practice might also include the collection and presentation of special-purpose data. In fact, much of the accounting data used by management are collected with a special purpose in mind. It must always be remembered that special-purpose accounting is exactly that—accounting that has a special purpose; it should not be used for purposes other than the one for which it was prepared.

Accounting systems are based on collection of historical data. This does not mean that accounting approaches cannot be used in estimating future financial values and results. Estimates of the future do not meet the requirement of objectivity of stewardship accounting, but they are the basic data ingredient which is necessary for any management decision. The really important figures in most business decisions are estimated future figures. Even though future estimates are subjective, a quantitative accounting measurement of the future can be very useful for many purposes.

FINANCIAL STATEMENTS

A financial statement is a presentation of basic accounting data for an organization as of a specific date or for a specified period of time. A great mass of financial records for an organization for a time period is integrated, consolidated, and condensed into more manageable form in financial statements. Accounting data in the form of financial statements are the most common source of information for the decision-making process in financial management as well as in lending and investing. The common financial statements are the statement of financial position (balance sheet), the income statement (profit and loss statement), and the flow of funds statement (source and application of funds statement).

The Statement of Financial Position

The statement of financial position, or balance sheet, describes the forms in which the firm's capital (assets) exists at any given point in time, and the sources of or claims to this capital. Since the claims to values in any self-contained organization cannot exceed the total of the values, a "balance sheet" always balances. The statement of financial position describes the basic accounting equation: assets equals liabilities plus net worth.

While the forms in which statements of financial position are presented vary substantially, the two most common forms are given in Figures 19–1 and 19–2. The balance in Figure 19–1 is between total assets

	September 30	
	1961	1960
ASSETS		
Current Assets:		
Cash	$ 31,301,157	$ 27,558,806
Accounts Receivable—principally from the United States government	245,649,576	141,829,364
Inventories, generally at cost, not in excess of market—less progress payments on contracts under which title to related inventories vests in the United States government: 1961—$129,420,359; 1960—$94,192,848	184,061,729	119,998,861
Prepaid Expenses—insurance, retirement plan costs, taxes, etc.	6,247,217	12,989,986
Total Current Assets	467,259,679	302,377,017
Investments—at cost	1,013,453	952,991
Property: Land, Improvements to Land and Leaseholds, Buildings, Machinery and Equipment, etc.— at cost	170,238,220	143,164,152
Less Accumulated Depreciation and Amortization	76,321,518	60,902,133
Net Property	93,916,702	82,262,019
Total	$562,189,834	$385,592,027

Fig. 19–1. Balance sheet,

and total claims against these assets, while the balance in Figure 19–2 is between net assets (after deducting liabilities) and stockholders' equity. Regardless of form, a statement of financial position is always as of an instant in time. Since the business assets and sources never stop changing, by the time any balance sheet is prepared, it is no longer an exact statement of the current position of the firm. The statement of financial position is, therefore, static rather than dynamic. It does not describe operations—it describes only the end result of an organization's operations at a point in time.

The individual asset items and the problems of evaluation of assets are discussed in Chapters 20 and 24. The nature of the liability items is covered in Chapters 7, 8, 21, 22, and 23. Stockholders' equity is discussed in Chapters 5, 6, and 25.

Users of the statement of financial position look to it for an indication of the strength and liquidity of the company's resources and the burden of the claims against these resources. Because of the emphasis on liquidity by the users of this statement, the usual listing of assets is in the order of their probable liquidation during the normal course of business operations. The claims against the assets are also normally listed in order of

	September 30	
	1961	1960
LIABILITIES		
Current Liabilities:		
Notes Payable to Banks—unsecured	$155,000,000	$ 50,000,000
Accounts Payable, Accrued Wages, etc.	152,726,277	97,396,281
Estimated Savings Refundable to the United States Government under Incentive-Type Contracts	3,510,637	4,543,767
United States Income Taxes	17,608,844	16,172,871
Dividends Payable	4,147,790	4,077,585
Total Current Liabilities	332,993,548	172,190,504
STOCKHOLDERS' EQUITY		
Capital Stock—Authorized, 12,000,000 shares of $1 each—outstanding: 1961—8,296,320 shares; 1960—8,155,669 shares	8,296,320	8,155,669
Paid-in Surplus (increase resulted from sale of 140,651 shares of capital stock to option holders)	49,569,591	45,220,635
Earnings Retained for Use in the Business	171,330,375	160,025,219
Total Stockholders' Equity	229,196,286	213,401,523
Total	$562,189,834	$385,592,027

North American Aviation, Inc.

maturity date from the shortest to the longest. Because of this, short-term creditors interested in repayment in the near future place emphasis upon the current assets and the current liabilities while longer-term creditors and stockholders must look at the total financial position. It is important to note that asset values are not based on current market prices but upon cost or cost less depreciation. Therefore, one should never use the statement of financial position in determining the value of the company in the event of a liquidation of all the assets.

	1961	1960
CURRENT ASSETS		
Cash	$ 228,588,000	$ 230,242,000
Marketable Securities, at lower of cost or market	1,200,024,000	1,157,695,000
Notes and Accounts Receivable, less estimated doubtful amounts	1,151,966,000	1,100,944,000
Inventories:		
Crude oil, products, and merchandise	750,069,000	699,760,000
Materials and supplies	159,779,000	187,756,000
Total Current Assets	3,490,426,000	3,376,397,000
LESS—CURRENT LIABILITIES:		
Notes and Loans Payable	294,632,000	236,380,000
Accounts Payable and Accrued Liabilities	979,010,000	928,959,000
Income Taxes Payable	421,583,000	452,642,000
Total Current Liabilities	1,695,225,000	1,758,416,000
Investments and Long-Term Receivables, at cost or less	531,710,000	482,419,000
Property, Plant and Equipment, at cost, less depreciation and depletion	6,267,018,000	6,061,278,000
Prepaid Charges and Other Assets	205,263,000	170,343,000
Total Assets Less Current Liabilities	8,799,192,000	8,472,456,000
Deductions:		
Long-Term Debt	816,449,000	807,791,000
Deferred Credits	175,353,000	146,088,000
Annuity, Insurance, and Other Reserves	410,074,000	400,706,000
Equity of Minority Shareholders in Affiliated Companies	305,482,000	288,690,000
Net Assets	$7,091,834,000	$6,829,181,000
SHAREHOLDERS' EQUITY:		
Capital	$2,375,657,000	$2,375,657,000
Earnings Reinvested and Employed in Business	4,716,177,000	4,453,524,000
	$7,091,834,000	$6,829,181,000

Fig. 19–2. Consolidated statement of financial position, December 31, 1961–1960, Standard Oil Company (New Jersey).

The Income Statement

The income statement, or profit and loss statement, is designed to show the results of business operations for a specific period of time. Operations are stated in terms of revenues (flows of values into the business) and expenses (flows of values out of the business). The difference between revenues and expenses is net profit or loss to the shareholders. The concept of profit is more fully discussed in Chapter 25.

The income statement includes items which are descriptive of the service of the firm to customers, employees, government, and the general public. In addition, this statement includes the profit figure, which is the primary objective of the stockholders and a collateral objective of management. Because the income statement is more closely related to the objectives of most users of financial statements, it is recognized as more significant than the statement of financial position. The income figure and its detailed determination is also commonly used as a measure of management's performance by outsiders as well as by management itself.

Figures 19–3 and 19–4 present statements of income for the two companies whose balance sheets were presented earlier. Items included indi-

	Year Ended September 30	
	1961	1960
INCOME:		
Net sales	$1,262,333,263	$964,162,496
Other	3,112,004	1,758,356
Total	1,265,445,267	965,920,852
COSTS AND EXPENSES:		
Cost of sales and other costs and expenses	1,203,982,470	917,036,472
Provision for United States income taxes	28,900,000	23,300,000
Interest expense	4,812,660	2,189,832
Total	1,237,695,130	942,526,304
NET INCOME FOR THE YEAR	$ 27,750,137	$ 23,394,548
EARNINGS RETAINED FOR USE IN THE BUSINESS AT BEGINNING OF THE YEAR	160,025,219	152,917,266
Total	187,775,356	176,311,814
Less Cash Dividends—$2.00 a share	16,444,981	16,286,595
EARNINGS RETAINED FOR USE IN THE BUSINESS AT END OF THE YEAR	$ 171,330,375	$160,025,219

Provision for depreciation and amortization amounted to $18,781,642 for 1961 and $16,897,709 for 1960.

Fig. 19–3. Statement of income and earnings retained for use in the business, North American Aviation, Inc.

cate relationships with customers (sales), with employees (wages, salaries, and employee benefits), with government (taxes), with creditors (interest), and with owners (net income). A specific discussion of the income and expense items which make up the income statement is included in Chapter 25.

Because a business does not start at the beginning of a fiscal year and stop at the end, the problem of determining periodic profitability is a significant one. Accounting judgments must be made concerning the accounting period to which various expense items and income items should be allocated. The accounting judgments would be easier if a business were accounted for only after its final liquidation. In that case, the accountant could add up all of the values taken out of the business,

	1961	1960
REVENUES:		
Sales and other operating revenue	$9,148,151,000	$8,695,805,000
Dividends, interest, and other revenue	208,236,000	219,199,000
	9,356,387,000	8,915,004,000
COSTS AND OTHER DEDUCTIONS:		
Crude oil, products, materials, and services	4,193,377,000	4,078,453,000
Taxes and other payments to governments	2,851,711,000	2,611,356,000
Wages, salaries, and employee benefits	922,970,000	916,797,000
Depreciation, depletion, and retirements	545,696,000	540,735,000
Interest and other financial charges	48,491,000	47,228,000
Income applicable to minority interests	36,059,000	31,862,000
	8,598,304,000	8,226,431,000
NET INCOME	$ 758,083,000	$ 688,573,000

Fig. 19–4. Consolidated statement of income for the years 1961 and 1960, Standard Oil Company (New Jersey).

subtract the amounts put in, and the difference would be the gains from business operation. However, since accounting data, and particularly profit information, are useful during the life of the business, it is necessary to have estimates of periodic profitability in order to make good business decisions. Much of the development of principles of accounting has been related to the problem of determining the period to which various costs should be charged.

Difficulties of objectivity in the valuation of cost of goods sold and in depreciation expense are discussed elsewhere in this text. It is emphasized here merely that the accounting approach used can significantly influence the stated results or profit for any given period of time.

The Flow of Funds Statement

A variety of titles is used for the financial statement that describes the inflow and outflow of funds. Among the more common names are the application of funds statement, the source and use of funds statement, the statement of changes in working capital, and the flow of funds statement.

Unfortunately, there is no universally accepted definition for the word *funds*. *Funds* have been defined as money or other means of payment, as the company's net resources, as net working capital, as current assets, as cash, and as values. The definition selected for funds determines the form of the flow of funds statement. Regardless of the definition, the general concepts are the same and the statement deals with movements of values into the firm, or from one type of asset to another, or out of the firm.

The flow of funds statement given in Figure 19–5 uses the net working capital as a definition of funds. This statement could be converted to one using cash as a definition by merely *adding* to or *subtracting* from the increase or decrease in working capital, *the changes* in inventory and accounts receivable and current liabilities. The statement as given in Figure 19–5 indicates the changes in permanent values in the organization and the sources of these changes. The example in Figure 19–6 indi-

	1961	1960
Total Revenue	$9,356	$8,915
Less Expenses		
Oil, products, materials, services, etc.	4,242	4,125
Taxes and other payments to governments	2,852	2,611
Wages, salaries, and employee benefits	923	917
Cash Earnings	1,339	1,262
Other Sources of Funds		
Proceeds from sales of properties	41	49
Net change in long-term debt	9	16
Total Funds Available	1,389	1,327
Disposition of Funds		
Additions to properties	795	720
Cash dividends to Jersey shareholders	495	485
Cash dividends to minority interests	27	27
Loss of working funds in Cuba	–	24
Other (net)	35	17
Total Funds Used	1,352	1,273
Increase (decrease) in Working Capital	$ 37	$ 54

Fig. 19–5. Summary of changes in working capital, Standard Oil Company (New Jersey) (000,000 omitted).

cates the changes in more liquid values, and actually describes the flow of cash and credit in the organization for the time period covered.

The flow of funds statement explains the origin of increases or decreases in funds over a period of time. This information can be used as a guide for working capital management in the future. In fact, projected flow of funds statements may be prepared. Knowledge of the total change in investments of funds over a period of time is no more important than knowledge of why and how the changes took place. The flow of funds statement provides this information. Major sources of funds are decreases in assets, increases in liabilities, and increases in net worth. More specifically, these sources include net income, depreciation, increase in current liabilities, sale of fixed assets, sale of securities, and reductions in inventory and receivables. Major uses of funds are increases in assets and decreases in liability and net worth. This includes the repayment of current liabilities, the retirement of long-term debts, repurchase of corporate securities, dividend payments, absorption of operating losses, purchase of fixed assets, and expansion of inventory and receivables.

APPLICATION OF FUNDS

FOR THE YEAR ENDING DECEMBER 31, 19x2

Source of Funds:			
Net Income			$ 480,540
Depreciation Charges			234,680
Sale of Preferred Stock			1,200,000
Increase in Current Liabilities			68,290
			$1,983,510
Use of Funds:			
Repayment of Mortgages		$500,000	
Purchase of Fixed Assets		986,440	
Preferred Dividends Paid		30,000	
Common Dividends Paid		266,800	1,783,240
Change in Working Capital (increase)			$ 200,270

Represented by:	19x2	19x1	Change
Cash	$ 436,200	$ 483,890	−$ 47,690
Accounts and Notes Receivable	1,132,230	781,060	+ 351,170
Inventories	802,340	905,550	− 103,210
Working Capital	$2,370,770	$2,170,500	+$200,270

Fig. 19–6.

The flow of funds statement can be used by the financial manager as an aid in preparing financial plans, particularly when the company experiences seasonal or cyclical changes. A study of past sources and uses during a period of change can indicate the use requirements in a coming period of change and give some indication of potential sources which could be used. The financial manager could prepare a flow of funds statement over the same portion of the past cycle that he is planning for in the current cycle and use this as a basis for predicting his needs for the immediate future. Normally the financial manager would be most interested in the changes from a maximum to a minimum and from a minimum to a maximum of the business cycle. These two periods would represent the greatest change in needs and uses of funds.

The flow of funds statement also calls the attention of management to unusual or significant changes which might deserve further investigation.

This statement may aid in the evaluation of past programs and in calling attention to past mistakes in order to avoid making the same mistakes in the future. The significant difference between the flow of funds statement and the income statement is its emphasis upon cash values and cash movements rather than upon accounting profits. Figures 19–4 and 19–5 are statements of the same company for the same time period and indicate clearly the difference between cash movements and earnings.

Creditors and stockholders also are interested in flow of funds statements because they reflect management's major financial policies, they reveal management's willingness to expand and the sources of funds used for expansion, and they indicate both management's willingness to accumulate liquid capital and the major financial changes of the company for the reporting period. This statement enables stockholders to focus attention on cash availability for dividend payment rather than on profits alone as indicated by the earnings statement. For creditors, this statement is useful in indicating direction of financial position.

RATIO ANALYSIS

Ratio analysis is the process of studying ratios to help predict the future for purposes of decision making. A ratio is simply one number expressed in terms of another. Ratios can be helpful because they present important segments of accounting data in related form. Often, two separate items of accounting data can be related to reveal an important fact usually not directly obvious from an examination of the items independently. Under many circumstances, the figures on financial statements have meaning for analysis purposes only when they are expressed relatively, or in the form of ratios, and then compared to some standard or norm. Ratio analysis increases the effectiveness of use of financial statements. For comparisons with other companies, ratios are often easier to use than absolute accounting figures from financial statements; also, they can be used to compare organizations of unlike size.

Let us consider the price-earnings ratio as an example of better analysis from use of relationships. If the XYZ Company stock is selling for $10 per share, an investor who is considering purchase of this stock would also want to know the amount of the earnings, since potential return is the reason for his purchasing the stock. The fact that the company earned $1.00 last year does not significantly help the investor make his decision unless he relates $1.00 to the $10 price of the stock. Thus he notes that the price-earnings ratio is 10 or that the earnings are 10% of the price. He then compares the price earnings ratio of 10, rather than either the price of $10 or the earnings of $1.00, to his other alternatives. A company whose stock is selling for $50 and earning $5.00 is comparable.

Uses of Ratio Analysis

Generally accepted approaches to mercantile credit analysis invariably include some elements of ratio analysis. Most national and regional credit organizations attempt to collect average ratios for use as standards in credit comparisons. Dun & Bradstreet, Inc. publishes fourteen important credit ratios for a wide variety of different industries. Robert Morris Associates also publishes standard ratios primarily for use by commercial banks in credit investigation. Ratio analysis by creditors has been used primarily for determining the liquidity and solvency of a firm. Because of the emphasis placed upon ratio analysis by creditors, other applications of this technique are often overlooked.

Stockholders and potential stockholders can make significant use of ratios in selecting from among alternate investments. Such ratios as earnings per share, price-earnings, and dividend yield are commonly quoted in connection with any potential investment. The investor might also utilize some of the creditors' approaches to ratio analysis in determining the liquidity and solvency of the firm in which he is considering investment. However, his major emphasis is on the portion of ratio analysis which tends to indicate relative profitability.

In this chapter, the primary concern is with management's use of ratio analysis. Because management must satisfy both creditors and owners, it is interested in the potential creditor's and owner's viewpoints. For purposes of determining potential credit availability, management would analyze its own operation from the point of view of the creditor. In planning how to attract additional stockholder funds, management would use an owner's analysis. However, management can also utilize ratio analysis for its own purposes of guiding the actions of the firm toward higher profitability, and studying the reasonableness of various types of costs incurred. It also uses ratio analysis in making financial structure decisions, in determining the level of investments in various assets, in determining areas of operation which should be studied for improvement, and in evaluating accounting data for purposes of decision making.

Standards for Comparison

The computation of a relationship between one fact and another leaves the analyst with very little real meaning unless he has a standard with which to compare the result. Thus, one can compute the current ratio of a firm (relationship of current assets to current liabilities) as 3-to-1. This, however, is meaningless unless the analyst can decide whether 3-to-1 is satisfactory. Is it too high or is it too low? The selection of a proper standard is probably the most important element in ratio analysis. The four most common types of standards used in ratio analysis in financial management are (1) absolute, (2) past record, (3) other companies' or industry average, and (4) budget or plan.

Absolute standards are those which have become generally recognized as being desirable regardless of the type of company, the time, the stage of the business cycle, or the objectives of the analyst. An example would be the standard of 2-to-1 for a current ratio. However, the fact that the electric utility companies have for years maintained current ratios significantly lower than this indicates that absolute standards are not very meaningful. The authors do not believe that there is an independent absolute standard which is desirable in all cases.

The company's own *past performance* can be used as a standard for the present or future. Thus, if a company's current ratio has been 3-to-1 in recent years and is now running 2-to-1 or less, a need for further investigation would be indicated. On the other hand, if the ratio had always been running less than 2-to-1 and was currently at the same level, the ratio would seem to meet the standard and there would be no need for further exploration. Past standards are useful insofar as the past is indicative of the future. If conditions are constant, past standards become very meaningful. The variance of present conditions from past conditions determines the reliability level in using past performance ratios as standards for current or future operations.

Other companies' or *industry average* ratios are commonly used in financial analysis as standards. Many trade associations collect accounting data from their members and prepare average industry ratios on the basis of these data. These industry standards are then available to the individual members for use in comparison. Dun & Bradstreet, Inc. and Robert Morris Associates have already been mentioned as sources of industry ratios. The problem in utilizing industry ratios or making up ratios for similar companies is that no two companies are exactly the same. Variations in accounting method could lead to significant differences in ratios. In addition, variability of product mix, geographic location, corporate objectives, and most other conditions under which a business operates lead to lack of comparability. Therefore, just because one firm's current ratio might be 2-to-1 when the industry average is 4-to-1, it should not be concluded that this company is in a poor financial position. Standards developed from other companies' data or from industry data are useful only in indicating areas where further analysis and study should be made.

A standard commonly used by management is the *planned* or *budgeted* standard. While this standard is not normally available to outsiders, it is particularly useful for management. The budget is a statement of what the company intends to do during a stated period of time. Ratios developed from actual performance can be compared to planned ratios in the budget in order to determine the degree of accomplishment of the budgeted or planned objectives of the firm. Budgeted or planned standards determined in advance, taking into account the conditions of the times and the specific company situation, can be very useful in financial analysis.

Limitations of Ratio Analysis

Ratio analysis can be only as valid as the basic data which are fed into the determination of the ratios. Thus, the selection of accounting method and the reliability of original financial figures are most important to good ratio analysis. The application of ratio analysis requires comparability and if the basic data are not comparable, the ratios themselves will not be.

There are certain mathematical problems in applications of ratios. For example, additions of a like dollar amount to both the numerator and denominator of the ratio will cause a change in the result unless the original ratio was 1-to-1. The problem of selection of the standard for comparison was mentioned above.

The most important limitation is in the analysis itself. Too often, too much meaning is read into a variance of a ratio from standard. Comparison of ratios serves only as a guide to areas in company operation which may be out of line. Further study is necessary before a definitive conclusion can be reached as to whether operations are as they should be.

Types of Ratios

The most commonly used ratios can be classified into three major groups: those used in connection with determination of profitability, those used for measurement of liquidity and solvency, and those used for measurement of resource utilization. A number of important management ratios are discussed elsewhere in the text. The ratios relative to profitability were covered in the preceding chapter. Ratios related to resource or asset utilization are discussed in Chapter 20.

Ratios used to determine solvency and liquidity have been developed primarily for creditor usage but are meaningful to management also, insofar as the company must remain solvent and satisfy the creditors to remain in business. A few of the more common liquidity ratios are discussed below.

Current Ratio. The *current ratio* is the ratio of current assets to current liabilities. Thus, if the current assets amount to $2,000,000, and the current liabilities are $1,000,000, this would be a ratio of 2-to-1. The current ratio is usually not expressed in ratio form, but rather as a simple number. In the above example, dividing the current liabilities into the current assets gives the resultant figure of "2" for the current ratio.

The current ratio expresses the ability of the company to pay its current liabilities. In the daily operation of a business it is the current liabilities that the management must be concerned about rather than a bond issue which may not come due for 20 years. The current liabilities are ordinarily repaid, not from the proceeds of a bond or stock issue, but rather from the cash on hand, or what will be collected from the accounts receivable or from the inventory. In other words, the current liabilities are repaid from the current assets. The current ratio shows the margin of safety of the company with regard to the payment of its short-term debts. Or, in other words, it shows how much the current assets may shrink without imperiling the ability of the company to meet these debts.

What constitutes an adequate current ratio would vary according to the particular industry, company, season of the year, and period of the business cycle. A company with a rapid current assets turnover will usually require a lower current ratio than one with a slow turnover. Furthermore, the amounts of the particular items that go to make up the ratio are of great importance. For example, a current ratio of 2-to-1 would undoubtedly be adequate if practically all the current assets were cash and equivalent, but it might be wholly inadequate if the bulk of the current assets were slow-moving merchandise or overdue receivables.

"Acid Test" Ratio. The *acid test* ratio is the relation of current assets after inventory has been deducted (sometimes called the *quick assets*) to the current liabilities. The amount of the cash and receivables (and marketable securities) indicates the ability of the company to meet its current liabilities better than when the inventory is added to the other current assets. The rule of thumb is that the cash (and equivalent) plus the receivables should be at least equal to the current liabilities. This ratio is sometimes referred to as the *quick ratio.*

Working Capital Turnover. The working capital turnover is found by dividing the average working capital (current assets) into the net sales for the year. The average working capital can be determined by taking one-half the sum of the working capital at the beginning of the year and at the end of the year.

The working capital turnover indicates the number of dollars of sales that are produced by each dollar of working capital. In other words, it shows the efficiency of the working capital. Generally speaking, the more rapid the turnover, the more efficient is the financial management of the concern. Too high a turnover, however, may result from insufficient cash or inventory and might prove to be embarrassing if raw material prices increase appreciably, or some other need for additional cash arises. The turnover figure may be compared with past turnover figures for the same company, and with those of similar companies in the same line of business.

Since the working capital position can be altered appreciably by a change in current liabilities, independent of the sales of the company, it might be advisable to calculate the turnover of the *net* working capital (current assets less current liabilities) instead of the *gross* working capital (current assets) turnover.

Debt to Equity. The relationship of the debt of the firm to owners' equity is an important credit ratio. If debt is substantial relative to equity, it means that a relatively small decrease in value of assets could wipe out owners' equity and remove protection from creditors. Owners' equity serves as a safety margin for creditors of the firm. Therefore, the relationship between the amount of creditors' claims and the amount of owners' equity is important in judging credit standing. A firm which has large amounts of owners' equity and only a minor amount of debt can more easily borrow in the event it gets into difficulty.

BUDGETING

A budget is a formal, written plan for future action. Financial budgets are plans stated in terms of dollar values. The budgeting process is the process of planning future dollar value flows in the organization. The financial budget is also very useful as a control tool for management.

The Budget as a Planning Tool

The reader should already be familiar with the importance of planning in business management. The budget becomes a tool of planning because, in order to budget, a company is forced to plan in advance. Furthermore, for financial budgets, the plan must be stated in dollar values. Preparing a written financial plan for the future requires thinking ahead. Management is forced to anticipate future external conditions which will affect the firm and to evaluate their effect upon operations. By so doing, management has more time to plan to meet changing external conditions. With more time available, more alternatives can be considered and, generally, better actions can be developed.

A written financial plan for the future requires coordination of the entire organization. It forces top management to select from among alternative actions which can be taken. This selection is done in advance of need so that it may be more carefully considered. Furthermore, if indicated results of the plan are not satisfactory, management has time to go back and reconsider operations so that they may be changed to produce desired results. The financial budget takes up where accounting statements leave off. The financial analysis discussed above dealt with the study of the past. Budgeting requires the development of financial plans for the future. Of particular importance to financial management, the budgeting process leads to the determination, significantly in advance of need, of additional future asset requirements. This gives financial management time to plan to meet the necessary asset requirements and to select the best possible means of financing. By arranging for financing in advance of need, waste and unsatisfactory action are avoided.

The Budget as a Control Tool

Once a financial plan is prepared and accepted as being the most realistic approach to objectives for the period under study, this plan can be used to determine how closely the firm is adhering to the plan. Thus, the financial budget becomes a control tool. The problem of use of standards was discussed above. The financial budget for a coming period of time becomes a type of standard to which actual operations may be compared. The major use of budgets for control is through variance analysis. That is, any significant variations in actual performance from planned performance are subject to scrutiny on the part of management. A decision must be made either to alter the plan or to make some adjustment in actual operations so that they can conform to plan.

A formal financial budgeting process allows better control of subordinates by management. If the budget is prepared in such a way that the various items in it are under the responsibility of different management elements, when variance occurs the responsible management is readily apparent.

Importance and Function of Budgets

With limited sources of capital, many companies would find themselves hard pressed for money on frequent occasions unless they anticipated their needs some time in advance. Practically all large businesses, which have thousands of employees and which turn out a variety of products from a large number of different departments, find that keeping budgets is essential to their successful operation. Most successful small corporations with few employees also maintain budgets although they are less complicated. Successful and profitable operation of a business can be obtained only when the various elements of the business are maintained in proper balance with each other.

The preparation of a budget coordinates the various departments of a business, and anticipates the capital requirements for various purposes. It is used as a standard for comparison of efficiency of actual operations to budgeted operations. Each department has to study its relation to the entire organization and to the ultimate profit of the enterprise. This advance planning and objective look at the department's place in the organization leads to better coordination between departments and to more profitable operations.

The budget, if properly prepared and operated, gives the financial officer of the company warning of new capital requirements so that he may provide for these requirements well in advance of their actual need. Without the budget, the financial officer would have difficulty in estimating and providing for future capital needs.

The budget establishes a standard of performance for the period against which actual results can be compared. The comparison of actual results with the budget may point out any weak spots in the organization.

The fact that a business maintains budgets and plans scientifically for future operations may aid in obtaining additional credit. If a concern can point out to a bank why it needs additional funds and where the money will come from to repay loans, that concern will receive more favorable treatment from the bank than a firm operating without advance planning. Proper use of budgeting is a sign of good management. In today's complicated business world, budgets are essential to efficient business management.

Forecasting

Before a budget or plan of future financial operation can be prepared, the total size of the operation involved must be forecast. The volume of sales determines production needs, which in turn determine the amount of many expense items. Cash inflow and cash outflow vary considerably with the volume of business transacted. The construction of any financial budget, therefore, has to start with the sales estimate. And, no budget is any better than the sales forecast on which it is based. Because of the importance of external factors in determining the level of sales, the sales forecast is normally the most difficult element in the budgeting process.

Several methods are used in attempting to forecast sales for a future period. A common technique is to project past results into the future, with some modifications for changed conditions, such as the introduction of new products, different competition, and the oscillations of the general business cycle. Another technique which is less commonly used is to sample the market for expressions of future buying intent. In certain lines, such as industrial goods, this method may be satisfactory, but it would be extremely difficult to follow in many consumer industries. Under this technique, the forecast is established on the basis of what selected customers state they intend to purchase during the coming period. If the sample is properly chosen, it should be indicative of the buying anticipations of other customers. Of course, anticipations and actual purchases do not necessarily coincide. A third, and more common, technique is based on anticipated future conditions. Generally, this involves an estimate of the total market potential and then of the individual company's share of that total market. In many instances, a combination of techniques is used along with a great deal of judgment on the part of the forecaster to set a figure for future sales or income.

Budget Preparation

The budgeting process varies substantially with the type of budget being prepared. The responsibility for budgeting also would vary with the type of budget. The cash budget is normally the responsibility of the chief financial officer while the operating budget would usually be the responsibility of top management. Most budgeting processes involve an element of build-up, that is, of collecting data from a variety of sources relative to future expectations and putting these data together to see what they look like as a combined unit. If the build-up as put together will apparently accomplish the objectives for the firm for the coming period, no further action is taken. More commonly, it is apparent from the first integration during the budget build-up that the over-all objectives of the firm will not be accomplished; new estimates are then obtained and plans are changed for the coming period.

A particular problem is that of selecting the time period for which the budget should be made. Some concerns budget operations for one year in advance, others for 6 months or quarterly. Some American corporations also project far into the future with budgets for 5, 10, or even 20 years in advance. It is obvious that the longer the period covered by the budget, the less accurate the budget may be. But even though it will be less accurate in forecasting corporate needs, long-term budgeting may be very useful as a guide for future planning. Budgeting projected far into the future will necessarily require revisions as conditions change and more information about the future becomes available.

In general, the decision on the period covered by the budget should be related to the time required to make effective planning possible. If the purpose of the budget is to determine cash requirements, 6 months or one year may be sufficient, for plans can be made and executed within a one-year period to meet cash variations. On the other hand, if the purpose of the financial plan is to determine the desirability of construction of an entirely new plant with a 20-year life, the plan requires estimates 20 years into the future. In this sense, the budget should be long-term. Many people will complain that it is impossible to budget far into the future, but if decisions are made which require estimates of the future, it is certainly possible to put these estimates down on paper in formal form.

There is less need for detail in long-term budgeting than in short-term budgeting, but the basic analysis of potential results must be there.

Flexible Budgeting

Because of potential errors in forecasting sales and production for periods of time in the future, any budget based on a single estimate of sales may be far from reality as the firm moves through the period of time for which the budget was prepared. A budget based on a sales estimate of $100,000 would certainly be meaningless for both planning and control if sales actually were only $60,000 or were $140,000 during the period for which the budget was prepared.

In situations where there is a small probability of meeting the sales forecast within a less than significant variation, *flexible* or *variable* budgeting may be used. This is the process in which separate sets of estimates are compiled for various forecasted levels of sales and production. If it appears that sales in the coming year may range anywhere from $75,000 to $125,000, three separate budgets may be prepared based on sales of $75,000, $100,000, and $125,000. As the year unfolds and it becomes apparent which of these three budgets is nearest to expected actual experience, that budget would be used for control purposes. Even after a budget is selected, it may require some change in planning also. When flexible budgeting is not used and the firm finds its actual experience varying significantly from budget, an entirely new budgeting process is required to plan for the period under operation. This requires time and the delay may cause the firm to move in the wrong direction before adjustments are made.

Budget Limitations

The whole purpose of budgeting as a management tool is to enable the firm better to accomplish its objectives. The budgeting tool is useful only insofar as the costs of its application do not exceed the savings which are provided.

Since most budgeting processes are based on a study of past operations and a projection of past operations into the future, it is often easy to carry forward past inefficiencies in the budgeted plan. In order to overcome this, some estimate of outside standards must be made for various items in the budget, and it should be periodically reviewed on a basis other than the firm's own past performance.

Another potential problem in budgeting, particularly as a control tool, is in improper management application of the budgeting process. If the budget becomes a vise within which management must operate regardless of circumstances, it defeats its basic purpose. The fact that a budget helps place responsibility on certain personnel for variance from budget should not stifle initiative on the part of these people to try new activities which could benefit the firm in the long run.

Finally, it must be remembered that the budget is a tool, not a goal in and of itself. The fact that a firm meets its budget exactly does not necessarily mean that it is doing the best job possible. The budget itself could be out of line. Furthermore, if too much credit is given for meeting a budget, the initial budgeting process tends to encourage a certain amount of built-in conservatism which enables management to meet the budget more readily than would be the case if it established goals which were reasonable but not quite so easily attainable.

Types of Budgets

The most commonly used type of budget in modern management is the *operating* or *income and expense* budget. This is a coordinated plan for revenues and expenses for all operating elements of the company. Various divisions and departments are forced to put their plans together for a joint company budget and discrepancies must be resolved. This forced coordination of the budgeting process is one of the most desirable features of this budget. In addition, when approved by top management, this budget becomes a statement of the planned accomplishment of the company's objectives for the coming period of time. In order to use this budget for control, expense and income data must be furnished periodically throughout its life so that variances from budgeted figures may be determined.

Other budgets used to some extent by modern management include the *cash* budget, *capital expenditures* budget, *production* budget, *materials purchased* budget, and *manpower* budget. The latter three are normally the responsibility of the production function of the business, and they will not be described here.

The capital budgeting process (discussed in Chapter 18) makes a choice between alternate projects. The capital expenditures budget, on the other hand, is a plan for the appropriation and expenditure of funds for fixed assets during the budget period. This budget requires a distinction between operating and capital expenditures. The capital budgeting process has already determined what projects will be undertaken. The capital expenditures budget is drawn up to show, in a time-phased fashion, how much money will actually be spent and the estimated dates on which it will be spent. This budget is useful in estimating cash requirements and in giving financial management sufficient advance notice to provide the necessary cash. In effect it becomes an adjunct to the cash budget which is discussed below.

CASH BUDGET

The primary purpose of the cash budget is to plan for the sources of cash necessary to meet the cash requirements during a given period of time. Therefore, the primary responsibility for this budget belongs with the chief financial officer who is responsible for the level of cash and the solvency of the firm. The cash budget is a prediction, based on careful analysis of past experience and anticipated conditions, of the flow of cash to and from the company. It differs from a projected profit and loss statement in that all non-cash incomes and expenses such as credit sales, depreciation, and amortization are eliminated from consideration. In addition, cash receipts and outlays which are not normally considered income and expense items from an accounting point of view are taken into account. These would include such things as purchase of assets, collection of accounts receivable, sales of securities, and payment of liabilities.

Cash Receipts

Weekly, monthly, or quarterly estimates will be made of the cash receipts from the following sources.

Sales. In drawing up a budget the logical place to start is with the sales department. The receipt and disbursement of cash depend upon the volume of sales. The sales for the budget period should be made out in terms of both the dollar volume and the unit volume. Then it will be necessary for someone to estimate what percentage of sales will be for cash and the percentage on credit. Credit sales are not an immediate source of cash. Only cash sales immediately enter into cash receipts.

Accounts Receivable. From the credit sales information an estimate of the accounts receivable (and notes receivable) will be made for each month. In order to determine when the cash from the accounts will be collected, it is necessary to consider the terms of sale. If payment of the accounts are to be made within 30 days from the date of sale, then sales on credit for one month will be collected the following month. Due consideration will have to be given, however, to estimated slow collections and bad debts.

Other Cash Receipts. Although the cash sales and collection of accounts and notes will make up practically all the total cash receipts, any other anticipated source will of course also be listed. These might include interest and dividends received as well as cash received from sale of assets or securities or from borrowing.

Cash Disbursements

To determine the total disbursements of cash, estimates will be made of the following disbursements.

Purchase of Materials. Based on the sales budget, the production department will be asked to submit a production schedule for the goods which are supposed to be sold. This will show the amount of materials or inventory which will go into the product and amount of direct labor cost. After giving effect to the inventory of raw materials, work in process, and finished goods on hand, to the minimum inventory which is to be maintained, and to the length of the production period, an estimate will be prepared of the amount of purchases which will have to be made each month. The terms of purchases will be taken into account and an estimate will be made of the amount of cash that will be needed each month to purchase the materials or to pay the accounts payable arising from the purchase.

Labor. From the production schedule an estimate will be computed of the amount of direct labor that will go into the product each month. Care should be taken, however, not to confuse the labor cost as shown on the production department's cost-accounting records, and the actual outlay of payroll cash. We are here interested in the latter. Due consideration will have to be given whether a week or two of wages are "held back" on the factory workers. It will also be found that, although there may be the same number of workdays in two different months, one month may contain four paydays, while the next month may have five.

Other Factory Expenses. In addition to the materials and direct labor costs, the manufacturing process will necessitate other expenses such as indirect labor, materials, and supplies. These go into the cost of the product as "indirect expenses" or "overhead." In making up the cash budget, however, we are concerned not with the overhead expenses as they appear on the cost records, but rather with the actual outlay of cash for these items.

Administrative and Selling Expenses. Administrative and selling expenses, which include salaries, supplies, rent, light, heat, insurance, advertising, etc., must, of course, also be taken into account. But here again, we do not use the same figures that appear in the income statement, but rather the estimate of monthly cash disbursements to cover these various items.

Other Cash Disbursements. The cash budget covers not only working capital items but also anything for which cash disbursements will have to be made such as payment of interest and dividends, purchase of fixed assets, and repayment of debt.

Cash Balance

At the bottom of the cash budget the difference between the total receipts and disbursements for each month will be shown. The cash on hand at the beginning of the period will be noted, and after giving effect to this and the difference between the monthly receipts and disbursements, a cumulative total of the cash balance should be written in. Business firms usually like to maintain a minimum cash balance of a certain amount. After considering this, we can calculate from the figures in the budget the amount of excess cash or deficiency which will be present at the end of each month. If a deficiency exists, then the company will know in advance when it must secure the cash through a bank loan or from some other source.

When budgets are made out on a monthly basis, the treasurer or disbursing officer is more interested in the day-by-day availability of funds than in the monthly totals. In other words, the budget may show that the excess of cash receipts over disbursements for a particular month may amount to, for example, $50,000, but this is no consolation to him if he has to meet a bill of $30,000 by the 10th of the month for purchases made the preceding month. Likewise, the total net cash receipts for the month of March, for example, will not be available to meet an income tax installment due March 15.

Uses of the Cash Budget

It was mentioned above that the primary use of the cash budget is to plan sources of cash to meet cash requirements, but there are other uses which are very meaningful to financial management. The cash balance in the cash budget, when related to the minimum cash requirement of the firm, indicates an excess or a shortage of cash. As the cash budget is projected for periodic intervals in the future, it indicates when a shortage will occur. In addition, the amount of the shortage of cash is indicated, as well as its duration. With these three pieces of information, the financial manager can plan the best possible sources to meet the cash shortage.

A second use of the cash budget is to enable the cash manager to do a better job of investing cash surpluses. Along with indicating the time, amount, and duration of shortages, the cash budget also indicates the time, amount, and duration of surpluses. With this information, proper short-term investments may be selected to utilize short-term surpluses of cash. Furthermore, the investment selected could be chosen with a maturity to coincide with the indicated need of the firm for cash for future operations. Cash budgets indicate the time and amount of funds needed to meet maturing obligations, tax payments, and dividend and interest payments. The cash budget may also be used as a control tool to indicate when actual operation varies from projected operation so that the plans for the future may be changed to meet changed actual conditions.

Limitations of the Cash Budget

The difficulty of preparing the cash budget must be considered as one of its limitations. Many assumptions must be made about the future—the most important of these is the sales and production estimate. In addition, there is some cost involved in the preparation of this budget. As the budget is based on future estimates, there is some level of probability that these estimates will not be met, and, therefore, the plans based on the budget must be changed as actual conditions indicate the changed requirements. Cash budgets must be flexible. Rather than ignore a budget once it is found to be out of line, good management will revise it and continue to use it for future planning. The importance of the cash budget to working capital management cannot be overemphasized.

Proforma Statements

Proforma statements are merely another way of stating financial budgets for the future. A proforma income statement is an estimated income statement for a coming period of time. It indicates the firm's planned profit and loss activities. A proforma balance sheet is an estimated balance sheet for some future date. It is based on the firm's estimate of the position it will be in at that date. Proforma statements can be used for control devices as it becomes recognized that the firm is varying from the planned estimates. Proforma statements are generally less useful than other types of budgets because they do not include periodic comparisons for variance analysis. Proforma balance sheets are useful insofar as they give the firm an indication as to what its balance sheet will look like in the future and they enable the firm to make a judgment in advance whether its financial position will be suitable to meet its needs, particularly in the eyes of creditors.

QUESTIONS

1. Discuss the differences in approach to financial analysis by creditors and management.
2. What is meant by stewardship accounting? What problems does stewardship accounting create for the financial manager?
3. What is meant by "conservatism" in accounting?
4. Describe the statement of financial position. What is its use in financial management?

5. What is the "flow of funds statement"? What are its uses in financial management?
6. Describe *ratio analysis*.
7. What are the four most common types of standards used in ratio analysis? Discuss each.
8. Differentiate ratios used for determination of profitability and those used for measurement of liquidity and solvency.
9. What is meant by the current ratio? What is an adequate current ratio?
10. What is meant by the "acid test" ratio? Do you think this is a more important ratio than the current ratio? Explain.
11. What is a budget? How do financial budgets differ from other budgets?
12. Differentiate the budget as a planning tool from the budget as a control tool.
13. What is meant by flexible budgeting? When should it be used?
14. Indicate the different kinds of budgets which may be kept by a large manufacturing company.
15. Indicate the importance of a cash budget and explain the procedure involved in making it out.

PROBLEMS

1. The Bord and Baylor Department Store is to open its doors for the first time on January 2, 19x1. Sales for the first 6 months are estimated as follows:

Month	Sales
January	$20,000
February	25,000
March	30,000
April	35,000
May	35,000
June	30,000

It is anticipated that 20 per cent of the sales will be cash and 80 per cent net 30 days. The gross profit on sales (profit before any expenses, except inventory) is expected to be 20 per cent. All purchases and expenses are to be paid immediately in cash. Fixed expenses will amount to $1,000 a month, and variable expenses will amount to 10 per cent of the sales. (Bad debts are included in variable expenses.) The company will start out with cash of $1,000 and inventory of $16,000, and it does not want these accounts reduced below these figures during any month. Make calculations below on a monthly rather than a daily basis. Assume that all estimates are correct. (Ignore federal income taxes, and assume that inventory sold in a particular month is purchased that month.) (a) Prepare a three-column report showing the cash income and cash outgo and the excess of one over the other, with proper notations as to source or purpose for each month. (b) If the company does not borrow any money, how much cash will it need at the start, exclusive of the original $1,000 in cash and the initial inventory of $16,000? How would this cash be obtained? (c) Assuming that no money is borrowed, list the individual current asset accounts as of the end of each month. (d) If the company could borrow at 7 per cent straight interest, would you recommend that money be borrowed for working capital? Why? If so, when should this be borrowed? (e) If the company has only the $1,000 in cash and the $16,000 inventory to begin business and has to borrow all the rest needed, indicate how much it would have to borrow and the duration of the loans if the total interest charges are kept at an absolute minimum. Assume the following for purposes of answering the question: straight 7 per cent interest paid at the beginning of each month on the loan of the previous month; the amount needed for a particular month is borrowed for that entire month; the excess of cash income over outgo for any particular month is available at the beginning of the month to pay off the loans; expenses stated above do not include interest charges. (f) If no money is borrowed, how much profit would the company make for the 6-month period? (g) As a practical matter, would you make any allowances for the possibility that the estimates given would not prove to be correct? Explain fully.

2. Wilson's Specialty Stores, Inc. presented the following balance sheet as of December 31, 19x1:

Assets		Liabilities and Net Worth	
Cash	$ 25,000	Accounts Payable	$100,000
Accounts Receivable	100,000	Long-Term Bank Note	100,000
Inventory	340,000	Capital Stock	300,000
Building & Equipment	300,000	Surplus	265,000
Total	$765,000	Total	$765,000

(a) Compute the current ratio. (b) Compute the "acid test" ratio. (c) Compute the equity-to-debt ratio.

3. The Rapid System Manufacturing Co. published the following financial statements:

Balance Sheet
As of December 31, 19x1

Assets		Liabilities and Net Worth	
Cash	$ 40,000	Accounts Payable	$ 310,000
Accounts Receivable	300,000	Bonds	800,000
Inventory	800,000	Capital Stock	1,500,000
Machinery	970,000	Surplus	500,000
Land and Buildings	1,000,000		
Total	$3,110,000	Total	$3,110,000

Income Statement
For the year ended December 31, 19x1

Sales		$10,000,000
Cost of Goods Sold		8,000,000*
Gross Margin		2,000,000
Expenses		
Administration	$ 700,000	
Selling	1,100,000	
Interest on Bonds	40,000	1,840,000
Net Income Before Taxes		$ 160,000

* Includes materials, labor, and overhead applicable to production department.

(a) What is the "current ratio" for this company? Is it too high or too low? Explain. (b) What is the "capitalization" of this company? How much "capital" does it have? (c) What is the "operating ratio"? (d) What is the margin of profit?

4. Assume that the company in the previous problem paid a federal income tax of 50 per cent, and a dividend of 4 per cent on its stock (par value $100). If you purchased some of the company's stock at the beginning of the year for $150 a share what would be the (a) "Earnings per share" on the stock? (b) Yield you received?

5. The Swift Co. had $40,000 in current assets and $20,000 in current liabilities. The company then paid off $10,000 of the current liabilities, thus increasing the current ratio from 2-to-1 to 3-to-1. Does the higher current ratio indicate that the company is in a better current position? Explain.

SELECTED READINGS

ANTHONY, ROBERT N. *Management Accounting*, rev. ed. Homewood, Ill.: Richard D. Irwin, Inc., 1960.

BIERMAN, HAROLD, JR. *Management Accounting*. New York: The Macmillan Co., 1959.

BLACK, HOMER E. and CHAMPION, JOHN E. *Accounting and Business Decisions*. Englewood Cliffs, N. J.: Prentice-Hall, Inc., 1961.

FOULKE, ROY A. *Practical Financial Statement Analysis*, 3d ed. New York: McGraw-Hill Book Co., Inc., 1957.

GUTHMANN, HARRY G. *Analysis of Financial Statements*, 4th ed. Englewood Cliffs, N. J.: Prentice-Hall, Inc., 1953.

HECKERT, J. BROOKS, and WILLSON, JAMES D. *Business Budgeting and Control*. New York: The Ronald Press Co., 1955.

HEISER, HERMAN C. *Budgeting—Principles and Practices*. New York: The Ronald Press Co., 1959.

HILL, THOMAS M., and GORDON, MYRON J. *Accounting: A Management Approach*, rev. ed. Homewood, Ill.: Richard D. Irwin, Inc., 1959.

JONES, RALPH C. *Effects of Price Level Changes*. New York: American Accounting Association, 1956.

MEYER, JOHN N. *Financial Statement Analysis*, 3d ed. Englewood Cliffs, N. J.: Prentice-Hall, Inc., 1961.

MILES, LAWRENCE D. *Techniques of Value Analysis and Engineering*. New York: McGraw-Hill Book Co., Inc., 1961.

O'DONNELL, JOHN L., and GOLDBERG, MILTON S. *Elements of Financial Administration*. Columbus: Charles E. Merrill Books, Inc., 1962.

SANZO, RICHARD. *Ratio Analysis for Small Business*. Small Business Management Series No. 20. Washington, D. C.: U. S. Government Printing Office, 1960.

TUCKER, SPENCER A. *Successful Managerial Control by Ratio Analysis*. New York: McGraw-Hill Book Co., Inc., 1961.

20

Asset Management

One of the major functions to be performed by financial management in the business organization is to raise funds to acquire operating assets. It is not really possible to completely segregate the raising of funds to finance assets from the management of those assets. Part of the problem in raising funds is determining how much to raise, and this depends upon the uses to which the assets are put and the efficiency of utilization of assets. In financing assets, the financial management of the business must know when the assets will initially be needed and how long this need will last.

In addition to this indirect interest in all assets, financial management has direct responsibility for certain assets. In almost all cases, the chief financial officer is directly responsible for the management of cash. In a large number of business firms he is also responsible for the management of marketable securities and accounts and notes receivable. He might also have responsibility for certain investment assets. In addition, he has a voice in the determination of the level of inventory to be carried and helps decide on the amount of fixed assets required for the firm. As a result, certain aspects of asset management must be considered in the financial management of a business enterprise.

Almost all activities of the business require utilization of cash in some way. Figure 20–1, which shows the flow of funds in a manufacturing firm, indicates the importance of cash in the acquisition of all other kinds of assets. It demonstrates the two-way flow from cash to other assets and from other assets back to cash during the operation of a business. Because financial management is responsible for cash, it strongly influences the management of all other assets of the business. When cash is short, great pressure may be placed upon the credit department for collection of receivables or on the sales department for the cash sale of inventory.

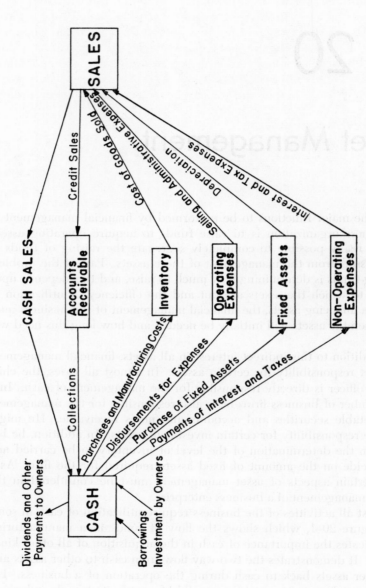

Fig. 20—1. Flow of funds in a business.

One of the main functions to be performed by financial management in the business concern is to provide funds to acquire the various assets. It is also important to control wisely both the inflow of funds to finance an increase in amount of total assets, and the reduction in assets brought by depreciation, manufacturing, and selling, upon the gradual sale of inventories, and upon the eventual collection of assets. Because the financial department of the business must know how to secure funds, it will be desirable to understand how the assets may be used.

In addition to its primary task of securing the financial management, it is also responsible to coordinate and oversee the chief financial officer in the sale of business operations and industries. In a large number of business firms, where the financial management of marketable securities and assets is important for the firm, he might also have responsibility for certain investment decisions. In them, he has a voice in the determination of the level of investment in the current and helps decide on the amount of fixed investment in the firm. As a result, certain aspects of asset management involves him directly in the financial management of a business enterprise.

Almost all activities of the business require the use of funds in some way. Figure 20—1, which shows the flow of funds in a business concern, illustrates the department of cash in the description of the various kinds of assets. It demonstrates the flow may readily other assets, and from other assets back to cash through the operation of a business. The cash management is responsible by which it through it closely influences the management of all other assets in the business. When cash is short, great pressure may be placed upon the credit department for collection of receivables or on the sales department for the cash sale of inventory.

When the firm has excess cash, it is more likely to approve a request from the manufacturing department for additional fixed assets or a request from the sales department for an expansion in inventory levels. While cash availability should not be the controlling factor in the determination of asset levels and asset management, the necessity for cash flow in a business is certainly an important consideration. Cash is necessary before almost any other assets can be acquired. The purpose of acquisition of assets is to aid in the flow of profits in the organization.

Asset Level Requirement

Both new and established businesses are faced with the problem of the amount of assets which should be provided and maintained for the efficient operation of the business. To maintain proper levels in the various asset accounts, constant management attention is required long after the initial decision is made as to how much is required to start the business. Asset requirements are constantly changing because of the expansion or contraction of sales, plant expansion, new product lines, changing wage and salary rates, pension plans, changing price levels, etc. The financial officer of the corporation should be constantly aware of any changes of this type and then should plan for proper adjustments in asset levels to meet the new requirements.

Attention to the maintenance of proper asset levels implies that too much could be invested in the assets of the firm as well as too little. The needs of the business are not met and the profit possibilities are lessened if inventory, fixed assets, and other investments are inadequate or if funds are insufficient to grant proper credit terms. On the other hand, excess assets must not be allowed to accumulate in unused form because of the adverse effect on the profitability of the firm. The major advantages of adequate assets are discussed below; from this discussion, the disadvantages which would result from an inadequate level of assets become apparent.

1. *Permits efficient operation.* A concern that has ample working capital will be able to operate efficiently. Raw materials in sufficient quantities will be obtainable. Purchasing in larger lots may mean lower prices. Payrolls can be met on time without worry or the necessity of borrowing at high rates of interest.

2. *Credit is maintained.* One of the most important factors in the success of many businesses is the maintaining of good credit with banks and suppliers of raw materials. Credit rating agencies classify business concerns on their capacity, willingness, and promptness in paying debts.

3. *Discounts may be taken.* The savings from taking advantage of cash discounts in purchase of goods may be substantial. Adequate cash

will enable a company to take these discounts and thus obtain materials at a lower price than that paid by other companies that are unable to purchase at discounts.

4. *Recessions may be weathered.* The chances of a company's weathering a recession are much better if it enters the period with ample working capital. When a recession hits, sales fall off and collections become slow. But the company's liabilities must be paid, and banks may call in loans sooner than would otherwise be the case.

5. *Emergencies and contingencies.* Emergencies of one kind or another such as lawsuits, adverse court decisions, increased taxes, and many other unexpected things may require additional assets. Companies also need some surplus cash to maintain minimum bank balances, and cash or liquid securities to meet their income tax payments. Ample cash or the equivalent enables a company to expand or to buy out other companies, effect mergers, branch out into more diversified lines, and carry on adequate research.

Certain disadvantages arise if a firm has too much invested in assets. This is particularly true if the unnecessary assets are cash or near-cash items. However, the theory of unused assets applies regardless of the type of asset. Too much investment in inventory or fixed assets as compared to the level of production being maintained could be just as inefficient as if there were excess cash on hand, and could lead to lower levels of profitability. The concept of unnecessary assets is called *redundancy*. By maintaining redundant assets within the firm, certain disadvantages may result.

1. *Return on investment may be low.* If a company has more assets than can be profitably employed, the return on the total assets of the company will be lower than would otherwise be the case. If all assets in regular use are earning 8 per cent, and the company has 25 per cent of its assets in surplus funds invested in 2 per cent government bonds, earnings on total assets would be only 6.5 per cent. Another company in the same field with no surplus funds may be earning 8 per cent on total assets.

2. *The management may become inefficient.* When managements have to work hard to meet payrolls, to take discounts, and to earn enough to carry on research and expand, they tend to be more efficient in many instances than when there is always cash at hand for all these purposes. Waste may creep in which otherwise would not be present.

3. *Relation with credit sources not maintained.* If a company always has plenty of cash on hand, it will not have to maintain close relations with banks and other possible sources of short-term capital. This may possibly result in the inability to get capital at some time in the future when adversity strikes.

While many firms consider it good financial management to carry more cash in liquid assets than is currently needed in the business, if it is found that there is no need for the surplus cash for any business purpose, the company should use it to reduce creditor obligations or pay it out to stockholders. In determining over-all asset levels, many firms would be interested in having some funds on hand to meet emergency requirements or unusual opportunities which might arise in the future. The determination of the proper level of assets to be maintained requires a compromise between the objectives of profitability and solvency, discussed in Chapter 17.

Types of Assets

Assets are usually classified as either *fixed* or *current* assets. *Current assets* are those which in the ordinary course of business will be turned into cash within an operating cycle (normally considered one year). The most important current asset accounts are cash, accounts and notes receivable, and inventory. Marketable securities may also be included. Current assets are also sometimes referred to as circulating capital, liquid assets, and working capital.

Fixed assets are those which will not be converted into some other form during the operating cycle of the business under normal business conditions. The common fixed asset accounts are land, buildings, plant and equipment, and other permanent investments. Over long periods of time, the fixed assets normally change form and are not entirely permanent in nature. Thus, a typewriter may be a fixed asset for a 10-year period of time. After that time period, the business may find that the typewriter is no longer suitable for its purposes, and it may be sold or disposed of in some way. Under normal circumstances, another typewriter would be acquired to replace the old one. Only land is of such a nature that it is generally considered a completely permanent investment for the business.

The terms *fixed* and *current* assets should not be considered interchangeable with *permanent* and *temporary* assets. While fixed assets are almost always considered permanent requirements of the firm, a large portion of current assets are, in reality, also a permanent requirement. The firm has a permanent requirement in inventory which cannot be considered temporary. As certain items of inventory are sold they must be immediately replaced if the firm is to continue operations. As a result, the inventory account never gets down to zero; it has a minimum level which is considered a permanent requirement. Thus, only the seasonal amounts of inventory carried to meet peak-season requirements are really temporary assets. This same analysis can be applied to accounts receivable and cash.

Working Capital

The term *working capital* is frequently used in corporate finance, but it does not always have the same meaning. It is important, therefore, to understand the several meanings of this term and to determine which meaning is being used in a specific application of the term. There are two common definitions of the term *working capital*. It refers either to the total of the current assets, or to the excess of the current assets over the current liabilities. This latter is sometimes called *net working capital* rather than *working capital*. In order that there will be no misunderstanding about the use of the term in this book, *working capital* will be used to refer only to total current assets. When the difference between current assets and current liabilities is discussed, the term *net working capital* or *net current assets* will be used.

In discussing working capital, it is convenient to divide the total into the following classes:

1. Fixed working capital
   a. Initial working capital
   b. Regular working capital
2. Variable working capital
   a. Seasonal working capital
   b. Special working capital

Fixed Working Capital. The *fixed working capital* is the minimum amount that is needed in the business. This amount varies among different businesses and within the same business depending upon managerial policies and the results of business operations. This kind of capital is divided into initial and regular working capital.

As the term indicates, the *initial working capital* is the amount needed when a business begins operations. A large amount of cash is required at this time in order to purchase all the items that are necessary. Inventories must be purchased and processed, but collections from the sale of such inventories may not take place for several months. Sufficient money will have to be on hand to meet the payrolls and pay the many other expenses for a relatively long period of time. It usually takes some time before a new business reaches a profitable stage. It is therefore necessary to provide working capital sufficient to absorb losses during this initial period.

After the business has gone through the formative stage and collections start rolling in, it will be found that a certain amount of working capital must be tied up in the business at all times to carry on a given volume of sales. This minimum amount necessary is called the *regular working capital*. It is true that cash will be collected from the sales and accounts receivable, but new inventories will have to be purchased and new credit granted.

The amount of regular working capital required varies greatly among different types of businesses. An electric light and power company, for example, has no "inventory" to sell, and since it does a cash business, it would require relatively less regular working capital than a retail furniture store or jewelry store doing practically all its business on credit.

Variable Working Capital. The *variable working capital* is an amount that is needed in addition to the regular working capital. It can be classified into seasonal and special working capital.

Some businesses are seasonal in nature; that is, their manufacturing or selling period is concentrated over only part of the year. A vegetable or fruit cannery and a manufacturer of Christmas toys are examples of such types of business.

The working capital needs of seasonal businesses fluctuate greatly during the year. As they are buying and processing or manufacturing to take care of the seasonal peak sales, the cash is constantly drained, inventories increase, and it may be necessary to borrow at the bank to take care of the purchases and expenses. Most businesses have some seasonal fluctuation in working capital needs. This extra seasonal amount is called *seasonal working capital.*

As orders start coming in, the inventory will be lessened and the cash and receivable accounts will increase. At the same time the need for cash for purchases and expenses lessens. As sales increase, this process continues, and the cash account will now show a large balance from the liquidation of the inventory and collection of the accounts, and the seasonal need for working capital will pass.

Any type of working capital other than initial, regular, and seasonal, is classed as *special.* Since cash is one of the items included in working capital, any need for additional cash would call for an increase in working capital. The following are among the more common needs for additional cash or other forms of working capital.

1. *Entering a period of prosperity.* Prosperity usually results in an increase in prices and sales for the more successful concerns. As prices increase, more cash is required to buy the same quantities of raw materials. Furthermore, sales are probably increasing at the same time, and this will require additional money for raw materials. At the same time, wages and other expenses are rising, and thus still more cash is required. Although this appears to be a special situation at the time, as long as prices and sales are maintained, such additional working capital becomes part of the regular working capital.

2. *Entering a period of recession.* From what has been said above, it may appear peculiar that special working capital may be needed when a recession hits. But such may be the case. Normally a company should cut down on its purchases when the business is headed into recession. But unfortunately, no one can be sure that such a period is at hand. Many companies will believe that what later proves to be a recession was only a slight setback in a period of prosperity. As a result they continue to expand inventories. As the recession gets under way, sales will begin slipping off, and collections will become slow. Unless purchases are cut and production schedules curtailed, the company will feel the need for additional working capital to carry the receivables and added inventory.

3. *Contingencies and emergencies.* Certain contingencies frequently arise which call for additional cash—shutting down of the plant for a long period due to strikes, floods, fires, etc.; uninsured property losses resulting from floods and fires which necessitate the investment of additional money in the business; litigation and unfavorable court decisions.

CASH

We all know the importance of cash for our personal needs; it is no less important to a business concern. Figure 20–1 indicates how all other asset items flow to and from cash. Cash is of particular importance because it is the most liquid of all assets. In cash form, value can readily be used to pay expenses or it can be converted to other forms of assets to meet business requirements. It is considerably more difficult to convert other assets than it is to convert cash. In fact, most other assets must first be converted to cash before they can be used for other purposes.

A business starts out with cash obtained from the sale of stocks or from the investment of the proprietor or the partners. This cash is used to buy fixed assets and inventory, and to pay the operating expenses. As the inventory is sold for credit, accounts or notes receivable take its place on the books of the company. Collection of the notes and accounts puts money into the cash account. This cash is again used to buy inventory, and the rotation starts all over again. It is thus seen that the current assets, or working capital, circulate in the business. This is why working capital is sometimes called "circulating capital."

The success of the business depends upon the expenditure or investment of the cash in such a way that it returns more cash or other assets to the business than was expended. Although it may merely be a symptom of some underlying major trouble, the immediate cause of failure of practically any business is insufficient cash.

The cash of a business consists of money or any medium of exchange that is generally accepted in payment of debt or in exchange for goods and services. The essence of cash is immediately available purchasing power. Included in cash assets would be the cash on hand at the location of the business, the petty cash accounts, cash in cash registers, cash in transit to banks, cash in banks, and cash in other institutions such as savings and loan associations and mutual savings banks. In addition, from the point of view of the financial manager, certain other assets are so readily marketable and available that they may be considered the same as cash for financial planning. The most common of these "near-cash" items are marketable government securities held as short-term investments in lieu of holding cash. The ability to convert these obligations to cash is sufficiently good to allow them to be considered along with cash in the planning process.

Table 20–1 indicates that government securities held by all industries actually exceed the total of cash for all industries. Most of the government securities are held by finance, insurance, and real estate institutions; thus cash is more important for non-financial firms than are government securities. Table 20–1 shows the relative importance of cash and near-cash items by industry classification. It should be noted that financial institutions carry a much higher percentage of total assets in cash than do other types of companies. In transportation and public utility companies, where

Table 20–1. Cash and Government Securities as a Percentage of Total Assets of Corporations by Major Industry Classification United States, 1958–59 (In Millions of Dollars)

Industry	Cash	Government Securities	Total	Per Cent of Total Assets
Finance, insurance, & real estate ...	$61,133	$112,845	$173,978	30.39
Construction	1,659	229	1,888	14.30
Mining	1,142	837	1,979	13.14
Manufacturing ...	16,231	11,133	27,364	11.60
Services	1,613	226	1,839	11.59
Wholesale & retail trade	7,484	1,031	8,515	10.73
Agriculture, forestry & fisheries ..	246	83	329	9.34
Transportation, communication, & public utilities	3,672	2,860	6,532	5.08
Total * ...	$93,248	$129,250	$222,498	20.90

* All industry, including some not classified into above classifications.
SOURCE: U. S. Treasury Department, Internal Revenue Service, *Statistics of Income 1958–59, Corporations* (Washington, D. C.: U. S. Government Printing Office, 1961), pp. 32–38.

large amounts of fixed assets are required and cash flows are relatively small, the percentage of total assets in cash and near-cash items is small. For all industries combined, in excess of 20 per cent of total assets is represented by cash and government securities.

Reasons for Holding Cash

Since cash is the most liquid of all assets, the obvious reason for holding it is for future conversion to another asset or for the purchase of some product or service. The primary use of cash is to meet the daily requirements of the business for payment for goods or services acquired. Certain amounts of cash are necessary to make change at cash registers and to maintain minimum bank accounts. In addition, cash disbursements do not exactly coincide with cash receipts; from time to time, large amounts of cash, in excess of immediate requirements, may be kept on hand in anticipation of additional cash requirements in the future. The basic use of cash is merely to meet the disbursement requirements of the firm.

Since cash is the most liquid of the assets, it is the safest one to hold for emergency purposes. In addition, cash items are fixed in value and are not subject to loss of principal other than through decline in buying power from inflation. Because of these features of cash, some surplus cash is often maintained for precautionary purposes.

Another use of cash is as a store for future investment. Opportunities often arise for special purchases at lower than normal cost. If the firm has sufficient cash on hand to take advantage of these opportunities, its profitability may be improved.

Other important uses of cash are for the maintenance of a credit rating or for reputation and prestige. Since cash is a safety factor for the firm, creditors often look to its amount of cash in judging the credit worthiness of a firm. The more cash a firm carries, the less its chance of getting into financial difficulty. Bank creditors particularly like to see a firm carry reasonable amounts of cash because these are usually deposited in banks and are therefore available for bank usage while in the firm's bank account. It is common practice in the United States to carry more cash than is immediately required. Very often this decision is at the instigation of bankers who offer more services to those business customers who carry larger amounts of cash. Banks are often more willing to lend to businesses that have large amounts of cash on hand.

Minimum Cash Level

In the discussion of cash budgeting, it was pointed out that there are certain periods of time when business transactions lead to excess cash, and other times when these same transactions lead to cash shortages. It is up to the financial manager to provide the cash necessary to meet the shortage, or to invest the excess available for the period of time when it is available. The cash budgeting process, however, requires that a minimum level of cash be established below which the financial manager should not go. The requirements over the minimum are determined primarily by the terms of purchase, terms of sale, and volume of sales of the business unit. The determination of the minimum level, however, is usually based on the reasons for holding cash given above.

In approaching the problem of determination of minimum cash level, first consideration has to be given to the actual amount of currency necessary to meet the buying and selling needs of the business. Certain businesses require a large amount of cash on hand for making change, but beyond these needs, the minimum requirement is very much influenced by banking relationships. In theory, it would not be necessary to carry any minimum cash balance in the bank and, at the lowest point in the cash account, the bank account could equal zero. However, most firms are too conservative to follow this practice and their planned minimum, as a safety factor, is an amount considerably higher than zero. In addition, by maintaining a minimum higher than zero, bank service charges are often reduced. Furthermore, a firm's credit rating can be influenced by the maintenance of a reasonable cash balance.

For obvious reasons, the minimum level is strongly influenced by outsiders and their requirements for the firm rather than by the firm's financial management. From a financial management point of view, it would be more profitable to invest all excess cash in income-producing investments of some type than to carry a minimum cash balance.

Cost of Cash Investment

The major disadvantage of carrying excess cash is its cost. This is an opportunity cost rather than an accounting cost but nonetheless it is real. If a firm has excess cash, that cash earns nothing for the firm. If the cash were invested in even a low-return investment such as short-term government securities, some additional income would be obtained and profitability would be improved. By having excess cash, the firm has more commitments to creditors or owners than would otherwise be the case.

When a firm reaches the point where it is permanently carrying excess cash in its minimum balance, it would be most advisable to find some long-run profitable investment for that cash or to repay it to creditors and owners. A decision on cash levels is another decision which requires a compromise between profitability and solvency.

Aiding Cash Flow

The financial manager has a variety of alternate actions at his disposal to improve his cash level or to increase his cash flow. One of these is the prevention of any "leaks" in cash. Since cash is the most liquid of assets, it is most subject to fraud and theft by employees, customers, and others with opportunities to gain access to it. Of all assets, cash has the most stringent security measures placed upon it. In most businesses the amount of cash lost through "leaks" is relatively small.

When a firm finds itself short of cash, a very common remedy is to attempt to speed up collections of accounts receivable, but this is only a temporary solution to a cash shortage problem. Furthermore, it could have the disadvantage of loss of customer goodwill. On the other hand, there is almost always some opportunity for speeding up collections through increased collection effort. In many firms, the collection of receivables one or two days earlier than in the past would lead to a very substantial increase in the average cash balance.

Another immediate approach to a cash shortage problem is to delay disbursements of cash. This approach also has a potential disadvantage in its effect upon the credit rating of the firm. To delay disbursements long beyond the expected payment time might actually lead to technical insolvency and liquidation of the business. Delays can also be costly in the loss of cash discounts. It is normally not possible to delay disbursements of payroll for any substantial period of time. However, some firms find that they can delay certain accounts payable for a considerable period. By reducing disbursement of funds, large amounts of cash can be accumulated rapidly in a firm, but this is only a short-run solution to the problem.

A more permanent solution to the problem of cash shortage would be to obtain permanent funds. If being short of cash is a permanent condition of a business, permanent measures rather than the temporary approaches discussed above must be taken. Permanent measures would include the increased use of long-term creditor capital, the expansion of owners' equity through reinvestment of earnings or through sale of stocks, or the sale of redundant assets. As will be seen in a later chapter, depreciation can also be a source of building of the cash account, along with retained earnings.

Short-Term Investment

The efficient financial manager will attempt to make his temporary excess cash work for him by investing it in some income-producing investment. Since the excess is of only a temporary nature, the investment must be temporary also. If long-term securities or stocks were purchased, the fluctuation in value in the market might more than offset any gains from dividends or interest earned during the time the investment was held. Most financial managers restrict themselves to very short-term securities for investment of excess short-term cash.

The available short-term securities are primarily government issues or securities of government agencies. It is normally considered wise to find securities with a maturity which will coincide with the need for the cash for other business purposes. While the return on very short-term investments is relatively low, it is greater than the amounts which would be earned were the cash lying idle in a bank account. Many financial managers would consider investing excess cash only if it were available for a minimum of a 3-month period. However, certain 30- and 60-day investments are also available and some financial managers go so far as to attempt to invest daily excess balances. This would be advisable only if the amounts involved were exceedingly large.

The selection of short-term investments is commonly one of the jobs of the financial manager of a firm. In order to make the selection, he has to know how much excess cash is to be available, when it will be available, and for how long. The answers to these questions are obtained from the cash budgeting process.

RECEIVABLES

The need for an investment in receivables arises through the ordinary business action of selling on credit. When a sale is made with promise of future payment by the buyer, the seller gives up his inventory and receives in return a promise to pay an account or note receivable. While it is not yet in cash form, this promise to pay has value to the firm and could be sold immediately to outside collection firms such as sales finance companies and factors. However, the normal business practice is for the seller to hold the account receivable until it is paid.

Table 20–2 indicates the percentage of total assets tied up in accounts and notes receivable by major industries. It can be seen that almost half of the assets of construction companies are receivables. If these companies could maintain the same volume without selling on credit, they would need over $6 billion less in assets for operation. However, credit sales are necessary to the operation of a construction business, and therefore, these firms must obtain the added capital to finance these receivables.

In excess of one-fifth of all assets of all American industry is represented by accounts and notes receivable. Notes are merely written evidences of the obligation. While notes make good evidence in the event of a legal question, from a practical point of view no distinction is made in this discussion between accounts receivable and notes receivable.

Proper Level of Receivables

A company that sells on credit will have costs over and above those of a company which sells strictly for cash. These costs of credit selling must be recovered in a charge for credit or in an increase in the selling price of the merchandise or in reducing other expenses due to economies of scale.

Table 20–2. Accounts and Notes Receivable as a Percentage of Total Assets of Corporations by Major Industry Classification United States, 1958–59

Industry	Accounts and Notes Receivable (In Millions)	Per Cent of Total Assets
Construction	$ 6,165	46.69
Wholesale & retail trade	24,356	30.70
Finance, insurance, & real estate	132,815	23.20
Manufacturing	40,405	17.13
Agriculture, forestry, & fisheries	480	13.62
Mining	1,996	13.25
Transportation, communication, & public utilities .	5,070	3.94
Total *	$214,322	20.13

* All industry including some not classified into above classifications.
Source: U. S. Treasury Department, Internal Revenue Service, *Statistics of Income 1958–59, Corporations* (Washington, D. C.: U. S. Government Printing Office, 1961), pp. 32–38.

The fact that so many business firms sell on credit indicates that they believe credit sales are to their advantage. Therefore, they must be recovering in some way all the additional costs of selling on credit which are not incurred by their competitors who sell for cash. The normal way in which these costs are recouped is through a larger volume of sales. Many customers cannot buy if they must immediately pay cash. These customers, therefore, must go to a credit seller. Many others prefer the convenience of credit purchasing even if they can purchase for cash. As a result, substantial volume is available to those who sell on credit which is not available to those who sell for cash only.

In many lines of business, practically all transactions are on a credit basis. If the firm is able to attract enough increased volume so that the efficiencies of larger-scale operation are sufficient to pay the added cost of credit, it is profitable to sell on credit and carry receivables. Firms selling on credit generally find that, due to substantially increased sales volume, their profits are higher even after extra credit costs than they would have been with cash sales only.

Thus, the proper level of receivables is not zero for most firms. It is, instead, that level at which the profit from the credit business equals or exceeds the cost of selling on credit. As soon as the costs of selling on credit exceed the incremental gross profit of the additional business, credit selling is not desirable. The profit maximization level varies from one type of business to another and from one firm to another within a given industry. In theory, a profit maximization approach should be taken in considering each credit application. Thus, if a potential sale of $1,000 is to be made on credit the firm must estimate the increased dollars of profit available from this sale after payment of all non-credit expenses of the transaction, and it must also estimate the cost of credit for this sale. If the incremental additional gross profit margin is $100 and the costs of credit (discussed below) are only $50, the credit sale should be made. If the incremental profit is $50 and costs are $100, the credit sale should not be made.

In practice, it is not easy to make the type of estimate discussed above nor is it practical to follow this analysis in each potential credit sale. As a result, certain credit policies are established by the firm on an over-all basis which tend to determine the level of receivables outstanding. These policies fall under the general headings of credit granting, credit terms, and collection policies.

Credit Granting

Each firm selling on credit has to determine which sales it will make on credit and for which ones it will require cash payment. The volume of *credit* sales is one of the most important factors in determining the over-all level of accounts receivable. A firm that is very strict in credit granting will have lower accounts receivable outstanding at any time than a firm that is very liberal. The policies established for the granting of credit should be closely geared to the philosophy of profit maximization. It is often found that sales departments, in their effort for greater sales, ordinarily are optimistic and inclined to recommend credit policies which are very liberal. Credit departments or finance departments, on the other hand, may tend to be too stringent. In order to maximize profits, a policy somewhere between the liberal and conservative attitudes should be followed.

In the granting of credit, the most important consideration is not whether the customer will pay or not; it is: Will the customer pay *as agreed?* Actual loss through bad debt (non-payment) is normally small. The major problems in credit costs are the length of time the credit is outstanding and the collection costs. To judge whether a customer will pay as agreed, the credit manager determines a credit rating for this purchaser. This credit rating is based on such things as the buyer's character, capacity, capital, and collateral, as discussed in Chapter 17.

The credit manager normally uses such tools as past payment record or present financial position of the applicant. The credit manager cannot know absolutely whether a customer will pay as agreed or not. It would be expected that in some small percentage of cases he would be wrong. Should a large percentage of the accounts be unsatisfactory, the credit-granting policies of the firm are probably in error. If the firm operates with absolutely no bad-debt losses and all customers paying on time, it would appear that the firm's credit-granting policies are too stringent.

Credit Terms

Another very important factor in determining the level of accounts receivable outstanding at any time is the credit terms offered by the company. Common credit terms state the date on which the account is due as well as any cash discounts offered. For example, the term *net 30* means that the account is due in 30 days from invoice date, and the required payment would be the same if the buyer paid now or waited the full 30 days. Terms of *2/10; net/30* mean the invoice amount is due in 30 days but if the customer pays within 10 days after invoice date, he may subtract 2 per cent from the billed amount and the account will be considered paid in full.

The terms of credit extended to customers vary considerably according to the kind of business and sometimes vary among different companies within the same industry. The cash discounts are offered as inducements for the buyer to pay his bills promptly. The more attractive the discount terms offered, the more likely that the buyer will pay within the discount period. Thus, there would be less capital needed to carry accounts receivable if very attractive cash discounts were offered by the seller.

The selling price of the goods, after deducting the cash discount, must cover all costs and profit to the seller. The extra income received by the seller when the discount is not taken is a contribution toward the seller's credit costs and should be sufficient to repay the seller for the cost of carrying the account for the longer period of time as well as for the potential additional collection cost and bad-debt losses.

In a purchase on terms *2/10; net/30* for $100, the real cost of the merchandise purchased is $98. This $98 must compensate the seller for all of his costs plus a reasonable profit. The extra $2 is a payment to the seller for extra credit granted the buyer. From the buyer's point of view, the $98 is the purchase price and if he does not take the discount and pays $100, he should consider the extra $2 as the cost of his own financing.

The length of the credit period is another portion of the credit terms. The longer the period of time granted buyers to pay receivables, the greater the need for capital to carry the receivables. For example, a firm granting 30-day terms will have more receivables outstanding at any one time than will a firm with the same amount of credit sales which grants only 15-day terms.

Collection Policies

The strictness of a firm's collection policy will also help determine the amount of the receivables outstanding. Those firms which pressure customers for collection immediately after the net credit period are likely to have fewer accounts outstanding for long periods of time. Special efforts devoted to collecting accounts when due will normally result in less ultimate bad-debt loss as well as in fewer overdue accounts. Many overdue accounts can be collected with the expenditure of some collection effort. While these collection efforts cost money to the firm, the cost is normally less than the cost of carrying the account receivable for a longer period of time or of the potential bad-debt loss of possible non-collection.

A certain amount of collection effort can be helpful in reducing capital needs for receivables. Collection procedures, however, must be tempered to maintain as much goodwill as possible. Collection efforts should be made only on buyers who are already past-due. These past-due accounts would normally tend to be less desirable customers, and they represent higher credit cost to the seller than other customers. If the seller could know in advance that the buyer was going to be past-due, he probably would not make the credit sale in the first place.

Cost of Credit Selling

There is a considerable cost involved in selling on credit. The obvious cost which most people think of first is the bad-debt loss. In practice, this cost is the smallest of the various credit costs. Most firms' actual bad-debt losses are relatively insignificant. Normal caution in credit granting can go a long way toward eliminating bad-debt losses as an important expense.

A much more important cost of credit is the cost of operating the credit department. Maintaining records of accounts receivable requires a fair amount of office help. In most firms, extra equipment is required, and certain personnel devote full time to the credit operation. All of these costs could be saved if the firm sold only for cash; also, there would be no requirement for monthly billing procedures.

The costs of operating a credit department may run anywhere from a negligible amount for firms dealing with only a few large credit customers, to 6 or even 10 per cent of sales for firms dealing with large numbers of small credit customers.

The time devoted to collection efforts by members of the credit department, and extra mailing and telephone expenses related to collection can be substantial. In addition, the costs associated with turning accounts over to an attorney or a collection agency are very high. While in most cases these accounts will probably eventually be collected, the costs of collection could run well in excess of 50 per cent of the total amount collected for long-overdue accounts.

Another important cost of credit operation is the cost of the capital tied up in receivables. This cost is often overlooked in decisions on profit maximization through credit sales. It is an important cost and certainly should be considered. If the firm averages $100,000 in outstanding receivables, it must recognize that it is paying for the use of that $100,000 to someone—either to creditors or to owners. Following the philosophy discussed under average cost of capital in Chapter 18, this cost may be somewhere around 10 per cent of average receivables outstanding, or in this case $10,000 per year. For a firm doing $1 million in sales, this cost alone is 1 per cent of sales. The longer receivables are outstanding, the higher the capital cost for each sale. For a receivable outstanding 6 months, this cost would probably be somewhere around 5 per cent.

Thus, it can be seen that the total cost of selling on credit varies from a negligible figure to as high as 10 or 12 per cent of a sale. On accounts which are paid within 10 days and billed only once, the only costs associated with credit would be the few costs of credit granting and one bookkeeping process plus the cost of capital for a 10-day period. These may total much less than 1 per cent of the sale. For an account outstanding 90 days, the cost of capital is substantially higher (for example, 2½ per cent), the bookkeeping costs are also higher, and no doubt some collection costs have been incurred for this account. If this 90-day-old account's incremental contribution to the profit of the company before consideration of credit is only 5 per cent, it is probably an unprofitable account.

Measurement of Receivables Management

Certain common practices are followed in attempting to measure the efficiency of the credit department of a specific firm. The proper measure for one firm is not necessarily suitable for another. The best and most reasonable measure is a comparison with the past experience of the same company.

One common credit analysis technique is the aging of accounts. This is a breakdown, at periodic intervals, of all accounts receivable outstanding, according to the length of time outstanding to date. The percentage of accounts over 60 days or over 90 days past-due is studied to indicate the effectiveness of the collection department. Firms selling on terms of net 30 days would normally expect to have only a very small percentage of accounts receivable outstanding beyond 90 days. All of these accounts would probably be receiving some collection attention.

Another efficiency measure for the credit department is the *receivables turnover,* which is calculated by dividing the annual net credit sales by the average monthly receivables. The receivables turnover can be used to check the efficiency of the credit and collections department, and also to determine the quality of the receivables.

Let us assume that a company has annual net sales of $1,500,000, of which $1,200,000 are credit sales made on the 2/10; net/30 basis, and that

the average monthly receivables is $100,000. Dividing $1,200,000 by
$100,000 gives a receivables turnover of 12 times a year. This means that
the average account is outstanding 30 days. We could conclude from this
that either no one took advantage of the discount, or that some did take
the discount but the accounts of some of the other customers have been
outstanding for more than 30 days, and have thus been overdue. The
latter would probably be the correct assumption. If turnover had averaged
15 times in the past, it is an indication of a slowing down in collections or
a change in credit-granting procedures which the firm might want to
correct.

Other measures are the delinquency ratio (the percentage of all receivables which are past-due) and the bad-debt ratio (the percentage of
bad debts to total credit sales). In many industries, this last ratio may
be as low as $\frac{1}{10}$ of 1 per cent or less. While $\frac{1}{2}$ of 1 per cent is the
standard rule of thumb in most retailing operations for the bad-debt
ratio, the ratio is usually less than that figure. In management of receivables, therefore, attention should be centered on past-due accounts
rather than bad debts. The greatest efficiencies are obtained by concentration on reduction of past-due accounts.

INVENTORY

In the case of merchandising and manufacturing companies, inventory is a very important part of total assets. Table 20–3 indicates that
inventory represents more than 30 per cent of total assets in wholesale

Table 20–3. Inventory as a Percentage of Total Assets of Corporations by
Major Industry Classifications
United States, 1958–59

Industry	Inventory (In Millions)	Per Cent of Total Assets
Wholesale & retail trade	$24,230	30.54
Manufacturing	49,643	21.05
Agriculture, forestry, & fisheries	395	11.21
Construction	1,303	9.87
Mining	828	5.50
Services	837	5.27
Transportation, communication, & public utilities..	2,710	2.11
Finance, insurance, & real estate	81	.01
Total *	$80,047	7.52

* All industry including some not classified into above classifications.
SOURCE: U. S. Treasury Department, Internal Revenue Service, *Statistics of Income 1958–59, Corporations* (Washington, D. C.: U. S. Government Printing Office,
1961), pp. 32–38.

and retail trade and in excess of 20 per cent in manufacturing. For other types of industry, inventory is considerably less important; it is practically negligible in finance, insurance, and real estate. Because of the importance of inventory in manufacturing and merchandising, success or failure of the business often depends upon the inventory policies of the firm. This is particularly true in times of fluctuating inventory prices.

Proper Level of Inventory

As is true with accounts receivable, the approach to determining the proper level of inventory is one of profit maximization. Inventory is necessary before sales can be made. It is through sales that profits are obtained by the firm. Therefore, if the desired inventory is on hand and ready for sale when the potential sale occurs, profits accrue to the firm. If the inventory is not available, the buyer normally will go elsewhere. Thus, each item of inventory has its potential profit for the firm. On the other hand, there is a cost of carrying inventory. The proper level of inventory investment would, therefore, be the level at which the profit realized by having the inventory on hand equates with the cost of carrying the inventory.

Underinvestment in inventory leads to shortages and reduction in sales. This can be costly to the firm in terms of profit. The firm which is constantly unable to deliver because of shortage of inventory is probably losing substantial profits. On the other hand, overinvestment in inventory has its negative features also. The cost of carrying excess inventory is substantial. A firm which is never short of inventory, never has a back order, or never loses a sale because of lack of inventory, is probably suffering from overinvestment in inventory.

There is often conflict between the sales and finance departments in judging proper inventory levels. Finance is overly conscious of the costs of carrying excess inventory and therefore tends to act in such a way as to lead to potential underinvestment in inventory. The sales department, on the other hand, is interested in making sales whenever possible, and its inventory policies often lead to overinvestment in inventory.

Costs of Carrying Inventory

The costs of carrying inventory will vary significantly from one firm to another. In manufacturing and merchandising, inventory costs are an important cost of operation. As is true of accounts receivable, a major cost of carrying inventory is the cost of the capital tied up. The cost of carrying an extra $100,000 in an inventory item for a 6-month period would be $5,000 at a 10 per cent cost of capital rate. The longer the inventory is held, the higher the cost of capital involved.

Space costs are also important in considering the cost of carrying inventory. Warehouses serve only one important function for business firms—the storage of inventory. All warehouse costs therefore become costs of carrying inventory. These costs would include rent, depreciation on building and equipment, utility costs, warehouse labor costs, etc. Sometimes included in warehouse costs are insurance and taxes. The more inventory carried, the higher the amount of insurance which must be carried and the greater the insurance cost. Many states impose an inventory tax of some type based on the valuation of inventory on hand.

Another category of inventory costs would be those related to pilferage and deterioration. If inventory were held only a very short period of time, practically no deterioration would take place. In some types of inventory, however, deterioration is quite rapid, and it is most important that it be held only a short period of time. In other inventories such as durable goods and metals, deterioration is much slower. Pilferage cost tends to be high where small unit value items which are readily marketable are car-ried in inventory. In certain lines of business, pilferage costs would be practically negligible.

Another potential cost of carrying inventory is the cost of obsolescence or of price decline. These costs are extremely difficult to estimate in advance. Where obsolescence potential is high, the cost of carrying inventory may be prohibitive. If a merchandising firm operated on a 25 per cent gross margin and one-fourth of its purchases became obsolete and worthless, the firm would have no gross profit margin after deducting obsolescence expense, which would equal 25 per cent of sales.

In certain lines of business, price declines can wipe out all gains potentially made by carrying inventory. When prices of raw materials or of purchased inventory are cut in the market, selling prices are also normally cut. If this is the case, and a firm is selling from inventory acquired at older, higher prices, its total net profit margin is often wiped out. While these price change costs are very subjective and difficult to determine, they can be very real costs. Good inventory management would require that some attention be paid to the potential of obsolescence or price decline in determining how much inventory to carry.

Types of Inventory

The three major types of inventory and the factors which determine the amount of each type that should be kept on hand are discussed below.

1. *Raw-materials inventory.* The proper size of the raw-materials inventory varies greatly among businesses. Under ordinary circumstances no larger inventory should be maintained than is needed to keep up with

the production schedule. In some instances, however, when the source of raw materials is uncertain, or when the time involved in getting the materials to the factory is not definitely known, or when prices are increasing, a larger amount may be invested in raw materials.

2. *Work-in-process inventory.* Generally speaking, the longer the production period, the greater will be the amount that will have to be tied up in work-in-process inventory. A shipbuilding company, for example, will have a relatively larger work-in-process inventory than a cannery.

3. *Finished-goods inventory.* Since the company is in business to make a profit from the sale of its product, it is obvious that the finished-goods inventory should at all times be sufficient to fill the orders as they come. In case of seasonal business, the inventory may have to be unusually large at certain periods in the year. In some instances a seasonal business will try to keep up the manufacturing process throughout the year in order to lessen overhead costs and to give steady employment to at least some of the workers. Thus, finished-goods inventories will accumulate throughout the year to be liquidated during the selling season. A company that sells from various distributing points throughout the country will have to maintain a much larger inventory than one which sells from only one place. The more sizes, shapes, and colors carried, the greater will be the need for a large finished-goods inventory.

Under normal circumstances the finished-goods inventory should not be much larger than the amount that can be turned out in the length of time that it will take to sell the inventory. In other words, if the company can turn out $100,000 in new products in a period of 3 months, and this is an economical run, and assuming the finished-goods inventory on hand can be sold within 3 months, the size of this inventory should not be much in excess of $100,000. Some allowance should be made for a breakdown or slow-up in production, and also for sales in excess of the estimate.

Inventory Turnover

One of the major measures used to judge the efficiency of inventory management is to determine the *inventory turnover.* The ideal turnover rate for any specific business is not necessarily that of its competitors or of the industry in general. Most business managers compare their turnover to their company's own past history and to the turnover rates of other similar companies. Some firms are highly profitable with a very high turnover rate; other firms in the same industry may do well with a very low turnover rate. If all other things were equal (never the case), most firms would prefer a higher turnover rate. The firms with low turnover rates must be able to sell more or sell at higher prices which will more than compensate for the reduced turnover rate. It is important to study each firm's turnover as an indication of inventory management efficiency.

The inventory turnover is calculated by dividing the average inventory into the cost of goods sold. If the inventory is "taken" only once a year, the average is found by adding the beginning and ending inventory, and dividing the sum by two. When monthly inventories are taken or calculated, an average of the monthly figures should be used.

It is to be noted that the sales are taken at their cost figure rather than at the "sales" figure, in order to eliminate the profit element from the sales figure. If the actual "cost of sales" figure is not obtainable, then the estimated "markup" is added to the average inventory figure, and this divided into the total "sales."

Let us assume that a company's beginning and ending inventories were $90,000 and $110,000 respectively, and that the sales expressed in cost were $400,000. Dividing $400,000 by $100,000 ($90,000 + $110,000 divided by 2) equals 4. Thus the company turned its inventory 4 times.

More significance is attached to the inventory figure in the case of merchandising concerns, such as retailers, jobbers, and wholesalers, than in the case of manufacturing companies. The latter have three kinds of inventory: raw materials, work in process, and finished goods. The work-in-process and finished-goods inventory valuations have labor and overhead costs included in addition to the raw materials. If inventory turnover is calculated for a manufacturing concern, it would have to be confined to the particular inventory under consideration. Each of the types of inventory turnover would be computed as follows:

$$\text{Raw material turnover} = \frac{\text{Raw materials going into work in process during period}}{\text{Average raw material inventory during period}}$$

$$\text{Work-in-process turnover} = \frac{\text{Work in process transferred to finished goods during period}}{\text{Average work-in-process inventory during period}}$$

$$\text{Finished goods turnover} = \frac{\text{Cost of goods sold during period}}{\text{Average finished goods inventory during period}}$$

The rate of turnover is highly significant. If we assume two companies with the same annual sales, the one with the faster turnover will require less capital tied up in inventory, and because of the smaller inventory, less space and therefore a smaller overhead. Or if two companies have the same inventory, the one with the quicker turnover will have larger sales and, assuming they have the same markup, larger profits. A company with a rapid turnover will ordinarily suffer fewer losses from obsolescence and shopworn merchandise.

Inventory Valuation

An important management decision in most businesses is the choice of an inventory valuation method. A number of different techniques are followed in practice. Each of these has a different effect on the valuation of working capital in the balance sheet, as well as on the amount of stated profits. After the physical inventory is taken at the end of an accounting period, the problem arises what dollar value to place on that inventory in the balance sheet. If a high dollar value is used (in other words if inventory is overvalued), profits will be overstated. If the ending inventory is overvalued, the actual cost of goods manufactured or sold will be less by the amount of the overvaluation, and the gross profit will be higher than if the proper valuation had been used. A higher gross profit means a higher net profit and results in higher income taxes.

Undervaluation has the opposite results on the profit. Undervaluation of balance sheet inventory means that cost of goods sold will actually be higher and profits will seem less with correspondingly reduced taxes. During periods of high taxes, many businesses are interested in undervaluation of balance sheet inventory so that taxes will be less. It is important that anyone studying the working capital position of a corporation or its profit picture have an understanding of the inventory valuation technique used and its effect on the amount of working capital and on profits and taxes.

Following are the major methods used in inventory valuation:

1. First-in, first-out
2. Average cost
3. Last-in, first-out
4. Cost, or cost or market (whichever is lower)
5. Inventory valuation reserves

1. *First-in, first-out.* Many businesses find it difficult to determine the actual cost of the inventory on hand. Where purchases of the same item are made several times during the inventory period at varying prices, it is difficult to tell which cost items are still on hand at the end of the period. One common practice used is to assume that the first items purchased were the first ones used in production or sold. This is the *first-in, first-out* inventory valuation method, which in practice is called FIFO. Actual cost figures are used for all items purchased during the period. It is then assumed that all items on hand in inventory were the last ones purchased and are priced accordingly. The result is that the book value of the inventory at any time is close to the existing market price. In periods of rising prices, this would mean that the inventory would be stated at higher prices than under other methods and that profits would also be higher with correspondingly higher taxes.

2. *Average cost.* Under the *average cost* method, a weighted average of the cost prices of an item is determined and this is used as the basis of the inventory valuation on the books. In periods of rising prices, this

method results in a lower valuation on balance sheet inventory and lower profits and income taxes than the FIFO method.

3. *Last-in first-out.* The *last-in, first-out* method of valuation is particularly popular in periods of rising prices because it results in a still lower value on balance sheet inventory and lower profits and income taxes. Under this system, which is called LIFO, cost prices are used and it is assumed that the last items purchased were the first items used or sold. Thus, the balance sheet inventory reflects earlier prices rather than the latest market prices. Under this method, the latest market prices enter the cost of goods sold, and, therefore, make cost and profits reflect current market prices of inventory. Valuation of inventory on the balance sheet under this method becomes out of line with existing inventory prices. Many firms changed to the LIFO method of inventory valuation for tax purposes during and after World War II when prices were rising sharply. In this way, profits reflected current costs and were therefore less than they would have been under average cost or FIFO. This technique results in lower taxes during inflation periods and higher taxes during deflation.

4. *Cost, or cost or market (whichever is lower).* When the cost prices of each individual item in inventory are available, companies do not have to worry about LIFO or FIFO or average cost as they know the actual costs involved. Some companies actually value their inventories at cost but others are more conservative and use the lower of cost or market. Under this method, profits from rising inventory values are not taken until the inventory is sold, but losses from declining inventory values are taken as the decline takes place. This is probably the most commonly used method of inventory valuation. In periods of rising prices, the inventory is still carried on the books at cost although replacement value would be much higher. This method results in a conservative statement of profits during periods of both rising and falling prices.

5. *Inventory valuation reserves.* Because of the possible loss or reduction in profits that may come from a reduction in prices, many companies will carry on their books a reserve for decline in inventory values. This reserve is often shown as a deduction from the inventory account on the books. This is conservative practice and is similar to the "cost or market, whichever is lower" method, stated above.

FIXED ASSETS

The major fixed asset accounts are plant, equipment, machinery, land, buildings, automobiles, delivery equipment, and furniture and fixtures. Table 20–4 indicates the importance of net (after reserves for depreciation) tangible fixed assets for major industries. It can be seen that in transportation, communication, and public utilities, fixed assets account for over 80 per cent of total assets. Fixed assets are significant in all industries with the exception of finance, insurance, and real estate. The quantity of fixed assets and their permanent nature make their management particularly important in furthering the profitability of the firm. Because of the permanent nature of these assets, they do not fluctuate in physical total from day to day during the normal operation of business. The major management decisions relative to fixed assets are at times of purchase and disposal. There is, of course, need for maintenance and protection in connection with certain fixed assets but the most important decision relative to a specific asset is its acquisition.

Table 20–4. Net Tangible Fixed Assets as a Percentage of Total Assets of Corporations by Major Industry Classification United States, 1958–59

Industry	Net Tangible Fixed Assets (In Millions)	Per Cent of Total Assets
Transportation, communication, & public utilities..	$103,586	80.50
Mining	7,661	50.86
Agriculture, forestry, & fisheries	1,758	49.90
Service	7,407	46.67
Manufacturing	86,812	36.81
Construction	2,307	17.47
Wholesale & retail trade	13,827	17.43
Finance, insurance, & real estate	34,104	5.96
All Industry	$257,571	24.20

SOURCE: U. S. Treasury Department, Internal Revenue Service, *Statistics of Income 1958–59, Corporations* (Washington, D. C.: U. S. Government Printing Office, 1961), pp. 32–38.

Because of the importance of the acquisition decision for fixed assets, this subject has been discussed separately in Chapters 17 and 18. The whole process of capital budgeting is related to an analysis of the maintenance of proper levels of assets. Profit maximization is the major determining factor in this analysis.

Costs of Fixed Assets

Like other assets, fixed assets involve a substantial capital cost. This capital cost is more important in connection with fixed assets because of their permanent nature. Ten per cent per year for capital cost on a $100,000 investment would equal the total investment over a 10-year period. If compound interest is taken into effect, the cost of capital would equal the total investment in approximately 8 years.

In addition to the very important cost of capital, certain other costs are inherent in the maintenance of any given amount of fixed assets. These are the same type of costs as those associated with maintaining inventory which is also a tangible asset. They would include the space costs, taxes and insurance, maintenance, and possible cost due to obsolescence and decline in price.

Valuation of Fixed Assets

Because of the specific problems encountered in attempting to place values on fixed assets once they have been acquired, a separate chapter is devoted to this subject. The problems of depreciation and depletion and their effect on fixed asset valuation are discussed in Chapter 24. Other approaches to valuation were discussed in Chapter 12.

QUESTIONS

1. What are the advantages of maintenance of an adequate level of assets?
2. What is meant by redundant assets? What is wrong with having redundant assets?
3. Differentiate current and fixed assets. Distinguish them from permanent and temporary assets.
4. Indicate the different kinds of working capital and state how each should be financed.
5. How is the minimum cash level determined?
6. How may cash flow be improved?
7. What should be done with temporary excess cash?
8. What factors determine the amount of working capital which will be tied up in accounts receivable?
9. Should the credit and collection policy of a company be such that no bad debts will be experienced? Explain.
10. How is the receivables turnover calculated? Of what significance is it?
11. What factors determine the amount of inventory which a manufacturing company must carry?
12. Indicate how a company computes its finished goods inventory turnover.
13. Indicate the various methods of inventory valuation. Which do you recommend? Why?
14. Describe the three major types of manufacturing inventory.
15. Discuss the varying importance of cash, accounts receivable, inventory, and fixed assets between major industry classes.

PROBLEMS

1. The inventory (at cost) of the Quality Department Store on January 1, 19x1, was $70,000. As of December 31 of the same year it was $80,000. Net

sales for the year as shown in the income statement amounted to $600,000. The average "markup" for the store was 25 per cent of the selling price. What was the inventory turnover for the year?

2. The Acme Manufacturing Co. follows the first-in, first-out method of inventory valuation. The inventory on hand on January 1 consisted of 600 units at an average cost of $1.00 per unit. It is the policy of the company to purchase additional inventory each 4 weeks (beginning in the fifth week of the year) sufficient in amount to last for a 4-week period. The first purchase was at $1.10 per unit, and the second purchase was at $1.20 per unit. The production schedule for the first quarter of the year calls for 100 units of inventory to go into production each week. Show in columnar form the purchases, issues, and balance on hand in terms of units, unit cost, and total cost, for the first 9 weeks of operations.

3. James White is considering building and operating a hot-dog stand near where a large atomic plant is being built. The contractor has agreed to build the stand for $4,600 complete with equipment. It is estimated that the construction of the plant will take 4 years, after which time it is thought that the stand would be practically worthless so far as business is concerned. White's father has agreed to lend him the $4,600 needed to build the stand. White estimated that he will gross $9,000 a year, and that his annual operating expenses will be $2,200 a year. He figures he will therefore net $6,800 a year. (a) Why would more than $4,600 probably be needed for this project? (b) What expenses were probably not given any consideration by White?

4. The Smith and Jones Specialty Shop sells men's and women's clothing at retail in a medium-sized Western city. Mr. Smith handles the selling function in the business and Mr. Jones looks after buying and finance. In recent years, Mr. Jones has become more and more cautious in credit granting and Mr. Smith claims that this is losing sales for the firm. Mr. Jones had tried to justify his policies on the basis of the low turnover of receivables and high bad-debt loss. Credit sales of the company have been running around $300,000 per year and average receivables outstanding have been approximately $50,000. Bad-debt losses over the past 3 years have averaged $1,000. Figure the receivables turnover and bad-debt loss ratio for the company. How would you determine whether these ratios are reasonable or not? If you were Mr. Smith, would you accept Mr. Jones' approach to the problem? If not, what counterarguments might you have?

5. Mr. Short, treasurer of the Standard Manufacturing Co., has just completed his cash budget projections for the coming year. In making his projections, he has set a minimum bank balance of $50,000. His projection indicates that his bank balance will rise substantially above this minimum in the spring and summer months. In the fall, he will need all of the excess cash plus some borrowing to finance purchase of seasonal inventory. His projections give cash balance at month-end only. His figures indicate that the excesses over minimum level will be as follows:

April, $25,000
May, $40,000
June, $90,000
July, $100,000
August, $75,000
September, $20,000

What do you recommend be done with the excess funds? Justify your decision.

SELECTED READINGS

BECKMAN, T. N. *Credits and Collections in Theory and Practice,* 7th ed. New York: McGraw-Hill Book Co., Inc., 1962.

CHAPIN, A. F., and HASSETT, GEORGE E., JR. *Credit and Collection Principles and Practices,* 7th ed. New York: McGraw-Hill Book Co., Inc., 1960.

CURTIS, EDWARD T. *Credit Department Organization and Operation.* American Management Association Research Studies No. 34. New York: American Management Association, 1958.

MAGEE, JOHN F. *Production Planning and Inventory Control.* New York: McGraw-Hill Book Co., Inc., 1958.

ROBINSON, ROLAND I. *The Management of Bank Funds,* 2d ed. New York: McGraw-Hill Book Co., Inc., 1962. Chapter 21.

SOLOMON, EZRA. *The Management of Corporate Capital.* Chicago: The Free Press of Glencoe, 1959.

TIMMS, H. L. *Inventory Management of Purchased Materials.* New York: National Association of Purchasing Agents, 1958.

WHITIN, THOMAS M. *The Theory of Inventory Management.* Princeton: Princeton University Press, 1953.

21

Unsecured Current Financing

Current financing means using sources of funds for which payment of principal is promised within one year. In the accounting statements, the current financing sources are listed as current liabilities. The most common current liability items are accounts payable, notes payable, accrued wages, accrued taxes, other accrued expenses, dividends payable, and current amounts payable on long-term liabilities. The sources of funds for accounts payable are normal trade creditors and other suppliers of goods and services. The funds represented by notes payable are generally obtained from banks, insurance companies, finance companies, factors, commercial paper houses, and others. The source of funds for the various accrued expenses is the supplier of the service for which the expense is incurred, such as the government, for taxes payable, or employees, for wages payable.

For many businesses, current sources are very important suppliers of funds. This is true for small businesses in particular. Current financing often represents the second most important source, after owners; sometimes it is the only other source. Almost every business organization makes some use of current financing. The use of current sources will vary from one season to another; at peak seasons current sources may represent 50 per cent or more of total funds for many businesses. Table 21–1 gives the percentage of current sources to total assets for various industries at the end of the fiscal year. Since most businesses close their fiscal year at the low point in inventory and receivables and in current financing sources, at the peak of the year current financing would be a much higher percentage of total assets.

Advantages of Current Financing

The various current sources of funds have certain advantages in common that the use of long-term creditor funds or owner financing does not

502

offer. One of the most important of these is availability. Certain current sources of funds are automatic or spontaneous and occur without any special action on the part of the business manager. Other current sources offer greater speed in obtaining funds than long-term suppliers of funds. Suppliers of current financing are likely to be more lenient in granting credit. Certain types of current financing are often available when all other sources of funds are not. Thus, current financing is often easier to obtain and is available with less advance planning on the part of the business manager.

Table 21–1. The Relative Importance of Types of Current Financing as a Percentage of Total Assets for Corporations by Major Industry Classes United States, 1959

Industry	Total Current Liabilities	Accounts Payable	Current Notes & Bonds Payable	Accrued Expenses	Other Current Liabilities
All corporations	25.0	5.6	3.5	2.1	13.8
Agriculture	26.6	8.6	11.9	1.9	4.2
Mining	19.7	9.4	4.2	4.1	2.0
Construction	52.6	22.3	7.6	4.0	18.7
Manufacturing	21.0	9.3	3.5	4.7	3.5
Transportation & utilities	11.4	3.1	1.8	3.5	3.0
Wholesale & retail trade	41.3	23.1	11.1	3.2	3.9
Services	32.3	13.0	9.7	4.1	5.5

SOURCE: U. S. Treasury Department, Internal Revenue Service, *Statistics of Income, 1958–59, Corporations* (Washington, D. C.: U. S. Government Printing Office, 1961), pp. 32–38.

Since payment to the suppliers of current financing is due in a shorter period of time, the risk of lending to a firm is generally thought to be less for current sources than for suppliers of longer-term capital. As a result, most current suppliers of funds are willing to settle for a lower interest rate or rate of return. While certain types of current financing may be very costly, under normal circumstances the same source, with the same control and risk provisions and with only the maturity changed, would require a still higher interest or rate of return for long-term maturities than for short-term maturities. It is a generally accepted principle of finance that risk to the lender is greater for long-term loans than for short-term loans.

Flexibility is generally a characteristic of dealing with suppliers of current financing. It is normally possible for the borrowing business to repay these funds at will without substantial penalty. Special arrangements are often made for adding to or subtracting from the use of the source of funds at the option of the borrower. These elements of flexibility are much more common in short-term sources than in more permanent sources.

Disadvantages of Current Financing

The major disadvantage to utilization of current financing sources is the responsibility it places on the borrower. When using current financing, the borrowing business commits itself to repayment at some stated time within 12 months. If it does not meet its commitment, it is in default. With longer-term maturities, there is more time to plan new sources of funds to meet payments. Since short-term obligations are low-risk to the supplier of funds, they would be high-risk to the borrower. No supplier of funds can cause financial embarrassment to the business unit until default occurs, and default cannot occur until the time for some promised action has passed. But the shorter the time in which an action is promised, the higher the possibility of default.

Control is another factor which is commonly considered in selecting sources of funds. It is difficult to generalize about the effect on control of the business by suppliers of short-term funds. In some cases, current creditors may exert a substantial influence on the operation of the business. More commonly, however, direct controls by suppliers of current financing are very limited.

The advantages and disadvantages of current financing as a source of funds vary with the specific current source being considered. The decision on which source to use depends on the circumstances of the individual firm. The decision would normally be made by weighing the varying effect of the factors discussed above under each given set of conditions. Most firms find it advantageous to utilize a variety of sources of current financing. Each of the more common sources will be discussed later with particular reference to its cost, risk, control, flexibility, and availability.

Determining Amount of Current Financing

It is a generally accepted principle of business finance that permanent needs should be permanently financed and temporary needs temporarily financed.

If temporary sources were used for permanent needs, the business would be required to meet early maturities by replacing them with other sources. The ability to obtain the new source to repay the old depends upon the decision of an outsider as well as the decision of a financial manager. Outside conditions may be such that a new source would not be available at the time needed. Thus, temporary financing of permanent needs is a very high-risk venture.

For example, should a firm decide to purchase a building and obtain the funds through 90-day bank notes, at the end of the first 90-day period, the firm would have to obtain an extension from the bank (at the bank's option) or find some new source of funds to pay off the 90-day bank note. Certainly, earnings would not be available during the 90 days to repay the entire note, nor would the owners probably have funds to put into the business, or they would not have borrowed 90 days earlier. Thus, the business is forced to rely on some other outside creditor. Particularly if conditions have changed since the original 90-day note was obtained, the business may find it very difficult to refinance and would thus be in a position of default should the bank refuse to extend the note. It is usually not the bank's intention to extend the note indefinitely, or it would have made more permanent arrangements originally.

Permanent financing of temporary needs is also undesirable in that it leads to the redundancy discussed in the preceding chapter. Permanent sources tend to be higher-cost sources than temporary ones. Thus, if some very short-term temporary need is financed with permanent funds, a higher-cost source would normally be used. In addition, when the need no longer exists, the firm would still have to pay for the use of the permanent funds. It would no doubt be forced to invest its excess funds in short-term low-yielding investments and the profitability of the firm would be reduced.

Thus, permanent financing of temporary needs leads to higher long-term cost for the firm and lower levels of profitability. Temporary financing of permanent needs, while it may be less costly in the short run, is a very high-risk operation. The above stated principle, therefore, is based on the assumption that the business firm does not want to accept the very high risk of financing permanent needs with temporary sources, nor does it want to lose the profitability of financing temporary needs with permanent sources.

Temporary and Permanent Needs and Sources

In order to apply the above principle, the financial manager must decide which needs are temporary and which are permanent. In most businesses, fixed-asset needs are thought of as permanent even though the assets depreciate and must be replaced in time. It is the general intention of firms to replace fixed assets as they wear out, and thus the physical need for the fixed asset continues throughout the life of the business. In the preceding chapter, the permanent and temporary portions of working capital were discussed. Minimum inventory levels and minimum amounts of accounts receivable and cash are necessary to most businesses at all times. Therefore, these become permanent needs.

The major example of temporary needs for most firms is seasonal requirements. These are needs which arise and become self-liquidating within a one-year period. An excellent example is the expansion of inventory for the Christmas season by retail stores. Just prior to Christmas, the inventory converts to accounts receivable, and later in the winter, the receivables convert to cash. At that point, there is no need in the business for the preceding higher level of assets. When the cash is obtained from the receivables, temporary sources of funds can be repaid and the firm will not suffer from redundant working capital during the slack summer season. In the fall, the process may be started over again for the temporary need of the next Christmas season.

The fact that current financing is defined as utilizing sources of funds with maturities of less than one year indicates that current financing is of a temporary nature in most instances. It, therefore, becomes the ideal source of funds for temporary needs. The maturity placed on the current source can be related to the time period of the need. Temporary needs are self-liquidating through the normal process of business operation by conversion from inventory to receivables to cash to provide the funds to meet payments on temporary financing. Thus, good business financial management would attempt to finance all temporary (seasonal) needs with current sources.

It must be recognized that some amount of current financing is spontaneous for the firm and that no normal business ever reaches a point where it is utilizing no current source of funds. The spontaneous sources of current financing should be utilized insofar as they are spontaneous. Thus, there is some permanent element in current liabilities just as there is a permanent element in inventories and accounts receivable. The permanent amount in current liabilities is generally very small, but it can be considered as a permanent source of funds for the firm. The truly temporary sources, therefore, are those over and above the spontaneous current liabilities.

The accounting distinction of one-year maturities in defining current liabilities is well-chosen and enables the business manager to study his temporary financing in relation to his temporary and permanent needs. Figure 21–1 illustrates temporary and permanent needs and temporary and permanent financing.

SPONTANEOUS SOURCES

Because of the way in which business activities are normally conducted, certain sources of funds become available spontaneously or automatically without any conscious effort on the part of the financial manager to obtain them. Under normal circumstances, spontaneous sources of funds may be thought of as no-cost sources.

The most common financial management decision regarding spontaneous sources is to utilize them whenever they occur automatically for as long as they are available at no cost. Once this decision is made, all the firm must do is attempt to determine the amounts available from these sources and subtract these amounts from total financial needs before deciding how much should be raised from other sources. Thus, spontaneous sources are automatically figured in cash budgeting—cash payments are planned only when due, not when the liability is incurred.

Trade Credit

For many businesses, the most important of the spontaneous sources of funds is normal trade credit. As can be seen in Table 21–1, accounts payable are an extremely important source of funds in certain lines of business and are significant for all lines. A large portion of the amounts listed in accounts payable are normal trade credit. For all U. S. corporations, accounts payable amounted to almost $60 billion or 5.6 per cent of total assets. For manufacturing, accounts payable amounted to $22 billion and 9.3 per cent of total assets, while for wholesale and retail trade they accounted for 23.1 per cent of total assets.

Trade credit occurs when business units sell and buy from each other with promise of future payment rather than immediate payment in cash. "Normal" trade credit is that portion of trade credit which is on open-book account and on which payment is made at the date which was agreed upon in the credit terms, and which requires the lowest dollar payment. Payment ordinarily would be made on the last day for taking the cash discount under terms providing for a cash discount or the net date under terms not providing for a cash discount. In normal trade credit, no money is saved by paying in advance of the cash discount or net dates.

There is a cost to the seller in granting "free" trade credit, for even a 10-day period of time involves some cost of capital. However, for buyers who pay bills on discount day, the cost to the credit seller is relatively small. The discount customer involves no collection expense for the seller, no bad-debt loss, relatively little bookkeeping expense, and a short period of time for the use of capital.

Because the costs to the seller are small, it is normally not possible for the buyer to buy for less by immediate payment of cash. If this is the case, the wise buyer will take advantage of the free use of funds up to the discount date or the net date if no discount is allowed. By so doing, the buyer's requirement for funds from other sources is less, and his over-all cost of capital is reduced.

The most common credit terms would require payment by the 10th of the next month in order to obtain the cash discount. For a purchase made on the 15th of a month (median date of purchase), these terms allow 25 days of "free" credit. Thus, a firm could average 7 per cent ($25 \div 365$) of its annual purchases in free trade credit. For many firms, this is a substantial source of funds—particularly in wholesale and retail trade.

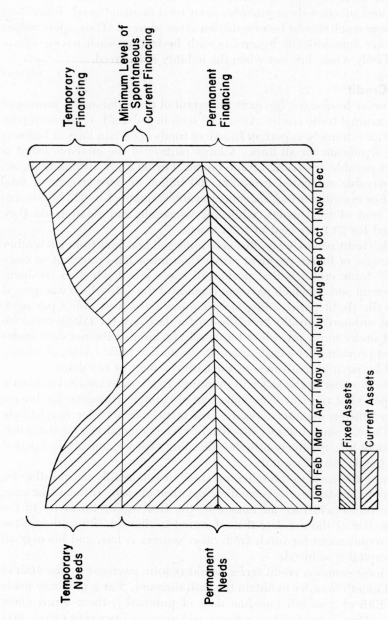

Fig. 21–1. Ideal relationship of needs and sources of funds.

Accruals and Deferred Items

The analysis applied above to normal trade credit is also applicable to various accruals and deferred items. It would normally be considered uneconomical for a firm to pay expenses such as taxes, wages, interest, etc., before due date. As a result, accruals of this nature are a spontaneous source of funds.

Accrued wages is one of the most important accruals. Employees are usually paid after they perform their services. In former times, it was common to pay workers at the completion of each day's work. Today, this is burdensome and unnecessary. Workers are normally paid weekly, bi-weekly, or monthly. The cost of handling payroll becomes much less when wages are paid less often. In addition, the business receives the use of the funds for a period of time until the wages are actually paid. If wages were paid daily instead of monthly, firms would have to have an increased amount of cash in order to meet the daily payments. Allowing wages to accrue for some period of time avoids an immediate drain upon cash. Thus, wages payable are an automatic or spontaneous source of funds to businesses.

The above discussion applies also to such items as accrued interest, accrued rent, and all other types of accruals. It applies also to dividends payable. While dividends are not considered an accounting expense, deferring payment of dividends allows the firm to conserve cash in the same way as deferring expenses.

Another very important spontaneous source of funds is federal income taxes payable. For many corporations, this is the largest current liability item at year-end. The tax liability to the federal government actually accrues during the entire year in which the company is earning profits. It may be difficult for many businessmen to accept the thought that the federal government is supplying them with funds. However, this is the case. If taxes had to be paid as incurred, businesses would need much more cash in order to meet the current tax payments. As is true with all spontaneous sources of funds, it would generally be considered poor management to pay federal income taxes in advance of due date. Heavy penalties are provided for late payment and nothing is to be gained by early payment. In the cash budgeting process, taxes payable are entered on due date rather than on the date on which the liability is incurred.

Many corporations have deferred income items. Cash is often received in advance of when it is earned. The cash received adds to the assets of the corporation and is available for general corporate use even though the goods and services for which the cash was paid are to be delivered at some future date. These items appear as current liabilities on corporate balance sheets. They represent a source of funds until payment is made in the form of transfer of goods and services to the supplier of these funds. Such items as gift certificates, sale of transportation service in advance of use, advance payments by customers, and special-order goods paid for in advance are examples of situations where deferred income represents a current source of funds. The basic source of supply for these funds is customers.

SUPPLIERS

Normal trade credit was discussed above. In many cases suppliers' funds are utilized beyond the time provided through normal trade credit. Many buyers of merchandise on credit do not pay on discount date; thus, they are using suppliers' funds for a period beyond the "no cost" time. Many other buyers of merchandise on credit do not pay on the agreed-upon net date. In addition, some sellers quote net terms which obviously include increased cost for financing over the period of time for which the credit is granted. In these cases, there should be alternate sources available where the merchandise or service could be purchased at lower cost for cash.

Many types of special arrangements exist between suppliers and customers in regard to use of suppliers' funds for short periods of time. All of these represent situations where the financial manager of a firm utilizes trade credit to obtain suppliers' funds beyond the amount considered spontaneous.

The financial manager's decision on utilization of these sources is different from his decision on spontaneous amounts. If he does not pay on discount date or net date or if he pays a higher purchase price in order to obtain credit, the financial manager should have determined that the cost, risk, control, flexibility, and availability factors were such as to make this the most suitable among the sources of funds available to him.

Cost

Although it may be hidden in many cases, there is a cost involved in obtaining trade credit. If the seller does not charge the buyer for the use of credit through an interest charge or similar fee, he must obtain his costs of granting credit through the selling price of the merchandise.

It is only under unusual circumstances that a seller charges interest for trade credit. Where no rate is charged and no cash discount included, the price of the merchandise includes the extra cost of the seller's granting of credit. If no discount is offered, the cost of using this credit will be determined by comparing prices with the cash prices of a similar seller. The cost of financing when cash discounts are offered is the amount of the discount.

An example of a term of sale which is widely used is 2/10; net/30. As noted in the previous chapter, this means that if the bill is paid within 10 days, a discount of 2 per cent will be allowed. If the bill is not paid within the 10 days, the full amount will be due at the end of 30 days. The time is computed from the date of the invoice. This discount rate figures out to be a high one when it is expressed on an annual basis. Assume that the goods are billed out at $100. If the buyer pays at the end of 10 days he will receive a discount of 2 per cent of $100, or $2. Thus he would pay only $98 for the goods. But if he waits 20 more days, he would have to pay the full $100. A charge of $2 for the use of $98 for 20 more days is equivalent to a charge of $36 (18 times 2) for the use of $98 for a year. This amounts to a rate of 36.73 per cent. (Note that if payment were made late, say on the 70th day, the cost would be only 12.25 per cent.)

Terms of this type represent very expensive financing. It would generally pay a buyer to obtain funds elsewhere to pay for the merchandise in 10 days rather than to take advantage of the extra 20 days offered at this extremely high interest rate.

Credit Terms

The credit terms granted by sellers are important in determining the use and the cost of trade credit. Terms vary substantially between various industries and even between companies in the same industry. Terms may also vary between individual buyers based on their credit rating and the seller's willingness to lend to various types of risk. Most industries have what are considered standard credit terms. These terms are based on the length of the customers' production or marketing period, the seasonal nature of the business, the nature of the article involved, the location of customers, and competitive conditions. Credit terms vary from Cash in Advance, or Cash on Delivery, in the case of buyers with very poor credit ratings, to 30-, 60-, 90-, or even 180-day terms in certain lines of business for better customers.

Risk, Control, and Flexibility

In using trade credit beyond the discount date, the buyer incurs no additional risk until the net date. However, if he does not pay at that time, he is actually in default, and the trade creditor may take foreclosure or other legal action against him. While trade creditors do not normally take legal recourse immediately upon default by buyers, non-payment to suppliers on the agreed date is very likely to affect a buyer's credit rating immediately. As discussed earlier, a good credit rating is one of the most important assets of a business.

Some suppliers do not expect certain buyers to pay on net date. If this is the case, it may be perfectly reasonable for the buyer to stretch out his payment beyond the date given in the credit terms. Commonly, he would receive a second bill 15 or 30 days later and perhaps another bill and/or a phone call after 60 days. If he pays at this point, no legal action is taken. However, in the eyes of the seller his credit rating has probably fallen, and this seller may make that information available to others.

In general, trade creditors exert very little control over their debtor customers. They have no legal rights to control the debtor's business beyond actions agreed to in the contract of sale. The normal trade credit contract calls for no control of any type over the debtor as long as the debt is not past-due. However, there is some implied control in all credit operations in that the debtor is interested in obtaining credit, and therefore, he must do those things in running his business which will satisfy the potential creditor that he is a good credit risk.

The use of trade credit meets the requirements of flexibility in that it can be repaid at any time as desired by the buyer. Normally, no penalty is suffered for advance payment. However, this source of funds is generally available only up to the amount of the purchases of goods and services. Therefore, the potential usage is limited.

UNSECURED COMMERCIAL BANK CREDIT

A primary purpose of commercial banks since their inception has been the aiding of commerce through the lending of money to finance commercial transactions—primarily the movement of goods through the channels of distribution. Commercial bank lending developed around a self-liquidating concept. This means that the usage to which the funds are put by the borrower will, through the normal operation of the borrower's business, produce the cash with which to repay the loan. An excellent example of this is the borrowing of money from a bank to purchase seasonal Christmas inventory.

The self-liquidating concept still influences much commercial bank lending policy today—particularly short-term unsecured lending. Commercial banks are generally not interested in providing a permanent source of funds under their short-term borrowing arrangements. These arrangements involve short-term maturities—the most common being 30, 60, or 90 days. A bank will often willingly renew its short-term notes once or twice, but it will only reluctantly renew them for periods in excess of one year.

The amount of funds available from banks varies with the credit of the borrower and with the lending bank. Banks have legal lending limits on the amounts they can lend each borrower. If a firm wants to borrow more than its bank's lending limit, it is possible for the firm to borrow from a number of different banks to overcome lending limit restrictions. Thus, in reality, the only limit on amount available from banks for short-term borrowing is the credit standing of the borrower.

In this section, only unsecured commercial bank credit will be discussed. Secured borrowing is covered in the next chapter. *Unsecured* means that there is no specific pledge of an asset in connection with the loan. Because of the short maturity involved in unsecured borrowing arrangements, commercial banks tend to have a very high payment priority under normal operating conditions.

Short-term lending by commercial banks has been one of the most important sources of funds throughout modern business history. However, changing economic conditions have altered the relative importance of this source to the firms using it and to the banks providing it. Prior to the First World War, short-term loans to business were the major investment of commercial banks. Table 21–2 indicates the importance of commercial loans to banks in the decade of the 1950's. While this aspect of bank lending increased in importance from the 1930's to the middle 1950's, it has leveled off at somewhat in excess of 20 per cent of total bank loans and investments.

Table 21–2. Total Loans and Investments and Commercial Loans Outstanding for All Commercial Banks

United States, 1950, 1955–1960

Year Ended December 31	Total Loans and Investments (In Millions of Dollars)	Commercial Loans (In Millions of Dollars)	Commercial Loans as a Per Cent of Total
1950	124,822	21,776	17.4
1955	160,881	33,245	20.7
1956	165,123	38,720	23.4
1957	170,068	40,526	23.7
1958	185,165	40,425	21.8
1959	190,270	40,174	21.1
1960	199,509	43,125	21.6

SOURCE: *Federal Reserve Bulletins.*

A large portion of the current notes and bonds payable (column 4 in Table 21–1) represents the amounts due commercial banks. The relative importance of current notes and bonds payable is indicated in this table. However, these figures are for fiscal year-end for corporations and this is the time when the corporation is most likely to have no bank borrowing. At certain times in the seasonal cycle of the firm, bank borrowing becomes a much more important source of funds than indicated by this table.

Line of Credit

The usual commercial bank loan is made on an unsecured note with a maturity ranging from 30 days to one year. Before obtaining a loan it is the usual custom for the bankers to go over the financial statements of the company and credit reports on the company, and after giving due consideration to the management, present status, and future prospects, to establish a *line of credit* for the company. This establishes a maximum amount which the company can borrow during a period of time without a credit recheck by the bank. The terms of the loan including the interest rate to be paid are included in this agreement. Since such loans are intended by the bank to be of a temporary nature, the bank likes to see all the loans paid off within a period of one year. Furthermore, it is preferred by the bank that this "cleanup" last for at least a 30-day period even though a new loan may be secured within a short period of time.

A line of credit has the advantage to the company of a known amount of obtainable credit. Even though it is not all needed at the time of the application, it can be taken up at any time during the year if the company needs the funds. Maturities on the notes can be established to allow repayment as desired. The line of credit saves credit checking each time a new amount is desired and gives the company a better basis for financial planning since it has an established known line of credit.

The line of credit agreement usually extends for a one-year period and may be renewed at the end of that time, or a new one with different provisions may be drawn up for the next year. Although the line of credit agreement does not force the bank to make the loan if conditions should materially change after it has been drawn up, the bank will usually abide by its terms, unless radical changes occur.

When a line of credit is not used, a business makes arrangements for a specific amount to be borrowed at a stated time with a definite maturity. The same type note as is used with a line of credit is signed by the borrower. If additional amounts are desired thereafter, the bank will make a completely new credit check in determining whether to lend these additional amounts to the borrower. Thus, the line of credit has substantial advantages to firms interested in varying the amount of bank loans outstanding during an annual period. Borrowing without a line of credit meets the requirements of those businesses borrowing for a specific purpose with no thought of additional use of bank credit during the year.

Cost

The cost of using short-term unsecured bank credit will vary with general economic conditions, the conditions of the specific business borrower, the size of the loan, the condition of the lending bank, and competitive rates of interest. The lowest cost would be the "prime" rate, which is the rate charged by leading New York banks to large borrowers of very high credit standing. This rate varies from time to time and has ranged from 3 to 5 per cent in recent years. Borrowers of smaller size or lower credit rating pay rates in excess of "prime," depending upon their particular conditions.

Table 21–3 gives annual average bank rates on short-term business loans by size of loan in 19 large cities in various years. It can be seen that, in every year, the rate was higher on smaller loans than on larger ones. In addition, it is interesting to note that the general trend of rates on all types of loans has been upward in recent years. However, the differential in rate between small and large loans has decreased during the period covered by the table.

Table 21–3. Annual Average Bank Rates on Short-Term Business Loans by Size of Loan, 19 Large Cities, 1945, 1950, and 1955–1960 (Per Cent Per Annum)

Year	All Loans	$1,000– $9,999	$10,000– $99,999	$100,000– $199,999	$200,000 and over
1945	2.2	4.3	3.2	2.3	2.0
1950	2.7	4.5	3.6	3.0	2.4
1955	3.7	5.0	4.4	4.0	3.5
1956	4.2	5.2	4.8	4.4	4.0
1957	4.6	5.5	5.1	4.8	4.5
1958	4.3	5.5	5.0	4.6	4.1
1959	5.0	5.8	5.5	5.2	4.9
1960	5.2	6.0	5.7	5.4	5.0

SOURCE: *Federal Reserve Bulletins.*

It is customary for a bank to "discount" the borrower's note. In other words, the bank will deduct the interest in advance from the principal amount of the loan, and credit the account of the borrower with the balance. Thus the effective rate paid by the borrower on the money that he actually gets to use will be higher than the rate of interest agreed upon. On a 180-day (6-month) loan, 6 per cent (annual rate) discounted is the equivalent to approximately 6.19 per cent since the borrower is paying $3.00 for the use of $97 instead of $100 for 6 months.

In the past, banks commonly required that the borrower maintain a minimum balance in his checking account of from 10 to 20 per cent of the principal amount of the loan. In such instances the effective rate of interest paid on the money that was actually available to the borrower was considerably in excess of the contract rate. If a 20 per cent balance were maintained on a 6-month, 6 per cent $100 loan, the borrower would be paying $3.00 interest but would receive the use of only $77. This would be an effective rate of 7.79 per cent. In recent years the practice has changed and many banks no longer require such minimum balances. But since banks usually require or expect that the borrower will maintain his checking account at that particular bank, certain balances will be maintained in order to meet the checks which are written in the ordinary course of business.

Risk, Control, and Flexibility

Short-term bank credit is normally considered a high-risk source of funds. The risk is high because of the short maturities which bring default if not paid as agreed. This is true of all short-term credit. In addition, bank credit is generally higher-risk than other short-term sources because banks are more careful in demanding compliance with agreements. Banks are trustees for other peoples' funds and are careful in the lending of these funds. Also, unlike the trade creditor who stands to gain from his relationship with the borrower through profit from sale of merchandise, commercial banks gain only in relation to the lending of funds. Commercial bank rates are low; therefore, only a very small amount of bad-debt loss can be absorbed by the banks. Also, commercial banks are supervised by federal and state agencies to insure prudent lending practices.

As a result, commercial banks are not likely to handle collection problems in the same manner as trade creditors, sending another bill or notice when payment is missed; nor are they likely to wait 30 or 60 days before making stringent collection efforts. In fact, commercial banks tend to take collection action as soon as the maturity date is passed. These actions normally involve immediate and stringent collection efforts if the bank and the borrower cannot agree upon an extension. Thus, the financial manager of the borrowing firm must make specific arrangements to meet every maturity with commercial banks. In many cases, this may be done by obtaining an extension from the bank but that would be strictly at the bank's option. A wise financial manager will not sign a note at a bank unless he has very clearly in mind the source of the funds for the repayment of the note at due date.

When the bank has some doubts about the ability of the company to repay the loan in the future, it may require certain contractual agreements which, in effect, control the activity of the borrower. One of these agreements may be the requiring of a pledge of specific assets. This will be discussed in the next chapter. Other types of control might include a requirement of the maintenance of certain financial statement ratios or the establishment of a maximum limit on salaries paid to officers or dividends paid to shareholders. Sometimes officers of the company are required to sign or indorse notes personally as a protection to the bank.

For good credit risks, however, banks generally exert very little control through contractual agreements. The major control occurs through the business's efforts to maintain a sufficient credit rating to enable it to borrow on an unsecured basis from the bank. As long as the business continues to meet the bank's credit rating standards, there is little likelihood that the bank would attempt to exert control measures.

Bank credit is highly flexible in usage. For a firm with a good credit rating, it is available on relatively short notice and in rather substantial amounts. Notes may be written to mature at times when funds are expected to be available. The interest paid is related only to the time that the notes are outstanding.

The substantial flexibility and low cost of bank credit relative to other sources of funds make this a very suitable source when repayment is certain. When repayment sources are not certain, the risk of utilizing short-term bank credit is so great as to make it normally undesirable.

Selecting a Bank

There are a variety of factors which the financial manager should consider in selecting a bank both for deposit and borrowing purposes. Generally, it would be desirable to carry checking accounts at the same bank where one borrows. There is no requirement that a borrower restrict himself to one bank. It would normally be desirable for a large business to deal with several different commercial banks.

In selecting a bank, one should look to its size and reputation. The bank should be large enough to handle normal loan expectations of the borrower. Lending policies are likely to vary among banks, so the borrower would be wise to deal with the bank whose lending policies come closest to meeting his requirements. It is generally more desirable for a business to deal with a bank in the locality of its operation than with one at a distance.

Sometimes a bank is chosen because of its convenience or because of certain personnel on its staff. In selecting a bank, services offered and the relative charges for these services are important. Lending rates for any one borrower may be different at different banks. Another factor to consider would be the ability to utilize correspondent banks of this bank. Most commercial banks maintain working arrangements with other banks in central cities for purposes of performing services that the individual bank could not do alone. The major factor, however, in selecting a bank is to choose one which will meet the business's borrowing needs.

COMMERCIAL PAPER HOUSES

Commercial paper is short-term unsecured notes of businesses. These notes are negotiable and carry a fixed maturity date. *Commercial paper houses* are middlemen who buy notes (commercial paper) from relatively large corporations and resell them to investors—primarily commercial banks. Commercial paper may be sold directly to the public (without the use of commercial paper houses) by the issuer, but this is done only when very large issues are involved. This technique has been utilized primarily by finance companies. Other types of businesses raising funds through the issuance of commercial paper generally use commercial paper houses.

Commercial paper houses actually buy the notes and resell them to investors. They do not indorse the notes, hence they are not liable in event the notes are not paid by the maker. From a practical standpoint, however, the houses, in order to stay in business, handle only notes of high quality issued by well-known corporations. Companies that use this means of obtaining capital are usually large or medium-sized.

Operations

The notes are made in even denominations such as $2,500, $5,000, $10,000, etc. The denominations may go as high as $100,000, or even higher. The total amount of the issue is usually greater than $100,000, and often runs into the millions. The notes usually have a maturity of 3, 4, or 6 months. They are made payable to the order of the borrower since it is not known at the time of issue who the creditor will be. They are signed and then indorsed by the borrower and are secured only by the credit of the borrower. In other words, they are not secured by a pledge of any property, and only the general credit of the issuing corporation is behind them.

These notes, which are referred to as "prime commercial paper," do not bear interest. They are sold at a discount to the commercial paper house. In addition, the commercial paper house receives a flat fee (commonly called "commission") of from ⅛ to ¼ of 1 per cent of the face value of the notes. Expressed on an annual basis a fee of the latter amount would be equivalent to 1 per cent on a 3-month note, and ½ of 1 per cent on a 6-month note. The principal compensation of the commercial paper house consists of this fee rather than the discount.

The commercial paper house sells the notes to investors at a slightly lower rate of discount, in other words at a higher price, than it paid for them. The notes are of course retired at maturity at their face value, so that as time goes on, assuming interest rates remain about the same, the value of the notes increases. If the commercial paper house holds the notes for a time before selling them, part of the discount would accrue to its benefit. The return to the ultimate holder of the note consists of the difference between his purchase price and the maturity value of the note.

In some companies the commercial paper operation consists of only one department; the other departments of these companies carry on a broker-age and investment banking business.

The volume of business of the commercial paper houses declined from 1920 to 1931. After 1931, the volume remained relatively stable until 1950. Since 1950, volume has risen substantially but has still not attained 1920 proportions. Most other financing institutions have volumes today far exceeding previous peaks.

Advantages

The advantages of using the commercial paper houses as compared with ordinary bank loans as a source of short-term capital follow.

1. *Lower cost.* The cost of borrowing through the commercial paper house is usually lower than for ordinary bank loans, although the differ-ence is narrower than in the past.

2. *Can obtain more capital.* In borrowing from a bank on an ordinary loan the amount of the loan is necessarily limited since the particular bank's resources are limited, and furthermore, the amount that it can lend to any one firm is limited. Through the sale of commercial paper the company can borrow from a number of banks. With the increase in mergers of large banks and the development of branch banking, how-ever, larger loans from a particular bank are now possible. Furthermore, the practice has developed of having several banks join in a particular loan to a large company.

3. *Borrower gets the use of all the money.* Some commercial banks still require or expect the borrower to keep a minimum bank account of from 10 to 20 per cent of the amount of the loan. With commercial paper the borrower gets the use of the full amount of the money borrowed.

4. *Ease of borrowing.* If the alternative to commercial paper borrow-ing is getting individual loans from several banks, then each bank will have to make its investigation of the borrower. In the case of commercial paper the one commercial paper house makes the examination.

5. *Prestige increased.* The sale of commercial paper to a number of banks in different sections of the country adds to the prestige of the bor-rower. His credit becomes known and established in localities other than where his factories or places of business are located. This wider market enables the borrower to take advantage of lower interest rates in certain sections of the country, and to obtain loans from banks in areas where the slack season is on.

Disadvantages

Some possible disadvantages of using commercial paper houses rather than ordinary bank loans are as follows.

1. *Ordinary banking connections may be neglected.* If a business relies too much on commercial paper for its short-term working capital needs, it may find sometime in the future that the paper is not marketable, and that an ordinary bank loan is difficult or impossible to secure because of the failure in the past to establish relations with the bank. For this reason it may be advisable to obtain part of the funds from ordinary bank loans even if some commercial paper is being sold. On the other hand, most businesses are able to establish relationships with banks by means of checking accounts and use of other bank services.

2. *Paper must be paid off at maturity.* When commercial paper is sold, the relationship between the borrower and the lender is an impersonal one. When the notes become due, the holders will demand payment. If a company on the other hand is unable to pay off an ordinary bank loan the bank and borrower can talk it over with the result that a new loan may be made, or the maturity of the old one, or part of it, may be extended.

3. *Can be used only by relatively large and successful companies.* Commercial paper houses will buy the notes only of companies that are medium- or large-sized and are well-established and successful. And these are the type of companies that can secure their needs from other sources. The commercial paper houses and their customers are not interested in the notes of new, small, or unsuccessful companies. Perhaps this point is not really a criticism of commercial paper itself; certainly it is not a disadvantage from the viewpoint of the large successful company.

OTHER UNSECURED SOURCES

Many businesses secure short-term loans from officers, stockholders, and friends. If these people have funds in liquid form and the business has short-term need of funds, it might be desirable to take advantage of this source. It is difficult to make generalizations about the cost or risk of borrowing from officers, owners, and friends. These sources are sometimes utilized on a secured as well as an unsecured basis.

An increasingly important potential source of funds is suppliers. This source was discussed above in connection with spontaneous sources and trade credit, but it also may be available apart from transfer of goods and services. A supplier does not want to lose his good customers, and he may make loans under certain circumstances to aid a good customer. Conversely, customers may also be suppliers of funds in that they like to be certain of good suppliers, and they may go so far as to help their suppliers over short periods of time with various loan arrangements.

Other sources of funds available for unsecured short-term financing would include government, factors, and finance companies. Because these lenders normally require a pledge of security, they are discussed in the next chapter.

QUESTIONS

1. Explain the relationship between permanent needs and permanent financing and the relationship between temporary needs and temporary financing.
2. What are examples of temporary needs?
3. What factors affect the decision on selecting the source of short-term financing?
4. What is meant by spontaneous sources of funds? Give some major examples of spontaneous sources.
5. What is meant by "trade credit"? Is it an important source of working capital to companies in the United States?
6. Indicate specifically why cash discounts are usually large when figured on an annual percentage basis.
7. Should a buying company show "Cash Discounts Taken" as an income item, or "Cash Discounts Not Taken" as an expense item? Explain.
8. If a company does not charge interest on credit sales, should it sell to cash customers at a lower price? Explain.
9. Describe the line of credit arrangement with commercial banks.
10. What is meant by the prime rate? Ascertain the current prime rate.
11. What does it mean when a bank discounts a loan? What does discounting do to the cost?
12. What is the effect of a compensating or minimum balance requirement in connection with a bank loan?
13. How would you go about selecting a specific bank for a business bank account?
14. Indicate the advantages and disadvantages to the borrower of selling notes through commercial paper houses.
15. How do commercial paper houses operate?

PROBLEMS

1. The balance sheet of the Randolph Co. on December 31, 19x2 was as follows:

Cash	$ 5,000	Accounts Payable	$ 20,000
Accounts Receivable—Net	40,000	Accruals	5,000
Inventory	60,000	Bank Loan Payable	25,000
Fixed Assets—Net	45,000	Mortgage Payable	25,000
		Equity	75,000
		Total Liabilities and Net	
Total Assets	$150,000	Worth	$150,000

Which items and how much of each might be considered permanent capital needs for this company? How much does the company have in permanent financing sources? What is the total of the current assets? What is the total of the current liabilities?

2. Assume that the Randolph Co. is a retailer of toys and that the above statement was as of November 30, 19x2. What needs would you consider temporary? How would you expect this company's balance sheet position to be different in the Spring of 19x3? Is this the time of year that you would expect to find a bank loan on the company's books?

3. The Plush Co. needs $20,000 for a 90-day period of time. In contacting the two local banks concerning a potential loan, Mr. White, treasurer of the Plush Co., found the following terms available: a 6 per cent discounted unsecured promissory note; a 5 per cent discounted unsecured promissory note with a requirement of a 20 per cent compensating balance. What is the effective rate of interest in each of these proposals? Which one would you select?

4. Determine the effective rate involved in passing the discount date and paying on the net date under the following terms: (a) 2/10; net/30. (b) 1/10; net/190. (c) 5/30; net/360. (d) 2/10; net/70. (e) net 180.

5. Make up a table, listing in the left-hand column spontaneous sources, suppliers, commercial banks, and commercial paper houses. Head the next five columns with the terms *Risk, Cost, Control, Flexibility, Availability.* Now fill in the spaces in the table with a statement appropriate for each source listed.

SELECTED READINGS

BECKHART, B. H. *Business Loans of American Commercial Banks.* New York: The Ronald Press Co., 1959.

DAVIS, RICHARD G., and GUTTENTAG, JACK M. "Are Compensating Balance Requirements Irrational?" *Journal of Finance,* March, 1962, pp. 121–26.

GOLDSMITH, RAYMOND W. *Financial Intermediaries in the American Economy Since 1900.* New York: National Bureau of Economic Research, Inc., 1958.

JACOBY, N. H., and SAULNIER, R. J. *Business Finance and Banking.* New York: National Bureau of Economic Research, Inc., 1947.

KATOMA, GEORGE. *Business Looks at Banks.* Ann Arbor: University of Michigan Press, 1957.

LIVINGSTON, H. J. *Management Policies in the American Banks.* New York: Harper & Row, Publishers, 1956. Chapters 2 and 3.

RICHTER, E. F. *How to Choose Your Banker Wisely.* Management Aids for Small Business, Annual No. 2. Washington, D. C.: U. S. Government Printing Office, 1956.

ROBINSON, R. I. *The Management of Bank Funds,* 2d ed. New York: McGraw-Hill Book Co., Inc., 1962.

22

Secured Current Financing

Although business borrowers in general, and many lenders would prefer to deal on an unsecured basis, a large portion of business loans made by commercial banks is secured, as is an even larger portion of loans made by certain other specialized financing institutions. A special study indicated that two-thirds of all business loans outstanding at federal reserve system member banks, and one-half of their total amount, were secured or indorsed.[1]

Credit is *secured* when something other than the debtor's general promise to pay is offered to the creditor in a credit transaction. Most commonly, the security pledged is some specific asset, in addition to the general promise to pay. Any asset of a business firm for which title could be transferred is a possible pledge in connection with secured credit. The other major type of security is the offering of someone else's promise to pay, in addition to that of the debtor. Normally in business borrowing, this latter form of security is used only for loans to very small businesses.

Reasons for Use

The reason for the use of security is primarily the reduction of the risk incurred by the lender. There is the obvious advantage for the lender that should the borrower default, the lender would have the right, prior to other creditors, to certain specific assets. This advantage, however, has meaning only in the event of default on the part of the borrower. Most lenders do not lend to firms when default seems a reasonable probability.

Lenders who require a pledge of some type receive advantages over and above the claims of other creditors. Security is normally required

[1] *Federal Reserve Bulletin*, September, 1959, p. 1114.

523

by the lender in cases where the borrower's credit standing is somewhat less than ideal. By requiring security, the lender places certain controls over the borrower. For example, when an asset is pledged to a lender, the borrower is prevented from using this specific asset to secure funds from some other lender. In addition, the borrower is unable to dispose of the pledged asset unless he repays the lender or at least obtains the lender's approval for this action. By requiring security, the lender can be more certain that the management of the borrowing firm will stay within certain boundaries in incurring other debt and disposing of assets.

Sometimes security is used to enable the lender to grant loans beyond his unsecured lending limit. Bank requirements generally allow larger loans to single borrowers when security of certain types is offered. In addition, security may be used when the borrower does not wish to give information regarding his operation. If the security is highly liquid and is a suitable pledge (such as marketable government securities), a lender will generally require little additional information on the financial status of the borrower.

From the borrower's point of view, security should normally be offered only when the lender requires it. The borrower gains little by offering security, other than the obtaining of specific funds. The offering of security restricts the borrower's actions regarding security pledged. It also affects his credit rating for additional borrowing. As a result, business financial managers tend to offer security only when it is demanded by the lender. This, however, occurs in a great many cases, particularly for small businesses.

In terms of future flexibility for management, it might be more desirable to pay a slightly higher rate of interest and obtain unsecured financing, but this is not usually possible. Generally, poor risks are asked to offer security, and there is no evidence to indicate that lower rates are obtained by the pledge of security of some kind. One study found that, for a particular period, the average rate on all unsecured loans of commercial banks was 4.5 per cent and the average on all secured loans of the same banks was 5.2 per cent.[2] Thus, the alternatives for the financial manager are usually either to agree to offer security to the lender or not to obtain the loan; rather than to agree to offer security to obtain a lower interest rate.

TYPES OF COLLATERAL

What constitutes good and suitable collateral for a secured loan from the viewpoint of the lender may not necessarily meet with the approval of the borrower. Thus, the collateral offered is generally a result of a

[2] *Federal Reserve Bulletin,* November, 1959, p. 1121.

compromise between the two diverse interests. In many cases, the lender demands a certain type of collateral as a condition of making the loan; in other cases, the borrower may have only one type of collateral available. From the lender's point of view, collateral is ideal if it is highly marketable and will have no substantial change in value. Marketable government securities rank high in this category. Other types of securities listed on organized exchanges would also be high in marketability. Fixed assets are generally very low in marketability; inventory is somewhat higher on the list.

The collateral pledged would have to have an element of durability—a life far in excess of the length of the loan. Its value must be sufficiently stable to enable the lender to dispose of the property without loss in the event of foreclosure. Thus, a lender may lend only 50 per cent on security with variable value but may go as high as 70, 80, or 90 per cent on security for which market value is much more stable.

In addition, the lender needs to be certain that the collateral pledged is not disposed of without his knowledge and approval. Thus, safeguarding techniques must be set up when the security pledged is inventory or equipment. The process of recording of mortgages tends to assure the lender of safety of title to real estate security. Similar protection must be devised for the lender in the event of a pledge of accounts receivable. Marketable securities may actually be placed in the lender's possession so that he is certain they are not sold without his knowledge.

From the above discussion, it is apparent that highly marketable, stable securities make the most desirable pledge from the lender's point of view. Real estate has the advantage of title protection but the potential disadvantage of substantial change in value. Accounts receivable and inventory may be subject to less change in value, but title protection becomes more difficult.

In offering security, the borrower takes quite a different point of view from the lender. By pledging an asset he is basically restricting his future actions relative to that asset. Thus, it would appear desirable for the borrower to pledge only items which he had no intention of liquidating during the life of the loan. The best example of these would be real estate. A borrower should only pledge inventory and receivables if a procedure is agreed upon to allow sale of the inventory and collection of the receivables. Marketable securities which the borrower does not intend to sell make an ideal pledge.

The borrower has to take into account the cost of the protection devices required by the lender on a pledge of security. The cost of a system protecting the lender on a loan made against receivables and inventory is much higher than the cost of a loan made against real estate or securities.

Accounts Receivable

Accounts receivable are becoming an increasingly important security behind short-term loans. Although the bulk of the accounts receivable financing is done by finance companies, factors, and commercial credit companies, an increasing portion is being handled by commercial banks. Most of these bank loans are made on the *non-notification* plan. That is, the person or firm that owes the account is not notified that it has been pledged as security for a loan. In the past particularly, and this still applies in many lines of business, persons or firms owing accounts interpret it as a sign of drastic financial weakness if the holder of the account pledges it as security for a loan. Furthermore, these persons owing the accounts would usually prefer to deal with the original party to the account.

In pledging receivables, the borrower will commonly make a formal agreement with the lender covering all the terms and conditions of the loan that is to be secured by the accounts receivable. Included in this will be the maximum percentage which will be lent on the accounts. This amount ordinarily varies between 65 and 90 per cent, with 75 to 80 being common. When the borrower needs money, he will prepare a list of the accounts to be assigned and will then execute a note to the lender for the amount of the loan. The lender will usually mark on the borrowing company's ledger that the particular accounts have been assigned. Some states require that this be done in order that the assignment be valid. Before drawing up the agreement, the lender will have taken into consideration the credit standing of both the company borrowing the money and the ones whose accounts are pledged, the size and age of the accounts, etc.

With an ordinary loan of this kind, the firm owing the account is not notified that it is pledged; thus it will make payments on the account directly to the immediate party to the account and the latter will turn his money over to the lender. If checks are given, they may be indorsed directly to the lender.

Since the borrower must sign a note in favor of the lender for the amount of the loan, if the accounts are not paid the borrower will be liable to the lender. If the borrower is unable to pay, and no other arrangement is worked out with the lender, the latter can as assignee of the account take whatever action the borrower could have taken against the parties owing the accounts.

Revolving Credit Arrangements. A revolving credit arrangement enables the borrower to substitute new accounts receivable for those collected. As long as he has pledged suitable receivables to some amount in excess of the loan (generally one-third more), the borrower does not need to make payments on the loan as specific receivables are collected. Instead, he merely substitutes a new receivable for the old one which has been paid. Under these arrangements, it is common for the borrower to take back pledged receivables which run beyond some stated time such as 60 days. He has to substitute new, acceptable receivables for these or make a payment to the lender.

Discounting Notes and Drafts. In some lines of business, such as the fur and jewelry trade, notes given by the buyer are often discounted by the seller with a lender. In this way the seller gets his money out of the goods immediately by paying the lender a discount or interest charge to hold the note until its maturity. The note will be indorsed by the seller, and thus both the buyer and seller can be held liable on the instrument. This is sometimes called "two-name" paper for this reason. Banks hesitate to do much business of this kind because in many instances a note is given by the buyer only after the account is past-due.

"Bills of exchange," "drafts," and "trade acceptances" may also be discounted by a lender. The seller draws a *bill of exchange*, or as it is more commonly called, a *draft* on the buyer for payment of goods on a debt due. The seller may draw this draft payable to himself. After signed acceptance by the buyer, the seller, not wishing to hold the draft until its maturity, indorses the draft and sells it to the bank at a certain discount.

Drafts that arise in connection with the purchase of goods, are accepted at the time of the sale, and have a maturity in conformity with the original terms of sale are called *trade acceptances*. Such a draft has a higher standing in banking circles than those given for overdue accounts or purposes other than the purchase of goods. Despite efforts of bankers and credit men to encourage the use of trade acceptances, they are not commonly used. Competition and custom cause businessmen to continue to use the open-book account.

Inventory

Table 22–1 indicates that inventory as collateral for bank loans is not nearly as common as receivables or fixed assets. The reason is that the arrangements necessary to protect the lender usually are very costly when inventory is pledged. Except where handling procedures are automatic, such as for shipment of merchandise, inventory financing is normally resorted to only as a last measure.

Chattel mortgages on inventory are rarely used as security for loans since the particular company will be constantly selling the inventory, and the legal difficulties involved in obtaining clear title under a chattel mortgage each time an item of inventory is sold would be too great. When inventory serves as security for a loan, the documents commonly used as collateral are bills of lading, trust receipts, warehouse receipts, and factors' liens.

Table 22–1. Type of Security of Member Bank Loans to Business, October 5, 1955

Type of Security	All Loans		Less Than One Year Maturity		More Than One Year Maturity	
	Number (In Thousands)	Amount (In Millions)	Number (In Thousands)	Amount (In Millions)	Number (In Thousands)	Amount (In Millions)
All loans	1,185	$30,805	820	$20,348	365	$10,457
Unsecured	386	15,105	347	10,839	39	4,266
Secured	799	15,700	473	9,510	326	6,190
Indorsement or comaker	186	2,755	153	2,266	33	489
Assignment of claims	53	2,813	43	1,758	10	1,055
Inventory	47	1,448	44	1,363	3	85
Equipment	218	2,194	78	646	140	1,548
Plant & real estate	164	3,592	43	1,255	121	2,337
U. S. Government securities	8	182	8	162	*	20
Other bonds	3	165	3	126	*	39
Stocks	39	1,002	37	765	2	237
Life insurance & savings accounts .	54	447	50	395	4	52
Other	26	1,102	15	772	11	330

* Less than five hundred.
SOURCE: *Federal Reserve Bulletin,* September, 1959, p. 1119.

Bill of Lading. A *bill of lading* is a document issued by a railroad or other common carrier when goods are delivered for shipment. This document serves as a receipt for the goods, a documentary evidence of title, and a contract to deliver the goods. A *straight* bill of lading passes title only to the consignee (buyer), is not negotiable, and therefore cannot be used as collateral for a loan. The *order* bill of lading gives title to the consignee or to anyone else to whom he may indorse the bill of lading. This type of bill of lading is thus negotiable, and can be indorsed to a lender as security for a loan. It is necessary to surrender the bill of lading to the common carrier in order for the buyer to get the goods.

The seller draws a *draft* or, as it is sometimes called, a *bill of exchange* on the buyer for the amount due for the goods. This draft orders the buyer to pay the money to the seller or to some other payee designated by the seller. The seller turns the draft and bill of lading over to his bank. The latter sends these instruments to the buyer's bank. If the draft is payable on sight, the buyer's bank collects the amount of the draft from the buyer, gives him the bill of lading, and remits the money to the seller's bank. Thus the buyer must pay the draft before he receives the bill of lading from the bank. Without the bill of lading, he cannot obtain the merchandise from the carrier. If it is a *time* draft, the "acceptance" of the buyer on the draft is obtained before he can get the bill of lading to claim the merchandise. The draft then comes back to the seller's bank. If the seller wants his money out of the draft before its maturity, the bank will discount it. That is, the bank will advance the seller the money after it has deducted the appropriate amount of interest. When the draft is payable to the seller, the latter will, of course, have to indorse it before the bank will give him the money.

Trust Receipts. *Trust receipts* for staple commodities and durable consumers' goods, such as automobiles, radios, televisions, refrigerators, and stoves, which are commonly sold to consumers on the installment plan, are often used as security for loans. This device is used in the following manner.

The buyer arranges with the bank for a loan sufficient in amount to pay for the particular merchandise. The buyer then orders the merchandise from the manufacturer and instructs him to draw a draft on the particular bank for the amount of the invoice, and to send this together with the bill of lading to the bank. Before releasing the bill of lading to the buyer, the bank will make him execute trust receipts in favor of the bank for the goods. The trust receipt specifies that the bank is the legal owner of the property and that the borrower will hold such property, or the proceeds from the sale of such property, in trust for the benefit of the bank. When the articles are sold the proceeds are used to repay the bank loan, and the particular trust receipts are canceled.

Warehouse Receipts. *Warehouse receipts* are used as security in about the same manner as trust receipts; in fact they may be used along with them. When the buyer gets the goods, if he stores them in a public warehouse he receives warehouse receipts. The latter are then turned over to the lender and the trust receipts are canceled. Reduced to its simplest definition, a warehouse receipt is a receipt for goods which are stored in a public warehouse. Such warehouses must be licensed and bonded. The receipts are made out in the form prescribed by the Uniform Warehouse Receipts Act, which also prescribes uniform procedures to be followed and rights of the parties to the instrument.

A warehouse receipt may be either negotiable or non-negotiable. In the case of the *negotiable* receipt the goods may be delivered to the designated person, or, if he has endorsed the receipt to someone else, to whoever is designated by the indorsement. If made out in favor of the purchaser of the goods the receipt by proper indorsement can be passed on to the lender to serve as security for a loan. When the *non-negotiable* warehouse receipt is used, the stored goods can be delivered only to the person designated in the receipt. If the buyer is designated, then a lender would not accept the receipt as security for a loan. But if the receipt is made out directly to the lender it can be used as collateral for a loan. In fact the non-negotiable form (made out to the bank or finance company) is more frequently used since the warehouse will release goods if the lender requests it by mail without the necessity of sending in the receipts each time some of the goods are to be released. When the negotiable form is used, the warehouse will require that the receipt be sent in each time any of the goods are to be released. Since the receipt through an indorsement may call for delivery of the goods to the bearer, there is danger of theft or loss when the lender parts with possession of the instrument.

Since independent public warehouses are not always near the place of business of the borrower, considerable time, expense, and trouble may be entailed in storing the goods. In recent years the practice of *field warehousing* has evolved as a practical means of financing, with inventory as security. Under this arrangement a designated part of the borrower's property is set aside and leased for a nominal rent to a field warehousing company. Appropriate signs must be posted indicating that the goods and space are under the control of the warehousing company. The company will put a designated custodian, properly bonded, in charge of the warehouse. Only the custodian may issue the receiving records from which the regional office of the warehousing company makes out the warehouse receipts, and no one else may release the goods on orders signed by the holders of the warehouse receipts. In short, the arrangement is designed to create an independent warehouse on the premises of the borrower.

Factors' Lien. The *factors' lien* is a document which assigns *all* of the firm's inventory to the financial institution to serve as collateral for the loan. This includes raw materials, work in process, and finished goods. This arrangement merely gives a particular creditor a preference over other creditors with respect to claims on inventory in the event of default. It does not prevent the borrower from using the inventory in the normal course of his business or from selling the finished goods inventory. Thus, this arrangement allows for frequent change in the quantity and type of goods pledged. The use of this device generally requires some kind of public notice to other creditors and is allowed only in states which have specific legislation providing for it.

Securities

Loans are often made to individuals with stock or bonds as collateral security. Banks commonly lend to investment bankers and security dealers on such security, but such loans are not ordinarily made to other types of businesses. If a company has marketable securities on hand it would normally liquidate them instead of securing a loan. In some instances, however, the company may have only a temporary need for the cash and would want to hold on to the securities as a more or less permanent investment. Or, the securities may represent investments made in subsidiary companies which are being held for control purposes. A loan secured by the securities may be preferred over their sale because the market value of the particular collateral may be relatively low at that time. In these cases, businesses may use loans secured by such collateral.

Securities which are listed on one of the leading exchanges, such as the New York Stock Exchange or the American Stock Exchange, are preferred by lenders since their market values are known constantly, and they can be liquidated in a matter of minutes if the loan is not repaid. Listing is particularly important when the security is a stock. Bankers, of course, will ordinarily accept only negotiable securities as collateral for a loan and will lend only a portion of the market value of the securities. The securities will have to be indorsed or they will have to be assigned to the bank by the completion of a separate assignment form.

Fixed Assets

Some businesses, particularly small concerns, find it necessary to mortgage their real estate or equipment as security for a loan. Real estate, however, is rarely used as security by large companies for the purpose of securing short-term funds. Small companies, or concerns with poor credit ratings, may find it necessary to pledge real property even for short-term needs because they are unable to obtain an unsecured loan and have no securities to pledge. This real property, must, of course, be free of other encumbrances.

The use of fixed assets for longer-term loans was discussed in Chapter 8. Table 22–1 indicates that almost $2 billion of fixed asset secured loans with short-term maturities were outstanding at commercial banks. Because of legal mortgage-recording processes and the stationary aspects of real estate, the lender needs to take less elaborate precautions to assure his claim when the pledged asset is real estate than when other kinds of business assets are offered as security. However, because of the specialized nature of such assets and their questionable market value, the amount of the loan secured by fixed assets is generally relatively small compared to the value of the asset.

Bankers' Acceptances

Bankers' acceptances are used almost exclusively in foreign rather than in domestic trade. The buyer of goods makes arrangements with his bank to "accept" by signature certain drafts drawn on the bank by the seller of the goods. The bank furnishes the buyer with a "letter of credit" indicating its agreement to accept the drafts up to a stated amount for specified merchandise, and this letter of credit is sent to the seller. Upon sale of the goods the seller draws the draft and sends it through an agent or other bank to the buyer's bank for acceptance. The bill of lading will commonly be attached to the draft. After the "accepted" draft has been returned to the seller, the latter may discount it at his bank or sell it in the open market. In the meantime the buyer will have made an arrangement with his bank to furnish the money needed to meet the draft at its maturity.

The buyer pays his bank a fee for accepting the draft, but it should be noted that this fee is only a commission for the bank's putting its credit behind the draft. The buyer presumably will have the money at the bank when the draft becomes due. Whoever buys the draft from the seller is the one who immediately furnishes the cash. The seller, of course, will have to pay a discount when he sells the draft, but since it has been accepted by a bank rather than an ordinary business, the discount rate will be relatively low.

Other Asset Pledges

As indicated in Table 22–1, approximately a half-million dollars in loans secured by life insurance policies or savings accounts were outstanding at commercial banks. The cash surrender value of a life insurance policy makes excellent collateral from both the lender's and the borrower's point of view. Many small businesses with buy-and-sell arrangements among executives have substantial officers' life insurance with fair amounts of equity which can be pledged as collateral for loans.

Other asset pledges would include patents, copyrights, government contracts, etc.

Comakers or Indorsers

The signature of a comaker or indorser as security on a note is somewhat different from the pledge of a specific asset. Instead of giving the lender a claim against assets, it allows the lender to attempt to collect on a general credit basis from the comaker if the original borrower is in default. In effect, the indorser says that if the original borrower does not pay, he (the indorser) will. Indorsed or cosigned notes to business are rather common as security for commercial bank loans, as indicated in Table 22–1.

Among security loans to business, they are exceeded only by loans on factories and real estate and by assignment of claims.

Cosigners or comakers are most commonly used in loans to small businesses where the individual owner or owners sign personally on a note for the business. However, cosigners are also used for a sale of merchandise; a supplier may sign on a buyer's note or a customer may cosign on a supplier's note. Generally, when a lender requires a cosigner on a business note, it is an indication that the lender questions the ability of the borrower to repay the note. Since cosignature usually indicates poor credit rating, it would appear desirable for any business firm to be very selective in deciding to cosign a note for any other business or individual.

SOURCES OF SECURED CURRENT FINANCING

Some of the sources discussed in Chapter 21 also make loans to businesses on a secured basis. This is particularly true of commercial banks. Some lenders, however, lend entirely or almost entirely on a secured basis. These include sales finance companies and factors. Since the commercial bank is particularly important both as a secured lender and as an unsecured lender it will be discussed here along with finance companies and factors.

Secured Bank Financing

Most of the discussion under types of collateral applies to the acceptance of collateral by commercial banks in lending to business enterprises. Banks have always been the major lenders on marketable securities and have more recently become important lenders on the pledge of accounts receivable and inventory as well.

In the past, banks hesitated to lend on the security of accounts receivable because they felt the risk was too great and the cost too high compared with other types of loans which they were able to make. Furthermore, the laws of some of the states, many of which have since been changed, would not permit the assignment of the accounts unless the persons owing the accounts were notified of their assignment. Due to the decline in ordinary bank loans in the 1930's, banks began giving more attention to lending on the security of accounts receivable. Furthermore, the lending business became more profitable when the banks were able to collect some additional charges for this type of arrangement. Table 22–1 indicates that almost $3 billion of loans secured by assignment of claims were outstanding at commercial banks.

The importance of other types of security as the bases for commercial bank lending is also indicated in Table 22–1. The pledging of fixed assets is particularly important in the longer-term maturities. Indorsement or the use of cosigners is among the most important types of security required for short-term bank loans. Techniques of pledging and the advantages and disadvantages of pledging various types of assets, as discussed earlier in this chapter, are applicable to banks as secured lenders.

Finance Companies

The nature of finance companies is commonly not understood because there are a number of different types of these companies, and they perform various functions. The situation is further aggravated by the fact that finance companies performing the same functions are referred to by different titles. The type of companies which we will briefly discuss here engages in one or both of the following types of business: (1) making loans on the security of accounts receivable, and (2) buying or lending on the security of installment paper. These companies may finance one or more of the following: manufacturers, wholesalers, retailers, and consumers.

In addition to being called *finance companies,* the following names are applied to these companies: *accounts receivable companies, automobile finance companies, commercial credit companies, discount companies, installment finance companies,* and *sales finance companies.* One type of "finance company" which is not included under this title is the *personal finance company* or, as it is sometimes called, the *small loan company,* or *consumer finance company,* which makes installment loans to consumers for purposes not directly connected with the purchase of goods.

Loans on Accounts Receivable. Borrowing money with the security of accounts receivable was discussed under bank loans, and the material there stated, which has equal application to loans obtained from finance companies, will not be repeated. Both the *non-notification* and the *notification* plans are used by finance companies, although the non-notification plan is more common. When the notification plan is used, payments on the accounts are made directly to the finance company which obtains power of attorney to indorse any checks, drafts, or notes made payable to the assignor of the accounts. The interest is computed daily and varies from 10 to 20 per cent, expressed on an annual basis. Where bank loans can be secured on the accounts, the rate of interest is usually lower than that charged by the finance company.

Discounting Installment Paper. The principal business of the finance company is discounting wholesale and retail installment paper, particularly in the automobile industry. For automobile and other similar paper, the finance companies lend to both the dealer and the consumer. The dealer puts up cash of from 10 to 20 per cent of the wholesale price of the cars and borrows the balance on his promissory note from the finance company. The manufacturer is instructed to draw a sight draft on the finance company for the balance due and to attach the bill of lading. In some instances the bill of sale is made out to the finance company. The finance company then releases the cars to the dealer under trust receipts. As the dealer sells the cars he remits to the finance company the amount due and the trust receipt is canceled.

When a purchaser buys a car he may make a down-payment of some amount, such as 33⅓ per cent, and may borrow the balance from the finance company. This is done when the purchaser enters into a contract with the dealer or finance company and signs a promissory note for the balance due. In some instances the purchaser will sign as many notes as there are monthly payments due. The payments may run over a period of up to 48 months. The car is either sold under a conditional sales contract, or under a chattel mortgage, depending upon which is favored in the particular state (laws relating to these two types of install-ment sales vary among the states). The contract and notes are sold by the dealer to the finance company, and payment on the notes is made by the purchaser directly to the finance company.

The dealer usually indorses the note "without recourse," which means that he will not be personally liable on the note if the maker is unable to pay it. Usually, however, the dealer makes an agreement that he will take over the car for resale after the finance company has repossessed it and pay the balance due the finance company. The dealer is in some in-stances required by the finance company to indorse the notes "with re-course" in the case of second-hand cars that are sold to poor credit risks. By the use of this unqualified indorsement the dealer can be held per-sonally liable on the note by the finance company if the purchaser of the car does not pay it.

Finance companies receive part of their funds from the same sources as other corporations, that is, through the sale of common and preferred stock and debenture bonds. But half or more of their funds are usually obtained from ordinary bank loans and through the sale of commercial paper. In the past, commercial banks have hesitated to lend directly on installment paper, but they have been willing to lend indirectly on it by lending to the finance companies which hold the paper. In recent years, however, banks have become interested in automobile paper particularly, and are now actively promoting this kind of business.

The principal business of the finance company is the buying of in-stallment paper and to a lesser extent, lending on the security of accounts receivable. In addition to these activities, many of them now also lend on inventories secured by trust and warehouse receipts, and on the security of equipment owned or purchased by a company.

Factors

We have already discussed the financing of accounts receivable by means of pledging them as security for a loan from a bank or a finance company. Another method of getting money from the accounts is to sell them to a factor. A *factor* is an individual or company that buys accounts outright. The process of buying accounts is called *factoring*. Factors often handle the entire credit process including approval, billing, and collection. Factors will lend against a pledge of receivables as well as purchase them outright.

Factoring started in the textile trade and is still used primarily in that field, although it has now spread to other industries; it is used both by manufacturers and wholesalers. When factoring first started it was carried on by a manufacturer's selling agent who was located in the large trading centers and who acted as the exclusive selling agent for a particular mill. The entire output of the mill was taken by the agent who undertook the actual selling, granting of credit, and collection of the accounts. The agent was in a better position to judge the credit risks and obtain financing aid than was the manufacturer.

At the present time the factor usually confines his activities to the financial rather than the selling end of the business. The manufacturer does the selling of the goods and then sells his accounts outright to the factor. Thus, the factor does the collecting, and any loss for uncollected accounts falls upon him. In other words, after the accounts are sold to the factor the manufacturer is no longer responsible. Customers of the manufacturer are notified to make payments on the accounts directly to the factor.

Since the factor stands to lose on poor accounts, when the manufacturer first makes an arrangement for the factoring of his accounts, the factor will go over the accounts carefully and purchase only those that appear to him to be good. Thereafter the factor will have to pass on the credit standing of all prospective purchasers before the sales can be made, and all accounts arising from sales will be purchased by him. The agreement between the manufacturer and the factor is usually for a one-year period, but in practice the arrangement continues until one of the parties wishes to withdraw.

For buying the accounts receivable the factor receives two different types of compensation: (1) a commission or fee, and (2) interest. The commission or fee is dependent upon the degree of risk involved and the collection costs, and is usually 1 or 2 per cent (the range is from $\frac{1}{4}$ to 4 per cent) of the face value of the accounts purchased the previous month. This is either paid in cash or deducted from the amount due from the factor for that particular month. This charge is intended to cover the risk which is assumed by the factor. The factor also receives interest, usually discounted at the annual rate of 6 per cent, on the amount of the accounts for the period equivalent to the credit period. If the seller of the accounts leaves part of the proceeds with the factor, the latter may pay him interest at the annual rate of from 2 to 6 per cent. This, of course, would offset at least part of the interest charged the seller.

Perhaps an example would make this discussion more understandable to the reader. Suppose that accounts with a face value of $10,000 are sold to the factor on June 1, for a commission of 2 per cent and interest at an annual rate of 6 per cent, with the terms of sale being 60 days. The factor would deduct interest of $100 (6 per cent interest on $10,000 for 60 days) and remit the seller the balance of $9,900 (less any fees due from the amounts purchased the previous month). The following month the fee of $200 (2 per cent of $10,000—note that the 2 per cent is not figured on an annual basis) will be paid to the factor. This is assuming that the seller leaves no funds with the factor.

Advantages. Following are the advantages of selling accounts to factors as compared to utilizing one of the other sources of short-term credit.

1. *May be the only source of funds available.* In some instances a firm can sell its accounts when it would be unable to borrow against them from a bank or finance company.

2. *No credits and collections department needed.* When accounts are sold to a factor it eliminates the need for and expense of a credits and collections department.

3. *Cost of credit definite and known.* When a firm sells on credit it never knows exactly what credit losses will be encountered as sales are being made. The costs of selling the accounts to the factor are known, and bad-debt losses will fall on the factor.

4. *Larger sales possible.* Selling the accounts permits larger inventories and possibly larger sales. When a company carries its own accounts, it may hesitate to sell a large amount to any particular customer because of the risk of losses. A factor may not hesitate to buy the accounts because they will probably constitute only a small percentage of the total accounts which he holds. Hence, larger individual sales may be made when it is known that the accounts are to be sold.

5. *Use of entire amount.* In comparison with a bank loan on the accounts, assuming a minimum balance to be maintained, sale of the accounts will give the company the use of the entire amount.

6. *Current working capital ratio may be improved.* A company may be able to improve its current working capital ratio by selling the accounts and using the proceeds to pay off bank loans or accounts payable. The following example will illustrate the point. Let us assume that the following is an abbreviated section of the current items on the company's balance sheet before sale of the accounts:

Before Sale

Accounts Receivable	$100,000	Accounts Payable	$100,000
Other Current Assets	300,000	Other Current Liabilities ..	100,000
Total	$400,000	Total	$200,000

If the accounts receivable are sold to the factor and the proceeds are used to pay off the accounts payable (factor's charges ignored), the same section of the balance sheet will be as follows:

After Sale

Current Assets	$300,000	Current Liabilities	$100,000

Before the sale of the accounts the company had a current ratio of only 2-to-1 ($400,000 compared to $200,000), but after the sale and payment of the accounts the current ratio was improved to 3-to-1 ($300,000 compared with $100,000). The improved current ratio may enable the company to obtain more goods on credit, or to obtain more in bank loans than before the sale, or a bank loan may be possible now although it was impossible before.

Disadvantages. The various ways of securing capital always have disadvantages as well as advantages when compared with other sources. The following are the principal disadvantages of selling accounts to factors:

1. *Relatively high cost.* The cost of obtaining short-term capital through the sale of accounts to factors is a relatively expensive way of obtaining working capital. We can illustrate this using the figures in the hypothetical situation stated above where the fee was 2 per cent, and the interest 6 per cent a year, with a credit period of 60 days. The fee of $200 added to the interest of $100 gives a total charge of $300. A charge of this amount is equivalent to a total charge of 18 per cent a year. ($300 for 2 months is equivalent to $1,800 for a year. A charge of the latter amount for the use of $10,000 would be at the annual rate of 18 per cent. The actual charge would be a little higher than this since the interest is discounted.)

It is recognized, however, that the total charge for factoring should not be compared with the interest charged on loans. The factoring charge includes an equivalent for the risk of bad debts and the billing and collection costs.

2. *Possibility of smaller sales.* Since the factor has to pass upon the credit standing of all prospective buyers, he may not permit sales to be made to certain firms, or he may limit the amount that may be sold to a particular firm.

3. *Unfavorable customer reaction.* Generally speaking, customers prefer to deal with the seller rather than with a factor. Furthermore, sale of accounts is sometimes taken to mean that the seller is in desperate financial condition. However, where factoring is common, as in the textile trade, most of the customers will probably understand and look upon it as standard practice.

Government

Beginning with the depression of the 1930's, government has also become a supplier of short- and intermediate-term funds to business. Short-term financing by government includes progress payments and advance payments to suppliers of goods and services for the government. In certain cases, this could be a very substantial source of funds. It is similar to the deferred credits discussed under spontaneous sources of credit.

In recent years, the Small Business Administration (SBA) has been an important source of loans to small business. While a majority of SBA loans are for more than a one-year period, the SBA is also a potential source of short-term financing. SBA loans are generally available only if bank credit is not available to the firm. They are normally much less flexible, involve more time for application and processing, and require more "red tape." SBA financing usually demands a pledge of specific assets.

Consumer Finance Companies

Very small business units needing amounts less than $1,000 or $2,000 may sometimes utilize consumer finance companies; the business owner would make the arrangements. The owner signs the note for the business and, in effect, offers his personal credit as collateral to obtain funds for his business. This type of financing is high-cost for most businesses and would generally be used only as a last resort and only by small businesses.

QUESTIONS

1. What is the advantage of unsecured, rather than secured, borrowing to the borrower?
2. What is the advantage to the lender of obtaining some pledge of collateral in connection with a business loan?
3. Discuss the importance of the various types of collateral in secured short-term borrowing.

4. What factors make for good collateral from a lender's point of view?
5. What factors make for good collateral from a borrower's point of view?
6. What is a revolving credit arrangement in connection with accounts receivable?
7. Discuss the procedure for borrowing with a pledge of a trade acceptance.
8. When a loan is made at a commercial bank on the collateral of accounts receivable, does the person owing the account know that it is pledged? Explain.
9. Explain the procedure involved in securing a loan on the collateral of warehouse receipts.
10. Indicate what is meant by field warehousing and the reason for its origin and use.
11. Distinguish between a straight and an order bill of lading. Can both be used as collateral for a loan? Explain.
12. What is the advantage to the lender and to the borrower of a pledge of marketable securities as compared to other types of security?
13. Explain what bankers' acceptances are and how they are used.
14. What different types of companies are known as finance companies? What different names are sometimes used for companies which handle automobile installment paper?
15. Indicate how the factor aids in working capital financing.

PROBLEMS

1. The balance sheet of the XYZ Co. on December 31, 19x1 was as follows:

Cash	$ 10,000	Accounts Payable	$ 25,000
Accounts Receivable	80,000	Bank Loan Payable	80,000
Inventory	120,000	Finance Company Note	60,000
Net Fixed Assets	90,000	Loan From Officer	100,000
		Equity	35,000
		Total Liabilities and Net	
Total Assets	$300,000	Worth	$300,000

On January 1st both the bank and finance company notes became due and the company was unable to pay. In liquidation, the following amounts were received:

Cash	$10,000	Inventory	$50,000
Accounts Receivable	$50,000	Fixed Assets	$10,000

The inventory was pledged to secure the bank loan and accounts receivable were pledged to the finance company. (a) How much will each class of creditor receive in dissolution? (b) What would the finance company have received had it not had a pledge of accounts receivable? (c) What would the bank have received had it not had a pledge of inventory? (Assume the accounts were pledged to the finance company.) (d) If you were the bank lending officer at the time of the loan, what requirement would you have made of the officers of the company?

2. The ABC Co. needs $50,000 for seasonal expansion of inventory and receivables. Sale of inventory and collection of receivables should provide the funds for repayment within a 6-month period. The following alternatives are

available: (a) Borrow from the bank at 6 per cent discounted on a 90-day note renewable for an additional 90 days. (b) Wait for 180 days to pay suppliers for the inventory received (terms of purchase are 2/10; net/30). (c) Pledge accounts receivable to a factor at the rate of 1 per cent per month on the amount outstanding with the loan value of the amounts pledged at 75 per cent of face.

Discuss the advantages and disadvantages of each of these techniques. Be sure to include cost, risk, and control. What other possible sources would you recommend?

3. What would you think of the ABC Co. (in Problem 2) putting the seasonal inventory purchased in a public warehouse and financing through pledging of warehouse receipts at the bank? Would field warehousing meet their needs? Could they utilize a bill of lading in financing?

4. The New Development Co. purchased some office furniture from the Easy Terms Furniture Co. The sale price was $120, but the furniture company agreed that this amount could be paid in six equal monthly installments, beginning one month after the date of sale. The company said that the New Development Co. would have to pay a carrying charge of 6 per cent, or $7.20, which amount was to be paid along with the final installment. What was the real rate charged by the furniture company? Would all of this carrying charge represent interest? Explain.

5. What is wrong with the financial structure of the XYZ Co. (Problem 1) as of December 31, 19x1? What recommended financial adjustments would you suggest? Could this firm be a profitable company?

SELECTED READINGS

BECKHART, B. H. *Business Loans of American Commercial Banks.* New York: The Ronald Press Co., 1959.

FOULKE, ROY A. *The Story of the Factor.* New York: Dun & Bradstreet, Inc., 1953.

GOLDSMITH, RAYMOND W. *Financial Intermediaries in the American Economy Since 1900.* New York: National Bureau of Economic Research, Inc., 1958.

JACOBY, N. H., and SAULNIER, R. J. *Accounts Receivable Financing.* New York: National Bureau of Economic Research, Inc., 1943.

———. *Business Finance and Banking.* New York: National Bureau of Economic Research, Inc., 1947.

———. *Financing Inventory on Field Warehouse Receipts.* New York: National Bureau of Economic Research, Inc., 1944.

LIVINGSTON, H. J. *Management Policies in American Banks.* New York: Harper & Row, Publishers, 1956. Chapters 2 and 3.

PHELPS, C. W. *Accounts Receivable Financing as a Method of Business Finance.* Baltimore: Commercial Credit Co., 1957.

———. *The Role of Factoring in Modern Business Finance.* Baltimore: Commercial Finance Co., 1956.

———. *The Role of the Sales Finance Companies in the American Economy.* Baltimore: Commercial Finance Co., 1952.

SEIDMAN, W. S. *Accounts Receivable and Inventory Financing.* Ann Arbor: Masterco Press, 1957.

SWEETSER, A. G. *Financing Goods.* Newton Highlands, Mass.: Albert G. Sweetser, 1957.

WARD, WILBERT, and HARFIELD, HENRY. *Bank Credits and Acceptances,* 4th ed. New York: The Ronald Press Co., 1958.

23

Intermediate Financing

To define intermediate-term financing is difficult because of the inexactness of the definition of long-term financing. Obviously, intermediate-term financing is between short-term and long-term; this means that it utilizes sources of funds which mature after one year but before 5, 10, 15, or 20 years. For purposes of discussion, a 10-year cut-off period will be used in this chapter. Thus, intermediate-term sources are those which will mature at some time between one and ten years from issue date.

Most intermediate-term sources are not readily renewable. As a result, intermediate-term sources include primarily those which the financial manager intends to repay on or before maturity by liquidation of assets or by refinancing through some entirely different source. Thus, maturity becomes very important in intermediate-term financing. It is not safe to rely upon obtaining some completely new source at the time the intermediate-term financing matures. As a result, only in recent years has American business turned to intermediate-term financing for substantial amounts of funds. In previous years, the average business would consider only temporary or permanent financing.

It is apparent that intermediate-term financing is ideal for financing those business needs which are temporary in nature but have a longer duration than seasonal needs; that is, those which would last for a period of one to ten years. The increasing use of intermediate-term financing in recent years has, however, been related to the financing of permanent rather than temporary needs. This means that the financial manager is committing himself to obtaining some other source of permanent financing to meet the maturity of the intermediate-term arrangement.

The common intention in this type of financing is to refinance through retained earnings accumulated during the period of the intermediate-term loan, and because of this intention, most intermediate-term financing involves some type of periodic payment. This arrangement is very workable since retained earnings accumulate over a period of time and are available for partial repayment of the intermediate-term source as they are retained. The intermediate-term sources discussed in this chapter all involve some type of periodic repayment of principal. The three major types of intermediate-term financing to be discussed are term loans, installment financing of equipment or buildings, and leasing.

From the lender's point of view, earning power becomes a much more important consideration in intermediate-term financing than in temporary financing. Liquidation of assets is not generally planned as a method of meeting the debtor's obligations in intermediate-term financing. The company's intention is usually to repay through retained earnings; thus its earning power must be sufficient to justify the use of this source.

Reasons for Use

Following the basic principle of financial management that temporary needs should be temporarily financed and permanent needs permanently financed, it would seem that intermediate needs should be intermediately financed. In practice, however, the typical business unit has very few intermediate needs; that is, it has a relatively low investment in assets that will be of a longer duration than seasonal needs but cannot be considered permanent.

It is true that buildings and equipment wear out eventually and that, therefore, the expected life of a specific piece of equipment or a building is actually only intermediate. However, since the general intention of business management is to replace the specific equipment or building at the end of its useful life, the financial requirement for fixed assets is a permanent one.

While certain firms experience temporary cyclical setbacks and therefore require less working capital during these periods of time, it is the general plan of these firms to regain or even to exceed their old level of sales; their minimum working capital requirements are therefore permanent.

The best example of intermediate requirements is financing of assets required for government projects during wartime. During the Second World War a large amount of expansion was undertaken with the knowledge that this expansion would no longer be needed at the end of the war. Thus, this investment in assets was basically intermediate. In peacetime, however, this situation rarely occurs. Most firms intend to continue in the foreseeable future to provide their present services at their current rate or at a greater rate. Therefore, except for seasonal requirements, the asset requirements of a firm are mainly permanent.

Because of the lack of truly intermediate needs, intermediate-term financing was not very popular prior to the Second World War. The greatly expanded use of intermediate financing since the war has been for the financing of permanent needs. Because these needs are permanent, liquidation of the assets acquired does not provide the funds for payment at maturity. As mentioned above, financial managers will then depend on the retained earnings of the firm to meet the maturity requirements. This might be considered *preinvestment* of future earnings.

The emphasis on this preinvestment of future earnings has come about because of the current federal tax structure, the increased stability of earnings, and an increasing recognition by lenders of the importance of earnings. A firm which is reasonably certain of some minimum amount of earnings in a coming 5-year period can finance its permanent requirements through an agreement that requires payment within 5 years, because its expected level of earnings will be more than sufficient to meet the payment requirements. The widespread use of intermediate-term financing in recent years has evolved from this type of situation.

Advantages and Disadvantages

The major advantage of preinvesting earnings is that intermediate financing generally costs less than long-term or permanent financing would cost for the period of time until retained earnings are available. Intermediate financing can be arranged to meet the specific term requirement of the borrowers, and it provides for some level of flexibility in repayment. While some control features are common in most intermediate-term financing arrangements, the level of control is often less than would be required from some permanent source of financing. For a permanent need, intermediate-term financing is less risky than temporary or short-term financing.

The major disadvantage of the use of intermediate-term financing for permanent needs is that the borrower must realize the expected level of earnings in the future in order to meet the agreed-upon maturities. Thus, there is some inherent risk in this approach to financing permanent needs. As long as the borrower has a reasonable expectation of future earnings, a sufficiently stable record of past earnings, and allows a margin of safety of expected earnings over repayment requirements, he can reasonably finance intermediate-term loans without assuming undue risk.

All of the general advantages of reinvesting of earnings (discussed in Chapter 25) apply to preinvestment of earnings. Because of the emphasis on reinvestment of earnings, preinvestment has gained increasing importance. The decision of financial management becomes one of weighing the increased risk of financing a permanent need with an intermediate source and planning on retained earnings to meet maturities against the cost and control advantages to be gained by taking this approach.

TERM LOANS

The *term loan* has become one of the most significant sources of intermediate-term financing in modern business. Much of the intermediate financing now used is in the form of term loans. The two leading sources of term loans are commercial banks and insurance companies. Both of these types of institutions became active in this field during the recovery from the depression of the 1930's.

Prior to 1930, commercial banks had operated primarily as sources of self-liquidating loans. While, in practice, many short-term bank loans were granted with the expectation of a whole series of renewals, the short-term maturity was still present. By making term arrangements which did not require short maturities, commercial banks made an important break with their prior practice. The major reason for their entry into this field was the reduction in short-term borrowing requirements of industry and the fact that banks had a surplus of funds to invest. A general realization of the suitable degree of safety and security offered by this type of lending was also an important factor.

During the same period, life insurance companies were having difficulty placing all of their available funds in the traditional long-term fixed-value investments. As a result, they were willing to move into the shorter-term maturities provided by term loans. With an acceptance by financial institutions of this type of financing and an increased desire on the part of business to preinvest earnings from the intermediate-term years in the future, the term loan became an ideal vehicle for financing, and is today an important technique for business finance.

Table 23–1 indicates that commercial banks which were members of the Federal Reserve System in October, 1957, had term loans outstanding in excess of $15 billion. (This figure does not include term loans of other

Table 23–1. Term Loans of Member Banks on Three Selected Dates, 1946, 1955, and 1957

Date	Term Loans Outstanding (In Millions)	Percentage Increase from Preceding Date	Term Loans as a Per Cent of Total Loans
November, 1946	$ 4,558	–	19.6
October, 1955	10,457	129.0	33.9
October, 1957	15,421	47.5	38.0

Source: *Federal Reserve Bulletin*, April, 1959.

financial institutions or of non-member banks.) These term loans constituted 38 per cent of all loans of these banks at that time. This table also indicates the growing importance of term loans in absolute amounts as well as in percentage of total loans.

The use of term loans varies rather substantially with the type of business. Table 23–2 gives an indication of usage by industry groups of term loans from Federal Reserve System member banks in October, 1957. Transportation and public utilities, and industrial products manufacturers were the larger users of member-bank term loans. Almost three-fourths of all loans of member banks to petroleum, coal, chemical, and rubber companies were term loans. Sales finance and various lines of trade are much smaller users of term loans from commercial banks.

Table 23–2. Amount of Term Loans of Member Banks, by Borrower Classification, October 16, 1957

Classification of Borrower	Millions of Dollars	Percentage Distribution	As a Per Cent of Total Loans
All Business	$15,421	100.0	38.0
Manufacturing & Mining			
Food, Liquor, & Tobacco	485	3.1	20.3
Textiles, Apparel, & Leather	314	2.0	18.6
Metals & Metal Products	1,905	12.4	34.5
Petroleum, Coal, Chemicals & Rubber ...	2,763	17.9	73.7
All Other	1,067	6.9	38.2
Trade			
Retail	1,387	9.0	30.2
Wholesale	600	3.9	20.1
Commodity Dealers	88	0.6	10.8
Other			
Sales Finance	266	1.7	8.6
Transportation & Other Public Utilities	2,839	18.4	68.1
Construction	596	3.9	30.1
Real Estate	1,307	8.5	43.9
Service	1,194	7.7	52.8
All Other	611	4.0	38.1

SOURCE: *Federal Reserve Bulletin*, April, 1959, p. 354.

Characteristics of Term Loans

The term loan has several distinguishing characteristics. First, it is of an intermediate-term length; that is, its maturity would be longer than one year but shorter than a time period which would be considered permanent. Second, a term loan provides for some type of periodic partial repayment of principal during the life of the loan. This installment payment feature is a substantial departure from normal short-term or long-term financing for business.

While maturities for term loans may run as high as 15 or 20 years, the great majority are for less than 10 years; for small businesses, most term loans have a final maturity of less than 5 years. However, in all cases, the stated maturity is for the final payment, not for the total payment of principal.

Installment arrangements vary substantially with specific contracts, but commonly the payment intervals would be monthly, quarterly, semiannually, or annually. In some cases, principal payments are not due during the first or second year of the contract but are due periodically thereafter. Often, payments during the early years are smaller than during the later years, or all payments are equal with the exception of the final payment which is substantially larger than the others. The timing of the payments should be established to coincide with the time in which the borrower will have cash available to make the payments. This requires careful planning when the term loan is initially negotiated; the timing and the amount of installment payments can be varied to meet the requirements of the specific situation.

In the normal term-loan arrangement, a note requiring installment payments is signed, or a series of notes, each with a different maturity, are signed at the time the loan is granted. The standard term-loan contract includes an acceleration clause which makes all installments due in the event of default in interest or in an installment of principal.

A pledge of some specific security is required more often for term loans than for short-term loans. Small businesses are more likely to be required to pledge assets than are large businesses. A study in 1955 indicated that 59.2 per cent of all term loans of Federal Reserve System member banks were secured. Over 90 per cent of all term loans to borrowers with assets of less than $1 million were secured, but only 22½ per cent of all term loans to borrowers in excess of $100 million were secured.[1]

All types of security have been used for collateral in term loans. The most common assets pledged are plant, real estate, or equipment. However, assignment of accounts receivable is also a common security for term loans. Inventory is a relatively uncommon type of collateral.

Protective Provisions

It is normal for the lender to include a number of "protective provisions" in the term-loan contract. Since the lender is committing his funds for longer than a seasonal period, he needs some assurance that the

[1] *Federal Reserve Bulletin*, April, 1959, p. 360.

general conditions under which the loan was made will not change during the life of the loan. The lender is obviously satisfied with the existing condition of the business at the time he makes the loan, or he would not make it; but he needs some protection against actions of management which might change these conditions before maturity occurs.

Major classes of protective provisions would include those which restrict the future use of credit by management, the disposal of assets, and the use of income, and those which are specifically related to the use of cash. Because of the importance of cash flow to meeting principal payments on term loans, the restrictions on cash tend to be the most universal.

A typical cash restriction would require the borrower to maintain a minimum current ratio throughout the life of the loan. Or, a certain dollar amount of net working capital may be required. The investment of cash in new fixed assets is often limited to some stated dollar amount unless approval of the lender is obtained for an increase in the amount. The firm is normally not allowed to redeem any of its outstanding stock, and restrictions are often placed on officers' salaries and on dividends.

To restrict the use of income, the most common protective provision would be one limiting the amount of dividend payments during the life of the loan. Dividends are often restricted to some stated dollar rate or to payment of amounts in excess of a minimum retained earnings account or minimum annual earnings.

Restrictions on management's power to dispose of assets might include the requirement that fixed assets over a certain dollar amount cannot be sold without prior approval of the lender. There may be a requirement for maintenance of a certain dollar amount in total assets. In addition, sufficient fire and theft insurance would have to be maintained on business assets.

A restriction that no assets could be pledged to others during the life of the loan would be an example of a protective provision restricting that agement in its future borrowing. The lender may also require a prohibition on the issuance of any additional fixed-debt securities during the life of the loan.

Other protective provisions of term-loan contracts could require that life insurance be maintained on major officers in an amount equal to the remaining principal payments on the loan. Almost all term-loan contracts include periodic reporting by the borrower to the lender. Some require audited reports by outside public accountants. Most contracts prohibit a substantial change in the operation of the business, such as a merger or consolidation.

Cost

The cost of term-loan financing varies with the size of the borrowing company and the amount of the loan. The normal procedure for determining the charge is to establish a rate such as 5 per cent or 6 per cent and charge that rate only on the unpaid principal balance. Interest would normally be due semiannually or at the time of periodic principal payments. In the few cases in which the interest is charged on the original balance rather than on the unpaid balance, the effective rate becomes much higher. The study of member-bank term loans referred to above (see Table 23–1) indicated that less than $1 billion of the $15 billion in term loans outstanding had the charge determined on the basis of the original balance. The average effective interest rate on these loans was 8.74 per cent. For the large majority of the loans in which the interest was figured on the remaining balance, the average effective rate was 4.52 per cent.[2]

Other Arrangements

Some term loans take the form of revolving credit. In this type of arrangement, loans may be made, paid off, and remade within the stated period of the loan (3, 5, or 10 years) as long as the total debt outstanding at any one time does not exceed the total commitment in the loan agreement. In these arrangements, the interest rate is often variable and will change as the prime rate or rediscount rate changes. Revolving credit arrangements offer substantial flexibility to the borrower.

Another type of intermediate-term financing is the standby arrangement. In this case, credit is set up at a bank, which the borrower may call upon as he sees fit. He may take it in whole or in part at any time within a given period of time. The borrower would normally pay a standby fee of a small amount (such as ½ of 1 per cent) for the use of this arrangement. In effect, he is paying an interest charge for money not borrowed but made available to him when he needs it.

Often, a term loan will have several lending participants. Where the credit is questionable or where the loan is too large for any one lender, a number of lenders may get together and each take a part of the term loan. Sometimes insurance companies participate with banks, or several banks or several insurance companies may participate in a term loan. It is also common for the federal Small Business Administration to participate with banks in granting term loans.

Term Loans from the Borrower's Point of View

Substitution of a term loan for short-term financing arrangements has several distinct advantages for the borrower. It substantially reduces the risk of meeting short-term maturities. Maturities in a term loan may be scheduled to coincide with the times in which funds are expected to be available for payment. The term loan may be a less costly arrangement in that there is not the constant need for renewal or refinancing of sources.

[2] *Federal Reserve Bulletin*, April, 1959, p. 360.

While the interest rate may be slightly higher than for short-term borrowing, it is generally less than for long-term borrowing. In addition to interest costs, however, costs of using a source of financing include the costs of obtaining it and these may be substantial for constantly renewed short-term financing. Long-term sources may also require substantial selling costs, registration costs, legal fees, etc.

Term loans can be designed to meet the specific needs of the borrower and therefore are highly flexible. This flexibility in the terms of the contract is very important in term loans. In addition, many term-loan arrangements provide for prepayment without any substantial penalty. It is often easier to negotiate term loans than long-term financing, and they can be obtained in smaller amounts than long-term loans. On the other hand, term loans often place a considerable number of control restrictions on the borrower. The borrower must be careful that his use of term loans does not significantly affect his short-term credit potential. He must also be reasonably certain of his repayment ability.

Sources of Term-Loan Financing

In certain cases customers will finance a supplier under a term-loan type of arrangement. More commonly, particularly in certain industries, suppliers will grant intermediate-term funds to customers who distribute their products, in order to insure themselves of good channels of distribution. The borrower repays the supplier through the earnings he makes from handling the supplier's products. The most important suppliers of term-loan financing, however, are still commercial banks, insurance companies, and government.

Commercial Banks. The above discussion has already treated term loans by commercial banks; they have been the major factor in the term-loan field for many years.

Insurance Companies. As contrasted to those of commercial banks, term loans made by insurance companies are often of longer maturity. However, insurance companies tend to require more restrictive provisions than do commercial banks, and insurance companies are not generally set up to make relatively small loans. As a result, most insurance company term loans are made to very large borrowers and are for large amounts. Insurance companies tend to do less unsecured term lending than do commercial banks.

Government Agencies. In recent years several government agencies have become sources of financing for many American corporations. These are discussed under intermediate financing because the term of the loans generally runs for more than one year, but for a period which would be considered less than long-term. The term loan is the common arrangement.

In an effort to aid business and pull the country out of the depression that was well under way, the federal government, in 1932, formed the Reconstruction Finance Corporation (RFC). The objectives of this corporation were "to provide emergency financing facilities for financial institutions, to aid in financing agriculture, commerce, and industry, and for other purposes."

The Small Business Administration (SBA) was set up in 1953 in place of the RFC, but it has neither the power nor the funds that were possessed by the RFC. As the title indicates, its loans are confined to small businesses and are designed to give aid where banks are unwilling or unable to provide needed intermediate financing. The SBA first attempts to get banks to grant the loans, or to have them grant a specific percentage of particular loans. Loans up to $250,000 may now be granted for a period of 10 years (in certain instances, 20 years) to businesses with less than 500 employees.

In recent years, the SBA has expanded its activities beyond financial assistance to small business. Today it offers government procurement assistance, disability loans under special programs, production and technical assistance, and management and research assistance. These are normally available without charge and in most cases are in the form of written publications.

Lending activities have also increased for the SBA in recent years. From its inception in 1953 through June, 1961, the SBA approved 25,351 loans for about $1.2 billion. Banks participated in over 60 per cent of all loans approved in 1960. In that year, slightly more than 50 per cent of all applications were approved. The major reason for turning down the other loans was "a lack of reasonable assurance of ability to repay the loans from earnings." The average amount of an SBA loan is $10,000 to $25,000. Approximately one-third of the loans are for the purpose of consolidation of obligations by the borrowers, another one-third are to increase working capital, and the remaining one-third are for the purchase of equipment and facilities. Retail trade has been the primary beneficiary of the Small Business Administration. Forty-seven per cent of all loans to 1961 were granted to retail establishments. Manufacturing was second in importance with 19 per cent, followed by service with 13 per cent, wholesale 10 per cent, construction 7 per cent, and all others 5 per cent.[3]

In 1958, Congress amended the Small Business Administration statutes by passing the Small Business Investment Act. The purpose of this Act is to stimulate and supplement the flow of private funds into channels of

[3] "Semi-Annual Report of the Small Business Administration" (Washington, D. C.: U. S. Government Printing Office, July, 1961).

equity capital and into long-term loans to small business. The primary purpose of using public funds is to stimulate the flow of private funds. Under this Act, the SBA licenses Small Business Investment Companies whose purpose is to make loans to and equity investments in small businesses. The SBA may lend up to $150,000 of the required $300,000 initial capital for each Small Business Investment Company (SBIC). In addition, the SBA may make additional loans for operating purposes up to 50 per cent of the combined capital and paid-in surplus of the borrowing SBIC. By restricting the amount of SBA (government) lending to SBIC's to an amount relative to the private investment in the SBIC, the investment of private funds in small business is stimulated. SBIC's are also given certain federal income tax advantages to stimulate investment in them by private interests.

From 1958 through June, 1961, 303 SBIC's were licensed. Of these, 298 companies remained operative in 1961 and had financing and loan situations totalling $78 million. The companies themselves had $240.5 million in capital at the end of June, 1961. Of this, $130.5 million was provided by public offerings after the SBIC's were established and $73.5 million came from initial capital. As of June, 1961, the Small Business Administration had bought $36.5 million in subordinated debentures in SBIC's. This is substantially below the amount to which it is tentatively committed.[4]

SBIC's either purchase stock or convertible debentures in small businesses or make long-term loans to these businesses. The long-term loans are substantially less important than the equity arrangements (convertible debentures). Ninety per cent of all the equity arrangements carry a cost to the small business of 9 per cent or less. The average cost to the small business of the long-term loans is substantially higher, with over 90 per cent of these loans being made at 13 per cent or less. The cost of equity arrangements is less because of the potential profit to be gained by conversion to common stock in the company and sale of this stock at a profit.

A large number of loan applications were outstanding on June 30, 1961, as were a large number (225) of license applications. While Small Business Investment Companies are a relatively new factor in the national economy, it is apparent that they could become an important financial institution in coming years.

INSTALLMENT FINANCING OF FIXED ASSETS

Installment financing of fixed assets fits into the intermediate-term category. Most installment purchase plans require final payment sometime after one year. For installment purchases of equipment, a maximum

[4] *Ibid.*

of 3, 4, or 5 years is common, although terms up to 10 years are possible. For installment purchases of land and buildings, maturities up to 10, 20, and 30 years may be common. Although installment purchases of buildings and real estate are commonly considered long-term, they may also be made with an intermediate-term arrangement, and since installment payments are planned for them, they logically fit into the intermediate category. While this discussion is concerned with installment financing of equipment, the same principles and procedures would apply to installment financing of buildings and real estate. Installment financing of railroad rolling stock was discussed in Chapter 8.

Installment financing of equipment for business is somewhat similar to consumer installment financing of automobiles and other durable goods. Equipment installment financing takes three general forms. First, the manufacturer of the equipment may sell it on installment terms to the purchaser. In this case, the manufacturer or distributor is directly financing the purchaser of the equipment. This is possible only if the manufacturers or distributors are well financed with available capital to carry accounts or notes receivable for a long period of time. Some manufacturers have set up their own financing subsidiaries, such as the General Electric Credit Corporation, to provide the funds for financing the sale of equipment by the parent company. Since this is not always the case, a second form of equipment financing is to borrow from a bank, with the equipment pledged as collateral for the loan used to pay off the manufacturer. In this case, the bank would be providing the purchaser of the equipment with capital to pay off the manufacturer. The third possibility is the sale or assignment of the account or note to a financial institution by the manufacturer. Under these circumstances, the financial institution is supplying the manufacturer with capital to carry his accounts or is actually carrying the accounts for him by purchasing them.

In all three of these arrangements, the loan is for the expressed purpose of financing the purchase of industrial or commercial equipment. The loan will require a down-payment of a sizable amount, under the philosophy that the purchaser should have sufficient equity in the equipment to make it financially desirable for him to continue payments. These down-payments commonly range from one-fifth to one-third, but may be as low as 10 per cent or as high as 50 per cent. The length of the payment period varies with the type of equipment, the needs of the purchaser, and the policies of the seller, but is normally limited by the years of use of the equipment and the possible obsolescence rate. The equipment financer should be fully repaid in advance of the full loss of the value of the equipment.

In keeping with the philosophy of repayment of intermediate-term sources from retained earnings and operating cash flow, equipment installment financing requires periodic payments. The planned source of funds for repayment is generally retained earnings and amounts retained from depreciation charges against the equipment.

Costs

Since the principal is amortized over the life of the loan, it makes a substantial difference whether the interest is charged on the original balance or on the remaining unpaid balance throughout the life of the loan. The more common procedure is to charge a rate on the original amount of the loan. Thus, if a firm purchases a piece of equipment for $10,000 and agrees to pay $3,000 down, the rate charged would normally be figured on a $7,000 balance. If the agreement were that the charge would be 6 per cent and that the total loan would be paid in two years, the interest charge would be $840 ($.06 \times \$7,000 \times 2$). This $840 would be added to the original $7,000 for a total of $7,840 to be paid in 24 equal monthly installments ($326.67 each). Since the original balance of $7,000 is outstanding only until the first payment is made and interest continues at the same rate throughout the life of the loan, the quoted rate of 6 per cent is highly misleading. The actual effective rate in this example is approximately 11.5 per cent.

A formula for determining the actual effective rate of interest in the case where installment payments are made is as follows:

$$r = \frac{2Ni}{P(n+1)}$$

in this formula, r equals the effective rate of interest, N equals the number of payments in a year, i equals the total dollar interest charge, P equals the original balance of the loan, and n equals the number of payments to be made. Note that N is the number of payments in a year regardless of the number of payments to be made. If payments are monthly, N is always 12; whereas n might be 6, 12, 24, etc. While this formula gives only an approximation, the result is close enough to the effective rate in most instances to suit the needs of the average businessman in attempting to determine relative costs.

In the above example,

$$r = \frac{2 \times 12 \times \$840}{\$7,000 \, (24+1)} = 11.52 \text{ per cent}$$

It is much more important to determine effective rate than to use quoted rate, in comparing costs of various types of financing. An effective interest cost of 11.5 per cent is a relatively high rate for a normal business to pay for the use of creditor funds. The same business may be able to finance through other sources at substantially lower average cost.

Since the cost of this type of financing is generally high, it is not normally recommended for a firm which has other sources of funds available for the time required. Should suppliers of equipment be willing to finance at a reasonable rate charged only on the declining unpaid balance, arrangements of this nature might be quite satisfactory compared to other alternatives. This type of financing is generally used by small businesses with a poor credit rating or with a limited number of alternate types of financing available.

Risk

Installment loans on equipment or buildings are almost always secured by the equipment or buildings being purchased. The collateral offered makes an important difference in determining the amount of the down-payment and the life of the financing agreement. The contract invariably offers repossession potential to the lender. Because of this, the borrower, or buyer, is risking the loss of use of the item purchased, in the event of default.

In almost all financial arrangements of this type, a note is also signed in which the buyer promises to pay the seller or financer a stated amount. These notes should be signed only when the buyer has certain knowledge of the source of funds necessary for repayment of the various installments as they come due. Conditional sale arrangements or chattel mortgages are common in equipment financing arrangements. The risk inherent in this type of financing relates to the stability of the cash flow and that portion of the cash flow which the buyer commits to the installment payments.

LEASING

If the firm leases assets instead of buying them, it does not need to finance these assets in the usual sense of the word. Thus, leasing in effect replaces other sources of funds which would be required were leasing not used.

Leased assets are not considered part of the financial position of the lessee only because of the accounting convention which emphasizes *ownership* in listing of assets. In reality, whether a building is owned or leased, it is the occupant (owner if owned, or lessee if leased) who has the use of this building as an operating asset. For financial planning purposes, therefore, leasing should be considered as a source of funds and as an alternative to other sources of funds such as borrowing, sale of stock, installment purchasing, etc. Sophisticated analysts of financial statements take into account the values of leased assets in studying assets, and the claims of lessors in studying liabilities.

Because a lease generally runs for an intermediate period of time, leasing is considered an intermediate-term source of financing. Leasing should not be considered a permanent source of funds because new arrangements must be made at the end of the lease, and because the lease requires, in effect, installment payments of principal. Of course a new lease may be signed at the expiration of the existing lease, but this is not necessarily a certain event, and if a new asset is not available on a lease arrangement, the firm must find some other source of funds to finance the purchase of the required asset. Leased assets are generally permanent requirements even though the financing arrangement is intermediate in form.

Leasing as an Alternative to Ownership of Assets

Although it has been general practice for businesses to own assets, throughout the history of modern business there have been many examples of leasing not only buildings but, in recent years, certain types of equipment as well. In the past, certain corporations (United Shoe Machinery Company and International Business Machines Corporation, for example) would not sell their products but would only lease them.

Many business firms have found it advantageous to lease certain fixed assets rather than to own them, while other firms in the same industries have found the reverse situation to be better. Thus, every problem has to be tackled independently to determine the advantages of owning and the advantages of leasing and decide which of these two approaches to take. The final decision would vary with the individual business firm, its overall cost of funds, the type of lease arrangements available, general business conditions, obsolescence factors, etc. Certain factors to be considered in these decisions can be discussed in general terms.

There are some situations where leasing is the only method available. This applies particularly in the case of certain desired locations which are only for rent—not for sale. Many retail establishments rent their locations because they are unable to purchase them even if they desire to do so. Another obvious use of a lease is for some asset which the firm wants for only a very short period of time. Ownership becomes obvious as an alternative to leasing in situations where a lease arrangement is not available for the asset desired.

In situations where both lease and ownership possibilities are available, the ultimate decision on which approach to take should be made on the basis of an analysis of cost, risk, control, and flexibility.

Characteristics of Leases

Because there is such a variety of lease arrangements available, it is difficult to generalize about leases as a source of funds; however, every lease involves some type of maturity date. For land and buildings, leases may run as long as 99 years (or even longer), although for commercial property in general, 20 or 30 years appears to be more common. In the leasing of equipment and other movable fixed assets, the more normal lease period may be from as little as one year to 5, 10, or 15 years. In addition to an initial leasing period, many lease arrangements provide for a renewal of the lease at the option of the lessee. Sometimes lease agreements offer a purchase option to the lessee.

All lease arrangements provide for some type of rental payments. The common requirement is for the rent to remain constant over the entire initial term of the lease. Rentals are usually paid on a monthly basis but may be paid quarterly, semiannually, or annually. Sometimes arrangements are worked out whereby rental payments are higher in the early period and lower in the later period. Most lease arrangements calling for renewals at the option of the lessee generally provide for a lower rental after the renewal than during the initial term of the lease.

The rental would have to be sufficient to cover all of the costs of the lessor including his depreciation costs and return on his investment. If the lessor pays maintenance, taxes, and insurance, these amounts also would have to be covered by the rental payments. It is important to note that costs to the lessor of such things as insurance, maintenance, and taxes may be different from the cost of these same items to the lessee.

Most lease arrangements involve restrictions on the use of the leased asset. Substantial alterations usually cannot be made without the approval of the lessor. Sometimes the lessee is restricted as to the geographical area in which he can use the leased asset. In other agreements, he may be required to utilize certain types of maintenance and maintenance procedures in connection with the asset. Most lease agreements make some arrangement for recovery by the lessor in the event that the lessee defaults on one or more of his rental payments.

Most leases make no reference to obsolescence. Should the fixed asset become obsolete after the life of the lease, the lessee has no obligation to purchase or absorb the obsolescence loss. On the other hand, should the fixed asset become obsolete during the life of the lease, the lessee is often required to continue to make his payments throughout the life of the lease. Some equipment leasing arrangements provide that the lease may be canceled by the lessee in the event of substantial obsolescence.

Advantages to the Lessee

Flexibility is the major potential advantage to the lessee. It is often possible for him to arrange the leasing of an asset for the specific time period necessary to meet his requirements, which means that he is not thereafter saddled with ownership and ownership problems. If he wants to substitute some other asset for the one involved in the lease, he need only wait until the lease expires, and does not have to make some arrangements for sale or disposal of an owned asset.

Another important advantage to the lessee is the complete financing potential through leasing. If the asset were purchased on installments, a down-payment would be required. If it were purchased outright with general funds of the business unit, a portion of these funds would obviously have to be from equity sources. Creditors usually do not provide 100 per cent of any operation. In a lease arrangement, however, the lessor (also a creditor, in effect) finances the total funds necessary to provide the asset.

Leasing of assets rather than financing them through loans or installment purchase generally leads to an improved balance sheet position. This is the case only if the person studying the balance sheet does not take the leases into account on both the asset and liability sides of the balance sheet. There is some evidence to indicate that in recent years more attention has been paid to the effect of leasing on the financial position of a business firm. However, standard accounting practice does not list the leased asset among the assets nor does it list the potential liability as a liability. As a result, since the leased asset is 100 per cent financed by creditor funds, to show neither the asset nor the liability portrays a better financial position than would be the case if both were shown. Because the financial position looks better, it may be possible for the business firm to obtain additional creditor sources of funds that would not be available if the asset were purchased and financed and appeared on the balance sheet.

Another possible advantage to the lessee is the lower total cost. This would occur where the rental payments are less than the total costs which the lessee would have incurred had he owned the specific asset. Lower costs are sometimes possible because the leasing company often has a lower cost of capital than the lessee. One of the major potential savings for the leasing company is in an improved tax status. The total rent payment is allowed as a deduction for federal income tax purposes (in the absence of a purchase agreement) whereas, if the asset were owned, only the depreciation expense (and interest on borrowed funds) would be deductible. In this way, the lessee is in effect able to depreciate land as well as buildings through rental payments while normal accounting procedures would allow no depreciation on the land. Furthermore, buildings may in effect be depreciated faster through the lease. The cost advantage does not accrue in all cases and so a specific study must be made to determine whether there is a cost advantage to leasing rather than owning a specific asset.

Disadvantages to the Tenant

The major disadvantage of leasing is the lack of control over the asset by the lessee. At the conclusion of the term of the lease, the lessee may be dispossessed and unable to replace the asset he had been using. Even during the life of the lease, the lessee is restricted in his potential usage of the specific asset. As long as the lease is operative, the lessee must continue to make his payments and has no right to sell the asset or to otherwise dispose of it.

A second major disadvantage of leasing is the risk involved. The entire rental payment becomes similar to a fixed charge on bonds. If the firm defaults, it is liable not only for the missed payments but for any losses the lessor would suffer throughout the remaining life of the lease. The lessor is, therefore, definitely a creditor of the lessee.

Sale and Leaseback

A special form of leasing is *sale and leaseback.* Under this arrangement, a business sells an asset which it owns (usually land or buildings) to another company which in turn leases it back to the original owner. This is, of course, only possible where the business has an asset of potential interest to a leasing company. Many industrial and commercial firms have had large amounts of money tied up in buildings and land. By the sale and leaseback arrangement, they have released large portions of funds for other uses. The sale and leaseback is basically no different from an original lease except that the company already has fixed assets and, therefore, the sale and leaseback provides cash rather than fixed assets. This cash may be used to repay financing sources or to acquire other assets.

The purchaser of the property is usually either a life insurance company or a non-profit organization, such as an educational institution or a charitable foundation. The rentals represent a higher return on the investment than could be obtained through the purchase of bonds. Furthermore, life insurance companies pay income taxes under a special formula which results in lower taxes than ordinary business corporations, and non-profit organizations pay no income taxes when they do not own the business outright.

In some of the older sales and leases, a clause was inserted giving the lessee the option to buy the property upon termination of the lease. The courts, however, have held that where such a clause is present, the original sale by the lessee was not a bona fide one, and that only the amount of the rental payments that would be equivalent to depreciation on the buildings could be charged for income tax purposes. In recent years there have been several instances where life insurance companies have entered into agreements with industrial concerns to build the plants themselves and lease them to the companies. For example, the New York Life Insurance Company built and leased properties costing $10,000,000 to the Continental Can Company.

QUESTIONS

1. Define intermediate-term financing.
2. What is meant by preinvestment of earnings?
3. Why has intermediate-term financing become more popular in recent years?
4. What are the major advantages and disadvantages of using intermediate-term financing?
5. Describe the term loan.
6. What are protective provisions? Discuss the major classes of protective provisions in term loans.
7. What is the standby arrangement?
8. What is meant by participation in a term loan?
9. What are the advantages and disadvantages of term loans from the lender's point of view?
10. What are the advantages and disadvantages of term loans from the borrower's point of view?
11. Describe a Small Business Investment Company.
12. Discuss installment financing of fixed assets.
13. Discuss leasing as an alternative to ownership of assets.
14. What are the possible advantages and disadvantages of leasing to the lessee?
15. Describe the sale and leaseback arrangement.

PROBLEMS

1. The Peerless Manufacturing Co. is about to launch an expansion program which will call for approximately $5,000,000 in funds for additional property and working capital needs. The board of directors has been considering an issue of common stock to obtain the money. The company has been paying a 6 per cent dividend on its $100 par value stock. The stock has been selling slightly in excess of its par value in the market for some time. Corporate income tax rates can be assumed to be 50 per cent.

Mr. Williams, who is the president of the Standard Life Insurance Co., is a friend of Mr. Henry, the chairman of the board of the Peerless Co., and suggested to Mr. Henry that he and his company consider the possibility of selling several of the plants to the insurance company in order to obtain the necessary amount of money. The plants could then be leased back for a long period of years.

Mr. Williams explained that all the rental payments could be deducted as an expense by the Peerless Co. before taxes, whereas none of the dividends on the stock could be deducted. He also called attention to the fact that as long as the Peerless Co. owned the plants, depreciation on only the buildings, and not the land, could be deducted for tax purposes. Mr. Williams explained that the insurance company would be content with 3½ per cent net return on its money if it could recover its investment within a 20-year period. The following proposal was worked out by the two executives and placed before the boards of directors of both companies:

1. Two plants to be sold to the insurance company for $5,000,000.
2. The Peerless Co. to pay all taxes, insurance, and maintenance on the plants.
3. The plants be leased to the Peerless Co. for a 20-year period for $337,500 a year.
4. An option be granted to the Peerless Co. to renew the lease for three additional 20-year periods at the nominal rent of $50,000 a year.

(a) Explain how the amount of the rental payments for the first 20 years would meet the objectives of the insurance company. (b) As a director of the Peerless Co. would you vote for the proposal to sell the plants and lease them back instead of issuing the additional common stock? Explain reasons for your answer and present figures to support it.

2. The Black and Green Co. is considering the purchase of a $20,000 drill press. It is anticipated that this press will have a 10-year life and there seems little chance for substantial loss through obsolescence. The manufacturer of the press has offered the following terms to the company. If the Black and Green Co. can make a 30 per cent down-payment, the manufacturer will deliver the equipment upon promise of monthly payments thereafter of $653.33 for 24 months. The manufacturer claims that this is at the rate of 6 per cent per year on the original amount borrowed. What is the effective rate of interest being charged? Would you take advantage of this arrangement?

3. In the above example, what would you think of leasing the drill press rather than purchasing it? What factors should be taken into consideration? What provisions would you expect to find in the lease agreement?

4. What would you think of a $5 million 6 per cent term loan for 5 years for the Peerless Manufacturing Co. described in Problem 1?

5. The Rubright Manufacturing Co. produces small electronic components. The company is only 8 years old and has grown very rapidly since its inception. Sales last year were in excess of $1 million and sales this year are $1.8 million. The management projects sales of $2.5 million next year and total sales in excess of $5 million for 5 years hence. The net profit margin has been averaging approximately 10 per cent after taxes and management expects to maintain this profit margin in the future. The company currently needs $3 million for plant expansion, additional equipment, and added working capital. What would you think of financing this on an intermediate-term basis for the next 5 years? Justify your answer.

SELECTED READINGS

Choate, Albert. "Security Purchases of Small Business Investment Companies," *Journal of Finance*, May, 1961, pp. 304–308.

Cohen, Albert H. *Long Term Leases*. Ann Arbor: University of Michigan Press, 1954.

Eiteman, W. J., and Davisson, C. M. *The Lease as a Financing and Selling Device*. Ann Arbor: Bureau of Business Research, University of Michigan, 1951.

Lewis, H. B. *Installment Financing of Industrial Equipment*. Industrial Marketing Series No. 17. New York: American Management Association.

JACOBY, N. H. and SAULNIER, R. J. *Term Lending to Business.* New York: National Bureau of Economic Research, 1942.

————. *Financing Equipment for Commercial and Industrial Enterprise.* New York: National Bureau of Economic Research, 1943.

PROCHNOW, H. B. *Term Loans and Theories of Liquidity.* Englewood Cliffs, N. J.: Prentice-Hall, Inc., 1949.

SAULNIER, R. J., HALCROW, H. G., and JACOBY, N. H. *Federal Lending and Loan Insurance.* Princeton: Princeton University Press, 1958.

SMALL BUSINESS ADMINISTRATION. Semi-Annual Reports. Washington, D. C.: U. S. Government Printing Office, all numbers.

24

Depreciation Policies

Depreciation is a decline or loss in value. It can be caused by a variety of factors including physical deterioration, market action, and obsolescence. In business and accounting circles, the term is more commonly restricted to loss in value due to some kind of physical deterioration. The term *depreciation* is commonly applied only to physical assets of a non-depletable nature. Depletion is defined later in the chapter.

Practically all the physical property used by a business, except land, wears out over a period of time. (From the standpoint of the farmer, even land wears out if it is not properly maintained.) The wearing-out process applies primarily to the fixed assets of businesses. This is because the physical items included in current assets are not normally held by the business long enough to experience any significant amount of depreciation. In practice, it is generally considered that all physical assets of a business except inventory and land depreciate.

This depreciation or wearing-out process results from two causes: (1) wear and tear from use, and (2) action of the elements—rain, ice, hail, freezing, thawing, heat, cold, etc. Often the more the asset is used, the greater will be the deterioration. The action of the elements goes on regardless of whether the property is used. Some property may deteriorate faster when it is not used if no efforts are made to maintain it.

MAINTENANCE POLICIES

One way to help reduce depreciation of physical assets is to provide for physical maintenance. Anything which can be done to increase the amount of useful service or increase the time over which useful service can be performed by an asset in effect increases value or, conversely, decreases depreciation of assets.

Included in the concept of maintenance is the problem of replacement of an asset at the most economic time, in order that the performance of service may be continued at a reasonable rate. A corollary problem is the disposal of assets which are no longer performing useful service or which, while they are capable of performing service, produce a service which the firm no longer needs.

Maintenance and Repairs

Maintenance work must constantly be done on machinery, equipment, plant facilities, and other fixed assets used in a business. Things are constantly going wrong with property which is in daily use and proper maintenance work must be done to keep it in proper operating condition. Even though machines are in running condition they have to be oiled, inspected, etc., to remain in good shape. When breakdowns occur, the machines must be repaired and put in proper running condition.

Maintenance and repairs are an expense of business and are normally charged as expenses against the period in which they occur. The theory of this approach is that the benefit from the maintenance and repair expenditures is received at the time the expenditure is made or shortly thereafter. Very often, major repairs to items of equipment or buildings will extend the useful life of the equipment or buildings a number of years into the future. It is generally considered proper to capitalize major repair expenditures and spread the cost out over the remaining useful life of the equipment or buildings. If a new roof is added to a building, the benefits of the new roof should last for a period of years in the future, and it would be unfair to charge all of the costs of the roof to the year in which the repair was made. Thus, periodic depreciation accounting is applicable for major maintenance and repair expenditures whose benefits last beyond an accounting period. The approach to this periodic charge would be the same as that applied to accounting for depreciation in fixed assets.

Replacements

Closely associated with maintenance and repairs are replacements of machines and equipment parts. In fact, maintenance and repairs frequently result in the replacement of certain parts of the equipment. Theoretically, if the replacement costs more than the depreciated value of the original part which is replaced, the excess should be charged to the appropriate asset account. In other words, the item should be "capitalized." The balance of the expenditure would be charged as an expense for the particular period. The annual depreciation charge for the particular asset in the future should be increased according to the amount capitalized. In view of the fact that large companies are constantly replacing worn-out parts, the time and expense involved in this added accounting are not justified by the results. It is therefore common for businesses to charge off replacements of parts to the repair or maintenance expense account for the period. In some instances companies charge off to expense all replacements which involve less than an arbitrary figure set by the particular company; costs exceeding that amount are charged to the asset account.

Replacement does not always occur at the time when the physical asset has completely deteriorated. It is often economically desirable to replace in advance of the complete loss of service output. The decisions on replacement of an asset or of a part of an asset would be made on the same basis as the original investment in fixed assets, discussed in Chapter 18. With changing costs of fixed assets, it would be expected that even replacement with a similar item will require a change in depreciation costs during the years of useful life of the new item. Under conditions of inflation, this change in depreciation cost is almost always upward.

Additions and Betterments

Some outlays of cash belong more appropriately under the heading of *additions* or *betterments* rather than replacements. These items add to the value of the property and therefore, from a theoretical standpoint, should be written up as assets or as an increase in the asset values rather than charged to expenses. From a practical standpoint, however, some companies adopt a policy similar to that followed in replacements; that is, if the item involves less than a fixed amount, it is charged off to expense for the particular period, otherwise it is added to the assets.

Decisions relative to adding to or bettering existing fixed assets would be treated in the same manner by management as decisions relative to the purchase of new fixed assets. If the additions and improvements contribute to future accounting periods as well as to the one in which they were purchased, it would be reasonable to capitalize these expenditures and to take the cost of them in the years in which they benefit the company. Therefore, additions and betterments commonly lead to higher depreciation charges in the future period.

Disposal

Assets should be disposed of when they are superfluous to the company. There is nothing to be gained by keeping on hand an asset for which the company anticipates no future use. If it is a depreciable asset, its value will consistently decline over the time it is held by the firm. In addition, certain insurance, space, and maintenance costs may be incurred for it. As a result, it is good management for the company to dispose of the asset rather than to hold it when it has no anticipated future use.

The decision on whether to dispose of the asset should consider the alternate uses the firm would have for the funds that would be obtained through liquidation of the asset and through reduced cash outlays in the future by not holding the asset. If alternate uses would be more productive to the firm than retaining the asset, it should be sold. Following this approach, it is often desirable for a firm to dispose of assets which it is using but which are yielding a very low return.

The reason for discussing maintenance, repairs, replacements, additions, betterments, and disposal is that these activities affect depreciation expense. For all of these items except disposal, if the particular item is treated as an expense, it is written off as such in the particular period in which it is incurred. But if the outlay is "capitalized," i.e., added to assets, it must be depreciated in future years. If assets are disposed of, the effect is immediate reduction in asset values and a lowering of depreciation charges in future years.

DEPRECIATION ACCOUNTING POLICIES

Despite proper maintenance and repairs, practically all fixed assets, except land, will eventually wear out; therefore proper depreciation charges should be made. It is sometimes argued that where the property consists of a large number of uniform small parts, and the replacement or repair of any one of them does not affect the life of the entire property, no depreciation charge is necessary since the property will never wear out. The roadbed of a railroad is an example. Ties and rails are being replaced constantly, and maintenance of the roadbed is continuous. The Interstate Commerce Commission, and generally the courts, however, do not agree with this viewpoint. Since 1943, railroads have had to charge depreciation, on the straight-line basis, on their "way and structures."

The problem of accounting for depreciation is the problem of allocation of the cost of the fixed asset to individual accounting periods during its useful life. If an asset were entirely expensed at the time of its purchase, the year of purchase would absorb much higher expenses than would seem reasonable, and profits for that year would be understated. The later years of use of this asset would include no charge for its use in the income statement, and, therefore, profits would be overstated.

The opposite extreme would be to capitalize the total cost of the asset and to make no charges against it until its useful life expired. Under this approach, profits would be overstated during all years of use of the fixed asset until the final year, in which profits would be sharply understated. Neither of these approaches seems reasonable to anyone interested in making decisions on the basis of the profit data of the firm. Thus, the standard approach to absorbing the cost of fixed assets in a firm is to allocate this cost in some manner over the estimated useful life of the fixed assets.

This allocation of cost of a long-lived asset to individual accounting periods should accomplish two objectives: (1) it should reflect the cost of the benefit which the current period receives from the use of the asset; and (2) it should result in carrying forward as an asset at the end of the current period only that part of the original cost which corresponds to service benefits expected from the asset in future periods.

Allocating Expense to Accounting Period

The value of the loss in substance of an asset is just as much an expense or cost of doing business as the amount spent for labor and materials. The finished product should, therefore, bear the depreciation expense just as any other expense. The only difference is that after the particular asset has been purchased there is no further outlay of cash demanded until the asset must be replaced.

In accounting, the annual depreciation to be charged to the "Depreciation" account appears as an expense in the income statement. The contra credit is to the "Reserve for Depreciation" account, which is a valuation reserve and is deducted from the asset account on the balance sheet. The trend in accounting practice is to get away from the use of the term "reserve" when applied to "valuation reserves" such as depreciation, since these "reserves" may be confused by the reader with "surplus reserves." The term *provision* (or *allowance*) *for depreciation* is now being used by many companies instead of *reserve*, and it is recommended that this term be used in the financial statements. For purposes of discussion, however, we will use the term *reserve*.

Proper Valuation of Assets

The actual current *market* value of the asset may be more or less than the depreciated value, but the accountant is not concerned with this. The fixed assets are going to be used in the business as long as they are useful to the business or until the company terminates, and the proper balance sheet value is considered to be cost less depreciation, rather than the current market value or the replacement value. From the standpoint of charging off depreciation as an expense, it is the actual cost (or cost less salvage value), not the current market or replacement cost, that is charged to expense over the life of the asset. The same amount as is charged off is added to the Reserve account.

The net fixed asset value (after deduction of reserve for depreciation) should represent that portion of the original cost which corresponds to service benefits expected from the asset in future periods. However, in times of inflation, the remaining portion of cost is far below any other measure which may be taken of remaining useful value.

Subjective Nature of Charge

The use of original cost presents particular problems when the value of the dollar is changing. In times of inflation, original cost tends to be substantially below current replacement cost or market value and also below a value based on future earning power of the asset to the firm. A number of studies have been made concerning different approaches to valuation of fixed assets but standard practice still recognizes only original cost.

The choice of original cost itself is subjective and many more subjective decisions must be made in determining the annual charge for depreciation. One of these subjective decisions regards the residual value of the asset. If an asset has a scrap value at the time of its disposal, the amount obtained from disposal should not be charged as depreciation expense during the useful life of the asset. Thus, most fixed asset accounting involves some determination of a residual value at the end of the period of time in which the firm plans to use the asset. Since this decision is based upon future values, it is very difficult to estimate accurately a residual or scrap value for a fixed asset some years in the future.

A more important subjective decision is the number of years of useful life—an estimate of the number of years during which the asset will be utilized by the firm in the future. If the length of useful life is estimated at 5 years rather than 10, the average depreciation charge over the 5 years will have to be twice as much as would be the case for a 10-year life. As this decision relates only to the future, no one knows exactly how many years an asset will be used. The very subjective nature of this decision has caused the Internal Revenue Service to establish average or reasonable lives for specific items under certain uses. Nonetheless, what may be a reasonable estimate of the future life for a given fixed asset under one set of circumstances is not necessarily reasonable under another set of circumstances. Table 24–1 gives the number of years of useful life for certain types of buildings suggested by the Internal Revenue Service.

The combination of future decisions required in determining the depreciation expense for an accounting period is such as to make the actual value chosen subject to substantial question. Therefore, the range of depreciation charges which could be justified under any specific set of circumstances is rather great. The depreciation expense chosen by management for its published statements is subject to close scrutiny by outsiders because of its very subjective nature.

Table 24–1. Suggested Years of Useful Life and Straight-Line Annual Depreciation Rates for Buildings, by Types
United States, 1962

Type of Building	Useful Life (Years)	Annual Depreciation Rate (Per Cent)
Apartments	40	2.5
Banks	50	2.0
Factories	45	2.2
Garages	45	2.2
Hotels	40	2.5
Loft Buildings	50	2.0
Office Buildings	45	2.2
Stores	50	2.0
Theaters	40	2.5
Warehouses	60	1.7

SOURCE: Internal Revenue Service, *Depreciation Guidelines and Rules*, Publication No. 456 (Washington, D. C.: U. S. Government Printing Office, 1962), p. 12.

Effect on Income Tax

Depreciation expense is a legitimate expense to be deducted before the determination of profit for income tax purposes. Because of the extremely high tax rates in recent years, considerable emphasis has been given to the effect on federal income taxes of the amount of depreciation charged. Since the charge is so subjectively determined, considerable variation could exist, and the Internal Revenue Service has been forced to set up certain rules and regulations to attempt to standardize the determination of depreciation charged by various business units. The more a business charges in depreciation expense, the less it pays in income taxes during the year of the charge. If the corporation is paying an income tax of 52 per cent, for example, every dollar charged as an expense of depreciation lessens the net taxable income by $1 and saves the business $.52 in income taxes in that year.

Overcharging depreciation in the early years of an asset's life results in lower income taxes for those years and higher taxes during the later years of the life of the asset. Undercharging during the early years has the opposite effect. The total amount of depreciation charged over the entire life of the asset is the same under both procedures—and this is exactly the same total charge as under the straight-line method. Most companies, however, would prefer to charge as much in depreciation as possible (under the Internal Revenue Service laws and regulations) during the early years in order that the early tax savings can be reinvested in the business and thus earn profits on it even though the tax bill will be heavier later on. In effect this amounts to borrowing some of the tax money from the government without paying any interest on it.

Some companies will prepare one income statement for the government and a different one for their shareholders. The one made out for the government may show the maximum depreciation charges possible. The published statement which goes to the shareholders may reflect a smaller depreciation charge, and therefore a larger net income.

Under certain circumstances a company will write down the value of its fixed assets for the purpose of lessening depreciation charges. The fixed assets, or at least part of them, may have been acquired during a period of high prices. This becomes an important matter when a recession hits and the earnings decline drastically. In order to make a better showing to the shareholders, and possibly the creditors or future creditors, a company may reduce the book value of the fixed assets and charge this off against the retained income or a type of surplus account. The annual depreciation charges in the future will accordingly be lessened with the result that the future deficit is decreased or the profit increased.

During the Second World War, a tremendous demand for war materials necessitated the building of new structures by many companies that had war contracts. As an inducement to extend the plant facilities, the government granted permission to the companies to write off the cost, or a substantial portion of the cost, of the new plants over a 5-year period. In other words, annual depreciation charges equivalent to about 20 per cent of the cost of the properties were permitted. This was done on the theory that the new plant facilities might be worthless after the war. The accelerated depreciation greatly reduced the amount that had to be paid in income taxes. The statutes provided that if the war ended before the 5-year period had expired, a company would be permitted to readjust the depreciation charges upward for the past years. When the war ended in 1945, many companies refigured their depreciation charges for the past several years and received tax refunds in substantial amounts. Many of the new buildings are just as good today as when built, and are in constant use in the production of ordinary products. After having written off the entire cost of the new buildings during a few years, some companies have later put the buildings back in the balance sheet at some figure which represented only normal depreciation rates. But since the entire cost of the new facilities had been written off for tax purposes, none of the new depreciation charges is tax deductible.

Effect on Replacement

Because of the effect of depreciation charges on the net profit figure, certain management and outsider actions are also affected by the amount of the depreciation charged. This is particularly true for payment of dividends and federal income taxes. The amount of the depreciation charge also affects the pricing of the firm if it prices on a basis of recovering total cost. Because of the uses of accounting data which include depreciation charges, the actual bookkeeping amount charged for depreciation influences the ability of a firm to replace assets.

Charging off depreciation as an expense, and setting up a "reserve" of similar amount, *does not directly* enable a company to replace the depreciated asset. The reserve account is merely an account, and all it consists of is some ink figures on the company's books. The reserve account may, for example, be for $10,000,000, but there is not one cent of cash or equivalent in the account.

The most that can be said in regard to the replacement of the particular asset is that the charging off of depreciation may result in less being paid out in the form of dividends and income taxes, and as a result the assets (of one type or another) may be larger than would have been the case if no depreciation charges had been made. This can best be explained through the use of figures.

Let us assume that Companies A and B both start out business operations on January 1, with property and net worth accounts as represented by the following abbreviated balance sheet:

Assets		Net Worth	
Machinery	$1,000,000	Capital stock	$5,000,000
Other assets	4,000,000		
Total	$5,000,000	Total	$5,000,000

We will make the following additional assumptions: the machinery will last 10 years, and have no scrap value; the other assets do not depreciate; each company will pay dividends equivalent to 80 per cent of the net income after federal income taxes; Company A will not charge off any depreciation on the machinery; Company B will annually charge off $100,000 depreciation on the machinery; and each company makes 10 per cent, before depreciation and taxes, on the original investment. The amount shown as taxes is according to the 1962 rates. The income statement would show the following for each year:

	Company A	Company B
Income before depreciation	$500,000	$500,000
Depreciation		100,000
Income after depreciation	500,000	400,000
Federal income taxes	254,500	202,500
Net income after taxes	245,500	197,500
Dividends	196,400	158,000
Retained income	$ 49.100	$ 39,500

After the end of the first year's operations the balance sheets for the two companies would appear as follows (if any liabilities were present, it is assumed that they were deducted from the gross assets):

Company A		Company B	
Assets		*Assets*	
Machinery	$1,000,000	Machinery	$1,000,000
		Less: Reserve for	
		depreciation	100,000
	1,000,000		900,000
Other assets	4,049,100	Other assets	4,139,500
Total assets	5,049,100	Total assets	5,039,500
Net Worth		*Net Worth*	
Capital stock	5,000,000	Capital stock	5,000,000
Retained income	49,100	Retained income	39,500
Total net worth	$5,049,100	Total net worth	$5,039,500

From a comparison of the two abbreviated income statements several things are apparent. By not charging off depreciation, Company A has paid $52,000 more in taxes than was necessary. Considering that $100,000 of the machinery was consumed in the year's operations, the *real* net income after taxes would be only $145,500. But dividends amounting to $196,400 were actually paid. It is thus apparent that $50,900 of the dividends actually were paid from the "Capital" of the company, rather than from the earnings. Also, after giving effect to the actual depreciation in the machinery, there is really a deficit of $50,900 present, rather than retained income of $49,100.

From the standpoint of the balance sheet, Company A's machinery account is overstated to the extent of $100,000 since there is no reserve for depreciation for that amount. The so-called retained income is reflected in the "Other Assets" account.

The financial statements of Company B reflect the correct accounting of the depreciation. The income tax base is lowered by the amount charged off as depreciation. Not only are taxes lower, but the 80 per cent dividends amount to less than in the case of Company A, because the charging of depreciation results in a lower income before taxes. This also accounts for lower retained earnings on the part of Company B.

In examining Company B's balance sheet it is seen that a "Reserve for Depreciation" account of $100,000 has been set up and this is deducted from the "Machinery" account to give a true current depreciated value of the machinery. It will be noted that the "Other Assets" of Company B increased by $100,000 more than retained earnings of $39,500. Ignoring the depreciation charge and the reserve for depreciation for the moment, Company B's net income was $297,500. The dividends would reduce this to $139,500. In other words the net assets (assets less liabilities) actually increased by $139,500 (aside from the reduced value of the machinery). That is why the "Other Assets" of Company B show an increase of that amount. The charging of $100,000 in depreciation does not take one cent out of the business; therefore, when we take the depreciation into account and lower the reported retained income by $100,000, the actual increase in the "Other Assets" account is $139,500.

To illustrate the situation at the end of 10 years, we will assume that the operating results and dividend policies of the two companies for each of the remaining 9 years is identical to that of the first year. Following is how the balance sheets (the assets shown are after any liabilities have been deducted) for the two companies would appear after 10 years:

Company A		Company B	
Assets		*Assets*	
Machinery	$1,000,000	Machinery	$1,000,000
		Less: Reserve for	
		depreciation	1,000,000
	1,000,000		0
Other assets	4,491,000	Other assets	5,395,000
Total assets	$5,491,000	Total assets	$5,395,000
Net Worth		*Net Worth*	
Capital stock	$5,000,000	Capital stock	$5,000,000
Retained income	491,000	Retained income	395,000
Total net worth	$5,491,000	Total net worth	$5,395,000

Since Company A did not charge off any depreciation for the entire 10-year period, the shortcomings expressed above for the first year's operations apply with equal force to each of the 10 years. The machinery is now worthless, according to our assumptions, and it must therefore be taken off the books. The elimination of this $1,000,000 from the assets will result in the obliteration of the entire retained earnings account of $491,000, and the creation of a "Deficit" account in the amount of $509,000. Thus, the failure to charge off the depreciation has resulted in the payment of excessive taxes, and the payment of dividends from capital, with the result that a deficit now must appear on the company's books.

The next question is, how can Company A replace its worn-out machinery? At the beginning of the 10-year period there were $4,000,000 in "Other Assets." Presumably this amount was needed in the business for inventory and other working capital and fixed capital assets, and is probably still needed. During the period the "Other Assets" have increased by only $491,000. So possibly this represents the maximum assets that may be withdrawn from the business in order to purchase a new machine. Assuming that the new machinery will cost the same as the old, it may be difficult to acquire the new machinery. Either the company will have to use part of its needed working capital, or part of the money to pay for the new machinery may have to be borrowed. And there is always the practical consideration whether the company would be able to borrow the amount needed. Such are the shortcomings of failure to handle depreciation of fixed assets correctly.

The advantages to Company B of charging off depreciation for the first year apply also to each of the other 9 years. And furthermore, Company B will be in a much better position to replace the worn-out machinery. It will be noted that the "Other Assets" of Company B increased by $1,395,000. The charging of depreciation not only reduced the amount of income taxes, but also made less available for dividend payments to the shareholders. Thus the increase in "Other Assets" was due in part to the accumulation of retained income, but $1,000,000 of it in effect resulted from charging off this amount as depreciation expense.

If only $4,000,000 in "Other Assets" is needed to run the business on its present scale of operation, then $1,395,000 in *assets of one form or another* would be available for the acquisition of new machinery. However, one point should be made clear: the charging of depreciation and the setting up of a "Reserve" account of a similar amount does not in itself put the company in a *cash* position to replace the old machinery. As we have stated above, the "Reserve" account is merely a bookkeeping entry—no cash or other assets are put into the reserve. It exists only as a bookkeeping account, and it should not be confused with a *fund* into which may be put cash or other assets. But the accounting for depreciation will result in the accumulation of additional assets in the business (unless deficits are suffered), and these additional assets will make it easier for the company to replace the machinery.

As a practical matter, if additional assets are acquired in the business as a result of operations, the business may expand constantly. Additional inventories or fixed assets may be acquired. Possibly, new machinery may be purchased gradually so that at the end of the 10-year period the old machinery, or part of it, will have been replaced.

We assumed that 80 per cent of the income after taxes was paid in dividends. This resulted in smaller dividends for Company B than for Company A. It might be thought by the reader that this in itself would enable Company B to replace its machinery more easily than Company A. But let us assume that Company B pays the same amount of dollars in dividends as Company A. This would reduce the annual retained income after dividends to $1,100, and reduce the annual increase in "Other Assets" to $101,100. The total increase in "Other Assets" for the 10-year period would be $1,011,000. Thus, the company would still have additional assets in excess of the amount needed for the replacement of the machinery.

It is interesting to note that the annual savings in income taxes of Company B as compared with Company A amounts to $52,000. In 10 years (assuming the same rates) the savings would be $520,000. (The effect of compounding would result in an even larger saving.) Thus, the tax savings resulting from charging of depreciation would result in the accumulation of additional assets over the period to pay for more than half the cost of the new machinery.

Use of Assets Resulting from Depreciation Charges

Although charging depreciation and setting up a reserve do not provide any cash with which to replace the assets, a company such as Company B might attempt to set aside $100,000 annually for the eventual replacement of the machinery. But it would seem uneconomical to take this amount out of the earning assets each year for a 10-year period. Of course, it might be invested in government bonds, but the rate of return on these would be relatively low. Commonly the amount equivalent to the reserve account just accumulates in the business and shows up as an increase in the inventory or other asset accounts. Naturally, it is the duty of the financial officer of the company to see to it that sufficient cash is available to replace the old machinery gradually or to replace it in its entirety at the end of the 10-year period.

If a company like Company B does all its business on a cash basis and does not expand or contract, its cash account should increase each year by not only the amount of the retained income after dividends, but also by the amount of the depreciation charges of $100,000. Therefore, in examining the company's statements to determine the ability of the company to stand interest charges or some other outlay of cash, it should be realized that the company will increase its cash by $139,500 a year, and not by $39,500.

Experience of American Manufacturing Corporations

Statistics relating to depreciation charges by American manufacturing corporations for selected years are shown in Table 24–2. It will be noted that the property accounts include land on which depreciation charges are not made. The percentage depreciation figures would, therefore, be higher if based on depreciable assets only.

As shown in the table the depreciation charges have increased considerably since pre-World War II, but that is to be expected in view of the appreciable increase in the property account. The latter has resulted both from the expansion in physical property in industry, and the higher prices at which the property has been acquired. But it will be noted that the 1939 depreciation was at the rate of about 4 per cent of the gross property valuation, whereas in 1960 it had increased to approximately 6¾ per cent. This percentage increase was due in large part to the stepped-up rate of depreciation permitted on certain types of properties since World War II.

Table 24–2. Property Accounts and Depreciation Charges of All Manufacturing Corporations
United States, Selected Years 1939–1960 (In Billions of Dollars)

Years Ended Dec. 31	Gross Prop. Acc't.[a]	Accrued Deprec. Res.[b]	Net Prop. Acc't.[a]	Annual Deprec. Charges [b]	Deprec. to Prop. Gross	Deprec. to Prop. Net
1939	$ 41.6	$18.5	$23.1	$ 1.6	3.9%	7.1%
1946	59.2	29.7	29.4	2.4	4.1	8.3
1948	74.0	32.8	41.2	3.9	5.2	9.4
1950	83.3	36.9	46.4	4.4	5.3	9.6
1952	100.6	42.8	57.7	6.0	6.0	10.4
1954	112.6	50.2	62.4	6.3	5.6	10.0
1955	114.9	50.3	64.6	7.8	6.8	15.5
1956	124.2	55.5	68.7	7.7	6.2	13.9
1957	137.0	60.8	76.2	8.5	6.2	14.0
1958	149.8	66.9	82.9	9.6	6.4	14.3
1959	160.6	73.8	86.8	10.5	6.5	14.2
1960	169.0	80.0	89.0	11.4	6.8	14.2

[a] Includes land.
[b] Includes amortization charges on defense facilities through 1954, and depletion charges every year.
Source: Data taken from U. S. Treasury annual "Statistics of Income" for 1939–60.

METHODS OF CHARGING DEPRECIATION

Under depreciation accounting, the cost of the particular asset is written off over the period of its usefulness. The usual method is to deduct the salvage or scrap value from the cost of the asset and the balance is the amount written off. For reasons of simplicity, we will assume in our discussion that the particular asset has no scrap value and that therefore the entire cost is to be written off.

The estimated life of the various types of assets will have to be determined before setting up the depreciation schedule. The past experience of the particular company or that of other companies is useful in estimating the probable life. Consideration will also have to be given to the Internal Revenue Service regulations for maximum percentage that may be written off annually so far as income taxes are concerned. (See Table 24–3.)

Some types of assets depreciate much faster than others. A company, for example, may depreciate its buildings over a period of from 40 to 50 years, and its machinery over a 6- or 10-year period. Dies, patterns, and jigs, on the other hand, might be written off over a period of from 1 to 5 years.

After having decided upon the period of time over which the asset is to be written off, the company must then decide upon what method will be used to determine the amount that will be written off each year, or each accounting period.

Table 24–3. Suggested Years of Useful Life and Straight-Line Annual Depreciation Rates for Production Machinery and Equipment in Selected Industries United States, 1962

Industry	Useful Life (Years)	Annual Depreciation Rate (Per Cent)
Aerospace	8	12.5
Air Transport	6	16.7
Cement	20	5.0
Chemicals	11	9.1
Electronics	8	12.5
Glass	14	7.1
Mining	10	10.0
Motor Vehicles	12	8.3
Radio Broadcasting	6	16.7
Recreation	10	10.0
Tobacco	15	6.7
Water Transportation	20	5.0
Wholesale Trade	10	10.0

SOURCE: Internal Revenue Service, *Depreciation Guidelines and Rules* (Washington, D. C.: U. S. Government Printing Office, 1962), pp. 14–20.

Production Method

Some companies charge depreciation according to the *production method.* The total number of operating hours possible for the machine is estimated and the depreciation is charged accordingly. Or, an estimate is made of the total number of units of product that can be turned out during the life of the machine, and the depreciation charged as so much per unit of output. Other methods depreciate over time rather than use.

This method recognizes the realistic fact that the greater the operation of the machine, the greater will be the wear and tear, and therefore, more depreciation will take place. This method, however, gives no consideration to the fact that some depreciation will take place even if the machinery is not in use. From a practical standpoint, this method has the advantage of having heavy depreciation charges when production is high and profits are probably large, and low charges during slack periods when profits fall off. This would tend to equalize the net income. At the outset it would be necessary to determine how many hours the machine can operate, or how many units it can turn out. This would be difficult to estimate. But under the time methods it might be equally difficult to estimate the number of years the machine will last. The production method of charging depreciation can conveniently be used when a company has a cost accounting system in operation.

Straight-Line Method

Under the *straight-line* method, each accounting year of estimated useful life is charged with exactly the same amount of depreciation. This was the method used in our hypothetical example above. It is the simplest and by far the most commonly used method. The ease of setting up and following the schedule under this method is enough to recommend it. Furthermore, it is approved by the Internal Revenue Service, the Interstate Commerce Commission, most of the state regulatory commissions, and generally by the courts.

Under the straight-line method it is more or less assumed that the value of the property depreciates by the same amount each year. The current market value, however, may not actually decrease exactly the same amount each year. But the purpose of charging depreciation is to charge each period with its share of the expense. This is done under the straight-line method. The property may actually decrease in market value less the second year than the first, but nevertheless the company got the same use of the property the second year as the first, and therefore, that year should bear as much of the cost as the first year.

If a company wants to have the total of the depreciation and maintenance or repair charges uniform during the entire period, the straight-line method would not be advisable since the maintenance charge on a machine, for example, is usually light when the machine is new, but heavy during the later years when the machine is old and constantly breaking down or necessitating greater maintenance.

Fixed-Percentage-of-Declining-Balance Method

The fixed-percentage-of-declining-balance method is similar to the straight-line method in that an estimate is made of the number of years the machine or other asset will last, but instead of charging off the same *amount* per year, the same *percentage* of the depreciated value is charged off each year. For example, if it is decided that the machine will last 10 years, it may be decided to apply the rate of 20 per cent ("double"-declining balance) a year on the depreciated value. Thus, if the machine cost $100,000, the depreciation for the first year would be $20,000. The depreciated value at the beginning of the second year would be $80,000, so during the second year it would be depreciated 20 per cent of $80,000, or $16,000. Continuing this process during the third, fourth, and fifth years it would be depreciated $12,800, $10,240, and $8,192, respectively. This "double"-declining-balance method was first approved for federal income tax purposes in 1954.

Applying the 20 per cent to a diminishing value will never result in the machine's being entirely written off since absolute zero is constantly being approached, but never reached. Therefore, it will be necessary to write off whatever balance remains during the last year the machine is used, or to switch to the straight-line method during the later years.

There are several arguments that might be used in favor of the fixed-percentage-of-declining-balance method. It results in heavy depreciation charges during the early years when the resale value would drop off relatively sharply. Also, the maintenance charges should be relatively light during the early years, but heavy during the later years. Thus the total cost or expense of the machine as represented by the sum of the depreciation charges and the maintenance expense would tend more toward equality during the life of the machine. Also, the larger income tax savings would result in the retention of more assets in the business at the beginning of the period.

The arguments opposing the method are that it is more difficult to figure the depreciation charges, and that since the company does not contemplate selling the machine, there is no reason for carrying it on the books at a figure more in line with the market value. Furthermore, if income tax rates increased during the later part of the life of the asset, the company would be harmed.

Sum-of-the-Year's-Digits Method

The "sum-of-the-year's-digits" method of charging depreciation was first approved by the Internal Revenue Service for income tax purposes also in 1954. Under this method the annual depreciation rate is represented by a fraction, the numerator of which is the number of years of useful life of the asset at the beginning of the particular year, and the denominator of which is the sum of years of useful life at the time the asset was acquired. This can also be best explained by the use of an illustration. Let us assume the same situation as above where a machine which cost $100,000 has an expected life of 10 years. The denominator of the depreciation rate fraction would be 55 ($10 + 9 + 8 + 7 + 6 + 5 + 4 + 3 + 2 + 1$). For the first year the numerator of the fraction would be 10. Thus, for the first year, $^{10}\!/_{55}$ of $100,000, or $18,181.82 in depreciation would be charged off. For the second year $^{9}\!/_{55}$ of $100,000 or $16,363.64 would be charged. This process would be continued until the tenth year when the charges would amount to only $1,818.18. It is to be noted that the depreciation rate each year, represented by the fraction, is applied to the original cost, and not to the declining balance, as in the method previously discussed.

This is an accelerated method of charging depreciation, somewhat similar to the fixed-percentage-of-declining-balance method described earlier, and therefore the same points there mentioned would apply to the "sum-of-the-year's-digits" method. Under the latter method, however, the entire cost of the asset will be charged off over the 10-year period without the necessity of switching over to the straight-line method.

First-Year-Extra-Allowance Method

Since 1958, the Internal Revenue Service has allowed businesses to deduct an extra 20 per cent of original cost of equipment (without regard to salvage value) as first-year depreciation over and above the normal first-year depreciation deductible. In order to use this extra first-year deduction, the asset must have been purchased since December 31, 1957, must have a useful life of at least 6 years, and must be tangible personal property rather than real estate. This extra first-year allowance may be taken only on a maximum of $10,000 ($20,000 for individuals filing a joint return) worth of equipment acquired in any one year. Thus the maximum extra first-year depreciation would be $2,000 for a corporation. The extra 20 per cent deduction may be coupled with any other accepted method of depreciation for the remaining 80 per cent of original cost (less salvage value).

Investment Tax Credit

In 1962 the tax laws were amended to permit a corporation to subtract from its regular income tax an amount equivalent to 7 per cent (3 per cent for public utilities and $3\frac{1}{2}$ per cent for savings and loan associations) of the cost of new (and used) equipment and machinery purchased within the year (not buildings) which have a life of 8 years or more (lesser percentages for equipment with shorter lives). The remaining 93 per cent of cost is then depreciated over the normal life of the equipment using any accepted method.

The maximum amount of the tax credit in any one year, however, cannot exceed $25,000 plus 25 per cent of the tax bill remaining after the $25,000 has been subtracted. Any "unused" part of the credit that cannot be taken in the year can be carried forward (and subtracted from taxes) for 5 years in the future (or carried back for one year in 1963, 2 years in 1964, and 3 years in 1965 and thereafter).

The following example will serve to illustrate how this works. Assume that a corporation, which has a tax bill of $520,000 for the particular year, purchases $3,000,000 of equipment (life of 8 years assumed). The investment credit would amount to 7 per cent of this, or $210,000. But for that year the maximum credit is $148,750.[1]

Subtracting this latter figure from the computed tax of $520,000, leaves a tax bill of only $371,250 for the year. The $61,250 "unused" part of the credit can be carried forward for the next 5 years.

Sinking-Fund Method

We have at several places pointed out that a fund represents the setting aside of cash or equivalent, while a *reserve* is merely a bookkeeping entry. The *sinking-fund* method of charging depreciation is a misnomer because usually no *fund* is set aside. Other titles sometimes used—the *compound-interest* and *annuity* methods—perhaps describe better the nature of this plan.

With the use of mathematical tables, it is ascertained what sum of money would have to be invested annually at interest of a predetermined rate compounded annually to equal the cost of the particular asset at the time it must be replaced. The amount of interest would increase each successive year due to the accumulation of annual installments and the compounding of interest on this increasing amount. As may be inferred from what has already been said, the annual installments are assumed to be equal in amount. But the sum of this given amount and the interest earned would increase each year due to the greater interest. A company using this method would charge depreciation, and credit the "Reserve for Depreciation" account each year with the sum of the installment and the interest. Thus, it is apparent that the amount of the depreciation charged (and the amount credited to the reserve) would increase each successive year.

Aside from being complicated to figure, this method throws a burden on later years because the higher depreciation charges come at a time when the maintenance charges on the particular asset will also be heavy. Also, despite the fact that the particular property being depreciated will probably not be sold, the actual decline in the resale value of the property would be relatively high, rather than low, during the early period of its life.

But there is something to be said in favor of this method of charging depreciation. As we have pointed out earlier in the chapter, the charging of depreciation results in the accumulation of assets equivalent to the amount of the depreciation, despite the fact that *no fund* is actually set aside. This amount is usually not set aside in a special account, but is to be found scattered among the various assets. Therefore, it constitutes part of the earning assets of the company. The amounts added to the assets as

[1] $520,000 less $25,000 equals $495,000. 25 per cent of $495,000 equals $123,-750. $25,000 plus $123,750 equals $148,750.

Table 24–4. Comparison of Results of Using Four Alternative Methods of Depreciation Accounting Over Eight Years for a $10,000 Asset

Year	Straight-Line		Double-Declining-Balance *		Sum-of-the-Year's-Digits		20% Extra First Year With Double Declining Balance *	
	Book Net Asset Value	Depreciation Expense	Book Net Asset Value	Depreciation Expense	Book Net Asset Value	Depreciation Expense	Book Net Asset Value	Depreciation Expense
Beginning	$10,000	$ –	$10,000	$ –	$10,000	$ –	$10,000	$ –
1	8,750	1,250	7,500	2,500	7,778	2,222	6,000	4,000
2	7,500	1,250	5,625	1,875	5,834	1,944	4,500	1,500
3	6,250	1,250	4,219	1,406	4,167	1,667	3,375	1,125
4	5,000	1,250	3,164	1,055	2,778	1,389	2,531	844
5	3,750	1,250	2,373	791	1,667	1,111	1,898	633
6	2,500	1,250	1,582	791	834	873	1,265	633
7	1,250	1,250	791	791	278	556	632	633
8	–0–	1,250	–0–	791	–0–	278	–0–	632

* Shift to straight-line method for the sixth year and after.

NOTE: It is assumed that scrap value after eight years will be zero.

a result of the charges for depreciation during the early years of the life of the particular asset are used in the business for a longer period than those which accumulate from the depreciation charges during the later years. Therefore, there is some justification for making the depreciation charges heavier during the later part of the asset's life.

The sinking-fund method of handling depreciation is rarely used by ordinary business corporations, but some public utilities have adopted it.

Other Methods

Another possible method is to annually revalue the asset at its *current* market value and charge off the difference between this and the figure at which it is carried on the books. This is rarely ever done in business. It would be time-consuming and difficult to determine the existing market value every year. Furthermore, since the fixed assets are not to be resold, there is no reason for carrying them at market values. When a company is being bought out, or combining with another company, it may be necessary to determine the existing market values of the fixed assets. Many people figure depreciation on their automobiles to be the same as the decline in the market value for the particular period.

Some companies, particularly in the past, have had no set depreciation policy. When earnings are large they charge off a large amount of depreciation and then when earnings fall off they cut down the depreciation charges. Although there may be some connection between the rate of depreciation and the extent of the use of the particular asset, there is little correlation between depreciation and net income before the depreciation charges. This method, however, has the advantage of charging depreciation according to the ability of the company to stand the charges, and thus it tends to stabilize the net income. But it is realized that the assets will have to be replaced sometime regardless of whether the company has any earnings. This *arbitrary* method is not recommended, and of course, it would not meet with the approval of the Internal Revenue Service.

Choice of Method

Due to the wide variety of methods which have been developed for measuring the depreciation expense in each accounting period, and the substantial variation in results obtained, the selection of the method used is an important decision of management. The major effect of selecting one method over another is the effect on the stated net income figure and the income taxes for the periods involved.

It would seem reasonable to evaluate depreciation methods in comparison to each other according to certain general criteria. The most important of these criteria would be which method provides the most useful information and which method is most likely to lead to the proper actions. Unfortunately, the net profit information has a number of different uses. In this sense, it would generally be considered good management practice to select the method for income tax purposes which leads to the lowest immediate income tax outlay. However, this decision for tax purposes may not be the best one for other purposes such as pricing, management evaluation, stockholder investment, and creditor evaluation.

With the growing importance of taxes and with accelerated depreciation allowed for tax purposes, businesses generally have tended toward selecting that method of depreciation which results in the lowest immediate outlay for taxes. The use of *accelerated methods* such as the sum-of-the-year's-digits or the double-declining-balance or the first-year-extra-allowance results in a tax deferral until future years. In fact, if the company continues to purchase assets periodically, the tax deferral may effectively be permanent.

The results obtained by the application of these accelerated methods for tax purposes may be misleading for other purposes. Managements and all analysts of accounting statements should be careful to evaluate reasonably the depreciation method used before drawing conclusions therefrom.

OBSOLESCENCE

Depreciation is a loss in value due to the physical deterioration of an asset. *Obsolescence,* on the other hand, is used to refer both to an asset's becoming outdated and to the *loss in value* due to its becoming outdated. In addition, obsolescence includes such things as unsuitability or inadequacy due to modern developments, an increase in the scale of operation, a change in the production process, or changes resulting from some governmental action.

Obsolescence and Depreciation

There is some difference of opinion whether depreciation and obsolescence can both take place at the same time, or whether the one that first causes the asset to be scrapped should bear the total charge. For example, even if a particular asset is becoming obsolete and eventually will have to be replaced, if it becomes worn out and fully depreciated before total obsolescence overtakes it, should there be any charges made for obsolescence? Or, suppose that the asset has to be replaced by a more efficient, new model when it is only half-depreciated. Should the entire cost of the asset be charged to obsolescence, or, since it has been half-depreciated, should only half of the cost be charged to obsolescence?

We are interested in indicating the problem here and not in offering a proper solution.

It is undoubtedly more difficult to predict obsolescence than depreciation. A new model machine on the market may make the old ones obsolete overnight. And often nothing is known about the new model until it is out. It would be conservative accounting practice to expect the worst and therefore be liberal in respect to obsolescence charges. In this respect it would be advisable to be conservative in estimating the life of assets so that if obsolescence overtakes the property, a relatively large part of it will have been charged off already.

Accounting Procedures

Most companies make no charge for obsolescence. In some instances they are liberal in charging off depreciation due to the fact that they include something in it for obsolescence. Some companies specifically recognize obsolescence, but lump together "Depreciation and Obsolescence" in the financial statements. Courts and governmental and regulatory bodies generally take the position that the "Depreciation" charge covers not only depreciation but obsolescence as well.

Since depreciation and obsolescence are caused by entirely different factors, it would seem only logical to separate them for purposes of charging the "Income" account. When this is done someone must decide just how much obsolescence is to be charged off. At best this must be guesswork, and perhaps that is why most companies either ignore obsolescence charges, or include them in the depreciation charge.

The accounting entries for obsolescence are the same as for depreciation; that is, it is charged as an expense and a "Reserve for Obsolescence" is credited. When depreciation and obsolescence are put into the same account, then the reserve is deducted from the appropriate asset account. When the reserve for obsolescence is set up separately, it still may be combined with the depreciation reserve. The purposes accomplished by charging obsolescence are similar to those for charging depreciation; that is, the current period is charged with the cost, the net value of the particular asset is correspondingly reduced, and other assets equivalent in amount to the charges will accumulate in the business since dividends are restricted to the extent of the charges.

DEPLETION

Depletion is the exhaustion of *wasting assets* on the part of companies that own timberlands, oil and gas wells, mines, and quarries. When the ore or minerals in a mine, for example, are exhausted, the property no longer has any value. When the minerals are sold, the difference between the income and expenses is not all profit. Part of the income represents the cost of the shrinking original property, that is, the gradual depletion of substance. Not to include this in the cost of the sales would be the same as not including the cost of the inventory on the part of an ordinary manufacturing or merchandising company. If a mining company did not make a charge for the minerals sold, and the total net income after taxes was paid to the shareholders in the form of dividends, part of the dividends would represent a return of capital, and eventually the mineral lands would have no value.

Accounting Procedure

Wasting asset companies prepare an estimate of the quantity of minerals, or whatever other material is involved, in the ground. Presumably this would be carried on the books at the cost figure. As the minerals are removed and sold, a *depletion* charge is made against the income for the cost per ton, or whatever other measure is used. The corresponding credit is made to either the particular asset account or to a "Reserve for Depletion" account, which is deducted from the asset accounts on the balance sheet. Accountants prefer that the credit be made to the Reserve account, particularly when "liquidating" dividends will later be paid to the shareholders.

The depletion charge accomplishes the same as the depreciation charge. The income for the particular period is charged with the proper amount, and since the dividends are restricted to this extent, other assets equivalent to the charge accumulate in the business. These might be constantly invested in new mineral lands to take the place of those which have been depleted.

Wasting asset companies may have to give special depreciation treatment to other assets. For example, a tipple at a particular mine will be worthless after the exhaustion of the ore; therefore, it should be completely depreciated by the time the ore is exhausted. Ordinary depreciation policies, however, would be applied to property such as a refinery if the company had numerous other sources to draw from in the event one ore deposit was exhausted.

Depletion and Income Taxes

If a wasting asset company did not make depletion charges then it would in part be paying income taxes on money that represented a return of its own capital. At the present time the federal tax laws permit oil and gas producing companies, coal and metal and certain other types of mines to charge depletion of 50 per cent of the *net income,* or 27½ per cent of the gross income from oil (15 per cent of the gross income for metal mines), whichever is lower.

When Assets Are Not To Be Replaced

If a company which operates only one mine is to be liquidated when the ore is exhausted, there is no reason for withholding from the shareholders the income that is represented by the depletion. In other words, part of the dividend would represent a return of capital. When such dividends are paid, the shareholders are informed as to what part of the dividend represents a return of capital. This should be done because the shareholder does not have to pay income taxes on that part of the dividends. According to the laws of most of the states, it is legal for a company with wasting assets to pay a dividend without first charging depletion.

AMORTIZATION

Many companies carry intangible fixed assets such as patents, copyrights, franchises, trade marks, and goodwill on the books at a stated value. These are usually amortized, in other words charged off, over a period of years. Patents last for only 17 years, and copyrights expire at the end of 28 years with an extension of another 28 years, so these should be completely written off by the time of their expiration. Quite often, however, their value ceases long before the exclusive legal right has terminated. Thus it would be conservative to write them off over a shorter period of time. Franchises also may be for only a limited time and should be written off during that period. Trade marks and goodwill do not legally terminate, but conservative accounting practice would call for writing these items off over a reasonable number of years.

It is generally considered good accounting practice to carry goodwill on the books only if it was purchased, and then it should not be valued at more than the cost price. Even though it may be purchased, some companies carry goodwill on the books at a nominal value of $1.

When intangible assets of the kind mentioned above are written off the books, the charge is ordinarily not called depreciation or obsolescence. The term *amortization* is usually used. Instead of setting up a reserve account, a credit is made directly to the asset account so that the book figure shows the net amortized value.[2]

---

[2] The term *intangible assets* is almost universally used to apply to such fixed assets as goodwill, patents, copyrights, franchises, etc. It is also used in connection with property taxes with a different meaning. The state may apply the tax to tangible personal property such as clothing, jewelry, automobiles, boats, etc., and/or to so-called *intangible* personal property such as stocks and bonds, bank accounts, etc. Where the tax is applied only to such things as stocks, bonds, bank accounts, money, etc., it is often called an *intangibles* tax. From the standpoint of a company's balance sheet, we would not consider stocks and bonds (owned), money, etc., to be *intangible* assets in the accounting sense. Unless otherwise indicated, we will use the term *intangible assets* to mean goodwill, etc. Securities will be treated as personal property, unless otherwise indicated.

QUESTIONS

1. Define *depreciation* and *depreciation accounting*.
2. What objectives are accomplished by the proper accounting handling of depreciation on the part of a business corporation?
3. Distinguish between maintenance or repairs, replacements, and additions or betterments. Why are they discussed in this chapter?
4. How should management approach the decision on whether to dispose of an asset?
5. When should fixed assets be replaced? Explain your answer.
6. What are the major problems involved in allocating fixed asset depreciation to accounting periods?
7. Does depreciation accounting lead to proper valuation of assets? Why or why not?
8. Does the overcharging of depreciation lessen the federal income tax? Explain.
9. Explain definitely how the proper accounting treatment of depreciation may result in the company's being better able to replace the depreciated asset than if no depreciation charges had been made.
10. Indicate the various methods of charging off depreciation. Which do you favor? Why?
11. (a) What situation may be encountered during a period of rising prices by a company which charges depreciation on the basis of cost? (b) What drawbacks might there be to a policy of charging depreciation on replacement costs during a period of rising prices? If this policy is followed should it be continued during a period of falling prices? Why or why not?
12. Distinguish between obsolescence and depreciation. Should the two be combined in the same account? Explain.
13. Assume that a half-depreciated asset is discarded because it becomes obsolete. What is the proper accounting procedure of writing off the asset and replacing it?
14. What accounting procedure should be followed in writing off intangible assets?
15. (a) Indicate the proper accounting handling of depletion charges. (b) What special income tax treatment is accorded companies which have wasting assets? (c) Indicate the shortcomings which may be encountered by a wasting asset company's not making the proper depletion charges.

PROBLEMS

1. The XYZ Co. has just purchased a new piece of equipment costing $10,000. The estimated useful life is 4 years. No scrap value is assumed. Determine the annual depreciation charge under each of the following methods: (a) Straight-line, (b) Double-declining-balance, (c) Sum-of-the-year's-digits.
2. In the above problem, which depreciation method would you select for pricing purposes? Why? Which method would you select for federal income tax purposes? Why?
3. The asset side of the balance sheet of both the Old Co. and the New Co. is as follows:

```
Cash ................ $    5,000
Inventory ............     95,000
Machinery ..........   1,000,000
Plant ...............   4,000,000
```

Both companies' average earnings before depreciation charges (and taxes) amount to $1,000,000 a year, and each of them follows a policy of paying out 90 per cent of their *net* income, after taxes, in the form of dividends, and investing half of the remaining income in United States government bonds. Assume federal income taxes to be 50 per cent.

Both companies state that the appreciation in the value of the plant will offset any depreciation, so no charge for the latter will be made. Both companies also agree that the machinery will be worthless in 10 years, but the Old Co. is not going to make any provision for depreciation or replacement "until the time comes when we have to replace it," whereas the New Co. will charge off machinery depreciation on a straight-line basis—treating this as an expense in the income statement and deducting a reserve of corresponding amount from the "Machinery" account on the balance sheet.

It is assumed that all the business is on a cash basis; that the liabilities remain the same; and that the "Plant," "Machinery" (except for "Reserve" account in case of the New Co.), and "Inventory" accounts remain the same as stated above.

(a) List the asset accounts for each company at the end of the 10 years. (b) Can the Old Co. replace its machinery? (c) Can the New Co. replace its machinery? If so, what account will furnish the money to buy it? (d) What becomes of the "Reserve for Depreciation" account? (e) Assuming that the plant would appreciate in value an amount equal to the depreciation, would that be a reason for not charging off depreciation on the plant? Explain.

4. Select a company whose stock is listed on the New York Stock Exchange and ascertain what policy it follows with relation to the depreciation of its various types of fixed assets.

5. The Adams Manufacturing Co. paid for all of its expenses, except depreciation, in cash, and received cash for all income items for the past 6 months. Raw material equal to that sold was purchased each month. Profits for the period after charging depreciation of $10,000, but before taxes, amounted to $200,000. Assume the federal income tax rate is 50 per cent. All items on the balance sheet except cash, reserve for depreciation, and surplus were the same at the end of the period as at the beginning. How much did the cash account (after taxes) increase during the period?

SELECTED READINGS

AMERICAN INSTITUTE OF CERTIFIED PUBLIC ACCOUNTANTS. *Accounting Trends and Techniques.* New York: American Institute of Certified Public Accountants. Published annually.

ANTHONY, ROBERT N. *Management Accounting.* Homewood, Ill.: Richard D. Irwin, Inc., 1960.

BLACK, HOMER A., and CHAMPION, JOHN E. *Accounting in Business Decisions.* Englewood Cliffs, N. J.: Prentice-Hall, Inc., 1961.

BROWN, E. C. *Effects of Taxation: Depreciation Adjustments for Price Changes.* Boston: Harvard University, Graduate School of Business Administration, 1952.

GRANT, E. L., and NORTON, PAUL T. *Depreciation.* New York: The Ronald Press Co., Revised Printing, 1955.

HILL, THOMAS M., and GORDON, MYRON J. *Accounting: A Management Approach,* rev. ed. Homewood, Ill.: Richard D. Irwin, Inc., 1959.

JONES, RALPH C. *Effects of Price Level Changes.* American Accounting Association, 1956.

RYAN, JOHN. *Current Depreciation Allowances.* New York: Fordham University Press, 1958.

TERBORGH, GEORGE. *Realistic Depreciation Policy.* Chicago: Machinery and Allied Products Institute, 1954.

25

Net Income and Retained Earnings

We have not yet carefully defined profit, or income, nor have we discussed its determination from an accounting point of view. An understanding of the true nature of profit is essential to a student of corporate finance. He must also appreciate the various ways in which the term *profit* is used by different groups in society. Further, and most importantly, he must be able to distinguish clearly between profit in its real sense and profit as measured by accounting.

The Meaning of Net Income

Throughout this chapter, the term *net income* will be used synonymously with the term *net profit*. The terms *profit* and *income* describe a concept of gain over a period of time. The term *income* itself is very descriptive for it obviously means values "coming in." *Net income* means the excess of gross income over out-go. The term *profit* also implies an excess or gain of values received over values disbursed. In attempting to measure income or profit for a firm, it is necessary first to determine which aspect of the firm will be emphasized. Thus, it has been common to use the term *net income* or *net profit* to describe the owners' gains from operations rather than the gains to other interested parties or to the business as a whole. The net gain to the business unit might be measured by the net increase in assets or by the amount of reinvested earnings. The net income or net profit figure used in accounting and by most businessmen is not the net to the business—it is the net gain to the owners of the business.

Gains and profits could be in a variety of forms: increase in inventory, increase in fixed assets, reductions in claims by others (liabilities), etc.

Because these potential gains and values take so many forms, a common denominator is necessary to measure increases or decreases in value. The common denominator normally used is the dollar, and the process of the determination of these changes in value and their measurements in dollar amounts is called financial accounting. Thus, the most commonly used definition of net income or net profit, as given above, is an accounting definition.

Because of the general acceptance of the accounting definition of profit, it will be emphasized in this book. However, it is important for the student to recognize that *real* profit or income could be substantially different from the measured profit developed by the accounting system. Net profit determination in accounting is the determination of the increase in value of the owners' equity in the assets of the corporation during a given period of time. In accounting, gross increases in owners' equity resulting from the operations of the business are called revenues or income and gross decreases are called expenses. The difference between revenues and expenses for a specified period of time is profit or net income (or net loss).

There is no implication in the accounting process that *net income* and *cash* are synonymous. Income arises from transactions that change owners' equity in a specified time period, but these same events would not necessarily cause changes in the cash position of the business. In cash accounting, only changes in the "Cash" account are described. The normal accounting used by modern business is accrual accounting, which takes into consideration all changes in value of the owners' equity during a given time. Increases in owners' equity could take the form of increases in cash, but could just as easily take the form of an increase in any other asset of the firm or a decrease in liabilities or both.

THE INCOME STATEMENT

The *income statement* is also called the "profit and loss statement," the "operating statement," or the "statement of operations." While this accounting statement was briefly described in Chapter 19, it is more fully discussed here because of the importance of the accounting process in measuring the net income of the firm. The income statement describes for a specific period of time the operations of the business which have led to net income or net loss. Thus, this statement shows the gross income received for the period, the expenses incurred, related to this income, and the net income after subtracting these expenses. Most large businesses prepare income statements at least quarterly, and some prepare them monthly. In smaller businesses, the income statement may be prepared only once a year. Because the income statement describes the results of operations for a period of time, it is an extremely useful management tool.

It should be emphasized that this statement shows all sales as income regardless of whether the goods sold have been paid for by the customers. All expenses incurred are listed even if there has not yet been an actual cash outlay for some specific items. The excess of income over expenses is the net income for the period, regardless of whether cash receipts exceeded cash disbursements by a similar amount. Even if the company does only a cash business and pays for all expenses in cash, it should not be concluded that the profit will show up in the "Cash" account at the end of the period. It may have been used to purchase additional inventory or fixed assets or to pay off liabilities. A typical but abbreviated income statement for a hypothetical manufacturing company is given below.

The Standard Manufacturing Company
INCOME STATEMENT
Year Ended December 31, 19x1

Gross Sales			$1,010,000
Less: Sales Returns and Allowances			10,000
Net Sales			$1,000,000
Cost of Goods Sold:			
Materials		$500,000	
Direct Labor		175,000	
Indirect Manufacturing Costs		25,000	700,000
Gross Margin (profit)			$ 300,000
Other Operating Expenses:			
Selling		$100,000	
Administrative		50,000	
Other		9,000	$ 159,000
Net Operating Income			$ 141,000
Non-operating Income:			
Interest Received	$ 500		
Rent Income	1,500	$ 2,000	
Non-operating Expenses:			
Interest Paid		1,000	1,000
Net Income (profit) Before Federal Income Tax			$ 142,000
Federal Income Tax			68,340
Net Income (profit) After Federal Income Tax			$ 73,660

Sales

The sales figure on an income statement includes all of the sales of the period regardless of whether collection has occurred. Some statements show the gross sales and a deduction for returns and allowances while other published statements merely show net sales after such deductions. Practice varies as to where "sales discount" is shown on the income statement. In some cases, the amount of the sales discounts is deducted from the gross sales. In other cases it is included as a deduction from sales along with returns and allowances, and in still other cases it is included as a non-operating expense. Sales would include only transfer of title of the "stock in trade" of the company. If some fixed asset is sold, the transaction is not normally included in sales, but the net result (gain or loss) from the sale is listed as a non-recurring item in "Other Expense" or "Other Income."

Cost of Goods Sold

To determine the cost of goods sold, a standard practice for merchandising companies is to add the purchases for the period to the inventory at the beginning of the period and then subtract the ending inventory. The problem is more complicated in processing or manufacturing firms because inventories include raw materials, work in process, and finished goods. However, some manufacturing firms use the same approach as merchandising companies.

Larger manufacturing firms will normally have cost accounting systems. These include in costs of goods sold not only the cost of the materials which went into the goods, but the direct labor costs and the indirect manufacturing costs. Materials withdrawn from the raw materials inventory are added to the work in process inventory, as is the cost of labor that was applied to the product during its processing stage. Also, indirect manufacturing costs (overhead or burden) are added to the work in process inventory as the goods go through the manufacturing process. The value of the completed product, including raw materials and direct labor and indirect costs, is subtracted from the work in process inventory and added to the finished goods inventory as soon as the production process is completed. When the item is finally sold, the value at which it was carried in the finished goods inventory is transferred to the cost of goods sold. Under this system, labor expense for goods which have not yet been sold is carried as part of the inventory value.

Like sales discounts, purchase discounts present a specific problem in accounting. Some companies will show cost of purchases net of purchase discount. Others will enter the gross price of the merchandise received and include purchase discount as a non-operating income item.

Other Operating Expenses

The Income Statement for the Standard Manufacturing Company (see page 593) shows the principal expenses that come under the heading of "Other Operating Expenses." Selling expense includes the salaries and commissions paid to salesmen, salesmen's traveling expenses, advertising, sales promotion, and other expenses which are allocated to the sales department. Administrative expenses include the salaries of the company's officers and other administrative employees, insurance, stationery, postage, rent, light, and heat expense allocated to administration, etc.

Under "Other" expenses would come any other operating expenses not listed under selling or administrative. Depreciation on the office furniture and fixtures might be one of these. In some instances, however, depreciation is included in the selling and administrative expenses.

Non-operating Income

Non-operating income is that income of the company which is not directly related to operations. In some cases the term *financial management income* is used instead of *non-operating income*, or that term may be applied to certain of the items that come under non-operating income.

Dividends received on stock and interest received on bonds held by the company are included in this item. It is desirable to separate the non-operating from the operating items in order that the income from the ordinary operations of the business can be clearly seen. Another item included in this section is any profit made from the sale of an asset other than "stock in trade" which is no longer needed in the business. Such an item is sometimes referred to as non-recurring income. A company, for example, may have been holding some real estate for a period of years thinking that use might be made of it sometime in the future. If this was sold at a large profit and the profit were included along with that from ordinary operations, the reader of the income statement would get a distorted picture of the relative efficiency of the company for that period. For these and other reasons, profit from an extraordinary transaction or non-recurring item should always be shown in the non-operating section. Another example of such an item would be income arising from the sale of securities of other companies which the company has been holding.

Non-operating Expenses

Expenses not related to operations are placed under "Non-operating Expenses." Interest paid on bank loans or on bonds outstanding are included in this section. The points stated above for non-operating income apply with equal force here. Any extraordinary or non-recurring loss, such as on sale of some asset other than stock in trade, would also be shown as non-operating expense.

Federal Income Taxes

The federal income tax is truly an expense and is shown as such on the income statement. But since it is based on the "net income," the latter figure is computed, as shown on the income statement, before the taxes are deducted. The "net income" figure then is commonly shown "before" and "after" federal income taxes.

Effect of Net Income on the Balance Sheet

To illustrate the possible effect of a year's operations on the balance sheet of a company, assume that the following was the balance sheet for the Standard Manufacturing Company at the beginning of the operating year.

The Standard Manufacturing Company
BALANCE SHEET
As of Beginning of Year 19x1

Assets			Liabilities and Net Worth		
Current Assets			Current Liabilities		
Cash		$ 20,000	Bank Loan		$ 25,000
Accounts Receivable		40,000	Accounts Payable		20,000
Inventory		208,000	Total Current Liabilities		$ 45,000
Total Current Assets		$268,000			
U. S. Bonds		20,000	Net Worth		
Fixed Assets			Capital Stock		$300,000
Machinery	$ 80,000		Retained Income		133,000
Less: Reserve for			Total Net Worth		$433,000
Depreciation	20,000	60,000			
Land and					
Buildings	$150,000				
Less: Reserve for					
Depreciation	20,000	130,000			
Total Fixed Assets		$190,000	Total Liabilities and		
Total Assets		$478,000	Net Worth		$478,000

After giving effect to the income and expenses for the year, as shown before in the income statement, the balance sheet for the end of the same year might appear as follows:

The Standard Manufacturing Company
BALANCE SHEET
Year Ended December 31, 19x1

Assets			Liabilities and Net Worth		
Current Assets			Current Liabilities		
Cash		$ 46,000	Accounts Payable		$ 25,000
Accounts Receivable		42,000	Federal Income Tax Payable		68,340
Inventory		316,000	Total Current Liabilities		$ 93,340
Total Current Assets		$404,000			
U. S. Bonds		20,000	Net Worth		
Fixed Assets			Capital Stock		$300,000
Machinery	$ 80,000		Retained Income		206,660
Less: Reserve for			Total Net Worth		$506,660
Depreciation	30,000	50,000			
Land and					
Buildings	$150,000				
Less: Reserve for					
Depreciation	24,000	126,000			
Total Fixed Assets		$176,000	Total Liabilities and		
Total Assets		$600,000	Net Worth		$600,000

It will be noticed that the retained income (surplus) shown on the balance sheet at the beginning of the year amounted to $133,000, but at the end of the year it stood at $206,660. This was an increase of $73,660.

This is exactly what the income statement shows the company made for the year, after taxes. This is to be expected for several reasons. If there are no appropriations of the net income to reserve accounts, and if no dividends are paid, the accountant transfers the net income for the year to the undivided profits account. The other explanation is that the increase in net assets during the year is the definition of net income.

It will be noted that the "Cash" account increased by $26,000, the "Accounts Receivable" account by $2,000, and the "Inventory" by $108,-000. This was a total increase in these assets of $136,000. But the machinery and buildings were depreciated (as noted from the increase in the reserve accounts) by $14,000. So the *net* increase in all the assets was $122,000. We find that, although the bank loan of $25,000 was paid off, the accounts payable increased by $5,000, and at the end of the year the company owed income taxes of $68,340. So the increase in the liabilities for the year amounted to $48,340. Subtracting this figure from the net increase in the assets gives us $73,660, which is the net income for the year after taxes as shown by the income statement. It appears from the statement that most of the profit for the year went into the purchase of additional inventory.

It is a little more difficult to attempt to follow through the transactions for the year from the cash standpoint. Undoubtedly all the accounts receivable on the books at the beginning of the year were collected by the end of the period. Also, probably all the accounts payable at the start of the year were paid off. Certainly we know that the bank loan of $25,000 was paid. But it is noted that the accounts receivable at the end were only $2,000 more than at the beginning of the year, and the accounts payable increased by only $5,000. Income tax for the year has not been paid. Of course, the depreciation charge of $14,000 did not call for a cash outlay. Since the interest income and rent income do not appear as assets, they have apparently been collected in cash. With these facts in mind we can follow through and account for the cash.

The excess of the increase in the accounts payable ($5,000) over the increase in accounts receivable ($2,000) means that $3,000 in cash must be accounted for. The profits would add $73,660. The profits would have been greater to the extent of $68,340 if income taxes (which are still owed) had not been charged as an expense. And if the depreciation charge of $14,000, which took no cash out of the business, had not been made, the profits would have been that much more. Adding these figures together shows us the net amount of cash to be accounted for.

Adjustment of accounts receivable and payable	$ 3,000
Net income for the year	73,660
Income taxes owed	68,340
Depreciation charges	14,000
Cash to be accounted for	$159,000

Referring to the two balance sheets, we find that the $25,000 bank loan was paid off, and that the inventory was increased by $108,000. This accounts for $133,000 of the cash. So we have to account for only $26,000 more. It will be noted that the cash account increased by exactly that amount. So, we have now accounted for all the increase in the cash. Following is a summary of what has just been said:

Payment of bank loan	$ 25,000
Increase in inventory	108,000
Increase in cash	26,000
Cash accounted for	$159,000

The reader should perhaps again be cautioned against confusing the net income and the cash. As we have just seen in the above example, the company earned a net income after taxes of $73,660, but the cash account increased by only $26,000. It is not recommended that the method we used above to account for the cash be used by the reader. To get a true picture of the flow of cash it would be necessary to give effect to every cash receipt and cash outlay. We can do this for the above company.

We will assume that the accounts receivable and accounts payable on the books at the beginning of the year are liquidated during the year. After comparing the inventories at the beginning and end of the year, and the cost of the materials which were sold, it is seen that the purchases must have been $608,000 for the year. But since $25,000 in accounts payable still remains on the books, only $583,000 in cash has been paid for the purchases. Since accounts receivable of $42,000 are on the books at the end of the year, only $958,000 of the net sales has been collected. To simplify matters, we will assume that the furniture was not carried at any value on the books, and that therefore the selling and administrative expenses did not include any depreciation. The depreciation totaling $14,000 was on the machinery and buildings, and is included in the indirect manufacturing costs. Following is a summary of the cash receipts and cash disbursements for the year:

Cash Receipts			*Cash Disbursements*	
Old Accounts	$ 40,000		Old Accounts	$ 20,000
Sales and New Accounts . . .	958,000		Bank Loan	25,000
Non-operating Income	2,000		Purchases and New Accounts	583,000
			Direct Labor	175,000
			Indirect Manufacturing Costs (other than Depreciation)	11,000
			Selling and Administrative Expenses	159,000
			Non-operating Expense . . .	1,000
			Total Disbursements . .	$ 974,000
			Excess of Receipts over Disbursements	26,000
Total	$1,000,000		Total	$1,000,000

As is seen from the above, the excess of cash receipts over disbursements for the year was $26,000, and this, as noted on the ending balance sheet, is the amount the cash account increased. In attempting to determine the cash items as we have done above, proper attention must be given to any income items in the income statement which have not been collected, and any expense items which have not been paid. In our example we considered that all the income items were actually received in cash, and that all the expense accounts were paid for, except depreciation and income taxes.

The reader should always be careful not to confuse cash receipts with income, or cash disbursements with expenses. As noted in the above example, cash was received from the collection of the old accounts, but this did not show as *income* on the income statement. Likewise, an item may be earned during the year and show on the income statement as income, but the cash for it may not have been received during that year. In like manner, we saw that cash was disbursed to pay off the old accounts and the bank loan, but the paying off of a debt is not an *expense*, and thus does not show in the income statement. Also, the income statement may show some expense such as taxes, but if it is not paid during the particular year there will be no cash outlay for it during that year.

Profit Distortion

Because accounting requires a great deal of application of judgment in measuring value changes, there are many potential areas of disagreement regarding the values and gains of a firm and, therefore, the profits of the firm as stated. Certain factors prevalent in today's economy have led to the possibility of a rather significant variation between "stated" profits and "real" profits.

Basic accounting conservatism calls for the recording of profits only when realized and of losses only when incurred. Thus, public accounting will accept write-downs of values of assets when conditions indicate that values have truly declined, but will not accept write-ups. This basic conservatism is designed to protect the outside user of accounting statements, but in times of rapidly changing prices it can lead to rather significant distortion in values as stated and, therefore, to a discrepancy between "stated" profit and "real" profit. In addition, accountants are reluctant to place value on intangible fixed assets because of the difficulty of measuring them. Thus, if these values are not recorded, the changes in these values do not affect stated net profits of the firm.

A much more important problem today in potential variation between stated profits and real profits is the effect of federal income taxation. Because taxes take such an important portion of profit before taxes, most firms are anxious to show as low a profit before tax as possible. This has led to an intentional understatement of profits wherever the tax laws would allow. Thus, many firms adopt depreciation techniques which lead to the statement of higher depreciation charges than has previously been the case, merely because these techniques are allowed for tax purposes and result in lower taxes. However, the user of these statements must also recognize that these depreciation methods result in lower statement of profits both before and after tax than would have otherwise been the case. Tax rules and regulations have become a significant factor in management decisions relating to accounting practices and methods. Therefore, stated profits often reflect tax considerations rather than attempts to measure true gains in owners' equity.

Profit Improvement

Management concentrates much of its effort on techniques for improving net profits. The two major approaches to increasing the dollar amount of net profits are to increase sales rapidly over the current amount of expenses, or to reduce expenses without a corresponding reduction in sales. Among other things, an efficient management is certainly interested in cutting costs. With the high price of labor, the introduction of labor-saving devices is one method of doing this. Anything that reduces expenses in relation to sales will result in a favorable change in net profit.

It is important to cut costs only where they may reasonably be cut from a long-run point of view. To reduce costs in the short run may lead to greater costs in the long run and an over-all poorer profit picture. The use of periodic accounting illustrates the importance of not overemphasizing the effect of an action on profit in any specific accounting period but considering instead its effect in the long run.

The immediate effect of cost reduction on net profit is normally much greater than the effect of an increase in sales. As long as cost reduction does not affect the the amount of sales, each dollar saved in cost results in a dollar increase in net profit before taxes. On the other hand, each dollar increase in sales would normally *not* result in a one-dollar increase in net profit before taxes. If the dollar sales increase is due to a price increase alone, the total may be carried to the net-profit-before-tax figure. However, if a dollar increase in sales is due to increased physical volume of sales, there would have to be a corresponding increase in cost of goods sold and the net effect on the net-profit-before-tax figure would be substantially less than the one-dollar increase in sales.

Fixed and Variable Costs

As sales increase, expenses will also increase, but usually the expenses should not increase in proportion to the sales. Every concern has certain *fixed* costs that are incurred regardless of whether the company operates or not, or regardless of the volume of sales. Depreciation on at least some of the fixed assets would be an example. The administrative expenses might not increase much, if at all, with a relatively large increase in sales. In some cases companies will actually operate at a loss if they can sell their products at such a price that at least some of the income can be applied toward the fixed expenses, even though they cannot get enough to cover all the fixed expenses. Not to operate at all might mean an even greater loss.

In addition to the fixed expenses, the company will have costs or expenses that vary with the volume of sales. For example, the cost of the raw materials and direct labor might be a more or less constant amount per unit of output, and thus vary directly with the volume produced and sold. These are called *variable* costs.

As production and sales increase, the total expenses will, of course, also increase. But due to the more or less fixed costs, the expenses will not increase in proportion to sales. In other words, a company may show an operating ratio of 85 per cent, for example, but an increase in the volume of production and sales may result in the ratio's falling to, for example, 80 per cent.

However, there may be a limit to which sales can be increased without increasing the fixed costs. After that point a slight increase in sales may call for additional facilities that would result in the fixed costs' increasing out of proportion to the increase in sales. However, after adding the new facilities which caused the total expenses to increase faster than the sales, a further increase in sales might be possible without an increase in fixed costs. In other words, a business might make less in profits for a while as a result of addition to the fixed costs, but this may still be done because it may enable the concern to secure even higher production and larger profits in the future.

In connection with the subject we are discussing, businessmen sometimes refer to the "break-even point." This is the point which must be reached before a profit is made. The *break-even* point represents the number of units that would be produced and sold if the company made neither a profit nor a loss. Because of the fixed costs, a profit will be earned after the break-even point has been passed. The break-even point for a particular company would vary from time to time as the selling price of its product is changed, or when the cost of raw materials and labor is changed.

In our discussion above we assumed that the unit sale price of the product remained constant. In many instances the unit cost of the product declines as more products are sold, with the result that the unit selling price for the product may be lowered.

RETAINED INCOME AND SURPLUS

After paying federal income taxes and dividends (if any) the balance of the net income shown on the income statement is carried to the net worth section of the balance sheet, and put into the account that represents the accumulated retained income from past years. The current retained income account in the income statement may be called, instead of "retained income," *net profit after dividends,* or *net earnings after dividends.* The account in the net worth section of the balance sheet into which the retained earnings entry is made is also known by different names: *retained income, retained earnings, accumulated income* or *earnings, earned surplus,* and *surplus.*

Accountants are getting many companies to eliminate the term *surplus* in the net worth section of the balance sheet, and to substitute a title such as *retained earnings,* when it represents the accumulation of earnings from operations. When the "surplus" represents something other than regular earnings, it is recommended that the source of the surplus be indicated along with the use of the word *surplus.*

In our discussion we will use the term *surplus,* because it covers not only the retained income, but also the "surplus" arising from any other source. It is thus a simple word and can be conveniently used in writing or in discussion. Even though the tendency is to get away from using the term, it is still used when referring in general to reserves that are set up from the "surplus." That is, all such reserves are called "surplus reserves."

Meaning of Surplus

The *surplus* of a company represents the excess of the assets over the sum of the liabilities and the par value or stated value (in the case of no-par stock) of the capital stock. Assuming that the "Capital Stock" account remains constant, any increase in the assets without as great an increase in the liabilities will result in an increase in the surplus. Also a decrease in the liabilities not accompanied by as great a decrease in the assets will increase the surplus. In other words, any increase in the *net* assets (assuming the capital stock account remains the same) results in an increase in the surplus.

It should be noted that the surplus is a net worth account, and it should be stressed that it is merely an "account" on the books of the company. It is never anything real or tangible. It appears only as an ink figure on the company's books and on the balance sheet. Let us assume that a company starts out by selling $1,000,000 in stock at its par value. No other assets are owned and we will assume, to simplify the discussion, that no liabilities are incurred. A simple balance sheet of the company would appear as follows:

Assets		Net Worth	
Cash	$1,000,000	Capital Stock	$1,000,000

As noted, the company has $1,000,000 in cash and not one cent in surplus. If all the cash was then spent for inventory, the company would have no cash and also no surplus. During the course of the year the company may sell this inventory and make a "net profit" after taxes of $100,000. We will assume that as the cash is received it is reinvested in additional inventory. The balance sheet would then appear as follows:

Assets		Net Worth	
Inventory	$1,100,000	Capital Stock	$1,000,000
		Surplus (retained income) .	100,000

The company now has $100,000 in "surplus," but not a cent in cash. Many people think that the "surplus" represents the *cash* which is not needed in the business. That is one of the reasons companies are getting away from using the term. From the simple example given above, it should be obvious that there is not necessarily any connection between the surplus account and the cash account. The surplus in a sense is a balancing account. It reflects any increase in the *net* assets for the period under consideration. If we are looking for the cash or other tangible property we must look to the assets section of the balance sheet and not to the net worth.

Meaning of Deficit

A *deficit* is the opposite of a surplus. A deficit exists when the assets are less than the sum of the liabilities and capital stock. For example, let us assume prices decline with the result that the company in the above example would have to sell its inventory at such a low price that it lost $200,000 during the second year of its operations. The balance sheet would then appear as follows:

Assets		Net Worth	
Cash (or Inventory)	$900,000	Capital Stock	$1,000,000
		Deficit	100,000
Total	$900,000	Total	$ 900,000

The effect of the operating loss is to wipe out the surplus entirely and to create in its place a deficit of $100,000. In some instances a company will list the deficit on the "assets" side, instead of subtracting it from the capital stock. Certainly a deficit is anything but an asset.

Earned Surplus or Retained Earnings

Commonly, the term *earned surplus* is taken to mean the surplus that arises from the net income which is retained in the business. In some instances the "earned surplus" is narrowly construed to mean only the earnings from ordinary operations, or at least not to include non-recurring profit such as that arising from the sale of a building no longer needed in the business. As commonly used however, and doubtless correctly so, "earned surplus" means all the retained net income regardless of the source. The terms *realized surplus, realized profits,* and *retained earnings* are used synonymously with *earned surplus.*

Capital Surplus

Surplus that arises from some source other than the retained net income is called *capital surplus.* Sometimes, the term *unearned surplus* or *unrealized surplus* is used to describe this type of surplus, but perhaps these phrases are misleading, because in some instances the capital surplus has been "realized" if not "earned." For example, if stock with a par value of $100 is sold for $120 a share by the issuing company, a capital surplus of $20 is thereby created. To say that this was unearned or unrealized might not convey the correct impression.

There are many sources of capital surplus, and the appearance of the balance sheet can be changed materially through the handling of capital surplus. It is only fair to the shareholders and others who may be interested in the balance sheet that the surplus which arises from retained net income be distinctly shown, and that it not be merged with the capital surplus. The management should also split the capital surplus up according to source, and use a title for the various accounts which reveals the source of each kind of surplus.

Following are some of the major sources of capital surplus:

1. Sale of stock for more than par or stated value
2. Forfeited subscriptions
3. Gifts made to company
4. Purchase of its own securities at less than par, stated, or face value
5. Reduction of "Capital Stock" account by reducing par or reducing number of shares
6. Reappraisal of assets upward
7. Mergers and consolidations
8. Recapitalizations and reorganizations
9. Elimination of certain reserves

Uses of Surplus

Since surplus is basically a balancing item between total assets and the sum of liabilities and capital stock accounts, surplus itself is nothing more than an accounting entry. The sum of the "Capital Stock" account and "Surplus" account shows the total of the owners' equity in the business. If the capital stock remains the same, changes in surplus represent changes in owners' equity. A discussion of uses of surplus is somewhat unrealistic because we cannot "use" an accounting entry; we can only use assets which the surplus represents. In order to use these assets, they must normally be in cash form. Common uses would then be the purchase of other assets or the payment of liabilities. At any point in time the accumulated surpluses of a business have already been used for the various asset items which the surpluses represent. Accounting makes no attempt to relate the surpluses to any specific asset accounts. The only real use of the amount listed on the balance sheet as surplus is in dividend determination. This is discussed in the following chapter.

RESERVES

A person not acquainted with accounting terminology is inclined to think of a "reserve" as cash or equivalent which is "reserved" or set aside for a particular purpose. This is not the way the term is used by accountants or businessmen in connection with balance sheets. The term *fund* is usually used in financial statements to apply to the account which represents an appropriation of cash or equivalent for some specific purpose. The *sinking fund* for the retirement of bonds is an example.

A *reserve* is a bookkeeping account. From an accounting standpoint, it is always a "credit." Assets, such as "funds," are always "debit" balance accounts. A reserve account may merely represent a deduction from an asset account, a liability of the company, or the earmarking of surplus.

Because of the misunderstanding in regard to the meaning of "reserve," many companies are eliminating use of this word and substituting such phrases as "provision for," "allowance for," or "appropriation for." This is recommended for purposes of published reports. For our purposes, however, it is much more convenient to use the term *reserve,* and we will continue to do so.

Reserves are usually divided into three general types, as follows:

1. Valuation reserves
2. Liability reserves
3. Surplus reserves

Valuation Reserves

In the preceding chapter we have already discussed valuation reserves when we considered the reserves for depreciation, obsolescence, and depletion. Another valuation reserve is the reserve for bad debts.

It will be recalled that the reserves are set up at the same time that the company makes a charge to the appropriate expense in the income statement. These reserves are deducted from the proper asset account to show the true depreciated or adjusted value of the particular asset. It is thus apparent that they are merely bookkeeping accounts.

Liability Reserves

Those who are not acquainted with accounting terminology would probably object more strenuously to calling a liability reserve a "reserve" than to applying the term to a valuation reserve. A liability reserve is actually a *liability*, or debt owed by the company. When used, it is applied to an expense which has actually been incurred, and for which a charge has been made in the income statement, but the cash has not yet been expended for it. A "reserve for interest" or "reserve for taxes," are examples. In some instances when the term *reserve* is applied to a liability, it is for an expense which has been incurred and is owed, but the exact amount owed is not definite at the time. This is sometimes the case with federal income taxes.

There is a trend away from the use of "Reserve" as applied to a liability. Even when the amount of the federal taxes owed is not definitely known, many companies are now using a title such as "Provision for Federal Income Taxes" to show the tax liability. In some instances the liability for taxes or other expenses is shown under the caption of "Accrued," followed by the name of the liability.

An increasing number of companies are establishing pension plans for their employees. In some instances annual amounts are paid to an insurance company or a trustee to cover the future payments. When this is done the plan is said to be *funded*. Other companies assume a liability for pensions but do not set up any separate fund at the time to cover the future payments. In some instances the balance sheet does not show any liability for the payments. In others a footnote is added to the balance sheet indicating the amount of the liability. Still other companies show the obligation under their liabilities. When the latter procedure is followed the liability may appear on the statements as a "Reserve for Pensions." In this case it is probable that the pension obligation was charged as an expense against the current income. Some companies set up a *surplus* reserve covering the pension. In some instances a company will set up a reserve for pensions covering the amount of the anticipated liability which is in excess of that which is funded with an insurance company or trustee.

Surplus Reserve

Surplus reserves represent the appropriation of surplus. In practically all instances it is an appropriation of *earned* surplus, that is, the *retained* income. These reserves represent nothing tangible. They merely earmark surplus. They are set up by debiting the surplus and crediting the reserve. Since the surplus itself is merely a balancing account and does not represent anything tangible, the reserve set up out of it likewise cannot be anything tangible.

The setting up of a surplus reserve accomplishes two purposes: (1) it specifically calls attention to the fact that the amount represented by the reserve is needed or may be needed for the purpose indicated in the reserve account title, and (2) it prevents the payment of dividends from that part of the surplus which is put into the reserve. If no surplus reserves were set up the "free" surplus would appear larger and the shareholders might think that the company should pay out more in the form of dividends. But the assets represented by the surplus may be needed for some specific purpose, and are therefore unavailable for dividends. Establishing the reserve and giving it a title that indicates the purpose for the retention of the surplus will result in better stockholder relations.

In some instances the surplus reserve is set up to show that assets of equivalent amount have been set aside in a separate fund for a specific purpose. The reserve for a sinking fund may be an example. In other instances such as the reserve for improvements, no cash or fund is set aside, but the reserve indicates that cash or other assets are not available for dividends and should be retained in the business to facilitate the expansion program. The more important surplus reserves are discussed below.

Reserve for Sinking Fund. This reserve was discussed in Chapter 7. Its purpose is to notify the company management and the shareholder that the company intends to retire bonded indebtedness with funds accumulated in the business from earnings. Therefore, the retained earnings or surplus is not available for dividend distribution or for other purposes. The reserve for sinking fund does not actually include the setting aside of assets to meet the bond liability.

A point that should be mentioned here is: What happens to the sinking fund reserve when the bonds are retired? The answer is that nothing happens to it. The use of cash or a sinking fund to retire the bonds reduces the assets, but the bond liability is reduced by the same amount. Therefore, the net worth of the company is not affected. The reserve has accomplished its purpose of indicating that assets of the same amount were being retained to retire the bonds, and preventing the payment of dividends to the extent of the amount appropriated. It is therefore put back into the surplus account by debiting the reserve and crediting the surplus. Dividends could then be legally paid from such surplus, but from a practical standpoint the use of cash to retire the bonds may make such dividends impossible.

Reserve for Expansion. The reserve for expansion may be so labeled, or it may be called a "Reserve for Additions, Betterments, and Improvements," or any one or more of these words may be used in the title. The purpose of this reserve is to show the purpose for retaining part of the surplus, and preventing dividends to the extent of the reserve, with the result that the company is in a better asset position to carry on an expansion program.

The expansion, however, merely means the substitution of one asset for another, and therefore the net worth of the company is not affected. In other words, the reserve is not consumed by the expansion. It may therefore be put back into the surplus account after the program has been completed. Although cash dividends could legally be paid from this surplus, the expansion may have depleted the cash. Since the amount formerly shown in the "Reserve" account is now permanently invested in fixed assets, it might be capitalized through a dividend payable in stock.

Reserve for Working Capital. The reserve for working capital is similar to the reserve for expansion, but attention is being called to the fact that the appropriation is for current rather than fixed assets. The restriction of dividends to the extent of the reserve does not of course automatically insure that the assets retained will find their way into additional working capital. The amount retained may be invested in additional fixed assets, or it might be used for debt retirement.

Reserve for Dividend Equalization. Certain advantages accrue from the payment of regular dividends. But earnings of most corporations fluctuate from year to year, particularly those which are more subject to the business cycle. Some companies will pay out a smaller proportion of their earnings when the net income is large than when it is relatively low. In this way they may be able to stabilize the rate of dividends on the stock from year to year. In order to facilitate this procedure the company may set up a reserve for dividend equalization when earnings are large, and then draw on this reserve for the payment of dividends when earnings fall off. It is obvious that when this reserve is used for dividend payments, it is consumed. This is in contrast to the surplus reserves discussed above which are put back into the surplus account after their purpose has been accomplished.

Reserve for Replacement of Assets. In our discussion of depreciation it was pointed out that depreciation was charged and reserves set up on the basis of the cost value, and that replacement was sometimes difficult during a period of rising prices. In addition to the usual method of handling depreciation, a surplus reserve equivalent in amount to the difference between the original cost and the replacement cost may be set up. Through the retention of earnings that otherwise may have been paid out in dividends, the company may be in a better asset position to replace the depreciated property. If the replacement does cost more than the original asset, the reserve account is not thereby consumed. The new asset will be carried on the books at the total cost price, and thus the net worth is not affected. The reserve account could then be put back into the surplus account, or it could be retained to aid in the replacement of other assets.

Reserve Against Decline in Asset Values. Many companies carry their raw materials inventory at cost or market, whichever is lower. If the market price declines after the goods are purchased, the inventories are marked down and the charge is made against current income for the loss. In some instances a company will want in addition to make some provision for the possible further decline of an indefinite amount in the inventory. This may be done by setting up a surplus reserve. If the decline actually takes place the loss is written off against the reserve. Otherwise, the reserve can be continued for the possible decline in future purchases, or it can be put back into the surplus account.

Reserve for Contingencies. Many companies carry a general surplus reserve called "Reserve for Contingencies." This is intended to take care of any losses for which provision has not otherwise been made. It may cover losses for which insurance is unobtainable, or possible losses in excess of the amount of insurance carried. In some instances a separate insurance reserve is set up.

Companies sometimes get involved in lawsuits relating to damages caused by the company's operations or possible patent infringements, and set up surplus reserves to cover adverse court decisions. It might be more conservative accounting to show some of these as current liabilities, particularly if it appears that the company will come out on the losing end of the case. In some instances a contingency reserve is set up to help the company during a period when its profits decline because of the invention of new industry methods or processes or the production of new models on the part of a competitor.

DEFICITS

When the liabilities of a company plus its "Capital Stock" account as shown on the books are greater than its assets, a deficit exists. A deficit represents a reduction in the owners' equity below the stated value of its stock. Deficits are relatively common in new companies. They usually come about through operating losses. If profits are made in the future and retained in the business, they wipe out the operating loss deficit.

Deficits may occur also from losses which may be considered non-recurring or non-operating. Examples would be physical destruction of property, or obsolescence of property. These non-operating losses are real, but would appear in the books as deficits only if they were recognized in the accounting process through a writing-down of the value of property. In addition, deficits may be created by accounting entries which reduce asset values or write up liabilities regardless of whether the write-down of assets or write-up of liabilities is realistic. Thus, book deficits are not necessarily real deficits, and vice versa.

Deficits may be eliminated in reality and from the books by retention of earnings in the amount of the deficits. This is the most common technique used to remove real deficits. In addition, deficits may be reduced or eliminated in the same way as a capital surplus may be created. These ways were listed earlier in this chapter.

REINVESTMENT

The decision on the reinvestment of earnings is actually a decision on the desirability of the firm's use of the earnings relative to paying them out to the stockholders, thereby letting the stockholders determine what use should be made of them. This decision is inherently tied into dividend policies, which are discussed in the next chapter. However, a portion of the decision is closely related to the firm's ability to utilize additional capital profitably through reinvested earnings, which have become a significant source of funds for business in recent years.

Table 25–1 gives the total amount of retained earnings and expenditures for new plant and equipment in billions of dollars for all American firms (except banks and insurance companies). This table indicates the importance of retained earnings as an internal source of funds to American business. In recent years, retained earnings have provided better than one-fourth of all new fixed capital investment by business. Thus reinvestment of earnings is one of the most important sources of funds for business today. The amount of retained earnings has exceeded net new security issues for American corporations in all but five of the twelve years from 1950 through 1961. In these twelve years, retained earnings totaled $104.8 billion while net new security issues totaled $90.9 billion.[1]

Purpose of Reinvestment

The purpose of reinvesting earnings should be the same as the purpose of any other management decision—the attainment of the objectives

[1] *Economic Report of the President, 1962* (Washington, D. C.: U. S. Government Printing Office, 1962), p. 283.

of the firm. If reinvested earnings are used to repay creditors rather than to expand the business, the apparent objectives of the decision are to improve the financial position of the firm and to add to its long-run financial stability.

Before earnings should be invested in expansion of assets of the firm, a determination should have been made that the expansion will meet the profitability objective of the firm. Earnings should be reinvested in additional assets only if the return on the investment is sufficient to compensate the owners for the retention of their earnings by the firm.

Table 25–1. Retained Earnings and Expenditures on New Plant and Equipment for All American Corporations Except Banks and Insurance Companies, 1950–1961 (In Billions of Dollars)

Year	Retained Earnings	Expenditures for New Plant and Equipment	Retained Earnings as a Per Cent of Expenditures
1950	$13.0	$16.9	76.9
1951	10.0	21.6	46.3
1952	7.4	22.4	33.0
1953	7.9	23.9	33.1
1954	6.3	22.4	28.1
1955	10.9	24.2	45.0
1956	10.5	29.9	35.1
1957	8.9	32.7	27.2
1958	5.7	26.4	21.6
1959	9.1	27.7	32.9
1960	7.4	30.8	24.0
1961	7.7	30.4	25.3

SOURCE: *Economic Report of the President, 1962* (Washington, D. C.: U. S. Government Printing Office, 1962), p. 283.

Reinvestment of earnings is only one of the sources of the funds available to most firms. Thus, the decision on expansion should be made separately from the choice of source of funds, and the decision to reinvest should be made after considering the other alternate sources of funds available to the firm. In the discussion of cost of capital, it was determined that reinvested earnings are a relatively expensive source of funds. However, they have the tremendous advantages of having no effect upon the control of the organization and of being minimum-risk funds. In addition, there is no cost involved in obtaining the funds such as would be required for the sale of additional securities. For these reasons, great emphasis has been placed on reinvestment of earnings as a suitable source of permanent capital for most American corporations. However, to justify reinvestment of earnings, the management must have determined that the use to which the funds will be put will be sufficiently profitable to compensate for the opportunity costs to the stockholder of not having these funds available for personal investment elsewhere.

Preinvestment of Earnings

In order to invest future earnings at the present time, the firm obviously must obtain funds elsewhere until the earnings materialize. Commonly, creditor sources are used to bridge the gap between the time of the investment in new assets and the retention of future earnings. Preinvestment of earnings has become increasingly common in recent years due to the increased stability of earnings for many corporations and the need for current expansion rather than waiting until earnings are available. Thus, the firms which preinvest earnings take advantage of expansion opportunities when they occur rather than when funds from earnings are available. The entire development of the intermediate-term loan in the post-war period has been related to the concept of preinvestment of earnings.

A decision to preinvest earnings should be made on the same basis as a decision to invest earnings which are currently on hand. It requires a commitment to withhold these earnings from the stockholder and, therefore, requires a planned level of profitability to compensate the stockholder in the future for the retention of earnings from him. A decision to preinvest earnings significantly affects future dividend decisions.

Because of the very close interrelationship between dividends and reinvestment of earnings, this subject will be discussed further in the next chapter in relation to the nature of dividend policy.

QUESTIONS

1. Define *profit* from an accounting point of view. Discuss other possible definitions of profit.
2. Indicate how the "cost of goods sold" might include different items, depending upon the particular company being considered.
3. Should "sales discounts" be subtracted from the "sales" in the income statement, or shown as a non-operating expense? Why?
4. Do you think "purchase discounts" should be subtracted from the cost of the purchases and the net shown under purchases, or should it be shown as a non-operating income item? Why?
5. When the net income of a corporation is reported for the year, is that before or after federal income taxes? Why?
6. Ascertain whether the financial manuals use the same terminology as used in this book for the various captions in the income statement.
7. (a) Indicate definitely what is meant by the "surplus" of a corporation.
   (b) How should a deficit be shown on the balance sheet?
8. Indicate the sources of capital surplus.
9. Distinguish among valuation reserves, liability reserves, and surplus reserves. Give two examples of each.

10. What disposition is finally made of each of the following reserves: reserve for improvements, reserve for bad debts, sinking fund reserve, reserve for federal income taxes?
11. What criticism is sometimes made of the use of the term *reserve?* What term might be substituted for it?
12. Should reserves for contingencies and reserves for taxes be shown as liabilities or in the net worth section of the balance sheet? Explain.
13. Define a *deficit*.
14. Indicate the various ways in which a deficit may be eliminated from the books. Which of these do you believe is the best? Explain.
15. How should a corporate board of directors approach the question of whether to reinvest corporate earnings?

PROBLEMS

1. Refer to the income statement and balance sheet for the Standard Manufacturing Co. (see pages 593 and 596). If the company doubled its gross sales in the next year, what might its income statement for the year 19x2 be like? Based on your estimated income statement for the year 19x2, make up a balance sheet for December 31, 19x2.

2. On January 1, 19x1, the net worth section of the balance sheet of the Peerless Metal Co. was as follows:

Capital stock	$3,000,000 (par $100)
Deficit	100,000

During the year the following transactions took place: $100,000 of the stock was donated back to the company, and half of this was sold for $80 a share; one of the plants was reappraised from $1,000,000 to $1,500,000; another plant was reappraised from $500,000 to $650,000; $1,000,000 (in par) of the unissued stock was sold for $120 a share; a new building was constructed at a cost of $200,000; $1,000,000 worth of the company's bonds were converted into unissued stock at $125 per share; earnings from ordinary operations were $400,000. (a) Indicate how the net worth section would appear at the end of the year. (The company's ledger has two surplus accounts: "Surplus" and "Capital Surplus.") (b) What can the company do with its "Capital Surplus"?

3. (a) Is surplus a tangible item? (b) Are cash dividends really paid from surplus? (c) The sales manager of a large industrial corporation, when asked how his company was going to finance the construction of a new office building, replied: "We are going to build it out of our surplus." When asked what he meant by "surplus," he pointed to the "Surplus" account on the balance sheet. Was the sales manager's statement technically accurate? Explain.

4. Indicate with respect to each of the following the general term that could be applied to that type of reserve account, the section of the balance sheet in which it should be placed, and contra "debit" entry that is made when the reserve is set up: (a) Reserve for Depreciation. (b) Sinking Fund Reserve. (c) Reserve for Betterments and Improvements. (d) Reserve for Dividend Equalization. (e) Reserve for Bad Debts. (f) Reserve for Obsolescence. (g) Reserve for Decline in Inventory Value. (h) Reserve for Federal Income Tax.

5. Look up the latest available financial statements of General Motors Corp. What reserves does this company have on its books? Attempt to ascertain how these reserves came into existence.

SELECTED READINGS

AMERICAN INSTITUTE OF CERTIFIED PUBLIC ACCOUNTANTS, STUDY GROUP ON BUSINESS INCOME. *Changing Concepts of Business Income.* New York: The Macmillan Co., 1952.

AMERICAN MANAGEMENT ASSOCIATION. *Improved Tools of Financial Management.* Financial Management Series, No. 111. New York: American Management Association, 1956.

————. *Modern Financial Planning and Control.* Financial Management Series, No. 110. New York: American Management Association, 1956.

DEWING, ARTHUR S. *Financial Policy of Corporations,* 5th ed. New York: The Ronald Press Co., 1953. Chapters 17-22, 25-26.

FOSTER, EDWARD, JR., and ROBBINS, SIDNEY. "Profit Planning and the Finance Function." *Journal of Finance,* December, 1957, pp. 451-67.

FOULKE, R. A. *Practical Financial Statement Analysis,* 3d ed. New York: McGraw-Hill Book Co., Inc., 1957.

GORDON, MYRON J. *The Investment, Financing, and Valuation of the Corporation.* Homewood, Ill.: Richard D. Irwin, Inc., 1962.

HATFIELD, H. R. *Surplus and Dividends.* Cambridge: Harvard University Press, 1943.

KENNEDY, RALPH D., and MCMULLEN, STEWART Y. *Financial Statements, Form, Analysis, and Interpretation,* 3d ed. Homewood, Ill.: Richard D. Irwin, 1957.

LEWIS, RONELLO B. *Accounting Reports for Management.* Englewood Cliffs, N. J.: Prentice-Hall, Inc., 1957.

OSBORNE, R. C. *Corporate Profits, War and Post-War.* Urbana: University of Illinois, Bureau of Economic and Business Research, 1954.

26

Dividends

After paying all expenses and income taxes, part of the net income of a corporation is usually paid out to the shareholders in the form of dividends, and the balance is transferred to the "Retained Earnings" or "Surplus" account. Either of these two accounts may be used, at least in part, to set up surplus reserve accounts. The balance left in the accounts may also be used in the future as a source of dividend payments.

This chapter is concerned with the types of dividends which may be paid, and the determination of dividend policies. Dividends paid by corporations take one of three forms: (1) those that are paid in cash or other property, (2) those that are paid in notes or bonds, and (3) those that are paid in stock of the company. It will be noted that each of these three different kinds of dividends affects different sections of the balance sheet. Following the discussion of stock dividends, we will take up *stock splits,* which are not dividends at all, but their similarity to stock dividends warrants their inclusion in this chapter. Following are the various kinds of dividends that fall into the three groups mentioned above:

1. Cash dividends
2. Property dividends
3. Scrip dividends
4. Bond dividends
5. Stock dividends

Cash Dividends

By far the most common form of dividends is cash dividends. Most of the discussion relating to this form of dividends will be reserved until later in the chapter when we take up dividend policies. It should be noted that "cash" dividends are not actually paid in cash but rather by checks. The larger companies have a bank or trust company act as their dividend-paying agent. Addressograph plates bearing the names and addresses of the shareholders are kept by the institution, and the latter has a record of the number and kind of shares held by each shareholder. All the detailed work in connection with making out the checks and sending them to the shareholders is handled by the institution.

Property Dividends

Dividends payable in assets or property other than cash are called "property" dividends. Usually this property takes the form of securities of other companies. In some instances such a dividend is referred to as a "security" dividend. In some cases the property or security dividend is a liquidation dividend, but in others such a dividend may be paid by a going concern. Some public utility holding companies have paid security dividends to their shareholders as a means of disposing of stock under the requirements of the Public Utility Holding Company Act. In anti-trust actions, when a corporation is ordered to divest itself of stock of other corporations, it will sometimes distribute that stock to its own shareholders. In some instances companies have paid dividends in government bonds which the company had been holding as an investment.

As an alternative to a security dividend, the company could sell the securities and pay a cash dividend. But the securities may be selling for more than the company paid for them, and the income tax would have to be paid on the profit. By paying the securities themselves out as dividends the corporation escapes the tax. The shareholders receiving such a dividend, however, would have to report them as ordinary earned income at the value existing on the day they are received. Another reason for not attempting to sell the securities is that it might unduly depress the price of the securities.

Occasionally dividends will be paid in property other than cash or securities. Building lots, liquor, and warehouse receipts for liquor have been distributed as dividends.

From an accounting standpoint the payment of a cash or property dividend results in a debit to the "Surplus," or "Retained Income" account, and a credit to the appropriate asset account.

A corporation will sometimes *spin off* the stock of a subsidiary to its own shareholders under conditions prescribed by the Internal Revenue Code which qualify it as tax-free to the recipient shareholders.

Scrip Dividends

Dividends that are paid in notes of the particular corporation are called *scrip* dividends. The notes usually bear interest and, when a definite due date is stated, are also negotiable. They are usually classified as current liabilities of the company, particularly when they mature within a period of one year. In event of failure of the company, the holders of the notes would be treated just as any other general creditor of the company, provided the dividend had been legally declared. Scrip dividends are rarely used.

The reason for the use of scrip dividends is that the company does not have the necessary cash available to pay a cash dividend; or it has the cash, but wants to use it for another purpose and still does not want to "pass" the dividend. Thus it declares and pays a scrip dividend. If a company has actual earnings, and the cash has not been collected yet but will be collected by the time the notes come due—then the scrip dividend may be justified. Or even if the cash is not now available but will be forthcoming from some other source, the dividend may be warranted. But in most instances when the scrip dividend has been used, the company should perhaps have passed the dividend at least until such time as it could pay a cash dividend. In some instances the earnings reported may not be real because of undercharging of depreciation or some other questionable accounting practice.

In a sense, the payment of a scrip dividend is an admission of the inability to pay a cash dividend. This situation should not be made worse by the assumption of an obligation in the form of the notes to pay cash at some future time.

Any obligation of the company to pay preferred dividends before the common dividends cannot be satisfied by the payment of a scrip dividend to the preferred shareholders, unless it is so specified in the stock contract or the preferred shareholders agree to such action.

Bond Dividends

Bond dividends are similar to scrip dividends except that the obligation assumes a longer maturity date. Both scrip and bond dividends result in the lessening of surplus and an addition to the appropriate liability account. Bond dividends, like scrip dividends, are rare.

In one way at least the bond dividend may be preferred over the scrip dividend. If the company cannot pay a cash dividend at the time, it may be unable to meet the short-term notes when they become due. A bond obligation of the same amount may be met, however, since the company has a longer period of time to secure the cash. In the meantime, however, interest will be continuing on the obligations.

It is not uncommon to see corporations paying cash dividends to their shareholders and at the same time selling bonds in the market. This would not seem much different in its effect on the corporation from retaining the cash instead of getting it through the sale of bonds, and declaring a bond dividend. A company might also consider a bond dividend as an alternative to a stock dividend. In each case the company retains the use of the money represented by the dividend. But before the earnings can be used to pay a dividend on the stock, income taxes must be paid on these earnings. But if a bond dividend is paid, the interest on the bonds is deductible before arriving at future net taxable income. Thus, in this respect, the corporation and its shareholders would benefit taxwise from the bond dividend. Any use of bond dividends on the part of close corporations for tax savings purposes, however, would undoubtedly be looked into by the Internal Revenue Service, and possibly the interest deduction would be disallowed.

STOCK DIVIDENDS

In relative importance, stock dividends rank next to cash dividends. A more lengthy discussion of stock dividends is advisable.

When a stock dividend is declared and paid, the "Surplus" or "Retained Earnings" account is debited, as in the case of any other kind of a dividend, and the "Capital Stock" account is credited. In order to pay the stock dividend the company would, of course, have to have sufficient authorized capital stock; otherwise, it would be necessary to go through the procedure—and pay the taxes and fees—for a charter amendment to get the necessary amount of authorized stock. When a stock dividend is paid, it should be noted that the par value or stated value of the outstanding stock is not changed, and the stock represented by the dividend possesses the same par or stated value as the stock on which the dividend is paid.

It should be apparent that so far as book values are concerned, the stock dividend does not give the shareholder anything he did not possess before. Let us assume that the net worth section of the balance sheet of a company appears as follows.

Capital Stock (par value $100)	$1,000,000
Surplus	2,000,000
Total Net Worth .....:..........	$3,000,000

The book value of the stock in the above example is $300 a share. If the company now pays a stock dividend of 100 per cent, the net worth would be changed as follows:

Capital Stock (par value $100)	$2,000,000
Surplus	1,000,000
Total Net Worth	$3,000,000

After the dividend each shareholder now has two shares of stock for each one share that he possessed before the dividend was paid. The book value per share, however, has been reduced from $300 to $150. So the shareholder now has two shares with a book value of $150 each, instead of one share with a book value of $300. In other words, the shareholder's equity is not changed at all by the stock dividend. It is similar to having two five-dollar bills instead of one ten-dollar bill (although the par value is not reduced).

Reasons for Paying Stock Dividends

The reasons for paying stock dividends are as follows.

1. *Money is Retained in the Business.* The stock dividend is the only kind of a dividend that may be paid without taking any money or other property out of the business at any time. As has been pointed out before, the earnings of a company are frequently not represented by cash; often they show up as more inventory and other assets. The earnings are said to be "plowed back" into the business. Perhaps a more accurate statement is to say they are absorbed by the business in the form of additions to the net assets. A company that uses its earnings for expansion purposes cannot, from a practical standpoint, pay cash dividends. The retained earnings or surplus is as permanent a part of the business as the assets represented by the capital stock. That being the case, there is no reason why the surplus should not be permanently capitalized by the payment of a stock dividend.

Even if the earnings were in the form of cash, but the company had a need for the funds in the near future, it would appear desirable not to pay the money out in the form of a cash dividend. The stock dividend may be recommended in such a situation.

2. *Pacify the Shareholders.* Shareholders expect to receive dividends when there are earnings. In the event the company has used or needs the money in the business, it can retain the money and still pay a stock dividend. In this way the shareholder is pacified.

In most instances, however, a stock dividend represents a special or extra dividend. At the time it is paid the company will usually also pay the regular dividend in cash. As a rule, the stock dividend is not used as a substitute for the regular cash dividend. But even though the regular cash dividends are paid, if the retained earnings are still relatively large, the shareholders may expect additional dividends. It is in a situation of this kind that the stock dividend is frequently used.

If the shareholder wants his additional dividend in the form of cash, he can sell the stock obtained as a dividend in the market. Of course, this would lessen the shareholder's proportionate interest in the business and his degree of control. Also, his right to future dividends, as well as his right to assets upon dissolution of the company, would be diluted.

3. *Reduce the Per-Share Earnings and Dividends.* If a company has a 100 per cent stock dividend, as in the example given above, since the number of shares is doubled without any new capital coming into the business, the earnings per share would tend to be reduced 50 per cent. Although a company likes to have large earnings per share, it does not want the figure to get too high. Extremely large earnings per share may cause labor, and particularly the labor unions, to think that the company is not paying high enough wages. Also, customers may wonder whether the company is charging too much for its products. Naturally, the total corporate earnings will tend to be just as large after the stock dividend, but the fact that the per-share earnings are less may cause some people to assume earnings are more reasonable than before.

If a company continues to pay out the same percentage of its earnings in the form of dividends, the 100 per cent stock dividend would tend to reduce the per-share dividends by 50 per cent. What was stated above in regard to the advantages of reducing the per-share earnings applies with equal force to the per-share dividends.

4. *Reduce the Market Price of the Stock.* In many instances the principal reason for declaring a stock dividend is to reduce the market price per share of the stock. That could also be accomplished with a stock split-up (discussed later in the chapter). Although companies like to see their stock selling for a relatively high price, there is a limit. Too high a price narrows the market. Fewer people can buy the stock, and its price is subject to greater fluctuations, at least from the standpoint of dollars-and-cents changes. Listed stocks selling for over $100 a share are good candidates for stock dividends or stock splits. Even $60, or $80, might be considered too high a price for a good market.

The market price of stock becomes of considerable importance when a new issue of stock is being considered. New shares will be sold (except under privileged subscriptions) at approximately the market price of the old stock. But a relatively high price may narrow the market so much that the company could not sell the stock for its real worth. Prior to the offering of the new stock, the company may therefore have a sizable stock dividend to reduce the market price of the stock, and thus enable the company to attract a wide market.

Practical Advantages to Shareholders

Perhaps in most instances shareholders actually benefit from the payment of stock dividends. The possible advantages are as follows.

1. *Favorable Future Outlook.* Corporate managements usually think through the consequences of a stock dividend before paying it. They realize that the per-share earnings and dividends will presently be re-

duced in proportion to the amount of new stock issued, and usually they would not authorize such dividends unless they thought that the future earnings were going to be as large or larger than those of the past. In some instances, particularly when the stock dividends are relatively small, the management indicates that it hopes to maintain the same *rate* of dividends on all the shares as it was paying on the old shares. This would necessitate more dollars to pay the future dividends. It is therefore probable that the managment expects earnings actually to increase in the future.

2. *Larger Dividends.* As stated above, in many instances the company continues to pay the same amount of dividends per share after a stock dividend has been paid. Since the shareholder holds more shares of stock after receipt of the stock dividend, his future cash dividends may be larger as a result of the stock dividend.

3. *Greater Market Value.* In many instances a stock dividend does not reduce the market price of the stock as much as its book value. This results from the fact that the stock will have a wider market, and the dividends may be maintained at the same rate. The shareholder, therefore, commonly finds that the market value of the aggregate of his holdings after the stock dividend is greater than it was before. Even if the immediate effect of the stock dividend is to reduce the market value of the stock per share, the market price often tends to work up toward the old price, for the reasons stated above.

4. *Tax Savings.* Cash dividends are taxable as ordinary income in the hands of the recipient stockholder. Stock dividends, on the other hand, are usually tax exempt. Taxability is the subject of the next section.

Taxability of Stock Dividends

It was stated above that a stock dividend does not give the shareholder anything that he did not possess before. It is for this reason that the Internal Revenue Code provides that a stock dividend is tax exempt unless: (1) it is paid to the preferred stockholders in lieu of their cash dividend for the current or preceding year, or (2) the stockholder has a choice whether to take his dividend in stock or in cash or other property. (This is sometimes called an *optional* dividend.) These rules apply regardless of whether the dividend is common stock paid on common or preferred, or vice versa.

When the stock dividend (other than one paid in preferred stock) is not taxable as ordinary income, the dividend reduces the *cost* price of the stock for purposes of computing the capital gain tax that must be paid upon sale of the stock. Thus, if a person paid $300 for a share of stock and subsequently the company had a 100 per cent non-taxable stock dividend, the cost price per share would be considered to be $150 a share. If one of the shares thereafter is sold for $180, a capital gain tax must be paid on the $30 gain. If only $200 had originally been paid for the stock, and one share was sold at $180 after the 100 per cent stock dividend had been paid, a capital gain tax would have to be paid on the per-share profit of $80. If the dividend had consisted of preferred stock, however, the proceeds from the sale would be taxed as ordinary income.

If the stock dividend is of the type that is taxable, then it will be taxed as ordinary income at its fair market value at the time the dividend is received. If the stock received is worth $150 a share (ex-dividends), that amount is included in the ordinary income of the shareholders. If this stock is later sold for $180 a share, for example, $30 would be considered a capital gain and taxed as such. If any of the old shares on which the stock dividend was paid are sold, however, their cost value would still be the amount actually paid for them regardless of the fact that their value had been diluted by the stock dividend.

The savings effected by having a stock dividend taxable (when the stock is sold) at the capital gain rate rather than having a cash dividend taxable as ordinary income is appreciable for persons who are in the higher income tax brackets. A person with a taxable (ordinary) income of from $50,000 to $60,000 (for those filing a joint return the income bracket should be doubled) must pay a tax of 75 per cent on the top $10,000. Those with taxable incomes in excess of $200,000 must pay a tax of 91 per cent on all income over $200,000. But any profit made on the sale of a tax-free (at the time of its receipt) stock dividend is subject to a maximum tax of 25 per cent (assuming it is a long-term capital gain).

The law, however, gives some relief to taxpayers with respect to ordinary taxable dividends. The first $50 ($100 under a joint return) of dividends received from domestic corporations may be excluded in reporting earned income. Then after computing the tax on the total reportable income, a credit is allowed from the tax of an amount equivalent to 4 per cent of the reported dividends from domestic corporations. (The amount of the credit, however, cannot exceed 4 per cent of the total taxable income.) The relative advantage of the stock dividend over the cash dividend discussed above should, therefore, be modified accordingly.

Fractional Share Warrants

When a company pays a stock dividend of anything less than 100 per cent, the problem of fractional shares arises. For example, if a company paid a 10 per cent stock dividend, shareholders holding less than 10 shares would not be entitled to a whole share. Or if the number of shares held was not divisible by 10, such as for example, 25 shares, the shareholder would be entitled to 2½ shares. The share dividend certificate would be made out for the number of whole shares. In the example just given the certificate would be for 2 shares.

The right to fractional shares is usually handled in one of two ways. The company either gives the shareholders cash equivalent to the value of the fractional shares they are entitled to, or a *warrant* is made out for the fractional shares. In the example just given the warrant would call for one-half of a share of stock. These warrants are made out to bearer and are transferable by delivery. They carry no voting rights and ordinarily are not entitled to any dividends or interest. It should be noted that these warrants are sometimes called *scrip,* but they should not be confused with the notes that are issued in connection with a *scrip dividend.*

Several things may be done with the warrants, and in some instances any of them could be used in a particular case, depending upon the terms announced by the company. In some instances the company will redeem the warrants for cash. Or cash of a sufficient amount may be sent in along with the warrants to enable the holder to get a whole share of stock. Commonly a market for warrants is maintained, and this is sometimes done by the issuing company or its transfer agent. Thus, a person holding a warrant for one-half of a share might either sell his warrant, or he could buy another warrant for one-half of a share and secure one whole share of stock. Usually a time limit, such as two or three years, is established for the exercise of the warrants; after that time they become void. It should be noted that these *warrants* give the shareholders *rights* to fractional shares, but they are *not* certificates of fractional shares of stock.

Stock Dividends Paid from Capital Surplus

Stock dividends may be paid from the retained earnings or from capital surplus. Some of the same principles governing the payment of cash dividends from capital surplus would apply with equal force to stock dividends, but in some instances a stock dividend, but not a cash dividend, would be recommended from certain types of capital surplus. If the surplus arises from the reappraisal upward of securities held as investments, it should not be capitalized through the payment of a stock dividend, since the market value of the securities may decline and accordingly the book value should then be marked down. If the amount representing the surplus has been invested in ordinary assets, the stock dividend would be warranted. In some states a stock dividend, but not a cash dividend, may be paid from the surplus arising from the revaluation of assets upward.

It is recommended that corporations inform their shareholders as to the source of the surplus from which stock dividends are paid. This is particularly true when the dividend is paid from capital surplus.

Readjustment of Capital Account

When stock dividends are used rarely by a company, particularly when the amount of the dividend is relatively large in relation to the shares outstanding, the shareholder should look upon the procedure not as a dividend but rather as a readjustment in the "Capital Stock" account in order to reduce the market price of the stock and/or to reduce the earnings per share.

Rescission of Stock Dividends

Unlike the declaration of a cash dividend, the declaration of a stock dividend does not create a liability on the part of the corporation. It therefore follows that after declaration of the dividend, but before its payment, the directors could rescind their action and the shareholders could do nothing about it. This is true even if the shareholders have been called upon to authorize additional stock for the dividend.

New York Stock Exchange Rules on Stock Dividends

The New York Stock Exchange believes that the payment of regular stock dividends of a relatively small amount (or, those on a "continuing basis") are misleading to shareholders unless such stock dividends are paid from profits earned during the particular period and unless the amount represented by the dividend is transferred from the "Earned Surplus" to the "Capital Stock" or "Capital Surplus" account. To this end, the Exchange, in 1953, adopted rules relating to the payment of such dividends.[1] If the stock dividend represents less than 25 per cent of the number of shares outstanding prior to the stock dividends (one new share for each four old shares would be a 25 per cent dividend), the Exchange will not approve the listing of the additional shares unless (1) the company transfers from the "Earned Surplus" to the "Capital Stock" or "Capital Surplus" account an amount equal to the fair value of the shares, which should closely approximate the current market price of the stock adjusted to reflect the issuance of the new shares, and (2) the earned surplus for the particular period covered by the dividend is sufficient in amount to cover the aggregate fair value of the stock dividend.

The above stated rules *apply also to a stock split-up* if the number of new shares is less than 25 per cent of the number of shares outstanding at the time of the split-up. For companies whose stock is listed on the

[1] *New York Stock Exchange Company Manual*, Sec. A 13.

NYSE, the accounting procedure for stock split-ups will therefore be different from that described below if the split-up is of the type that falls under the NYSE rules. If the stock dividend or split-up comes under the NYSE rules and a cash dividend is also paid at the time, the earnings should be sufficient in amount to cover both the stock and the cash. The Exchange, however, believes that the split-up should be not less than 2-for-1, in which case the above stated NYSE rules would not be applicable.

If the stock dividend or stock split-up involves shares representing 100 per cent or more of the number of shares outstanding prior to the distribution, the NYSE rules or requirements stated above are not applicable. For stock distributions representing from 25 to 99 per cent of the number of shares outstanding, the presumption is that the NYSE rules are not applicable, but the particular circumstances present will be taken into account to determine the validity of the assumption.

STOCK SPLITS

Stock split-ups or, as they are sometimes called, *stock splits* are not dividends at all, but their similarity to stock dividends warrants their inclusion in this chapter. As the name indicates, a stock split-up results in the replacement of the company's shares with a larger number of shares. But, unlike a stock dividend, the "Surplus" account is not affected. Furthermore, the split-up does not increase the aggregate amount shown under "Capital Stock" in the balance sheet. But the split-up does necessitate a reduction in the par value or stated value per share of the capital stock. If a company which has stock outstanding with a par value of, for example, $100, splits its stock 2-for-1, it will be necessary to reduce the par value per share from $100 to $50. A comparison of the relative effects on the balance sheet of a stock dividend and a stock split-up are shown below.

BEFORE STOCK DIVIDEND OR STOCK SPLIT-UP

Capital Stock (par value $100)	$1,000,000
Surplus	2,000,000
Total Net Worth	$3,000,000

AFTER 100 PER CENT STOCK DIVIDEND		AFTER 2-FOR-1 SPLIT-UP	
Capital Stock		Capital Stock	
(par value $100)	$2,000,000	(par value $50)	$1,000,000
Surplus	1,000,000	Surplus	2,000,000
Total Net Worth	$3,000,000	Total Net Worth	$3,000,000

Since the surplus is not affected by the stock split-up, a company could conceivably have a stock split-up when no surplus existed, but it would be impossible to have a stock dividend under these circumstances. However, it is highly improbable that a split-up would occur if no surplus existed. A company may want to reduce the market price of its shares but still retain the advantage of showing the same surplus on the balance sheet. This could be accomplished with the split-up.

A stock dividend increases the number of shares on which future dividends will be paid, and at the same time lessens the surplus from which the dividend may be paid. If the same *rate* (expressed in percentage of par value) of dividends is continued after a stock split-up, the future dividends would demand no more cash disbursements than before, and furthermore, the surplus from which such dividends may be paid is not reduced by virtue of the split-up. In other respects the stock dividend and stock split-up accomplish similar purposes. Since the par value or stated value of the stock must be reduced in event of a split-up, this will necessitate approval of the shareholders for a charter amendment (assuming in the case of no-par stock that the stated value is specified in the charter [2]). But a stock dividend does not call for a charter amendment unless additional authorized shares are necessary for the payment of the dividend.

As stated above in connection with stock dividends, if the split-up falls under the NYSE rules, the accounting for the split will be the same as for a stock dividend.

Stock Splits and Taxation

Since stock split-ups do not result in any income to the shareholder, they are not taxable. For purposes of the capital gain tax upon the sale of the shares after a split-up, the original cost of the shares is apportioned to the new shares. For example, if $200 was paid for a share of stock and the company subsequently had a 2-for-1 split-up, the cost of the new shares would be considered to have been $100 for each share.

Advantages of Stock Splits

Following is a summary of the reasons for or advantages of a stock split-up. Since most of these same points apply to stock dividends, and were discussed in that connection, we will merely list the points.

1. The per-share earnings and dividends may be reduced.
2. The market price of the stock will be reduced.
3. The surplus of the company is not affected.

Shareholders may actually benefit from stock split-ups in the same way as stock dividends. That is, the split-up is interpreted as indicating

---

[2] If a $100 par stock is split 2-for-1, the issuing company usually sends the stockholders one new $50 par share for each old share held, and in addition sends him a $50 par "stamp" to be pasted over the $100 par designation on each old stock certificate.

that the management of the company is optimistic about the future, and although the market price of the stock will probably be reduced immediately after the split-up, it may tend to go back to its old price. If the dividends are continued at the same amount per share as before, the shareholder would get more in dividends. Stock splits were frequently used in the late 1920's and during the prosperous period following World War II.

Reverse Stock Split-ups

Many companies whose stock rose to relatively high prices in the prosperous 1920's, found that their stock fell to extremely low prices in the depression of the early 1930's. The split-ups, of course, resulted in the per-share prices' falling lower than otherwise would have been the case. In many instances the stock sold so low that it was in the "cat and dog" class. Many companies had acquired assets at inflated prices and the heavy depreciation charges were making a bad situation worse so far as earnings were concerned. To reduce the future depreciation charges it would be necessary to reduce the valuation of the assets. This would reduce the badly depleted surplus, or add to a deficit. To correct the situation many companies had a "reverse stock split-up," that is, they would, upon proper authorization, call the old stock in and replace it with fewer shares. In this way the market price per share would be increased. But if two shares of $50 par, for example, were replaced with one share of $100 par stock, the surplus of the company would not be affected. At the time the new shares were issued some companies did not change the par value per share. Many issued a lesser number of low-par shares to take the place of no-par stock. This would add to the surplus and make possible the write-off of some of the book valuations of the assets and thus permit lower depreciation charges.

DIVIDEND TERMINOLOGY

In the above discussion, dividends were classified according to the medium in which they are paid. The following terminology is also applied to dividends.

Regular Dividends

Preferred stock carries a preferential dividend, expressed either in per cent or dollars per share, and this may be considered the regular dividend even though the stock may receive additional amounts if it is participating in some form. The term "regular dividend," however, is commonly used with reference to the common stock.

Classified common stock ordinarily carries a stated dividend rate in a manner similar to preferred stock, but again, the term *regular dividend* is usually applied to the ordinary common stock. Ordinary common stock does not carry a stated dividend rate, nor is any expressed in the charter or bylaws. But in practice the board of directors by their action in declaring a fixed amount of dividends at regular intervals establish what is thought of as the "regular dividend." This is commonly a quarterly dividend, although sometimes it may be semiannual or annual. In some instances the term *regular dividend* is printed on the dividend check. In many cases the directors and officers of the company refer to the dividend by this term, and a conscious effort is made to have a regular dividend rate established. Most of the stocks of the leading companies listed on the New York Stock Exchange have what is looked upon as regular dividend rates on their common stock.

In practically all instances the regular dividend is paid in cash, although in a few cases a more or less "regular" dividend has been paid in stock or the regular stock dividend is paid in addition to the regular cash dividend.

Extra Dividends

When companies which have established a regular dividend rate on their stock pay more than this amount in dividends, they usually label the additional dividend an "extra" dividend. The dividend is specifically called extra because the company does not want the shareholders to expect that this amount will be paid regularly in the future. In many instances a separate check, different in color, and in some cases marked "extra dividend," will be made out for the extra dividend.

Some corporations pay their regular dividends during the first three quarters of the year, and then after viewing the results for the entire year, pay an extra amount in addition to the regular dividend at the end of the last quarter.

Although in most instances the extra dividend is paid in cash, in some cases it consists of a stock dividend or occasionally a dividend in property other than cash.

Declaring and paying dividends is sometimes referred to as "cutting a melon," and the dividends may be called "melons." In some instances this terminology is applied only to an extra or special dividend, and in others it is applied only to a dividend of appreciable amount.

Interim and Final Dividends

When corporations follow the practice referred to above of paying a regular dividend or a relatively small one during the first three quarters and then paying the regular dividend plus an extra, or a relatively large dividend, at the end of the year, the first three quarterly dividends are sometimes referred to as *interim* dividends, and the last one is called the *final* dividend.

Special Dividends

An extra dividend is sometimes referred to as a "special" dividend. In some instances the term is applied not to the extra dividend as described above, but rather to an isolated or occasional dividend which is paid from the profits from some special or non-recurring item such as the sale of some real estate which is not needed in the business.

Liquidating Dividends

The distribution of cash or other property made to shareholders upon liquidation of the company is referred to as a "liquidating" or "liquidation" dividend. Usually it represents merely a return of part of the original capital contributed by the shareholders, and is sometimes called a "capital" dividend. Occasionally, however, the business may be sold for more than the amount of the capital stock, in which case part of the dividend would represent the surplus or profits of the company. In most instances, however, all such dividends consist of "capital." In the case of holding companies that are broken up as a result of a court order, or those being dissolved under the provisions of the Public Utility Holding Company Act of 1935, the dividend may, in part at least, consist of the securities of other companies.

In some instances the part of the dividend paid by a going concern which represents the depletion of a wasting asset company is referred to as a liquidating dividend.

Liquidating dividends, being a return of capital, are treated differently from ordinary dividends for income tax purposes. The part of a dividend which represents a liquidation dividend is not reported as ordinary income, but rather it is deducted from the cost of the stock. Thus, when the stock is sold, any profit made (as measured by the difference between the selling price and the adjusted cost price) is taxed as a capital gain.

Liquidating dividends may also be treated differently from ordinary dividends when preferred stock is outstanding. The provisions of the preferred stock contract concerning its right to assets upon dissolution will govern the right of the stock to liquidating dividends, rather than the clauses that relate to its right to ordinary dividends.

DECLARATION OF DIVIDENDS

One of the powers of the board of directors of a corporation is the declaration of dividends. Naturally the cash position of the company, its need for funds, the earnings, amount of surplus shown on the books, the dividend policy followed by the company, etc., all have an important bearing on how much in dividends, if any at all, will be declared. The president of the company or the finance committee of the board of directors often suggests or recommends how much should be declared, but the final authority for the declaration of dividends is the board of directors.

Even if the earnings are relatively large, the board is under no obligation to pay dividends. The judgment of the board of directors is usually final in regard to dividends. If the directors believe the earnings are needed in the business for possible future contingency or for expansion purposes, the shareholders ordinarily can do nothing about it. In exceptional cases the shareholders may appeal to a court of equity to compel the declaration of dividends.

In the case of preferred stock, if the contract calls for the payment of dividends each year in which profits are earned, which is a rare type of contract, the courts might compel the payment of the dividend if profits are earned. If dividends are declared on the common before the arrears on the preferred or the current preferential dividend is paid, recourse could be had to the courts to have the dividend rescinded, or to compel the declaration of the preferred dividend.

Declared Dividends Are Debts

After the board of directors has declared a cash dividend, it constitutes a debt of the corporation. After declaration, but before payment, the dividend should show as a current liability of the company. If the company should fail, and assuming the dividend was properly and legally declared, the shareholders would be treated as general creditors with respect to the declared dividend. If, however, money was set aside in a special fund or bank account for the payment of the dividend, the shareholders would be treated as preferred creditors with respect to that fund. If a stock dividend is declared and has not yet been paid, the amount of the stock dividend should be shown along with the outstanding stock in the net worth section of the balance sheet.

Remedies for Improper Dividends

The statutes of particular states must be consulted to determine the remedies that are available in event the directors improperly or illegally declare and pay a dividend. If such a dividend has been only declared and not paid, shareholders cannot get the court to force its payment. The directors could rescind the dividend and the shareholders would have no right against the corporation or the directors with respect to the dividend.

In many states directors are personally liable for the payment of illegal dividends. Usually receivers or trustees or a new management of the corporation can sue the directors to recover for the company any amounts paid in illegal dividends. As a rule, the statutes specify penalties for the payment of dividends from "capital." In some states, including New York, it is a misdemeanor, while in others it is a criminal offense. Usually the directors are not liable for improper dividends if they acted in good faith, and used reasonable care in the selection of the officers and others responsible for the preparation of the financial statements. If a director believes that a dividend is being illegally declared he should go on record in the minutes of the meeting as opposing the dividend; otherwise he may be held liable.

The ability to recover an illegal dividend from the shareholders is another matter. If the improper or illegal dividend causes insolvency, or causes the company to fail, it can be recovered in a number of states. If this does not result and if the shareholders were innocent and received the dividend in good faith, in a number of states recovery may not be had.

FACTORS AFFECTING DIVIDEND POLICIES

We will be concerned here primarily with cash dividends. The problem of whether dividends can or should be declared by the directors is influenced by a number of factors, chief among which are the following:

1. Law and regulation
2. Contractual arrangements
3. Nature of company business
4. Age and size of company
5. Stock distribution
6. Tax considerations
7. Earnings
8. Cash flows and liquidity
9. Attempt to maintain stable dividend

Common Law

It is a common-law rule that dividends cannot be paid from "capital." The "capital" of a corporation, as used in this sense, is usually defined to mean the capital stock. More specifically, it means the par or stated value of the stock, or the amount shown under "Capital Stock" in the net worth section of the balance sheet. Some courts have said that the capital is a "trust fund" or it is like a trust fund for the benefit of creditors. This, of course, is an inaccurate statement since there is no property set aside in trust. Furthermore, operating losses may reduce the capital of a company and nothing can be done about it by the creditors. Although the law looks upon the capital stock to be the legal "capital" of a corporation, from a practical standpoint the capital of a company consists of its assets. Dividends actually cannot be paid from the "Capital Stock" account. Dividends paid in cash or other assets are actually paid from "capital" (as we defined the term earlier in the book), but there must be profits or surplus on the books at least equivalent to the amount of the dividends before they may be paid.

What the law means therefore when it says that dividends cannot be paid from capital, is that no dividends can be paid if the net assets (assets less liabilities) are less than the amount of the capital stock as shown in the balance sheet, or if the payment of such dividends would reduce the net assets below the capital stock figure. The law reasons that creditors or prospective creditors grant credit on the strength of the amount shown as the "capital" of the corporation, and that it would be unfair or injurious to them if the directors paid dividends which would impair this capital.

The cases sometimes say that dividends can be paid only from the profits or accumulated profits of the company. This is not strictly true since usually at common law dividends can be paid to the extent of the company's surplus, regardless of the source of the surplus.

Statutory Law

The statutory provisions can be conveniently discussed under the following headings.

Dividends from Surplus. The typical statutory provision states that dividends can be paid only from "surplus," or as some phrase it, dividends can be paid only from the excess of assets over the liabilities plus the legal or stated capital. In defining surplus or net assets the statutes of a number of the states provide that proper deductions must be made for depreciation and bad debts. Some provide that deduction will also have to be made for depletion in the case of wasting asset businesses, although in some states no deduction need be made if so provided in the articles of incorporation.

The statutes of many of the states are silent about the availability for dividends of surplus arising from the upward reappraisal of assets. In Ohio the statutes specifically prohibit cash dividends from this source, but permit stock dividends.

Unless specifically prohibited by statutes, a dividend can legally be paid out of capital surplus. The statutes of some states, however, including California, Pennsylvania, Illinois, and Michigan, limit such dividends to stock dividends and those paid on preferred stock. In some states, if a dividend is paid from a source other than "earned" surplus, the shareholders must be notified as to its source.

The statutes of Delaware permit a dividend to be paid from the current earnings or those of the previous year even if a deficit exists on the books.[3] Such dividends, however, cannot be paid if the net assets are

---

[3] Similar statutes are found also in California, Minnesota, and New Jersey. Dividends paid from current earnings with a deficit present are sometimes called "nimble dividends." Such dividends are permitted also in England.

less than the preferred stock's preference as to assets, or if the dividend would reduce the net assets below that amount.

No Dividends When Insolvent. The statutes of about one-third of the states, including California, Illinois, Massachusetts, and Ohio, specifically state that a dividend cannot be paid when the company is insolvent or when the dividend would cause it to become insolvent. This raises the question as to what is meant by insolvency. Ordinarily, "insolvency" refers to a situation where the assets are less than the liabilities plus stated capital.[4] As used in this way the rule is merely stating that a surplus must be present before a dividend may be declared. But in Massachusetts and Ohio, "insolvency," as used in the particular statute, means the inability to meet debts as they become due. This is using the term in the "equity" sense. Thus, in these states, even if a surplus is present, the statutes say that dividends cannot be paid if the company is insolvent or if the dividend would cause the company to become insolvent. But even in the absence of such statutes, equity courts in most of the states, if they were called upon to do so, would prohibit a dividend under these circumstances.

Restrictions Imposed by Commissions and Regulation

The Public Utility Holding Company Act of 1935 provides that before dividends may be paid from capital or unearned surplus by a registered holding company or its subsidiary, approval must be obtained from the Securities and Exchange Commission. Any provisions in the state statutes or Commission regulation relating to public utilities or financial institutions must be observed. Various accounting provisions concerning dividends are contained in the following legislation and must be followed by corporations subject to these particular statutes: Federal Communications Act, Federal Water Power Act, Interstate Commerce Act, and the Motor Carrier Act.

Contractual Arrangements

Restrictions on the payment of dividends are frequently found in the company's charter, bylaws, and bond indentures. Where preferred stock is present and has cumulative rights to dividends, all dividends in arrears and those for the current year must be paid before any dividends may be paid on the common stock. In event of liquidation the contractual right of the preferred with respect to any preference as to accrued dividends must be observed.

In some instances dividends may be paid only from earnings that arise after the particular securities have been issued. Preferred stock and bond

---

[4] Although in a strict "bankruptcy" definition insolvency means that the value of the assets are less than the amount of the debts.

contracts and agreements with other types of creditors sometimes contain provisions which prohibit dividends if the effect of their payment would be to reduce the net current assets below a specified figure, or if it would lower the current ratio below the specified one.

Nature of Company Business

The nature of the business conducted by the particular company commonly influences the dividend policy. Generally speaking, a company whose earnings are subject to wide fluctuations, such as many industrial companies, should follow a more conservative dividend policy than one whose earnings are more certain and regular. A public utility would illustrate the latter.

A company that comes under the head of a growth industry will constantly have need of funds for expansion purposes. This does not mean, however, that such a company will retain a relatively large part of the earnings. In many instances the earnings would not provide sufficient funds for expansion, so new securities must be sold from time to time. In order to maintain a good market for its securities the company may find it beneficial to follow a more liberal dividend policy.

Age and Size of Company

A young or small company cannot ordinarily obtain funds from the sale of securities in the market. Reinvested earnings may be the only source of additional funds open to the company. In some instances bank loans may be obtained, but in many cases even these are unobtainable by new or small companies. Such companies must, therefore, follow a very conservative dividend policy if they expect to have the necessary funds for expansion purposes.

Stock Distribution

The fact that the stock of a corporation is closely held may have a profound effect on the dividend policy of the company. If the stock is held by a relatively small number of shareholders who are the officers and directors of the company and who need the income of the company for living purposes, the tendency would be to withdraw the "income" of the company in the form of salaries to the maximum extent permitted by the Internal Revenue Service, rather than in the form of dividends. The reason for this is, of course, to minimize the amount of the combined federal corporate and personal income tax.

If, on the other hand, the stock of a close corporation is held by wealthy people who are in a high income tax bracket, they may prefer not to withdraw the corporate income either in the form of salaries or dividends. If profitable use can be made of the retained earnings, the stock would increase in value. Should part of the stock be sold, the profit realized would be subject to the maximum long-term capital gain rate of only 25 per cent. Or, the shareholder may prefer to pass along the stock in his estate to his beneficiaries and thus not have it subjected to any form of income tax.

When the stock, or at least part of it, is widely distributed, the directors may find it profitable to follow a dividend policy which will result in the best future stockholder relations.

Tax Considerations

The favorable tax treatment accorded stock dividends was mentioned earlier in the chapter when we discussed stock dividends. The impact of taxes on dividend policies of close corporations was discussed in the above section. Care should be taken, however, to avoid retaining earnings beyond the "reasonable" needs of business. In addition to the regular corporate income tax, the Internal Revenue Code imposes an additional tax on any earnings (after an accumulated $100,000 exemption) which are retained beyond the "reasonable anticipated needs" of the business. Any such improper retained earnings can be taxed at the rate of 27½ per cent on the first $100,000 (beyond the total accumulated $100,000 exemption), and 38½ per cent on the amount in excess of $100,000. In determining if earnings beyond the reasonable needs of the business have been retained, the government gives consideration to the following: whether the stock is closely held by a family or other small group, whether loans have been made to company officers or the shareholders out of money that could have been used for dividend purposes, and whether money has been invested in securities which have no relation to the normal business activities of the company.

It should be made clear that the retention of a relatively large portion of the earnings does not automatically subject the company to the additional taxes. The government must initiate the action, and the company is given the right to explain the reasons for the retention. The company policy may be justified by the fact that the money was needed for the purchase of additional inventory, for expansion purposes, for replacement of equipment, for contingency reserves, etc.

Earnings

Dividends may legally be paid only when the corporate books show the presence of earnings or a surplus. The surplus may have arisen from a type of capital surplus or from accumulated earnings. Rarely are cash dividends paid from capital surplus. Surplus built up from accumulated past earnings is ordinarily invested in current or fixed assets which are needed in the business. So, in the final analysis, cash dividends are ordinarily paid from current earnings. Thus, any dividend policy will be based on or closely related to the current earnings.

Many boards of directors have the philosophy that they should "plow back" (really retain) into the company $1 in earnings for each $1 paid in dividends. This would result in a dividend pay-out ratio of 50 per cent. Actually the pay-out ratio for the typical industrial concern averages between 50 and 60 per cent. But, as we have already pointed out, many young or small companies or growth concerns may pay out much less than this—in some cases, of course, they pay out nothing even though they have earnings. Other factors discussed previously such as the stock distribution pattern, etc., would influence the dividend pay-out ratio.

Cash Flows and Liquidity

Although we say that a dividend is paid from earnings or surplus, from a practical standpoint it is obvious that a cash dividend is paid from cash. So, the availability of cash, and the effect on the liquidity of the company of the use of this cash for a dividend, are important considerations in the determination of dividend policy.

In the first place we should recognize that there is not necessarily any relationship between the "net earnings" of a company and the size of its cash account. Earnings appear on the income statement even though they may be represented on the balance sheet by accounts or notes receivable, and not cash. Even though the receivables arising from the earnings may have been collected, the cash may have been used to purchase additional inventories or even sunk into fixed assets.

On the other hand, the cash account may increase by an amount much greater than the net earnings of the company for the particular period. Non-cash expenses, such as depreciation and depletion, reduce the net earnings from what they would have been had such changes not been made, but they do not reduce the cash. These charges may increase the cash account by an amount greater than that which is generated from the "net earnings."

From what has just been said it is obvious that the cash budget may form the basis for the cash dividend policy. When the payment of regular dividends is included as an item in the budget, it will become apparent how much, if any, outside capital will be needed to maintain the dividend. A company will strive to maintain a liquid position, even if it means cutting or passing the dividend. A carefully prepared budget, however, may enable a company to maintain its dividend even if it is necessary to borrow the money to do so.

When the net cash which is generated from the business is absolutely required for some purpose other than for dividends, the availability of outside capital and cost of such capital, if obtainable, may determine the dividend policy.

In the determination of a dividend policy not only are the current earnings and cash flows important, but careful thought must be given to the probable future earnings and cash flows.

Attempt To Maintain Stable Dividends

There is a strong inclination on the part of boards of directors to pay a regular amount in dividends annually even though the earnings may fluctuate from year to year. This means that in prosperous years the dividend pay-out ratio will decline, but in poor years it will increase. As a company continues to increase its earnings, it may tend to still pay out the same interim quarterly dividend as in the past, but then add an extra dividend in the final quarter. Only after it becomes apparent that the increased earnings have become more or less permanent will the typical company incorporate the extra into the regular dividend. Following are the advantages of a stable dividend policy.

1. *Stock is Less Speculative.* The stock tends to become known more as an *investment* stock rather than a *speculative* stock. The so-called investor class, including some institutions, will buy it. This gives stability to the stock and widens its market.

2. *Aids Future Financing.* As a result of the stability in price and wider market for the stock, future stock financing is made easier. The stock will usually sell at a high price in relation to the dividends being paid, so the cost of the money obtained from the sale of additional stock will be relatively low.

3. *Bonds May Be Classified as Legal Investments.* The laws of the various states prescribe requirements which must be met by a company, in order that its bonds may be purchased by savings banks and other fiduciaries in the state. One of the requirements frequently found is that the company must have maintained an unbroken dividend record for a specified length of time, such as five years. Bonds that qualify as *legals* attract a relatively wide market and sell on a relatively low-yield basis. Thus, future financing through the sale of additional bonds is relatively easy and cheap.

4. *Future Planning Made Easier.* A company knows at all times just how much will be required in the future to meet dividend payments. With this in mind the officials can better plan future financial requirements.

5. *Improves Stockholder Relations.* To an increasing extent corporations are realizing the importance of establishing and maintaining good relations with their stockholders. Nothing accomplishes this better than a policy of liberal and stable dividends.

Perhaps the best example of a stable dividend policy is that followed by the American Telephone and Telegraph Company. This company has paid dividends of some amount in each year since 1881. Beginning in

1922, and continuing to 1959, a regular dividend of $9 a year ($2.25 quarterly) was paid. This was done despite the fact that during the depression of the 1930's, earnings on several occasions dipped below the amount of the dividend. In 1959 the stock was split 3-for-1 and the per-share annual dividend was set at $3.30. In 1961 the dividend was raised to $3.60. A selected list of companies that have paid dividends every quarter for 50 years or more is shown in Table 26–1.

Table 26–1. Selected List of Companies Listed on the New York Stock Exchange Paying Cash Dividends in Every Quarter for 50 Years or More

Company	Year Quarterly Dividend Began
American Brake Shoe	1904
American Electric Power	1910
American Natural Gas	1904
American News	1864
American Snuff	1903
American Telephone and Telegraph	1882
Baltimore Gas and Electric	1911
Beech-Nut Life Savers	1903
Boston Edison	1892
Burroughs Corporation	1906
City Products	1909
Cleveland Electric Illuminating	1912
Commonwealth Edison	1890
Consolidated Edison Company of New York	1892
Detroit Edison	1909
duPont de Nemours (E. I.)	1905
Eastman Kodak	1902
General Cigar	1909
General Electric	1899
International Harvester	1910
Kroger	1910
National Biscuit	1899
National Lead	1906
New England Telephone and Telegraph	1886
Otis Elevator	1911
Owens-Illinois Glass	1907
Parke-Davis and Company	1897
Pittsburgh Plate Glass	1899
Procter & Gamble	1898
Pullman Inc.	1867
Reynolds (R. J.) Tobacco	1901
Singer Manufacturing	1890
Texaco	1903
Union Pacific Railroad	1907
United Shoe Machinery	1899
United States Playing Card	1896
Washington Gas Light	1885
West Virginia Pulp and Paper	1895
Westinghouse Air Brake	1884
Yale & Towne	1904

SOURCE: *Exchange*, The New York Stock Exchange, July, 1962.

QUESTIONS

1. Indicate the three general forms of dividends, each of which affects the balance sheet in different ways. Indicate the names of the various types of dividends.
2. Distinguish between bond and scrip dividends. When would the payment of such dividends be justified?
3. Indicate how a 100 per cent stock dividend and a 2-for-1 stock split-up are similar and how they differ.
4. Indicate the various reasons why a corporation might pay a stock dividend.
5. If the object is to reduce the market price of the stock would you as a director vote for a stock dividend or a stock split-up? Give reasons for your answer.
6. Would you favor the payment of a regular stock dividend? Why or why not?
7. Indicate whether a stock dividend is taxable as income in the hands of the recipient stockholder. If the dividend is not taxable indicate how the capital gain or loss would be computed when the holder sold the stock.
8. In the long run do you think that a stockholder has a good chance of gaining from a stock dividend or a stock split-up? Explain.
9. How do corporations handle the situation when a stock dividend is declared and the shareholder does not hold sufficient stock to obtain a whole share in dividends?
10. Explain the NYSE rules relating to stock dividends and stock splits.
11. Explain what is meant when it is said that dividends cannot be paid from "capital."
12. (a) Can a corporation pay a dividend from capital surplus? Explain. (b) Can a corporation pay a dividend from income other than "earned"? Explain.
13. Should a large successful company that constantly needs funds for expansion follow a conservative or liberal dividend policy? Explain.
14. Indicate the advantages of a stable dividend policy to the company.
15. Indicate how the income tax laws might influence the dividend policy of a corporation.
16. Are directors under any obligation to declare dividends? Explain.
17. Are dividends ever a debt of the corporation? Explain.
18. Indicate the various factors which determine whether a company can or will pay a dividend in any given year.
19. What is meant when it is said that a corporation "cut a melon"?
20. How often do large corporations, which follow a regular dividend policy and whose stock is listed, pay dividends?

PROBLEMS

1. The following is a condensed balance sheet of the Smith Corp. as of December 31, 19x1:

Assets		Liabilities and Net Worth	
Current Assets	$ 3,000,000	Liabilities	$ 1,000,000
Fixed Assets	8,000,000	Capital Stock	5,000,000
		Surplus	5,000,000
Total	$11,000,000	Total	$11,000,000

The par value of the stock is $50 per share, and it is selling in the market for its approximate book value. The company is contemplating an expansion program that will necessitate the raising of $2,000,000 through the sale of new stock to the public. Financial advisors have suggested that the new financing could be more successfully carried out if the offer price were somewhat less than $100 per share. When the expansion program was considered by the directors, several of them favored a 100 per cent stock dividend before the sale of the new stock; others favored a 2-for-1 stock split-up. During the past 5 years the company has earned an average of 10 per cent on its net assets and has paid a regular dividend of $6 per share. (a) Could this proposed new stock issue be sold to the public without first offering it to the stockholders? Explain. (b) Why might it be desirable to offer the new stock to the public at less than $100 per share? (c) Why were the stock dividend and stock split-up proposed at the directors' meeting? (d) Explain why you as a director might favor the stock dividend instead of the split-up. (e) Explain why you as a director might favor the split-up instead of the stock dividend. (f) Would either the stock dividend or the split-up necessitate a charter amendment? Explain.

2. At the meeting of the directors of the Jones Corp. it was proposed that a scrip dividend be declared. Director Brown objected to this, saying that the paying of a scrip dividend was the same as declaring a cash dividend and not paying it; director Johnson objected on the ground that the declaring of such a dividend adversely affected the corporation in two ways: first, that it added to the liabilities, and second, that it also reduced the surplus of the company. (He stated that if a scrip dividend of $100,000 were declared, the liabilities would be increased $100,000, and the surplus reduced $100,000, thus affecting the company to the extent of $200,000.) (a) Under what conditions would you as a director vote for the declaration of a scrip dividend? (b) Criticize Mr. Brown's statement. (c) Criticize Mr. Johnson's statement.

3. Ascertain the common-stock dividend policy of the Commonwealth Edison Co. since 1958. (a) What advantages accrue to the company from paying part of the dividend in stock rather than paying a larger cash dividend? (b) How may the common stockholders benefit from this dividend policy? (c) Is anyone harmed by such a dividend policy? (d) What advantages does this policy offer to both the company and its shareholders as compared to paying a higher cash dividend only, and then selling more common stock to the common shareholders through the privileged subscription? (e) Do you believe that other companies should adopt a similar dividend policy? Why do you think they have not done so?

4. The following questions refer to the Peerless Metal Co. as of January 1, 19x2. (See Problem 2, Chapter 25.) (a) How much could the company pay out legally in the form of cash dividends? (b) Which particular source of surplus could better be used as a basis for a stock rather than a cash dividend? Why? (c) Which particular sources of surplus do you think inadvisable as a basis for cash dividends? Why? (d) List the additional information that you would desire before deciding upon any dividend action for the company. (e) Do the stockholders have any right against the corporation in respect to dividends? Explain.

5. The question of dividend action was before the directors of the Wear-Forever Corp. at their January meeting in 19x1. The company had recently tied up a considerable amount of money in inventories and was not in a cash position to meet the regular dividend. The president recommended that $90,000 be borrowed at the bank to enable the company to pay the regular

6 per cent dividend—a rate that had been paid for the past 13 years. (a) Is it legal to declare dividends when there is insufficient cash on hand to pay the dividend? (b) Do you think the president's recommendation might have been sound? Why? (c) Would the 13-year dividend experience of the company have any influence on you as a director in voting on the president's recommendation? Explain. (d) What additional information would you as a director want before acting on the president's recommendation?

SELECTED READINGS

BOGEN, JULES I. (ed.). *Financial Handbook,* 3d ed. New York: The Ronald Press Co., 1952, Section 19.

CAMPBELL, JAMES A., and BERANEK, WILLIAM. "Stock Price Behavior on Ex-Dividend Dates," *Journal of Finance,* December, 1955, pp. 425–29.

DORIS, LILLIAN (ed.). *Business Finance Handbook.* Englewood Cliffs, N. J.: Prentice-Hall, Inc., 1953, Chapter 13.

DURAND, DAVID, and MAY, ALAN M. "The Ex-Dividend Behavior of American Telephone and Telegraph Stock," *Journal of Finance,* March, 1960, pp. 19–31.

GORDON, MYRON J. *The Investment, Financing, and Valuation of the Corporation.* Homewood, Ill.: Richard D. Irwin, Inc., 1962.

SUSSMAN, M. RICHARD. *The Stock Dividend.* Ann Arbor: Bureau of Business Research, The University of Michigan, 1962.

WALKER, ERNEST W., and BAUGHN, WILLIAM H. *Financial Planning and Policy.* New York: Harper & Row, Publishers, 1961, Chapter 11.

WALTER, JAMES E. "Dividend Policies and Common Stock Prices," *Journal of Finance,* March, 1956, pp. 29–41.

WESTON, J. FRED (ed.). *Readings in Finance From* Fortune. New York: Holt, Rinehart and Winston, Inc., 1958. Selection 24.

V

EXPANSION AND ADJUSTMENT

27

Expansion

Growth and bigness are common American goals. Size measures are used as standards to judge success. Many businessmen would place growth alongside service and profit as a primary objective of their firms. Although the United States is one of the newer countries among the nations of the world, its commercial and industrial development has exceeded that of any other country. This has meant that in a relatively short span of time old businesses have had to expand, and new businesses have been formed. The population of the country has steadily increased, and the standard of living of the people has been improving at the same time. It is sometimes said that a business must go forward to keep from going backward; it cannot stand still. Of course there are many business units, particularly in the services and merchandising, that tend to remain about the same size, but in the larger retail and wholesale organizations and the industrial world, expansion has been the rule.

The increase in population and improved standard of living have called for the production and sale of more products. Companies that are already established in business often have the production facilities, management, experience, and financial resources to expand their capacity to meet an increased demand for goods far better than a new company just coming into the field. Therefore, expansion of existing businesses in the United States has taken place at a rapid tempo.

With the increased demand for goods, the typical businessman wants to increase his production to take advantage of the additional sales possibilities. Larger-scale operations often result in decreased costs of one kind or another. In order to stay in business, competitors will find it necessary to expand their plant facilities and produce on a larger scale in order to reduce their costs to the point where they can sell their products in the competitive market. Furthermore, businessmen do not like to see their competitors enjoying the personal triumph that goes with bigness while they remain in obscurity.

Increasing costs of both labor and materials have also been a factor in expansion. These make it increasingly advantageous to obtain the economies of large-scale production. Some companies have not only increased the production and sales of their regular products, but, in order to absorb the higher costs of operations, they have also taken on additional products and new lines. In times of prosperity and during war periods, plant facilities are expanded rapidly to take care of the additional demand for goods. This results in a tremendous increase in plant capacity. When the extra demand has been satisfied and more or less normal times have returned, competition becomes increasingly keen.

Purpose of Expansion

As is true of other management decisions, a decision to expand a business should be guided by the objectives of the firm. If the objective is profitability, the effect of the proposed expansion upon future profits and future investment must be analyzed, and the decision to expand should only be made if the expected results include increased profitability for the firm. If the firm's major objective is growth, all expansion would fit within the general area of this objective, and therefore, this firm has made a permanent decision to continue expansion. The only question in this case is one of direction. However, relatively few firms would have growth alone as an objective. Thus, most expansion decisions are closely related to potential for making future profits. This is generally true even when the firm states that service is its primary objective.

A number of specific motives for expansion have been offered by various business firms. Most of these would lead to improvement of future profitability over the level of profit expected if expansion does not take place. Some of the typical motives for expansion are summarized below. It should be noted that all of these motives, except the last one, affect the profit of the firm. When the decision to expand is based on personal ambition, it is management's own decision, based on its personal objectives rather than on the objectives of the firm. However, it is very difficult to separate management from the firm which it manages and unquestionably personal objectives of management influence business decisions.

1. *Desire for Larger Income.* In a capitalistic economy such as ours the principal function of management is to make profits for the owners. Managements that are able to pay their shareholders relatively large dividends need not have fear of not being reelected or reappointed. Competition among executives for jobs, even in the higher echelons of man-

agement, is always present to a sufficient extent to keep executives on their toes and make them give a good accounting of their stewardship.

In addition to keeping their jobs, many corporate executives have additional incentives for working toward the end of larger earnings for the company. In many companies the directors and officers have relatively large holdings of the company stock. Larger profits mean larger dividends. In some instances the executives hold options to purchase the company's stock at a set price. The higher the market price of the stock goes as a result of favorable earnings, the greater will be the value of the options and consequently the profit from the sale of the stock. Larger corporate profits often result in larger salaries to the officers. Also, in addition to salary, many officers get an annual bonus based on the company's earnings. Shareholders are usually more willing to vote liberal pensions to officers if they are able to produce good earnings for the company.

2. *Competition.* Competition in most lines of business is such that a particular company may have to expand to be able successfully to compete with other concerns in the same line of business. This obviously is another way of stating the profit motive.

3. *Lower Costs.* The desire for lower costs could be interpreted to mean the same as larger profits. If expansion could bring about the production of a larger number of products at a decreasing cost per unit, that much more in profits would be earned. Or, the reduced costs may enable the company to reduce the selling price of the product, and this may result in additional profits from an increased volume of sales.

4. *Absorb Competitors.* When competition gets too keen for a particular company it may attempt to buy out or combine with another company or companies. Life might be more pleasant and profits higher with less competition.

5. *Personal Ambition.* It is often difficult to determine just what makes some of the leading executives of our large corporations tick. Perhaps many of them do not know either. It is apparent that something besides money spurs them on. But just what? Business leaders are human beings and like other people they want to be successful and command the esteem of their fellowmen. They get a kick out of being the head of a large business, and many of them like the feeling of having the final word in dealing with other people. The creative urge or a lust for power is present in many people. The businessman may want to become more important in order that he can climb socially and become a member of an élite business group or become acceptable to people in higher social strata.

It is not uncommon for top-level executives to leave high-paying jobs in order to accept an important governmental post at a moderate salary.

People sometimes will give up good business positions in order to engage in one of the professions, which pay much less for their services. Motives other than money may be the primary ones.

Perhaps we should not forget the executive's wife. In many cases she is the one who does the pushing. And her motive may be economic, but she may love riches mainly as a means to conspicuous consumption, because her highest ambition may be to belong to an élite group and be envied by others.

Measures of Expansion

Business size is measured in many different ways; thus, expansion, or change in business size, is also measured in a variety of ways. Sometimes size is measured in physical terms such as units of plant capacity, number of employees, units of production, etc. However, the much more common measures of size and expansion involve the use of dollar values. Dollar measurements include sales, total assets, owners' equity, profits, capital structure, and value added. Table 27–1 gives sales and assets figures for nine leading American corporations in 1939 and 1961. The percentage of increase in sales is also indicated.

There are many problems inherent in using dollar values as measures of growth and expansion. Unfortunately, the dollar is not a stable value in and of itself. The dollar's value in 1939 was much greater than the dollar's value in 1961. Practically every American firm expanded in dollar sales from 1939 to 1961. However, a firm which merely doubled its sales in this 22-year period actually experienced a decrease in physical sales volume, since prices were more than twice as high in 1961 as they were in 1939. Measuring growth and expansion over long periods of time with absolute dollars becomes unrealistic in periods of changing prices. Adjusting the 1961 sales volume figures for the firms listed in Table 27–1 to 1939 values gives a very different picture of rate of growth for these companies. It becomes apparent that Pennsylvania Railroad had a decrease in volume over this 22-year span and two other companies did not double in adjusted sales. On an adjusted basis, the sales increase for International Business Machines was 600 per cent rather than 1600 per cent.

All selected companies doubled assets during this period except Pennsylvania Railroad, which is the company whose volume actually decreased. However, this company's assets increased by $500 million. The increase in asset values for these nine firms was necessary to support increased dollar sales volumes. It indicates that in times of inflation, firms must expand the dollar investment even if they are merely holding their own in terms of physical output. From an accounting point of view, much of the gains of these firms came from reinvested earnings but, in reality, this earnings reinvestment was necessary merely to maintain a relatively similar plant for some of these companies rather than to provide for real physical expansion. From the point of view of society, physical expansion is the important measure rather than increased dollars when the new dollars are worth less than the old dollars. From the point of view of the firm, real growth takes place only if the expansion in dollar measures is great enough to compensate for any inflation which might have taken place during the period under study. It is estimated that half of the growth in dollar value of assets and in dollar sales in the post–World War II period for the nation as a whole was due to changing dollar values rather than to real growth.

Advantages and Disadvantages of Expansion

Assuming a profit objective for the firm, the major advantage of expansion is that it can lead to increased profits. If the firm is really interested in profit maximization or profitability, it should be careful not to pay too much attention to increasing dollar profits. To justify an expansion from a return-on-investment point of view, the increased dollar profits expected in the future must be sufficient to compensate reasonably for the additional investment required. Thus, the real advantage of expansion to any firm with profitability as a goal is based on the determination that the future profits accruing from the expansion will justify the additional investment required for the expansion. Approaches to this determination are discussed in Chapters 17 and 18.

Expansion means increase in size. Most commonly it would be an increase in size of operations. This would involve additional assets for the purpose of increasing sales volume. Expansion of existing firms is often an attempt to increase the scale of operations. Many businessmen have assumed that large-scale operations are more economical, and therefore more profitable, than small-scale operations. While economic theory tells us about the economies of larger-scale operations, there are certainly many instances where larger-scale operations have not led to greater efficiency and greater profit. Increasing the scale of operations will almost invariably affect profit in some way. Sometimes it leads to decreased profit rather than to increased profit. Potential advantages and disadvantages of large-scale operations relative to their effect on profit are discussed below.

The following is a rather exhaustive list of advantages of larger-scale operations. Rarely would all of these points be applied to a particular situation. In many instances actually no advantages accrued from an expansion movement. It is believed that the points listed are self-ex-

Table 27–1. Growth in Sales and Assets of Selected Corporations Adjusted for Changing Dollar Values
United States, 1939 and 1961

Corporation	Sales 1939 (In Millions of Dollars)	Sales 1961 (In Millions of Dollars)	Sales 1961 Adjusted * (In Millions of 1939 Dollars)	1961 Sales As a Per Cent of 1939 Sales In Unadjusted Dollars	1961 Sales As a Per Cent of 1939 Sales In Adjusted Dollars	Total Assets 1939 (In Millions of Dollars)	Total Assets 1961 (In Millions of Dollars)
Consolidated Edison	$ 251	$ 699	$ 294	278	117	$1,064	$3,191
General Electric	304	4,456	1,876	1,463	616	392	2,677
General Foods	145	1,160	488	797	335	90	549
General Motors	1,376	11,395	4,797	828	349	1,706	8,272
Goodyear Tire & Rubber	200	1,473	620	736	310	191	1,085
International Business Machines	9	1,694	713	1,717	722	79	1,768
Pacific Gas & Electric	107	695	292	650	273	786	2,644
Pennsylvania Railroad	457	875	368	191	81	2,359	2,873
United States Steel	904	3,301	1,390	365	154	1,768	5,072

* Adjusted for changes from 1939 to 1961 in the Wholesale Price Index of the Department of Labor.
SOURCE: *Moody's Manuals.*

planatory, so no discussion will be given. The advantages can conveniently be classified under the following headings:

Purchasing

1. Reduced costs due to large-scale buying
2. Possibility of obtaining more and cheaper credit
3. Buying from original sources and elimination of profit of middlemen
4. Control of sources of raw materials

Production

1. Reduced costs due to large-scale production
2. Use of expensive labor-saving machinery
3. Economies of specialization
4. Use of technical experts
5. Stabilization of production
6. More effective utilization of byproducts

Selling

1. Lower selling costs
2. More effective use of salesmen
3. More effective use of advertising media
4. Possible elimination of middlemen
5. Saving in transportation costs
6. Possibility of foreign sales

Administration

1. Affording better management
2. Better utilization of specialized experts
3. Management costs per unit of product may be less, due to large sales volume
4. Better utilization of accounting and statistical methods and machines
5. Affording extensive research
6. Better methods and procedures which may result in better labor relations and smaller labor turnover

Finance

1. Better credit
2. Raising funds through sale of securities to investment bankers and others
3. More effective control over credits and collections
4. More efficient use of money
5. Greater possibility of stabilized earnings and dividends
6. Ability to compete effectively with other companies
7. Ability to buy out competitors

In spite of the economies of large-scale operations stated above, there are certain disadvantages. In some cases the expansion proves disastrous and the company fails. Following are the possible disadvantages of large-scale operations. No attempt has been made to classify them.

1. The hoped-for economies of purchasing, producing, administration, and financing may not be realized.
2. The management may not be able to cope with a large-scale business.
3. The personal element may be lost, or its effectiveness lessened.
4. Possibility of encountering public hostility due to large size.
5. Greater probability of regulation and intervention on the part of the government.
6. Possibility of more labor trouble.

TYPES OF EXPANSION

Approaches to expansion can be classified in a variety of ways. One common classification is internal or external. A second classification is by method of financing the expansion—through internal sources, sale of securities, borrowing, etc. A third classification is by direction of the expansion, that is, on the same level of production and distribution or on other levels, or in the manufacture of the same type of products or other products.

Internal and External Expansion

When a company enlarges its facilities without taking over or controlling other companies or buying operating assets of other companies, this is called internal expansion. This expansion may be financed from internal or external sources such as retained earnings or sale of securities, but it is still considered an internal expansion.

If the expansion takes the form of buying the controlling stock interest in another company or of combining with another company in some way or buying its assets, it is referred to as external expansion regardless of the source of funds used to finance the purchase or combination.

Internal expansion, therefore, adds new productive capacity to the total economy; external expansion is expansion for the firm alone at the expense of some other firm, and therefore, the total productive capacity of the economy is unchanged. In looking at society from the macro point of view, internal expansion is the only important kind of expansion. From the business unit's point of view, however, either type of expansion can aid in the accomplishment of its objectives.

Internal expansion is not confined to the enlargement of existing plant or facilities. If the company expands through construction of new plants or the addition of new distribution facilities, this is still classed as internal expansion. The increasing emphasis upon diversification and decentralization has led to a significant amount of internal expansion in entirely new facilities in new locations.

Approaches to external expansion are discussed in the following chapter. Decisions on internal expansion are top-management decisions rather than financial management decisions. Financial management is charged with the responsibility of providing the funds needed, once the expansion decision has been made. The addition of new facilities would be made only after the production and marketing areas determined the efficiency and profitability advantages and the sales potential for the product of the new facilities.

Methods of Financing Expansion

The type and extent of new financing depend, of course, upon the type of expansion or combination. Reference will also be made to types of financing in the next chapter when we discuss various forms of external expansion.

Internal expansion and some forms of external expansion require new funds for the corporation. Small companies that cannot sell securities through investment bankers will normally have to depend on retained earnings and depreciation charges for expansion purposes. Large companies also rely on these sources to a much greater extent than they rely on the sale of new securities. This means that expansion for many companies will probably occur only at the rate at which profits are available for reinvestment.

The importance of internally generated funds relative to external sale of securities is indicated in Table 27–2. It can be seen from these data that corporations in the United States depend to a great extent upon depreciation and depletion reserves as a source of funds for new fixed assets. The second most important source of funds for these firms from 1950 through 1961 has been retained earnings, closely followed by new security issues. While these data are for old and new concerns, new firms could account for only a very small portion of any of the figures. Thus, the data in Table 27–2 describe the approach taken to expansion by existing firms.

Annual permanent financing (column 7 in Table 27–2) has risen steadily in recent years. Firms are expanding at a greater dollar rate. While most of the funds obtained have been put into plant and equipment (column 11), permanent additions to working capital (column 12) are becoming increasingly important. The need for expanded working capital as capacity grows is indicated by this information. Working capital has grown much more than indicated by the table, for the table does not include additions from current financing sources.

Table 27–2. Expansion and Financing Data for All American Corporations Except Banks and Insurance Companies, 1950–1961 (In Billions of Dollars)

Year	(1) Earnings After Taxes	(2) Depreciation	(3) Retained Earnings	(4) Total Internal Sources (2)+(3)	(5) Dividend Payments	(6) Net New Security Issues	(7) Total Permanent Financing (4)+(6)	(8) Depreciation as a Per Cent of Financing (2)÷(7)	(9) Retained Earnings as a Per Cent of Financing (3)÷(7)	(10) Net New Security Issues as a Per Cent of Financing (6)÷(7)	(11) Expenditures for New Plant and Equipment	(12) Permanent Additions to Working Capital (7)−(11)
1950	$22.8	$ 7.8	$13.0	$20.8	$ 9.2	$ 3.7	$24.5	31.8	53.1	15.1	$16.9	$ 7.6
1951	19.7	9.0	10.0	19.0	9.0	6.3	25.3	35.6	39.5	24.9	21.6	3.7
1952	17.2	10.4	7.4	17.8	9.0	7.9	25.7	40.5	28.8	30.7	22.4	3.3
1953	18.1	11.8	7.9	19.7	9.2	7.1	26.8	44.0	29.5	26.5	23.9	2.9
1954	16.8	13.5	6.3	19.8	9.8	5.9	25.7	52.5	24.5	23.0	22.4	3.3
1955	23.0	15.7	10.9	26.6	11.2	6.9	33.5	46.9	32.5	20.6	24.2	9.3
1956	23.5	17.3	10.5	27.8	12.1	7.9	35.7	48.5	29.4	22.1	29.9	5.8
1957	22.3	19.1	8.9	28.0	12.6	10.6	38.6	49.5	23.1	27.4	32.7	5.9
1958	18.8	20.3	5.7	26.0	12.4	9.4	35.4	57.4	16.1	26.5	26.4	9.0
1959	23.7	21.5	9.1	30.6	13.4	7.8	38.4	56.0	23.7	20.3	27.7	10.7
1960	22.7	22.9	7.4	30.3	14.1	8.0	38.3	59.8	19.3	20.9	30.8	7.5
1961	22.8	24.4	7.7	32.1	14.4	9.4	41.5	58.8	18.6	22.6	30.4	11.1

SOURCE: *Based on Economic Report of the President, 1962* (Washington, D. C.: U. S. Government Printing Office, 1962), pp. 279 and 283.

Columns 8, 9, and 10 give a percentage breakdown of total permanent financing into the three major sources—depreciation, retained earnings, and new security issues. The growing importance of depreciation as a source of funds for new assets is clearly indicated. Retained earnings has actually declined in relative importance in this 12-year period. Proceeds from new security issues have remained more stable and have produced slightly under 25 per cent of requirements. Internal sources of funds have been three times as important as sale of new security issues.

Direction of Expansion

Regardless of whether expansion is carried on internally or externally or how it is financed, expansion may be in one of several directions. The terms applied to these types of expansion are *horizontal, vertical,* and *circular* expansion. When the expansion is effected through a combination of one type or another then these terms are applied to the combination.

Horizontal Expansion. When the expansion takes the direction of acquiring more assets or other companies of a similar nature and in the same stage of production and distribution, in order to increase the production and sale of the original line of products, it is called *horizontal* expansion. If control of other companies is acquired in the process it is called "horizontal combination." The horizontal method is usually the way that most companies expand their operations. The motive behind it is, of course, the desire to make more profits. This may be brought about through decreasing costs resulting from large-scale operations. Advertising and selling may also be more effective with a larger volume of sales. In some instances the desire to control the market may be present. Greater stabilization of sales may result from a wider diversification of the sales territory. Typical examples of companies that have expanded their operations by this method are the following: American Tobacco Company, Chrysler Corporation, Colgate-Palmolive Company, National Dairy Products Corporation, and Federated Department Stores.

Vertical Expansion. When the expansion takes the direction of reaching back to the source of raw materials, or forward to the further processing of the products produced by the company, or sales of the finished product, it is called *vertical* expansion. When this is accomplished by the union of one or more companies it is called a "vertical combination." Expanding in the direction of raw materials may be done to insure the source of the materials essential to the operations of the company, and in some instances the functions performed by the original supplier can be performed more cheaply by the company itself. When plant facilities or companies are acquired to further process the company's products and distribute them to the public, better control of the market may be had.

Whenever the expansion takes the direction of carrying on any additional step from the source of the raw materials to the ultimate sale of the products to consumers, economies may be effected which will lessen costs. If the functions of the various steps can be carried on at no greater cost than formerly, the profit of the middleman may be eliminated.

The United States Steel Corporation is a good example of a company that has expanded vertically. Through its subsidiaries it owns and operates mines, transportation systems, processing plants, manufacturing companies, and selling organizations. The Ford Motor Company has done likewise, but the various processes are carried on by divisions of the company instead of subsidiaries. Richman Brothers Company, and the Singer Sewing Machine Company are examples of manufacturing companies that have acquired their own retail outlets.

Circular Expansion. When additional products or lines of products are taken on which are somewhat different from those being produced or sold, but involve the same channels of distribution, it is termed *circular* expansion. Similarly, when this is accomplished through a type of combination it is referred to as a "circular combination." The products involved in this type of expansion are said to be *complementary*, or supplementary, to the original line. The products are not directly competitive, but are sold through the same outlets. If a company selling ice takes on the sale of coal, or vice versa, it is referred to as circular expansion. Circular expansion resembles horizontal more than vertical expansion. It is undertaken primarily for the hoped-for economies in distribution.

A good example of circular expansion was the formation of the General Foods Corporation to effect a combination of companies selling food products. In the hard goods industry the combination of the American Radiator Company and the Standard Sanitary Manufacturing Company to form the American Radiator & Standard Sanitary Corporation in order to offer a more complete line of building products, illustrates the circular combination. The General Motors Corporation can be classed as a circular combination, since it involved the combination of companies producing other automobiles, at least some of which were sold through the same outlets.

FINANCIAL MANAGEMENT AND EXPANSION

A decision on whether to expand and the extent and direction of the planned expansion is a tremendously important management decision. Many businesses have passed out of existence or have been absorbed by others because of their failure to keep pace with an expanding and changing economy. Others, on the other hand, have failed because of unwarranted or unwise expansion. The large public utility holding companies developed in the 1920's became unwieldy and uneconomic (as well as illegal) and have gone by the wayside, leaving sound operating companies which are smaller but more efficient. On the other hand economies of scale are important in many industries and the efficient public utility operating plant today is significantly larger than the corresponding plant in the 1920's.

While expansion is a top-management decision, it involves problems in all phases of business, such as purchasing, production, selling, and finance. Inability of any of these areas properly to handle its end of the expansion program may wreck the entire program and cause the business to fail. In the final analysis, the ability of management on all levels to cope with the problems arising from expansion is most important and the failure of any single department can generally be attributed to poor management.

Financial management has certain specific responsibilities in an expansion program. These are discussed below.

Determination of Profitability. One of the most important elements in the expansion decision for an existing business unit is to determine the potential future profitability resulting from the proposed expansion. In many cases, financial management has this responsibility. In other cases, it shares this responsibility with other departmental areas in the business. In any case, the determination of profit is a financial determination and financial management must be satisfied as to the potential effect on profits of a proposed expansion. The return on investment approach to making alternate investment decisions is the recommended one for determining the profitability of an expansion.

Selection of Sources of Funds. Selection of sources of funds for financing of the expansion is a financial decision. Top financial management must weigh the potential risks involved in the project and its estimated return in judging which sources of funds would be most suitable for financing the proposed expansion. The only difference between selecting sources of funds for expansion of existing businesses and selecting sources for a new business is that the decision approach begins with the existing financial structure for an established business. The present structure becomes the base for judging what additional sources of funds to use. The problems of balancing risk, cost, and control are the same in either case. The approach to the determination of capital structure discussed in Chapter 11 for new business, would apply also for an expansion of an established business.

Achieving the Plan. An additional responsibility of financial management in expansion is establishing measurements useful for controlling the level of investment in the expansion and for the subsequent operations and profits. If the decision to expand is based on estimates of profitability, these estimates become a budget against which the actual results of expansion can and should be compared. Furthermore, the profitability estimates require an estimate of the level of investment required for expansion. Good financial management should collect data on actual investments in expansion as they are made and compare them against the required level that was estimated when the decision was made to invest. By comparing the variance of actual experience from the original estimates, financial management is able to pinpoint deviations and to encourage adjustments in operations which would help bring actual results into line with the original plan. Controlling the results of the expansion program and the level of investment in expansion is similar to control processes used for all operations and investment.

Expansion Problems for Financial Management

Certain specific areas of financing of expansion can create substantial problems for financial management. Five of the specific problem areas are discussed below.

Maintenance of Adequate Working Capital Position. The immediate reason that companies fail is a lack of cash. The real reasons for failure are all those factors which result in inadequate cash. The management of a company must keep close watch over the relationship between the current assets and the current liabilities. Although the current assets may increase, this may be accompanied by an even greater increase in the current liabilities; also, the current assets may be inflated with obsolete and overvalued inventory and uncollectible accounts.

It is a more or less normal process for a business to expand through an increase in sales. But the company may soon be hard-pressed for cash and unable to meet its accounts and notes payable, if the additional profits earned are invested in additional fixed assets. Its mistake would be its failure to realize that a permanent increase in the volume of sales necessitates additional working capital in the form of inventories to be tied up permanently in the business. Such companies may find their fixed asset expansion programs to be disastrous, because they were financed out of needed working capital.

Avoidance of Excess Debt. The rate of interest that will have to be paid on bonds is usually less than the dividend rate that must be promised on the stock in order to raise capital for expansion purposes. Thus, in order to benefit from trading on the equity, a company may prefer a bond to a stock issue. Unless the use to which the funds are put results in additional earnings, a company may find difficulty in meeting the bond interest, and the principal when it becomes due. Hoped-for profits from the expansion are not always realized. Furthermore, the increased maintenance and depreciation charges on the additional facilities add to the expense incurred by the company.

Expansion takes place usually in a period of prosperity. In most instances interest rates are relatively high then, and thus the fixed charges may become a burden to the company.

Avoidance of Excess Stock Issues. A stock issue will not get a company into the trouble that may result from a bond issue. But an excessive amount of stock outstanding may produce a strain on the company to pay dividends. And the reduction of the dividend rate, or the passing of a dividend, adversely affects the company's credit and makes for poor stockholder relations.

Expansion usually occurs in a period of high prices. When the next recession hits, the maintenance and depreciation charges on the added facilities may prove to be burdensome, and the lower earnings make it difficult to maintain dividends.

Retention of Control. Large corporations that are controlled by the management through the proxy system need give little thought to the matter of control in deciding upon the means of financing expansion. But small- and medium-size companies often plan their financing so that there is little or no danger of losing control. When a company is controlled by an individual or a small group of persons, non-voting preferred stock or bonds may be sold instead of common stock in order not to disrupt control. Even non-voting preferred stock may not be issued because it is more or less necessary to include in the contract a provision giving it voting rights if dividends are in arrears for a specified number of quarterly periods.

In some instances the owners and managers of a company will hesitate to sell additional common stock to the public even if the amount sold is sufficiently small to enable the management to retain control. The reason is that they do not want to be bothered with minority shareholders. The sale of additional common stock through the privileged subscription method, of course, would not alter control, but naturally it would necessitate additional investment on the part of the present owners.

It is obvious that the issuance of bonds for the purpose of retaining control would be an unwise act if in the circumstances the company should not be able to stand the fixed charges and additional debt.

Tax Considerations. It was pointed out earlier that the issuance of bonds rather than stock would reduce the income taxes that a company would have to pay. This encourages some companies to use bond financing for expansion.

In some instances a sale or purchase of a business is prompted by tax considerations. A company may buy out another one at a relatively small price in order to write off against its profits the losses that have been incurred by the company which is purchased. Corporations can write off losses against the profits of the past three years (carryback), or against the profits of the next five years (carryover).

Opportunities also may exist where owners of a small corporation may be desirous of selling or exchanging their shares for the purpose of lessening the estate taxes that would be levied against their estate upon their death. When shares of a company are not listed and have no market, upon death of the owner the tax appraisers may arrive at a fair value by capitalizing the past earnings or valuing the stock at the book figures. Either of these may result in a relatively high valuation for tax purposes. Anticipating this, the owners may seek opportunities of exchanging their shares for those of a large corporation whose shares are listed and have frequent sales that indicate their market value. Or, the owners of the small business may want to sell their shares for cash and pay the relatively smaller capital gains. In either case, the families of the owners would be in a better position to pay or to get the cash necessary to pay the estate taxes upon the death of the owners.

QUESTIONS

1. What is the underlying reason for growth in most American corporations?
2. List the various specific motives that account for expansion of American business concerns.
3. Discuss the advantages and disadvantages of large-scale operations.
4. What is the shortcoming of measuring growth in dollar values rather than physical units?
5. Differentiate *internal* and *external expansion.*
6. Define *vertical expansion* and give an example.
7. Indicate the difference between *horizontal* and *circular expansion.*
8. Under which of the three types of expansion or combination (by direction) would you put the following companies: General Motors Corporation? United States Steel Corporation? General Foods Corporation?
9. Generally speaking, what type of companies can rely on retained earnings for expansion and what type cannot?
10. If a company whose stock is widely held is in constant need of funds for expansion purposes, should it pay out a relatively large percentage of its earnings in dividends or retain a relatively large percentage? Explain.
11. Generally speaking, are there any limits to the size which a company may attain and still operate efficiently?
12. Indicate several of the financial problems that arise in connection with an expansion program.
13. What are the specific responsibilities of financial management in expansion decisions?

14. Discuss the problem of retention of control, in an expanding business.
15. What tax considerations are involved in expansion decisions?

PROBLEMS

1. The Elephant Manufacturing Co. is 100 per cent owned by Mr. Jacob Wellman and his family. The company has been profitable over the years and produces a complete line of household paints. All manufacturing is in one plant and distribution is regional in the Middle Atlantic and New England states. Mr. Wellman believes that there is substantial opportunity for sales in the East North Central states but realizes that this will require the building or purchase of a new plant in that area. The investment required in the new plant will be approximately equal to that in the existing plant and working capital requirements will also be equal. The Elephant Manufacturing Co.'s current structure is 20 per cent current liabilities, 20 per cent long-term notes and 60 per cent equity.

How would you suggest that the proposed expansion be financed? How would the problem of retention of control affect your answer? How might tax considerations affect your answer? Under what conditions should the expansion be undertaken?

2. The following information is available about the operations of the Standardized Part Co. for the year 19x1. The company sold 10,000,000 of its units for $1 each, on which it made a net profit before income taxes of 5 per cent on sales. Half of the sales price of the product was made up of materials cost. The unit labor cost was equal to 40 per cent of the materials cost, and the overhead costs were equal to 50 per cent of the labor costs. Administrative expenses were $500,000, and advertising and selling expenses made up the balance of the expenses. (Disregard income taxes in this problem.)

The sales manager of the company estimated that the sales volume (units) could be doubled if the selling price were reduced to $0.90 per unit. The president called in the department heads and had them prepare a budget for their respective departments based on this production schedule. It was found that the expenses would be as follows: unit materials cost reduced 10 per cent because of larger-scale buying; unit labor cost unchanged; overhead costs increased 50 per cent; administrative expenses increased 10 per cent; and advertising and selling expenses increased 50 per cent. In addition to these expenses, the company would have to pay annual interest of $120,000 on the money borrowed to acquire the additional equipment necessary to carry on this scale of operations. (Depreciation on the new equipment was considered in the increased overhead charges.)

The president then asked the sales manager to make an estimate of the price at which 30,000,000 units could be disposed of annually. This was reported back at $0.80 per unit. On this production schedule the budget committee gave the following estimate of costs: materials unit cost, $0.43; labor, $6,000,000; overhead, $3,000,000; administrative expenses, $600,000; advertising and selling expenses, $2,000,000; and interest expenses, $300,000. (a) Draw up an income statement for each of the three scales of operations. (b) As president of the company how many units would you order the production department to manufacture? (c) What would the total unit cost of the product be in each case? (d) If the product could be sold at $1 and the total unit cost was $0.96, how many units would have to be sold in order to make the same total net profit as was made in 19x1? (e) Should the company push production to the point where the unit cost of the product is least? Explain.

3. Classify the following as to type of combination: (a) A company making starting, lighting, and ignition equipment is merged into an automobile manufacturing company. (b) A bank stock holding company acquires all the stock, except qualifying directors' shares, of three banks. (c) A company making airplane motors buys out a company that makes airplane propellers. (d) A company that manufactures fighting planes buys up all the stock of a concern that makes small pleasure airplanes. (e) A coffee company, a chocolate company, and a breakfast food company combine.

4. Pennsylvania Electronics Co. is a distributor of electronic products in Allegheny County, Pennsylvania. The company has grown very rapidly since its inception and has reinvested all of its earnings. At the present time, the company controls about one-third of the total volume in the region; its five competitors share the remaining two-thirds of the volume. The managers of the company believe that by carrying a significantly larger inventory, they could pick up an additional volume in the county and perhaps pull their position up to 50 per cent of total industry sales in the area.

Sales for the company last year were $1,500,000. The company has total assets of $450,000. These are financed by accounts payable $200,000, notes to suppliers $100,000, bank note $50,000, and common stock and retained earnings $100,000. The company has been netting after tax about 1.5 per cent of sales, and its net profit to owners' equity is 22 per cent. The company estimates that about $15,000 in additional investment is necessary to pick up the additional sales.

Do you think the company should expand? Explain your answer.

5. Using *Moody's Manuals,* select several companies which have expanded vertically in the past 10 years. Also select several companies which have expanded horizontally and several which have used circular expansion during the past decade.

SELECTED READINGS

AMERICAN INSTITUTE OF CERTIFIED PUBLIC ACCOUNTANTS. *Business Combinations.* Accounting Research Bulletin No. 40. New York: American Institute of Certified Public Accountants, 1951.

AMERICAN MANAGEMENT ASSOCIATION. *Integration Policies and Problems in Mergers and Acquisitions.* Financial Management Series, No. 113. New York: American Management Association, 1957.

BUTTERS, J. K., and LITNER, JOHN. *Effect of Federal Taxes on Growing Enterprises.* Cambridge: Harvard University Press, 1945.

BUTTERS, J. K., and others. *Taxation and Business Concentration.* Princeton, N. J.: Tax Institute, Inc., 1952.

FEDERAL TRADE COMMISSION. *Report on Corporate Mergers and Acquisitions.* Washington, D. C.: U. S. Government Printing Office, 1955.

KAPLAN, A. D. H. *Big Enterprise in a Competitive System.* Washington: The Brookings Institution, 1954.

LARSON, H. M. *Guide to Business History.* Cambridge: Harvard University Press, 1950.

LEWIS, RONELLO B. *Financial Analysis for Management.* Englewood Cliffs, N. J.: Prentice-Hall, Inc., 1959.

MARTING, ELIZABETH. *Management for the Small Company.* New York: American Management Association, 1959.

NATIONAL ASSOCIATION OF MANUFACTURERS. *Major Tendencies in Business Fnance.* Economic Policy Division Series No. 57. New York: National Association of Manufacturers, 1953.

OSBORN, R. C. *Effects of Corporate Size on Efficiency and Profitability.* Champaign: University of Illinois, Bureau of Economics and Business Research, 1950.

WESTON, J. FRED. *The Role of Mergers in the Growth of Large Firms.* Berkeley: University of California Press, 1953.

28

Combinations

One important approach to expansion utilized by industry has been the acquisition of other existing enterprises rather than the creation of new facilities. While the techniques used in combination and the forms and results have varied, the major portion of the expansion of many existing large firms has been accomplished through the acquisition of other companies.

Because the American economic system is founded on competition, and because of the obvious implications of competition for various kinds of acquisitions and combinations of existing companies, government has taken a hand in restricting acquisitions and combinations. The legality of different forms of combinations has varied substantially over the years and is still in a process of change. As certain approaches to combinations are ruled out by government, others are developed. The legal restrictions on combinations are discussed later in this chapter.

Historical Development of Combinations

While some efforts have been made to expand through combination during all periods of modern business history, certain periods stand out. As would be expected, most expansion and combination periods begin after a recovery from a depression, and end with a panic, depression, or recession. The first period began about 1885, with the prosperous years following the depression, and ended abruptly with the panic of 1893. The most important of the early combinations was the Standard Oil Trust which was organized in 1879. Another early combination resulted in the formation of the American Sugar Refining Company in 1892. Fearful of the effects that might result from these and other combinations, a number of the states enacted statutes to outlaw trusts. In 1890, Congress enacted the Sherman Anti-Trust Act. This legislation, however, did not immediately stop the formation of monopolies. The National Lead Company was formed later in 1890, and in 1892, the General Electric Company and the United States Rubber Company were formed. But the panic of 1893 and the ensuing depression, rather than legislation, brought this first period of combination to an end. In contrast to some of the later periods, the combinations formed during this first cycle were promoted by businessmen for the purpose of effecting economies in the production and distribution of goods and for the purpose of controlling the production and distribution of goods through monopolies.

The depression which began in 1893 had completed its course by the Autumn of 1896 and the second period of expansion took place from 1897 to 1903. The election of President McKinley, who was in sympathy with big business, was an important factor and created a favorable climate for combinations. Exports were increasing, security prices began to rise, and a period of business prosperity was at hand. Among the combinations formed at this time were the Otis Elevator Company, United States Steel Corporation, Eastman Kodak Company, and the American Can Company. The decline in number of combinations at the end of this period was accounted for by the disappearance of profits made by existing combinations, the decline in stock market activity, court decisions upholding the Sherman Anti-Trust Act, and the panic of 1903. The "trust" form of organization had been used in the first period of combinations, but it later was outlawed by both legislation and court decisions. During the second period the holding company device was the favorite method of effecting the combinations.

With the ending of World War I in 1918, the third period of combinations got under way. Although in the previous periods combinations were limited to the railroad and industrial fields, this period embraced almost every line of business, including public utilities, financial institutions, and merchandising concerns. Although trusts and the holding companies were the principal means of effecting combinations in the earlier periods, the third cycle made use of holding companies, mergers, consolidations, and other forms of combination. The investment banker, who was one of the types of promoters in the combination period which ended in 1903, occupied an even more important place in effecting combinations during this third period. Many of the combinations which took place in the late 1920's were not effected for sound economic reasons. Often, the only reason for their existence was the desire of investment bankers to make more money from the sale of securities. Businesses and business combinations became overextended. The stock market crash in the Autumn of 1929 brought an end to this period of combination.

Since 1940, there have been two pronounced waves of combinations, the 1946–1947 period, and the one from 1954 to date. The most comprehensive study of the combination movement was published by the Federal Trade Commission in 1955, covering the period 1948–1954.[1] The study indicated that from the limited evidence available it appeared that "outside interests" played an important role in the combination movement. These included legal and economic consultants, banks, and investment bankers. The non-electrical machinery industry led the field in numbers with 249 acquisitions of companies during the period. This was followed by the food products field which showed 243 instances of combinations. These two industries accounted for more than one-fourth of the total of 1,773 combinations in manufacturing and mining.

The merger movement has continued unabated since 1954. While no major comprehensive studies of this movement are available at this time, it is apparent that this is one of the broadest based of all of the combination periods. In the latter half of the 1950's a substantial number of mergers took place among financial institutions. Several banks merged with other banks and a number of mergers also occurred in sales finance, personal finance, savings and loan associations, and insurance companies. Combinations were also very prevalent in retailing and wholesaling. A number of the industrial combinations of this period took the form of very heterogeneous organizations uniting very dissimilar industrial operations.

FORMS OF COMBINATION

American combinations have followed many different patterns. Some of the first forms used are no longer legal, but other forms have developed to take their place. The following forms of combinations will be discussed in this chapter: the purchase of assets, mergers and consolidations, holding companies, leases, trade associations, interlocking directorates, communities of interest, trusts, pools, and gentlemen's agreements.

Purchase of Assets

The term *purchase of assets* has a special meaning in situations where a purchase of assets results in a form of combination of enterprises. When a company acquires assets through the "purchase-of-assets method," it acquires assets that are not ordinary stock in trade of the seller, and it acquires all or a substantial part of the total assets of the seller.

The board of directors has the power to do all things necessary to carry out the purposes for which the corporation was formed. This includes the purchase of assets needed in the business or desired for expansion purposes. Thus only the board of directors, and not the shareholders, of the purchasing corporation need approve the purchase of assets.

[1] *Report on Corporate Mergers and Acquisitions,* Federal Trade Commission, (Washington, D. C.: U. S. Government Printing Office, May, 1955).

The power given to the directors does not include that of selling all or a substantial part of the total assets of the company. Thus the selling corporation must have the sale of assets approved not only by the board of directors but by the stockholders also. Statutory provisions have been adopted in most of the states which specify the percentage of the voting shares that would have to authorize the sale. Even if the required vote authorizing the sale has been obtained, dissenting shareholders can demand that the corporation buy back their shares. The statutes provide for a "fair cash value" for the shares.

Ordinarily, the creditors have no voice in the sale of assets, and unless special circumstances exist, they have no claim against the assets acquired by the purchaser. If the creditors have a lien on the assets, however, this lien continues on the property after it has been acquired by the purchaser. The purchasing corporation acquires the new property *subject* to any existing mortgages. It does not *assume* the issue, unless it is so agreed, or unless the issuing company goes out of existence at the time the assets are sold. If stock of the purchasing corporation instead of cash is given for the assets, and if the seller cannot secure the cash from this stock and has no other assets from which the creditors can be paid, the courts may hold that the purchaser is liable for the debts.

Since the purchase-of-assets method of combination is similar to the merger or consolidation, the advantages of the purchase of assets usually listed are in comparison with these other methods.

1. Normally, the approval of only the shareholders of the selling company is necessary to effect a purchase of assets. Mergers and consolidations call for the approval of the shareholders of both affected companies.
2. The laws of some of the states do not permit their corporations to merge or consolidate with a corporation organized in another state.
3. Only the desired assets are acquired, whereas in a merger or consolidation all the property is involved.
4. It is usually easier to reach an agreement on the purchase price of specific assets than for the total business, which would be necessary for a merger or consolidation.
5. The liabilities of the selling company need not be assumed by the purchasing company, but in event of a merger or consolidation they must be assumed unless they have been paid off.
6. Certain tax advantages may be realized.

Mergers and Consolidations

A merger results when an existing company acquires all of the assets and the liabilities of another company and the latter company passes out of existence. A consolidation results when a company newly formed for this particular purpose takes over the assets and liabilities of two or more other companies, and the latter pass out of existence as separate entities. This is usually accomplished by the new company's exchanging its shares with the shareholders of the other companies for their shares, and then canceling the latter shares upon dissolution of the companies.

It is apparent that although the merger and consolidation differ in some respects, they are very similar. In the case of a consolidation, two or more companies are fused ("merged" in a sense) into a new company, whereas a merger results when one or more companies are fused ("merged") into an already existing company. Because the difference is one of form more than of substance, the two methods of combination are often not distinguished. About two-thirds of the states have general statutes authorizing either mergers or consolidations or both. Usually mergers of railroads, public utilities, and financial institutions are covered by special regulation.

Several points of difference between a sale of assets and a merger have been stated above. Another difference can be in the method of effecting the legal transfer of assets. In the case of sale of assets, title to the property is transferred by means of a deed or bill of sale, which is the usual way of transferring property, whereas in a merger the transfer is accomplished by the execution and filing of the merger agreement.

In many instances a company will acquire a substantial stock interest in the company which it expects to acquire by means of a merger. The approval of a designated percentage of the shares of the selling company is necessary to effect a merger. Shares sufficient to give control may be acquired prior to negotiations for the merger. Not only does this aid in getting the approval of the required amount of stock, but it may also lessen the amount to be paid to shareholders who dissent to the merger. If all the stock is acquired, no problems can arise.

Advantages. Following are the principal advantages of the merger or consolidation as a type of combination:

1. It results in the elimination of the merged company or companies as separate entities, and thus no corporate taxes must be paid on them.
2. There are no minority stock interests of other companies to deal with.
3. It is a permanent form of combination.
4. Management is centralized in one company.
5. If properly handled, the shareholders of the merged company will not have to pay any taxes on the exchange of securities.
6. The statutes usually provide that the surviving company succeeds to all the rights and privileges of the companies that are merged into it.

Procedures. Before a merger or consolidation may be effected it is necessary to get the approval of the boards of directors of all the constituent companies. A plan will have been worked out specifying the basis for the exchange of shares, the policies to be followed until the combination is effected, and, in the case of a consolidation, the list of proposed directors and officers. The boards of the various companies will adopt resolutions approving the combination and calling for meetings of the shareholders of their respective companies to vote on the proposal. Usually a special meeting of the shareholders of the various companies is called for the purpose of voting on the combination proposal.

After the merger or consolidation has been approved by the shareholders, the appropriate corporate officers sign the merger or consolidation agreement, and it is filed in the required state office where the original articles of incorporation were filed. If the agreement conforms to the law and the proper taxes and fees are paid, it will be approved, and the state will issue a certificate of merger or consolidation, which makes the combination complete.

The recourse for dissenting shareholders is to go to court to oppose the merger or to demand the fair cash value for their shares. The statutes authorizing the merger or consolidation will provide the procedure to be followed. In order not to be forced to pay an excessive amount to dissenting shareholders, the merger or consolidation plan often provides that the combination will not be effective if shares in excess of a specified number dissent.

In some instances the current assets, or part of them, are used to pay off the general unsecured creditors of some or all of the constituent companies before the combination is effected. In that event only the fixed assets and fixed or long-term debt are taken over by the consolidated or surviving company. Where the above procedure is not followed, the consolidated or surviving company would automatically assume all the debts, both secured and unsecured, of the constituent companies. Bonds of the constituent companies which are secured by a lien on property retain that lien after the combination has taken place. They also assume the security of the general credit of the consolidated or surviving company. If any of the bonds of the companies that lose their identity are convertible into stock, in the absence of provision otherwise, the courts have usually held that the conversion right is extinguished by the merger or consolidation.

General creditors of the constituent companies become general creditors of the consolidated or surviving company. But the determination of the relative position of such creditors with respect to the assets of the former constituent companies is not always easy. Equity holds that the rights of creditors shall not be impaired in any way by a merger or consolidation, and most statutes agree. Furthermore, the courts have taken the position that the capital of a corporation is a "trust fund" for the benefit of creditors. Courts of equity have accordingly held that both secured and unsecured creditors of a constituent company have a prior right to the assets of the old company ahead of either the secured or unsecured creditors of one of the other constituent companies to the combination, provided the specific assets can be identified. If they have been sold, then no such priority would exist. In any event, however, the secured creditors would have a senior claim to any property which specifically comes under their lien.

Promotion. In promoting a combination it is advisable to reduce to a minimum the possibility that a substantial number of shareholders will dissent to the plan. The promotion will usually take one of two forms, the *option method* or the *bargaining method*.

Under the *option method* the promoter deals with each of the companies separately. For a consideration, which is usually cash, he buys from the particular company an option to purchase all its assets or stock at a stipulated price within a stated period of time. If the option is not exercised by the expiration date it is void and the company retains the money paid for the option.

In recent years, the *bargaining method* rather than the option method has been used to effect combinations. As the term suggests, under this method the promoter, who may be the president of a large company, approaches a smaller company and attempts to interest it in combining with the large company through a merger or consolidation.

When it has been established that a combination is possible or probable, a valuation of the worth of the respective companies must be made in order to know how much to pay for the properties, or to determine the basis for the exchange of securities, or to give those taking the initiative the information which is needed for bargaining.

Although the exact treatment given the various companies or their security holders will depend in part on the bargaining ability of the parties concerned, the price paid for the properties or the basis for the exchange of securities will tend to depend upon the relative worths of the companies. The relative values of the companies are usually arrived at by taking into consideration the value of the net tangible assets, the earnings record, and the market value of the securities. These factors were discussed in Chapter 12.

Holding Companies

The holding company device has perhaps been the easiest and cheapest, and at the same time one of the most effective ways, of forming combinations in the United States. It was used in the early railroad combinations; industrial companies made extensive use of it starting in the 1890's; and public utilities since the turn of the century have built up tremendous systems through its use. Many of our largest combinations today operate under the holding company system.

As the term is generally used, a holding company is one that owns sufficient voting stock of another company to have *working control* over it. Working control would ordinarily be assumed to be control over the election of a majority of the board of directors. Where the controlling shares of holding companies which own controlling interest in operating companies are owned by still another holding company, the latter is referred to as a *top* holding company, and the other holding companies are called *intermediate* holding companies. This process of superimposing holding companies upon holding companies is referred to as *pyramiding*.

Advantages. There are many advantages of the holding company device both from the standpoint of comparison with the separate control and operation of the various companies concerned, and in comparison with other forms of combinations.

1. *Operating Economies.* The holding company can afford to hire expert managers, and can pass along their advice to the various operating companies. This applies also to specialized phases of business operations such as accounting, engineering, financial, and legal. It may also carry on research better and more cheaply than the various operating companies. Economies may also come from standardized and quantity purchases. These economies are derived from combination, and they may also be effected through one or more of the other forms of combinations.

2. *Cheaper Financing.* A large, well-known holding company can secure additional capital more easily and more cheaply than if the capital were sought directly by the subsidiary companies. Here again, we are stating an advantage of combination. If all the companies forming the system were merged into one company, or were consolidated, the same advantage would be enjoyed.

3. *Ease of Forming Combinations.* The holding company device is perhaps the easiest and quickest method of forming combinations. To get control of other companies it is necessary to secure only a majority of the voting stock, although in the case of large companies control can be gained on a much smaller percentage.

4. *Less Funds Required To Form Combination.* If the stock necessary to effect a combination must be purchased, it would require much less to acquire the controlling stock interests through the holding company device than to effect a merger or consolidation. Furthermore, no funds would be required to deal with dissenters. Considerably less cash

would be required through the use of the holding company than if assets were purchased which would call for cash equivalent to the value of the property acquired.

5. *Debts of Other Companies Not Assumed.* Under ordinary circumstances, the holding company can acquire control of the various companies without paying off their debts, or without assuming their debts. Furthermore, the holding company is not liable for future debts of or judgments against the subsidiary companies. When the business being transacted by the subsidiary is unsuccessful and the creditors cannot be paid, the holding company may merely discard the company and leave the creditors without any recourse except their right against the defunct subsidiary.

6. *Laws or Regulation More Favorable to Domestic Subsidiary.* Some states favor their own corporations over those formed in other states. In order to prevent the necessity of paying the taxes and being treated as a foreign corporation, the company may organize a small domestic subsidiary in the state and then subject it to the taxation and regulation applicable to domestic corporations.

7. *Other Reasons for Separate Subsidiary.* A corporation which manufactures and sells a high-quality product may wish to broaden its market by starting to make and sell, or by combining with other companies which handle, a similar but cheaper product. The company may not want to manufacture and sell the product itself or combine with the other companies through a merger or consolidation, because of the fear that it may lose its reputation for the high-quality product.

Where goodwill or a valuable trade name has been built up by a company in a particular community, rather than effect a merger or consolidation, it would probably be better to acquire controlling shares in the company and let it continue to operate as a local concern officered by local people and retaining the same name. In carrying on foreign operations, a business may be so different from the domestic business that a separate corporation would be indicated. Furthermore, the subsidiary may be incorporated in the foreign country in order to lessen the possibility of incurring the shortcomings of prejudices against alien companies. A separate subsidiary corporation may be formed by a company, or group of companies, for the purpose of carrying on some specialized operations such as construction, real estate transactions, financing, insurance, and holding and leasing patents. Where several companies plan to build and operate a common property, such as a railroad terminal, it is customary for them to organize a separate subsidiary to take title to and operate the property.

Disadvantages. Some of the possible disadvantages of the holding company as compared to other forms of combination follow.

1. *States' Taxes and Fees.* A state organization tax and an annual franchise fee must be paid by every corporation in the holding company system, including the holding company itself, in the state in which it is organized. If any of these corporations transact intrastate business within another state, the foreign corporation tax will have to be paid in that state. The amount of all these taxes may be more than would have to be paid if the combination had been effected through a merger or consolidation.

2. *Federal Income Tax.* The holding company system of combination results in heavier federal income taxes than if the merger or consolidation method were used. The various subsidiaries will have to pay federal income tax on their incomes. Then the holding company will have to pay income tax on 15 per cent of the dividends received from the subsidiaries. Thus, part of the income of the subsidiaries that is paid to the holding company as dividends is taxed twice. The holding company may file a consolidated income tax return for the group if it owns at least 80 per cent of the subsidiaries' voting stock, and at least 80 per cent of the subsidiaries' non-voting stock. A penalty of 2 per cent must be paid for filing a consolidated return. (This penalty is waived in the case of railroads and regulated utilities.)

3. *Other Expenses.* Ascertaining the various taxes and amounts that must be paid, and preparing the many tax forms cost money. Setting up and operating accounting systems for the various companies will probably be more expensive than if the combination was all one company. The sending-out of notices of the shareholders' and directors' meetings, and the holding of these many meetings, entail some expense.

4. *Minority Interests.* When the holding company does not own all the stock of the subsidiaries, the minority interest may cause trouble and expense. Although the holding company may actually own over half of the stock of the subsidiaries, courts of equity stand ready to protect minority interests.

5. *Possibility of Loss of Control.* Companies acquired by merger or consolidation are acquired for good. But in some instances a holding company may lose control of one of its subsidiaries. For example, if control was exercised on less than a majority of the voting stock, some other faction may quietly buy-in enough shares on the market to take control away from the holding company.

6. *Coordination More Difficult.* Due to the decentralization of management among the companies comprising the holding company system, there is a possibility of less coordination among the various companies than if one company had been formed by means of merger or consolidation.

7. *Regulation in the Public Utility Field.* Holding companies in the gas and electric utility field are subject to the Public Utility Holding Com-

pany Act of 1935, and the regulations that have been promulgated under this legislation. Since the Act covers combinations formed through only the holding company device, those formed under the merger or consolidation are not subject to this regulation.

Abuses of the Holding Company Device. The ease and cheapness of using the holding company device as a means of combination, and the profits that could be made by the insiders, have resulted in many abuses of the holding company device. This has been particularly true in the electric power and gas field. All of the abuses below were found particularly in the utility field, but some of them are applicable to any field.

1. *Uneconomical Structures.* Combinations have been built by the holding company device that cover companies operating in such widely scattered sections of the country and of the world that few if any operating economies could be realized. The capital structures became unduly complicated, and intercorporate relations were not understandable to the security holders or regulatory authorities. All of this made it possible for some organizers and insiders to defraud the companies and to profit personally at the expense of those whose properties they were supposed to administer.

2. *Concentration of Economic Power.* The pyramiding of public utility holding company systems took place to such an extent that before legislation compelled their dissolution, a comparative few top holding companies controlled most of the production and distribution of gas and electric power in the United States.

3. *Stock Watering.* In most instances relatively high prices were paid to acquire the controlling stock interest in the various companies that were desired in the combination. In order to get the money necessary to buy the stock, the holding company would have to issue large amounts of its own stock. To make the books balance, the stock or property of the subsidiaries would be carried at high valuations on the books of the holding company, and in its consolidated statements.

4. *Top-heavy Capital Structures.* Among the public utility holding company systems particularly, the practice was to issue not only excessive amounts of stocks, but excessive amounts of senior obligations as well; in fact, the amounts of these were commonly out of proportion even to the excessive stock issues.

5. *Milking the Subsidiaries.* A favorite practice carried on by many holding companies in the public utility field was popularly called "milking the subsidiaries." The holding company would charge the subsidiaries excessive management fees. Not only did such exorbitant charges harm the shareholders but in some instances these charges, along with other expenses, resulted in failure of the company and resultant losses to creditors.

6. *"Upstream" Loans.* In some of the utility holding company systems, the holding company securities were issued in such excessive quantities, and on such highly inflated values, that the holding company in need of funds would "borrow" from one of its prosperous subsidiaries.

7. *Manipulation of Accounts.* In the past many holding companies manipulated their own accounts and those of their subsidiaries to accomplish the desired purposes. In many instances the depreciation and maintenance accounts were handled in such a way as to make a better showing for the weak companies. Secret reserves were built up through improper accounting practices. In some systems intercompany sales of products, assets, and securities were made at such prices that the earnings of the prosperous companies were lessened and those of the less successful companies increased. In many cases the accounts were juggled in such a way as to show larger subsidiary earnings so that the holding company could get more in dividends on the stock of the subsidiaries.

8. *Evasion of Control.* The public utility companies were under the control of the public utility commission, or similar body, in the states in which they were formed and operated. But the companies organized to hold the stock of the public utilities were holding companies, and not public utilities; hence they did not come under the jurisdiction of the regulatory body.

9. *Excess Rates to Consumers.* Property values were greatly inflated by the practices of some of the holding companies. Securities were issued in excessive amounts and fixed charges on the bonds and dividends on the preferred stock required large sums of money. The excessive management fees charged by the holding companies added to the expense of the subsidiaries. All of these factors would tend to prevent a reduction in rates charged the consumer, or cause an actual increase in rates.

Leases

Leasing of assets as a means of financing was discussed in Chapter 23. In Chapter 8, the leasing of railroad equipment by a trustee was described. These types of leasing are not used as a form of combination. Instead, the lease as a form of combination is a long-term lease of all or a substantial part of the assets of a company for purposes of combination. Railroads have made the most extensive use of the lease as a method of combination.

The major advantage of the lease in effecting a combination is that the lessee obtains the use of the entire properties of another company without any outlay of cash. Leases may provide for either fixed or variable rent—the fixed rent lease is much more common in the use of leasing for combination purposes. The amount of the fixed rent is determined after giving consideration to taxes of the lessor, interest on bonds, dividends at a specified rate, and any other fixed expenses that would have to be paid by the lessor.

The acquiring of other companies through the lease method is somewhat similar to selling bonds and buying property with the proceeds. Fixed rental payments covering the bond interest, dividends, and taxes of the lessor are comparable to the payment of interest on bonds that might have been issued by the lessee. However, leasing the property does not call for the repayment of a principal amount. Bonds would appear as a liability on the balance sheet of the company but its obligation to pay rent under a lease does not show. It is apparent, therefore, that leasing the property of another company is another method of trading on the equity.

The lease usually provides that the lessee must guarantee the payment of interest and principal on the bonds of the lessor. Thus, the bonds retain whatever lien they may have had on the property of the lessor, and in addition the guarantee of the lessee makes them in effect debenture bonds of the lessee. Directors cannot rent the corporate property without the consent of the shareholders. The statutes of practically all the states, however, provide for leasing the property if some specified percentage of the stockholders agree. One of the provisions of the lease is that the lessee guarantees the dividends on the lessor's stock. Thus, in effect the shareholders of the lessor become creditors of the lessee with respect to the dividends on their stock.

In the case of long-term leases of this kind, it is a matter of common law that the lessee shall make the necessary repairs in connection with the leased properties. The lease itself, however, usually specifically provides that the lessee will make all necessary repairs and otherwise maintain the property in operating condition, and will carry proper insurance on the properties. It is also common law that any improvements or additions made to leased property by the tenant shall revert to the landlord upon termination of the lease. This, however, is not a serious matter to the lessee in most instances, because the lease may have, for example, 500 years yet to run. The great probability is that any improvements made to the property will have fully depreciated or become obsolete before that time.

Advantages to Lessor.

1. A fixed income is assured regardless of the volume of business or the expenses incurred.
2. The bondholders benefit from the additional security of the general credit of the lessee.
3. The shareholders become general creditors of the lessee with respect to their dividends.

Disadvantages to Lessor.

1. The company gives up its independent control and earning power, and its future is thus dependent upon the lessee.
2. Future prosperity will not result in any direct benefit, except in the few instances where the rental payments are based on income or earnings.
3. The purchasing power of the money received by the shareholders may decline due to inflation.

Advantages to Lessee.

1. Use of the property is obtained without the outlay of any funds or the issuance of additional securities.
2. Control over the properties may enable the entire system to benefit.
3. Future prosperity will benefit the company, particularly when the rental payment is fixed.
4. The company will tend to benefit from inflation.
5. The lease may be more easily disposed of, in event of failure of the lessee, than an obligation to bondholders who might come into existence as a result of raising money to buy the properties as an alternative to leasing.
6. The obligation assumed under the lease does not show up as a liability on the balance sheet of the lessee. If bonds were issued to finance the purchase of the properties they would appear as a liability on the balance sheet.

Disadvantages to Lessee.

1. The rental payments may become a burden if profitable use cannot be made of the properties, or if earnings in general decline.
2. Deflation would tend to harm the lessee.
3. Improvements made may revert to the lessor upon termination of the lease.
4. The taxes and fees to maintain the lessor as a separate company must be paid.
5. Separate reports of various kinds must be filed for both companies.
6. The leased property cannot be used by the lessee as direct security for bonds, although the leasehold may possibly be accepted as security.

Other Forms of Combinations

The earliest arrangement which resulted in a type of combination was the *gentlemen's agreement*. This constituted the principal type of combination used until about 1875. Gentlemen's agreements were merely oral agreements between the executives of two or more companies to maintain prices, restrict output, divide the market, or follow some other common policy. Being merely oral agreements, it is obvious that they were a weak, decentralized form of combination. Agreements between companies are not in themselves necessarily illegal, but since these agreements concerned price maintenance, restriction of production, and limitation of the market, they were illegal.

Pools were similar to gentlemen's agreements and were formed for the same purposes, but they were somewhat more formal in nature and were usually reduced to writing. Penalties were usually provided for violation of these agreements, but since the arrangements were illegal, the courts would not enforce the penalties or award damages for violation of these agreements. Pools covered a wider range of activity than gentlemen's agreements. They are no longer common except in the export field, where they are legal.

The word *trust* is applied by many to any form of combination which is in restraint of trade. It is because the trust arrangement was one of the earliest and most effective forms of combinations in restraint of trade, that the term is now often applied to any form of illegal combination. A *trust* was formed when the shareholders of two or more corporations transferred their shares, or the controlling shares, to a group of trustees. The trustees in turn gave the shareholders trust certificates to represent their shares. These trust certificates were transferable in the same manner as the stock. The trustees held the controlling stock interests in the various corporations and thus could elect the same people or some of the same people, to the board of directors of these companies. Or if the same individuals were not elected to the boards, the trustees could still control the companies through the election of directors who would follow their dictates.

When the policies of two or more companies, not otherwise combined or affiliated, can be influenced or controlled by a small group of persons who are members of the same family, or who hold controlling shares in the companies or otherwise dominate control, a *community of interest* is said to exist. This is, of course, an informal arrangement, but control over the companies may nevertheless be obtained the same as if the companies were combined in a more formal way. Monopolies effected through the community of interest are often difficult to break up; the presence of this type of control is sometimes concealed since no outward evidences of combination appear and there are no written agreements.

When one or more of the same persons serve on the board of directors of two or more corporations, it is referred to as *interlocking directorates*. The Clayton Act prohibits interlocking directorates in large national banks and large industrial corporations that compete with each other. The Banking Act of 1933 prohibits interlocking directorates in investment banks and commercial banks that are members of the Federal Reserve System.

A *trade association* is a non-profit organization formed to promote the mutual interests of individuals or companies engaged in the same line of business. It is a service organization, and does not engage in any business transactions on its own account. The trade association differs from the other forms of combinations in that its activities usually are only indirectly related to the principal business carried on by the members, while the other combinations are formed for the primary purpose of fixing prices, limiting production, lessening competition, or effecting economies in connection with the primary purpose for which the businesses operate. In some instances, however, trade associations have been used as a means of limiting production or fixing prices or restricting competition in other ways. When this has been brought to the attention of the courts, such activities have been held to be illegal.

COMBINATIONS AND THE LAW

According to the early common law, all contracts in restraint of trade were void regardless of whether the restraint was *reasonable* or *unreasonable*. Thus, if a party to such an agreement broke it and the other parties brought action in damages against him, the courts would not lend themselves to the enforcement of something which they considered to be illegal, and would not, therefore, award damages. The courts and state and federal officials had no right to take the initiative and break up any such agreements. So long as the parties to the contract abided by its terms, the agreement or combination in restraint of trade continued. This constituted the inherent weakness of the common law in regard to agreements or combinations in restraint of trade.

The opposition of the people to agreements in restraint of trade finally found expression through the enactment in various states of statutes or constitutional provisions prohibiting such agreements. The state legislation did not prove effective in breaking up agreements or combinations in restraint of trade. Some of the states did little to enforce the statutes. If one state prohibited a company from carrying on its business in that state, the concern would go to a more liberal state.

The Sherman Anti-Trust Act of 1890

Many of the combinations carried on interstate commerce throughout the country, and the federal government through the Constitution had the power to regulate interstate commerce. After several unsuccessful attempts to get Congress to act, the Sherman Anti-Trust Act was passed in

1890. But little was done by the government to enforce the Act during the years immediately following its passage.

The first important industrial case under the Sherman Act to reach the Supreme Court of the United States was that of *United States v. E. C. Knight Company*,[2] which was decided in 1895. The Supreme Court, however, held that the combination was not in violation of the Sherman Act. The court admitted that the company had a monopoly in the manufacture of sugar, but it said that the Sherman Act referred to monopolies in *trade or commerce*, not in manufacturing.

The next important case to be decided by the Supreme Court under the Sherman Act was that of *United States v. Trans-Missouri Freight Association*,[3] which was decided in 1897. This case was of considerable importance at the time, because the court said that the Sherman Act applied to every contract in restraint of trade, and that it therefore was applicable to railroads; and also that the Act specified that all contracts in restraint of trade, whether they were reasonable or unreasonable, came under the prohibition of the Act.

The case of *Northern Securities Company v. United States*,[4] which was decided by the Supreme Court in 1904, was the first case tried under the Sherman Act which involved a holding company. The Court ruled that the Sherman Act covered holding companies, and that the Northern Securities Company, which was a railroad holding company, was in violation of the Act and had to be dissolved.

The Supreme Court, in a unanimous decision[5] handed down in 1911, held that the Standard Oil Company had violated the Sherman Act, and ordered its dissolution. The importance of the *Standard Oil* case is due in part to the fact that the Court set up the "rule of reason." This in effect modified the Sherman Act by judicial decree. The Act, as originally passed by Congress, stated that "every" contract or combination or conspiracy was illegal. The Court, in the *Standard Oil* case, interpreted the Act to state that every "unreasonable" contract or combination or conspiracy was illegal. This case marked a turning point in the enforcement of the Sherman Act as all later cases under the Act had to take into account the reasonableness of the combination. In spite of the "rule of reason" interpretation in this case, the Standard Oil Company of New Jersey was deemed an unreasonable combination and ordered dissolved.

In 1911, the government brought action against the United States Steel Corporation on the grounds that it was violating the Sherman Act. Before the case was decided, World War I had begun, and at the request

[2] 156 U.S. 1 (1895).
[3] 166 U.S. 290 (1897).
[4] 193 U.S. 197 (1904).
[5] Standard Oil Company of New Jersey v. United States, 221 U.S. 1 (1911).

of the government, the case was postponed. After the war ended, the action was resumed. The suit had originally been brought against the company because of its large size. But the court said that size alone did not mean that the company had violated the antitrust laws, and that so long as the company did not restrain trade or effect a monopoly, its activities were legal.[6]

A somewhat new philosophy was projected by the Court in its decision since it indicated that the public interest would best be served by letting the company continue to exist. This virtually changed the court's "rule of reason" into a "rule of business expediency." The Court specifically stated that "the mere size of a corporation, or the existence of unexerted power unlawfully to restrain competition, does not of itself make such a corporation a violator of the Sherman Anti-Trust Act."[7] This decision that size alone is not the criterion for prosecution under the Sherman Act has been the subject of much controversy in recent years.

The Clayton Act of 1914

It was felt that if certain practices which led to monopoly were outlawed, the need for dealing with the monopolies after they were an accomplished fact would be reduced. The agitation for strengthening the Sherman Act finally resulted in the enactment, in 1914, of the Clayton Act, and the Federal Trade Commission Act. The latter created the Federal Trade Commission to aid in the prevention and elimination of practices which are in restraint of trade. The Clayton Act contained more detailed provisions than the Sherman Act. The principal ones follow.

1. *Price Discrimination.* Price discrimination was prohibited where its effect was substantially to lessen competition or where it tended to create a monopoly in any line of commerce.

2. *Tying Contracts.* A "tying contract" refers to the situation where a company sells or leases its products only on condition that the purchaser agree not to buy or lease any of the products handled by a competitor. The Clayton Act specifically provides that such contracts are illegal where they substantially lessen competition or tend to create a monopoly in any line of commerce.

3. *Labor.* The Clayton Act specifically states that the labor of a human being is not a commodity or article of commerce, and that nothing in the antitrust laws shall be construed as forbidding or making illegal non-profit labor organizations.

4. *Intercorporate Shareholding and Holding Companies.* Corporations engaged in commerce were forbidden to acquire the shares of

[6] United States v. U. S. Steel Corp., 251 U.S. 417 (1920).
[7] *Ibid.* at 451.

another corporation engaged in commerce where the effect of such stock acquisition would substantially lessen competition between the companies, or restrain the commerce in any community, or tend to create a monopoly in any line of commerce.

5. *Interlocking Directorates.* The Act provided that no person could be a director in two or more industrial corporations engaged in commerce, if any one of the corporations had capital, surplus, and undivided profits of more than $1,000,000, if the companies had been in competition, or if the elimination of competition by agreement between them would violate the antitrust laws.

The Public Utility Holding Company Act of 1935

Although the right to form corporations was reserved for the various states, the federal government, in the Constitution, was granted the right to regulate interstate commerce. Even though the holding company was organized in a particular state, its activities and control of subsidiaries crossed state boundaries and thus were of the nature of interstate commerce. The financing of the holding companies involved the use of the mails and was an interstate commerce transaction. The stock market crash of 1929, and the ensuing depression, brought to light many of the abuses that had been practiced. Because of this, the government enacted legislation to restrict and control the activities of the public utility holding companies.

The Public Utility Holding Company Act of 1935 requires all companies subject to the Act to register with the Securities and Exchange Commission. Companies subject to the Act are those which are engaged in interstate commerce, and which own or control at least 10 per cent of the voting stock of an electric or gas utility, or of a holding company which comes under the Act, or persons that exercise such controlling influence over utility companies or utility holding companies that in the public interests they should come under the Act. Excluded from the Act are those companies whose activities are predominantly intrastate in nature, or those which hold the securities for a special reason such as selling or liquidating them, or those in which the utility business comprises only a very small part of their total activities.

The Act required that every registered holding company file with the Commission a voluntary plan of reorganization to conform with the provisions of the Act. The purpose of the reorganization was to simplify the holding company systems, and to make each one a single, integrated system. In connection with simplification, the capital structures of the holding companies and the subsidiaries should not be unduly complicated. The reorganization plan must provide for the elimination of senior securities from the top-heavy capital structures so that the subsidiaries can provide proper maintenance, depreciation reserves, reasonable rates to consumers, and dividends to the investors. Adequate provision must be made to squeeze the water out of the highly saturated asset values. The plan must also provide for a fair distribution of voting power among the shareholders and for a fair election of directors, with the result that control over the operations would be exercised by the local managements in the particular communities. The reorganization plan must provide for the elimination of useless intermediate holding companies. In connection with the intercorporate holding of stock, the Act provides that there shall be not more than three layers of companies in the system. Registered holding companies can retain the shares of only those subsidiaries which constitute a single system both geographically and functionally. The Commission has interpreted this to mean that the operating companies must be in a similar line of business in one or more adjoining states.

The Securities and Exchange Commission must approve all security issues of registered holding companies and their subsidiaries. Before the Commission will approve the issue it makes certain that the particular issue is necessary for the efficient operation of the company, that it is reasonably adapted to the security structure of the company and the system, that a proper relationship exists between the security issues and the earnings of the company, and that the terms of sale are reasonable and not detrimental to the public, investors, or consumers.

The Act provides that no registered holding company or its subsidiaries may acquire additional securities of other companies or properties without approval of the Commission. This permission will be granted only when the Commission is satisfied that the consideration asked is reasonable, and that it will not unduly complicate the capital structure or result in too great a concentration of control.

The Act specifically prohibits upstream loans. Loans may be made by the holding company to the subsidiaries subject to the regulations of the Commission. Service companies may be set up within the system for purposes of sales, service, or construction, but they must be of an "operating" nature, and the services must be those which the operating company could not perform for itself. The charges made for the services must be fair and distributed among the companies in accordance with the services actually rendered. All other intercompany transactions, such as the purchase or sale of securities or property, must conform to the regulations adopted by the Commission. The payment of dividends on the common stock is also subject to the regulations of the Commission, and proper maintenance and reserves for depreciation must be provided before dividends will be approved.

The 1950 Legislation

Section 7 of the Clayton Act was so written that only monopoly combinations of corporations which were accomplished through the acquisition of stock in competing companies were illegal. For some time, the Federal Trade Commission had been complaining to Congress that this section had limited application. Instead of acquiring the stock of competing companies, businesses merely bought the assets of their competitors to accomplish the same objective and thus avoid prosecution under the Clayton Act. After considerable review of the Clayton Act and its interpretation, Congress passed an amendment in 1950 with the purpose of preventing corporations from acquiring another corporation by means of the acquisition of its assets, where under the present law it is prohibited from acquiring the stock of that corporation.[8]

Anti-Trust Exemption

From time to time, Congress has seen fit to enact legislation which exempts certain types of agreements or combinations from the Sherman and Clayton Acts. The Webb-Pomerene Act, which was adopted in 1918, exempted from the Sherman Act those associations which are formed for the purpose of export trade, provided they do not restrain trade within the United States. The Capper-Volstead Act, passed in 1923, had as a purpose the exemption of certain actions of farm cooperative organizations from antitrust Acts. The Emergency Transportation Act of 1933 exempted certain types of railroad agreements from the antitrust laws. The National Industrial Recovery Act of 1933, which has since been declared unconstitutional by the Supreme Court, did the same for industrial corporations. The Agricultural Adjustment Act of 1933 exempted from the antitrust laws certain agreements providing for the marketing of agricultural products. Labor was first mentioned for exemption in the Clayton Act, but it was not until the Norris-LaGuardia Act of 1932, and the Wagner Act of 1935, that labor became completely exempt from federal antitrust legislation.

Present Status of Combinations and the Law

While some business practices and certain mergers and combinations are clearly illegal under the present law and its interpretation, there is a wide area of action in which grave doubt exists concerning legality or illegality. It is doubtful whether the law can ever be so clearly interpreted as to remove all question regarding each individual action. A major problem today is that of size and monopoly. Is large size alone sufficient evidence of restraint of trade to be a violation of antitrust law? The Court has not given a clear-cut decision on this matter.

[8] Public Law 899, Sec. 7; 81st Congress, 2d Session (December 29, 1950).

Considering the nature of the various antitrust laws and the court decisions that have been rendered under them, it is difficult to define the present attitude of the government and the courts toward large companies and combinations. Businessmen are also uncertain about how far they can go without danger of their action's being later declared illegal. The enforcement of the antitrust legislation has varied substantially with changes in the executive branch of the government. The internal growth of corporations often results in situations which are very much unsettled in law. Every large corporation today must keep in mind the effects of its actions on the competitive situation in its field if it wants to steer clear of antitrust prosecution. Even with the constant guidance of good legal advice, corporations may perform some act which the government might consider a violation of antitrust legislation.

QUESTIONS

1. In the case of a combination effected through the "purchase of assets" is the approval of the shareholders of both the seller and the buyer necessary? Explain.
2. Are dissenting shareholders entitled to any relief when all or a substantial part of the corporation's assets are sold? Explain.
3. Explain the rights of creditors of both the selling and buying corporation with respect to the specific property which is sold.
4. Distinguish between mergers and consolidations.
5. (a) What is meant by a holding company? (b) What different types of holding companies are found in business?
6. Indicate the advantages of forming a combination through the use of the holding company device as compared with a merger or consolidation.
7. What are the possible disadvantages to the parties concerned of using the holding company to effect a combination as compared with a merger or consolidation?
8. (a) What are the advantages to the lessee of the lease method of combination as compared to the outright purchase of the properties? (b) In what field have leases been a common method of combination? (c) What type of securities commonly arise in connection with a railroad lease?
9. What is meant by a community of interest? In what different ways may it be effected?
10. What is meant by *interlocking directorates*? When are they illegal?
11. How do trade associations differ from other forms of business combinations?
12. What was the attitude of the common law with respect to combinations in restraint of trade? Could the common law break them up?
13. Indicate the important point in regard to the Supreme Court's attitude toward combinations that is contained in each of the following cases: the *Knight* case, the *Trans-Missouri Freight Association* case, the *Standard Oil Company* case, and the *United States Steel Corporation* case.
14. Indicate the principal provisions of the Clayton Act.
15. Explain what is meant by "tying contracts," and indicate whether they are legal.

PROBLEMS

1. Mr. A. Wizard has worked out a plan for the promotion of a number of utilities in South America. He wants to control all these utilities on a small amount of capital. His present plan calls for the construction of four utilities in each of four South American countries (a total of 16 companies). An intermediate holding company is to be formed in each of the countries to control each of the four utilities operating within that country, and a top holding company is to be organized to control the four intermediate holding companies.

The gross income of each of the operating companies is expected to be $20,000,000 annually, and profit before bond interest is paid is expected to be 8 per cent of the gross income. Sufficient operating company securities will be sold to construct the necessary plants, etc., and pay for the costs of selling all the securities, including those issued by the holding companies.

In determining the capitalization of the operating companies it has been decided that only one bond issue will be sold for each company and that the bond interest should be earned exactly four times. Common stock will be issued in an amount equal (in par value) to the bonds sold, and half of this common stock will be non-voting. Preferred stock dividends will take only 20 per cent of the amount available for such dividends. The bonds of all the operating and holding companies will bear an interest rate of 5 per cent, and all the preferred stock issued will be 6 per cent non-participating and non-voting. Two-thirds of the amount available for operating company common-stock dividends will be paid as dividends on the common shares. All the stock of both operating and holding companies has a par value of $100 per share, and all the bonds, a face value of $1,000 each.

The intermediate holding companies will sell securities in an amount necessary to acquire a 50 per cent interest in the voting common stock of the operating companies. All securities of both operating and holding companies will be sold at their par value. The intermediate holding companies will issue the same amount of non-voting common stock as voting common stock; preferred stock equal (in par value) to the common stock will be issued; and the amount of bonds issued will be equal to the common and preferred stock combined. The intermediate holding companies have no assets other than the stock of the operating companies. Their only income is the dividends paid by the operating companies, and all this is paid out to the security holders in the form of interest and dividends.

The top holding company owns only a 50 per cent interest in the voting stock of the intermediate holding companies. Its only income is the dividends paid by the intermediate holding companies, and all this is paid out to the security holders in the form of interest and dividends. The top holding company issues bonds, preferred stock, and voting and non-voting common stock in an amount necessary to acquire at par value the 50 per cent interest in the voting stock of the intermediate holding companies, and the amounts of these securities issued bear the same relation to its total capitalization as in the case of the intermediate holding companies. (a) Indicate the financial structure of an operating company, an intermediate holding company, and the top holding company. (b) Prepare an income statement for each type of company, showing the amount of dividends paid. (c) Assume 50 per cent of the voting stock to be controlling interest, how much stock of the top holding company would Mr.

Wizard have to have in order to control all the operating companies? Explain. What percentage dividend would he receive? (d) What were the earnings per share on the operating company's common stock? (e) If both the gross income and the expenses (other than interest) of the operating companies declined 10 per cent and they continued to pay out two-thirds of the amount available for common dividends, how much in dividends would Mr. Wizard receive based on part (c)? Assume that the capitalizations remained the same and that the holding companies continued their same dividend policies.

(In the foregoing problem the foreign taxes [assume no income taxes] and other expenses, except bond interest, of the holding companies are assumed to be paid by the operating companies in return for the managerial services furnished by the holding companies, and they are included in the expenses of the operating companies.)

2. Look up a "consolidated" balance sheet of a holding company system (in which the holding company owns no operating properties directly) in whatever source is available to you. (a) The property accounts of what companies appear on the statement? (b) Do the securities of the operating companies owned by the holding company appear as assets? Why or why not? (c) What consideration is given to the securities of operating companies which are not owned by the holding company?

3. The Standard Automobile Accessory Co. buys a number of its parts from other companies and assembles them for sale mainly to automobile manufacturing companies. One of its suppliers is the Acme Metal Co. The materials obtained from this company are so vital to the Standard Co. that the latter has given some consideration to the acquisition of some kind of control over the Acme Co. The Standard Co. does not have sufficient funds to buy the Metal Co. or to buy controlling interests in it. Because of several circumstances, it will not attempt to do any new financing. It has been suggested that the Standard Co. lease the Acme Co. under a long-term lease whereby the rental payments would be sufficient in amount to pay all the expenses of the Acme Co. and to allow a liberal dividend to its shareholders. List the possible advantages to the Standard Co. of the lease as compared to other methods of combination.

4. What other forms of combinations might be available to the Standard Automobile Accessory Co. in the above problem? What are the advantages and disadvantages of these various forms? Had the Standard Co. been willing to take on new financing, what additional forms of combinations might have been feasible?

5. Mr. Atwood is a stockholder in the Jonesville Press which buys paper from the Meadville Paper Manufacturing Co., a company in which Mr. Atwood is both a stockholder and a director. The Jonesville Press has asked him if he would accept a directorship in their company, but Mr. Atwood is afraid that to do so would be in violation of the antitrust laws. Do you think it would be in violation of these laws? Might any other type of objection be raised? What precaution could be taken against the latter?

SELECTED READINGS

AMERICAN MANAGEMENT ASSOCIATION. *Corporate Mergers and Acquisitions.* New York: American Management Association, 1958.
———. *Legal, Financial, and Tax Aspects of Mergers and Acquisitions.* New York: American Management Association, 1957.

FEDERAL TRADE COMMISSION. *Report on the Merger Movements*. Washington, D. C.: U. S. Government Printing Office, 1948.

————. *Industrial Concentration and Product Diversification in the 1,000 Largest Manufacturing Companies, 1950*. Washington, D. C.: U. S. Government Printing Office, 1957.

————. *Report on Corporate Mergers and Acquisitions*. Washington, D. C.: U. S. Government Printing Office, 1955.

MARTIN, DAVID D. *Mergers and the Clayton Act*. Berkeley: University of California Press, 1959.

NELSON, RALPH L. *Merger Movements in American Industry*. Princeton: Princeton University Press, 1959.

WESTON, J. FRED. *Readings in Finance from* Fortune. New York: Holt, Rinehart and Winston, Inc., 1958. Section X.

29

Failure and Equity Receivership

While all businesses plan to be successful, not all firms accomplish their objectives. Those which do not are known as "failures." Long before the general public becomes aware that a business is a failure, internal management may recognize that the firm is not moving in the direction of accomplishment of its objectives. Management may then attempt to take certain actions to change the direction of the firm and to prevent failure. One approach is reorganization in some form.

While it is hoped that the readers of this book will be working with successful organizations, it must be recognized that a large number of business firms become failures. Therefore, it is appropriate in a book of this kind to discuss the subject of business failure and potential reorganizations that might help prevent failure.

The reader's interest, of course, should not be in the failures themselves, but rather in the events leading toward failure or the causes of failure. An understanding of these factors can be important in formulating procedures and policies that may prevent failure. Further, a study of failures indicates that firms may be reorganized and move on toward accomplishment of objectives after failure is recognized. Failure does not necessarily require dissolution. An understanding of possible approaches to reorganization may indicate a method by which a failure may be converted into a success.

FAILURE

The term *failure* has different meanings to different people. The term *insolvency*, which also has different interpretations, is sometimes used interchangeably with the word *failure*, and at other times a distinction is made between the two terms. We will not attempt to give an exact definition of these words, since no generally accepted meaning has been formulated. But we will explain how the terms are commonly used.

Economic Failure

It is generally stated that a business is an *economic failure* when it is unable to earn a satisfactory return on the investment of the owners after giving effect to the degree of risk involved. From an economic standpoint, therefore, it must be apparent that many companies are economic failures. Many firms during their early life fail to earn a satisfactory return on the investment. In fact many of them operate at losses from time to time, but the state of their working capital is such that they are able to continue in business. But we would not classify them as economic failures unless, over a long period of time, they failed to have adequate earnings.

It is not common to refer to an economic failure as an actual failure. So long as a company pays its bills as they become due, it may remain in business for years even though it is an economic failure.

Financial Failure

Many businesses at various times have debts coming due that cause considerable loss of sleep on the part of the owners or managers. They may have a special sale for the purpose of getting cash immediately to pay their debts. Or, perhaps a bank loan may be obtained. If the need is for long-term funds, a stock issue or a bond issue may be arranged. In some instances assets other than the stock in trade may be liquidated in order to obtain funds. But as long as the funds are obtained and the debts are paid, we would not classify the business as a financial failure.

As the term is generally used, *financial failure* occurs when the business is unable to pay its debts. The business may thereupon liquidate and close its doors, or some cooperative arrangement may be worked out to keep the business going, or it may go through a drastic reorganization. Some writers state that financial failure occurs when some loss falls on the creditors—regardless of whether the business is terminated. Some use the term *legal failure* to mean the same as *financial failure,* but others apply it to the situation where the failure has been confirmed or adjudicated by the court, and a receiver or trustee has been appointed, or where the business has been declared bankrupt. When we use the term *failure* hereafter we will be referring to *financial failure,* that is, the inability to meet debts as they become due.

A concern may operate as an economic failure for a number of years without actually failing (financial failure). It is likewise true that a company may be earning a satisfactory return on its investment, in other words it is not an economic failure, but the inability of the company to meet a bank loan or a maturing bond issue may cause it to fail actually (from a financial point of view).

Insolvency. The term *insolvency* is often used to apply to the situation where a business is unable to meet its debts as they fall due; in other words, the same meaning as *financial failure*. From a statutory standpoint, however, *insolvency* applies to the situation where the assets, at a fair valuation, are insufficient to pay the debts. This is the way the term is defined in the Bankruptcy Act. We will use the latter meaning, particularly when the term is applied to a particular company or individual that is bankrupt or is about to become bankrupt.

When prices of property and securities decline, many companies would be unable to pay all their obligations if they were forced to liquidate. In other words, from the statutory viewpoint they are insolvent. But so long as they can meet their debts as they come due, they are not regarded by businessmen as being a failure or insolvent. Likewise, a company's total assets may exceed its debts; in other words the company is not insolvent, but it may fail (using the term in its financial sense) because of inability to meet a bond maturity.

Real vs. Apparent Causes of Failure

The immediate reason for practically all failures is the inability to pay debts. In other words, the reason is lack of cash or its equivalent. But this is merely a superficial sign. The real reasons for failure are those underlying factors which result in the weak cash position. It is in these underlying causes that we are interested.

Although we do not consider a company to have failed until it is unable to meet its debts, or is forced to undergo some compromise settlement with its creditors, or is reorganized or closes its doors, the factors causing the failure may have been at work for many years. It is therefore often difficult to determine the real cause of the failure. Furthermore, there may be a number of different factors which caused the failure.

There can be no doubt that the most important single cause of failure of most business enterprises is incompetent and inefficient management. In fact, during the same period a number of companies will be operating under similar circumstances, but some will fail and others will survive. If we were to trace back the real cause of the failures we could probably attribute it to the managements. Listed here are a number of causes of failure, but it is realized that in most instances the particular cause would not have resulted in failure if the management had been on its toes and had insured against the calamity or had taken the proper steps to prevent or to correct the shortcomings before it was too late.

Causes of Failure

There are about as many causes of failure as there are books dealing with the subject. The length of the classification depends upon how minutely the causes are listed.

The causes of failure are usually classified as "external" or "internal," depending on whether they arise outside or inside the business. Since this is a book on finance, we will separate the financial causes from the other internal factors. In the following classification management is included as an internal cause, but it is really an influence on all other factors.

    I. *External causes*
       1. Excessive competition
       2. The general business cycle
       3. Change in public demand
       4. Governmental acts
       5. Adverse acts of labor
       6. Acts of God
    II. *Internal causes*
      A. Non-financial
         1. Poor over-all management
         2. Unwise promotion
         3. Unwise expansion
         4. Inefficient purchasing
         5. Inefficient production
         6. Inefficient selling
         7. Overextension of inventories
      B. Financial
         1. Poor management
         2. Excessive fixed charges
         3. Excessive funded debt
         4. Excessive floating debt
         5. Overextension of credit
         6. Unwise dividend policy
         7. Inadequate maintenance and depreciation

Table 29–1 gives another listing of causes of failure and their relative importance.

External Causes of Failure

External causes are those which originate outside the business. They occur because of changing political, economic, weather, and demand conditions, and are not the result of acts of management. Management must accept these external changes as they occur and attempt to adjust the firm's operations to meet the changes.

Table 29–1. Why Businesses Fail

Apparent Causes	Industry Group (In Per Cent)*					
	Mfg.	Whol.	Ret.	Const.	Comm. Serv.	Total
Neglect	2.1	3.3	2.7	3.1	2.8	2.7
Fraud	1.4	3.0	1.3	1.0	1.4	1.4
Inexperience, incompetence ..	93.9	91.8	91.1	90.4	90.1	91.5
Inadequate sales	53.7	49.0	51.9	34.3	52.0	48.9
Heavy operating expenses.	8.1	4.2	3.3	11.5	6.0	5.8
Receivables difficulties....	13.8	17.6	5.3	16.1	7.2	9.9
Inventory difficulties	5.5	16.2	10.5	2.0	1.6	7.4
Excessive fixed assets	10.0	3.5	5.5	4.8	13.3	6.6
Poor location	0.4	0.6	4.0	0.2	1.0	2.2
Competitive weaknesses ..	16.8	21.5	22.4	28.8	18.7	22.1
Other	4.1	3.6	3.2	5.1	3.4	3.7
Disaster	0.9	0.8	1.0	0.4	0.6	0.8
Reason unknown	1.7	1.1	3.9	5.1	5.1	3.6
Total number of failures	2,763	1,622	7,960	2,800	1,445	16,590

* Compiled by Dun & Bradstreet, Inc. Classification based on opinion of creditors and information in credit reports. Since some failures are attributed to a combination of causes, percentages do not add up to 100 per cent.

SOURCE: *Dun's Review: and Modern Industry,* September, 1961, Vol. 78, No. 3. New York: Dun & Bradstreet Publications Corp., p. 15.

Excessive Competition. Competition is often cited as the reason for failure of many concerns. Normal competition, however, usually helps to keep businessmen on their toes and in many instances is a healthy factor. The mere fact that the cause of failure is attributed to competition in itself may be more or less a confession that other companies have been more successful in pricing policies, selling, or service rendered. When the competition, however, gets to the cutthroat stage where price wars are being waged by the large, strong companies against the smaller and financially weaker concerns, it can be ruinous.

The Business Cycle. A recession is often given as the reason for many failures. It is true that most businesses are adversely affected by falling prices, a drop in sales, and slow collections, and many of them fail as an immediate result of some or all of these factors. It must, however, be admitted that if a company is strong financially, has liberal reserves, good management, and makes a useful product which can be sold at a fair price, it has a good chance of surviving a recession.

Change in Public Demand. A business can be successful only when it sells a product or service which the public wants and can afford to buy. As advances are made in the arts and sciences, and research results in the creation of new products which the public prefers to the old products, a company that continues to manufacture only the obsolete product is doomed to failure. We have seen the automobile replace the horse, but not all carriage or wagon manufacturers failed. Those who changed their line of products to answer the public demand remained in existence. Many companies constantly carry on research so that they might be able to lead in the introduction of new and better products. As the public demand changes, the better managed companies usually change their production to conform to what is wanted.

Governmental Acts. The enactment of certain laws, particularly federal statutes, and some court decisions occasionally result in the failure of certain companies. The enactment, in 1918, of the 18th Amendment to the Constitution resulted in the failure of many concerns in the beer and liquor industries. The lowering or elimination of protective tariffs sometimes affects an industry so much that many companies may fail. Business taxes have in some cases caused a failure. The chain store taxes that exist in some states are an example. In wartime or periods of emergency certain governmental restrictions may cause some companies to fail because of their inability to get raw materials for the manufacture of their products. Price and wage regulations may also work severe hardship on some concerns.

Adverse Acts of Labor. In recent years the demands of some labor unions have resulted in the failure of business concerns. Unreasonable wages may result in such excessive costs that it becomes impossible for the company to compete in the market. This is true particularly in small companies and those in which labor costs comprise a relatively large percentage of the total cost of the product. In some instances prolonged strikes in plants supplying the raw materials used by a particular company may force that company to close its doors. A sound labor relations policy and program is essential for modern business.

Acts of God. Certain fortuitous factors, which the law terms "acts of God," are the cause of some failures. These include fires, earthquakes, tornadoes, explosions, and floods. The financial loss from some of these calamities may be eliminated if proper insurance is maintained. Insurance against all sorts of losses, however, would be too costly.

Non-financial Internal Causes of Failure

Internal causes of failure are those which could have been prevented or changed by some internal action in the company. Internal causes may all be laid at management's door. Different past decisions by management would have eliminated these causes of failure. Because of the importance of internal *financial* causes of failure, these are discussed separately from non-financial causes.

Unwise Promotion. Some concerns start business under such conditions that they are almost certain to fail. Adequate consideration should be given to the nature of the product to be manufactured, or service to be rendered; the costs should be well worked out, and pricing and the market should be known; attention should be given to the location, source of raw materials, and labor. Two important requisites are always needed for success: good management and adequate finances.

Unwise Expansion. Many companies are successful as long as they operate as small or medium-sized concerns, but fail when they expand their production, sales, and plant facilities. In some instances the management is unable to cope with the problems that arise from large-scale operations or the market may not be able to absorb the output. Sometimes the expansion is made when prices are too high, or the financing may have been too expensive. The expansion may take the form of branching out into other lines with which the management is not familiar. Some businesses run into the law of diminishing returns; as the number of units of output increases, the costs per unit may become higher.

Inefficient Purchasing. A company often does not have adequate funds on hand to take advantage of discounts offered on purchases. This may prove to be disastrous particularly when the discounts are relatively large. Other companies will be taking the discounts and therefore will be in a position to undersell those companies which do not take the discounts.

Inefficient Production. Inefficient production may result in such high costs that a particular company may not be able to sell its products in competition with lower-cost producers. This may result from inadequate or obsolete machinery and equipment. In some cases not enough of the production is mechanized and, as a result, direct labor comprises too high a percentage of the total cost of the product. Or the trouble may be inadequate foreman supervision, poor lighting, too high a labor turnover, excessive waste, improper inspection, or a host of other internal factors in the production department.

Inefficient Selling. American industry is noted for its emphasis on advertising and selling. Materials well purchased and produced mean nothing until and unless they are sold. Considerable emphasis must therefore be put on proper selling in order to make money. Efficient selling calls for attractive, well-placed advertising, the careful selection and training of salesmen, adequate supervision of the sales force, and a proper knowledge of the market and potential market. Inadequacy in any of these factors may cause a company to fail.

Overextension of Inventories. Overextension of inventories is the immediate cause of many companies' failure, particularly in the merchandising field. Some of the causes of failure stated above, such as the general business cycle, or the improper estimate of sales, may result in the accumulation of excessive inventories, but failure resulting from excessive inventories sometimes occurs when it cannot be blamed on the sales department or the business cycle. This is such a common cause of failure that it must be listed separately. Funds tied up in inventory commonly come from other working capital sources. When too much is invested in such assets, the company will be hard pressed for cash. Such a situation can easily cause failure.

Internal Financial Causes of Failure

Only creditors are in a legal position to force dissolution of a firm over the objections of management and owners. Thus, in preventing failure, we place great emphasis on meeting creditors' claims. Financial decisions include the determination of the amount of creditors' funds which will be utilized by the firm, and therefore, failure is often closely related to previous financial decisions.

Poor Financial Management. Perhaps most of the internal financial causes of failure can be attributed to weak financial management. A fundamental error of having too much of the capitalization in bonds, and too little in stock, can easily wreck a company. Incorrectly estimating the capital needs can do likewise. Improper terms of sale and slack collection policies can cause considerable trouble. The selection of the wrong type of securities to sell at a particular time, or the improper timing of a security sale can be disastrous to a business. Unwise dividend policies, and inadequate maintenance and depreciation can eventually cause a company to fail. Some of these are listed below as separate causes of failure. Probably most of them could be traced back to poor financial planning.

Excessive Fixed Charges. The presence of too large an amount of bonds outstanding can result in such excess fixed charges that the company is unable to meet them and failure results. Many railroads have failed because of this. The companies could have possibly refunded the obligation at maturity, but the immediate inability to pay the fixed charges resulted in failure.

Excessive Funded Debt. Some companies can successfully meet their current fixed charges, but their inability to meet a large bond maturity causes them to fail. It is easy to say that the management should have been anticipating the bond maturity and provided for it. In many cases, however, the earnings are inadequate to provide the funds, and other sources of capital may have been exhausted. A company might not really be insolvent, that is, its assets may exceed its liabilities, but the working capital position may be so weak that it is unable to provide the funds to meet the bonds, and failure results.

Excessive Floating Debt. By "floating debt" is meant the current liabilities. Aside from the possibility of a real estate mortgage, this is the only kind of debt that practically all small companies have outstanding. The floating debt is usually owed to either banks or trade creditors, or both. Most failures result immediately from a lack of cash coupled with too much current debt. It sometimes occurs because a business is prosperous. It is a normal desire of businesses to want to expand their sales. If a company attempts to expand its sales volume without the addition of any new permanent capital in the business, financial difficulties probably will be encountered. The additional working capital investment will drain the cash, and the current liabilities will pile up.

Overextension of Credit. Many companies fail because of their inability to collect what is owed them in time to meet their own obligations. In some instances the failure of the company's debtor will cause a particular company to fail. For that reason, too much credit should not be granted one individual or one company.

Unwise Dividend Policy. Many companies do not reduce their dividend rate in the face of declining profits. Some pay dividends out of accumulated surplus even when deficits for the particular period exist. Some companies may be justified in following such a policy, but the great majority of them are not in a financial position to follow this course of action. In some instances liberal dividends are paid right up to the time that failure is admitted. And in many of these cases it would appear that if the dividends had not been paid the company could have prevented the failure.

Inadequate Maintenance and Depreciation. Too liberal a dividend policy may result at least in part from the fact that a company undercharges maintenance and depreciation. Dividends may thus have been paid partly from capital rather than from profits. A long-continued policy of this kind will result in the eventual wearing-out of the property, and no cash will be available with which to replace it. To stay in business it is necessary to keep the properties in proper repair. Adequate provision should constantly be made during the life of the property to replace it when it is no longer of any use to the company. During a period of inflation companies find that to replace a particular piece of equipment may require upwards of twice the original cost. Depreciation charges and depreciation reserves are usually calculated on the original cost basis. Thus, even if cash or its equivalent equal to the depreciation reserve is available for the replacement of equipment, the new equipment may require twice that amount.

COMPROMISES

In many instances of failure creditors will lose less if some kind of a compromise settlement can be worked out between them and the owners or managers. Forced liquidation of a business results in the sale of the assets at sacrifice prices. Both the creditors and owners may lose less if the business is allowed to continue in operation.

If the business should be reorganized, it may also be to the advantage of both the owners and creditors to avoid legal or judicial reorganization. When a reorganization takes place through equity receivership or the Bankruptcy Act, it is costly and time-consuming. Every effort should be made to work out some kind of an understanding for the rehabilitation or liquidation of the business without resorting to court action. Under the latter, the referees, trustees, and lawyers may benefit more than the business and its creditors.

Extensions

Extension of maturities is a common type of compromise settlement when a debtor is technically insolvent but has long-run potential for payment. Extensions are possible for short-term notes and accounts payable as well as for long-term liabilities. New notes or bonds with longer maturities may be issued to replace outstanding obligations. An extension of any kind requires agreement of both debtor and creditor as it involves a change in a legal contract.

It might be to the advantage of creditors to grant the debtor a little extra time to pay his debts rather than attempt to force him to pay by legal action. An extension is more probable when the business is small or the number of creditors not large, when the management appears to be sound, and the financial trouble only temporary.

The success of an extension depends upon agreement of all the creditors. Since he has a legal right to receive payment, any creditor who does not agree to the extension can sue and receive judgment against the debtor and then levy on the business property for the satisfaction of his claim. This may force receivership or bankruptcy. In some instances when several of the small creditors will not agree to the extension plan, they will be bought out by the larger creditors. Larger creditors are more likely to recognize that it is to their advantage to keep the business in operation. Smaller creditors might realize this too, but may feel that they can benefit by being dissenters if they believe the larger creditors will buy them out. One of the disadvantages of extension is that it is not final in law unless *all* parties agree. This is one reason why extensions are difficult to effect.

Composition

A composition settlement is a common-law arrangement whereby the creditors agree among themselves and with the debtor to accept less than the full amount of their claims in discharge of the debts. Like an extension, a composition is used when the creditors believe they will in the long run get more out of the debtor than if they immediately forced liquidation or receivership or reorganization. But unlike the situation where extensions are made, the debtor is in a more drastic financial position and probably has an excess of liabilities over assets.

Like the extension, the composition settlement can ordinarily be used only when the business is relatively small, and when there are not many creditors. In order to effect a composition there must be at least two creditors entering into the agreement. As a practical matter it is desirable that all the creditors join in. A composition, however, may be worked out by only part of the creditors, such as the unsecured creditors, for example. Creditors not entering into the agreement could proceed against the debtor in the regular way, but those agreeing to the composition would be held to their agreement, even though they got less than the other creditors.

Commonly, the composition settlement does not provide for complete payment in cash of the agreed amount at the time of the composition. Sometimes the entire payment is deferred for the future. In other cases part of the settlement is made in cash and the balance is represented by notes that mature at a later date.

The above applies to common-law compositions. Under the Bankruptcy Act, compositions which are called "arrangements" may be worked out under court supervision. Unlike the common-law composition, the arrangement is binding on all the unsecured creditors after it has been approved by a majority of each class of creditors and by the court.

Assignments

Small concerns are sometimes liquidated through an *assignment* of the assets for the benefit of the creditors. This may be done under either the common law or the statutes of the particular state. Under common law, the assignment is not recorded, and the administration of the assets is under the supervision of the creditors rather than the court.

If one or more of the creditors takes aggressive action ahead of the other creditors, the debtor may effect an assignment so that all the creditors will be treated equally. The debtor may prefer assignment to equity receivership or bankruptcy because less publicity is involved and because his future credit rating may suffer less. Usually the creditors receive a larger percentage of their claims under an assignment than through bankruptcy proceedings because more time is available to find good buyers for assets, a foreclosure sale is not necessary, and court and legal costs are substantially reduced.

The procedure is for the debtor to assign the assets to a trustee, who is referred to as the "assignee." The assignee is often one of the creditors or a group of creditors. In other cases he may be a disinterested third party. The assignee administers and sells the property in an orderly fashion, and distributes the proceeds to the creditors proportionately according to the amount of their claims.

As a practical matter it is usually necessary for all the creditors to be satisfied with the assignment. Since the Bankruptcy Act provides that an assignment constitutes an "act of bankruptcy," any creditor not agreeing to the assignment can file a petition in bankruptcy. It is for this reason that the assignment is rarely used today. Since the concern may end up in bankruptcy, it would be better in those instances where this appears probable, to dispense with the assignment and start action under the Bankruptcy Act. If the costs of bankruptcy are to be incurred in the future anyway, there is no point in adding the costs and time of an attempted assignment.

Creditors' Committee

Company ownership and management may enter into an agreement with creditors whereby the management of the company is turned over to a group of the creditors called a creditors' committee. This agreement may last for a given period of time or until the creditors are paid their amounts due. The committee may operate the business itself, or it may bring in some outside business expert, or it may actually use a present officer of the company. The committee is usually composed of some of the principal creditors who are thought to be good managers. The committee may ask existing creditors to grant extensions or to subordinate their claims in favor of new financing to allow the committee to get the company back on its financial feet. If a reorganization appears necessary, the creditors' committee may formulate the plan, or if liquidation is indicated, the committee may supervise it.

Creditors' committees avoid unfavorable publicity and are normally less costly than legal proceedings to settle debts. However, creditors' committees have no legal authority to set aside questionable claims, and they are powerless to prevent a dissatisfied creditor from throwing the company into receivership or bankruptcy. These weaknesses make it difficult for a creditors' committee to accomplish its task of putting the business back on its feet without legal proceedings.

EQUITY RECEIVERSHIP

A friendly arrangement cannot always be worked out for the continuation, reorganization, or liquidation of a business. This is particularly true when the concern is large and has a large number of creditors. Creditors who have a lien on the company property, such as mortgage bondholders, might take steps to foreclose their liens and thereby, when it is to their advantage, leave the company stripped of its most valuable assets. Or some of the unsecured creditors might be impatient with the other creditors and with the debtor, and take aggressive action ahead of the other creditors by suing and obtaining judgment against the debtor. With the judgment, they then get a lien on the company property. They may then have the sheriff seize and sell the property for the satisfaction of the claim.

Forced sale of the kind just mentioned usually results in the property's being sold for a relatively small percentage of its book value. Furthermore, creditors who have reduced their claims to judgments and liens are entitled to 100 cents on the dollar before the other creditors get anything. This procedure obviously results in liquidation or partial liquidation of the company. Not only are the assets sold at sacrifice prices, but the going-concern value of the company is destroyed.

The primary purpose of receivership is to place the company under the protection of the court so that creditors possessing judgments and liens cannot foreclose and seize the company property. In the meantime, under the protection of the court, some equitable solution to the company's problem may be worked out, and it may be allowed to continue in business even though a reorganization may be necessary.

Because of changes which have been made in the Bankruptcy Act, beginning in 1933, which permit reorganization in addition to liquidation, companies now select bankruptcy proceeding rather than equity receivership in practically all instances when financial difficulties force them to choose between these courses of action. Receivership is still used occasionally under circumstances of financial difficulty, but it is more likely to be used when there is some other need for court jurisdiction, such as dispute among the shareholders over the election of a board of directors, or when the company officers are charged with fraud. Since receivership following financial difficulties is more involved than when it results from other causes, in the following discussion we will assume that the receivership is brought about by financial troubles.

Equity Receivership Procedure

Since receivership is an equitable rather than a legal action, petition for the appointment of a receiver comes under the equity courts. That is why it is referred to as *equity receivership*. The receiver may be appointed by either a state or a federal court, depending upon where the petition is filed. Federal rules are uniform and have been more carefully worked out than those in most of the states.

The receiver appointed may be a lawyer in whom the court has confidence, or it may be an official of the company. Quite often both are appointed as co-receivers. The lawyer would be familiar with the many legal problems and procedures involved, while the company official would be experienced in the company's affairs.

A creditor might on his own initiative file a petition for the appointment of a receiver. But in most instances, in order to prevent the foreclosure of any liens, the corporate management itself would initiate the action by arranging with a "friendly" creditor to file the petition. In order to get federal court jurisdiction, the claim of the creditor would have to be in excess of $3,000. Since actions between citizens of different states can originate in the federal courts, the creditor would be a citizen of a state other than the one in which the corporation was organized. When the corporation itself initiates the action, it is called a voluntary receivership. When a creditor or group of creditors initiates the action, it is called *involuntary receivership*. Voluntary receivership is much more common than involuntary.

The creditor will file a complaint that the corporation is unable to meet its debts as they mature, that some of the creditors have secured judgments against the company or are about to secure judgments, and that if a receiver is not appointed the creditors will seize the assets with resultant losses to all. At the same time, the corporation files an answer admitting the allegations and asks that a receiver be appointed. A court hearing will then be held and, if the court believes that a receiver is needed, one will be appointed.

Powers and Duties of Receiver

Receivership places the property under the jurisdiction of the court, and the receiver is the agent of the court appointed to administer the property. Major actions on the part of the receiver will be taken only upon court order, although the order may follow requests made by the receiver. Generally the powers and duties of the receiver are as follows.

1. *Receive and Conserve the Assets of the Company.* The primary function of the receiver is to take over the assets of the company for the

purpose of keeping them intact. The receiver serves during the period in which some plan of reorganization is being worked out. He is supposed to see to it that as much of the property as possible is still available at the time the receivership is vacated. He prevents the payment of any of the assets to old creditors. In this way, certain creditors cannot benefit at the expense of others by being paid off while others are trying to work out some kind of settlement. One reason for receivership is the prevention of foreclosure of liens in order that all assets be available for continued operation or for payment to all creditors after a solution to the particular problem is worked out.

2. *Manage and Operate the Company.* In most instances, the best way to conserve the assets is to continue to operate the company. Continued operation may help change the assets into more liquid form as well as maintain customers and suppliers for future operation. Under receivership the receiver becomes the chief executive of the company. He may decide, however, to retain the principal officers of the company in order to obtain the benefits of their past experience. The receiver may also hire experts to help him in the operation of the business. The receiver will take in the money from operations and apply it to the operating expenses. It is his duty also to collect the debts owed the company. Funds, if available, may also upon court order be applied toward the debts owed by the company.

3. *Raise New Money.* Regardless of what may have been the fundamental or underlying cause of the failure of the company, the immediate cause is always the lack of cash. The receiver will have the use of any money that the company takes in during receivership. But commonly this will not furnish enough funds to meet the needed requirements. In view of the financial condition of the company, new money cannot be obtained from the sale of stock, or borrowed in the ordinary way. The court may therefore authorize the issuance of *receiver's certificates.*

Although receiver's certificates are considered to be obligations of the receiver, they are his obligations in an official rather than a personal capacity. The certificates, like other obligations of the company, must be repaid from the property of the company. If the assets of the company are not sufficient to satisfy the obligations, the receiver has no personal liability for them. The claim or lien of the receiver's certificates is specified by the court. As a practical matter it will be necessary to give them sufficient priority over other obligations of the company in order that they may be sold. Commonly this means that they will be placed ahead of all defaulted obligations, but not necessarily ahead of some or all of the obligations in which default has not occurred. In the case of a reorganization, receiver's certificates may be paid off from the proceeds of the sale of new securities, or in part or entirely from the assessments made upon shareholders, or the holders may take some longer-term claim against the reorganized company.

4. *Validate Claims and Handle Payments.* When creditors file their claims it will be up to the receiver, subject to approval by the court, to determine which claims are valid and to what extent. In paying any claims, the current expenses of receivership will be taken care of first. Any balance of funds may be used to pay certain earlier creditors as designated by the court. The court, for example, after giving consideration to the priority of liens, may authorize the payment of bond interest, to the extent that it is earned.

5. *Action on Company Contracts.* It is an important function and duty of the receiver to examine all contracts and leases made by the company with the view toward determining their profitableness. One of the objectives of receivership is to restore the company to efficient operations. If it develops that the company has taken some leases of property or given guaranties with respect to subsidiaries or their securities, in which the benefits received are less than the amount the company is paying out on the lease or guaranty, the receiver will ask the court that these agreements be canceled. This, of course, is an important objective that could never be accomplished by the company without the benefit of the courts. The other party to the contract, however, may file a claim in the final reorganization for any damages sustained by him as a result of the cancellation of the contract. But in order for the claim to be recognized it will be necessary for him to prove that he has been harmed by the cancellation.

6. *Report on the Condition of the Company.* It is the duty of the receiver to report to the court the condition of affairs of the company. This report does not make suggestions for disposition of property or any plan of reorganization, or settlement of claims. It merely discusses the value of the property and the future possible results of operations. The final report can be made only after the company has been under the receiver's jurisdiction sufficiently long for him to have arrived at a final conclusion in regard to the company property and prospects. This report is of great value to the court since the latter will, on the basis of the contents of the report, decide what action shall be taken in regard to the company.

Receivership Compared With Compromise Settlements

Receivership has certain advantages over compromise settlements. One of these is that cooperation of the creditors and their agreement to receivership are not required. Under receivership, claims of creditors are properly evaluated and validated. In receivership, new money may be raised through the issuance of receiver's certificates. Receivership permits operation of the company until sufficient time has elapsed to determine what is wrong with the company and what is needed.

Receivership, however, publicly acknowledges to the world that the company has failed. If the company gets back on its feet, much goodwill and credit will have been destroyed by such action. Receivership is the most costly and time-consuming method of reorganizing or liquidating a company.

Procedure Following Receivership

Although receivership may last many years, it is merely a temporary action pending the determination of the final solution to the problem. One of the following three courses of action will be taken following the lifting of receivership.

1. *Rehabilitation.* In rare instances the financial difficulties are resolved under receivership, and the company is returned to its owners in a solvent condition.

2. *Liquidation.* If the company cannot be rehabilitated and also cannot be reorganized, it may be decided that the situation is hopeless, and the court may order liquidation.

3. *Reorganization.* In most instances the two extremes stated above are not followed, but the company is reorganized instead and continues in business.

REORGANIZATION FOLLOWING RECEIVERSHIP

The term *reorganization* is sometimes used to mean any recasting of the financial structure because of failure or threatened failure; that would include some of the recapitalizations and adjustments and compromise settlements discussed above. The term has also been used in a more restricted way to apply to only those instances in which a new company is formed to take over the properties of the old company through a court sale following receivership.

Usually the term *reorganization* is not used when the readjustment called for is minor in nature. We will not apply it here to those situations which were included under recapitalizations, readjustments, and compromise settlements. But when financial difficulties are so serious in nature that adjustments of this kind cannot successfully be made, and it is necessary to recast the financial structure through receivership or the Bankruptcy Act, we will then use the term *reorganization*.

Reorganization Procedure

The various classes of security holders have antagonistic positions in a reorganization since the settlement given one class may be at the expense of another class. The management, due to their election by the shareholders and also because they are usually important shareholders in the company, will probably look after the interests of the shareholders, particularly the common shareholders, more than the interests of the creditors. Some of the large bondholders, or the investment bankers who handled the particular bond issue, may take the initiative and form a committee for the protection of that particular class of creditors. Other classes of creditors will also probably form protective committees. In some instances several different groups will compete with each other to represent the interests of a class of creditors.

Each of the protective committees makes a call for the deposit of securities representing the class of security holders the committee was set up to protect. The deposit of securities gives the committee authority to represent the security holders.

The various committees cannot hope to effect a reorganization plan themselves. Thus, representatives of the various committees form a *reorganization committee* for the purpose of formulating a suitable plan of reorganization. Several of the individuals may be designated as "managers" of the reorganization committee. This committee will try to effect some feasible plan. With the protective committees representing divergent interests, they will be asked to compromise on many points.

When a plan has been worked out, the protective committees will ask that various security holders sign a *ratification* agreement, which binds them to the plan. Those not agreeing can usually ask for a return of their securities. If all of the security holders would agree to the plan, it could be put into immediate operation without the necessity of a court sale of the properties. But such one hundred per cent agreement would rarely be possible. Before the court will approve a reorganization plan it will be necessary to get a substantial majority of the various classes of security holders to agree to the plan. The court is interested primarily in the satisfaction of all those with legal claims against the company. Any creditor dissatisfied with the proposed plan will have to receive equitable treatment before the court will approve the plan.

After having arrived at a value of the corporate property, the court will establish an *upset price*. This is the minimum price acceptable by the court for the corporate properties. At the time and place specified by the court the public sale of the properties will take place. The reorganization committee uses the securities which have been deposited with the protective committee as part of the consideration to be used in bidding on the properties. The court will also specify the minimum amount that must be paid in cash by the committee. The reorganization committee, through its control of the securities, will probably be the only bidder at the sale and will pay for the property by turning in the securities it controls plus the required amount of cash. From a legal standpoint, the sale represents a foreclosure of all the liens possessed by the securities held by the reorganization committee as well as those possessed by other creditors.

The sale price of the property establishes the equity of security holders who do not agree to the plan. Let us assume that a corporation had outstanding a $10,000,000 first mortgage bond, a $5,000,000 second mortgage bond issue, and a $5,000,000 debenture bond issue. We will furthermore assume that the corporate properties are sold for $15,000,000, the amount established as the upset price. Of this amount $10,000,000 is paid for properties securing the mortgages and $5,000,000 for other properties. The first and second mortgage and debenture bondholders who agreed to the reorganization would get whatever the plan called for. Dissenting first mortgage bondholders, however, would be entitled to 100 cents on the dollar since the pledged property brought this amount. Dissenting holders of the second mortgage bonds and of the debentures would get 50 cents on the dollar.

The upset price should be sufficiently high to allow the dissenters a fair value for their securities, but not so high as to prevent the sale of the properties. In some instances where there is no bidder, the court is forced to lower the upset price. The upset price must be low enough to cause the reorganization committee to submit a bid. The committee will submit a bid only if it feels that the price paid for the properties would be low enough to permit profitable operation in the future.

Upon court sale of the properties, the reorganization committee buys the properties and turns them over to a new corporation which is formed for that purpose. The old corporation and its securities pass out of existence, and the new securities are distributed to those who agreed to the reorganization plan.

Reorganizations commonly call for new cash. This is needed to pay off dissenters, retire receiver's certificates, pay reorganization expenses, and provide new working capital for the reorganized company. A major problem of the reorganization committee is the raising of this needed new cash. One of the best ways is through assessment of present interested parties. The stockholders of the company may be asked to pay-in a certain amount of cash if they wish to maintain any interest in the new company. Even creditors may be assessed in certain instances. Sometimes new securities are sold by the reorganized company to obtain needed cash. In this event, old security holders are generally the major parties interested in the new securities.

Shortcomings of Equity Reorganizations

Following are the more important shortcomings of reorganization under the equity courts which have led to increased use of reorganization under the Bankruptcy Act (discussed in Chapter 30).

1. *Cost.* Equity receiverships and reorganizations are the most costly of the various methods of readjustment or reorganization. The procedure followed must conform to the law, and lawyers have an active part in the work. The protective committees also collect compensation. Court costs must be paid along with the receiver's fees and all his expenses.

2. *Time-consuming.* Equity receiverships and reorganizations are long, drawn-out affairs, which, of course, adds to their cost. Some companies have been in a receiver's hands for a quarter of a century or longer, and then after emerging from one receivership they may sink back again into another protracted one.

3. *Appointment of Ancillary Receivers.* If the receiver is appointed by the state court, receivership proceedings will have to be started in the various states in which the corporate property is located. This is costly and complicates the procedure of receivership. When action is brought in the federal court, ancillary actions will be necessary in the other federal court districts in which the property is located.

4. *Little Control over Protective Committees.* The protective committees are formed through the initiative taken by some of the creditors, shareholders, or investment bankers. Although they are supposed to represent the particular group of security holders whose securities they received on deposit, in some instances the management of the corporation controls them. In some cases the committees appear to be more interested in the fees and expenses they collect than in protecting the security holders.

5. *Court Has Little Control over Reorganization Plan.* The reorganization plan is drawn up by the reorganization committee. This committee may be dominated by one class of creditors, or it may be controlled by the common shareholders. Whoever controls this important committee may receive preferential treatment in the final plan. This lack of control on the part of the court over the formulation of the reorganization is sometimes mentioned as the most serious objection to equity reorganizations.

6. *Court Lacks Authority To Replace Liens.* Aside from giving priority to those who grant credit for the receivership expenses, and the giving of some priority to receiver's certificates, the court lacks the authority to subordinate any liens in favor of new creditors. This makes it impossible to secure any new funds except through the issuance of receiver's certificates.

7. *Problem of Dissenters.* Dissenters can destroy any plan set up by the reorganization committee regardless of its fairness or reasonableness. The court has no authority to force dissenters to agree to any plan. They are entitled to their payment or they can force bankruptcy regardless of long-range advantages of reorganization to themselves as well as to other creditors. Paying off dissenters in equity receivership reorganizations places a cash burden on the reorganized company at a time when it is already short of cash for operations and other needs.

QUESTIONS

1. (a) Distinguish between economic failures and financial failures. (b) Distinguish between the terms *failure* and *insolvency*.
2. Indicate how a company might be considered insolvent but not a financial failure, and vice versa.
3. Indicate what is meant by the distinction between the real and the apparent causes of failure.
4. The operation of the business cycle is often given as the reason for failure of business concerns. Do you believe that this is more of an apparent cause than a real cause? Can the probable future trend of business be predicted now any better than 25 or 30 years ago? Explain.
5. Is the consent of all creditors necessary to effect an extension in the maturity of a debt? Explain.
6. (a) Indicate the situation under which a composition settlement might be effected. (b) Is 100 per cent agreement necessary to effect such a settlement? Explain.
7. (a) Indicate the circumstances under which an assignment for the benefit of creditors might be successfully used. (b) If this action is taken could the debtor be thrown into bankruptcy? Explain.
8. (a) Indicate the circumstances under which creditors' committee management and reorganization might be accomplished. (b) What are the relative advantages and disadvantages of this form of reorganization as compared with reorganization following receivership or trusteeship under the Bankruptcy Act?
9. Indicate the procedure for placing a company in the hands of a receiver in equity.
10. Indicate what is accomplished while a company is in the hands of a receiver.
11. Indicate the procedure followed under receivership pointing toward the final reorganization of the company.
12. (a) Under whose authority are receiver's certificates issued? (b) What determines the lien possessed by receiver's certificates?
13. What are the relative advantages and disadvantages of equity receiverships as compared with the other forms of adjustments previously discussed?
14. Explain the meaning of the term *reorganization* as used in this chapter to distinguish this form of reconstruction from the other types previously described.
15. Indicate what is meant by the *upset price*, who establishes it, and what is accomplished by setting such a price.

PROBLEMS

1. The Householder Supply Co. has operated at a loss for a number of years. In spite of cutbacks in activities and consolidation of efforts, the firm was forced to apply for reorganization proceedings. The reorganization committee has developed a plan for reorganizing the company which involves lowering the interest rate on the first mortgage bonds, an extension and 25 per cent reduction in face value on the second mortgage bonds, conversion of past-due accounts payable into 6-month non-interest-bearing notes, and exchange of preferred stock for common stock. Common stockholders will be offered rights to purchase shares in the new company but the old common stock will be wiped out entirely. There are a number of dissenting claimants in each class of creditor and owner. The approved claims are as follows:

First mortgage bonds......	$1,500,000
Second mortgage bonds	1,000,000
Accounts payable	1,000,000
Preferred stock	2,000,000
Common stock	Residual

The court has placed an upset price of $1,500,000 on the mortgaged property and $500,000 on the remainder of the assets.

If the assets sell for their upset price, what claim will the dissenters in each group have? If the mortgaged assets sell for $500,000 above upset price and other assets for $500,000 above upset price, what claim will the dissenters in each group have?

2. The following are the balance sheets of the A, B, C, and D companies as of June 30, 19x1, when stock prices were lower than they had been for many years:

Balance Sheets
(in thousands)

	Co. A	Co. B	Co. C	Co. D
Cash	$ 5	$ 10	$ 0	$ 5
Receivables	50	80	40	50
Inventory	200	400	180	300
Fixed Assets	1,000	3,500	1,600	800
Total	$1,255	$3,990	$1,820	$1,155
Current Liabilities	$ 800	$ 20	$ 20	$ 5
Fixed Liabilities	0	1,000	0	0
Capital Stock	300	2,000	2,000	1,000
Surplus	155	970	−200°	150
Total	$1,255	$3,990	$1,820	$1,155

° Deficit.

Company A has been able to meet obligations to date. Its current liabilities represent notes which come due July 31, 19x1. The directors considered selling all the assets to pay off the notes. In an independent appraisal it was found that the gross assets would bring only $650,000.

Company B has been earning 9 per cent on its capital stock for the past three years. Its fixed liabilities represent bonds which came due June 30, 19x1, and which the company was unable to pay off or make other provisions for settlement.

Company *C* has been earning 7 per cent on its stock for the past 3 years. There has been no occasion to have an appraisal made of the corporate property. All obligations have been paid when due.

Company *D* enjoyed large earnings before the depression, but earnings fell off materially in the two years previous, and in the first 6 months of 19x1 the company suffered a deficit. It has, however, met all obligations when they fell due. The company's stock was selling in the market for $30 a share at the date of the above balance sheet. The par of the stock is $100. It is to be noted that the stock was selling for an amount which was less than the net current asset value of the company. There has been no occasion for an appraisal of the property.

(a) Indicate in the case of each company whether it is insolvent or a financial failure and the reasons why it is or is not. (b) Indicate whether you think any of the companies should dissolve, and state your reasons.

3. The Anderson Co. presented the following balance sheet as of December 31, 19x1:

Assets		Liabilities and Net Worth	
Cash	$ 5,000	Accounts Payable	$ 150,000
Receivables	110,000	Notes Payable	300,000
Inventory	685,000	Accrued Taxes	50,000
Machinery	1,500,000	First Mortgage	1,000,000
Plant	5,000,000	Second Mortgage	1,000,000
Deficit	200,000	Debenture Bonds	1,000,000
		Common Stock	3,000,000
		Preferred Stock	1,000,000
Total	$7,500,000	Total	$7,500,000

The notes bear interest at the rate of 7 per cent. The interest rates of the bond issues are as follows: First, 5 per cent; Second, 6 per cent; Debentures, 7 per cent. The capital stock has a par value of $100 per share. The inventory valuation should be discounted about 10 per cent, and it is probable that 3 per cent of the accounts receivable are uncollectible. The notes come due June 30, 19x2; the first mortgage bonds are due December 31, 19x1; the second mortgage bonds mature December 31, 19x4; and the debentures come due December 31, 19x2. The preferred stock is 7 per cent cumulative, but the dividends on this stock have not been paid for the past 4 years.

The company was very successful many years ago. The debentures were issued some years ago to get money for expansion purposes. The mortgages were later sold to secure funds to acquire another plant. The company was hard-hit in the deflation period but came back fairly well in the following prosperous period. But the company has never recovered from the depression. Earnings before interest charges for the past 2 years have averaged only $80,000. Interest was paid in part in these years from the sale of some real estate that the company owned in the business section of the city.

The company manufactures two products, similar in nature, which are purchased by consumers. It started out manufacturing product *A*, which is high-grade and expensive. When the public later demanded a cheaper product, the president of the company, who has served in that capacity since the company was formed, refused to lower the quality of his product. Later he was forced to give in, and he started manufacturing product *B* under a different trade name. He has, however, insisted on still making product *A*, although the losses suffered on this product have had to be borne by the profit made on product *B*. List in general the things that should be done in an attempt to put this company back on its feet as a successful business enterprise.

4. The following question relates to the Anderson Co. described in Problem 3. Do you think the company should be reconstructed through a creditors' committee, or consent operation? Give reasons for your answer.

5. This problem also relates to the Anderson Co. in Problem 3. Assuming that the various creditors' committees decide to reorganize the company and attempt to continue operations, what plan for reorganization would you establish? Include in your plan any additional cash requirements and potential sources of this cash as well as the kinds of payments or securities which should be offered to existing claimants in the company.

SELECTED READINGS

CLARK, RALPH E. *A Treatise on the Law and Practice of Receivers.* Cincinnati: Anderson, 1959.

COLLIER, W. M. *Bankruptcy Act.* Albany: Matthew Bender & Co., Inc., 1960.

DEWING, ARTHUR S. *The Financial Policy of Corporations,* 5th ed. New York: The Ronald Press Co., 1953. Vol. 2, Chapters 39–43.

GRIFFITHS, OSWALD. *The Law Relating to Bankruptcy, Deeds of Arrangement, Receiverships and Trusteeships,* 5th ed. London: Textbooks, 1953.

HOLZMAN, R. S. *Corporate Reorganizations: Their Federal Tax Status,* 2d ed. New York: The Ronald Press Co., 1955.

WESTON, J. FRED. *Readings in Finance from* Fortune. New York: Holt, Rinehart and Winston, Inc., 1958. Section XI.

30

Reorganization, Bankruptcy, and Termination

The first bankruptcy laws were enacted by the Romans as early as 313 B.C. The first statute of this kind in England came in 1542, but this law was for the benefit of creditors and not debtors. It was not until 1705 that provision was made in the English law for the discharge of the debtor from his obligations under bankruptcy proceedings.

At the time of the formation of the federal government in the United States there was considerable difference of opinion whether the right to enact bankruptcy laws should be delegated to the federal government or retained by the various states. Those favoring the federal government finally won. Several other federal statutes enacted subsequently were of short duration. Finally the federal government, in 1898, enacted the Bankruptcy Act, which with its amendments is still the law of the land today.

The Bankruptcy Act of 1898

The Bankruptcy Act of 1898 provided for the liquidation, and not the reorganization, of an insolvent company. Due to the public necessity for the services rendered by railroads and public utilities, they were exempt from the Bankruptcy Act. Although other types of corporations could avail themselves of the bankruptcy law, many of these companies resorted to equity receivership and reorganization rather than bankruptcy, which could lead only to liquidation.

Due to the shortcomings of equity receivership and reorganization, Congress, in 1933, amended the Bankruptcy Act through the enactment of Section 77, to permit railroads to *reorganize* under the Bankruptcy Act.

713

In 1934, Section 77B was added to the Act to permit all other types of corporations to *reorganize* under the Bankruptcy Act. In 1938, Section 77B was supplanted by the Chandler Act, which is sometimes referred to as Chapters X and XI of the Bankruptcy Act. Chapter XI was designed for the reorganization of small concerns with only bank and merchandise creditors, while Chapter X pertains to larger corporations which have securities outstanding.

It should be kept in mind that we are discussing *reorganizations* under the Bankruptcy Act. We will also briefly consider liquidation under the Bankruptcy Act, which before 1933 was the only action possible under this statute.

THE CHANDLER ACT

Reorganization under Chapter X (Chandler Act) may be accomplished by any corporation other than a railroad, bank, savings and loan association, or municipal corporation. The company may voluntarily instigate the proceedings, or involuntary proceedings may be started by three or more creditors whose claims against the company aggregate $5,000 or more, or by a trustee under the indenture of a bond issue. When the company files a voluntary petition it must be stated that the company is insolvent or unable to pay its debts as they mature. When involuntary action is brought the petition must show that the company was adjudged to be bankrupt, or that a "proceeding to foreclose a mortgage" or similar action had been undertaken.

Appointment of Trustee

After the petition has been approved, the judge must appoint a trustee, or trustees, to conduct the necessary business of the company. If the liabilities of the company amount to $250,000 or more, the judge must appoint a "disinterested" trustee. In order to qualify as a disinterested party, a trustee cannot be (a) a stockholder or creditor of the company, (b) an underwriter of any of the company's outstanding securities, or an underwriter of any of the company's securities within a period of 5 years prior to the filing of the petition, (c) director, officer, attorney, or employee of the company, or underwriter or attorney of an underwriter of the company at the time, or within 2 years prior to the filing of the petition, or (d) any other person directly or indirectly connected with the company or underwriter and who might have an interest materially adverse to the interests of any class of creditors or shareholders. When the total indebtedness is less than $250,000, the judge may appoint a disinterested trustee or he may at his discretion allow the company to continue in possession of its property.

Duties of the Trustee

The trustee in bankruptcy has more duties to perform, and plays a much more active part in the reorganization of the company than the receiver in equity. In addition to running the business, Chapter X states that the trustee shall perform the following duties.

1. Collect the essential information in regard to the company's financial position, condition of its property, operation of the business, and the desirability of continuing the operations, and report the findings to the judge, the stockholders, creditors, and the Securities and Exchange Commission.
2. Investigate the past conduct of the officers and directors and report to the judge any evidence of fraud, mismanagement, or irregularities.
3. Invite the various classes of creditors, bondholders, and shareholders to submit plans for the reorganization of the company.
4. Prepare a reorganization plan and file it with the court within the time limit set by a judge. If a reorganization is not recommended a report must be filed setting forth the reasons.

It will be recalled that under equity receivership the receiver has nothing to do with the reorganization plan. In a reorganization under Chapter X, the trustee is charged with the drawing-up of the reorganization plan. Since the trustee is the agent of the court, it follows that the latter will supervise the reorganization procedure.

Protective Committees

Protective committees—and in some instances a "reorganization" committee—are used in reorganizations under Chapter X, but they are under court control, and have less power and authority than under equity receivership reorganization. Chapter X provides that the court may require full disclosure of the lists of stockholders and bondholders, so that interested parties may proceed to form protective committees.

The members of the protective committees or the reorganization committee may formulate a plan for the reorganization and submit it to the trustee. Although each class of security holders will be interested in getting the most for its particular class of securities, it is realized that an inequitable plan would be unacceptable to the trustee and to the court. It will be recalled that under Chapter X the trustee, and not the committees, is charged with the duty of drawing-up the reorganization plan.

Work Preliminary to Plan

Before a reorganization plan can be formulated it is necessary to know what caused the company to fail. The reorganization plan should take the cause of failure into consideration in an attempt to prevent such occurrence in the future.

Engineering reports on the condition of the physical plant are necessary to determine productive capacities and repair and replacement policies. A study of the debtor's industry and its relative place in that industry should be made in order to determine the desirability of continued operation by the company. Estimates should also be made of the amount of money needed for improvements and working capital to enable the company to compete successfully with others in the field.

Intensive legal work must be done. The various contracts and leases made by the company should be searchingly examined to determine their legality and profitableness. From the examination of the company it should be possible to determine what are the profitable and unprofitable units. The relative position of the various liens will be determined, and from this it will be possible to arrive at some conclusion on the sacrifices which must be made by any class of security holders.

Mandatory Provisions of Reorganization Plan

Chapter X provides that certain provisions shall be in every reorganization plan, and specifies others that may be included. The following are included in the mandatory provisions.

1. Provisions calling for the payment of all costs and expenses of administration and other allowances approved by the court.
2. Provisions for the rejection of any executory contract except contracts in the public authority.
3. Provisions in the charter prohibiting the issuance of non-voting stock, and insuring equitable distribution of voting power among the various classes of stock.
4. Adequate provisions relating to the execution of the reorganization plan, including any sale of the corporate property, merger with one or more corporations, or other procedure for the carrying-out of the plan.
5. Certain provisions for changes must be listed in the plan if they are to take effect. All alterations or modifications in the rights of any class of creditors or stockholders, either through the issuance of new securities or otherwise, must be spelled out.
6. Provisions relating to the treatment of any class of creditors where the required two-thirds majority assent to the plan is not obtained.

Objectives To Be Accomplished

Due to differing circumstances, the exact nature of the reorganization plan varies with each reorganization. The purpose of any reorganization, however, is to eliminate whatever is wrong and get the company back on its feet as a going concern. The principal objectives to help accomplish this are listed as follows.

1. Correction of any managerial defects
2. Reduction of fixed charges
3. Reduction of floating debt
4. Collection of new money

Treatment of Interested Parties

Under the Bankruptcy Act, the claim of the United States, or a political subdivision thereof, for taxes is entitled to priority. Certain employees to whom wages were due within 3 months before legal bankruptcy proceedings were started are entitled to preference up to $600 each. Expenses and debts incurred by a receiver in equity or a trustee in bankruptcy also receive preferred treatment. Creditors having a *preferred* status are usually paid off during receivership or during the period the property is under the jurisdiction of the bankruptcy court. If not, the reorganization plan makes provision for their payment.

Trustee's certificates are issued in reorganization under Chapter X in the same manner and for the same reason that receiver's certificates are issued under equity receivership. The relative standing of the certificates depends upon the lien given them by the court. If they are given a claim prior to the first mortgage bonds, they would rank immediately after the preferred creditors. They are commonly paid off from the proceeds of the sale of new securities or from assessments made on the old security holders.

Generally speaking, the *secured bonds* of a company would receive better treatment in the reorganization than the unsecured obligations. Their actual treatment would depend upon the exact nature of their lien, and the value to the company of the property which constitutes their security. Where the company would not be expected to earn enough to pay the interest on the old senior bonds, they would have to undergo sacrifices similar to those for junior bonds.

Greater sacrifices must be made by bondholders who are *junior* to those stated above. Where the worth of the properties is less than the amount of the first and second mortgage, bonds having a claim junior to these, and debenture bonds, may be asked to exchange their bonds for stock. Or they may be asked to stand an assessment of, for example, 20 per cent of the face value of their bonds, for which they will receive a junior bond. Even though a particular bond issue might be undisturbed in a reorganization, the new bonds exchanged for the old may have a maturity much farther in the future.

Where the corporate property is worth no more than the amount represented by the senior claims, the *general creditors* may be given the "opportunity" to buy new securities, in some instances junior bonds. They may also be offered some stock free as an inducement to buy the other securities. In the case of some industrial reorganizations where there are no bonds outstanding, the general creditors may be given bonds for their claims.

According to Chapter X, all classes of security holders must be given consideration in the reorganization plan. But this does not mean that the old stock interest cannot be eliminated. In some instances the *preferred stockholders* are given common stock and the old common stock is eliminated. The preferred stockholders may be given a combination of both preferred stock and common stock or they may be "assessed" a designated amount of dollars per share for which they are given a new bond equal in par value to the amount of the assessment, and then they are also given a certain amount of either new preferred or common shares. The *common shareholders* may be "assessed" a proportionately larger amount, and may also be given a proportionately smaller amount of new common stock. Shareholders, of course, cannot be compelled to pay assessments. But if they do not do so, their old stock interest is wiped out, and they receive nothing in the reorganization. When they are "assessed," it amounts to giving them the "opportunity" to buy new securities in the company. Perhaps the shareholder should realize that under these circumstances his old equity is gone, and now he is merely being asked to buy new securities in a company which has been in financial difficulty.

Control

In order to prevent the old management from exercising control or new groups from taking over, the court may decide that the voting stock of the reorganized company should be placed in the hands of a voting trust for a designated period of years. The court will appoint trustees to hold and vote the stock. Voting trust certificates, rather than the stock itself, will be distributed to the security holders. In this way continuity of the management is gained until the company can get back on its feet, and the purposes of reorganization are accomplished.

Procedure Under Chapter X

Within the time specified by the court, the trustee will submit the reorganization plan to the court. A hearing will then be held at which time the creditors or shareholders may present objections to the plan, amendments to it, or they may present reorganization plans of their own.

Chapter X provides that if the indebtedness of the company exceeds $3,000,000, the judge must request an advisory report from the Securities and Exchange Commission before he can approve or disapprove the plan. By this request the SEC becomes a party to the reorganization. It will make a searching examination of the company's position, and will be represented at all hearings. The Commission will then file a report with the judge indicating its recommendations with respect to the reorganization plans. It should be made clear, however, that the Commission acts in an advisory capacity only. The judge can follow the suggestions of the Commission, or he may ignore them entirely.

After receiving the report of the SEC, if requested, the judge will enter an order approving one or more of the plans presented by the trustees, or others. In so doing the judge will make sure that the plan: (1) conforms to the requirements of the Bankruptcy Act, (2) is fair and equitable to the various classes of creditors and shareholders, and (3) is feasible and practical.

The judge then sets a time within which the creditors and shareholders affected by the plan may accept it. Those who are undisturbed in the reorganization, and those whose equity is wiped out, are not required to act. The judge will indicate into which class the particular creditors and shareholders are to be put. This is important since they vote on the plan by class.

Following approval of a plan by the court, the trustee is required to send to all those affected by the plan: (1) a summary of the plan approved by the court, (2) the opinion of the judge approving the plan, (3) the report, if any, filed by the SEC, and (4) any other material which the judge deems desirable.

The voting by the security holders is done under the supervision of the trustee. When *two-thirds in amount* of each class of creditors has voted in favor of the plan, and these acceptances in writing are filed with the court, the plan is binding on *all* creditors of that class, regardless of whether they voted or how they voted on the plan. If the company is insolvent, the shareholders have no vote on the plan, but if it is solvent, the approval of the plan by a majority in amount of each class of stock will make the terms binding on all the other shareholders in that class.

After the necessary favorable vote on the reorganization plan has been accomplished and this information is filed with the court, the latter will call a hearing to consider final confirmation of the plan. After the court is satisfied as to the validity of the plan, it will finally approve it and issue a final decree: (1) discharging the company from its debts and terminating the rights of shareholders, except as provided in the plan, (2) discharging the trustee, (3) making such other provisions as may be equitable, and (4) closing the estate.

Receivership Under Chapter X Compared With Equity Receivership

The major change in receivership under the Bankruptcy Act has to do with the problem of dissenters. Under equity receivership, dissenters can demand their full payment. In this way, some creditors can benefit at the expense of others who take a long-range rehabilitation point of view. Under the Chandler Act, dissenters may be bound by the actions of others of their class. The law takes away certain rights of creditors to demand their legal claim in bankruptcy. Since Chapter X states that all of a class of creditors will be bound by a reorganization plan if two-thirds of that class agree, certain safeguards for fairness are written into the Act. Under equity receivership, all the court looked for was approval of the plan by interested parties.

In Bankruptcy Act reorganizations, the court, trustee, and SEC consider the fairness of the proposed plan to interested parties as well as the satisfaction of those parties. The Chandler Act prevents a small group of dissenters from holding up reorganization. It also usually reduces the need for payment of cash to dissenters, thus allowing the new corporation to get a better start with less new cash required.

Advantages of Reorganization Under the Bankruptcy Act

1. *Foreclosure Sale Eliminated.* Following equity receiverships, a court sale of the property is necessary in order to freeze out those whose equity was gone, and to establish a basis for settling with those who did not agree to the plan. Under the Bankruptcy Act, when the required two-thirds approval of each class of creditors, and a majority approval of each interested class of stock is obtained, the reorganization plan is made binding on all the security holders. This eliminates the necessity of court sale.

2. *Ancillary Receiverships Eliminated.* It will be recalled that when action is brought for the appointment of a receiver in a federal court, if some of the property of the company is located in other court districts, it will be necessary to bring ancillary receivership actions for the appointment of receivers in the various court districts. Under the Bankruptcy Act, the one trustee (or co-trustees) is all that is necessary.

3. *Protective Committees Under the Supervision of the Court.* Under the Bankruptcy Act, lists of security holders must be made public and the activities of the protective committees are under the supervision of the court.

4. *Reorganizations Accomplished in Less Time.* Under equity proceedings receiverships often drag out over a long period of years. The procedure provided under the Bankruptcy Act shortens the time of court jurisdiction.

5. *Reorganization Plan Formulated by Trustees.* Under equity receiverships reorganization plans are drawn up by the reorganization committee, which represents the various protective committees. Under the Bankruptcy Act the independent trustee is charged with the duty of formulating the plan.

6. *Reduction of Problem of Dissenters and Reduced New Cash Needs.* These points were discussed under the comparison of Chapter X reorganizations with equity receivership proceedings.

Arrangements Under Chapter XI

This legislation is designed for the adjustment of smaller companies with only unsecured debts, whose financial difficulties have not reached a drastic situation. Chapter XI provides for an "arrangement" rather than a complete reorganization of the company. According to the law, an *arrangement* is a "plan of a debtor for the settlement, satisfaction, or extension of the time of payment of his unsecured debts." An arrangement is similar to a composition settlement or extension, except that it is carried out under the bankruptcy statutes and has the approval of the courts.

Only the debtor corporation can petition for an arrangement. The petition must state either that the company is insolvent or that it is unable to meet its debts as they become due. If the court deems it necessary, a receiver will be appointed for the company. If no receiver or trustee is appointed, the debtor company will continue in possession of its property.

The court then calls a meeting of the creditors and other interested parties. At the meeting the judge hears witnesses, receives proofs of claims and allows or disallows them, examines the debtor company, and, if they are willing, receives the acceptances of the creditors to the arrangement.

If the arrangement is accepted by all the creditors at this first meeting, the court will confirm the plan. If 100 per cent agreement cannot be obtained at this meeting, the court will not confirm the arrangement until it has been accepted in writing by a majority of the creditors representing a majority in amount of the claims (or if they are divided into classes, a majority in number and amount of each class of creditors). The debtor company must pay into the court any money or securities to be distributed to the creditors in accordance with the plan before the court will give its final confirmation. With the approval indicated above, the plan becomes binding on all the creditors regardless of whether they voted for the arrangement.

If the required approval of the creditors cannot be obtained, the court may dismiss the action and direct that proceedings be instigated against the company under other provisions of the Bankruptcy Act.

RAILROAD REORGANIZATION

Railroad reorganization is governed by Section 77 of the Bankruptcy Act. The general procedure is somewhat similar to that discussed above for other types of corporations, so only the major differences will be indicated.

The petition to the court can be made voluntarily by the railroad with the approval of the Interstate Commerce Commission, or by creditors with claims aggregating 5 per cent or more of the total indebtedness of the company. If the petition is approved, the court will appoint the trustee who must be approved by the Interstate Commerce Commission.

The reorganization plan may be presented by the company, the trustee, or 10 per cent in amount of any class of creditors or shareholders. These plans are presented, not to the court, but directly to the Interstate Commerce Commission. The latter holds hearings on the plans and then files a report indicating its acceptance of one of the plans, or it may formulate its own plan of reorganization. Hearings are then held on this plan and the Commission files the final report with the court. If the court rejects the plan it is referred back to the Commission and the same procedure as before takes place.

Upon approval of the final plan by the court, the Interstate Commerce Commission will conduct the voting on the plan by the various classes of security holders. To make the plan effective it must be approved by two-thirds in amount of each class of creditors, and if the company is solvent, a majority in amount of each class of shareholders. But even if less than these majorities vote in favor of the plan, the court may nevertheless approve the plan if it conforms to the requirements of the law, and if it is thought that fair and equitable treatment is given to those rejecting the plan, and that the rejection is not reasonably justified. After confirmation by the court the plan is put into operation under the supervision of the Interstate Commerce Commission.

The Mahaffie Act

Despite the advantages of reorganization of railroads under Section 77 as compared with that following equity receivership, it is nevertheless costly and time-consuming. In an effort to facilitate reorganizations of certain kinds, Congress in 1948 enacted the Mahaffie Act, which added Section 20b to the Interstate Commerce Act.

The Mahaffie Act provides for the voluntary recapitalization or read-justment of the funded indebtedness of railroads without going through the lengthy and costly reorganization procedure under Section 77. Under this new legislation the company may, with the permission of the Interstate Commerce Commission and the required approval of the security holders affected, alter any provision of a mortgage, indenture, charter, or other instrument of any class of securities. Before submitting the proposed alterations to the security holders, the Commission must hold public hearings and make sure that the proposed alterations are (1) within the provisions of the law, (2) in the public interest, (3) in the best interests of the railroad, each class of shareholders, and each class of security holders involved, and (4) not adverse to the interests of any class of creditors not affected by the alterations.

After approval by the Commission, the plan is submitted to each class of security holders which is affected by the proposed alterations. To make the plan effective it is necessary to secure the approval of at least 75 per cent in amount of each class of security holders affected by the proposed alterations.

It should be noted that readjustments under the Mahaffie Act cannot be instigated by the general unsecured creditors, nor can their rights be altered in any respect under this legislation.

TERMINATION WITHOUT FAILURE

The final phase in the life of any concern is dissolution. The term *dissolution* means the legal termination of the life of the corporation. The charter of the company is surrendered and all the rights, powers, and duties conferred upon the corporation by the statutes and the charter are brought to an end.

In contrast to dissolution, *liquidation* refers to the winding-up of the business affairs of the corporation, the conversion of the assets into cash, and the distribution of the cash to the proper creditors and security holders.

In many instances involving failures, corporations are dissolved and liquidated at the same time. But this does not necessarily have to take place. A corporation that has failed may go through a reorganization and give up its old charter (thus being dissolved), but continue in business with a new corporate structure. In such a case it cannot be said that the business was liquidated. A company may liquidate by distributing its assets to its owners, but remain in existence as a corporate shell. Thus it has not been dissolved.

Reasons for Voluntary Dissolution or Liquidation

In most instances a company is liquidated because it is insolvent, is unable to pay its debts, or is unable to earn a satisfactory return. In some cases, however, the business is terminated for other reasons. These reasons are as follows:

1. Desire of owners to retire from business
2. Liquidation prompted by legislation
3. Dissolution to lessen taxes
4. Inordinate labor demands

5. Liquidation due to decreasing profits
6. Exhaustion of resources
7. Simplification of corporate structure
8. Dissolution resulting from antitrust and holding company laws

Procedure of Voluntary Dissolution

Dissolution is a statutory procedure and can be accomplished only by following the steps prescribed by the statutes. These vary among the states, but the following are typical.

1. *Vote by Shareholders.* In some states the voluntary proceedings may be initiated by the written approval of all the shareholders. If a meeting is called for the purpose of voting on the dissolution, the notice may have to be sent to all the shareholders, regardless of whether they possess voting rights. The usual vote required is two-thirds of the voting power.

2. *Filing of Certificate.* The officers or shareholders then file a certificate of dissolution or statement of intent to dissolve with the proper state official, usually the secretary of state.

3. *Notice of Dissolution.* All the shareholders and creditors are advised of the dissolution by the appropriate corporate officials.

4. *Liquidating Agents.* The board of directors or trustees appointed by the shareholders may act as liquidating agents.

5. *Sale of Property and Distribution of Proceeds.* The liquidating agents then proceed to sell the property in accordance with the statutes, pay the creditors off according to the degree of their claims, and any balance left is distributed to the shareholders.

6. *Surrender of Stock Certificates.* In some states the statutes provide that upon receipt of the final liquidating dividend, the shareholders shall surrender their stock certificates for cancellation.

7. *Certificate of Dissolution.* Some statutes prescribe that after the final winding-up of the affairs has occurred, articles of dissolution must be filed, and the state will then issue a certificate of dissolution which officially extinguishes the corporation.

Dissolution Initiated by State

Since the state, through its laws, creates the corporation, it can also by its laws dissolve it. Following are the reasons why a state may dissolve a corporation.

1. *Revocation by Legislature.* When special charters by the legislature are permitted, they may contain a clause giving the legislature the power to dissolve the corporation. If such power is not given, the legislature has no authority to dissolve a corporation unless it has violated the contract or the laws of the state.

2. *Dissolution Based on Contingency*. The statutes in some of the states provide that certain acts or their omission on the part of the corporation will dissolve it.

3. *Dissolution from Misuse or Non-Use*. In some of the states the statutes provide that if the corporation misuses its rights and privileges, such as by performing *ultra vires* acts, the state might bring action in the courts to dissolve the corporation. The non-use of the corporate franchise may also give rise to court action to dissolve the company.

4. *Dissolution Due to Expiration of Charter*. In some states the life of a corporation is limited, and the duration must be stated in the charter. Unless the charter is renewed, the company will be legally dissolved.

Partial Liquidation

In some instances a corporation will undergo merely partial liquidation, and therefore will not dissolve. For one reason or another the securities of the company may be selling in the market at a relatively low price. If the company nevertheless has adequate working capital it might take advantage of the situation and use part of its cash to retire part of the bonds or stocks that may be outstanding. Even if the securities of a corporation are not selling at a relatively low price in the market, if surplus cash is on hand, perhaps some of the senior securities should be retired either by their purchase in the market, the exercise of any call feature, or the asking for tenders from the security holders.

TERMINATION FOLLOWING FAILURE

Friendly Liquidation

In the case of small concerns with a relatively small number of creditors, it may be possible to have a friendly liquidation following failure. If all the creditors agree, the debtor company may be left in charge of its properties and its officers may proceed with an orderly liquidation of these properties, and the application of the proceeds on the debts owed. If the management is honest and fairly efficient, and the creditors have confidence in them, this may prove to be the most satisfactory method of dissolution since it eliminates all the expenses of court action and may consume much less time than some of the judicial proceedings.

Compositions and Assignments

Composition settlement and assignments were discussed in Chapter 29, and are included here merely for the sake of completeness. Such settlements also are of a friendly character since if 100 per cent agreement cannot be obtained, dissenters, if not bought off, could throw the concern into receivership or bankruptcy.

Liquidation Following Receivership

In the preceding chapter, we discussed equity receivership. There it was pointed out that the outcome of receivership might be the rehabilitation or reorganization of the corporation, but that if neither of these was possible, the court might, except in the case of public service companies, order the liquidation of the corporation. Also in event of an attempted reorganization under Chapter X, if the required agreement of the security holders cannot be obtained, action may be brought for liquidation through bankruptcy proceedings.

BANKRUPTCY

Bankruptcy means that debts cannot be paid and that a court procedure is necessary for the discharge of the debtor's remaining debts and for the proper settlement of obligations with available assets. Bankruptcy is a last-resort measure to obtain a discharge for the debtor and a fair treatment of creditors after all other possibilities have disappeared.

Purpose of Bankruptcy

Bankruptcy proceedings may be to the advantage of both the debtor and the creditor. If a person fails, not only may all his assets be exhausted by the creditors, but they may get deficiency judgments against him for the balance of whatever may be owed. If the debtor attempts to continue in business, or to start in anew, he can get nowhere because his old creditors may attach his property. Thus he may be prevented from ever getting back on his feet. Through bankruptcy proceedings, although his assets will be taken to apply to the debts, he is discharged from the balance still owed. This permits him to re-enter business or accumulate other property free from interference from his old creditors.

From the standpoint of the creditors, a debtor may conceal part of his property that should go to them. Or certain creditors may be preferred over others with the result that some will get more than they are entitled to while others will get less. Furthermore, the method of liquidation may be such that less will be available for the creditors. If bankruptcy proceedings are begun all the assets of the debtor must be reported under the penalty of criminal action. The assets will be sold in an orderly fashion, and the creditors will be paid off according to their legal rights and preferences.

If a debtor goes through bankruptcy, he is prevented from doing so again within a period of 6 years. The bankruptcy laws apply to both individuals and corporations.

Initiating the Action

Bankruptcy proceedings may be started voluntarily by the debtor or involuntarily by the creditors. Any person, or corporation, except a railroad, moneyed, or municipal corporation, may initiate a *voluntary* bankruptcy proceeding by filing a petition in the federal court stating that he is unable to meet his debts and asking that he be declared bankrupt.

Involuntary action can be brought by creditors against any person, partnership, or corporation owing debts of $1,000 or over, except railroad, moneyed, or municipal corporations, and wage earners and farmers. If there are 12 or more creditors, the petition must be filed by three or more of the creditors having claims aggregating $500 or more above any specific security for their claims. If there are less than 12 creditors, the petition may be filed by one creditor having claims of $500 or more in excess of any specific security. The petition must state that the debtor is totally insolvent and that an *act of bankruptcy* has been committed within 4 months from the time the petition is filed. Insolvency is defined by the statute to mean that the total assets, at a fair valuation, are insufficient to pay the debts.

Acts of Bankruptcy

A creditor can ordinarily force a debtor to commit an act of bankruptcy by obtaining a lien against his property, if the debt involved is not satisfied within 30 days. A simplified statement of these acts follows:

1. Transferring, concealing, or removing any property with intent to hinder, delay, or defraud creditors
2. Transferring any property to one or more creditors with intent to prefer them over other creditors
3. Permitting any creditor to obtain a lien on the property through legal proceedings and not vacating or discharging the lien within 30 days
4. Making a general assignment for the benefit of creditors
5. Permitting or suffering either voluntarily or involuntarily the appointment of a receiver or trustee while insolvent or unable to pay the debts as they became due
6. Admitting in writing inability to pay the debts and expressing a willingness to be adjudged bankrupt

Further Procedure

If the petition for bankruptcy has been filed voluntarily by the debtor, the action cannot be disputed, and the court will immediately adjudicate him bankrupt. If it is an involuntary action, the debtor will be served with a subpoena and a copy of the petition. A hearing will be held and the court will then either dismiss the action because of lack of evidence that the debtor is insolvent and has committed an act of bankruptcy, or the court will adjudicate him bankrupt.

At any time between the filing of the petition and the selection of a trustee, if the court deems it necessary, it may appoint a *receiver in bankruptcy* to take charge of the bankrupt's property and run the business until the petition is dismissed or a trustee selected. The functions and duties of this receiver are similar to those of a receiver in equity, except that he ordinarily serves for a shorter period of time.

The court will assign one or more *referees* to administer the case. A referee is a judicial officer who is appointed by the court for a term of years to administer bankruptcy cases. The referee acts practically as the judge in the case. He usually, however, does not have authority to discharge the bankrupt, and his actions are at all times subject to review of the court. The referee will call a meeting of the creditors at which time their claims are proved and the bankrupt's position is examined. The creditors will be given the opportunity of selecting one or three *trustees* to take over the corporate property. The trustee must receive the approval of the referee or the court, and he is considered an officer of the court. If the creditors do not select a trustee, the referee or court will appoint one. Title to all the bankrupt's property passes to the trustee, and it is his duty to collect all the property of the bankrupt, convert it into cash, pay to the creditors the dividends (the term used in the law) declared by the referee, and render the required reports to the referee.

Priority of Claims

Since the property of the bankrupt will bring an amount insufficient to pay off all the creditors' claims, it is of importance to know the order of priority under bankruptcy. The statute specifies the following order of priority:

1. The actual and necessary expenses of preserving the bankrupt estate—this includes filing fees, cost of recovering transferred or concealed property, and other administrative costs
2. Wages due workmen or servants of the bankrupt, earned within 3 months before filing of the petition for bankruptcy, but not to exceed $600 a person
3. Reasonable costs of creditors resulting in refusal, revocation, or setting-aside an arrangement, a bankrupt's discharge, or conviction of a person for an offense under the statute
4. Taxes due the United States, a state, county, district, or municipality
5. Secured creditors with respect to the amount received from the specific security
6. Rent owed a landlord, and accrued within 3 months prior to the bankruptcy

7. General, or unsecured, creditors, such as debenture bondholders and trade and bank creditors, and balances, if any, owed secured creditors after they have received the proceeds from the sale of the specific pledged property

Debts Not Affected by Discharge

A discharge in bankruptcy discharges only those debts which are incurred before bankruptcy, and only those that are provable. Unless the following debts, however, are paid off in closing the estate, they are not discharged through bankruptcy.

1. Taxes due the United States, or a subdivision thereof
2. Liabilities for obtaining property under false pretenses or for willful and malicious injuries to the person or property of another, or for alimony due or to become due, or for support of wife or child
3. Debts that are not scheduled in time for proof, if known to the bankrupt, unless the creditors had knowledge of the bankruptcy proceedings
4. Debts created by the bankrupt's fraud, embezzlement, or misappropriation while acting as an officer or in any fiduciary capacity
5. Wages due workmen or servants, which have been earned within 3 months prior to the bankruptcy proceedings
6. Money received from an employee and retained to secure faithful performance by the employee of his contract

Bankrupt's Exemptions

The various states have statutes which exempt certain property of debtors from seizure by judicial process. In many of the states a *homestead* exemption up to a specified amount is permitted. In some states *personal property* such as household furniture and articles, tools, and clothing up to a specified value are exempt. Although the Bankruptcy Act is a federal statute, the exemptions allowable by the laws of the particular state will be observed if the proper procedure is followed. Generally, exemptions apply only to individuals, not to corporations.

Advantages of Bankruptcy

The advantages of bankruptcy are the same as the reasons for bankruptcy laws stated earlier in the chapter. They are repeated here as a summary. If bankruptcy was not possible, a debtor might use his assets to pay some creditors, and the others would get little or nothing, although they might be on an equal footing with the repaid creditors. Or, the debtor might continue in business, even though he is running into debt further each day, until all the assets are exhausted and there is little or nothing left for the creditors.

From the standpoint of the debtor, bankruptcy discharges him from any amounts owing to creditors after the property has been exhausted. This enables him to acquire property or a business in the future without interference from earlier creditors. He thus is given another chance to make good.

Shortcomings of Bankruptcy

In some instances bankruptcy has been used by unscrupulous persons as a means of getting out of paying their just debts. Debtors may conceal property in one way or another, and thus be discharged from their debts and still retain some of their property. The Bankruptcy Act is federal law, and the intentional concealment of property is a federal offense for which a person may be punished by imprisonment for a period not exceeding 5 years, or fined not to exceed $5,000, or both.

The expenses of bankruptcy proceedings are extremely high. In a great many cases all the property of the bankrupt is consumed by these expenses, and the creditors get nothing. Almost any type of judicial proceeding is costly. The forced liquidation resulting from the proceedings is also another factor in accounting for the relatively small amounts that are received by the creditors.

QUESTIONS

1. (a) Does the Bankruptcy Act provide for liquidation or reorganization of a company? Explain. (b) When was reorganization under the Bankruptcy Act first possible?
2. Indicate the procedure followed under Chapter X to effect a reorganization.
3. Indicate in general the relative treatment accorded various classes of creditors in a reorganization under Chapter X.
4. What are the usual objectives to be accomplished in a reorganization?
5. Compare reorganization under Chapter X of the Bankruptcy Act and under the equity courts.
6. (a) Explain what part, if any, is played by the Securities and Exchange Commission in a reorganization under Chapter X. (b) What advantages may be secured by reorganizing under Chapter X.
7. How does the reorganization of railroads under Section 77 differ from the reorganization of industrial companies under Chapter X?
8. (a) Distinguish between liquidation and dissolution. (b) How can a company liquidate without dissolving?
9. List the reasons why a company might liquidate and dissolve even if it did not fail or was about to fail.
10. For what reasons may a state initiate dissolution proceedings against a corporation?
11. Distinguish between voluntary and involuntary bankruptcy and state the ways that such actions may be initiated.
12. Indicate what is meant by an act of bankruptcy and give a list of such actions.

13. What debts are not discharged by bankruptcy?
14. Can all of a person's property be used to apply toward his debts under bankruptcy? Explain.
15. What advantages to the debtor might result from dissolution following bankruptcy rather than without such legal action?

PROBLEMS

1. The following questions relate to the Anderson Co. mentioned in Problem 3 in Chapter 29. It is assumed that the company went into receivership; that 100 per cent agreement could not be obtained from the security holders; and that a court sale was necessary. Assume, further, that the taxes due have been paid off from the collection of accounts receivable; that there are no preferred general creditors; and that the security holders follow their strict legal rights. (a) At what figure do you think the "upset" price should be set? Why? (b) If the court sale takes place at the upset price stated by you in part (a), indicate how much will be received by each class of security holders. (c) If the average earnings were $110,000, at what figure do you think the property would sell? (d) If the property were bought at court sale for $1,500,000, how much on the dollar would be received by each class of security holders?

2. Assume that the Anderson Co. is undergoing reorganization under Chapter X of the Bankruptcy Act and that the reorganization plan should give consideration to the collection of new capital through the assessment of security holders. Assume that the average earnings for the past 3 years have been $90,000; that the taxes have been paid off; that there are no preferred general creditors; and that the property is considered to be worth about $1,667,000. Draw up a reorganization plan for this company indicating the treatment that you would recommend for the various classes of security holders.

3. The following questions relate to Problem 2 in Chapter 29. (a) Do you believe that any of the companies should go through bankruptcy and dissolve? Explain. (b) Do you believe any of the companies should be reorganized under the Bankruptcy Act? Explain. (c) Do you believe that any of the companies could get along without the necessity for reorganization or liquidation? Explain.

4. If the company or companies that you recommended bankruptcy and dissolution for in the above question were unincorporated, would you be more inclined or less inclined to recommend bankruptcy and dissolution? Explain.

5. Immediately prior to liquidation, the balance sheet of the Davidson Co. was as follows:

Assets		Liabilities and Net Worth	
Cash	$ 60,000	Accounts Payable	$150,000
Accounts Receivable, net	200,000	Taxes Payable	10,000
Inventory	150,000	First Mortgage Bonds	150,000
Fixed Assets, net	500,000	Second Mortgage Bonds	100,000
		Debenture Bonds	200,000
		Preferred Stock	100,000
		Common Stock	300,000
		Deficit	(100,000)
Total	$910,000	Total	$910,000

After all expenses of liquidation, the accounts receivable brought $100,000 in cash, the inventory brought $50,000, and the fixed assets brought $200,000. These amounts, along with the $60,000 cash originally on hand, gave $410,000 to be distributed. The mortgage bonds were secured by all the fixed assets. Under bankruptcy proceedings, how would the $410,000 be distributed?

SELECTED READINGS

COLLIER, W. M. *Bankruptcy Act*. Albany: Matthew Bender & Co., Inc., 1960.

DEWING, ARTHUR S. *The Financial Policy of Corporations*, 5th ed. New York: The Ronald Press Co., 1953. Vol. 2, Chapters 39–43.

DODD, E. M., and BILLYOU, DEFOREST. *Cases and Materials on Corporate Reorganization*. Brooklyn: The Foundation Press, 1950.

HOLZMAN, R. S. *Corporate Reorganizations: Their Federal Tax Status*, 2d ed. New York: The Ronald Press Co., 1955.

MACLACHLAN, JAMES A. *Handbook of the Law of Bankruptcy*. St. Paul: West Publishing Co., 1956.

MOORE, JAMES W. *Debtors' and Creditors' Rights*. Albany: Matthew Bender & Co., Inc., 1951.

———, and others. *Bankruptcy Act*. Albany: Matthew Bender & Co., Inc., 1952.

WESTON, J. FRED. *Readings in Finance from* Fortune. New York: Holt, Rinehart and Winston, Inc., 1958. Section XI.

Index

Absolute standards, 457
Accelerated depreciation, 584
Acceleration clause, 143, 547
Acceptances, 527–32
  bankers', 532
  trade, 527, 528–29
Accounting, 9–11, 445–55, 566–90
  data, 445–47
  deferred, 445
  department, 9
    of an investment bank, 313
  depreciation, 566–90; *see also* Depreciation
  financial statements, 447–55, 469
  method of return on investment, 419, 423, 427
  relation of, to finance, 10–11
  stewardship, 445, 447
  use of data, 447
Accounts receivable, 466, 485–91, 526–27
  aging, 490
  collateral, 526–27
  collection, 488–89
  companies, 534–36
  cost of, 489–90
  credit granting, 487–88
  credit terms, 488
  estimate of, 466
  loans by finance companies, 534
  management measurement, 490–91
  proper level of, 485–87
  turnover, 490–91
Accruals, 509–10
Accrued dividends, 279–80, 509
Accrued interest, 509
Accrued taxes, 509
Accrued wages, 509
Accumulation plans, 380–82
Acid-test ratio, 459
Act of bankruptcy, 700–27
Acts of God, 694
Additions, 565, 608
Adjustment bonds, 190
Administrative law, 12
After-acquired property clause, 170–72

Agency powers, 18
Agent, 231
Aging of accounts, 491
Agreement
  among purchasers, 314–15
  buy-and-sell, 24, 532
  selling group, 316
Agricultural Adjustment Act of 1933, 684
Allied members, 346, 347
Allowance for depreciation, 565
American Institute of Certified Public Accountants, 445
American Stock Exchange, 343, 347–48, 531
Amortization, 587
Analysis, 443–60
  by creditors, 443–44
  by owners, 444
  of statements, 447–55
  ratio, 455–60
Ancillary receivership, 708, 720
Annuity method of charging depreciation, 581
Anthony, Robert N., 424, 425
Anti-dilution clause, 121, 212
Anti-monopoly, 35
Anti-trust laws, 35, 679–85
  Clayton Act of 1914, 681–82
  exemptions from, 684
  1950 legislation, 684
  present status of, 684–85
  Sherman Anti-Trust Act, 679–81
Apparent power, 75
Application of funds statement, 452
Arbitrage, 296
Arbitrary method of charging depreciation, 583
Arrangements, 699, 721
Articles of Association, 50
Articles of Incorporation, 50
Assessments, 718
Asset value, 267–68
Assets
  basis for capitalization, 272
  cash, 480–85

733

Assets (*Continued*)
current, 237, 477
fixed, 236–37, 477, 497–98; *see also*
Fixed assets
intangible, 587
inventory, 490–97
level of, 475–77
management of, 473–501
marshaling of, 20
permanent, 477
purchase of, 666–67
receivables, 485–91
redundant, 476
replacement of, 608
requirement, 475–77
reserve for replacement of, 608
temporary, 477
types of, 477–80
valuation of, 267–68
wasting, 585
working capital, 478–80
Assignee, 700
Assignment, 85, 699–700, 725
as an act of bankruptcy, 700, 727
form, 85
Associate brokers, 347
Associate members, 347
Association
articles of, 50
business, 36
partnership, 31–32; *see also* Partnership, association
trade, 678
Assumed bonds, 185
Assuming a mortgage, 167
Auditor, 9, 77
Authentication, 142
Authorized stock, 83–84
Automobile finance companies, 534–36
Availability of capital, 252, 504
Average cost inventory valuation, 496–97
Average cost of capital, 438–40

Baby bonds, 132
Bad debt ratio, 491
Bad debts, reserve for, 605
Balance sheet, 448–50
effect of net income on, 595–99
Balanced investment fund, 374
Bank
commercial, 307, 512–17; *see also* Commercial banks
investment, 307–38; *see also* Investment banking
line of credit, 514
loans, 512–17
cost, 514–16

discounting, 515
secured, 533–34
term, 545–46, 550
unsecured, 512–17
Bankers' acceptance, 532
Bankers' shares, 125–26
Banking Act of 1933, 678
Bankruptcy, 726–30
acts of, 727
advantages of, 729
debts not affected by, 729–30
exemptions, 729
initiating action, 727
involuntary, 727
priority of claims in, 728–29
procedures, 727–28
purpose of, 726
receiver in, 728
referee, 728
reorganizations, in, 713–22; *see also*
Reorganization
shortcomings of, 730
trustee, 728
voluntary, 727
Bankruptcy Act, 187, 260, 691, 700, 701,
713–22, 726–30
Chapter X, 714–21; *see also* Reorganization, under the Bankruptcy Act
Chapter XI, 714, 721; *see also* Reorganization, under the Bankruptcy
Act
definition of failure, 691
1933 amendment, 713
of 1898, 713
provision for liquidation, 726–30
Section 77, 713–14
Section 77B, 714
Bankrupt's exemptions, 729
Bargaining method, 670
Bear, 359
Beneficiary, 34
Best-effort commitment, 314
Betterments, 565, 608
Big board, 343
Bill of exchange, 527, 528
Bill of lading, 528–29, 532
Blanket issue, 174
Block offerings, 363–65
Block sales, 364
Blue-sky laws, 231, 324
Board of directors, 9, 53, 69–74; *see also*
Directors
Bond, 131
brokers, 347
dealers, 347
dividend, 617–18
fund, 375

houses, 311
indentures, 142–44, 282
interest, 137
investment fund, 375
power of attorney, 139
premium, 151
quotation, 136–37
trustee, 140–42
yield, 134–36
Bonds, 130–63, 164–96, 197–222
adjustment, 190
after-acquired property clause, 170–72
assumed, 185
authentication, 142
baby, 132
blanket, 175
bridge, 173
callable, 150
car trust, 179
closed issue, 167
collateral trust, 175–77; *see also* Collateral trust bonds
compared with stock, 130–31
consolidated, 174
conversion, 148
convertible, 197–222; *see also* Convertible bonds
cost of capital, 434–35
coupon, 139–40
debenture, 188–90
denomination, 132
direct lien, 173
divisional, 173
dock, 173
endorsed, 185
equipment, 177
equipment obligations, 177–83; *see also* Equipment, obligations
extension, 154, 174
features of, 132–33
first mortgage, 172
general, 175
guaranteed, 185–86
improvement, 174
income, 190–92
interest rates, 137–38
joint, 187
junior, 165–67, 174, 717
land trust, 183–84
leasehold mortgage, 184–85
long-term, 133
maturity of, 133
medium-term, 133
mortgage, 164–75; *see also* Mortgage, bonds
open issue, 169–70
participating, 192–93

preference, 190
premium, 151
prices, 137–38
prior-lien, 173–74
profit sharing, 192–93
purchase money, 171
quotations, 136–37
real estate, 172
reasons for selling, 144–48
redemption feature of, 148–51
refunding, 151–54
refunding mortgage, 175
registered, 138–39
registered-coupon, 140
retirement of, 148–60; *see also* Retirement of bonds
sale through privileged subscriptions, 303–4
second mortgage, 166, 174, 717
secured debenture, 190
senior, 174
serial, 159–60
short-term, 133
sinking fund, 142
special direct lien, 173
subordinated debenture, 189–90
terminal, 173
third, 166, 174
types of, 164–96
underlying, 173
unified, 174
unsecured, 185–93; *see also* Unsecured bonds
warehouse, 173
yield on, 134–36
Bookkeeper, 9
Book value, 95–98
Bradley, J. F., 113
Break-even point, 601
Break-even price in convertible bonds, 203–4
Bridge bonds, 173
Broker, 307–8, 346–47
associate, 347
bond, 347
commissions, 346
commissions charged, 360–61
floor, 346
odd-lot, 347
two-dollar, 346
Brokerage fees to bankers, 323–24
Budget committee, 10
Budget standards, 457
Budgets, 460–69
as a planning tool, 460–61
capital, 427, 465
capital expenditures, 465

Budgets (*Continued*)
  cash, 465, 466–69; *see also* Cash,
    budget
  control tool, 461
  flexible, 464
  forecasting, 462–63
  function of, 461–62
  importance of, 461–62
  income and expense, 465
  limitations, 464–65
  manpower, 465
  materials purchased, 465
  operating, 465
  preparation, 463–64
  production, 465
  sales, 467
  types of, 465
  variable, 464
Bull, 359
Business
  associations, 36
  commercial, 5
  executive promoter, 229
  expediency, rule of, 681
  finance, 3–7; *see also* Finance
  industrial, 5
  law, 10–12
  organization, forms of, 2-80, 246
    corporation, 40–60; *see also* Corpora-
      tion
    individual proprietorship, 16–17
    joint stock company, 33–34
    Massachusetts trust, 36–37
    non-corporate, 5, 16–39
    partnership, 17–33; *see also* Partner-
      ship
    trust arrangements, 34–37
  trust, 36
Buy-and-sell agreement, 24, 532
Buying and selling securities, 353–65
  block offerings, 364–65
  brokers' commissions, 360–61
  dollar averaging, 362–63
  margin buying, 356–57
  monthly investment plan, 362
  odd lots, 357–58
  secondary distribution, 363–64
  short-selling, 358–60
  transfer taxes, 362
  types of orders, 354–56
    limited, 354–55
    market, 354
    stop-loss, 355–56
Buying department of an investment bank,
    312
Bylaws, 52–54
  amendment, 54

  definition of, 52
  provisions of, 53–54

C's of credit, 407
Call, 150
  yield to, 136
Callable
  bonds, 150
    yield on, 136
  preferred, 118, 122
  serial bonds, 160
Calls, 215
Capacity, 407
Capital, 84, 271, 407, 631
  budgeting, 427–28, 465
  circulating, 480
  cost of, 431–40; *see also* Cost of capital
  distinguished from capitalization, 271
  expenditures budget, 465
  gains tax, 385
  outside, 246
  stock, 51–52, 83–102, 103, 271; *see
    also* Stock
    distinguished from capitalization, 271
    minimum, 51
  structure, 244–63
    choice of, 251–54
    factors in choosing, 245–49
    financial corporations, 260–61
    importance of, 245
    industrial corporations, 255–57; *see
      also* Industrial companies
    insurance corporations, 260–61
    patterns, 254–61
    principles, 249–51
    public utilities, 257–59; *see also* Pub-
      lic utilities
    railroads, 259–60; *see also* Railroads
    real estate corporations, 260–61
    top-heavy, 674
  surplus, 604, 623–24
  turnover, 419
  working, 478–80; *see also* Working
    capital
Capitalism, 13
Capitalization, 264–65, 271–76
  bases of, 271–74
  distinguished from capital, 271
  distinguished from capital stock, 271
  distinguished from capital structure, 271
  of earnings, 270
  over-, 274–75
  policy, 423
  under-, 275–76
Capitalizing earnings, 270
Capper-Volstead Act, 684
Car trust certificates, 179

Cash, 480–85, 636
  balance, 468
  budget, 465, 466–69
    cash balance, 468
    cash disbursements, 467–68
    cash receipts, 466
    limitations of, 469
    uses of, 468–69
  cost of, 483
  differentiated from net income, 592
  disbursements, 467–68
  discount, 488
  dividends, 615–16
  flow, 483–84, 636
  in advance, 511
  investment of, 484–85
  leaks, 483
  minimum, 468, 482–83
  on delivery, 511
  reasons for holding, 482
  receipts, 466
  redundant, 89
  restriction, 548
  surrender value of life insurance, 532
Caveat emptor doctrine, 324
Census of Shareowners in America, 340–41
Certificates
  equipment trust, 177–83
  land trust, 183–84
  of dissolution, 724
  of incorporation, 50
  receivers', 187–88
  stock, 84–85
  trustees', 187–88
Certification of the trustee, 142
Cestui que trust, 34
Cestuis que trustent, 34
Chairman of the board, 9, 76
Chandler Act, 714–21; *see also* Bankruptcy Act, Chapter X and Chapter XI
Character, 407
Charter, corporate, 50–52
  contents of, 50–52
  duration of, 52
  purpose clause, 51
  special provisions, 52
Chattel mortgage, 175, 527, 555
Circular combination, 656
Circular expansion, 656
Circulating capital, 480
Class voting, 66–67
Classified stock, 67, 124, 628
Clayton Act of 1914, 678, 681–82, 684
  1950 Amendment, 684
Cleanup, 514

Close corporation, 274
Closed-end investment companies, 372–73
  buying charges, 377–78
  market price of, 378–79
Closed-end mortgage, 167
Code of regulations, 52
Cohan, Avery B., 318, 320, 321
Collateral, 175, 407, 408, 524–32
Collateral objectives, 399
Collateral trust bonds, 175–77
  payment of interest, dividends, and principal on pledge securities, 176–77
  reasons for issuance, 175–76
  substitution of pledged securities, 177
  types of securities pledged, 175–76
  voting pledged stock, 177
Collection policies, 488–89
Collective rights, 61
Comakers, 532–33
Combinations, 664–88
  and the law, 679–85
    anti-trust exemption, 684
    Clayton Act of 1914, 681–82
    1950 legislation, 684
    present status, 684–85
    Public Utility Holding Company Act of 1935, 682–83
    Sherman Anti-Trust Act, 679–81
  circular, 656
  forms of, 666–79
    communities of interest, 678
    consolidations, 667–70; *see also* Mergers
    gentlemen's agreements, 677
    holding companies, 670–75; *see also* Holding companies
    interlocking directorates, 678
    leases, 675–77
    mergers, 667–70; *see also* Mergers
    pools, 678
    purchase of assets, 666–67
    trade associations, 679
    trust, 35, 678; *see also* Trust
  historical development of, 664–66
  horizontal, 655
  periods of, 664–66
  vertical, 655
Commercial banks, 307, 512–17, 550
  differing from investing banking, 307
  selecting, 517
  term loans, 545, 550
  unsecured loans, 512–17
Commercial credit companies, 534–36
Commercial paper, 518
Commercial paper houses, 518–20
Commission, 317

Commission broker, 346
Commissions on stock, 346, 360–61
Commitment, in investment banking, 313–14
  best-effort, 314
  firm, 313
  stand-by, 313
Common law, 11
  on dividends, 631–32
  trust, 36
  voting, 63
Common stock, 83–102, 103–4, 277–78; *see also* Stock
  book value of, 96
  cost of, 436–37
  investment fund, 375
  recapitalization, 277–78
  theory of investment, 104
  treatment in reorganization, 718
Community of interest, 678
Companies Act of 1844, 41
Company, 19
Comparability, 446
Compensation of investment bankers, 317–18
Competitive bidding, 319–21
Complementary products, 656
Compositions, 699, 725
Compound interest method of depreciation, 581
Compromises, 698–701, 704–5
  assignment, 699–700
  compared with receivership, 704–5
  composition, 699
  creditors' committee management, 700–1
  extensions, 698–99
Comptroller, 9, 394
Compulsory redemption, 118–19
Concentration of economic power in holding companies, 674
Conditional sale plan, 178, 555
Conditions, 408
Conservatism, 446, 447
Consistency, 446
Consolidated bond, 174
Consolidation, 667–70; *see also* Mergers
Constitution of the United States, 682, 694
Consultants, 230
Consumer finance, 4
Consumer finance company, 534, 539
Contingencies, reserve for, 609
Contribution, right of, 20, 21
Control, 68–70, 248, 251, 253–54, 431, 504, 718
  methods of continuing, 68–70

point, 431
  retention in expansion, 659
  tool, 461
Controller, 9, 74, 77, 394–96
Controlling, 7, 8
Conversion, 148
  as a method of retiring bonds, 148
  period, 207–8
  price, 202
  rate, 202
  ratio, 121, 202–3
  value, 203–4
Convertible bonds, 197–210, 212–13
  adjustment for interest and dividends, 206
  advantages to buyer, 201–10
  as a hedge for short selling, 209
  compared with warrants, 212–13
  conclusions on, 209
  conversion period, 207–8
  conversion ratio, 202–3
  disadvantages to buyer, 201–2
  disadvantages to issuer, 200–1
  extent of use, 197–98
  price pattern of, 203–4
  protection against dilution, 208–9
  subordinated debentures, 207
  uneven number of shares, 206–7
  when to convert, 204–6
  why sold, 199–200
Convertible preferred stock, 120–22
Convertible securities, 120–22, 197–222
Conveyance of title, 165
Cooling period, 330
Copyrights, 240–41, 532, 587
Corporate bonds, 130–96, 197–222; *see also* Bonds
Corporate finance, 3–7; *see also* Finance
Corporate stock, 83–102; *see also* Stock
Corporation, 17, 26–29, 40–60
  attributes of, 44
  bylaws, 52–54; *see also* Bylaws
  charter, 50–52; *see also* Charter, corporate
  classification, 43
  close, 274
  definition of, 44
  directors, 71–74; *see also* Directors
  domestic, 42
  duration, 52
  foreign, 42, 46, 55
  history of, 40
  importance of, 17
  laws, 41
  life of, 45
  limited liability of, 45–46
  location of principal office, 51

management of, 46, 61–80; *see also* Management
name, 50
non-profit, 42, 43, 44
non-stock, 42, 43, 44
officers, 74–78; *see also* Officers
perpetual, 52
private, 42, 43
profit, 42, 43, 44
public, 42, 43
purpose of, 51
relative importance, 17
state of incorporation, 46–50
stock, 42, 43, 44
stockholders, 61–71; *see also* Stockholders
taxation, 26–29
temporary, 274
transacting business in other states, 54–58
transferability of shares in, 45
types of, 42–44
valuation, 413–15
Cosigner, 532–33
Cost, 265–66, 504
of bank credit, 514–16
of capital, 251, 253, 431–40
average, 438–40
bonds, 434–35
common stock, 436–37
preferred stock, 435–36
retained earnings, 437–38
of cash, 483
of fixed assets, 498–99
of goods sold, 594
of installment financing, 554–55
of inventory, 492–93
of receivables, 489–90
of suppliers' funds, 510–11
of term loans, 548–49
Cost or market inventory valuation, 497
Costs
fixed, 600–1
variable, 600–1
Coupon bonds, 139–40
Covenants, 143
Creator, 34
Credit
analysis, 443–44
C's, 407
department, 9
granting, 487–88
line, 514
manager, 9, 487
rating, 406–8
from creditor's viewpoint, 407–8
importance of, 406–7

revolving, 526–27, 549
sales, 485–91; *see also* Accounts receivable
terms, 488, 511
trade, 507
Creditors, 21, 443–44
analysis, 443–44
general, 717
inside, 21
outside, 21
preferred, 717
Creditors' committee management, 700–1
Cum-dividends, 87
Cum-rights, 294
Cumulative dividends, 108–10
Cumulative preferred stock, 108–10
Cumulative voting, 63–66
Curb Exchange, 343; *see also* American Stock Exchange
Current asset value, 98
Current assets, 237, 477
Current financing, 502–41; *see also* Short-term financing
Current market method of charging depreciation, 583
Current ratio, 116, 458–59
Current yield, 136
Customers, 444, 520
Cutting a melon, 628

Dartmouth College case, 44
Debenture bonds, 188–90
protective provisions, 189
secured, 190
subordinated, 189–90
Debenture stock, 126
Debit balance, 356
Debt readjustment, 281–82
elimination of burdensome provisions, 282
extension of maturity, 281
reduction of interest rate, 281–82
reduction of principal, 282
Debt to equity ratio, 460
Decision making, 14, 442
Declaration of dividends, 629–31
Deed of trust, 36, 142
Default, 253
Defeasance clause, 165
Deferred items, 509–10
Deferred stock, 126
Deficit, 603, 609–10
Delectus personae, 23
Delinquency ratio, 491
Delivery, regular-way, 86, 137
Denomination of bonds, 132
Depletion, 585–87, 605

Depreciation, 563–90
  accounting policies, 566–76
  allocating expense to accounting period, 567
  and obsolescence, 584–85
  charges, 575, 576
    use of assets resulting from, 575
  effect on income tax, 569–70
  effect on replacement, 570–75
  experience of American manufacturing corporations, 575–76
  in wasting asset companies, 586
  inadequate, 697
  methods of charging, 576–84
    accelerated, 584
    annuity, 581
    arbitrary, 583
    choice of, 583–84
    compound interest, 581
    current market, 583
    first year extra allowance, 580
    fixed-percentage-of-declining-balance, 578–79
    investment tax credit, 580–81
    production, 577–78
    sinking fund, 581–83
    straight-line, 578
    sum-of-the-year's-digits, 579–80
  rates, 569
  reasons for charging, 566–75
    allocating expense to accounting period, 567
    lessening income tax, 569–70
    proper valuation of assets, 567–68
    replacement of depreciated assets, 570–75
  reserve, 565, 605
  subjective nature of, 568
  valuation of assets, 567–68
Detachable warrants, 211, 213–14
Differential, 357
Dilution, 208–9
Direct lien bonds, 173
Direct negotiation, 319–21
Directorates, interlocking, 678, 682
Directors, 9, 53, 69–70, 71–74
  chairman of board, 9
  classification, 69, 72
  committees of, 53, 73
  finance committee, 9
  interlocking, 678, 682
  liabilities of, 73–74
    avoidance of, 74
  meetings, 53
  powers of, 72–73
  qualifications of, 72
  staggered terms for, 69–70

Discount, 317, 515
  bank loans, 515
  cash, 488
  companies, 534–36
  sales, 593
Discounting, 515
  drafts, 527, 532
  installment paper, 534–36
  notes, 515, 527
Disinterested trustee, 714
Disposal of assets, 565–66
Dissenters, 669, 709, 720
Dissolution, 723–26
  after failure, 725–26
  based on contingency, 725
  certificate of, 724
  contrasted with liquidation, 723
  due to expiration of charter, 725
  from misuse or non-use, 725
  initiated by state, 724–25
  notice of, 724
  partial, 725
  through bankruptcy, 726–30; see also Bankruptcy
  voluntary, 723–24
    procedure, 724
    reasons for, 723–24
Distribution, 8
Diversified common stock investment fund, 375
Divided account, 315
Dividends, 615–41
  accrued, 279–80, 509
  bond, 617–18
  bylaw provisions on, 54
  cash, 615–16
  cum, 87
  cumulative, 108–10
  declaration of, 629–31
  equalization, reserve for, 608
  ex-, 86
  extra, 628
  final, 628–29
  from surplus, 632–33
  illegal, 630
  improper, 630
  interim, 628
  liquidating, 586, 629
  non-cumulative, 109–10
  optional, 621
  policies, 631–38
    factors affecting, 631–36
      age of company, 634
      cash flow, 636–37
      common law, 631–32
      contractual arrangements, 633–34
      earnings, 635–36

liquidity, 636–37
nature of company business, 634
reserves, 117
restrictions of commissions, 633
size of company, 634
statutory law, 632–33
stock distribution, 634
tax considerations, 635
stable, 637–39
unwise, 697
preference, 107
preferred, 107–12
property, 616
quarterly, 628
reduction of rate, 280
regular, 627
reinvestment of, 382–83
restrictions, 189, 548
scrip, 616–17
security, 616
special, 629
stable, 637–39
stock, 277, 618–25; see also Stock, dividend
terminology, 627–29
types of, 615
when insolvent, 633
Divisional bonds, 173
Dock bonds, 173
Dollar averaging, 362, 380–81
Domestic corporation, 42
Double-declining-balance, 579
Drafts, 527, 528–29, 532
Dun & Bradstreet, Inc., 407, 456, 457, 693
Dusk-to-dawn sales, 364

Earned surplus, 602–5; see also Surplus
Earning power valuation, 265, 267, 268–71
Earnings, 247–48; see also Net income
as a basis for capitalization, 247–48, 272–73
capitalizing, 270
evaluation of future, 265, 267, 268–71
per share, 98
preinvestment of, 544
statement, 450–52; see also Income, statement
Economic failure, 690
Economic society, 13–14
Economics, 10, 14
Effective date, 330–31
Emergency Transportation Act of 1933, 684
Employees, 444
Engineers, 230

Enterprise Development Corp., 230
Entity, 45
Entrepreneurship, 16
Equipment
bonds, 177
installment financing, 552–55
mortgage plan, 177–78
obligations, 177–83
conditional sale plan, 178
investment worth of, 182–83
mortgage plan, 177–78
Philadelphia plan, 178–83; see also Philadelphia plan
use, 183
trust certificates, 179; see also Equipment, obligations
Equitable title, 165
Equity, 11, 145
actions, 11
courts, 11
of redemption, 165
receivership, 701–9; see also Receivership
securities, 11
Estate, incorporation of, 274
Estimating, 462–63
Ex-dividend, 86
Ex-rights, 294
Exchange acquisitions, 365
Exchange distributions, 364
Exchanges, stock, 341–67; see also Stock, exchanges
Exempt securities, 325, 328
Exempt transactions, 325, 329
Exemptions of bankrupt, 729
Expansion, 645–63
achieving the plan, 657–58
advantages of, 649–51
determination of profitability, 657
direction of, 655–56
disadvantages of, 652
external, 652–53
financial management, 656–60
financial problems of, 658–60
avoidance of excess debt, 658–59
avoidance of excess stock issues, 659
maintenance of adequate working capital position, 658
retention of control, 659
tax consideration, 659–60
financing methods, 653–55
internal, 652
measures of, 648–49
purpose of, 646–48
reserve for, 608
selection of source of funds, 657

Expansion (*Continued*)
  types of, 652–56
    circular, 656
    external, 652–53
    horizontal, 655
    internal, 652
    vertical, 655–56
  unwise, 695
Extension, 154, 281, 698–99
Extension bonds, 174
External causes of failure, 692–94
External leverage, 146
External standards, 428
Extra dividends, 628

Face-amount installment certificate investment company, 371–72
Face value, 132
Factor, 536–39
  advantages of, 537–38
  disadvantages of, 539–40
  types of compensation, 536
Factoring, 536
Factors' lien, 530
Failure, 689–98
  apparent, 691
  causes of, 692–98
  economic, 690
  external causes, 692–94
  financial, 405, 690
  financial causes, 696–98
  internal causes, 694–98
  legal, 690
  non-financial internal causes, 694–96
  real, 691
Fair cash value for shares, 667
Federal Bankruptcy Act, 713–22, 726–30; see also Bankruptcy Act
Federal Communications Act, 633
Federal income tax, 146–48, 569–70, 586, 595
  and depletion, 586
  and depreciation charges, 569–70
  and holding companies, 673
  and stock dividends, 621–22
  and stock split-ups, 626
  bond interest deducted before computing, 146, 148
  on corporation, 26–29
  on general partnership, 24–29
Federal Power Commission, 319
Federal Reserve Bulletin, 513, 515, 524, 528, 545, 546, 547, 548
Federal Reserve System, 545, 547, 679
  Board of Governors, 350, 356
Federal Securities Act of 1933, 326–36; see also Securities Act of 1933

Federal Trade Commission, 12, 328, 666, 681, 684
Federal Trade Commission Act, 681
Federal transfer tax, 362
Federal Water Power Act, 633
Fergusson, Donald A., 113, 122
Field warehousing, 530
FIFO, 496
Final dividend, 628–29
Finance, 3–15
  areas of, 3–7
  automobile, 5
  business, 3, 4, 5, 6
  committee, 394
  companies, 534–36
  consumer, 4, 6
  consumption, 5
  corporate, 3, 4, 6
  corporations, 260–61
  definition of, 3–7
  department, 9, 393
  federal, 4, 6
  function, 7–10, 392–95
  in an economic society, 13–14
  international, 4, 6
  inventory, 5
  local, 4, 6
  macro, 14
  micro, 14
  non-profit, 4, 5, 6
  organization, 391–95, 397; see also Financial organization
  personal, 5
  place of, in business, 392
  private, 3, 5–7
  public, 3–5, 6
  real estate, 5
  receivables, 5
  state, 4, 6
  vice-president of, 9, 395
Financial corporations, 5, 42, 43, 44
Financial executives, 394–95, 397
Financial failure, 405, 690
Financial management, 7–10, 390–641, 656–60
  defined, 391
  income, 595
  objectives, 399–400
  of expansion, 656–60
  place of, 9–10
  problems, 9
  tools, 442–72
Financial markets, 13–14
Financial mix, 408–9
Financial organization, 391–95, 397
  duties of financial executives, 395–97
  internal structure, 394–95

organization level, 393
relation to other functions, 392–93
Financial plan, 244; *see also* Capital, structure
Financial risk, 252
Financial statements, 447–55, 469
application of funds, 452
balance sheet, 448
flow of funds, 452–55
income, 450–52
profit and loss, 450
source and use of funds, 452
statement of changes in working capital, 452
statement of financial position, 448–50
Financial structure, 244; *see also* Capital, structure
Finder, 323
Finished goods inventory, 494
turnover of, 495
Firm commitment, 313
First mortgage bonds, 165, 172
First year extra allowance method, 580
First-in, first-out inventory valuation, 496
Fixed assets, 236–37, 477, 497–99
as collateral, 531
costs of, 498–99
estimates, 236–37
installment financing of, 552–55
tangible, 498
valuation, 499
Fixed charges, 149, 696–97
elimination of, 149
excessive, 696–97
reduction of, 149
savings on, through refunding, 152–53
Fixed costs, 600–1
Fixed investment company, 372
Fixed-percentage-of-declining-balance method of charging depreciation, 578–79
Fixed trust, 372
Fixed working capital, 478–79
Flat quotation, 192
Flexibility, 251, 254, 504
Flexible budgets, 464
Floating debt, 697
Floor broker, 346
Floor trader, 347
Flow of funds, 473–75
Flow of funds statement, 452–55
Forecasting, 462–63
Foreclosure, 720
Foreign corporations, 42, 46
Foreign investment fund, 376

Forms of business organizations, 2–80, 246; *see also* Business, organization, forms of
Founders' shares, 126
Fractional share warrants, 216, 622–23
Franchise, 587
amortization of, 587
tax, annual, 48
Free surplus, 607
Free trade credit, 507
Friendly creditor, 702
Friendly liquidation, 725
Front-end load, 381
Fully paid stock, 88
Fully participating stock, 111
Fund, 154–58, 574, 605
differentiated from reserve, 158, 574, 605
retirement, 119
sinking, 154–58; *see also* Sinking fund
Funded, 606
Funded debt, 151
Funds, 452–55
definition, 452
flow of, 452–55, 473–75

General bonds, 175
General creditors, 717
General incorporating laws, 41
General manager, 74, 77–78
General mortgage bonds, 174
General partnership, 17–29; *see also* Partnership, general
General rights, 61
Gentlemen's agreements, 677
Goodwill, 587
Government, 444
Government agencies, as a source of working capital, 539, 550–52
Graham, Benjamin, 260
Grantor, 34
Groups, 314–17; *see also* Syndicate
Guaranteed bonds, 185–86
Guaranteed stock, 124, 186

Hall v. Geiger-Jones Co., 324
Hedge for short selling, 209, 214
Holding companies, 42, 68–69, 670–75
abuses of, 674–75
advantages of, 671–72
disadvantages of, 672–74
intermediate, 671
Public Utility Holding Company Act of 1935, 673–74
taxation of, 673
top, 671
Homestead exemption, 729

Horizontal combination, 655
Horizontal expansion, 655
Humphreys v. Winons Co., 70

Illegal dividend, 630
Immediate participating stock, 112
Improper dividends, 630
Improvement bonds, 174
Incidental power, 75
Income, 591–601; *see also* Net income
and expense budget, 465
   bonds, 190–92
      compared with preferred stock, 191–
         92
      interest provision in, 191
      quotation, 192
      recent uses, 192
   determination, 592–95
   method of valuation, 265, 267
   statement, 450–52, 592–95
      cost of goods sold, 594
      federal income taxes, 595
      non-operating expenses, 595
      non-operating income, 595
      other operating expenses, 594–95
      sales, 593–94
   taxes, 146–48, 569–70, 586, 595; *see
      also* Federal income tax
   state, 49
Incorporation, 40–60
   articles of, 50
   certificate of, 50
   organization meeting, 54
   procedure, 50–54
   restrictions imposed on, 49
   selecting state of, 46–50
   tax, 47–48
Incorporators, 50
Indenture, 142–44, 282
Individual proprietorship, 16–17
Indorsers, 532–33
Industrial companies, 5, 8, 255–57
Industry standards, 457
Inherent power, 75
Initial working capital, 478
Injunction, 333
Inside creditors, 21
Insiders, profit by, 351
Insolvency, 405, 633, 689, 691
Inspection of the books, right of stock-
   holders, 70–71
Installment
   finance companies, 534–36
   financing of fixed assets, 552–55
   investment plan companies, 371–72
   paper, 534–36
   term loans, 547

Insurance companies, 260–61, 545, 550
Intangible assets, 587
Interest, 137–38
   accrued, 509
   bond, 137
   rate reduction, 281–82
   relationship to bond price, 137–38
Interim dividends, 628–29
Interlocking directorates, 678, 682
Intermediate financing, 542–62
   advantages and disadvantages, 544–45
   reasons for use, 543–44
   term loans, 545–52
Intermediate holding company, 671
Intermediate term, 542
Internal expansion, 652
Internal leverage, 146
Internal Revenue Code, 25, 621, 635
Internal Revenue Service, 12, 384, 481,
   486, 489, 498, 503, 569, 577, 634
Internal standards, 429
Interstate commerce, 54, 56–58
Interstate Commerce Commission, 249,
   260, 294, 319, 326, 566, 722
Interstate Commerce Commission Act,
   633, 722
Intrastate commerce, 54, 56–58
Inventor, 230
Inventory, 491–97, 527–30
   as collateral, 527–30
   cost of carrying, 492–93
   finished-goods, 494
   loans, 527–30
   proper level of, 492
   raw-materials, 493–94
   turnover, 494–95
   types of, 493–94
   valuation, 494–97
      reserves, 497
   work-in-process, 494
Investment, determining amount, 412–
   16
Investment Advisors Act of 1940, 349
Investment bankers, 216, 230
   advantages of, to investors, 309–10
   as promoters, 230
   brokerage fees to, 323–24
   compensation paid to, 317–18
   receipt of stock options, 216
   services performed by, 308–9
   types of, 311
Investment banking, 307–38
   advantages to investors, 309–10
   competitive bidding, 319–21
   departments of, 312–13
   differs from brokerage, 307–8
   differs from commercial banking, 307

private placement, 321–24
regulation of, 324–36
syndicates, 313–19
Investment companies, 368–88
  accumulation plans, 380–82
  charges for buying, 376–79
  history of, 369–71
  investment in, 379–80
  management fees, 379
  market price of, 378–79
  nature of, 368–71
  non-regulated, 384
  regulated, 384, 385
  regulation, 383–84
  reinvestment of dividends, 382–83
  systematic withdrawal plans, 383
  taxation of, 384–86
  types of, 371–76
    balanced fund, 374
    bond fund, 375
    closed-end, 372–73, 377–79
    diversified common stock fund, 375
    face-amount installment certificate,
      371–72
    fixed, 372
    foreign, 376
    installment investment fund, 372
    management, 374
    mutual, 373
    non-resident-owned, 376
    open-end, 373–74, 376–77
    preferred stock fund, 375
    semi-fixed, 372
    special situation, 376
    specialized fund, 376
    unit, 372
Investment Company Act of 1940, 349,
  370, 373, 383–84
Investment dealer, 311
Investment fund, 372
Investment plans, 380–82
  accumulation, 381–82
Investment stock, 637
Investment tax credit, 580–81
Investment trust, 35, 368–88; see also In-
  vestment companies
Investors, 309–10
Involuntary bankruptcy, 727
Involuntary liquidation, 115
Involuntary receivership, 702
Issued stock, 83–84

Janney Appellant v. Philadelphia Trans-
  portation Co., 70
Joint and several liability, 19
Joint bonds, 187
Joint liability, 19

Joint Stock Companies Registration Act,
  41
Joint stock company, 33–34
Joint venture, 32–33
Junior mortgage, 165–67, 174
Justice, 11

Land trust certificates, 183–84
Last-in first-out inventory valuation,
  497
Law, 10–12
  administrative, 12
  combinations and the, 679–85; see also
    Combinations, and the law
  common, 11, 631–32
  general incorporating, 41
  relation to finance, 10–12
  statutory, 12, 632–33
Lawyers, 230
Leasehold mortgage bonds, 184–85
Leases, 170, 178, 185, 238–39, 555–60
  advantages of, 557
  alternative to ownership, 556
  as means of combination, 675–77
  characteristics of, 556–57
  disadvantages of, 559
  equipment, 178–83
  in promotion, 238–39
  plan, 178
  sale-and-leaseback, 559–60
  terms of, 179–81
Legal
  entity, 45
  failure, 690
  form of organization, 246
  investment, 637
  title, 165
Lessee, 238
Lessor, 238
Letter of credit, 532
Letter of deficiency, 331
Leverage, 106, 147, 251
Liability, 19–21
  civil, 333–34
  criminal, 333–34
  in Massachusetts trust, 36–37
  joint, 19
  joint and several, 19
  limited, 31, 41, 45–46
  of directors, 73–74
    avoidance of, 74
  of incoming partners, 22–23
  of outgoing partners, 22
  of partners, 19–21
  of promoters, 231
  of stockholders, 87–88
  reserves, 606

Liability (*Continued*)
under Federal Securities Act of 1933, 333–35
unlimited, 19, 21, 33
Lien, theory of mortgage, 165
Liens, 165
Life insurance, cash surrender value, 532
Life tenant, 34
LIFO, 497
Limited liability, 31, 41, 45–46
account, 315
Limited open-end mortgage, 169
Limited order, 354–55
odd-lot, 357
Limited partnership, 29–31
Limited partnership association, 31
Line activity, 392
Line of credit, 514
Liquidating dividend, 586, 629
Liquidation, 115, 705, 723–26; *see also* Dissolution
contrasted with dissolution, 723
following receivership, 705, 726
friendly, 725
involuntary, 115
partial, 725
value, 266
voluntary, 115, 723
Liquidity, 251, 405, 636
Listed stocks, 348
Listing requirements, 344
Living trust, 34
Loading charge, 377
Long-term bonds, 133

Macro finance, 14
Mahaffie Act, 722–23
Mail Fraud Act of 1909, 326
Maintenance, 563–64
inadequate, 697
of fixed assets, 563–66
of market, 310
of ratios, 116
Management, 8, 46, 61–80, 390–641
corporate, 46, 61–80
fees, 379
financial, 390–641
good, 69
investment companies, 374
of assets, 473–501
representative, 46
scientific, 442
shares, 126
task of, 8
tools, 442–72
Manipulation
in holding companies, 675
prohibition of, 350

Manpower budget, 465
Manufacturing, 8
Margin
buying, 356–57
of profit ratio, 403
requirements, 350
Market
financial, 13–14
maintenance, 310
order, 354
odd-lot, 357
over-the-counter, 339–40, 353
over-the-telephone, 339
security, 339–67; *see also* Stock exchanges
support, 90, 309
system, 13
valuation, 265, 266–67
value, 268
value of stock, 98
Marketing, 10
Marketing organization, 393
Marshaling of assets, 20
Marshall, John, 44
Massachusetts trust, 36–37
Materials purchased budget, 465, 467
Maturity of bonds, 133
extension of, 154, 281
yield to, 135
McKinley, William, 665
Medium-term bonds, 133
Meetings
directors, 53
stockholders, 53
Melon, 628
Mergers, 170–71, 667–70
advantages of, 668
agreement, 669
procedures, 669
promotion of, 670
Micro finance, 14
Middleman, 308
Midwest Stock Exchange, 349
Milking the subsidiaries, 674
Minimum cash balance, 468, 482–83
Mining partnership, 32
Minority, 68
in consolidation, 673
interest, 68
Monopoly, 35
Monthly investment plan, 362
Moody's Manuals, 650
Morgan, J. P., 3
Morris, Robert, Associates, 456, 457
Mortgage, 164–75
and deed of trust, 142
assuming a, 167
bonds, 164–75

types of, 172–75
chattel, 175, 527
closed-end, 167
consolidated, 174–75
divisional, 173
equipment, 177
first, 165, 172
general, 174–75
junior, 165–67, 174
limited open-end, 169
nature of, 164–65
open-end, 169–70
  restrictions on, 169–70
prior-lien, 173–74
purchase money, 171
real estate, 172
recording, 531
refunding, 174–75
second, 166, 174
senior, 174
third, 166, 174
Mortgagee, 164
Mortgagor, 164
Motor Carrier Act, 633
Multiplier, 272
Mutual funds, 368–88; *see also* Investment companies
Mutual investment companies, 368–88; *see also* Investment companies

National Association of Investment Companies, 382
National Association of Security Dealers, Inc., 317, 353, 384
National Industrial Conference Board, Inc., 395, 397, 398
National Industrial Recovery Act of 1933, 684
National Stock Exchange, 348
Near-cash, 481
Negotiable receipt, 529
Negotiation, 319–21
Net current assets, 478
Net income, 247–48, 591–601
  determination, 592–95; *see also* Income, statement
  differentiated from cash, 592
  distortion, 599–600
  effect on balance sheet, 595–99
  estimating, 234–35
  improvement, 600
  meaning of, 591–92
Net profit, 591–601; *see also* Net income
Net tangible asset value, 95
Net tangible fixed assets, 498
Net working capital, 478
New York Curb Exchange, 343
New York Mercantile Exchange, 348

New York state transfer tax, 362
New York Stock Exchange, 29, 67, 85, 86, 113, 120, 121, 137, 208, 294, 343–47, 372, 531, 624–25, 627
  advantages of listing on, 344–45
  advantages of listing to investor, 345–46
  composition of membership, 346–47
  listing application, 121
  monthly investment plan, 362
  1962 Census of Shareholders, 340–42
  rule against non-voting common, 67
  rule on non-voting preferred, 113
  rules on stock dividends, 624–25
  rules on stock splits, 624–25
No-par stock, 93–95, 278
  advantages of, 94–95
  change to par, 278
  stated value of, 94
  tax disadvantages of, 95
Nominal basis for capitalization, 273–74
Nominal yield, 134
Non-cumulative dividends, 109–10
Non-cumulative preferred stock, 109–10
Non-detachable warrants, 211
Non-negotiable warehouse receipt, 530
Non-notification plan, 526, 634
Non-operating expenses, 595
Non-operating income, 595
Non-participating stock, 110, 115, 289
Non-profit organizations, 5, 42, 43, 44
Non-regulated investment companies, 384
Non-resident-owned investment companies, 376
Non-stock corporations, 42, 43, 44
Non-voting stock, 67, 113, 289
Normal trade credit, 507
Norris-LaGuardia Act of 1932, 684
Northern Securities Co. v. United States, 680
Northwestern-Stockham Cases, 54
Notes
  discounting, 527
  receivable, 485–91; *see also* Accounts receivable
Notification, 324, 526, 534

Objectives, 9, 396–400
  financial management, 399–400
  permanence, 399
  profit, 398–99
  service, 396–98
Objectivity, 446
Obsolescence, 584–85, 605
Odd-lot, 347, 357–58
  broker, 347
  buying and selling, 357–58
  dealer, 347

Odd-lot (*Continued*)
  differential, 357
  houses, 357
  short selling, 360
Of record, stockholder, 86
"Off-the-board" offerings, 364
Offering circular, 328
Officers, 53, 74–78, 217
  duties of, 75–78
  executive, 75
  general manager, 74, 77–78
  liability of, 78
  powers of, 75–78
  president, 74, 75–76
  qualifications of, 75
  receipt of stock options, 217
  secretary, 74, 77
  treasurer, 74, 77
  vice-president, 76
Open order, 355
Open-book account, 527
Open-end investment company, 373–74
  buying charges, 376–78
Open-end mortgage, 169–70
  restrictions, 169–70
Operating budget, 465
Operating company, 42
Operating expenses, 594–95
Operating profit margin, 403–4
Operating ratio, 402–3
Operating statement, 592–95; *see also* Income statement
Option method of promotion, 670
Optional dividends, 621
Optionee, 239
Optioner, 239
Options, stock purchase, 215–19, 239–40
  distinguished from warrants, 215–16
  given to corporate officers, 217
  given to corporate promoters, 216
  given to investment bankers, 216
  in promotion, 239–40
  problems in connection with, 219
  restricted, 218
  tax status of, 218–19
Order bill of lading, 528
Orders, types of, 354–56
Ordinary shares, 103
Organic functions, 392
Organization
  expense, 236
  forms of, 2–80
  meeting, 54
  of finance function, 391–95, 397; *see also* Financial organization
  tax, 47–48, 236

Organized security exchanges, 341–67; *see also* Stock, exchanges
Organizing, 7
Original cost, 265–66
Outside capital, 246
Outside creditors, 21
Outstanding stock, 83–84
Over-the-counter market, 339–40, 353
  regulation of, 353
Over-the-telephone market, 339
Overcapitalization, 274–75, 282
Owner analysis, 444
Owner-promoter, 229

Par value, 92, 93, 277–78
  change to no-par, 278
  changes in, 277
  disadvantages of, 92–93
  stock, 92–93
Partial liquidation, 725
Participating bonds, 192–93
Participating preferred stock, 110–12
  fully, 111
  immediate, 112
  simple, 111
  special, 112
Partners, 17–33
  agency powers of, 18
  general, 17–29
  incoming, liability of, 22–23
  limited, 29–33
  loans to business, status of, 22
  nature of liability, 19–21
  outgoing, liability of, 22
  special, 30
Partnership, 17–33
  association, 31–32
  general, 17–29
    agency powers in, 18
    buy-and-sell agreement, 24
    contract, 18
    liability, nature of, 19–21; *see also* Liability
    marshaling of assets, 20
    name, 19
    sharing of profits, 21–22
    stability of, 23–24
    taxation of, 24–29
    termination of, 23
    use of, 29
  importance of, 17
  joint venture, 32–33
  limited, 29–31
  mining, 32
Past performance standards, 457
Patents, 240, 532
Pay-back, 402

Pay-out ratio, 637
Pension reserve, 606
Permanence as an objective, 399
Permanent assets, 477
Permanent needs, 505
Permanent sources, 505
Personal finance, 5
Personal finance companies, 534
Personal property tax, 49
Philadelphia plan, 178–83
  investment worth of certificates, 182–83
  security behind obligation, 181–82
  terms of lease, 179–81
  use, 183
Pilcher, C. James, 121, 198, 208
Planned standards, 457
Planning, 7, 430
  tool, 460–61
Pledged securities, 175–77
  payment of, 176–77
  substitution of, 177
  voting, 177
Pools, 678
Post, 353
Postponability, 401–2
Power of attorney, 86, 139, 534
  bond, 139
  stock, 86
Powers, 75
  apparent, 75
  incidental, 75
  inherent, 75
Pre-emptive rights, 70, 219, 288–90
Preference
  bonds, 190
  shares, 104
Preferred creditors, 717
Preferred stock, 103, 104–23, 279–81
  and pre-emptive rights, 289–90
  anti-dilution clause, 121
  book value of, 96
  callable feature, 118, 122
  compared with income bonds, 191–92
  compulsory redemption, 118–19
  convertible, 120–22
  cost of capital, 435–36
  cumulative, 108–10
  dividend preference, 107–8
  elimination of, 279
  elimination of accrued dividends, 279–80
  elimination of provisions, 280–81
  investment fund, 375
  investment worth of, 122–23
  legal nature of, 106
  liquidation rights, 114–15
  maintenance of certain ratios, 116

non-cumulative, 109–10
non-participating, 110, 115, 289
non-voting, 113, 289
participating, 110–12
  fully, 111
  immediate, 112
  simple, 111
  special, 112
protective provisions, 115–17
ratios, 116
recapitalization of, 279–81
redemption of, 117–22
reduction of dividend rate, 280
right to assets upon dissolution, 114–15
rights, 122
sale through privileged subscription, 304–5
sinking funds, 119–20
treatment in reorganization, 718
voting right of, 112–14
why issued, 105–6
yields, 107
Preinvestment of earnings, 544, 612
Preliminary prospectus, 331
Premium on bonds, 151
Prepaid charge plan, 381
Present value, 424–25; *see also* Time value
President, 9, 74, 75–76
Price
  bond, 137–38
  conversion, 202
  discrimination, 681
  stabilization, 318–19
  upset, 706
Price-earnings ratio, 98, 401
Primary distribution, 339
Primary service function, 397
Prime commercial paper, 518
Prime rate, 515
Prior-lien, 125, 173–74
  bonds, 173–74
  stocks, 125
Priority of claims, 728
Private corporation, 7, 42, 43, 44
Private finance, 3, 5–7
Private placement, 321–24
  advantages of, 323
  disadvantages of, 323
  reasons for, 322–23
Privately owned businesses, 7, 43
Privileged subscriptions, 287–306
  conditions for success, 300–3
  practical reason for, 290–91
  procedure, 291–92
  reasons for use, 287–91
  sale of preferred stock and bonds, 303–4

Privileged subscriptions (*Continued*)
  underwriting of, 303
  value of right, 292–99
Product performance, 429–30
Production, 8, 10
Production budget, 465
Production method of charging depreciation, 577–78
Professional promoter, 229
Profit, 398–99, 400, 591–601; *see also* Net income
  and loss statement, 450–52, 592–95; *see also* Income, statement
  as an objective, 398–99
  corporations, 42, 43, 44
  distortion, 599–600
  estimating, 234–35
  improvement, 600
  margin, 403, 419
  planning, 430–31
  real, 592, 599
  secret, 232
  stated, 599
Profit-sharing bonds, 192
Profitability, 400–4, 408, 412–31; *see also* Return on investment
Proforma statements, 469
Promoter, 216, 226, 228–33
  business executive, 229
  compensation for, 231–33
  inventor, 230
  investment banker, 230
  legal position of, 231
  liability of, 231
  owner, 229
  professional, 229
  receipt of stock options, 216
  types of, 229–30
  venture capital firms, 230
Promoters' shares, 126
Promotion, 225–43
  estimating, 234–37
    costs, 234–35
    current assets, 237
    fixed assets, 236–37
    funds, 237
    profits, 234–35
    promotion expenses, 236
    revenues, 234
  expenses, 236
  in a new field, 226–27
  in an established field, 227
  legal aspects of, 238–41
    copyrights, 240–41
    leases, 238–39
    options, 239–40
    patents, 240

meaning of, 225
of a combination, 227–28
  bargaining method, 670
  option method, 670
of major changes, 228
purpose of, 241
stages in, 233–38
  assembly, 237–38
  discovery of the idea, 233
  financing, 235–37
  investigation, 233–35
unwise, 695
Property dividend, 616
Property tax, 49
  personal, 49
Proprietorship, 16, 17
Prospectus, 328, 331–33
  preliminary, 331
  red-herring, 331
Protective committee, 706, 708, 715
Protective provisions, 115–17, 169–70, 189, 547–48, 720
  debenture bonds, 189
  open-end bond issues, 169–70
  preferred stock, 115–17
  term loans, 547–48
Provision for depreciation, 565
Proxies, 66, 351–52
  committee, 66
  regulations, 66, 351–52
  voting, 66
Public corporation, 7, 42, 43, 44
Public finance, 3–5, 6
Public utilities, 5, 42, 43, 44, 257–59
  capital structure, 257–59
Public Utility Holding Company Act of 1935, 259, 319, 349, 616, 629, 633, 673–74, 682–83
Publicly owned businesses, 43
Purchase agreement, 314–15
Purchase group, 314–16
Purchase money mortgage, 171
Purchase of assets, in combination, 666–67
Purpose clause, 51
Puts, 215
Pyramid, 356
Pyramiding, 671

Qualification, 324
Quick assets, 459
Quick ratio, 459
Quotations
  bonds, 136–37
  income bonds, 192

Railroads, 5, 42, 43, 44, 259–60
  capital structure, 259–60

equipment trust obligations, 177–83
reorganization, 721–23
Ratification agreement, 706
Ratios, 402–4, 455–60
acid-test, 459
analysis, 455–60
bad-debt, 491
conversion, 202–3
current, 116, 458–59
debt-to-equity, 460
delinquency, 491
earnings per share, 98
inventory turnover, 494–95
limitations, 458
liquidity, 458
maintenance of, 116
margin-of-profit, 403
of assets to preferred stock, 116
of earnings to preferred dividends, 116
operating, 402
operating profit margin, 403
payout, 637
preferred to common stock, 117
price-earnings, 98, 401
profit margin, 403
profitability, 458
quick, 459
receivables turnover, 490
resource utilization, 458
return-on-investment, 404
solvency, 458
standards for comparison, 456–58
types of, 458–60
uses of, 456
utilization, 458
working-capital, 538
working capital turnover, 459–60
Raw-materials inventory, 493–94
turnover, 495
Readjustment, 276–83; *see also* Recapitalization
Real estate, as collateral, 525, 531
Real estate bonds, 172
Real estate corporations, 260–61
Real estate finance, 5
Real profit, 592–99
Real value, 99, 275
of assets, 275
Realized profits, 604
Realized surplus, 604
Reason, rule of, 680–81
Recapitalization, 264–65, 276–83
common stock, 277–78
methods of, 277–78
changes in par, 277–78
conversion, 278
reclassification, 278

reverse split-ups, 277
stock dividends, 277
stock split-ups, 277
debt readjustment, 281–82; *see also*
Debt, readjustment
overcapitalized companies, 282
preferred stock, 279–81
elimination of accrued dividends,
279–80
elimination of burdensome provisions, 280–81
elimination of issue, 279
reduction of dividend rate, 280
undercapitalized companies, 283
Receipts
trust, 529–30
warehouse, 529–30
Receivables, 485–91; *see also* Accounts
receivable
turnover, 490
Receiver, 702–4, 728
ancillary, 708
in bankruptcy, 728
in equity, 702–4
powers and duties of, 702–4
Receivers' certificates, 187–88, 703
Receivership, 701–9, 719–20
compared with Bankruptcy Act reorganization, 719–20
compared with compromise settlement,
704–5
equity, 701–9
involuntary, 702
powers and duties of receiver, 702–4
procedure, 702
procedure following, 705
reorganization following, 705–9
voluntary, 702
Reclassification of stock, 278
Reconstruction Finance Corporation, 551
Record date, 291, 294
Recourse, 535
Red-herring prospectus, 331
Redemption, 117–22, 148–51
as a means of bond retirement, 148–51
at maturity, 148–50
before maturity, 150–51
disadvantages to bondholders of, 151
methods of, 150–51
compulsory, 118–19
of preferred stock, 117–22
Redundancy, 476
Redundant cash, 89
Redundant working capital, 506
Referee in bankruptcy, 728
Refunding, 151–54
bonds, 174–75

Refunding (*Continued*)
  inducements for, 153–54
  mortgage bonds, 174–75
  reasons for, 151–52
  savings through, 152–53
  use of warrants in, 215
Regional stock exchange, 349
Registered bonds, 138–39
Registered-coupon bonds, 140
Registration
  of exchanges, 349
  of listed securities, 350
    termination of, 352–53
  of stock, 329–31
  statement, 328, 329–31
    effective date of, 330–31
Regular dividends, 627–28
Regular members, 347
Regular way
  delivery, 86, 137
  rights, 294
Regular working capital, 478–79
Regulated investment company, 384, 385
Regulation, 249
  of investment companies, 383–84
  of security issues, 324–36
    by states, 324–26
      exempt securities, 325
      exempt transactions, 325
      of financial institution securities, 326
      of public utility securities, 326
      weaknesses of, 325–26
    Federal Securities Act of 1933, 326–36; *see also* Securities Act of 1933
  of security markets, 349–53
    Federal Securities Exchange Act of 1934, 349–53; *see also* Securities Exchange Act of 1934
  proxy, 351–52
Regulations, 52
Rehabilitation, 705
Reinvestment of dividends, 382–83
Reinvestment of earnings, 610–12
Remainderman, 34
Reorganization, 215, 277, 705–9, 715–22
  committee, 706, 715
  following receivership, 705–9
    procedure, 706–7
    shortcomings of, 708–9
  Mahaffie Act, 722–23
  plan, 706, 708, 715–16, 720
    court control over, 708
    mandatory provisions of, 716
    objectives of, 716
    work preliminary to, 715–16
  railroad, 721–23

  under the Bankruptcy Act, 714–22
    advantages of, 720–21
    appointment of trustee, 714
    Chapter X procedures, 718–20
    Chapter XI arrangements, 721
    control, 718
    duties of trustee, 715
    protective committee, 715
    railroad, 721–22
    reorganization plan, 715–16
    Section 77, 713–14, 721–22
    treatment of interested parties, 717–18
  use of warrants in, 215
Repairs, 564
Replacement
  cost, 265–66
  effect of depreciation, 570–75
  of assets, 564–65
  reserves, 608
Rescission, 624
Research department of an investment bank, 312
Reserves, 158, 605–9
  bad debts, 605
  contingency, 609
  depletion, 586, 605
  depreciation, 567, 574, 605
  dividend, 117, 608
  expansion, 608
  inventory valuation, 497
  liability, 606
  obsolescence, 605
  pensions, 606
  replacement of assets, 608
  sinking fund, 158, 607
  surplus, 117, 602, 606–9; *see also* Surplus, reserves
  taxes, 606
  valuation, 497, 605–6
  working capital, 608
Restraint of trade, 679
Restricted stock option, 218
Restrictions
  on further issues, 116
  on mortgage indebtedness, 169
Retailing, 8
Retained earnings, 437–38, 602–5; *see also* Surplus
Retained income, 437–38, 602–5; *see also* Surplus
Retirement fund, 119; *see also* Sinking fund
Retirement of bonds, 148–60
  at maturity, 154
  before maturity, 148–54
    conversion, 148

disadvantages to bondholder of, 151
  methods of, 148–52
  redemption, 148–51
  refunding, 151–54
Return on investment, 404, 412–31
  accounting method, 419, 426–27
  determination of investment, 412–16
  determination of return, 416–17
  effect of capitalization policy, 423
  relating return to investment, 417–19
  time value, 419–27
  uses of, 427–31
Reverse stock split-up, 277, 627
Revolving credit, 526–27, 549
Right of contribution, 20, 21
Rights, 216, 291–300
  action by outsiders, 299
  actual price of, 296–97
  effect on stock price in long run, 297–98
  preferred stock, 122
  quotations of, 294–95
  taxation of, 299
  value of, 292–99
    actual, 296
    determining, 292–93
    explanation of, 293–94
    theoretical, 296
    when stock ex-rights, 295–96
  what to do with, 298–99
  when issued, 294
Rights of preferred stockholders, 122
Rights of stockholders, 61–71
  collective, 61
  general, 61
  inspection of the books, 70–71
  list of, 62
  pre-emptive, 70, 288–90
  voting, 62–70
Rights-on, 294
Risk, 251, 252–53, 504
  financial, 252
Robert Morris Associates, 456, 457
Rockefeller, John D., 3
Rockefeller Brothers, Inc., 230
ROI, 404
Rule of business expediency, 681
Rule of reason, 680–81

Sale and lease-back arrangement, 559–60
Sales, 466, 593–94
  budget, 467
  department of an investment bank, 312
  discount, 593
  forecast, 466
Sales finance companies, 534–36
SBIC, 552
Scientific management, 442

Scrip dividends, 616–17
Seasonal working capital, 478, 479
Seat on exchange, 346
Second mortgage bonds, 166
Secondary distribution, 313, 339, 363–64
Secondary offering, 364
Secret profit, 232
Secretary, 9, 77
Secured current financing, 523–41; see
  also Short-term financing
Secured debenture, 190
Secured obligations, 164–88, 523–41
  current financing, 523–41
  mortgage bonds, 164–75
  other obligations, 175–88
    collateral trust bonds, 175–77; see
      also Collateral trust bonds
    equipment obligations, 177–83; see
      also Equipment, obligations
    land trust certificates, 183–84; see
      also Land trust certificates
    leasehold mortgage bonds, 184–85
Securities, 130
  as collateral, 525, 531
  bonds, 130–96; see also Bonds
  buying and selling, 353–65; see also
    Buying and selling securities
  convertible, 197–222; see also Convert-
    ible bonds
  corporate, 83–196
  exchanges, 341–67; see also Stock, ex-
    changes
  exempt from regulation, 325, 328
  listed, 348
  listing, 344
  over-the-counter, 339–40
  pledged, 175–77; see also Pledged se-
    curities
  registration of listed, 350
  regulation, 326–36, 349–53; see also
    Regulation
  stock, 83–129; see also Stock
Securities Act of 1933, 78, 231, 322, 326–
  36, 384
  administration of, 328
  avoidance of liability, 335
  basic purpose of, 327
  effective date of registration statement,
    330–31
  evaluation of, 335–36
  exempt securities, 328–29
  exempt transactions, 329
  penalties provided, 333–34
  persons liable, 334–35
  prospectus, 331–33
  provisions of, 328
  red-herring prospectus, 331

Securities Act of 1933 (*Continued*)
  registration statement, 329–31
  value of civil liability provisions, 335
Securities and Exchange Commission, 66,
    78, 141, 143, 152, 249, 291, 294,
    319, 322, 328, 331–36, 349–53, 362,
    370, 383, 384, 633, 682, 683, 715,
    718
Securities Exchange Act of 1934, 78, 319,
    328, 349–53, 363
  information on stock holdings, 351
  manipulation prohibition, 350
  margin requirements, 350
  over-the-counter market, 353
  periodic reports, 352
  proxy regulations, 351–52
  registration of exchanges, 349
  registration of securities, 350
  segregation, 350–51
  short-term profits of insiders, 351
  termination of registration, 352–53
Security, 523–41; *see also* Collateral
Security buyers, 309–10
Security dividends, 616
Security exchanges, 339–67; *see also* Stock,
    exchanges
Security issues, regulation of, 324–36; *see
    also* Regulation of security issues
Security markets, regulation of, 349–53
Segregation, 350–51
Selling group, 314, 316–17
  agreement, 316
Selling short, 358–60
Selling syndicate, 314, 316–17
Semi-fixed investment company, 372
Senior bonds, 174
Senior stock, 125
Serial bonds, 159–60
Service, 397–98
Service companies, 8
Service of process, 52, 57
Several liability, 19
Shareholders, 340–41
Shares of stock, 83; *see also* Stock
  bankers', 125–26
Sherman Anti-Trust Act, 35, 664, 665,
    679–81, 684
Short selling, 209, 214, 358–60
Short-term bonds, 133
Short-term financing, 502–41
  advantages of, 502–4
  commercial bank, 512–17
  commercial paper houses, 518–20
  customers, 520
  determining amount of, 504–5
  disadvantages of, 504
  secured, 523–41

  spontaneous sources, 506–10; *see also*
    Spontaneous sources
  suppliers, 510–12
  temporary sources, 505–6
  unsecured, 502–22
Short-term investment, 484–85
Simple participating stock, 111
Sinking fund, 119, 120, 142, 154–58, 605
  distinguished from sinking fund re-
    serve, 159
  installments, 155–56
    optional, 156
  investments, types of, 157–58
  method of charging depreciation, 581–
    83
  payments, 156–57
    obligation for, 157
    substitutes for, 156
  preferred stock, 119–20
  reasons for, 154–55
  reserve, 158, 607
  trustees, 157
Small business, 26
Small Business Administration, 7, 539,
    549, 551–52
Small Business Investment Act, 551–52
Small Business Investment Companies,
    552
Small loan company, 534
Sole proprietorship, 16–17
Solvency, 400, 404–9
Source and use of funds statement, 452
Special
  bids, 365
  direct lien bonds, 173
  dividend, 629
  offerings, 364
  participating stock, 112
  partners, 30
  situation, 376
  working capital, 478, 479–80
Specialist block purchases, 365
Specialist block sales, 365
Specialists, 346
Specialized investment fund, 376
Speculative stock, 637
Spin-off, 616
Split-ups, 277, 624–27; *see also* Stock
  split-ups
Spontaneous sources of funds, 506–10
  accruals and deferred items, 509–10
  trade credit, 507
Spread, 317
Spreads, 215
Stabilization of price, 318–19
Staff activity, 392
Staff evolution, 392

Stamped bonds, 185
Stand-by arrangement, 549
Stand-by commitment, 313
Stand-by fee, 303
Stand-by syndicate, 303
Standard Oil Co. of New Jersey v. United States, 680
Standard Oil Trust, 35
Standards for comparison, 428–29, 456–58
State of incorporation, 46–50
State regulation of securities, 324; *see also* Regulation
Stated profit, 599
Stated value, 94
Statement of changes in working capital, 452
Statement of financial position, 448–50, 595–99
Statement of operations, 592
Statistical department of an investment bank, 312
Statutory law, 12, 632–33
Stevens, W. H. S., 113
Stewardship accounting, 445–47
Stock, 53–54, 83–102, 103–29, 130–31, 277–78
  assignment form, 85
  authorized, 83–84
  bankers', 125–26
  book value of, 95–98
  buying and selling, 353–65; *see also* Buying and selling securities
  bylaws provisions on, 53–54
  capital, 51, 83–102, 103, 271; *see also* Capital, stock
  certificates, 84–85
  classified, 67, 124
  common, 83–102, 103–4; *see also* Common stock
  compared with bonds, 130–31
  convertible, 120–22
  corporations, 42, 43, 44
  cost of, 435–37
  cum-dividend, 87
  cumulative, 108–10
  current asset value of, 98
  debenture, 126
  deferred, 126
  dividend, 277, 618–25
    advantages to stockholders, 620–21
    differs from stock split-up, 625–26
    fractional share warrants, 622–23
    New York Stock Exchange rules on, 624–25
    optional, 621
    paid from capital surplus, 623–24

readjustment of capital account, 624
reasons for, 619–20
regular, 628
rescission of, 624
taxability of, 621–22
ex-dividend, 86
exchanges, 341–67
  American, 347–48; *see also* American Stock Exchange
  buying and selling on, 353–65; *see also* Buying and selling securities
  National, 348
  New York, 343–47; *see also* New York Stock Exchange
  Regional, 349
  registration of, 349
  regulations of, 349–53
founders', 126
fully paid and non-assessable, 88
guaranteed, 124, 125
investment, 637
issued, 83, 84
listed, 348
management, 126
market, 339–67; *see also* Stock, exchange
market value of, 98–99
minimum, 51
nature of, 83
no-par, 93–95, 278; *see also* No-par stock
non-cumulative, 109–10
non-participating, 110, 115
non-voting, 67, 113
of record, 86
options, 215–19; *see also* Options, stock
ordinary, 103
outstanding, 83–84
par, 92–93, 277–78; *see also* Par value, stock
participating, 110–12
power of attorney, 86
preference, 104
preferred, 103, 104–23, 279–81; *see also* Preferred stock
price, effect of rights on, 297, 298
prior-lien, 125
promoters', 126
purchase warrants, 210–15; *see also* Warrants, stock purchase
real value of, 99
reasons for reacquiring, 89–90
reclassification, 278
redemption, 117–22
rights, 216
senior, 125
speculative, 637

Stock (*Continued*)
split-up, 277, 624–27
advantages of, 626–27
differs from stock dividend, 625–26
New York Stock Exchange rules on, 624–25
reverse, 627
taxation, 626
stated value, 94, 277
tenders, 90
transfer, 85–88
transfer tax, 362
treasury, 88–92; *see also* Treasury stock
unlisted, 348
watering, 674
Stockbroker, 308
Stockholders, 53, 61–71, 340–41
analysis, 444
control, 68–70
entitled to vote, 87
liability of, 87–88
meetings, 53
rights, 61–71; *see also* Rights
treatment in reorganization, 718
Stop order, 331, 333
Stop-loss order, 355–56, 358, 360
in short selling, 360
odd-lot, 358
Straddles, 215
Straight bill of lading, 528
Straight voting, 63
Straight-line method, 578
Stumpage charge, 156
Subordinated debenture, 189–90
Subscription
privileged, 287–306; *see also* Privileged subscriptions
warrants, 291–92
Subshares, 125
Subsidiary, 171
Substitution cost, 265–66
Sum-of-the-digits method of charging depreciation, 579–80
Suppliers, 444, 445, 510–12, 520
Support of the market, 309
Surplus, 244, 602–5
capital, 604, 623–24
cost of, 437–38
earned, 602
free, 607
meaning of, 602–3
realized, 604
reserves, 158, 602, 606–9
against decline in asset values, 609
for contingencies, 609
for dividend equalization, 608

for expansion, 608
for preferred dividends, 117
for replacement of assets, 608
for working capital, 608
sinking fund, 158, 607
unrealized, 604
uses of, 604–5
Sweetener, 211
Syndicate, 312, 313–19
department of an investment bank, 312
purchase, 314–16
selling, 316–17
underwriting, 314
Syphers v. McCune, 70
Systematic withdrawal plans, 383

Take-down, 316
Tangible asset value, 95
Tangible fixed assets, 498
Taxation, 4, 10, 12–13
capital gains, 622
expansion, 659–60
of corporations, 26–29
of holding companies, 673
of investment companies, 384–86
of joint stock companies, 33–34
of Massachusetts trusts, 37
of partnerships, 24–29
of restricted stock options, 218
of rights, 299–300
of stock split-ups, 626
Taxes, 248
dividend considerations, 635
federal income, 569–70; *see also* Federal income taxes
federal stock transfer, 362
holding company, 673
state, 47–49
franchise, 48
income, 49
incorporation, 47–48
New York stock transfer, 362
organization, 47–48
personal property, 49
property, 49
stock dividend, 621–22
Technical insolvency, 405
Temporary assets, 477
Temporary corporations, 274
Temporary needs, 505
Temporary sources, 505
Tenants in common, 32
Tenders, 90
Tennessee Valley Authority, 43
Term loans, 545–52
Terminal bonds, 173

Termination, 723–26
Terms
  of credit, 488, 511
  of sale, 488
Testamentary trust, 34
Third mortgage bonds, 166
Time draft, 529
Time value, 419–27
  method, 421, 426, 427
Timeliness, 446
Timing patterns, 420–21
Title, 165
Title theory, 165
Tools of financial management, 442–72
Top holding company, 671
Total insolvency, 405
Trade
  acceptance, 527, 528–29
  association, 678
  credit, 507–12
  marks, 587
Trading department of an investment
    bank, 312
Trading on the equity, 106, 145–47
  with bonds, 145–47
  with preferred stock, 147
Transfer, 85–88
  of stock, 85–88
  tax, 362
Transferability of shares, 45
Treasurer, 9, 74, 77, 394–95, 397
Treasury stock, 88–92, 289
  and pre-emptive rights, 289
  definition of, 88
  legal right to acquire, 91–92
  reasons for acquiring, 89–90
  ways of acquiring, 90
Triangular relationship, 419
Trust
  agreement, 142
  as a means of combination, 35, 678
  business, 36
  certificates, 178–84
    equipment, 178–83
    land, 183–84
  combinations formed by, 35, 678
  common law, 36
  deed, 36
  devise, 35
  duration of, 34
  fixed, 372
  fund theory, 91, 119
  investment, 35, 368–88; see also Invest-
    ment companies
  living, 34
  Massachusetts, 36–37, 369

receipts, 529–30
semi-fixed, 372
testamentary, 34
unit, 372
voting, 35, 69
Trust Indenture Act of 1939, 141, 143,
    156, 349
Trustee, 34, 140–42, 714–15
  appointment of, 714
  certification of the, 142
  disinterested, 714
  duties of, 715
  in bankruptcy, 714–15, 728
  of a bond issue, 140–42
  under the Bankruptcy Act, 714–15
Trustees' certificates, 187–88, 717
Trustor, 34
Truth in Securities Act, 327; see also Se-
    curities Act of 1933
Turnover
  capital, 419
  inventory, 494–95
  receivables, 490–91
  working capital, 459–60
Two-dollar broker, 346
Two-name paper, 527
Tying contract, 681

Ultra vires act, 51, 725
Undercapitalization, 275–76, 283
Underlying bonds, 173
Underwriting, 303; see also Investment
    banking
  privileged subscriptions, 303
  syndicate, 314
Undivided account, 315
Unearned surplus, 604
Unified bonds, 174
Uniform General Partnership Act, 22–23
Uniform Negotiable Instruments Act, 88
Uniform Stock Transfer Act, 88
Uniform Warehouse Receipts Act, 529
Unit investment company, 372
United States Treasury Department, 481,
    486, 489, 498, 503, 576
United States v. E. C. Knight Co., 680
*United States v. Trans-Missouri Freight
    Ass'n*, 680
United States v. U. S. Steel Corp., 681
Unlimited liability, 19–21, 33
  account, 315
Unlisted trading, 348
Unrealized surplus, 604
Unsecured bonds, 185–93
  adjustment, 190
  assumed, 185

Unsecured bonds (*Continued*)
   debenture, 188–90
   guaranteed, 185–86
   income, 190–92
   joint, 187
   participating, 192–93
   preference, 190
   receivers' certificates, 187–88
   secured debentures, 190
   subordinated debentures, 189–90
   trustees' certificates, 187–88
Unsecured current financing, 502–21
Upset price, 706

Valuation, 264–71, 413–16
   asset, 267–68, 567–68
   based on both assets and earnings, 271
   cost, 265–66
   division, 415–16
   entire corporation, 267–71, 413–15
   fixed assets, 499
   income, 265, 267
   inventory, 495–97
   market, 265, 266–67
   principles of, 265–67
   reserves, 496, 497, 567, 605–6
Value
   asset, 267–68
   book, 95–98
   current asset, 98
   face, 132
   investment, 412–16
   market, 98–99
   net tangible asset, 95
   no-par, 93–95, 278; *see also* No-par
     stock
   par, 92–93, 277–78; *see also* Par value
   present, 424–25
   real, 99, 275
   stated, 94, 277
   tangible asset, 95
   time, 419–27
Variable budget, 464
Variable costs, 600–1
Variable working capital, 478, 479–80
Venture, joint, 32–33
Venture capital firms, 230
Vertical combination, 655
Vertical expansion, 655
Vice-president of finance, 9, 76
Voluntary bankruptcy, 727
Voluntary dissolution, 723–24
Voluntary liquidation, 115
Voluntary receivership, 702
Voting, 62–70, 177
   class, 66–67
   common law, 63

contingent, 67
cumulative, 63–66
fractional, 67
multiple, 67
pledged stock, 177
proxy, 66
rights of preferred stockholders, 112–14
stockholder entitled to, 87
straight, 63
trust, 35, 69
   certificates, 35

Wabash Ry. Co. v. Barclay, 109, 110
Wagner Act of 1935, 684
Warehouse bonds, 173
Warehouse receipts, 529–30
Warehousing, field, 530
Warrants, 210–15, 216, 219, 291–92, 622–23
   fractional share, 216, 622–23
   problems in connection with, 219
   stock purchase, 210–15
     anti-dilution provision, 212
     compared with convertible privilege, 212–13
     detachable, 211, 213–14
       price of, 213–14
     distinguished from options, 215
     duration of, 211–12
     hybrid form, 214
     non-detachable, 211
     price of stock with, 211
     reason for use, 211
     types of securities carrying, 210
     use as a hedge in short selling, 214
     use in refunding, 215
     use in reorganization, 215
   subscription, 291–92
Wasting assets, 585
Watered stock, 674
Webb-Pomerene Act of 1918, 684
Weissman, Rudolph L., 370
When issued, 294
Whetten, Leland C., 65, 70
Whitney, J. H., & Co., 230
Wholesaling, 8
Wi, 294
Wiesenberger, Arthur, 369, 370, 373, 379
With recourse, 535
Without recourse, 535
Wolfson v. Avery, 69
Work-in-process inventory, 494
   turnover, 495
Working capital, 478–97
   fixed, 478–79
   gross, 460

initial, 478
items, 480–97
   cash, 480–85
   inventory, 491–97
   receivables, 485–91
kinds of, 478
maintenance of, in expansion, 658
net, 460, 478
ratios, 538
regular, 478–79
reserve for, 608
seasonal, 478, 479

special, 478, 479–80
turnover, 459–60
variable, 478, 479–80

Yield, 134–36, 400
bond, 134–36
computing, 134–36
current, 136
nominal, 136
preferred stock, 107
to call date, 136
to maturity, 135